PENGUIN CLASSICS

LEVIATHAN

THOMAS HOBBES, the son of a curate, was born in Malmesbury, Wiltshire, in 1588. He studied at Oxford and spent most of his life employed by the aristocratic Cavendish family, whose younger members he accompanied on European tours. He published his translation of Thucydides' *History of the Peloponnesian War* in 1629, and in the 1630s his interests increasingly concerned themselves with modern science and philosophy. In 1640, in the context of political turmoil in England, Hobbes fled to Paris, where he lived throughout the Civil War. It was here that he began work on his masterpiece, *Leviathan*. In January 1649, Charles I was executed and England was subsequently declared a Commonwealth; *Leviathan* was published in 1651, and Hobbes returned home from France several months later. His comprehensive philosophical system was presented in his trilogy, *De Corpore* (1655), *De Homine* (1658) and *De Cive* (1642). In his eighties, Hobbes wrote an autobiography in Latin verse and translated the whole of Homer's *Odyssey* and *Iliad*. He died at Hardwick Hall in Derbyshire, aged ninety-one.

CHRISTOPHER BROOKE is a lecturer at Cambridge University in the Department of Politics and International Studies, and author of *Philosophic Pride: Stoicism and Political Thought from Lipsius to Rousseau* (2012).

Contents

Chronology

5 April 1588 Birth of Thomas Hobbes, the son of a curate, in Malmesbury, Wiltshire.

1603 Death of Queen Elizabeth. King James VI of Scotland succeeds to the English throne. About this time, Hobbes begins studying in Oxford, at Magdalen Hall.

1608 Hobbes completes his Bachelor of Arts degree and enters the employment of the Cavendish family, for whom he works for almost his entire adult life, first as a tutor to William Cavendish.

1614–15 Hobbes spends a year in Venice with William Cavendish, with a side visit to Rome.

1620 Anonymous publication of *Horae subsecivae* ('Leisure Hours'), a volume of essays, three of which have been attributed to Hobbes, including a lengthy 'Discourse upon the beginning of Tacitus'.

1622 Hobbes acquires a share in the Virginia Company, and becomes involved in its business.

1625 Death of King James. His son Charles succeeds to the throne.

1629 Hobbes publishes his translation of Thucydides' *History of the Peloponnesian War*. King Charles dissolves Parliament, beginning an eleven-year period known as the Personal Rule.

1629–30 Hobbes travels in France and Switzerland with a new pupil, Gervase Clifton. There is a striking encounter with Euclid's geometry in a library in Geneva. Hobbes's scientific interests continue to grow.

1634–6 Hobbes travels to Paris, Rome and Florence with his first pupil's son, also called William Cavendish.

1640 King Charles summons a new Parliament. Hobbes fails to be elected for Derby. The 'Short' Parliament meets in April and is dissolved in May. Hobbes writes *The Elements of Law*. Another Parliament is summoned. The 'Long' Parliament meets for the first time in November. Hobbes flees to Paris.

1641 René Descartes' *Meditations on First Philosophy* are published, together with a set of objections from Hobbes and Descartes' replies.

1642 Hobbes publishes *De Cive* ('On the Citizen'). Civil war begins in England.

1646 The sixteen-year-old Prince of Wales arrives in exile in Paris, where Hobbes teaches him mathematics.

1647 Hobbes is seriously ill. Around this time – possibly later – he begins work on *Leviathan*.

1649 King Charles is executed on 30 January. Parliament declares the Commonwealth in May.

1651 Publication of *Leviathan* in the spring. Hobbes leaves France in December to return to England.

1655 Publication of *De Corpore* ('On Body').

1658 Publication of *De Homine* ('On Man'). Death of Oliver Cromwell.

1660 Restoration of the monarchy. Hobbes's former pupil becomes King Charles II.

1668 The Latin *Leviathan* – Hobbes's own translation – is published.

1672 Hobbes composes an autobiography in Latin verse.

1679 Death of Hobbes, at Hardwick Hall, Derbyshire, aged ninety-one.

Introduction

I

Ever since its first publication in 1651, *Leviathan* has provoked strong and mostly critical reactions. It is usually read as an apology for authoritarian monarchy – yet authoritarian monarchists hated it, insofar as it denied the divine right of kings (as this was conventionally understood, at least), and grounded its argument in a set of claims that they viscerally rejected about the natural equality of all. But if Hobbes shared his foundational premises with the radicals, they in turn rejected the arguments he built on that shared foundation that concentrated political authority at a single point – the Sovereign – and rejected almost all limits on that authority.

That unsettling ability to get under the skin of both sides of the most significant political arguments reverberates down to the present. From one point of view, Hobbes looks like a modern liberal, with his emphases on self-interest, the plurality of judgements, the consent of the governed, representation, scepticism about the existence of a robust common good, politics organized around the search for a peaceful modus vivendi, perhaps even religious toleration, and a thoroughgoing methodological individualism. And from another point of view, he just doesn't, with his sharp opposition to the kind of constitutionalism that seeks to divide or limit political power, his subordination of the rights of private property to the requirements of politics, his attacks on the authority of the institutions of what we might call civil society, including the churches, or his insistence that the Sovereign will be in charge of the meaning of language itself.

Both in the seventeenth century and much more recently, the suspicion recurs that those who attack Hobbes most stridently may be those who are in certain respects following him most closely. And at least in part in virtue of this ability to provoke – which in turn generates a demand on the provoked to be a bit clearer about just what they themselves think and why they think it – *Leviathan* remains a permanent fixture on academic syllabi in political philosophy and the history of political thought, just as Hobbes wanted it to be, for as he writes on almost the very last page, 'I think it may be profitably printed, and more profitably taught in the Universities' (p. 597).

II

Thomas Hobbes was born in the Wiltshire town of Malmesbury on 5 April 1588. His father was also named Thomas Hobbes, a curate in a nearby village; his mother was Catherine née Middleton, who, in the words of Hobbes's friend and biographer John Aubrey, 'fell in labour with him upon the fright of the Invasion of the Spaniards', having heard news of the forthcoming Armada that sailed against England that year, such that, as Hobbes was much later to write, 'she gave birth to twins, myself and fear'.[1] Several members of Hobbes's family were affluent clothiers, one of whom, his uncle Francis, a glover, was to pay for his education. His father's life went less well: he was summoned before the archdeacon's court in 1602 and the bishop's court in 1603, and was excommunicated after failing to do penance and to pay a fine arising out of an altercation with the vicar of nearby Foxley. Early in 1604 he encountered his enemy who (according to Aubrey's brother William, in a letter) 'provoked him ... at the church doore, soe Hobs stroke him and was forcd to fly for it', later to die 'in obscurity beyound London'.[2]

The younger Hobbes was initially taught Latin and Greek by a local schoolmaster, Robert Latimer, of whom Aubrey wrote that he was 'a good Graecian, and the first that came into our Parts hereabout since the Reformation'.[3] When Hobbes was about fourteen – so round about the time his father's troubles began – he went to study for his undergraduate degree at Magdalen Hall in Oxford, where, Aubrey tells us, he 'did not much care for Logick, yet he learnd it, and thought himselfe a good Disputant'.[4] In 1608, having completed his BA, Hobbes entered the employment of the aristocratic Cavendish family, with whom he would be associated for the rest of his life, working at various times as a tutor, secretary, agent – or being left alone to get on with his studies. His first duties concerned the education of William Cavendish, the future 2nd Earl of Devonshire, culminating in a European tour that took Hobbes to Venice in 1614–15. There were subsequent tours with Gervase Clifton to France and Switzerland in 1629–30, and with his first pupil's son – also William Cavendish, the 3rd Earl of Devonshire – to Rome, Florence and Paris between 1634 and 1636.

We know frustratingly little about Hobbes's intellectual development throughout this period, or the evolution of his views about politics. A handful of texts have been scrutinized for the clues they may afford to Hobbes's thinking. *Horae subsecivae* ('Leisure Hours') was an anonymous volume of essays published in 1620, of which three pieces have been attributed to Hobbes following the use of a technique of computer analysis known as 'wordprinting', one of which is an interesting extended discussion of the opening passages of Tacitus' *Annals*.[5] More recently, an unpublished translation by Hobbes of an anonymous 1626 Latin pamphlet in the

Machiavellian or *raison d'état* ('reason of state') tradition, '*Altera secretissima instructio . . .*' ('A second most secret instruction'), has come to light.[6] But there is not a great deal with which to work. Much more significant is Hobbes's first major publication, in 1629, a superb translation of Thucydides' *History of the Peloponnesian War*. Hobbes's interest in this work is often interpreted as a sign of his commitment to the monarchy, given Thucydides' alertness to the dangers that demagogues pose to the democratic polity. More intriguingly, it can be read as criticism of the politicians in 1620s England – including the Duke of Buckingham, Francis Bacon, and Hobbes's own Cavendish employer – who had been lobbying for war with France and Spain.[7]

Hobbes's broadly humanist early style was to change quite drastically, apparently following a chance encounter in a 'Gentleman's Library' in Geneva in 1630 with a copy of the ancient geometer Euclid's book, the *Elements*, open at the page that explained Pythagoras' theorem. Aubrey recounts this famous episode:

> He read the Proposition. *By G—*, sayd he (he would now and then sweare an emphaticall Oath by way of emphasis) *this is impossible!* So he reads the Demonstration of it, which referred him back to such a Proposition; which proposition he read. That referred him back to another, which he also read. *Et sic deinceps* [and so on] that at last he was demonstratively convinced of that trueth. This made him in love with Geometry.[8]

Whether or not there was such an epiphany, Hobbes became increasingly preoccupied with scientific topics in the 1630s, and he paid close attention to the work of French contemporaries as the decade wore on. He was particularly interested in René Descartes, whose interests paralleled his own, whose *Discourse on Method* was published in 1637, and with whom he ended up quarrelling over which of them had what ideas first.

A scientific manuscript from this period known as the 'Short Tract' may or may not be by Hobbes, and he was certainly the author of a Latin treatise on optics some time around the end of the decade.

Politics, however, took over his attention in 1640. After dissolving Parliament in 1629, King Charles had governed England for eleven years through the Royal Prerogative. His main difficulty concerned raising sufficient revenue. The Crown's options were limited in the absence of Parliamentary consent, and the King's recourse to 'Ship Money', a tax on the coastal counties to support the navy, was unpopular. There were also problems with the Scottish Church. Charles's father, James I (of England) and VI (of Scotland), had reintroduced episcopacy – i.e. the bishops – to the Church of Scotland, and Charles was keen for further reforms to the liturgy to bring Scottish practice closer to that of the Church of England. This provoked a great deal of opposition in Scotland, and a movement for the restoration of Presbyterianism – i.e. no bishops – which led to rival armies confronting each other in 1639, though without any major military engagements. A new English Parliament was then summoned, in the hope that anti-Scottish patriotic feeling would generate adequate supply to support the resumption of war. It was in this context, at the behest of his employer, that Hobbes unsuccessfully stood as a candidate for Derby.

The Short Parliament, as it came to be called, met in April. Parliament wanted reforms before it would authorize new funds, the King insisted on Parliament dealing with finance before he would turn his attention to other matters, and in the end he broke the stand-off by dissolving Parliament in May. Around the same time, Hobbes completed a manuscript in English known as *The Elements of Law*, various copies of which were circulated, in which he set out his distinctive political theory for the first time. This earned him a reputation as a staunch supporter of the King, so when a new

Parliament – the Long Parliament, as it would later come to be known – met in November and began to flex its muscles, Hobbes fled to Paris, where he was to live for the next decade.

Early on during his time in France, Hobbes produced a new version of his political argument, this time for publication in Latin, as *De Cive* ('On the Citizen'), in 1642. But his focus on politics was not exclusive, and around this time he also prepared, at the instigation of his friend, the friar Marin Mersenne, a set of objections to Descartes' *Meditations on First Philosophy*, which were published in 1641 together with the author's replies, as well as a lengthy unpublished critique of the philosopher Thomas White (now known as the *Anti-White*). Hobbes's main project, however, was to work on *De Corpore* ('On Body'), which he saw as the first part of a trilogy that would include *De Homine* ('On Man') as well as the already published *De Cive*. *De Corpore* and *De Homine* were eventually to appear in the 1650s.

Fighting between the forces of the King and the Parliament began in 1642, and as the tide of the war turned against the Royalists, Paris became increasingly populated with exiles, including the sixteen-year-old Prince of Wales, who arrived in 1646, and to whom Hobbes was engaged to teach mathematics. In 1647 Hobbes experienced a period of serious illness, and the following year his old friend Mersenne died and the Prince left Paris. It was around this time, or afterwards, that Hobbes turned his attention to the composition of *Leviathan*. Just when he began work on the book is unclear. In his much later verse autobiography, Hobbes insinuated that its origins lay in 1646. But he may not have started before the second half of 1649, as there is a letter to Samuel Sorbière in June of that year saying that he was still working on *De Corpore* then.[9] The most solid contemporary evidence we have is a remark in a letter of May 1650 from Robert Payne to Gilbert Sheldon, reporting that Hobbes had already written thirty-seven chapters of 'Politiques, in English', out of an anticipated fifty.[10]

We don't know exactly when *Leviathan* was written, and there is also disagreement over why it was written. The two problems intersect. Those who think that Hobbes, perhaps drawn back into Royalist circles through his connection to the Prince of Wales, sought to present another uncompromisingly monarchical statement of his political theory are more likely to favour an earlier date for his turn to its composition. But when Edward Hyde (later the 1st Earl of Clarendon) asked Hobbes why he was publishing *Leviathan*, he replied, 'The truth is, I have a mind to go home.'[11] Those who think that Hobbes in writing *Leviathan* sought an accommodation with the new regime following the execution of the King on 30 January 1649 are more likely to think that he began sustained work on the project only later – in which case, in light of the finished book's sheer length and the fact that it appeared in print in 1651, it must have been composed at a very brisk rate indeed.

III

Leviathan is best known to this day for its account in the thirteenth chapter of what has come to be called the 'state of nature' – though Hobbes's own formulation was the 'naturall condition of Mankind' (p. 100). Most particularly, it is famous for just one phrase, the remark that in such a condition human life would be 'nasty, brutish, and short' (p. 103). But Hobbes himself does not seem to have been as struck by the phrase as those who have come after him. When he subsequently came to translate *Leviathan* into Latin there was no attempt to preserve the triad; 'nasty' dropped out, to become 'bruta & brevis'.

What is a state of nature? It's tempting to think of it as the way human beings lived 'in the beginning', and certainly before the development of political institutions, but Hobbes pushes back against this with his remark that 'I believe it was never generally so, over all the world', and that 'there are many places, where they live so now'. In *Leviathan* he gave the example of 'the savage people in many places of *America*' (p. 104) – and, more cryptically, in correspondence he appears to have used the example of 'soldiers who serve in different places and masons who work under different architects'.[12] Certainly, however, the nightmare of the state of nature is a condition into which Hobbes thinks it possible to fall, should political institutions fail. Analytically, we can say that according to Hobbes two individuals are in a state of nature with respect to one another if and only if they lack a common authority standing over them.

Hobbes also asserts that the state of nature is a state of war – not that it has a tendency to become one, but that that's what it is. How does his argument proceed? It begins with a claim about human equality. Because Hobbes thinks we're all roughly the equals of one another, there's an equality of vulnerability about our lives in the condition of nature. The 'weakest has strength enough to kill the strongest,' he writes, 'either by secret machination, or by confederacy with others, that are in the same danger with himselfe' (p. 100). The facts of human equality also mean that we are liable to come into conflict with one another. An 'equality of ability' gives rise to an 'equality of hope in the attaining of our Ends' (p. 101). No one has a reason to defer to anybody else. And there are three distinct routes by which individuals end up in conflict: *competition*, when 'two men desire the same thing' (p. 101) which they cannot both have; *diffidence*, when someone who is only concerned for their own safety attacks another, just in case that person should subsequently attack them, and *glory*, when violence results from someone's concern that they are not valued as highly by another as they think that they ought to be. And a world in which violence may result from these separate mechanisms is, Hobbes argues, a 'condition which is called Warre; and such a warre, as is of every man, against every man' (p. 102). There doesn't have to be constant fighting. Indeed, Hobbes analogizes the condition of war to the drizzly English weather:

> For as the nature of Foule weather, lyeth not in a showre or two of rain; but in an inclination thereto of many dayes together: So the nature of War, consisteth not in actuall fighting; but in the known disposition thereto, during all the time there is no assurance to the contrary. (pp. 102–3)

In the following chapter, Hobbes introduces a new language, that of the 'Right of Nature' and the 'Laws of Nature'. The former – following the Dutch philosopher Hugo Grotius – is the idea that we have a right to do what we judge to be necessary for our self-preservation. The latter are principles discoverable by reflection which, if followed, will conduce to self-preservation. The 'Fundamentall' law of nature is *'to seek Peace, and follow it'* – but if we judge that peace is unavailable, then we are entitled to *'seek, and use, all helps, and advantages of Warre'* (p. 106) as we strive to keep ourselves alive. So the troubling predicament of the state of nature isn't generated by the idea that our rights are being violated, but rather by the thought that we are all acting in accordance with our natural right. If everyone is making their own judgements about when they have to act violently in order to secure themselves, that makes the situation much more dangerous for everybody. And so the first law of nature and the right of nature combine as the basis for the derivation of Hobbes's second law of nature, which is that the interests of peace require us to *'lay down'* (p. 106) our natural right, if it can be done in a coordinated way with others, and such that each can enjoy the same liberty as everybody else. And from there Hobbes proceeds to spin out a whole series of other laws of nature – there are nineteen in total – such as the third,

'*That men performe their Covenants made*' (p. 117); or the fifth, '*That every man strive to accommodate himself to the rest*' (p. 124); or the fifteenth, '*That all men that mediate Peace, be allowed safe Conduct*' (p. 127).

Of particular interest is the ninth law of nature, against pride. Hobbes reasserts the natural equality with which he began chapter thirteen, and observes that 'The inequallity that now is, has bin introduced by the Lawes civill'. He then makes a joke about Aristotle, who had mistakenly thought that some people were by nature 'more worthy to Command, meaning the wiser sort (such as he thought himselfe to be for his Philosophy;) others to Serve, (meaning those that had strong bodies, but were not Philosophers as he)' (p. 125). This provides a good moment to remind ourselves of the extent to which Hobbes's theory rejects some of the fundamentals of Aristotelian political thought, which had argued for a *summum bonum*, or highest good, at which all aim, or ought to aim, and which we might actually attain. According to Hobbes, human beings are instead restless machines, striving for 'Power after power' whose desires 'ceaseth onely in Death' (p. 80). Aristotle had argued that human beings were not naturally equal – that free adult men were superior in their capacity to reason than women, children and slaves – and also that a human being was not just a gregarious but also a 'political animal' (*zoon politikon*). This latter claim Hobbes directly contradicted with his insistence that life in the state of nature was 'solitary' (as well as 'poore, nasty, brutish, and short'). That may in fact be rhetorical overstatement, partly in light of the obvious consideration that young children need parenting, but also insofar as Hobbes doesn't think that humans are entirely asocial: if we were, it would be hard to explain why we get pleasure out of the perception that we are superior to others, as Hobbes thinks we do. But this is a thin kind of natural sociability, and hardly one that provides the foundation for a large and lasting political society – not least because the concern with glorying over others is one of the causes of conflict mentioned above. Hence, the laws of nature teach that we must disclaim the quest for glory and regard one another instead as being our equals. 'If Nature therefore have made men equall, that equalitie is to be acknowledged', Hobbes writes, before slipping in the intriguing twist that even 'if Nature have made men unequall; yet because men that think themselves equall, will not enter into conditions of Peace, but upon Equall termes, such equalitie must be admitted'. And he concludes, 'The breach of this Precept is *Pride*' (p. 126).

The laws of nature, Hobbes goes on to explain, aren't really laws, strictly speaking, because there aren't any sanctions for breaking them – though he does think that when rulers systematically violate the laws of nature they risk rousing their subjects to rebellion, or being overthrown, or conquered. So although they bind us in conscience (or, as he says, *in foro interno*) – we always ought to want to live in a world in which all the laws of nature are followed by everybody – they can't actually be expected to regulate our behaviour (*in foro externo*) in the absence of effective sanctions, since to keep our promises when no one around us is doing so is simply to make ourselves 'a prey to others' (p. 129). So we need to turn from nature to artifice, in order to find a way out of the predicament of the natural condition of mankind, and the artificial mechanism that Hobbes theorizes is a covenant – or, as it is called in later literature, a social contract.

The aim is to get ourselves in a situation in which principles like the laws of nature might reliably govern our behaviour, so we can live peacefully with our fellows. For that to happen, we need to live under laws that carry a sanction if we disobey them. And since much of the violence in the state of nature is provoked by individuals' decisions about what's needed for their self-preservation, we need – as far as possible – to take those judgements out of the hands of the individuals themselves. Hobbes's idea, then, is that a group of individuals in the state of nature might covenant together, one with another, to submit to the authority of a third party. In particular, it's that third party – who is called the Sovereign – who makes the necessary judgements about what threats are posed to the people whom we can now call the subjects. The heart of the argument is presented in chapter seventeen:

> This is more than Consent, or Concord; it is a reall Unitie of them all, in one and the same Person, made by Covenant of every man with every man, in such manner, as if every man should say to every man, *I Authorise and give up my Right of Governing my selfe, to this Man, or to this Assembly of men, on this condition, that thou give up thy Right to him, and Authorise all his Actions in like manner*. This done, the Multitude so united in one Person, is called a COMMON-WEALTH, in latine CIVITAS. This is the Generation of that great LEVIATHAN, or rather (to speake more reverently) of that *Mortall God*, to which wee owe under the *Immortall God*, our peace and defence. For by this Authoritie, given him by every particular man in the Common-Wealth, he hath the use of so much Power and Strength conferred on him, that by terror thereof, he is inabled to forme the wills of them all, to Peace at home, and mutuall ayd against their enemies abroad. (p. 140)

In agreeing to submit to authority, we take ourselves out of the state of nature, making possible a life of peace and prosperity, or, as Hobbes calls it elsewhere, 'commodious living' (p. 105).

At this point it is worth emphasizing three things about Hobbes's argument. First, to reiterate, the Sovereign is not a party to the covenant. There is a sense in which there's a fundamental exchange at the heart of Hobbes's political theory, that of obedience for protection (p. 597). But the obligations that arise out of the covenant are obligations that the covenanting parties owe to one another, and the Sovereign stands apart from that network of obligation. The relationship that the subjects have to the Sovereign is one of submission, rather than any reciprocal or contractual obligation. Second, although Hobbes himself was a partisan of monarchy, his Sovereign does not have to be an individual, but might just as well be a group of people, which would make the regime an aristocracy; or a popular assembly, which would make the regime a democracy (p. 151). (Jean-Jacques Rousseau would argue in the eighteenth century that the mistake Hobbes made was to think that sovereignty could be transferred to an external third party; from his point of view, Hobbesian sovereignty had to be the republican sovereignty of a popular assembly.) Third, the story Hobbes tells about the covenant turns out not to be the only story about how one might end up the subject of a Sovereign. In addition to 'Common-wealth by Institution' there is also 'Common-wealth by Acquisition', which is 'where the Soveraign Power is acquired by Force' (p. 162), after someone gives in to threats of violence from another. The former is arguably more interesting from the point of view of abstract political theory, as it illuminates how sovereignty might be established through the reciprocal action of equals in a state of nature. Some interpreters, however, have focused on the latter's alternative story of the origin of government, one founded in submission to conquest rather than covenant. And the sovereignty that results, Hobbes insists, is the same on both accounts.

Whether instituted or acquired, then, we now have subjects and their Sovereigns. The Sovereign is the 'Soveraign Representative', whom the subjects have authorized, and this means that the subjects themselves are, properly speaking, the authors of the actions of the representative, which in turn means that 'nothing the Soveraign Representative can doe to a Subject, on what pretence soever, can properly be called Injustice, or Injury' (p. 174). Although modern politics is by no means fully Hobbesian, we nevertheless use a similar language of representation – ours is a 'representative democracy', we say – and it is interesting to consider our own institutions in the light of Hobbes's argument. But that argument also packed a particular polemical punch in Hobbes's own time. There were influential members of the House of Commons in 1640 who, in their quarrel with the King, argued that it was the Commons that represented the people – that *looked like* the people – and that gave it a certain authority that the Crown and the Lords could not exercise on their own. But Hobbes's reply was that it was the monarch, not the Commons, that was the true representative of the people. It didn't matter that he wasn't elected, or that he didn't look much like his subjects. The King was the Sovereign representative, and the Parliament – Lords and Commons alike – was at best an advisory body which he invited to assist him in the work of governing his kingdom.

The authority of the Sovereign, on Hobbes's account, is far-reaching, since the Sovereign – if it chooses to be – is the judge of anything that might fall into dispute. In particular, the Sovereign is the ultimate authority over the meanings of the words that we use. (In his earlier presentation of his political theory, *The Elements of Law*, Hobbes had written about how the quarrels of the state of nature might arise from disagreements about 'the names and appellations of things . . . as for example: of what is to be called right, what good, what virtue, what much, what little, what *meum* and *tuum* [mine and thine], what a pound, what a quart, &c. For in these things private judgments may differ, and beget controversy'.[13]) Sovereign authority, furthermore, must be concentrated at a single point, for 'a Kingdome divided in it selfe' through some kind of constitutional division of sovereignty 'cannot stand' (p. 148); any ambiguity about where political authority ultimately resides risks a slide down a slippery slope into civil war and a return to the state of nature.

Even sovereignty, however, has its limit. Submission to a Sovereign means that we allow its judgement to take the place of our own. But we can never fully relinquish our right of nature to the Sovereign. As Hobbes explains, the transfer of right 'is a voluntary act: and of the voluntary acts of every man, the object is some *Good to himselfe*'. One cannot therefore give up 'the right of resisting them, that assault him by force, to take away his life; because he cannot be understood to ayme thereby, at any Good to himselfe' (p. 108). Although the Sovereign doesn't do me any injustice when it seeks to have me killed, I will nevertheless resist to the best of my ability when it becomes clear that this is what it is aiming to achieve. That's why 'they lead Criminals to Execution, and Prison, with armed men, notwithstanding that such Criminals have consented to the Law, by which they are condemned' (pp. 114–15). Some commentators have argued that, read at only a slight angle, we can in fact spin quite an extensive right of resistance out of Hobbes's argument, and make it look a lot more like an argument more usually associated with Hobbes's younger contemporary, the philosopher John Locke. But as the example itself suggests, Hobbes's thought is that the moment at which we reach the outer limit of sovereignty is also the moment at which resistance is futile. There are other moments in *Leviathan*, too, where Hobbes hints at the limits of the Sovereign's authority. The Sovereign can demand that I supply it with a soldier, but it does not have to be me, if I can pay someone to take my place (p. 178). And the Sovereign's authority may run out on the field of battle itself, where 'every one may use his own reason in time of danger, to save his own life, either by flight, or by submission to the enemy, as hee shall think best' (p. 167).

For a number of years, commentators have been struck by the parallels between Hobbes's state of nature and the so-called 'prisoner's dilemma', a popular piece of 'game theory'. Imagine that the police have two suspects in custody, in separate cells, who can each either remain silent or implicate the other in a crime they have jointly committed. Each is best off if they betray their comrade, who remains silent. In that circumstance, they will be released immediately, whilst their partner will receive a very long prison sentence. If both remain silent, they will both receive a short prison sentence. And if each betrays the other, they will both receive a long prison sentence. The theory of rational choice dictates that in these circumstances, both suspects (if they are above all concerned to minimize their time in prison) will betray their partner, even though the outcome – the long prison sentence – is worse for both of them than what would have happened had they both remained silent. To see why, consider the matter from the point of view of the first suspect: if her partner remains silent, she gets the best outcome available to her by betraying him; and if he betrays her, she is still better off betraying him than if she remains silent. And since the logic of the game is symmetrical, we can be confident that each will betray the other. Is the Hobbesian state of nature like this, where the logic of the situation drives each 'player' to violence, resulting in a nightmare for everybody, when they all would have been better off had they managed to restrain themselves?

Perhaps it is. But it is worth being cautious. Richard Tuck has pushed back against this approach to interpreting Hobbes by reminding us that Hobbes's concern was not so much with how we do behave but with how we have a right to behave, and that this normative concern tends to fall out of the picture when we employ an analytical framework that is only really comfortable operating on the terrain of personal interests.[14] More generally, one of the problems with the push to reinterpret Hobbes through the lens of game theory is that we may end up thinking that what's valuable in Hobbes is the extent to which he seems to anticipate developments in twentieth-century social theory, which would not only be to render *Leviathan* somewhat flat and relatively uninteresting, but also to risk losing sight of those parts of his argument that can't be assimilated so easily to a rational-choice perspective. We become a bit too interested, perhaps, in the 'competition' and 'diffidence' stories, which can be more easily modelled in game-theoretic terms than can 'glory'. As Philip Pettit has recently written, 'Those who cherish the utterly implausible idea that our rational self-interest will generally block any otherwise unproductive concern with position and status sometimes describe themselves as Hobbesians. Their self-description couldn't be further off the mark. Hobbes would have regarded their psychology as shallow, and the policies it suggests as silly and dangerous.'[15]

The rational actors of conventional game theory aim to maximize their pay-offs, and if they always want more than they have got, they can sound a lot like Hobbes's individuals, always striving for 'Power after power'. But Hobbesian individuals are especially concerned with where they stand in relation to those around them: I am more powerful than you, you are richer than me. This is the glory story, and it's cashed out in the language of honour, pride and vainglory, to which Hobbes repeatedly returns. In the second recension of his political theory, *De Cive*, glory is of decisive importance: 'Every pleasure of the mind is either glory (or a good opinion of oneself), or ultimately relates to glory.'[16] There is no claim quite as sweeping as this in the later work, but it would be misleading to shunt it into the margins; Gabriella Slomp has argued, for example, that 'the significance of glory in *Leviathan* cannot be overemphasised'.[17]

Keeping our eye on glory, furthermore, allows us to do something quite striking, which is to turn Hobbes into something of a recognition theorist, alert to the thoroughgoing extent to which our own sense of self is bound up with our beliefs about how we appear in the eyes of others, and the affirmation that we perceive ourselves to receive from them. The philosopher G.W. F.

Hegel usually dominates discussion of the moral psychology of 'recognition', the key text being his 1807 work
The Phenomenology of Spirit, with its famous passage
on the so-called 'master–slave dialectic'. More recently,
there's been some scholarly interest in exploring the
variety of self-love that Jean-Jacques Rousseau called
amour-propre in similar terms, most notably from
Frederick Neuhouser.[18] But in a significant respect it is
Hobbes who stands at the head of a long line of writers – Rousseau and Hegel, but also Bernard Mandeville
and Immanuel Kant – in supplementing a crude model
of self-seeking individualism with an awareness of
just how powerful is our desire to have standing in
the eyes of others, and the strikingly reflexive psychology of the constant self-policing of our actions with
an eye on the responses of others to which this gives
rise.

One of the classic objections to Hobbes's argument
takes aim at the importance he ascribed to glory. In the
middle of the eighteenth century, Montesquieu argued
that ideas of empire and domination were so complex
that they could not be among the most elementary human
ambitions.[19] Rousseau, who was in some ways Montesquieu's disciple, wrote that 'the Philosophers' had gone
back to find their natural men, but not far enough, and
that the men thus depicted were not so much 'natural'
men, but men who were already thoroughly socialized –
seventeenth-century Englishmen, perhaps.[20] But it may
very well be that Hobbes had anticipated just that kind of
objection, and had already moved to meet it. Philip Pettit
has argued persuasively that Hobbes's state of nature is
not offered at all as an account of pre-social humankind,
but as an account of human beings at some moment in
their history once they have already acquired language,
which is an accidental, contingent discovery that they
have made. In Pettit's account, it's when humans started
to communicate with one another that Hobbes believed
their relations became conflictual; their passions began

to be inflamed, giving rise to the state of war. It may well be that the account of human development presented in Rousseau's *Discourse on the Origin of Inequality* – in which the acquisition of language is also the stage that takes us from peaceable, solitary, orang-utan-like forest living to something much more troublesome – is far closer to Hobbes's own view of the matter than is generally supposed.[21]

When Hobbes offers an explanation of his book's title, at the end of chapter twenty-eight, ideas about pride, comparison and pre-eminence take centre stage, along with the eponymous biblical sea-monster itself:

> Hitherto I have set forth the nature of Man, (whose Pride and other Passions have compelled him to submit him-selfe to Government;) together with the great power of his Governour, whom I compared to *Leviathan*, taking that comparison out of the two last verses of the one and fortieth of *Job*; where God having set forth the great power of *Leviathan*, calleth him King of the Proud. *There is nothing*, saith he, *on earth, to be compared with him. He is made so as not to be afraid. Hee seeth every high thing below him; and is King of all the children of pride.* (p. 263)

The first part of the quotation from Job also appears as part of *Leviathan*'s famous frontispiece (which is repro-duced at the head of this edition): *non est potestas super terram quae comparetur ei.*

In the event, then, that the proud can be induced to submit to civil government – and they may have to be induced rather forcibly, since those who suffer from the delusions of vainglory overestimate their own powers and abilities, and so may be less inclined to seek the security of mutual covenanting for mutual protection – so the Sovereign extinguishes their pride by dominating them. They are made so fearful of the Sovereign's sword when they contemplate going against its will, and so conscious of their inferiority in power and might to the Sovereign, that they cannot any longer delude themselves into thinking that they are its equal or superior. The disparity between individual subject and Sovereign is too vast for that, and the result is that the proud are chastened and rendered – at last – governable. According to the old Christian hymn the Magnificat, it is God's role to humble the proud, but here it is the Leviathan, the mortal god, that performs this vital task.

Many people dislike Hobbes's theory, because of the centrality it ascribes to fear. It may seem awful to think that fear plays such a powerful role in fleshing out an account of political obligation. It is awful, indeed, in the old sense of that word: the Leviathan inspires awe. Many later writers – including contractarian thinkers like Locke and his successors – insist that there must be a normative distinction between promises we make uncoerced and promises we make when we are in fear of our lives. The Hobbesian thought is that promises are always made for fear of the consequences of not making them, and that fearing imminent death is just a particularly vivid instance of the much more general phenomenon. But we can push the objection to Hobbes a little further than by simply expressing a dislike of a politics of fear. Hobbes's Sovereign can dictate the content of our ideas of justice, determine the meanings of the words we use, tell us which religions we will be permitted to practise, which books can be taught in the universities, what we cannot say in public. To twentieth- and twenty-first-century eyes, Hobbes appears to be defending an Orwellian vision of the all-powerful state, which strikes many readers today as repugnant. So what might be said on behalf of this politics of fear? And why is Hobbes so keen to defend such an extensive zone of unchallengeable state authority?

Let's start with fear. According to Hobbes's mechanistic psychology, to desire something is literally to be drawn towards it, whereas to fear something is to shy

away from it; and on the whole we fare better on the
self-preservation front when we shy away from things.
So we fear the Leviathan, and it is our shared fear of
the Leviathan's power which keeps us in line and makes
human society tolerable, peaceable, governable. The passions of love, by contrast, can be very dangerous indeed.
When people are in love, they do foolish things, dangerous both to themselves and to the people around them.
(From this point of view it was typical that in the love
poetry Hobbes wrote in old age, he rhymed the words
'cupid' and 'stupid'.) Romance is a problem for Hobbes,
for it inflames the imagination; so too is the popular
seventeenth-century habit of reading romantic literature:
Victoria Kahn has explored Hobbes's treatment of *Don
Quixote* as a book that encourages the weak-minded
to indulge in fantasies of vainglory.[22] Classical literature
was especially dangerous, because of its tendency to grip
the moral imaginations of the young, who come to think
falsely that there is a distinction between the legitimate
king and an illegitimate tyrant, for example, and that
it is permissible or even laudable to kill the latter. A tyrant, Hobbes tells is, is merely a monarch 'misliked' (p.
151). When we love a charismatic leader, we follow and
are willing to die for them. When we love our God and
think that he can only be worshipped properly in one
way, we are willing not only to risk our own lives but to
kill other people. These are troubling outcomes for
Hobbes. In the well-ordered Hobbesian state, the affec-
tionate passions will no longer be able to disrupt the life of
the wider society. They will be largely confined to private
life, where they are less likely to do serious harm. Indeed,
Richard Tuck has made the case that Hobbesian citizens
will not be especially passionate creatures at all – since
the passions, on Hobbes's view, arise in various ways out
of our concern for self-preservation, and if that concern
has been satisfactorily addressed through the institution
of sovereignty, then our emotional responses will not be
what they once were.[23]

Whereas liberals today generally tend to defend civil society against the predations of the state, Hobbes's judgement ran in the other direction. Early modern society was full of corporate bodies of one kind or another, many of which descended from mediaeval times, which sought to advance the interests of their members at the expense of others, and claimed their own rights and privileges, often in the face of the Crown. Hobbes was intensely concerned that the power of the state should be able to chasten such groups. The aristocrats, for example, had to learn that the honour over which they obsessed was simply a reflection of the honour of the Sovereign, which it permitted them to enjoy. They did not have any independent site of authority from which they might challenge a monarchical Sovereign. No amount of custom and practice, however far it stretched back, could infringe upon the prerogatives of sovereignty. There were companies that claimed monopolies over certain aspects of economic life, guilds which regulated the practice of various trades, cities with their charters that gave them exemptions from paying particular taxes. In all these cases, Hobbes's point is the same: that such privileges are granted by the authority of the Sovereign, and can be just as easily revoked on the same authority.

A part of Hobbes's assault on corporate life was directed against the idea that professional expertise could legitimate authority. His insistence that law was the declared will of the Sovereign was, among other things, directed against the English lawyers who claimed an authority for the common law, of which they were the most knowledgeable and through which they would inevitably have the greatest influence. He distrusted the universities, and argued that the scholastic Aristotelian philosophy they propounded was full of meaningless jargon, all of which filled students' heads with confusion, and encouraged them to defer to the authority of the dons. In *Leviathan*, he remarks of the universities that 'since the Authority of Aristotle is onely current there, that study is not properly Philosophy, (the nature whereof dependeth not on Authors,) but Aristotelity' (p. 560). Hobbes thought that what was taught at Oxford and Cambridge was one of the causes of the English Civil War; and *Leviathan* ends with a recommendation that it become a university textbook (p. 597). In later life, Hobbes was acutely suspicious of what went on at the Royal Society, where scientific experiments were conducted behind closed doors.

Hobbes generally viewed these corporate bodies as if they were conspiracies directed against the interests of the broader society for the benefit of well-placed elites, and he compares them to 'wormes in the entrayles of a naturall man' (p. 274). And if he was especially concerned by the activities of those who were able to exploit their position to shape the ways in which subjects thought about matters of the highest importance, his polemic was particularly directed against the churches. Like other corporate bodies in England, Hobbes believed that the Church had had too much power for a very long time. He thought it had been a critical error of William the Conqueror, for example, 'when he took an Oath, not to infringe the liberty of the Church' (p. 265). In the age of the Reformation, the dangers posed by religion were multiplied. Germany had been racked by war in the first half of the sixteenth century; the French wars of religion filled much of its second half; both the long conflict between the Dutch rebels and the Spanish monarchy and the Thirty Years War in central Europe had an inescapably religious dimension – as did the English Civil War and the related conflicts in Scotland and Ireland, even if these were never simply reducible to a conflict between episcopacy and Presbyterianism, or between Protestants and Catholics.

Even those who accepted the truth of Christianity – as Hobbes was willing to do in *Leviathan*, though there were many who suspected him of atheism – had to answer the question as to how they recognized what counted as authoritative religion. The Catholic hierarchy asked its flock to place its trust in the authority of the Roman Catholic Church and its institutions, headed by the Pope, to interpret the meaning of Scripture. But by what signs can we tell the difference between a Pope and an antipope? Some Protestants might deny the authority of such an ecclesiastical hierarchy to do that, and insist on the importance of the encounter between the individual Christian and the biblical text. But the sceptical question just recurs: how do we know that the vernacular translation is accurate? Or what the original text says, when there are competing manuscript versions? Or that the Greek or Hebrew texts have been reliably transmitted from antiquity? Discussion of the problems of Scripture and religion filled the second half of *Leviathan*, and, for Hobbes, the only solution to these various dilemmas was – as usual – to concentrate authority in the Sovereign: it would adjudicate theological disputes, if it judged it to be necessary to do so, just as much as it would adjudicate such civil disputes as might arise.

From Hobbes's perspective, the churches were not just one set of troublesome corporate bodies amongst others. They claimed an allegiance on Christian souls that always threatened to pose a challenge to the authority of the state. Ecclesiastics were very good indeed at manipulating the passions of love and fear in order to get people to do what they wanted them to be doing. One reason why they were quite so effective is that they were able to persuade people to fear divine punishment after death. So one significant part of Hobbes's project was an attempt to redirect popular fear, away from the fear of invisible spirits, and towards the fear of the Sovereign's visible sword. In chapter thirty-eight of *Leviathan*, he hammers away at arguments for the existence of Hell, showing that various passages of Scripture cannot bear the traditional weight that has been placed on them, and that references to hell-fire should be understood not literally but metaphorically. The churches placed great emphasis on their martyrs, and so Hobbes worked to undermine confidence in these. Etymologically, 'martyr' means 'witness', and, for Hobbes, those who actually witnessed the risen Christ were the authentic martyrs, 'whereas they which were not so, can Witnesse no more, but that their antecessors said it, and are therefore but Witnesses of other mens testimony' (p. 416).

Hobbes clearly argued that the Sovereign was entitled to enforce uniformity of religious observance, and to have a state church whose dogmas – beyond the bare claim that Jesus is the Christ – were ultimately to be determined by political authority. But it remains less clear that that was his preferred religious option, and the closing pages of *Leviathan* contain an interesting argument on behalf of religious freedom, reminding us that Hobbes was far more hostile towards ecclesiastical power than he was towards religion itself. In a remarkable passage towards the end of chapter forty-seven, he describes the recent unravelling of the religious settlement in England, where first the 'Power of the Popes was dissolved totally' under the Tudors (p. 581); more recently, in 1646, the Presbyterians 'obtained the putting down of Episcopacy'; and 'almost at the same time, the Power was taken also from the Presbyterians' – i.e., the authority of church congregations to determine doctrine. This ushered in a situation much like that of the early, or 'Primitive', Christians, who were able 'to follow Paul, or Cephas, or Apollos, every man as he liketh best'. As long as this did not give rise to 'contention' (in this context, theological quarrels) or to 'measuring the Doctrine of Christ, by our affection to the Person of his Minister', Hobbes suggested that this state of affairs 'is perhaps the best', with Christians listening to the preachers they preferred and no significant church structures existing whatsoever. He gave two reasons for his preference: 'First, because there ought to be no Power over the Consciences of men, but of the Word it selfe, working Faith in every one'; and second,

> because it is unreasonable in them, who teach there is
> such danger in every little Errour, to require of a man
> endued with Reason of his own, to follow the Reason
> of any other man, or of the most voices of many other
> men; Which is little better, then to venture his Salvation
> at crosse and pile (pp. 581–2)

– or, as we would say, on the toss of a coin. A magnificent
burst of sarcasm directed against the apologists for ecclesiastical power concludes the passage, and *Leviathan*'s final
chapter closes with an extended comparison between the
Papacy and the Kingdom of the Fairies (pp. 582–4).

IV

In the Review and Conclusion, Hobbes underscores
the immediate political teaching of his book: the Parliamentarians have conquered, and the new regime in
England is to be obeyed. The 'point of time, wherein
a man becomes subject of a Conquerour, is that point,
wherein having liberty to submit to him, he consenteth,
either by expresse words, or by other sufficient sign, to
be his Subject' (p. 589), and that point arrives when the
old order is no longer able to offer protection to those
who were once its subjects. That point of time was also
fast approaching for Hobbes. His publisher Andrew
Crooke entered *Leviathan* in the Stationers' Register in
January 1651, the book was published in the spring, a
fair copy of the manuscript was presented to the Prince
of Wales in Paris in the autumn, Hobbes's relations with
the exiled Court deteriorated rapidly, and in the Winter
of 1651–2 he left Paris and returned to England, where
he was to live for the rest of his very long life. He died
aged ninety-one, in 1679.

NOTES

1. John Aubrey, 'Thomas Hobbes' in *Brief Lives*, Oliver Lawson Dick, ed., with an introduction by Ruth Scurr (London: Penguin, 2016), p. 147. Hobbes's remark comes from the verse autobiography that he wrote in 1672.

2. *Brief Lives*, p. 148.

3. *Ibid*.

4. *Ibid*., p. 149.

5. Thomas Hobbes, *Three Discourses: A Critical Modern Edition of Newly Identified Work of the Young Hobbes*, Noel B. Reynolds and Arlene W. Saxonhouse, eds. (Chicago: University of Chicago Press, 1995).

6. Noel Malcolm, *Reason of State, Propaganda, and the Thirty Years' War: An Unknown Translation by Thomas Hobbes* (Oxford: Oxford University Press, 2007).

7. See Kinch Hoekstra, 'Hobbes's Thucydides' in A. P. Martinich and Kinch Hoekstra, eds., *The Oxford Handbook of Hobbes* (Oxford: Oxford University Press, 2016).

8. *Brief Lives*, p. 150.

9. Noel Malcolm, ed., *The Correspondence of Thomas Hobbes* (Oxford: Clarendon Press, 1994), Letter #61, vol. 1, pp. 176–7.

10. British Library, Harleian MSS, 6942, no. 128.

11. Edward Hyde, *A Brief View and Survey of the Dangerous and Pernicious Errors to Church and State in Mr. Hobbes's Book, entitled Leviathan* (Oxford, 1676), p. 8.

12. *Correspondence*, Letter #110 (François Peleau to Hobbes), vol. 1, pp. 422–5.

13. Thomas Hobbes, *The Elements of Law, Natural and Politic*, J. C. A. Gaskin, ed. (Oxford: Oxford University Press, 1999), p. 180.

14. Richard Tuck, *Hobbes: A Very Short Introduction* (Oxford: Oxford University Press, 2002), pp. 120–3.

15. Philip Pettit, *Made with Words: Hobbes on Language, Mind, and Politics* (Princeton: Princeton University Press, 2008), p. 3.

16. Hobbes, *On the Citizen*, Richard Tuck and Michael Silverthorne, eds. (Cambridge: Cambridge University Press, 1998), p. 23.

17. Gabriella Slomp, 'Hobbes on Glory and Civil Strife' in

Patricia Springborg, ed., *The Cambridge Companion to Hobbes's Leviathan* (Cambridge: Cambridge University Press, 2007), p. 181.

18. See, especially, Frederick Neuhouser, *Rousseau's Theodicy of Self-Love: Evil, Rationality, and the Drive for Recognition* (Oxford: Oxford University Press, 2008).

19. Montesquieu, *The Spirit of the Laws*, Anne Cohler, Basia Miller and Harold Stone, eds. (Cambridge: Cambridge University Press, 1989), p. 6.

20. Jean-Jacques Rousseau, 'Discourse on the Origin and Foundations of Inequality among Men' in Rousseau, *The Discourses and Other Early Political Writings*, Victor Gourevitch, ed. (Cambridge: Cambridge University Press, 1997), p. 132.

21. Pettit, *Made with Words*, ch. 6, pp. 94–7 and ch. 7, esp. p. 98.

22. Victoria Kahn, *Wayward Contracts: the Crisis of Political Obligation in England, 1640–1674* (Princeton: Princeton University Press, 2004).

23. Richard Tuck, 'The Utopianism of *Leviathan*', in Tom Sorell and Luc Foisneau, eds., *Leviathan After 350 Years* (Oxford: Oxford University Press, 2004).

Further Reading

For Hobbes's biography, the classic treatment is by John Aubrey in his *Brief Lives*, Oliver Lawson Dick, ed. (Penguin, 2016). On the biographer himself, see Ruth Scurr's remarkable recent volume, *John Aubrey: My Own Life* (Chatto & Windus, 2015). The best recent short biography is by Noel Malcolm in the *Oxford Dictionary of National Biography*. A longer treatment is A. P. Martinich, *Hobbes: A Biography* (Cambridge University Press, 1999).

Handy collections of essays by various scholars include Patricia Springborg, ed., *The Cambridge Companion to Hobbes's Leviathan* (Cambridge University Press, 2007), A. P. Martinich and Kinch Hoekstra, eds., *The Oxford Handbook of Hobbes* (Oxford University Press, 2016), Tom Sorell, ed., *The Cambridge Companion to Hobbes* (Cambridge University Press, 1996) and Nancy J. Hirschmann and Joanne H. Wright, eds., *Feminist Interpretations of Thomas Hobbes* (Pennsylvania State University Press, 2012), together with two volumes produced to mark significant anniversaries: G. A. J. Rogers and Alan Ryan, eds., *Perspectives on Thomas Hobbes* (Oxford University Press, 1988) for Hobbes's 400th birthday, and Tom Sorell and Luc Foisneau, eds., *Leviathan After 350 Years* (Oxford University Press, 2004).

Excellent recent books on Hobbes include Noel Malcolm, *Aspects of Hobbes* (Oxford University Press, 2002), Philip Pettit, *Made With Words: Hobbes on*

Language, Mind, and Politics (Princeton University Press, 2008), Jeffrey Collins, *The Allegiance of Thomas Hobbes* (Oxford University Press, 2005), Gabriella Slomp, *Thomas Hobbes and the Political Philosophy of Glory* (New York: St Martin's Press, 2000), Jon Parkin, *Taming the Leviathan* (Cambridge University Press, 2007), and three books by Quentin Skinner, all published by Cambridge: *Reason and Rhetoric in the Philosophy of Hobbes* (1996), *Hobbes and Republican Liberty* (2008) and the papers collected in the third volume of his *Visions of Politics* (2002).

Books that are not narrowly focused on Hobbes but still contain much valuable scholarship include Richard Tuck, *Philosophy and Government, 1572–1651* (Cambridge University Press, 1993), Ross Harrison, *Hobbes, Locke, and Confusion's Masterpiece* (Cambridge University Press, 2003) and Victoria Kahn, *Wayward Contracts: the Crisis of Political Obligation in England, 1640–1674* (Princeton University Press, 2004). Some works from the 1980s that are still well worth reading are Richard Tuck, *Hobbes: A Very Short Introduction* (Oxford University Press, 2002; originally published as a Past Master in 1989), Steven Shapin and Simon Schaffer, *Leviathan and the Air-Pump: Hobbes, Boyle, and the Experimental Life* (Princeton University Press, 1985), Gregory S. Kavka, *Hobbesian Moral and Political Theory* (Princeton University Press, 1986) and Jean Hampton, *Hobbes and the Social Contract Tradition* (Cambridge University Press, 1986). Still older studies that repay attention include Leo Strauss, *The Political Philosophy of Hobbes: Its Basis and Its Genesis* (Oxford University Press, 1936) and Michael Oakeshott, *Hobbes on Civil Association* (Oxford University Press, 1975). Two forthcoming studies that promise to be well worth the wait are Arash Abizadeh, *Thomas Hobbes and the Two Dimensions of Normativity* (Cambridge University Press) and Kinch Hoekstra, *Thomas Hobbes and the Creation of Order* (Oxford University Press).

A useful reference work is A. P. Martinich, *A Hobbes Dictionary* (Blackwell, 1995). Essential for further serious work on *Leviathan* is Noel Malcolm's critical edition of both the English and the Latin texts in three volumes (Clarendon Press, 2012).

A Note on the New Edition

The roots of this Penguin edition of *Leviathan* now go back half a century. C. B. Macpherson's unannotated edition was published as a Pelican Classic in 1968, and was reissued as part of the Penguin English Library in 1981, before becoming a Penguin Classic in 1985. The text was based on a copy of the first edition of *Leviathan* in the library at the University of Toronto, where Macpherson worked. That 1651 edition is known as the 'Head', to distinguish it from two other seventeenth-century editions that are known as the 'Bear' and the 'Ornaments' editions, both of which present themselves as having also been printed by Andrew Crooke 'at the Green Dragon is St Paul's Church-yard' in 1651, but which were in fact published considerably later. ('Head', 'Bear' and 'Ornaments' describe the different printer's ornaments that appear on the title-page of these editions; the numbers in square brackets that appear throughout the text of this edition refer to the pagination of the 'Head'.)

Macpherson's edition has been invaluable for generations of readers, but it has in recent years been showing its age. The introduction still offers a well-informed, well-written, engaging and intelligent discussion of Hobbes's political theory, but it does read now as something of a period piece: Macpherson's idiosyncratic version of Marxism is somewhat out of fashion these days, with its concern to identify the various ways in which Hobbes is a distinctively 'bourgeois' thinker, and

to explore the question of why the bourgeoisie nevertheless rejected his argument.

The text of the new Penguin *Leviathan* is based
on Macpherson's edition, but with over 200 minor
alterations. What kind of changes have been made?
Transcription errors which have accidentally mod-
ernized some spellings have been corrected, some
punctuation marks have been adjusted, some capital
letters have been either added or removed, some ital-
ics either added or removed, and so on. But in general,
I have kept editorial interventions to a fairly minimal
level. I have inserted a closing parenthesis when this
seems to be missing, and corrected small errors in Hobbes's Greek diacritics. On the other hand, I've let his
biblical references stand even where these are inaccu-
rate; and where the right reference would be hard to
find, based on what Hobbes supplies – i.e., it is more
than a few verses out – I have inserted a note.

The notes perform a variety of functions. Among
other things, they briefly identify many of the historical
and mythical figures that Hobbes mentions in his text
on their first appearance, supply missing biblical references, provide some references to Aquinas to illuminate
some of the scholastic arguments to which Hobbes
refers, translate snippets of Latin that Hobbes himself does not, note some words whose meanings have
shifted quite a bit since Hobbes's time, or elucidate some
phrases or historical allusions that might otherwise be
obscure. When it comes to references to Roman and
Greek texts, I have supplied these in standard forms that
ought to make it easy to look them up on, for example, the online Perseus Digital Library (and I encourage
readers to do so). These notes do not aim to supply any
kind of detailed philosophical commentary on Hobbes's
argument, and there is obviously a great deal more that
might be said about the details of the text of *Leviathan*
that is left unsaid in what follows.

In preparing this text and these notes, I have benefited

in particular from consulting the apparatus of the critical edition of *Leviathan* edited by Karl Schuhmann and G. A. J. Rogers (Bristol: Thoemmes Continuum, 2003); the notes that J. C. A. Gaskin appended to his 1996 edition of *Leviathan*, which is part of the Oxford World's Classics series; and, especially, the extraordinary work of Noel Malcolm in his three-volume edition of *Leviathan* for the Clarendon edition of the works of Hobbes, to which all Hobbes scholars will be vastly indebted for a very long time to come.

My thanks to Teresa M. Bejan, Paul Sagar and Samuel Garrett Zeitlin for their invaluable assistance.

Non est potestas Super Terram quæ Comparetur ei. Iob. 41. 24

LEVIATHAN
Or
THE MATTER, FORME
and POWER of A COMMON-
WEALTH ECCLESIASTICALL
and CIVIL.

By THOMAS HOBBES
of MALMESBVRY.

London
Printed for Andrew Crooke
1651

LEVIATHAN,

OR

The Matter, Forme, & Power

OF A

COMMON-WEALTH

ECCLESIASTICALL

AND

CIVILL.

By THOMAS HOBBES *of* Malmesbury.

LONDON,

Printed for ANDREW CROOKE, at the Green Dragon
in St. *Pauls* Church-yard, 1651.

TO

MY MOST HONOR'D FRIEND

Mr *FRANCIS GODOLPHIN*

of *Godolphin*

Honor'd Sir,

Your most worthy Brother Mr *Sidney Godolphin*,[1]
when he lived, was pleas'd to think my studies something, and otherwise to oblige me, as you know, with
reall testimonies of his good opinion, great in themselves, and the greater for the worthinesse of his person.
For there is not any vertue that disposeth a man, either
to the service of God, or to the service of his Country, to
Civill Society,[2] or private Friendship, that did not manifestly appear in his conversation, not as acquired by
necessity, or affected upon occasion, but inhærent, and
shining in a generous constitution of his nature. Therefore in honour and gratitude to him, and with devotion
to your selfe, I humbly Dedicate unto you this my discourse of Common-wealth. I know not how the world
will receive it, nor how it may reflect on those that shall
seem to favour it. For in a way beset with those that contend, on one side for too great Liberty, and on the other
side for too much Authority, 'tis hard to passe between
the points of both unwounded. But yet, me thinks, the
endeavour to advance the Civill Power, should not be by
the Civill Power condemned; nor private men, by rep-
rehending it, declare they think that Power too great.
Besides, I speak not of the men, but (in the Abstract) of
the Seat of Power, (like to those simple and unpartiall
creatures in the Roman Capitol,[3] that with their noyse
defended those within it, not because they were they,
but there,) offending none, I think, but those without,

or such within (if there be any such) as favour them.
That which perhaps may most offend, are certain Texts
of Holy Scripture, alledged by me to other purpose than
ordinarily they use to be by others. But I have done it
with due submission,[4] and also (in order to my Subject)
necessarily; for they are the Outworks of the Enemy,
from whence they impugne the Civill Power. If notwithstanding this, you find my labour generally decryed,
you may be pleased to excuse your selfe, and say I am
a man that love my own opinions, and think all true
I say, that I honoured your Brother, and honour you,
and have presum'd on that, to assume the Title (without
your knowledge) of being, as I am,

SIR,

Paris, *April* 15/25 1651.   Your most humble, and
                                      most obedient servant,
                                      THO. HOBBES

THE INTRODUCTION

Nature (the Art whereby God hath made and governes the World) is by the *Art* of man, as in many other things, so in this also imitated, that it can make an Artificial Animal. For seeing life is but a motion of Limbs, the begining whereof is in some principall part within; why may we not say, that all *Automata* (Engines that move themselves by springs and wheeles as doth a watch) have an artificiall life? For what is the *Heart*, but a *Spring*; and the *Nerves*, but so many *Strings*; and the *Joynts*, but so many *Wheeles*, giving motion to the whole Body, such as was intended by the Artificer? *Art* goes yet further, imitating that Rationall and most excellent worke of Nature, *Man*. For by Art is created that great LEVIATHAN called a COMMON-WEALTH, or STATE, (in latine CIVITAS) which is but an Artificiall Man; though of greater stature and strength than the Naturall, for whose protection and defence it was intended; and in which, the *Soveraignty* is an Artificiall *Soul*, as giving life and motion to the whole body; The *Magistrates*, and other *Officers* of Judicature and Execution, artificiall *Joynts*; *Reward* and *Punishment* (by which fastned to the seate of the Soveraignty, every joynt and member is moved to performe his duty) are the *Nerves*, that do the same in the Body Naturall; The *Wealth* and *Riches* of all the particular members, are the *Strength*; *Salus Populi* (the *peoples safety*) its *Businesse*; *Counsellors*, by whom all things needfull for it to know, are suggested unto it, are the *Memory*; *Equity* and *Lawes*, an artificiall

Reason and *Will*; *Concord*, *Health*; *Sedition*, *Sicknesse*; and *Civill war*, *Death*. Lastly, the *Pacts* and *Covenants*, by which the parts of this Body Politique were at first made, set together, and united, resemble that *Fiat*, or the *Let us make man*, pronounced by God in the Creation.

[2] To describe the Nature of this Artificiall man, I will consider

> First, the *Matter* thereof, and the *Artificer*; both which is *Man*.
> Secondly, *How*, and by what *Covenants* it is made; what are the *Rights* and just *Power* or *Authority* of a *Soveraigne*; and what it is that *preserveth* and *dissolveth* it.
> Thirdly, what is a *Christian Common-wealth*.
> Lastly, what is the *Kingdome of Darkness*.

Concerning the first, there is a saying much usurped of late, That *Wisedome* is acquired, not by reading of *Books*, but of *Men*. Consequently whereunto, those persons, that for the most part can give no other proof of being wise, take great delight to shew what they think they have read in men, by uncharitable censures of one another behind their backs. But there is another saying not of late understood, by which they might learn truly to read one another, if they would take the pains; and that is, *Nosce teipsum*, *Read thy self*:[1] which was not meant, as it is now used, to countenance, either the barbarous state of men in power, towards their inferiors; or to encourage men of low degree, to a sawcie behaviour towards their betters; But to teach us, that for the similitude of the thoughts, and Passions of one man, to the thoughts, and Passions of another, whosoever looketh into himself, and considereth what he doth, when he does *think*, *opine*, *reason*, *hope*, *feare*, &c, and upon what grounds; he shall thereby read and know, what are the thoughts, and Passions of all other men, upon the like occasions. I say the similitude of

Passions, which are the same in all men, *desire*, *feare*, *hope*, &c; not the similitude of the *objects* of the Passions, which are the things *desired*, *feared*, *hoped*, &c: for these the constitution individuall, and particular education do so vary, and they are so easie to be kept from our knowledge, that the characters of mans heart, blotted and confounded as they are, with dissembling, lying, counterfeiting, and erroneous doctrines, are legible onely to him that searcheth hearts. And though by mens actions wee do discover their designe sometimes; yet to do it without comparing them with our own, and distinguishing all circumstances, by which the case may come to be altered, is to decypher without a key, and be for the most part deceived, by too much trust, or by too much diffidence; as he that reads, is himself a good or evil man.

But let one man read another by his actions never so perfectly, it serves him onely with his acquaintance, which are but few. He that is to govern a whole Nation, must read in himself, not this, or that particular man; but Man-kind: which though it be hard to do, harder than to learn any Language, or Science; yet, when I shall have set down my own reading orderly, and perspicuously, the pains left another, will be onely to consider, if he also find not the same in himself. For this kind of Doctrine, admitteth no other Demonstration. [3]

PART ONE

OF MAN

CHAP. I

Of SENSE

Concerning the Thoughts of man, I will consider them first *Singly*, and afterwards in *Trayne*, or dependance upon one another. *Singly*, they are every one a *Representation* or *Apparence*, of some quality, or other Accident of a body without us; which is commonly called an *Object*. Which Object worketh on the Eyes, Eares, and other parts of mans body; and by diversity of working, produceth diversity of Apparences.

The Originall of them all, is that which we call SENSE; (For there is no conception in a mans mind, which hath not at first, totally, or by parts, been begotten upon the organs of Sense.) The rest are derived from that originall.

To know the naturall cause of Sense, is not very necessary to the business now in hand; and I have else-where written of the same at large.[1] Nevertheless, to fill each part of my present method, I will briefly deliver the same in this place.

The cause of Sense, is the Externall Body, or Object, which presseth the organ proper to each Sense, either immediatly, as in the Tast and Touch; or mediately, as in Seeing, Hearing, and Smelling: which pressure, by the mediation of Nerves, and other strings, and membranes of the body, continued inwards to the Brain, and Heart, causeth there a resistance, or counter-pressure, or endeavour of the heart, to deliver it self: which endeavour because *Outward*, seemeth to be some matter without. And this *seeming*, or *fancy*, is that which men call *Sense*; and consisteth, as to the Eye, in a *Light*, or *Colour figured*; To the Eare, in a *Sound*; To the Nostrill, in an *Odour*; To the Tongue and Palat, in a *Savour*; And to the rest of the body, in *Heat, Cold, Hardnesse, Softnesse*, and such other qualities, as we discern by *Feeling*. All which qualities called *Sensible*, are in the object that causeth them, but so many several motions of the matter, by which it presseth our organs diversly. Neither in us that are pressed, are they anything else, but divers motions; (for motion, produceth nothing but motion.) But their apparence to us is Fancy, the same waking, that dreaming. And as pressing, rubbing, or striking the Eye, makes us fancy a light; and pressing the Eare, produceth a dinne; so do the bodies also we see, or hear, produce the same by their strong, though unobserved action. For if those Colours, and Sounds, were in the Bodies, or Objects that cause them, they could not bee [4] severed from them, as by glasses, and in Ecchoes by reflection, wee see they are; where we know the thing we see, is in one place; the apparence, in another. And though at some certain distance, the reall, and very object seem invested with the fancy it begets in us; Yet still the object is one thing, the image or fancy is another. So that Sense in all cases, is nothing els but originall fancy, caused (as I have said) by the pressure, that is, by the motion, of externall things upon our Eyes, Eares, and other organs thereunto ordained.

But the Philosophy-schooles, through all the Universities of Christendome, grounded upon certain Texts of *Aristotle*, teach another doctrine;[2] and say, For the cause of *Vision*, that the thing seen, sendeth forth on every side a *visible species* (in English) a *visible shew, apparition*, or *aspect*, or *a being seen*; the receiving whereof into the Eye, is *Seeing*. And for the cause of *Hearing*, that the thing heard, sendeth forth an *Audible species*, that is, an *Audible aspect*, or *Audible being seen*; which entring at the Eare, maketh *Hearing*. Nay for the cause of *Understanding* also, they say the thing Understood sendeth forth *intelligible species*, that is, an *intelligible being seen*; which comming into the Understanding, makes us Understand. I say not this, as disapproving the use of Universities: but because I am to speak hereafter of their office in a Common-wealth, I must let you see on all occasions by the way, what things would be amended in them; amongst which the frequency of insignificant Speech is one.

CHAP. II

Of IMAGINATION

That when a thing lies still, unlesse somewhat els stirre it, it will lye still for ever, is a truth that no man doubts of. But that when a thing is in motion, it will eternally be in motion, unless somewhat els stay it, though the reason be the same, (namely, that nothing can change it selfe,) is not so easily assented to. For men measure, not onely other men, but all other things, by themselves:[3] and because they find themselves subject after motion to pain, and lassitude, think every thing els growes weary of motion, and seeks repose of its own accord; little considering, whether it be not some other motion, wherein that desire of rest they find in themselves, consisteth. From hence it is, that the Schooles say, Heavy bodies fall downwards, out of an appetite to rest, and to conserve their nature in that place which is most proper for them; ascribing appetite, and Knowledge of what is good for their conservation, (which is more than man has) to things inanimate, absurdly.

When a Body is once in motion, it moveth (unless something els hinder it) eternally; and whatsoever hindreth it, cannot in an instant, but in time, and by degrees

quite extinguish it: And as wee see in the water, though
the wind cease, the waves give not over rowling for a
[5] long time after; so also it happeneth in that motion,
which is made in the internall parts of a man, then, when
he Sees, Dreams, &c. For after the object is removed, or
the eye shut, wee still retain an image of the thing seen,
though more obscure than when we see it. And this is
it, the Latines call *Imagination*, from the image made
in seeing; and apply the same, though improperly, to
all the other senses. But the Greeks call it *Fancy*; which
signifies *apparence*, and is as proper to one sense, as to
another. IMAGINATION therefore is nothing but *decaying sense*; and is found in men, and many other living
Creatures, aswell sleeping, as waking.

The decay of Sense in men waking, is not the decay of
the motion made in sense; but an obscuring of it, in such
manner, as the light of the Sun obscureth the light of the
Starres; which starrs do no less exercise their vertue by
which they are visible, in the day, than in the night. But
because amongst many stroaks, which our eyes, eares,
and other organs receive from externall bodies, the predominant onely is sensible; therefore the light of the Sun
being predominant, we are not affected with the action
of the starrs. And any object being removed from our
eyes, though the impression it made in us remain; yet
other objects more present succeeding, and working on
us, the Imagination of the past is obscured, and made
weak; as the voyce of a man is in the noyse of the day.
From whence it followeth, that the longer the time is,
after the sight, or Sense of any object, the weaker is the
Imagination. For the continuall change of mans body,
destroyes in time the parts which in sense were moved:
So that distance of time, and of place, hath one and the
same effect in us. For as at a great distance of place,
that which wee look at, appears dimme, and without
distinction of the smaller parts; and as Voyces grow
weak, and inarticulate: so also after great distance of
time, our imagination of the Past is weak; and wee lose

(for example) of Cities wee have seen, many particular Streets; and of Actions, many particular Circumstances. This *decaying sense*, when wee would express the thing it self, (I mean *fancy* it selfe,) wee call *Imagination*, as I said before: But when we would express the *decay*, and signifie that the Sense is fading, old, and past, it is called *Memory*. So that *Imagination* and *Memory*, *Memory* are but one thing, which for divers considerations hath divers names.

Much memory, or memory of many things, is called *Experience*. Againe, Imagination being only of those things which have been formerly perceived by Sense, either all at once, or by parts at severall times; The former, (which is the imagining the whole object, as it was presented to the sense) is *simple Imagination*; as when one imagineth a man, or horse, which he hath seen before. The other is *Compounded*; as when from the sight of a man at one time, and of a horse at another, we conceive in our mind a Centaure.[4] So when a man compoundeth the image of his own person, with the image of the actions of an other man; as when a man imagins himselfe a *Hercules*, or an *Alexander*,[5] (which happeneth often to them that are much taken with reading of Romants) it is a compound imagination, and properly but a Fiction [6] of the mind. There be also other Imaginations that rise in men, (though waking) from the great impression made in sense: As from gazing upon the Sun, the impression leaves an image of the Sun before our eyes a long time after; and from being long and vehemently attent upon Geometricall Figures, a man shall in the dark, (though awake) have the Images of Lines, and Angles before his eyes: which kind of Fancy hath no particular name; as being a thing that doth not commonly fall into mens discourse.

The imaginations of them that sleep, are those we call *Dreams*. And these also (as all other Imaginations) have *Dreams* been before, either totally, or by parcells in the Sense. And because in sense, the Brain, and Nerves, which are the necessary Organs of sense, are so benummed in sleep, as not easily to be moved by the action of Externall Objects, there can happen in sleep, no Imagination; and therefore no Dreame, but what proceeds from the agitation of the inward parts of mans body; which inward parts, for the connexion they have with the Brayn, and other Organs, when they be distempered, do keep the same in motion; whereby the Imaginations there formerly made, appeare as if a man were waking; saving that the Organs of Sense being now benummed, so as there is no new object, which can master and obscure them with a more vigorous impression, a Dreame must needs be more cleare, in this silence of sense, than are our waking thoughts. And hence it cometh to passe, that it is a hard matter, and by many thought impossible to distinguish exactly between Sense and Dreaming. For my part, when I consider, that in Dreames, I do not often, nor constantly think of the same Persons, Places, Objects, and Actions that I do waking; nor remember so long a trayne of coherent thoughts, Dreaming, as at other times; And because waking I often observe the absurdity of Dreames, but never dream of the absurdities of my waking Thoughts; I am well satisfied, that being awake, I know I dreame not; though when I dreame, I think my selfe awake.

And seeing dreames are caused by the distemper of some of the inward parts of the Body; divers distempers must needs cause different Dreams. And hence it is, that lying cold breedeth Dreams of Feare, and raiseth the thought and Image of some fearfull object (the motion from the brain to the inner parts, and from the inner parts to the Brain being reciprocall:) And that as Anger causeth heat in some parts of the Body, when we are awake; so when we sleep, the over heating of the same parts causeth Anger, and raiseth up in the brain the Imagination of an Enemy. In the same manner;[6] as naturall kindness, when we are awake causeth desire; and desire makes heat in certain other parts of the body;

so also, too much heat in those parts, while wee sleep, raiseth in the brain an imagination of some kindness shewn. In summe, our Dreams are the reverse of our waking Imaginations; The motion when we are awake, beginning at one end; and when we Dream, at another.

The most difficult discerning of a mans Dream, from his waking [7] thoughts, is then, when by some accident we observe not that we have slept: which is easie to happen to a man full of fearfull thoughts; and whose conscience is much troubled; and that sleepeth, without the circumstances, of going to bed, or putting off his clothes, as one that noddeth in a chayre. For he that taketh pains, and industriously layes himself to sleep, in case any uncouth and exorbitant fancy come unto him, cannot easily think it other than a Dream. We read of *Marcus Brutus*, (one that had his life given him by *Julius Cæsar*, and was also his favorite, and notwithstanding murthered him,) how at *Philippi*, the night before he gave battell to *Augustus Cæsar*, hee saw a fearfull apparition, which is commonly related by Historians as a Vision: but considering the circumstances, one may easily judge to have been but a short Dream.[7] For sitting in his tent, pensive and troubled with the horrour of his rash act, it was not hard for him, slumbering in the cold, to dream of that which most affrighted him; which feare, as by degrees it made him wake; so also it must needs make the Apparition by degrees to vanish: And having no assurance that he slept, he could have no cause to think it a Dream, or any thing but a Vision. And this is no very rare Accident: for even they that be perfectly awake, if they be timorous, and superstitious, possessed with fearfull tales, and alone in the dark, are subject to the like fancies; and believe they see spirits and dead mens Ghosts walking in Churchyards; whereas it is either their Fancy onely, or els the knavery of such persons, as make use of such superstitious feare, to passe disguised in the night, to places they would not be known to haunt.

Apparitions or Visions

From this ignorance of how to distinguish Dreams, and other strong Fancies, from Vision and Sense, did arise the greatest part of the Religion of the Gentiles in time past, that worshipped Satyres, Fawnes, Nymphs, and the like; and now adayes the opinion that rude people have of Fayries, Ghosts, and Goblins; and of the power of Witches. For as for Witches, I think not that their witchcraft is any reall power; but yet that they are justly punished, for the false beliefe they have, that they can do such mischiefe, joyned with their purpose to do it if they can: their trade being neerer to a new Religion, than to a Craft or Science. And for Fayries, and walking Ghosts, the opinion of them has I think been on purpose, either taught, or not confuted, to keep in credit the use of Exorcisme, of Crosses, of holy Water, and other such inventions of Ghostly men.[8] Neverthelesse, there is no doubt, but God can make unnaturall Apparitions: But that he does it so often, as men need to feare such things, more than they feare the stay, or change, of the course of Nature, which he also can stay, and change, is no point of Christian faith. But evill men under pretext that God can do any thing, are so bold as to say any thing when it serves their turn, though they think it untrue; It is the part of a wise man, to believe them no further, than right reason makes that which they say, appear credible. If this superstitious fear of Spirits were taken away, and with it, Prognostiques from Dreams, false Prophecies, and many other things depending thereon, by [8] which, crafty ambitious persons abuse the simple people, men would be much more fitted than they are for civill Obedience.

And this ought to be the work of the Schooles: but they rather nourish such doctrine. For (not knowing what Imagination, or the Senses are), what they receive, they teach: some saying, that Imaginations rise of themselves, and have no cause: Others that they rise most commonly from the Will; and that Good thoughts are blown (inspired) into a man, by God; and Evill thoughts by the

Divell: or that Good thoughts are powred (infused) into a man, by God, and Evill ones by the Divell. Some say the Senses receive the Species of things, and deliver them to the Common-sense; and the Common Sense delivers them over to the Fancy, and the Fancy to the Memory, and the Memory to the Judgement, like handing of things from one to another, with many words making nothing understood.

Under-standing

The Imagination that is raysed in man (or any other creature indued with the faculty of imagining) by words, or other voluntary signes, is that we generally call *Understanding*; and is common to Man and Beast. For a dogge by custome will understand the call, or the rating of his Master; and so will many other Beasts. That Understanding which is peculiar to man, is the Understanding not onely his will; but his conceptions and thoughts, by the sequell and contexture of the names of things into Affirmations, Negations, and other formes of Speech: And of this kinde of Understanding I shall speak hereafter.

CHAP. III

Of the Consequence or TRAYNE *of Imaginations*

By *Consequence*, or TRAYNE of Thoughts, I understand that succession of one Thought to another, which is called (to distinguish it from Discourse in words) *Mentall Discourse*.

When a man thinketh on any thing whatsoever, His next Thought after, is not altogether so casuall as it seems to be. Not every Thought to every Thought succeeds indifferently. But as wee have no Imagination, whereof we have not formerly had Sense, in whole, or in parts; so we have no Transition from one Imagination to another, whereof we never had the like before in our Senses. The reason whereof is this. All Fancies are Motions within us,

reliques of those made in the Sense: And those motions
that immediately succeeded one another in the sense,
continue also together after Sense: In so much as the former comming again to take place, and be prædominant,
the later followeth, by coherence of the matter moved, in
such manner, as water upon a plain Table is drawn which
way any one part of it is guided by the finger. But because
in sense, to one and the same thing perceived, sometimes
one thing, sometimes another succeedeth, it comes to
passe in time, that in the Imagining of any thing, there is
[9] no certainty what we shall Imagine next; Onely this
is certain, it shall be something that succeeded the same
before, at one time or another.

Trayne of   This Trayne of Thoughts, or Mentall Discourse, is of
Thoughts two sorts. The first is *Unguided, without Designe,* and
unguided inconstant; Wherein there is no Passionate Thought, to
govern and direct those that follow, to it self, as the end
and scope of some desire, or other passion: In which
case the thoughts are said to wander, and seem impertinent one to another, as in a Dream. Such are Commonly
the thoughts of men, that are not onely without company, but also without care of any thing; though even
then their Thoughts are as busie as at other times, but
without harmony; as the sound which a Lute out of tune
would yeeld to any man; or in tune, to one that could
not play. And yet in this wild ranging of the mind, a man
may oft-times perceive the way of it, and the dependance of one thought upon another. For in a Discourse of
our present civill warre, what could seem more impertinent, than to ask (as one did) what was the value of a
Roman Penny? Yet the Cohærence to me was manifest
enough. For the Thought of the warre, introduced the
Thought of the delivering up the King to his Enemies;
The Thought of that, brought in the Thought of the
delivering up of Christ; and that again the Thought of
the 30 pence, which was the price of that treason: and
thence easily followed that malicious question; and all
this in a moment of time; for Thought is quick.[9]

The second is more constant; as being *regulated* by *Trayne of* some desire, and designe. For the impression made by *Thoughts* such things as wee desire, or feare, is strong, and perman- *regulated* ent, or, (if it cease for a time,) of quick return: so strong it is sometimes, as to hinder and break our sleep. From Desire, ariseth the Thought of some means we have seen produce the like of that which we ayme at; and from the thought of that, the thought of means to that mean; and so continually, till we come to some beginning within our own power. And because the End, by the greatnesse of the impression, comes often to mind, in case our thoughts begin to wander, they are quickly again reduced into the way: which observed by one of the seven wise men, made him give men this præcept, which is now worne out, *Respice finem*;[10] that is to say, in all your actions, look often upon what you would have, as the thing that directs all your thoughts in the way to attain it.

The Trayn of regulated Thoughts is of two kinds; One, when of an effect imagined, wee seek the causes, or means that produce it: and this is common to Man and Beast. The other is, when imagining any thing what-soever, wee seek all the possible effects, that can by it be produced; that is to say, we imagine what we can do with it, when wee have it. Of which I have not at any time seen any signe, but in man onely; for this is a curiosity hardly incident to the nature of any living crea-ture that has no other Passion but sensuall, such as are hunger, thirst, lust, and anger. In summe, the Discourse of the Mind, when it is governed by designe, is noth-ing but *Seeking*, or the faculty of Invention, which the Latines call *Sagacitas*, and [10] *Solertia*; a hunting out of the causes, of some effect, present or past; or of the effects, of some present or past cause. Sometimes a man seeks what he hath lost; and from that place, and time, wherein hee misses it, his mind runs back, from place to place, and time to time, to find where, and when he had it; that is to say, to find some certain, and limited time and place, in which to begin a method of seeking.

Again, from thence, his thoughts run over the same places and times, to find what action, or other occasion *Remem-* might make him lose it. This we call *Remembrance*, or *brance* Calling to mind: the Latines call it *Reminiscentia*, as it were a *Re-conning* of our former actions.

Sometimes a man knows a place determinate, within the compasse whereof he is to seek; and then his thoughts run over all the parts thereof, in the same manner, as one would sweep a room, to find a jewell; or as a Spaniel ranges the field, till he find a sent; or as a man should run over the Alphabet, to start a rime.

Prudence   Sometime a man desires to know the event of an action; and then he thinketh of some like action past, and the events thereof one after another; supposing like events will follow like actions. As he that foresees what wil become of a Criminal, re-cons what he has seen follow on the like Crime before; having this order of thoughts, The Crime, the Officer, the Prison, the Judge, and the Gallowes. Which kind of thoughts, is called *Foresight*, and *Prudence*, or *Providence*; and sometimes *Wisdome*; though such conjecture, through the difficulty of observing all circumstances, be very fallacious. But this is certain; by how much one man has more experience of things past, than another; by so much also he is more Prudent, and his expectations the seldomer faile him. The *Present* onely has a being in Nature; things *Past* have a being in the Memory onely, but things *to come* have no being at all; the *Future* being but a fiction of the mind, applying the sequels of actions Past, to the actions that are Present; which with most certainty is done by him that has most Experience; but not with certainty enough. And though it be called Prudence, when the Event answereth our Expectation; yet in its own nature, it is but Presumption. For the foresight of things to come, which is Providence, belongs onely to him by whose will they are to come. From him onely, and supernaturally, proceeds Prophecy. The best Prophet naturally is the best guesser; and the best guesser, he that is most

versed and studied in the matters he guesses at: for he
hath most *Signes* to guesse by.

A *Signe*, is the Event Antecedent, of the Consequent;   *Signes*
and contrarily, the Consequent of the Antecedent, when
the like Consequences have been observed, before: And
the oftner they have been observed, the lesse uncertain
is the Signe. And therefore he that has most experience
in any kind of businesse, has most Signes, whereby to
guesse at the Future time; and consequently is the most
prudent: And so much more prudent than he that is new
in that kind of business, as not to be equalled by any
advantage of naturall and extemporary wit: though perhaps many young men think the contrary.

Neverthelesse it is not Prudence that distinguisheth
man from [11] beast. There be beasts, that at a year old
observe more, and pursue that which is for their good,
more prudently, than a child can do at ten.

As Prudence is a *Præsumtion* of the *Future*, contracted   *Conjecture of*
from the *Experience* of time *Past*: So there is a Præsum-   *the time past*
tion of things Past taken from other things (not future
but) past also. For he that hath seen by what courses
and degrees, a flourishing State hath first come into civil
warre, and then to ruine; upon the sight of the ruines of
any other State, will guesse, the like warre, and the like
courses have been there also. But this conjecture, has
the same incertainty almost with the conjecture of the
Future; both being grounded onely upon Experience.

There is no other act of mans mind, that I can remember, naturally planted in him, so, as to need no other
thing, to the exercise of it, but to be born a man, and live
with the use of his five Senses. Those other Faculties, of
which I shall speak by and by, and which seem proper
to man onely, are acquired, and encreased by study and
industry; and of most men learned by instruction, and
discipline; and proceed all from the invention of Words,
and Speech. For besides Sense, and Thoughts, and the
Trayne of thoughts, the mind of man has no other
motion; though by the help of Speech, and Method, the

same Facultyes may be improved to such a height, as to distinguish men from all other living Creatures.

Whatsoever we imagine, is *Finite*. Therefore there is no Idea, or conception of anything we call *Infinite*. No man can have in his mind an Image of infinite magnitude; nor conceive infinite swiftness, infinite time, or infinite force, or infinite power. When we say any thing is infinite, we signifie onely, that we are not able to conceive the ends, and bounds of the thing named; having no Conception of the thing, but of our own inability. And therefore the Name of *God* is used, not to make us conceive him; (for he is *Incomprehensible*; and his greatnesse, and power are unconceivable;) but that we may honour him. Also because whatsoever (as I said before,) we conceive, has been perceived first by sense, either all at once, or by parts; a man can have no thought, representing any thing, not subject to sense. No man therefore can conceive any thing, but he must conceive it in some place; and indued with some determinate magnitude; and which may be divided into parts; nor that any thing is all in this place, and all in another place at the same time; nor that two, or more things can be in one, and the same place at once: For none of these things ever have, or can be incident to Sense; but are absurd speeches, taken upon credit (without any signification at all,) from deceived Philosophers, and deceived, or deceiving Schoolemen. [12]

CHAP. IV

Of SPEECH

Originall of The Invention of *Printing*, though ingenious, compared
Speech with the invention of *Letters*, is no great matter. But who was the first that found the use of Letters, is not known. He that first brought them into *Greece*,[11] men

say was *Cadmus*, the sonne of *Agenor*, King of Phæni-
cia. A profitable Invention for continuing the memory
of time past, and the conjunction of mankind, dispersed
into so many, and distant regions of the Earth; and with
all difficult, as proceeding from a watchfull observation
of the divers motions of the Tongue, Palat, Lips, and
other organs of Speech; whereby to make as many differences of characters, to remember them. But the most
noble and profitable invention of all other, was that
of SPEECH, consisting of *Names* or *Appellations*, and
their Connexion; whereby men register their Thoughts;
recall them when they are past; and also declare them
one to another for mutuall utility and conversation;
without which, there had been amongst men, neither
Common-wealth, nor Society, nor Contract, nor Peace,
no more than amongst Lyons, Bears, and Wolves. The
first author of Speech was *God* himself, that instructed
Adam how to name such creatures as he presented to
his sight;[12] For the Scripture goeth no further in this
matter. But this was sufficient to direct him to adde more
names, as the experience and use of the creatures should
give him occasion; and to joyn them in such manner by
degrees, as to make himself understood; and so by succession of time, so much language might be gotten, as he
had found use for; though not so copious, as an Orator
or Philosopher has need of. For I do not find any thing in
the Scripture, out of which, directly or by consequence
can be gathered, that *Adam* was taught the names of all
Figures, Numbers, Measures, Colours, Sounds, Fancies,
Relations; much less the names of Words and Speech, as
Generall, *Speciall*, *Affirmative*, *Negative*, *Interrogative*,
Optative, *Infinitive*, all which are usefull; and least of
all, of *Entity*, *Intentionality*, *Quiddity*, and other insignificant words of the School.

But all this language gotten, and augmented by *Adam*
and his posterity, was again lost at the tower of *Babel*,[13]
when by the hand of God, every man was stricken for
his rebellion, with an oblivion of his former language.

And being hereby forced to disperse themselves into severall parts of the world, it must needs be, that the diversity of Tongues that now is, proceeded by degrees from them, in such manner, as need (the mother of all inventions) taught them; and in tract of time grew every where more copious.

The use of Speech The generall use of Speech, is to transferre our Mentall Discourse, into Verbal; or the Trayne of our Thoughts, into a Trayne of Words; and that for two commodities; whereof one is, the Re[13]gistring of the Consequences of our Thoughts; which being apt to slip out of our memory, and put us to a new labour, may again be recalled, by such words as they were marked by. So that the first use of names, is to serve for *Markes*, or *Notes* of remembrance. Another is, when many use the same words, to signifie (by their connexion and order,) one to another, what they conceive, or think of each matter; and also what they desire, feare, or have any other passion for. And for this use they are called *Signes*. Speciall uses of Speech are these; First, to Register, what by cogitation, wee find to be the cause of any thing, present or past; and what we find things present or past may produce, or effect: which in summe, is acquiring of Arts. Secondly, to shew to others that knowledge which we have attained; which is, to Counsell, and Teach one another. Thirdly, to make known to others our wills, and purposes, that we may have the mutuall help of one another. Fourthly, to please and delight our selves, and others, by playing with our words, for pleasure or ornament, innocently.

Abuses of Speech To these Uses, there are also foure correspondent Abuses. First, when men register their thoughts wrong, by the inconstancy of the signification of their words; by which they register for their conceptions, that which they never conceived; and so deceive themselves. Secondly, when they use words metaphorically; that is, in other sense than that they are ordained for; and thereby deceive others. Thirdly, when by words they declare that to be their will, which is not. Fourthly, when they use them to grieve one another: for seeing nature hath armed living creatures, some with teeth, some with horns, and some with hands, to grieve an enemy, it is but an abuse of Speech, to grieve him with the tongue, unlesse it be one whom wee are obliged to govern; and then it is not to grieve, but to correct and amend.

The manner how Speech serveth to the remembrance of the consequence of causes and effects, consisteth in the imposing of *Names*, and the *Connexion* of them.

Of Names, some are *Proper*, and singular to one onely thing; as *Peter, John, This man, this Tree*: and some are *Common* to many things; as *Man, Horse, Tree*; every of which though but one Name, is nevertheless the name of divers particular things; in respect of all which together, it is called an *Universall*; there being nothing in the world Universall but Names; for the things named, are every one of them Individuall and Singular. *Names Proper & Common*

Universall

One Universall name is imposed on many things, for their similitude in some quality, or other accident: And wheras a Proper Name bringeth to mind one thing onely; Universals recall any one of those many.

And of Names Universall, some are of more, and some of lesse extent; the larger comprehending the lesse large: and some again of equall extent, comprehending each other reciprocally. As for example, the Name *Body* is of larger signification than the word *Man*, and comprehendeth it; and the names *Man* and *Rationall*, are of equall extent, comprehending mutually one another. But here wee [14] must take notice, that by a Name is not alwayes understood, as in Grammar, one onely Word; but sometimes by circumlocution many words together. For all these words, *Hee that in his actions observeth the Lawes of his Country*, make but one Name, equivalent to this one word, *Just*.

By this imposition of Names, some of larger, some of stricter signification, we turn the reckoning of the consequences of things imagined in the mind, into a reckoning of the consequences of Appellations. For example, a man that hath no use of Speech at all, (such, as is born and remains perfectly deafe and dumb,) if he set before his eyes a triangle, and by it two right angles, (such as are the corners of a square figure,) he may by meditation compare and find, that the three angles of that triangle, are equall to those two right angles that stand by it. But if another triangle be shewn him different in shape from the former, he cannot know without a new labour, whether the three angles of that also be equall to the same. But he that hath the use of words, when he observes, that such equality was consequent, not to the length of the sides, nor to any other particular thing in his triangle; but onely to this, that the sides were straight, and the angles three; and that that was all, for which he named it a Triangle; will boldly conclude Universally, that such equality of angles is in all triangles whatsoever; and register his invention in these generall termes, *Every triangle hath its three angles equall to two right angles*. And thus the consequence found in one particular, comes to be registred and remembred, as an Universall rule; and discharges our mentall reckoning, of time and place; and delivers us from all labour of the mind, saving the first; and makes that which was found true *here*, and *now*, to be true in *all times* and *places*.

But the use of words in registring our thoughts, is in nothing so evident as in Numbering. A naturall foole that could never learn by heart the order of numerall words, as *one*, *two*, and *three*, may observe every stroak of the Clock, and nod to it, or say one, one, one; but can never know what houre it strikes. And it seems, there was a time when those names of number were not in use; and men were fayn to apply their fingers of one or both hands, to those things they desired to keep account of; and that thence it proceeded, that now our numerall words are but ten, in any Nation, and in some but five, and then they begin again. And he that can tell ten, if he recite them out of order, will lose himselfe, and not know when he has done: Much lesse will he be able

to adde, and substract, and performe all other operations of Arithmetique. So that without words, there is
no possibility of reckoning of Numbers; much lesse of
Magnitudes, of Swiftnesse, of Force, and other things,
the reckonings whereof are necessary to the being, or
well-being of man-kind.

When two Names are joyned together into a Consequence, or Affirmation; as thus, *A man is a living
creature*; or thus, *if he be a man, he is a living creature*, If the later name *Living creature*, signifie all that
the former name *Man* signifieth, then the affirmation,
or conse[15]quence is *true*; otherwise *false*. For *True*
and *False* are attributes of Speech, not of Things. And
where Speech is not, there is neither *Truth* nor *Falshood*.
Errour there may be, as when wee expect that which
shall not be; or suspect what has not been: but in neither
case can a man be charged with Untruth.

Seeing then that *truth* consisteth in the right ordering   *Necessity of*
of names in our affirmations, a man that seeketh precise   *Definitions*
truth, had need to remember what every name he uses
stands for; and to place it accordingly; or else he will find
himselfe entangled in words, as a bird in lime-twiggs;[14]
the more he struggles, the more belimed. And therefore
in Geometry, (which is the onely Science that it hath
pleased God hitherto to bestow on mankind,) men begin
at settling the significations of their words; which settling of significations, they call *Definitions*; and place
them in the beginning of their reckoning.

By this it appears how necessary it is for any man that
aspires to true Knowledge, to examine the Definitions of
former Authors; and either to correct them, where they
are negligently set down; or to make them himselfe. For
the errours of Definitions multiply themselves, according
as the reckoning proceeds; and lead men into absurdities, which at last they see, but cannot avoyd, without
reckoning anew from the beginning; in which lyes the
foundation of their errours. From whence it happens,
that they which trust to books, do as they that cast up

many little summs into a greater, without considering
whether those little summes were rightly cast up or not;
and at last finding the errour visible, and not mistrusting
their first grounds, know not which way to cleere themselves; but spend time in fluttering over their bookes;
as birds that entring by the chimney, and finding themselves inclosed in a chamber, flutter at the false light of
a glasse window, for want of wit to consider which way
they came in. So that in the right Definition of Names,
lyes the first use of Speech; which is the Acquisition of
Science: And in wrong, or no Definitions, lyes the first
abuse; from which proceed all false and senslesse Tenets; which make those men that take their instruction
from the authority of books, and not from their own
meditation, to be as much below the condition of ignorant men, as men endued with true Science are above
it. For between true Science, and erroneous Doctrines,
Ignorance is in the middle. Naturall sense and imagination, are not subject to absurdity. Nature it selfe cannot
erre: and as men abound in copiousnesse of language;
so they become more wise, or more mad than ordinary.
Nor is it possible without Letters for any man to become
either excellently wise, or (unless his memory be hurt by
disease, or ill constitution of organs) excellently foolish.
For words are wise mens counters, they do but reckon
by them: but they are the mony of fooles, that value
them by the authority of an *Aristotle*, a *Cicero*, or a
Thomas,[15] or any other Doctor whatsoever, if but a man.

Subject to   *Subject to Names*, is whatsoever can enter into, or be
Names considered in an account; and be added one to another
to make a summe; or substracted one from another, and
leave a remainder. The Latines called [16] Accounts of
mony *Rationes*, and accounting, *Ratiocinatio*: and that
which we in bills or books of account call *Items*, they
called *Nomina*; that is, *Names*: and thence it seems to
proceed, that they extended the word *Ratio*, to the faculty of Reckoning in all other things. The Greeks have
but one word λόγος, for both *Speech* and *Reason*; not

that they thought there was no Speech without Reason; but no Reasoning without Speech: And the act of reasoning they called *Syllogisme*; which signifieth summing up of the consequences of one saying to another. And because the same things may enter into account for divers accidents; their names are (to shew that diversity) diversly wrested, and diversified. This diversity of names may be reduced to foure generall heads.

First, a thing may enter into account for *Matter*, or *Body*; as *living, sensible, rationall, hot, cold, moved, quiet*; with all which names the word *Matter*, or *Body* is understood; all such, being names of Matter.

Secondly, it may enter into account, or be considered, for some accident or quality, which we conceive to be in it; as for *being moved*, for *being so long*, for *being hot*, &c; and then, of the name of the thing it selfe, by a little change or wresting, wee make a name for that accident, which we consider; and for *living* put into the account *life*; for *moved, motion*; for *hot, heat*; for *long, length*, and the like? And all such Names, are the names of the accidents and properties, by which one Matter, and Body is distinguished from another. These are called *names Abstract*; because severed (not from Matter, but) from the account of Matter.

Thirdly, we bring into account, the Properties of our own bodies, whereby we make such distinction: as when any thing is *Seen* by us, we reckon not the thing it selfe; but the *sight*, the *Colour*, the *Idea* of it in the fancy: and when any thing is *heard*, wee reckon it not; but the *hearing*, or *sound* onely, which is our fancy or conception of it by the Eare: and such are names of fancies.

Fourthly, we bring into account, consider, and give names, to *Names* themselves, and to *Speeches*: For, *generall, universall, speciall, æquivocall*, are names of Names. And *Affirmation, Interrogation, Commandement, Narration, Syllogisme, Sermon, Oration*, and many other such, are names of Speeches. And this is all the variety of Names *Positive*; which are put to mark *Use of Names Positive* somewhat which is in Nature, or may be feigned by the mind of man, as Bodies that are, or may be conceived to be; or of bodies, the Properties that are, or may be feigned to be; or Words and Speech.

Negative   There be also other Names, called *Negative*; which
Names with   are notes to signifie that a word is not the name of the
their Uses   thing in question; as these words *Nothing*, *no man*, *infinite*, *indocible*, *three want foure*, and the like; which are nevertheless of use in reckoning, or in correcting of reckoning; and call to mind our past cogitations, though they be not names of any thing; because they make us refuse to admit of Names not rightly used.

Words insig-   All other Names, are but insignificant sounds; and
nificant   those of two [17] sorts. One, when they are new, and yet their meaning not explained by Definition; whereof there have been aboundance coyned by Schoole-men, and pusled[16] Philosophers.

Another, when men make a name of two Names, whose significations are contradictory and inconsistent; as this name, an *incorporeall body*, or (which is all one) an *incorporeall substance*, and a great number more. For whensoever any affirmation is false, the two names of which it is composed, put together and made one, signifie nothing at all. For example, if it be a false affirmation to say *a quadrangle is round*, the word *round quadrangle* signifies nothing; but is a meere sound. So likewise if it be false, to say that vertue can be powred, or blown up and down; the words *In-powred vertue*, *In-blown vertue*, are as absurd and insignificant, as a *round quadrangle*. And therefore you shall hardly meet with a senselesse and insignificant word, that is not made up of some Latin or Greek names. A French-man seldome hears our Saviour called by the name of *Parole*, but by the name of *Verbe* often; yet *Verbe* and *Parole* differ no more, but that one is Latin, the other French.

Under-   When a man upon the hearing of any Speech, hath
standing   those thoughts which the words of that Speech, and

their connexion, were ordained and constituted to signifie; Then he is said to understand it: *Understanding*
being nothing else, but conception caused by Speech.
And therefore if Speech be peculiar to man (as for ought
I know it is,) then is Understanding peculiar to him
also. And therefore of absurd and false affirmations,
in case they be universall, there can be no Understanding; though many think they understand, then, when
they do but repeat the words softly, or con them in their
mind.

What kinds of Speeches signifie the Appetites, Aversions, and Passions of mans mind; and of their use
and abuse, I shall speak when I have spoken of the
Passions.

The names of such things as affect us, that is, which *Inconstant*
please, and displease us, because all men be not alike *names*
affected with the same thing, nor the same man at all
times, are in the common discourses of men, of *inconstant* signification. For seeing all names are imposed to
signifie our conceptions; and all our affections are but
conceptions; when we conceive the same things differently, we can hardly avoyd different naming of them. For
though the nature of that we conceive, be the same; yet
the diversity of our reception of it, in respect of different
constitutions of body, and prejudices of opinion, gives
everything a tincture of our different passions. And
therefore in reasoning, a man must take heed of words;
which besides the signification of what we imagine of
their nature, have a signification also of the nature, disposition, and interest of the speaker; such as are the
names of Vertues, and Vices; For one man calleth *Wisdome*, what another calleth *feare*; and one *cruelty*, what
another *justice*; one *prodigality*, what another *magnanimity*; and one *gravity*, what another *stupidity*, &c.
And therefore such names can never be true grounds of
any ratiocination. No more can Metaphors, and Tropes
of speech: but these are less dangerous, because they
profess their inconstancy; which the other do not. [18]

CHAP. V

Of REASON, and SCIENCE

Reason what When a man *Reasoneth*, hee does nothing else but
it is conceive a summe totall, from *Addition* of parcels; or
conceive a Remainder, from *Substraction* of one summe
from another: which (if it be done by Words,) is conceiv-
ing of the consequence of the names of all the parts, to
the name of the whole; or from the names of the whole
and one part, to the name of the other part. And though
in some things, (as in numbers,) besides *Adding* and *Substracting*, men name other operations, as *Multiplying*
and *Dividing*; yet they are the same; for Multiplication,
is but Adding together of things equall; and Division,
but Substracting of one thing, as often as we can. These
operations are not incident to Numbers onely, but to
all manner of things that can be added together, and
taken one out of another. For as Arithmeticians teach
to adde and substract in *numbers*; so the Geometricians
teach the same in *lines*, *figures* (solid and superficiall,)
angles, *proportions*, *times*, degrees of *swiftnesse*, *force*,
power, and the like; The Logicians teach the same in
Consequences of words; adding together *two Names*,
to make an *Affirmation*; and *two Affirmations*, to
make a *Syllogisme*; and *many Syllogismes* to make a
Demonstration; and from the *summe*, or *Conclusion* of
a *Syllogisme*, they substract one *Proposition*, to finde
the other. Writers of Politiques, adde together *Pactions*,
to find mens *duties*; and Lawyers, *Lawes*, and *facts*, to
find what is *right* and *wrong* in the actions of private
men. In summe, in what matter soever there is place for
addition and *substraction*, there also is place for *Reason*; and where these have no place, there *Reason* has
nothing at all to do.

Reason   Out of all which we may define, (that is to say deter-
defined mine,) what that is, which is meant by this word *Reason*,

when wee reckon it amongst the Faculties of the mind. For REASON, in this sense, is nothing but *Reckoning* (that is, Adding and substracting) of the Consequences of generall names agreed upon, for the *marking* and *signifying* of our thoughts; I say *marking* them, when we reckon by our selves; and *signifying*, when we demonstrate, or approve our reckonings to other men.

And as in Arithmetique, unpractised men must, and Professors themselves may often erre, and cast up false; so also in any other subject of Reasoning, the ablest, most attentive, and most practised men, may deceive themselves, and inferre false Conclusions; Not but that Reason it selfe is always Right Reason, as well as Arithmetique is a certain and infallible Art: But no one mans Reason, nor the Reason of any one number of men, makes the certaintie; no more than an account is therefore well cast up, because a great many men have unanimously approved it. And therefore, as when there is a controversy in [19] an account, the parties must by their own accord, set up for right Reason, the Reason of some Arbitrator, or Judge, to whose sentence they will both stand, or their controversie must either come to blowes, or be undecided, for want of a right Reason constituted by Nature; so is it also in all debates of what kind soever: And when men that think themselves wiser than all others, clamor and demand right Reason for judge; yet seek no more, but that things should be determined, by no other mens reason but their own, it is as intolerable in the society of men, as it is in play after trump is turned, to use for trump on every occasion, that suite whereof they have most in their hand.[17] For they do nothing els, that will have every of their passions, as it comes to bear sway in them, to be taken for right Reason, and that in their own controversies: bewraying their want of right Reason, by the claym they lay to it.

The Use and End of Reason, is not the finding of the summe, and truth of one, or a few consequences, remote

Right Reason where

The use of Reason

from the first definitions, and settled significations of names; but to begin at these; and proceed from one consequence to another. For there can be no certainty of the last Conclusion, without a certainty of all those Affirmations and Negations, on which it was grounded, and inferred. As when a master of a family, in taking an account, casteth up the summs of all the bills of expence, into one sum; and not regarding how each bill is summed up, by those that give them in account; nor what it is he payes for; he advantages himself no more, than if he allowed the account in grosse, trusting to every of the accountants skill and honesty: so also in Reasoning of all other things, he that takes up conclusions on the trust of Authors, and doth not fetch them from the first Items in every Reckoning, (which are the significations of names settled by definitions), loses his labour; and does not know any thing; but onely beleeveth.

Of Error and Absurdity   When a man reckons without the use of words, which may be done in particular things, (as when upon the sight of any one thing, wee conjecture what was likely to have preceded, or is likely to follow upon it;) if that which he thought likely to follow, followes not; or that which he thought likely to have preceded it, hath not preceded it, this is called ERROR; to which even the most prudent men are subject. But when we Reason in Words of generall signification, and fall upon a generall inference which is false; though it be commonly called *Error*, it is indeed an ABSURDITY, or senselesse Speech. For Error is but a deception, in presuming that somewhat is past, or to come; of which, though it were not past, or not to come; yet there was no impossibility discoverable. But when we make a generall assertion, unlesse it be a true one, the possibility of it is unconceivable. And words whereby we conceive nothing but the sound, are those we call *Absurd, Insignificant,* and *Non-sense*. And therefore if a man should talk to me of a *round Quadrangle*; or *accidents of Bread in Cheese*; or *Immateriall Substances*; or of *A free Subject*; *A free-Will*;[18] or any *Free*, but free from being hindred by opposition, I should not say he were in an Errour; but that his words were without meaning; that is to say, Absurd.

[20] I have said before, (in the second chapter,) that a Man did excell all other Animals in this faculty, that when he conceived any thing whatsoever, he was apt to enquire the consequences of it, and what effects he could do with it. And now I adde this other degree of the same excellence, that he can by words reduce the consequences he findes to generall Rules, called *Theoremes*, or *Aphorismes*; that is, he can Reason, or reckon, not onely in number; but in all other things, whereof one may be added unto, or substracted from another.

But this priviledge, is allayed by another; and that is, by the priviledge of Absurdity; to which no living creature is subject, but man onely. And of men, those are of all most subject to it, that professe Philosophy. For it is most true that *Cicero* sayth of them somewhere; that there can be nothing so absurd, but may be found in the books of Philosophers.[19] And the reason is manifest. For there is not one of them that begins his ratiocination from the Definitions, or Explications of the names they are to use; which is a method that hath been used onely in Geometry; whose Conclusions have thereby been made indisputable.

The first cause of Absurd conclusions I ascribe to the want of Method; in that they begin not their Ratiocination from Definitions; that is, from settled significations of their words: as if they could cast account, without knowing the value of the numerall words, *one*, *two*, and *three*. *Causes of absurditie 1*

And whereas all bodies enter into account upon divers considerations, (which I have mentioned in the precedent chapter;) these considerations being diversly named, divers absurdities proceed from the confusion, and unfit connexion of their names into assertions. And therefore

The second cause of Absurd assertions, I ascribe to *2*

the giving of names of *bodies*, to *accidents*; or of *accidents*, to *bodies*; As they do, that say, *Faith is infused*, or *inspired*;[20] when nothing can be *powred*, or *breathed* into any thing, but body; and that, *extension* is *body*; that *phantasmes* are *spirits*, &c.

3   The third I ascribe to the giving of the names of the *accidents* of *bodies without us*, to the *accidents* of our *own bodies*; as they do that say, the *colour is in the body; the sound is in the ayre*, &c.

4   The fourth, to the giving of the names of *bodies*, to *names*, or *speeches*; as they do that say, that *there be things universall*; that *a living creature is Genus*, or *a generall thing*, &c.

5   The fifth, to the giving of the names of *accidents*, to *names* and *speeches*; as they do that say, *the nature of a thing is its definition; a mans command is his will*; and the like.

6   The sixth, to the use of Metaphors, Tropes, and other Rhetoricall figures, in stead of words proper. For though it be lawfull to say, (for example) in common speech, *the way goeth, or leadeth hither, or thither, The Proverb sayes this or that* (whereas wayes cannot go, nor Proverbs speak;) yet in reckoning, and seeking of truth, such speeches are not to be admitted.

7   The seventh, to names that signifie nothing; but are taken up, and [21] learned by rote from the Schooles, as *hypostatical, transubstantiate, consubstantiate, eternal-Now*, and the like canting of Schoolemen.[21]

To him that can avoyd these things, it is not easie to fall into any absurdity, unlesse it be by the length of an account; wherein he may perhaps forget what went before. For all men by nature reason alike, and well, when they have good principles. For who is so stupid, as both to mistake in Geometry, and also to persist in it, when another detects his error to him?

Science   By this it appears that Reason is not as Sense, and Memory, borne with us; nor gotten by Experience onely, as Prudence is; but attayned by Industry; first in apt imposing of Names; and secondly by getting a good and orderly Method in proceeding from the Elements, which are Names, to Assertions made by Connexion of one of them to another; and so to Syllogismes, which are the Connexions of one Assertion to another, till we come to a knowledge of all the Consequences of names appertaining to the subject in hand; and that is it, men call SCIENCE. And whereas Sense and Memory are but knowledge of Fact, which is a thing past, and irrevocable; *Science* is the knowledge of Consequences, and dependance of one fact upon another: by which, out of that we can presently do, we know how to do something else when we will, or the like, another time: Because when we see how any thing comes about, upon what causes, and by what manner; when the like causes come into our power, wee see how to make it produce the like effects.

Children therefore are not endued with Reason at all, till they have attained the use of Speech: but are called Reasonable Creatures, for the possibility apparent of having the use of Reason in time to come. And the most part of men, though they have the use of Reasoning a little way, as in numbring to some degree; yet it serves them to little use in common life; in which they govern themselves, some better, some worse, according to their differences of experience, quicknesse of memory, and inclinations to severall ends; but specially according to good or evill fortune, and the errors of one another. For as for *Science*, or certain rules of their actions, they are so farre from it, that they know not what it is. Geometry they have thought Conjuring: But for other Sciences, they who have not been taught the beginnings, and some progresse in them, that they may see how they be acquired and generated, are in this point like children, that having no thought of generation, are made believe by the women, that their brothers and sisters are not born, but found in the garden.

But yet they that have no *Science*, are in better, and

nobler condition with their naturall Prudence; than
men, that by mis-reasoning, or by trusting them that
reason wrong, fall upon false and absurd generall rules.
For ignorance of causes, and of rules, does not set men
so farre out of their way, as relying on false rules, and
taking for causes of what they aspire to, those that are
not so, but rather causes of the contrary.

To conclude, The Light of humane minds is Perspicuous Words, [22] but by exact definitions first snuffed, and
purged from ambiguity; *Reason* is the *pace*; Encrease
of *Science*, the *way*; and the Benefit of man-kind, the
end. And on the contrary, Metaphors, and senslesse
and ambiguous words, are like *ignes fatui*;[22] and reasoning upon them, is wandering amongst innumerable
absurdities; and their end, contention, and sedition, or
contempt.

Prudence &   As, much Experience, is *Prudence*; so, is much Sci-
Sapience, ence, *Sapience*. For though wee usually have one name
with their of Wisedome for them both; yet the Latines did always
difference distinguish between *Prudentia* and *Sapientia*; ascribing
the former to Experience, the later to Science. But to
make their difference appeare more cleerly, let us suppose one man endued with an excellent naturall use,
and dexterity in handling his armes; and another to
have added to that dexterity, an acquired Science, of
where he can offend, or be offended by his adversarie, in
every possible posture, or guard: The ability of the former, would be to the ability of the later, as Prudence to
Sapience; both usefull; but the later infallible. But they
that trusting onely to the authority of books, follow the
blind blindly, are like him that trusting to the false rules
of the master of Fence,[23] ventures præsumptuously upon
an adversary, that either kills, or disgraces him.

Signes of   The signes of Science, are some, certain and infallible;
Science some, uncertain. Certain, when he that pretendeth the
Science of any thing, can teach the same; that is to say,
demonstrate the truth thereof perspicuously to another:
Uncertain, when onely some particular events answer to

his pretence, and upon many occasions prove so as he
sayes they must. Signes of prudence are all uncertain;
because to observe by experience, and remember all
circumstances that may alter the successe, is impossible.
But in any businesse, whereof a man has not infallible Science to proceed by; to forsake his own naturall
judgement, and be guided by generall sentences read in
Authors, and subject to many exceptions, is a signe of
folly, and generally scorned by the name of Pedantry.
And even of those men themselves, that in Councells of
the Common-wealth, love to shew their reading of Politiques and History, very few do it in their domestique
affaires, where their particular interest is concerned;
having Prudence enough for their private affaires: but in
publique they study more the reputation of their owne
wit, than the successe of anothers businesse. [23]

CHAP. VI

Of the Interiour Beginnings of Voluntary Motions;
commonly called the PASSIONS.
And the Speeches by which they are expressed.

There be in Animals, two sorts of *Motions* peculiar to   *Motion Vitall*
them: One called *Vitall*; begun in generation, and con-   *and Animal*
tinued without interruption through their whole life;
such as are the *course* of the *Bloud*, the *Pulse*, the *Breath-*
ing, the *Concoction*,[24] *Nutrition*, *Excretion*, &c; to which
Motions there needs no help of Imagination: The other
is *Animall motion*, otherwise called *Voluntary motion*;
as to *go*, to *speak*, to *move* any of our limbes, in such
manner as is first fancied in our minds. That Sense, is
Motion in the organs and interiour parts of mans body,
caused by the action of the things we See, Heare, *&c*;
And that Fancy is but the Reliques of the same Motion,
remaining after Sense, has been already sayd in the first

and second Chapters. And because *going, speaking*, and the like Voluntary motions, depend alwayes upon a precedent thought of *whither, which way*, and *what*; it is evident, that the Imagination is the first internall beginning of all Voluntary Motion. And although unstudied men, doe not conceive any motion at all to be there, where the thing moved is invisible; or the space it is moved in, is (for the shortnesse of it) insensible; yet that doth not hinder, but that such Motions are. For let a space be never so little, that which is moved over a greater space, whereof that little one is part, must first be moved over that. These small beginnings of Motion, within the body of Man, before they appear in walking, speaking, striking, and other visible actions, are com-

Endeavour monly called ENDEAVOUR.

This Endeavour, when it is toward something which *Appetite* causes it, is called APPETITE, or DESIRE; the later, being *Desire* the generall name; and the other, oftentimes restrayned to signifie the Desire of Food, namely *Hunger* and *Hunger* *Thirst*. And when the Endeavour is fromward some-*Thirst* thing, it is generally called AVERSION. These words *Aversion* *Appetite*, and *Aversion* we have from the *Latines*; and they both of them signifie the motions, one of approaching, the other of retiring. So also do the Greek words for the same, which are ὁρμὴ, and ἀφορμὴ. For Nature it selfe does often presse upon men those truths, which afterwards, when they look for somewhat beyond Nature, they stumble at. For the Schooles find in meere Appetite to go, or move, no actuall Motion at all: but because some Motion they must acknowledge, they call it Metaphoricall Motion; which is but an absurd speech: for though Words may be called metaphoricall; Bodies, and Motions cannot.

Love That which men Desire, they are also sayd to LOVE: *Hate* and to HATE those things, for which they have Aversion. So that Desire, and [24] Love, are the same thing; save that by Desire, we alwayes signifie the Absence of the Object; by Love, most commonly the Presence of the

same. So also by Aversion, we signifie the Absence; and
by Hate, the Presence of the Object.

Of Appetites, and Aversions, some are born with men;
as Appetite of food, Appetite of excretion, and exoneration,[25] (which may also and more properly be called
Aversions, from somewhat they feele in their Bodies;)
and some other Appetites, not many. The rest, which are
Appetites of particular things, proceed from Experience,
and triall of their effects upon themselves, or other men.
For of things wee know not at all, or believe not to be,
we can have no further Desire, than to tast and try. But
Aversion wee have for things, not onely which we know
have hurt us; but also that we do not know whether they
will hurt us, or not.

Those things which we neither Desire, nor Hate, we
are said to *Contemne*: CONTEMPT being nothing else
but an immobility, or contumacy of the Heart, in resisting the action of certain things; and proceeding from that
the Heart is already moved otherwise, by other more
potent objects; or from want of experience of them. *Contempt*

And because the constitution of a mans Body, is in
continuall mutation; it is impossible that all the same
things should alwayes cause in him the same Appetites,
and Aversions: much lesse can all men consent, in the
Desire of almost any one and the same Object.

But whatsoever is the object of any mans Appetite or
Desire; that is it, which he for his part calleth *Good*:
And the object of his Hate, and Aversion, *Evill*; And
of his Contempt, *Vile* and *Inconsiderable*. For these
words of Good, Evill, and Contemptible, are ever used
with relation to the person that useth them: There being
nothing simply and absolutely so; nor any common
Rule of Good and Evill, to be taken from the nature of
the objects themselves; but from the Person of the man
(where there is no Common-wealth;) or, (in a Common-
wealth,) from the Person that representeth it; or from
an Arbitrator or Judge, whom men disagreeing shall by
consent set up, and make his sentence the Rule thereof. *Good*
Evill

The Latine Tongue has two words, whose significations approach to those of Good and Evill; but are not
Pulchrum precisely the same; And those are *Pulchrum* and *Turpe*.
Turpe Whereof the former signifies that, which by some apparent signes promiseth Good; and the later, that, which
promiseth Evil. But in our Tongue we have not so generall names to expresse them by. But for *Pulchrum*, we say
in some things, *Fayre*; in others *Beautifull*, or *Handsome*,
or *Gallant*, or *Honourable*, or *Comely*, or *Amiable*; and
for *Turpe*, *Foule*, *Deformed*, *Ugly*, *Base*, *Nauseous*, and
the like, as the subject shall require; All which words, in
their proper places signifie nothing els, but the *Mine*, or
Countenance, that promiseth Good and Evil. So that of
Good there be three kinds; Good in the Promise, that is
Pulchrum; Good in Effect, as the end desired, which is
Delightfull called *Jucundum*, *Delightfull*; and Good as the Means,
Profitable which is called *Utile*, *Profitable*; and as many of Evil: For
Evill, in Promise, is that they call *Turpe*; Evil in Effect,
Unpleasant and [25] End, is *Molestum*, *Unpleasant*, *Troublesome*;
Unprofitable and Evill in the Means, *Inutile*, *Unprofitable*, *Hurtfull*.

As, in Sense, that which is really within us, is (as I
have sayd before) onely Motion, caused by the action
of externall objects, but in appearence; to the Sight,
Light and Colour; to the Eare, Sound; to the Nostrill,
Odour, &c: so, when the action of the same object is
continued from the Eyes, Eares, and other organs to the
Heart; the reall effect there is nothing but Motion, or
Endeavour; which consisteth in Appetite, or Aversion,
to, or from the object moving. But the apparence, or
Delight sense of that motion, is that wee either call DELIGHT, or
Displeasure TROUBLE OF MIND.

This Motion, which is called Appetite, and for the
Pleasure apparence of it *Delight*, and *Pleasure*, seemeth to be, a
corroboration of Vitall motion, and a help thereunto;
and therefore such things as caused Delight, were not
improperly called *Jucunda*, (*à Juvando*,) from helping
Offence or fortifying; and the contrary, *Molesta*, *Offensive*, from
hindering, and troubling the motion vitall.

Pleasure therefore, (or *Delight*,) is the apparence, or sense of Good; and *Molestation* or *Displeasure*, the apparence, or sense of Evill. And consequently all Appetite, Desire, and Love, is accompanied with some Delight more or lesse; and all Hatred, and Aversion, with more or lesse Displeasure and Offence.

Of Pleasures, or Delights, some arise from the sense of an object Present; And those may be called *Pleasures of Sense*, (The word *sensuall*, as it is used by those onely that condemn them, having no place till there be Lawes.) Of this kind are all Onerations[26] and Exonerations of the body; as also all that is pleasant, in the *Sight, Hearing, Smell, Tast, or Touch*; Others arise from the Expectation, that proceeds from foresight of the End, or Consequence of things; whether those things in the Sense Please or Displease: And these are *Pleasures of the Mind* of him that draweth those consequences; and are generally called JOY. In the like manner, Displeasures, are some in the Sense, and called PAYNE; others, in the Expectation of consequences, and are called GRIEFE.

Pleasures of sense

Pleasures of the Mind

Joy

Paine

Griefe

These simple Passions called *Appetite, Desire, Love, Aversion, Hate, Joy*, and *Griefe*, have their names for divers considerations diversified. As first, when they one succeed another, they are diversly called from the opinion men have of the likelihood of attaining what they desire. Secondly, from the object loved or hated. Thirdly, from the consideration of many of them together. Fourthly, from the Alteration or succession it selfe.

For *Appetite* with an opinion of attaining, is called HOPE.

Hope

The same, without such opinion, DESPAIRE.

Despaire

Aversion, with opinion of *Hurt* from the object, FEARE.

Feare

The same, with hope of avoyding that Hurt by resistence, COURAGE.

Courage

Sudden *Courage*, ANGER.

Anger

Constant *Hope*, CONFIDENCE of our selves.

Confidence

Constant *Despayre*, DIFFIDENCE of our selves.[27]

Diffidence

[26] *Anger* for great hurt done to another, when we conceive the same to be done by Injury, INDIGNATION.

Indignation

Benevolence *Desire* of good to another, BENEVOLENCE, GOOD

Good Nature WILL, CHARITY. If to man generally, GOOD NATURE.

Covetous- *Desire* of Riches, COVETOUSNESSE: a name used

nesse always in signification of blame; because men contending for them, are displeased with one anothers attaining them; though the desire in it selfe, be to be blamed, or allowed, according to the means by which those Riches are sought.

Ambition *Desire* of Office, or precedence, AMBITION: a name used also in the worse sense, for the reason before mentioned.

Desire of things that conduce but a little to our ends; And fear of things that are but of little hindrance,

Pusillanimity PUSILLANIMITY.

Magnanimity *Contempt* of little helps, and hindrances, MAGNANIMITY.

Valour *Magnanimity*, in danger of Death, or Wounds, VALOUR, FORTITUDE.

Liberality *Magnanimity*, in the use of Riches, LIBERALITY.

Miserable- *Pusillanimity*, in the same WRETCHEDNESSE, MIS-

nesse ERABLENESSE; or PARSIMONY; as it is liked, or disliked.

Kindnesse *Love* of Persons for society, KINDNESSE.

Naturall Lust *Love* of Persons for Pleasing the sense onely, NATURALL LUST.

Love of the same, acquired from Rumination, that is,

Luxury Imagination of Pleasure past, LUXURY.

The passion *Love* of one singularly, with desire to be singularly

of Love beloved, THE PASSION OF LOVE. The same, with fear

Jealousie that the love is not mutuall, JEALOUSIE.

Revengeful- *Desire*, by doing hurt to another, to make him con-

nesse demn some fact of his own, REVENGEFULNESSE.

Curiosity *Desire*, to know why, and how, CURIOSITY; such as is in no living creature but *Man*: so that Man is distinguished, not onely by his Reason; but also by this singular Passion from other *Animals*; in whom the appetite of food, and other pleasures of Sense, by prædominance, take away the care of knowing causes; which is a Lust of the mind, that by a perseverance of delight in the continuall and indefatigable generation of Knowledge, exceedeth the short vehemence of any carnall Pleasure.

Feare of power invisible, feigned by the mind, or imagined from tales publiquely allowed, RELIGION; not allowed, SUPERSTITION. And when the power imagined, is truly such as we imagine, TRUE RELIGION. *Religion* *Superstition* *True Religion*

Feare, without the apprehension of why, or what, PANIQUE TERROR; called so from the Fables, that make *Pan*[28] the author of them; whereas in truth, there is alwayes in him that so feareth, first, some apprehension of the cause, though the rest run away by Example; every one supposing his fellow to know why. And therefore this Passion happens to none but in a throng, or multitude of people. *Panique* *Terrour*

Joy, from apprehension of novelty, ADMIRATION; proper to Man, because it excites the appetite of knowing the cause. *Admiration*

Joy, arising from imagination of a mans own power and ability, [27] is that exultation of the mind which is called GLORYING: which if grounded upon the experience of his own former actions, is the same with *Confidence*: but if grounded on the flattery of others; or onely supposed by himself, for delight in the consequences of it, is called VAINE-GLORY: which name is properly given; because a well grounded *Confidence* begetteth Attempt; whereas the supposing of power does not, and is therefore rightly called *Vaine*. *Glory* *Vain-glory*

Griefe, from opinion of want of power, is called DEJECTION of mind. *Dejection*

The *vain-glory* which consisteth in the feigning or supposing of abilities in our selves, which we know are not, is most incident to young men, and nourished by the Histories, or Fictions of Gallant Persons; and is corrected oftentimes by Age, and Employment.

Sudden Glory, is the passion which maketh those *Sudden Glory*

Laughter   *Grimaces* called LAUGHTER; and is caused either by some sudden act of their own, that pleaseth them; or by the apprehension of some deformed thing in another, by comparison whereof they suddenly applaud themselves. And it is incident most to them, that are conscious of the fewest abilities in themselves; who are forced to keep themselves in their own favour, by observing the imperfections of other men. And therefore much Laughter at the defects of others, is a signe of Pusillanimity. For of great minds, one of the proper workes is, to help and free others from scorn; and compare themselves onely with the most able.

Sudden   On the contrary, *Sudden Dejection*, is the passion that
Dejection causeth WEEPING; and is caused by such accidents, as
Weeping suddenly take away some vehement hope, or some prop of their power: And they are most subject to it, that rely principally on helps externall, such as are Women, and Children. Therefore some Weep for the losse of Friends; Others for their unkindnesse; others for the sudden stop made to their thoughts of revenge, by Reconciliation. But in all cases, both Laughter, and Weeping, are sudden motions; Custome taking them both away. For no man Laughs at old jests; or Weeps for an old calamity.

    Griefe, for the discovery of some defect of ability,
Shame is SHAME, or the passion that discovereth it selfe in
Blushing BLUSHING; and consisteth in the apprehension of some thing dishonourable; and in young men, is a signe of the love of good reputation; and commendable: In old men it is a signe of the same; but because it comes too late, not commendable.

    The *Contempt* of good Reputation is called
Impudence IMPUDENCE.

Pitty   *Griefe*, for the Calamity of another, is PITTY; and ariseth from the imagination that the like calamity may befall himselfe; and therefore is called also COMPASSION, and in the phrase of this present time a FELLOW-FEELING: And therefore for Calamity arriving from great wickedness, the best men have the least Pitty;

and for the same Calamity, those have least Pitty, that think themselves least obnoxious to the same.

Contempt, or little sense of the calamity of others, is that which [28] men call CRUELTY; proceeding from Security of their own fortune. For, that any man should take pleasure in other mens great harmes, without other end of his own, I do not conceive it possible. *Cruelty*

Griefe, for the successe of a Competitor in wealth, honour, or other good, if it be joyned with Endeavour to enforce our own abilities to equall or exceed him, is called EMULATION: But joyned with Endeavour to supplant, or hinder a Competitor, ENVIE. *Emulation* *Envy*

When in the mind of man, Appetites, and Aversions, Hopes, and Feares, concerning one and the same thing, arise alternately; and divers good and evill consequences of the doing, or omitting the thing propounded, come successively into our thoughts; so that sometimes we have an Appetite to it; sometimes an Aversion from it; sometimes Hope to be able to do it; sometimes Despaire, or Feare to attempt it; the whole summe of Desires, Aversions, Hopes and Fears, continued till the thing be either done, or thought impossible, is that we call DELIBERATION. *Deliberation*

Therefore of things past, there is no *Deliberation*; because manifestly impossible to be changed: nor of things known to be impossible, or thought so; because men know, or think such Deliberation vain. But of things impossible, which we think possible, we may Deliberate; not knowing it is in vain. And it is called *Deliberation*; because it is a putting an end to the *Liberty* we had of doing, or omitting, according to our own Appetite, or Aversion.

This alternate Succession of Appetites, Aversions, Hopes and Fears, is no lesse in other living Creatures then in Man: and therefore Beasts also Deliberate.

Every *Deliberation* is then sayd to *End*, when that whereof they Deliberate, is either done, or thought impossible; because till then wee retain the liberty of doing, or omitting, according to our Appetite, or Aversion.

In *Deliberation*, the last Appetite, or Aversion, immediately adhæring to the action, or to the omis-*The Will* sion thereof, is that wee call the WILL; the Act, (not the faculty,) of *Willing*. And Beasts that have *Deliberation*, must necessarily also have *Will*. The Definition of the *Will*, given commonly by the Schooles, that it is a *Rationall Appetite*, is not good.[29] For if it were, then could there be no Voluntary Act against Reason. For a *Voluntary Act* is that, which proceedeth from the *will*, and no other. But if in stead of a Rationall Appetite, we shall say an Appetite resulting from a precedent Deliberation, then the Definition is the same that I have given here. *Will* therefore *is the last Appetite in Deliberating*. And though we say in common Discourse, a man had a Will once to do a thing, that neverthelesse he forbore to do; yet that is properly but an Inclination, which makes no Action Voluntary; because the action depends not of it, but of the last Inclination, or Appetite. For if the intervenient Appetites, make any action Voluntary; then by the same Reason all intervenient Aversions, should make the same action Involuntary; and so one and the same action, should be both Voluntary & Involuntary.

[29] By this it is manifest, that not onely actions that have their beginning from Covetousnesse, Ambition, Lust, or other Appetites to the thing propounded; but also those that have their beginning from Aversion, or Feare of those consequences that follow the omission, are *voluntary actions*.

Formes of The formes of Speech by which the Passions are *Speech, in* expressed, are partly the same, and partly different from *Passion* those, by which wee expresse our Thoughts. And first generally all Passions may be expressed *Indicatively*; as *I love, I feare, I joy, I deliberate, I will, I command*: but some of them have particular expressions by themselves, which neverthelesse are not affirmations, unlesse it be when they serve to make other inferences, besides that of the Passion they proceed from. Deliberation is expressed *Subjunctively*; which is a speech proper to signifie suppositions, with their consequences; as, *If this be done, then this will follow*; and differs not from the language of Reasoning, save that Reasoning is in generall words; but Deliberation for the most part is of Particulars. The language of Desire, and Aversion, is *Imperative*; as *Do this, forbeare that*; which when the party is obliged to do, or forbeare, is *Command*; otherwise *Prayer*; or els *Counsell*. The language of Vain-Glory, of Indignation, Pitty and Revengefulness, *Optative*: But of the Desire to know, there is a peculiar expression, called *Interrogative*; as, *What is it, when shall it, how is it done*, and *why so?* Other language of the Passions I find none: For Cursing, Swearing, Reviling, and the like, do not signifie as Speech; but as the actions of a tongue accustomed.

These formes of Speech, I say, are expressions, or voluntary significations of our Passions: but certain signes they be not; because they may be used arbitrarily, whether they that use them, have such Passions or not. The best signes of Passions present, are either in the countenance, motions of the body, actions, and ends, or aimes, which we otherwise know the man to have.

And because in Deliberation, the Appetites, and Aversions are raised by foresight of the good and evill consequences, and sequels of the action whereof we Deliberate; the good or evill effect thereof dependeth on the foresight of a long chain of consequences, of which very seldome any man is able to see to the end. But for so farre as a man seeth, if the Good in those consequences, be greater than the Evill, the whole chaine is that which Writers call *Apparent*, or *Seeming Good*. And contrarily, when the Evill exceedeth the Good, the whole is *Apparent*, or *Seeming Evill*: so that he who hath by Experience, or Reason, the greatest and surest prospect of Consequences, Deliberates best himself; and is able when he will, to give the best counsell unto others. *Good and Evill apparent*

Continuall successe in obtaining those things which a man from time to time desireth, that is to say, con-
Felicity tinuall prospering, is that men call FELICITY; I mean the Felicity of this life. For there is no such thing as per-petuall Tranquillity of mind, while we live here;[30] because Life it selfe is but Motion, and can never be without Desire, [30] nor without Feare, no more than without Sense. What kind of Felicity God hath ordained to them that devoutly honour him, a man shall no sooner know, than enjoy; being joyes, that now are as incomprehen-sible, as the word of School-men *Beatificall Vision* is unintelligible.

The forme of Speech whereby men signifie their opin-
Praise ion of the Goodnesse of any thing, is PRAISE. That
Magnification whereby they signifie the power and greatnesse of any thing, is MAGNIFYING. And that whereby they signifie the opinion they have of a mans Felicity, is by the Greeks
μαχαρισμός called μακαρισμός, for which wee have no name in our tongue.[31] And thus much is sufficient for the present purpose, to have been said of the PASSIONS.

CHAP. VII

Of the Ends, *or Resolutions of* DISCOURSE

Of all *Discourse*, governed by desire of Knowledge, there is at last an *End*, either by attaining, or by giving over. And in the chain of Discourse, wheresoever it be interrupted, there is an End for that time.

If the Discourse be meerly Mentall, it consisteth of thoughts that the thing will be, and will not be; or that it has been, and has not been, alternately. So that wheresoever you break off the chayn of a mans Dis-course, you leave him in a Præsumption of *it will be*, or, *it will not be*; or *it has been*, or, *has not been*. All which is *Opinion*. And that which is alternate Appetite,

in Deliberating concerning Good and Evil; the same is
alternate Opinion, in the Enquiry of the truth of *Past*,
and *Future*. And as the last Appetite in Deliberation, is
called the *Will*; so the last Opinion in search of the truth
of Past, and Future, is called the JUDGEMENT, or *Reso-* *Judgement,*
lute and *Finall Sentence* of him that *discourseth*. And as *or Sentence*
the whole chain of Appetites alternate, in the question *final*
of Good, or Bad, is called *Deliberation*; so the whole
chain of Opinions alternate, in the question of True, or
False, is called DOUBT. *Doubt*

No Discourse whatsoever, can End in absolute knowledge of Fact, past, or to come. For, as for the knowledge
of Fact, it is originally, Sense; and ever after, Memory.
And for the knowledge of Consequence, which I have
said before is called Science, it is not Absolute, but Conditionall. No man can know by Discourse, that this, or
that, is, has been, or will be; which is to know absolutely: but onely, that if This be, That is; if This has been,
That has been; if This shall be, That shall be: which is
to know conditionally; and that not the consequence of
one thing to another; but of one name of a thing, to
another name of the same thing.

And therefore, when the Discourse is put into Speech,
and begins with the Definitions of Words, and proceeds
by Connexion of the same into generall Affirmations,
and of these again into Syllogismes; [31] the End or last
summe is called the Conclusion; and the thought of the
mind by it signified, is that conditionall Knowledge, or
Knowledge of the consequence of words, which is commonly called SCIENCE. But if the first ground of such *Science*
Discourse, be not Definitions; or if the Definitions be not
rightly joyned together into Syllogismes, then the End or
Conclusion, is again OPINION, namely of the truth of *Opinion*
somewhat said, though sometimes in absurd and senslesse
words, without possibility of being understood. When
two, or more men, know of one and the same fact, they
are said to be CONSCIOUS of it one to another; which *Conscience*
is as much as to know it together. And because such are

fittest witnesses of the facts of one another, or of a third; it was, and ever will be reputed a very Evill act, for any man to speak against his *Conscience*; or to corrupt or force another so to do: Insomuch that the plea of Conscience, has been alwayes hearkened unto very diligently in all times. Afterwards, men made use of the same word metaphorically, for the knowledge of their own secret facts, and secret thoughts; and therefore it is Rhetorically said, that the Conscience is a thousand witnesses. And last of all, men, vehemently in love with their own new opinions, (though never so absurd,) and obstinately bent to maintain them, gave those their opinions also that reverenced name of Conscience, as if they would have it seem unlawfull, to change or speak against them; and so pretend to know they are true, when they know at most, but that they think so.

When a mans Discourse beginneth not at Definitions, it beginneth either at some other contemplation of his own, and then it is still called Opinion; Or it beginneth at some saying of another, of whose ability to know the truth, and of whose honesty in not deceiving, he doubteth not; and then the Discourse is not so much concerning the Thing, as the Person; And the Resolution *Beliefe* is called BELEEFE, and FAITH: *Faith, in* the man; *Beleefe*, *Faith* both *of* the man, and *of* the truth of what he sayes. So that in Beleefe are two opinions; one of the saying of the man; the other of his vertue. To *have faith in*, or *trust to*, or *beleeve a man*, signifie the same thing; namely, an opinion of the veracity of the man: But to *beleeve what is said*, signifieth onely an opinion of the truth of the saying. But wee are to observe that this Phrase, *I beleeve in*; as also the Latine, *Credo in*; and the Greek, πιστέυω εις, are never used but in the writings of Divines. In stead of them, in other writings are put, *I beleeve him*; *I trust him*; *I have faith in him*; *I rely on him*: and in Latin, *Credo illi*; *fido illi*: and in Greek, πιστέυω ἀυτῷ: and that this singularity of the Ecclesiastique use of the word hath raised many disputes about the right object of the Christian Faith.

But by *Beleeving in*, as it is in the Creed, is meant, not trust in the Person; but Confession and acknowledgement of the Doctrine. For not onely Christians, but all manner of men do so believe in God, as to hold all for truth they heare him say, whether they understand it, or not; which is all the Faith and trust can possibly be had in any person whatsoever: But they do not all believe the Doctrine of the Creed.

[32] From whence we may inferre, that when wee believe any saying whatsoever it be, to be true, from arguments taken, not from the thing it selfe, or from the principles of naturall Reason, but from the Authority, and good opinion wee have, of him that hath sayd it; then is the speaker, or person we believe in, or trust in, and whose word we take, the object of our Faith; and the Honour done in Believing, is done to him onely. And consequently, when wee Believe that the Scriptures are the word of God, having no immediate revelation from God himselfe, our Beleefe, Faith, and Trust is in the Church; whose word we take, and acquiesce therein. And they that believe that which a Prophet relates unto them in the name of God, take the word of the Prophet, do honour to him, and in him trust, and believe, touching the truth of what he relateth, whether he be a true, or a false Prophet. And so it is also with all other History. For if I should not believe all that is written by Historians, of the glorious acts of *Alexander*, or *Cæsar*; I do not think the Ghost of *Alexander*, or *Cæsar*, had any just cause to be offended; or any body else, but the Historian. If *Livy* say the Gods made once a Cow speak, and we believe it not; wee distrust not God therein, but *Livy*.[32] So that it is evident, that whatsoever we believe, upon no other reason, then what is drawn from authority of men onely, and their writings; whether they be sent from God or not, is Faith in men onely.

Of the VERTUES commonly called
INTELLECTUAL; and their contrary DEFECTS

Intellectuall VERTUE generally, in all sorts of subjects, is somewhat
Vertue that is valued for eminence; and consisteth in compari-
defined son. For if all things were equally in all men, nothing
would be prized. And by *Vertues* INTELLECTUALL, are
always understood such abilityes of the mind, as men
praise, value, and desire should be in themselves; and go
commonly under the name of a *good witte*; though the
same word *Witte*, be used also, to distinguish one certain ability from the rest.

Wit, Naturall,   These *Vertues* are of two sorts; *Naturall*, and
or Acquired *Acquired*. By Naturall, I mean not, that which a man
hath from his Birth: for that is nothing else but Sense;
wherein men differ so little one from another, and from
brute Beasts, as it is not to be reckoned amongst Vertues.
But I mean, that *Witte*, which is gotten by Use onely,
and Experience; without Method, Culture, or Instruc-
Naturall Wit tion. This NATURALL WITTE, consisteth principally in
two things; *Celerity of Imagining*, (that is, swift succession of one thought to another;) and *steddy direction* to
some approved end. On the Contrary a slow Imagination, maketh that Defect, or fault of the mind, which is
commonly called DULNESSE, *Stupidity*, and sometimes
by other names that signifie slownesse of motion, or difficulty to be moved.

[33] And this difference of quicknesse, is caused by the
difference of mens passions; that love and dislike, some one
thing, some another: and therefore some mens thoughts
run one way, some another; and are held to, and observe
differently the things that passe through their imagination. And whereas in this succession of mens thoughts,
there is nothing to observe in the things they think on,
but either in what they be *like one another*, or in what

they be *unlike*, or *what they serve for*, or *how they serve to such a purpose*; Those that observe their similitudes, in case they be such as are but rarely observed by others, are sayd to have a *Good Wit*; by which, in this occasion, is meant a *Good Fancy*. But they that observe their differences, and dissimilitudes; which is called *Distinguishing*, and *Discerning*, and *Judging* between thing and thing; in case, such discerning be not easie, are said to have a *good Judgement*: and particularly in matter of conversation and businesse; wherein, times, places, and persons are to be discerned, this Vertue is called DISCRETION. The former, that is, Fancy, without the help of Judgement, is not commended as a Vertue: but the later which is Judgement, and Discretion, is commended for it selfe, without the help of Fancy. Besides the Discretion of times, places, and persons, necessary to a good Fancy, there is required also an often application of his thoughts to their End; that is to say, to some use to be made of them. This done; he that hath this Vertue, will be easily fitted with similitudes, that will please, not onely by illustration of his discourse, and adorning it with new and apt metaphors; but also, by the rarity of their invention. But without Steddinesse, and Direction to some End, a great Fancy is one kind of Madnesse; such as they have, that entring into any discourse, are snatched from their purpose, by every thing that comes in their thought, into so many, and so long digressions, and Parentheses, that they utterly lose themselves: Which kind of folly, I know no particular name for: but the cause of it is, sometimes want of experience; whereby that seemeth to a man new and rare, which doth not so to others: sometimes Pusillanimity; by which that seems great to him, which other men think a trifle: and whatsoever is new, or great, and therefore thought fit to be told, withdrawes a man by degrees from the intended way of his discourse.

In a good Poem, whether it be *Epique*, or *Dramatique*; as also in *Sonnets*, *Epigrams*, and other Pieces, both

Good Wit, or Fancy

Good Judgement

Discretion

Judgement and Fancy are required: But the Fancy must be more eminent; because they please for the Extravagancy; but ought not to displease by Indiscretion.

In a good History, the Judgement must be eminent; because the goodnesse consisteth, in the Method, in the Truth, and in the Choyse of the actions that are most profitable to be known. Fancy has no place, but onely in adorning the stile.

In Orations of Prayse, and in Invectives, the Fancy is prædominant; because the designe is not truth, but to Honour or Dishonour; which is done by noble, or by vile comparisons. The Judgement does but suggest what circumstances make an action laudable, or culpable.

[34] In Hortatives, and Pleadings, as Truth, or Disguise serveth best to the Designe in hand; so is the Judgement, or the Fancy most required.

In Demonstration, in Councell, and all rigourous search of Truth, Judgement does all; except sometimes the understanding have need to be opened by some apt similitude; and then there is so much use of Fancy. But for Metaphors, they are in this case utterly excluded. For seeing they openly professe deceipt; to admit them into Councell, or Reasoning, were manifest folly.

And in any Discourse whatsoever, if the defect of Discretion be apparent, how extravagant soever the Fancy be, the whole discourse will be taken for a signe of want of wit; and so will it never when the Discretion is manifest, though the Fancy be never so ordinary.

The secret thoughts of a man run over all things, holy, prophane, clean, obscene, grave, and light, without shame, or blame; which verball discourse cannot do, farther than the Judgement shall approve of the Time, Place, and Persons. An Anatomist, or a Physitian may speak, or write his judgement of unclean things; because it is not to please, but profit: but for another man to write his extravagant, and pleasant fancies of the same, is as if a man, from being tumbled into the dirt, should come and present himselfe before good company. And 'tis the want of Discretion that makes the difference. Again, in profest remissnesse of mind, and familiar company, a man may play with the sounds, and æquivocall significations of words; and that many times with encounters of extraordinary Fancy: but in a Sermon, or in publique, or before persons unknown, or whom we ought to reverence, there is no Gingling[33] of words that will not be accounted folly: and the difference is onely in the want of Discretion. So that where Wit is wanting, it is not Fancy that is wanting, but Discretion. Judgement therefore without Fancy is Wit, but Fancy without Judgement not.

When the thoughts of a man, that has a designe in hand, running over a multitude of things, observes how they conduce to that designe; or what designe they may conduce unto; if his observations be such as are not easie, or usuall, This wit of his is called PRUDENCE; and *Prudence* dependeth on much Experience, and Memory of the like things, and their consequences heretofore. In which there is not so much difference of Men, as there is in their Fancies and Judgements; Because the Experience of men equall in age, is not much unequall, as to the quantity; but lyes in different occasions; every one having his private designes. To govern well a family, and a kingdome, are not different degrees of Prudence; but different sorts of businesse; no more then to draw a picture in little, or as great, or greater then the life, are different degrees of Art. A plain husband-man is more Prudent in affaires of his own house, then a Privy Counseller in the affaires of another man.

To Prudence, if you adde the use of unjust, or dishonest means, such as usually are prompted to men by Feare, or Want; you have that Crooked Wisdome, which is called CRAFT; which is a signe of [35] Pusillanimity. *Craft* For Magnanimity is contempt of unjust, or dishonest helps. And that which the Latines call *Versutia*, (translated into English, *Shifting*,) and is a putting off of a present danger or incommodity, by engaging into a greater, as when a man robbs one to pay another, is but a shorter sighted Craft, called *Versutia*, from *Versura*, which signifies taking mony at usurie, for the present payment of interest.

Acquired Wit   As for *acquired Wit*, (I mean acquired by method and instruction,) there is none but Reason; which is grounded on the right use of Speech; and produceth the Sciences. But of Reason and Science, I have already spoken in the fifth and sixth Chapters.

The causes of this difference of Witts, are in the Passions: and the difference of Passions, proceedeth partly from the different Constitution of the body, and partly from different Education. For if the difference proceeded from the temper of the brain, and the organs of Sense, either exterior or interior, there would be no lesse difference of men in their Sight, Hearing, or other Senses, than in their Fancies, and Discretions. It proceeds therefore from the Passions; which are different, not onely from the difference of mens complexions; but also from their difference of customes, and education.

The Passions that most of all cause the differences of Wit, are principally, the more or lesse Desire of Power, of Riches, of Knowledge, and of Honour. All which may be reduced to the first, that is Desire of Power. For Riches, Knowledge and Honour are but severall sorts of Power.

And therefore, a man who has no great Passion for any of these things; but is as men terme it indifferent; though he may be so farre a good man, as to be free from giving offence; yet he cannot possibly have either a great Fancy, or much Judgement. For the Thoughts, are to the Desires, as Scouts, and Spies, to range abroad, and find the way to the things Desired: All Stedinesse of the minds motion, and all quicknesse of the same, proceeding from thence. For as to have no Desire, is to be Dead: so to have weak Passions, is Dulnesse; and to have *Giddinesse* Passions indifferently for every thing, GIDDINESSE, and *Distraction*; and to have stronger, and more vehement

Passions for any thing, than is ordinarily seen in others, is that which men call MADNESSE.   *Madnesse*

Whereof there be almost as many kinds, as of the Passions themselves. Sometimes the extraordinary and extravagant Passion, proceedeth from the evill constitution of the organs of the Body, or harme done them; and sometimes the hurt, and indisposition of the Organs, is caused by the vehemence, or long continuance of the Passion. But in both cases the Madnesse is of one and the same nature.

The Passion, whose violence, or continuance maketh Madnesse, is either great *vaine-Glory*; which is commonly called *Pride*, and *selfe-conceipt*; or great *Dejection* of mind.

Pride, subjecteth a man to Anger, the excesse whereof, is the Madnesse called RAGE, and FURY. And thus it   *Rage* comes to passe [36] that excessive desire of Revenge, when it becomes habituall, hurteth the organs, and becomes Rage: That excessive love, with jealousie, becomes also Rage: Excessive opinion of a mans own selfe, for divine inspiration, for wisdome, learning, forme, and the like, becomes Distraction, and Giddinesse: The same, joyned with Envy, Rage: Vehement opinion of the truth of any thing, contradicted by others, Rage.

Dejection, subjects a man to causelesse fears; which is a Madnesse commonly called MELANCHOLY, appar-   *Melancholy* ent also in divers manners; as in haunting of solitudes, and graves; in superstitious behaviour; and in fearing some one, some another particular thing. In summe, all Passions that produce strange and unusuall behaviour, are called by the generall name of Madnesse. But of the severall kinds of Madnesse, he that would take the paines, might enrowle a legion. And if the Excesses be madnesse, there is no doubt but the Passions themselves, when they tend to Evill, are degrees of the same.

(For example,) Though the effect of folly, in them that are possessed of an opinion of being inspired, be not visible alwayes in one man, by any very extravagant action, that proceedeth from such Passion; yet when many of them conspire together, the Rage of the whole multitude is visible enough. For what argument of Madnesse can there be greater, than to clamour, strike, and throw stones at our best friends? Yet this is somewhat lesse than such a multitude will do. For they will clamour, fight against, and destroy those, by whom all their lifetime before, they have been protected, and secured from injury. And if this be Madnesse in the multitude, it is the same in every particular man. For as in the middest of the sea, though a man perceive no sound of that part of the water next him; yet he is well assured, that part contributes as much, to the Roaring of the Sea, as any other part, of the same quantity: so also, though wee perceive no great unquietnesse, in one, or two men; yet we may be well assured, that their singular Passions, are parts of the Seditious roaring of a troubled Nation. And if there were nothing else that bewrayed their madnesse; yet that very arrogating such inspiration to themselves, is argument enough. If some man in Bedlam[34] should entertaine you with sober discourse; and you desire in taking leave, to know what he were, that you might another time requite his civility; and he should tell you, he were God the Father; I think you need expect no extravagant action for argument of his Madnesse.

This opinion of Inspiration, called commonly, Private Spirit, begins very often, from some lucky finding of an Errour generally held by others; and not knowing, or not remembring, by what conduct of reason, they came to so singular a truth, (as they think it, though it be many times an untruth they light on,) they presently admire themselves; as being in the speciall grace of God Almighty, who hath revealed the same to them supernaturally, by his Spirit.

Again, that Madnesse is nothing else, but too much appearing Passion, may be gathered out of the effects of Wine, which are the same with those of the evill disposition of the organs. For the varie[37]ty of behaviour in

men that have drunk too much, is the same with that of
Mad-men: some of them Raging, others Loving, others
Laughing, all extravagantly, but according to their severall domineering Passions: For the effect of the wine, does
but remove Dissimulation; and take from them the sight
of the deformity of their Passions. For, (I believe) the
most sober men, when they walk alone without care and
employment of the mind, would be unwilling the vanity
and Extravagance of their thoughts at that time should
be publiquely seen: which is a confession, that Passions
unguided, are for the most part meere Madnesse.

The opinions of the world, both in antient and later
ages, concerning the cause of madnesse, have been
two. Some, deriving them from the Passions; some,
from Dæmons, or Spirits, either good, or bad, which
they thought might enter into a man, possesse him, and
move his organs in such strange, and uncouth manner, as mad-men use to do. The former sort therefore,
called such men, Mad-men: but the Later, called them
sometimes *Dæmoniacks*, (that is, possessed with spirits;) sometimes *Energumeni*, (that is, agitated, or moved
with spirits;) and now in *Italy* they are called not onely
Pazzi, Mad-men; but also *Spiritati*, men possest.

There was once a great conflux of people in *Abdera*,
a City of the Greeks, at the acting of the Tragedy of
Andromeda,[35] upon an extream hot day: whereupon, a
great many of the spectators falling into Fevers, had this
accident from the heat, and from the Tragedy together,
that they did nothing but pronounce Iambiques, with
the names of *Perseus* and *Andromeda*; which together
with the Fever, was cured, by the comming on of Winter:
And this madnesse was thought to proceed from the Passion imprinted by the Tragedy. Likewise there raigned a
fit of madnesse in another Græcian City, which seized
onely the young Maidens; and caused many of them to
hang themselves.[36] This was by most then thought an act
of the Divel. But one that suspected, that contempt of
life in them, might proceed from some Passion of the

mind, and supposing they did not contemne also their
honour, gave counsell to the Magistrates, to strip such
as so hang'd themselves, and let them hang out naked.
This the story sayes cured that madnesse. But on the other
side, the same Græcians, did often ascribe madnesse, to
the operation of the Eumenides, or Furyes; and sometimes of *Ceres, Phœbus*, and other Gods:[37] so much did
men attribute to Phantasmes, as to think them aëreal living bodies; and generally to call them Spirits. And as the
Romans in this, held the same opinion with the Greeks:
so also did the Jewes; For they called mad-men Prophets, or (according as they thought the spirits good or
bad) Dæmoniacks; and some of them called both Prophets, and Dæmoniacks, mad-men; and some called the
same man both Dæmoniack, and mad-man. But for the
Gentiles, 'tis no wonder; because Diseases, and Health;
Vices, and Vertues; and many naturall accidents, were
with them termed, and worshipped as Dæmons. So that
a man was to understand by Dæmon, as well (sometimes) an Ague, as a Divell. But for the Jewes to have
such opini[38]on, is somewhat strange. For neither
Moses, nor *Abraham*[38] pretended to Prophecy by possession of a Spirit; but from the voyce of God; or by a Vision
or Dream: Nor is there any thing in his Law, Morall,
or Ceremoniall, by which they were taught, there was
any such Enthusiasme; or any Possession. When God
is sayd, *Numb.* 11. 25. to take from the Spirit that was
in *Moses*, and give to the 70. Elders, the Spirit of God
(taking it for the substance of God) is not divided. The
Scriptures by the Spirit of God in man, mean a mans
spirit, enclined to Godlinesse. And where it is said *Exod.*
28.3. *Whom I have filled with the spirit of wisdome to
make garments for Aaron*,[39] is not meant a spirit put
into them, that can make garments; but the wisdome of
their own spirits in that kind of work. In the like sense,
the spirit of man, when it produceth unclean actions, is
ordinarily called an unclean spirit; and so other spirits,
though not alwayes, yet as often as the vertue or vice

so stiled, is extraordinary, and Eminent. Neither did the other Prophets of the old Testament pretend Enthusiasme; or, that God spake in them; but to them by Voyce, Vision, or Dream; and the *Burthen of the Lord*[40] was not Possession, but Command. How then could the Jewes fall into this opinion of possession? I can imagine no reason, but that which is common to all men; namely, the want of curiosity to search naturall causes; and their placing Felicity, in the acquisition of the grosse pleasures of the Senses, and the things that most immediately conduce thereto. For they that see any strange, and unusuall ability, or defect in a mans mind; unlesse they see withall, from what cause it may probably proceed, can hardly think it naturall; and if not naturall, they must needs thinke it supernaturall; and then what can it be, but that either God, or the Divell is in him? And hence it came to passe, when our Saviour (*Mark* 3.21.) was compassed about with the multitude, those of the house doubted he was mad, and went out to hold him: but the Scribes said he had *Belzebub*, and that was it, by which he cast out divels; as if the greater mad-man had awed the lesser. And that (*John* 10.20.) some said, *He hath a Divell, and is mad*; whereas others holding him for a Prophet, sayd, *These are not the words of one that hath a Divell*. So in the old Testament he that came to anoynt *Jehu*,[41] 2 *Kings* 9.11. was a Prophet; but some of the company asked *Jehu*, *What came that mad-man for?* So that in summe, it is manifest, that whosoever behaved himselfe in extraordinary manner, was thought by the Jewes to be possessed either with a good, or evill spirit; except by the Sadduces,[42] who erred so farre on the other hand, as not to believe there were at all any spirits, (which is very neere to direct Atheisme;) and thereby perhaps the more provoked others, to terme such men Dæmoniacks, rather than mad-men.

But why then does our Saviour proceed in the curing of them, as if they were possest; and not as if they were mad? To which I can give no other kind of answer, but that which is given to those that urge the Scripture in like manner against the opinion of the motion of the Earth. The Scripture was written to shew unto men the kingdome of God, and to prepare their mindes to become his obedient [39] subjects; leaving the world, and the Philosophy thereof, to the disputation of men, for the exercising of their naturall Reason. Whether the Earths, or Suns motion make the day, and night; or whether the Exorbitant actions of men, proceed from Passion, or from the Divell, (so we worship him not) it is all one, as to our obedience, and subjection to God Almighty; which is the thing for which the Scripture was written. As for that our Saviour speaketh to the disease, as to a person; it is the usuall phrase of all that cure by words onely, as Christ did, (and Inchanters pretend to do, whether they speak to a Divel or not.) For is not Christ also said (*Math*.8.26.) to have rebuked the winds? Is not he said also (*Luk*.4.39.) to rebuke a Fever? Yet this does not argue that a Fever is a Divel. And whereas many of those Divels are said to confesse Christ; it is not necessary to interpret those places otherwise, than that those mad-men confessed him. And whereas our Saviour (*Math*.12.43.) speaketh of an unclean Spirit, that having gone out of a man, wandreth through dry places, seeking rest, and finding none; and returning into the same man, with seven other spirits worse than himselfe; It is manifestly a Parable, alluding to a man, that after a little endeavour to quit his lusts, is vanquished by the strength of them; and becomes seven times worse than he was. So that I see nothing at all in the Scripture, that requireth a beliefe, that Dæmoniacks were any other thing but Mad-men.

Insignificant   There is yet another fault in the Discourses of some *Speech* men; which may also be numbred amongst the sorts of Madnesse; namely, that abuse of words, whereof I have spoken before in the fifth chapter, by the Name of Absurdity. And that is, when men speak such words, as put together, have in them no signification at all; but are fallen upon by some, through misunderstanding of the words they have received, and repeat by rote; by others, from intention to deceive by obscurity. And this is incident to none but those, that converse in questions of matters incomprehensible, as the Schoole-men; or in questions of abstruse Philosophy. The common sort of men seldome speak Insignificantly, and are therefore, by those other Egregious persons counted Idiots. But to be assured their words are without any thing correspondent to them in the mind, there would need some Examples; which if any man require, let him take a Schoole-man into his hands, and see if he can translate any one chapter concerning any difficult point; as the Trinity; the Deity; the nature of Christ; Transubstantiation; Free-will, &c. into any of the moderne tongues, so as to make the same intelligible; or into any tolerable Latine, such as they were acquainted withall, that lived when the Latine tongue was Vulgar. What is the meaning of these words. *The first cause does not necessarily inflow any thing into the second, by force of the Essentiall subordination of the second causes, by Which it may help it to worke?* They are the Translation of the Title of the sixth chapter of *Suarez* first Booke, *Of the Concourse, Motion, and Help of God.*[43] When men write whole volumes of such stuffe, are they not Mad, or intend to make others so? And particularly, in the question [40] of Transubstantiation; where after certain words spoken, they that say, the White*nesse*, Round*nesse*, Magni*tude*, Quali*ty*, Corruptibili*ty*, all which are incorporeall, &c. go out of the Wafer, into the Body of our blessed Saviour, do they not make those *Nesses*, *Tudes* and *Ties*, to be so many spirits possessing his body? For by Spirits, they mean alwayes things, that being incorporeall, are neverthelesse moveable from one place to another. So that this kind of Absurdity, may rightly be numbred amongst the many sorts of Madnesse; and all the time that guided by clear Thoughts of their worldly lust, they forbear disputing, or writing thus, but Lucide Intervals. And thus much of the Vertues and Defects Intellectuall.

Of the Severall SUBJECTS of KNOWLEDGE

There are of KNOWLEDGE two kinds; whereof one is *Knowledge of Fact*: the other *Knowledge of the Consequence of one Affirmation to another*. The former is nothing else, but Sense and Memory, and is *Absolute Knowledge*; as when we see a Fact doing, or remember it done: And this is the Knowledge required in a Witnesse. The later is called *Science*; and is *Conditionall*; as when we know, that, *If the figure showne be a Circle, then any straight line through the Center shall divide it into two equall parts*. And this is the Knowledge required in a Philosopher; that is to say, of him that pretends to Reasoning.

The Register of *Knowledge of Fact* is called *History*. Whereof there be two sorts: one called *Naturall History*; which is the History of such Facts, or Effects of Nature, as have no Dependance on Mans *Will*; Such as are the Histories of *Metals*, *Plants*, *Animals*, *Regions*, and the like. The other, is *Civill History*; which is the History of the Voluntary Actions of men in Common-wealths.

The Registers of Science, are such *Books* as contain the *Demonstrations* of Consequences of one Affirmation, to another; and are commonly called *Books of Philosophy*; whereof the sorts are many, according to the diversity of the Matter; And may be divided in such manner as I have divided them in the following Table. [41]

SCIENCE, that is, Knowledge of Consequences; which is called also PHILOSOPHY.

- **Consequences from the Accidents of Bodies Naturall; which is called naturall Philosophy.**
  - **Consequences from the Accidents common to all Bodies Naturall; which are Quantity, and Motions.**
    - Consequences from Quantity, and Motion Indeterminate; which being the Principles, or first foundation of Philosophy, is called *Philosophia Prima.* → **PHILOSOPHIA PRIMA.**
    - Consequences from Quantity, and Motion determined.
      - Consequences from Quantity, and Motion determined.
        - By Figure, ... } *Mathematiques,* → **GEOMETRY.**
        - By Number, ... } → **ARITHMETIQUE.**
      - Consequences from the Motion, and Quantity of Bodies *in speciall.*
        - Consequences from the Motion, and Quantity of the great parts of the World, as the *Earth and Starres.* — *Cosmography,* → **ASTRONOMY. GEOGRAPHY.**
        - Consequences from the Motion of *Special* kinds, and Figures of Body. — *Mechaniques, Doctrine of Weight.* → *Science of* **ENGINEERS. ARCHITECTURE. NAVIGATION.**
  - **PHYSIQUES, or Consequences from Quality.**
    - Consequences from the Qualities of Bodyes Transient, such as sometimes appear, sometimes vanish, ... → **METEOROLOGY.**
    - Consequences from the Qualities of Bodies *Permanent.*
      - Consequences from the Qualities of *Starres.*
        - Consequences from the *Light* of the Starres. Out of this, and the Motion of the Sunne, is made the Science of .... → **SCIOGRAPHY.[44]**
        - Consequences from the *Influence* of the Starres, ... → **ASTROLOGY.**
      - Consequences from the Qualities of Bodies *Terrestriall.*
        - Consequences from the parts of the Earth, that are *without Sense.*
          - Consequences from the Qualities of *Minerals,* as *Stones, Metalls, &c.*
          - Consequences from the Qualities of *Vegetables,*
        - Consequences from the Qualities of *Animals.*
          - Consequences from the Qualities of *Animals in generall.*
            - Consequences from *Vision,* .... → **OPTIQUES.**
            - Consequences from *Sounds,* .... → **MUSIQUE.**
            - Consequences of Consequences from the rest of the senses.
          - Consequences from the Qualities of *Men in speciall.*
            - Consequences from the Passions of men, ... → **ETHIQUES.**
            - Consequences from *Speech,*
              - In *Magnifying, Villifying, &c.* ...... → **POETRY.**
              - In *Reasoning,* .... → **RHETORIQUE.**
              - In *Perswading,* .... → **LOGIQUE.**
              - In *Contracting,* .... → The Science of **Just and Unjust.**

- **Consequences from the Accidents of Politique Bodies; which is called POLITIQUES, and CIVILL PHILOSOPHY.**
  - 1. Of Consequences from the *Institution* of COMMON-WEALTHS, to the *Rights,* and *Duties* of the *Body Politique,* or *Sovereign.*
  - 2. Of Consequences from the same, to the *Duty,* of and *Rights,* of the *Subjects.*

Of POWER, WORTH, DIGNITY, HONOUR, *and* WORTHINESSE

Power The POWER *of a Man*, (to take it Universally,) is his present means, to obtain some future apparent Good. And is either *Originall*, or *Instrumentall*.

Naturall Power, is the eminence of the Faculties of Body, or Mind: as extraordinary Strength, Forme, Prudence, Arts, Eloquence, Liberality, Nobility. *Instrumentall* are those Powers, which acquired by these, or by fortune, are means and Instruments to acquire more: as Riches, Reputation, Friends, and the secret working of God, which men call Good Luck. For the nature of Power, is in this point, like to Fame, increasing as it proceeds; or like the motion of heavy bodies, which the further they go, make still the more hast.

The Greatest of humane Powers, is that which is compounded of the Powers of most men, united by consent, in one person, Naturall, or Civill, that has the use of all their Powers depending on his will; such as is the Power of a Common-wealth: Or depending on the wills of each particular; such as is the Power of a Faction, or of divers factions leagued. Therefore to have servants, is Power; To have friends, is Power: for they are strengths united.

Also Riches joyned with liberality, is Power; because it procureth friends, and servants: Without liberality, not so; because in this case they defend not; but expose men to Envy, as a Prey.

Reputation of power, is Power; because it draweth with it the adhærence of those that need protection.

So is Reputation of love of a mans Country, (called Popularity,) for the same Reason.

Also, what quality soever maketh a man beloved, or feared of many; or the reputation of such quality, is

Power; because it is a means to have the assistance, and service of many.

Good successe is Power; because it maketh reputation of Wisdome, or good fortune; which makes men either feare him, or rely on him.

Affability of men already in power, is encrease of Power; because it gaineth love.

Reputation of Prudence in the conduct of Peace or War, is Power; because to prudent men, we commit the government of our selves, more willingly than to others.

Nobility is Power, not in all places, but onely in those Common-wealths, where it has Priviledges: for in such priviledges consisteth their Power.

Eloquence is power; because it is seeming Prudence.

Forme is Power; because being a promise of Good, it recom[42]mendeth men to the favour of women and strangers.

The Sciences, are small Power; because not eminent; and therefore, not acknowledged in any man; nor are at all, but in a few; and in them, but of a few things. For Science is of that nature, as none can understand it to be, but such as in a good measure have attayned it.

Arts of publique use, as Fortification, making of Engines, and other Instruments of War; because they conferre to Defence, and Victory, are Power: And though the true Mother of them, be Science, namely the Mathematiques; yet, because they are brought into the Light, by the hand of the Artificer, they be esteemed (the Midwife passing with the vulgar for the Mother,) as his issue.

The *Value*, or WORTH of a man, is as of all other *Worth* things, his Price; that is to say, so much as would be given for the use of his Power: and therefore is not absolute; but a thing dependant on the need and judgement of another. An able conductor of Souldiers, is of great Price in time of War present, or imminent; but in Peace not so. A learned and uncorrupt Judge, is much Worth in time of Peace; but not so much in War. And as in other things, so in men, not the seller, but the buyer determines the Price. For let a man (as most men do,) rate themselves at the highest Value they can; yet their true Value is no more than it is esteemed by others.

The manifestation of the Value we set on one another, is that which is commonly called Honouring, and Dishonouring. To Value a man at a high rate, is to *Honour* him; at a low rate, is to *Dishonour* him. But high, and low, in this case, is to be understood by comparison to the rate that each man setteth on himselfe.

The publique worth of a man, which is the Value set on him by the Common-wealth, is that which men *Dignity* commonly call DIGNITY. And this Value of him by the Common-wealth, is understood, by offices of Command, Judicature, publike Employment; or by Names and Titles, introduced for distinction of such Value.

To Honour   To pray to another, for ayde of any kind, is *to* HON-
and Dis- OUR; because a signe we have an opinion he has power
honour to help; and the more difficult the ayde is, the more is the Honour.

To obey, is to Honour; because no man obeyes them, whom they think have no power to help, or hurt them. And consequently to disobey, is to *Dishonour*.

To give great gifts to a man, is to Honour him; because 'tis buying of Protection, and acknowledging of Power. To give little gifts, is to Dishonour; because it is but Almes, and signifies an opinion of the need of small helps.

To be sedulous in promoting anothers good; also to flatter, is to Honour; as a signe we seek his protection or ayde. To neglect, is to Dishonour.

To give way, or place to another, in any Commodity, is to Honour; being a confession of greater power. To arrogate, is to Dishonour.

To shew any signe of love, or feare of another, is to Honour; [43] for both to love, and to feare, is to value. To contemne, or lesse to love or feare, then he expects, is to Dishonour; for 'tis undervaluing.

To praise, magnifie, or call happy, is to Honour; because nothing but goodnesse, power, and felicity is valued. To revile, mock, or pitty, is to Dishonour.

To speak to another with consideration, to appear before him with decency, and humility, is to Honour him; as signes of fear to offend. To speak to him rashly, to do anything before him obscenely, slovenly, impudently, is to Dishonour.

To believe, to trust, to rely on another, is to Honour him; signe of opinion of his vertue and power. To distrust, or not believe, is to Dishonour.

To hearken to a mans counsell, or discourse of what kind soever, is to Honour; as a signe we think him wise, or eloquent, or witty. To sleep, or go forth, or talk the while, is to Dishonour.

To do those things to another, which he takes for signes of Honour, or which the Law or Custome makes so, is to Honour; because in approving the Honour done by others, he acknowledgeth the power which others acknowledge. To refuse to do them, is to Dishonour.

To agree with in opinion, is to Honour; as being a signe of approving his judgement, and wisdome. To dissent, is Dishonour; and an upbraiding of errour; and (if the dissent be in many things) of folly.

To imitate, is to Honour; for it is vehemently to approve. To imitate ones Enemy, is to Dishonour.

To honour those another honours, is to Honour him; as a signe of approbation of his judgement. To honour his Enemies, is to Dishonour him.

To employ in counsell, or in actions of difficulty, is to Honour; as a signe of opinion of his wisdome, or other power. To deny employment in the same cases, to those that seek it, is to Dishonour.

All these wayes of Honouring, are naturall; and as well within, as without Common-wealths. But in Common-wealths, where he, or they that have the supreme Authority, can make whatsoever they please, to stand for signes of Honour, there be other Honours.

A Soveraigne doth Honour a Subject, with whatsoever Title, or Office, or Employment, or Action, that he
himselfe will have taken for a signe of his will to Honour him.

The King of *Persia*, Honoured *Mordecay*,[45] when he
appointed he should be conducted through the streets
in the Kings Garment, upon one of the Kings Horses,
with a Crown on his head, and a Prince before him, pro-
clayming, *Thus shall it be done to him that the King will
honour*. And yet another King of *Persia*, or the same
another time, to one that demanded for some great
service, to weare one of the Kings robes, gave him leave
so to do; but with this addition, that he should weare
it as the Kings foole; and then it was Dishonour.[46] So
that of Civill Honour, the Fountain is in the person of
the Common-wealth, and dependeth on the Will of the
Soveraigne; and is therefore temporary, and called *Civill
Honour*; such as are Magi[44]stracy, Offices, Titles; and
in some places Coats, and Scutchions[47] painted: and men
Honour such as have them, as having so many signes of
favour in the Common-wealth; which favour is Power.

Honourable   *Honourable* is whatsoever possession, action, or quality, is an argument and signe of Power.

And therefore To be Honoured, loved, or feared of
many, is Honourable; as arguments of Power. To be
Dishonour- Honoured of few or none, *Dishonourable*.
able   Dominion, and Victory is Honourable; because acquired by Power; and Servitude, for need, or feare, is
Dishonourable.

Good fortune (if lasting,) Honourable; as a signe of the
favour of God. Ill fortune, and losses, Dishonourable.
Riches, are Honourable; for they are Power. Poverty,
Dishonourable. Magnanimity, Liberality, Hope, Courage, Confidence, are Honourable; for they proceed from
the conscience of Power. Pusillanimity, Parsimony, Fear,
Diffidence, are Dishonourable.

Timely Resolution, or determination of what a man
is to do, is Honourable; as being the contempt of

small difficulties, and dangers. And Irresolution, Dishonourable; as a signe of too much valuing of little impediments, and little advantages: For when a man has weighed things as long as the time permits, and resolves not, the difference of weight is but little; and therefore if he resolve not, he overvalues little things, which is Pusillanimity.

All Actions, and Speeches, that proceed, or seem to proceed from much Experience, Science, Discretion, or Wit, are Honourable; For all these are Powers. Actions, or Words that proceed from Errour, Ignorance, or Folly, Dishonourable.

Gravity, as farre forth as it seems to proceed from a mind employed on some thing else, is Honourable; because employment is a signe of Power. But if it seem to proceed from a purpose to appear grave, it is Dishonourable. For the gravity of the former, is like the steddinesse of a Ship laden with Merchandise; but of the later, like the steddinesse of a Ship ballasted with Sand, and other trash.

To be Conspicuous, that is to say, to be known, for Wealth, Office, great Actions, or any eminent Good, is Honourable; as a signe of the power for which he is conspicuous. On the contrary, Obscurity, is Dishonourable.

To be descended from conspicuous Parents, is Honourable; because they the more easily attain the aydes, and friends of their Ancestors. On the contrary, to be descended from obscure Parentage, is Dishonourable.

Actions proceeding from Equity, joyned with losse, are Honourable; as signes of Magnanimity: for Magnanimity is a signe of Power. On the contrary, Craft, Shifting, neglect of Equity, is Dishonourable.

Covetousnesse of great Riches, and ambition of great Honours, are Honourable; as signes of power to obtain them. Covetousnesse, and ambition, of little gaines, or preferments, is Dishonourable.

Nor does it alter the case of Honour, whether an action (so it be [45] great and difficult, and consequently a signe of much power,) be just or unjust: for Honour consisteth onely in the opinion of Power. Therefore the ancient Heathen did not thinke they Dishonoured, but greatly Honoured the Gods, when they introduced them in their Poems, committing Rapes, Thefts, and other great, but unjust, or unclean acts: In so much as nothing is so much celebrated in *Jupiter*, as his Adulteries; nor in *Mercury*, as his Frauds, and Thefts: of whose praises, in a hymne of *Homer*, the greatest is this, that being born in the morning, he had invented Musique at noon, and before night, stolne away the Cattell of *Apollo*, from his Herdsmen.[48]

Also amongst men, till there were constituted great Common-wealths, it was thought no dishonour to be a Pyrate, or a High-way Theefe; but rather a lawfull Trade, not onely amongst the Greeks, but also amongst all other Nations; as is manifest by the Histories of antient time. And at this day, in this part of the world, private Duels are, and alwayes will be Honourable, though unlawfull, till such time as there shall be Honour ordained for them that refuse, and Ignominy for them that make the Challenge. For Duels also are many times effects of Courage; and the ground of Courage is alwayes Strength or Skill, which are Power; though for the most part they be effects of rash speaking, and of the fear of Dishonour, in one, or both the Combatants; who engaged by rashnesse, are driven into the Lists to avoyd disgrace.

Coats of   Scutchions, and Coats of Armes hæreditary, where
Armes   they have any eminent Priviledges, are Honourable; otherwise not: for their Power consisteth either in such Priviledges, or in Riches, or some such thing as is equally honoured in other men. This kind of Honour, commonly called Gentry, has been derived from the Antient Germans. For there never was any such thing known, where the German Customes were unknown. Nor is it now any where in use, where the Germans have not inhabited. The antient Greek Commanders, when they

went to war, had their Shields painted with such Devises as they pleased; insomuch as an unpainted Buckler was a signe of Poverty, and of a common Souldier: but they transmitted not the Inheritance of them. The Romans transmitted the Marks of their Families: but they were the Images, not the Devises of their Ancestors. Amongst the people of *Asia*, *Afrique*, and *America*, there is not, nor was ever, any such thing. The Germans onely had that custome; from whom it has been derived into *England*, *France*, *Spain* and *Italy*, when in great numbers they either ayded the Romans, or made their own Conquests in these Westerne parts of the world.

For *Germany*, being antiently, as all other Countries, in their beginnings, divided amongst an infinite number of little Lords, or Masters of Families, that continually had wars one with another; those Masters, or Lords, principally to the end they might, when they were Covered with Arms, be known by their followers; and partly for ornament, both painted their Armor, or their Scutchion, or Coat, with the picture of some Beast, or other thing; and also put some eminent [46] and visible mark upon the Crest of their Helmets. And this ornament both of the Armes, and Crest, descended by inheritance to their Children; to the eldest pure, and to the rest with some note of diversity, such as the Old master, that is to say in Dutch,[49] the *Here-alt* thought fit. But when many such Families, joyned together, made a greater Monarchy, this duty of the Herealt, to distinguish Scutchions, was made a private Office a part. And the issue of these Lords, is the great and antient Gentry; which for the most part bear living creatures, noted for courage, and rapine; or Castles, Battlements, Belts, Weapons, Bars, Palisadoes, and other notes of War; nothing being then in honour, but vertue military. Afterwards, not onely Kings, but popular Commonwealths, gave divers manners of Scutchions, to such as went forth to the War, or returned from it, for encouragement, or recompence to their service. All which, by an observing Reader, may be found in such ancient Histories, Greek and Latine, as make mention of the German Nation, and Manners, in their times.

Titles of   Titles of *Honour*, such as are Duke, Count, Mar-
Honour quis, and Baron, are Honourable; as signifying the value set upon them by the Soveraigne Power of the Common-wealth: Which Titles, were in old time titles of Office, and Command, derived some from the Romans, some from the Germans, and French. Dukes, in Latine *Duces*, being Generalls in War: Counts, *Comites*, such as bare the Generall company out of friendship; and were left to govern and defend places conquered, and pacified: Marquises, *Marchiones*, were Counts that governed the Marches, or bounds of the Empire. Which titles of Duke, Count, and Marquis, came into the Empire, about the time of *Constantine* the Great,[50] from the customes of the German *Militia*. But Baron, seems to have been a Title of the Gaules, and signifies a Great man; such as were the Kings, or Princes men, whom they employed in war about their persons; and seems to be derived from *Vir*, to *Ber*, and *Bar*, that signified the same in the Language of the Gaules, that *Vir* in Latine; and thence to *Bero*, and *Baro*: so that such men were called *Berones*, and after *Barones*; and (in Spanish) *Varones*. But he that would know more particularly the originall of Titles of Honour, may find it, as I have done this, in Mr. *Seldens* most excellent Treatise of that subject.[51] In processe of time these offices of Honour, by occasion of trouble, and for reasons of good and peaceable government, were turned into meer Titles; serving for the most part, to distinguish the precedence, place, and order of subjects in the Common-wealth: and men were made Dukes, Counts, Marquises, and Barons of Places, wherein they had neither possession, nor command: and other Titles also, were devised to the same end.

Worthinesse   WORTHINESSE, is a thing different from the worth,
Fitnesse or value of a man; and also from his merit, or desert; and consisteth in a particular power, or ability for that,

whereof he is said to be worthy: which particular ability, is usually named FITNESSE, or *Aptitude*.

For he is Worthiest to be a Commander, to be a Judge, or to have any other charge, that is best fitted, with the qualities required to the [47] well discharging of it; and Worthiest of Riches, that has the qualities most requisite for the well using of them: any of which qualities being absent, one may neverthelesse be a Worthy man, and valuable for some thing else. Again, a man may be Worthy of Riches, Office, and Employment, that neverthelesse, can plead no right to have it before another; and therefore cannot be said to merit or deserve it. For Merit, præsupposeth a right, and that the thing deserved is due by promise: Of which I shall say more hereafter, when I shall speak of Contracts.

CHAP. XI

Of the difference of MANNERS

By MANNERS, I mean not here, Decency of behaviour; as how one man should salute another, or how a man should wash his mouth, or pick his teeth before company, and such other points of the *Small Moralls*; But those qualities of man-kind, that concern their living together in Peace, and Unity. To which end we are to consider, that the Felicity of this life, consisteth not in the repose of a mind satisfied. For there is no such *Finis ultimus*, (utmost ayme,) nor *Summum Bonum*, (greatest Good,) as is spoken of in the Books of the old Morall Philosophers.[52] Nor can a man any more live, whose Desires are at an end, than he, whose Senses and Imaginations are at a stand. Felicity is a continuall progresse of the desire, from one object to another; the attaining of the former, being still but the way to the later. The cause whereof is, That the object of mans desire, is not

What is here meant by Manners

to enjoy once onely, and for one instant of time; but to assure for ever, the way of his future desire. And therefore the voluntary actions, and inclinations of all men, tend, not only to the procuring, but also to the assuring of a contented life; and differ onely in the way: which ariseth partly from the diversity of passions, in divers men; and partly from the difference of the knowledge, or opinion each one has of the causes, which produce the effect desired.

A restlesse desire of Power, in all men   So that in the first place, I put for a generall inclination of all mankind, a perpetuall and restlesse desire of Power after power, that ceaseth onely in Death. And the cause of this, is not alwayes that a man hopes for a more intensive delight, than he has already attained to; or that he cannot be content with a moderate power: but because he cannot assure the power and means to live well, which he hath present, without the acquisition of more. And from hence it is, that Kings, whose power is greatest, turn their endeavours to the assuring it at home by Lawes, or abroad by Wars: and when that is done, there succeedeth a new desire; in some, of Fame from new Conquest; in others, of ease and sensuall pleasure; in others, of admiration, or being flattered for excellence in some art, or other ability of the mind.

Love of Contention from Competition   Competition of Riches, Honour, Command, or other power, en[48]clineth to Contention, Enmity, and War: Because the way of one Competitor, to the attaining of his desire, is to kill, subdue, supplant, or repell the other. Particularly, competition of praise, enclineth to a reverence of Antiquity. For men contend with the living, not with the dead; to these ascribing more than due, that they may obscure the glory of the other.

Civil obedience from love of Ease   Desire of Ease, and sensuall Delight, disposeth men to obey a common Power: Because by such Desires, a man doth abandon the protection might be hoped for *From feare of Death, or Wounds* from his own Industry, and labour. Fear of Death, and Wounds, disposeth to the same; and for the same reason. On the contrary, needy men, and hardy, not contented with their present condition; as also, all men that are ambitious of Military command, are enclined to continue the causes of warre; and to stirre up trouble and sedition: for there is no honour Military but by warre; nor any such hope to mend an ill game, as by causing a new shuffle.

Desire of Knowledge, and Arts of Peace, enclineth men to obey a common Power: For such Desire, containeth a desire of leasure; and consequently protection from some other Power than their own. *And from love of Arts*

Desire of Praise, disposeth to laudable actions, such as please them whose judgement they value; for of those men whom we contemn, we contemn also the Praises. Desire of Fame after death does the same. And though after death, there be no sense of the praise given us on Earth, as being joyes, that are either swallowed up in the unspeakable joyes of Heaven, or extinguished in the extreme torments of Hell: yet is not such Fame vain; because men have a present delight therein, from the foresight of it, and of the benefit that may redound thereby to their posterity: which though they now see not, yet they imagine; and any thing that is pleasure in the sense, the same also is pleasure in the imagination. *Love of Vertue, from love of Praise*

To have received from one, to whom we think our selves equall, greater benefits than there is hope to Requite, disposeth to counterfeit love; but really secret hatred; and puts a man into the estate of a desperate debtor, that in declining the sight of his creditor, tacitely wishes him there, where he might never see him more. For benefits oblige; and obligation is thraldome; and unrequitable obligation, perpetuall thraldome; which is to ones equall, hatefull. But to have received benefits from one, whom we acknowledge for superiour, enclines to love; because the obligation is no new depession: and cheerfull acceptation, (which men call *Gratitude*,) is such an honour done to the obliger, as is taken generally for retribution. Also to receive benefits, though from an equall, or inferiour, as long as there is hope of requitall, *Hate, from difficulty of Requiting great Benefits*

disposeth to love: for in the intention of the receiver, the
obligation is of ayd, and service mutuall; from whence
proceedeth an Emulation of who shall exceed in benefit-
ing; the most noble and profitable contention possible;
wherein the victor is pleased with his victory, and the
other revenged by confessing it.

And from   To have done more hurt to a man, than he can, or is
Conscience of willing to expiate, enclineth the doer to hate the sufferer.
deserving to For he must expect re[49]venge, or forgivenesse; both
be hated which are hatefull.

Promptnesse   Feare of oppression, disposeth a man to anticipate,
to hurt, or to seek ayd by society: for there is no other way by
from Fear which a man can secure his life and liberty.

And from   Men that distrust their own subtilty, are in tumult,
distrust of and sedition, better disposed for victory, than they that
their own wit suppose themselves wise, or crafty. For these love to
consult, the other (fearing to be circumvented,) to strike
first. And in sedition, men being alwayes in the procincts
of battell, to hold together, and use all advantages of
force, is a better stratagem, than any that can proceed
from subtilty of Wit.

Vain under-   Vain-glorious men, such as without being conscious
taking from to themselves of great sufficiency, delight in supposing
Vain-glory themselves gallant men, are enclined onely to osten-
tation; but not to attempt: Because when danger or
difficulty appears, they look for nothing but to have
their insufficiency discovered.

    Vain-glorious men, such as estimate their sufficiency
by the flattery of other men, or the fortune of some precedent action, without assured ground of hope from
the true knowledge of themselves, are enclined to rash
engaging; and in the approach of danger, or difficulty,
to retire if they can: because not seeing the way of
safety, they will rather hazard their honour, which may
be salved with an excuse; than their lives, for which no
Ambition, salve is sufficient.

from opinion   Men that have a strong opinion of their own wisdome
of sufficiency in matter of government, are disposed to Ambition.

Because without publique Employment in counsell or magistracy, the honour of their wisdome is lost. And therefore Eloquent speakers are enclined to Ambition; for Eloquence seemeth wisedome, both to themselves and others.

Pusillanimity disposeth men to Irresolution, and consequently to lose the occasions, and fittest opportunities of action. For after men have been in deliberation till the time of action approach, if it be not then manifest what is best to be done, 'tis a signe, the difference of Motives, the one way and the other, are not great: Therefore not to resolve then, is to lose the occasion by weighing of trifles; which is pusillanimity. *Irresolution, from too great valuing of small matters*

Frugality, (though in poor men a Vertue,) maketh a man unapt to atchieve such actions, as require the strength of many men at once: For it weakeneth their Endeavour, which is to be nourished and kept in vigor by Reward.

Eloquence, with flattery, disposeth men to confide in them that have it; because the former is seeming Wisdome, the later seeming Kindnesse. Adde to them Military reputation, and it disposeth men to adhære, and subject themselves to those men that have them. The two former, having given them caution against danger from him; the later gives them caution against danger from others. *Confidence in others from Ignorance of the marks of Wisdome and Kindnesse*

Want of Science, that is, Ignorance of causes, disposeth, or rather constraineth a man to rely on the advise, and authority of others. For all men whom the truth concernes, if they rely not on their own, must rely on the opinion of some other, whom they think wiser than themselves, and see not why he should deceive them. *And from Ignorance of naturall causes*

[50] Ignorance of the signification of words; which is, want of understanding, disposeth men to take on trust, not onely the truth they know not; but also the errors; and which is more, the non-sense of them they trust: For neither Error, nor non-sense, can without a perfect understanding of words, be detected. *And from want of Understanding*

From the same it proceedeth, that men give different
names, to one and the same thing, from the difference of
their own passions: As they that approve a private opinion, call it Opinion; but they that mislike it, Hæresie:
and yet hæresie signifies no more than private opinion;
but has onely a greater tincture of choler.

From the same also it proceedeth, that men cannot
distinguish, without study and great understanding,
between one action of many men, and many actions of
one multitude; as for example, between the one action
of all the Senators of *Rome* in killing *Catiline*,[53] and the
many actions of a number of Senators in killing *Cæsar*;
and therefore are disposed to take for the action of
the people, that which is a multitude of actions done
by a multitude of men, led perhaps by the perswasion
of one.

Adhærence   Ignorance of the causes, and originall constitution
to Custome,   of Right, Equity, Law, and Justice, disposeth a man to
from Ignor-   make Custome and Example the rule of his actions; in
ance of the   such manner, as to think that Unjust which it hath been
nature of   the custome to punish; and that Just, of the impun-
Right and   ity and approbation whereof they can produce an
Wrong   Example, or (as the Lawyers which onely use the false
measure of Justice barbarously call it) a Precedent; like
little children, that have no other rule of good and evill
manners, but the correction they receive from their
Parents, and Masters; save that children are constant
to their rule, whereas men are not so; because grown
strong, and stubborn, they appeale from custome to
reason, and from reason to custome, as it serves their
turn; receding from custome when their interest requires
it, and setting themselves against reason, as oft as
reason is against them: Which is the cause, that the
doctrine of Right and Wrong, is perpetually disputed,
both by the Pen and the Sword: Whereas the doctrine
of Lines, and Figures, is not so; because men care not,
in that subject what be truth, as a thing that crosses
no mans ambition, profit, or lust. For I doubt not, but

if it had been a thing contrary to any mans right of dominion, or to the interest of men that have dominion, *That the three Angles of a Triangle should be equall to two Angles of a Square*; that doctrine should have been, if not disputed, yet by the burning of all books of Geometry, suppressed, as farre as he whom it concerned was able.

Ignorance of remote causes, disposeth men to attribute all events, to the causes immediate, and Instrumentall: For these are all the causes they perceive. And hence it comes to passe, that in all places, men that are grieved with payments to the Publique, discharge their anger upon the Publicans, that is to say, Farmers, Collectors, and other Officers of the publique Revenue; and adhære to such as find fault with the publike Government; and thereby, when they have engaged themselves beyond hope of justification, fall also upon the Supreme [51] Authority, for feare of punishment, or shame of receiving pardon. *Adhærence to private men, From ignorance of the Causes of Peace*

Ignorance of naturall causes disposeth a man to Credulity, so as to believe many times impossibilities: For such know nothing to the contrary, but that they may be true; being unable to detect the Impossibility. And Credulity, because men love to be hearkened unto in company, disposeth them to lying: so that Ignorance it selfe without Malice, is able to make a man both to believe lyes, and tell them; and sometimes also to invent them. *Credulity from Ignorance of nature*

Anxiety for the future time, disposeth men to enquire into the causes of things: because the knowledge of them, maketh men the better able to order the present to their best advantage. *Curiosity to know, from Care of future time*

Curiosity, or love of the knowledge of causes, draws a man from consideration of the effect, to seek the cause; and again, the cause of that cause; till of necessity he must come to this thought at last, that there is some cause, whereof there is no former cause, but is eternall; which is it men call God. So that it is impossible to *Naturall Religion, from the same* make any profound enquiry into naturall causes, without being enclined thereby to believe there is one God Eternall; though they cannot have any Idea of him in their mind, answerable to his nature. For as a man that is born blind, hearing men talk of warming themselves by the fire, and being brought to warm himself by the same, may easily conceive, and assure himselfe, there is somewhat there, which men call *Fire*, and is the cause of the heat he feeles; but cannot imagine what it is like; nor have an Idea of it in his mind, such as they have that see it: so also, by the visible things of this world, and their admirable order, a man may conceive there is a cause of them, which men call God; and yet not have an Idea, or Image of him in his mind.

And they that make little, or no enquiry into the naturall causes of things, yet from the feare that proceeds from the ignorance it selfe, of what it is that hath the power to do them much good or harm, are enclined to suppose, and feign unto themselves, severall kinds of Powers Invisible; and to stand in awe of their own imaginations; and in time of distresse to invoke them; as also in the time of an expected good successe, to give them thanks; making the creatures of their own fancy, their Gods. By which means it hath come to passe, that from the innumerable variety of Fancy, men have created in the world innumerable sorts of Gods. And this Feare of things invisible, is the naturall Seed of that, which every one in himself calleth Religion; and in them that worship, or feare that Power otherwise than they do, Superstition.

And this seed of Religion, having been observed by many; some of those that have observed it, have been enclined thereby to nourish, dresse, and forme it into Lawes; and to adde to it of their own invention, any opinion of the causes of future events, by which they thought they should best be able to govern others, and make unto themselves the greatest use of their Powers. [52]

OF RELIGION

Seeing there are no signes, nor fruit of *Religion*, but in Man onely; there is no cause to doubt, but that the seed of *Religion*, is also onely in Man; and consisteth in some peculiar quality, or at least in some eminent degree thereof, not to be found in other Living creatures. *Religion, in Man onely*

And first, it is peculiar to the nature of Man, to be inquisitive into the Causes of the Events they see, some more, some lesse; but all men so much, as to be curious in the search of the causes of their own good and evill fortune. *First, from his desire of knowing Causes*

Secondly, upon the sight of any thing that hath a Beginning, to think also it had a cause, which determined the same to begin, then when it did, rather than sooner or later. *From the consideration of the Beginning of things*

Thirdly, whereas there is no other Felicity of Beasts, but the enjoying of their quotidian Food, Ease, and Lusts; as having little, or no foresight of the time to come, for want of observation, and memory of the order, consequence, and dependance of the things they see; Man observeth how one Event hath been produced by another; and remembreth in them Antecedence and Consequence; And when he cannot assure himselfe of the true causes of things, (for the causes of good and evill fortune for the most part are invisible,) he supposes causes of them, either such as his own fancy suggesteth; or trusteth to the Authority of other men, such as he thinks to be his friends, and wiser than himselfe. *From his observation of the Sequell of things*

The two first, make Anxiety. For being assured that there be causes of all things that have arrived hitherto, or shall arrive hereafter; it is impossible for a man, who continually endeavoureth to secure himselfe against the evill he feares, and procure the good he desireth, not to be in a perpetuall solicitude of the time to come; So *The naturall Cause of Religion, the Anxiety of the time to come* that every man, especially those that are over provident, are in an estate like to that of *Prometheus*.[54] For as *Prometheus*, (which interpreted, is, *The prudent man*,) was bound to the hill *Caucasus*, a place of large prospect, where, an Eagle feeding on his liver, devoured in the day, as much as was repayred in the night: So that man, which looks too far before him, in the care of future time, hath his heart all the day long, gnawed on by feare of death, poverty, or other calamity; and has no repose, nor pause of his anxiety, but in sleep.

Which makes
them fear
the Power
of Invisible
things
This perpetuall feare, always accompanying mankind in the ignorance of causes, as it were in the Dark, must needs have for object something. And therefore when there is nothing to be seen, there is nothing to accuse, either of their good, or evill fortune, but some *Power*, or Agent *Invisible*: In which sense perhaps it was, that some of the old Poets said, that the Gods were at first created by humane Feare: which spoken of the Gods, (that is to say, of the many Gods [53] of the Gentiles) is very true.[55] But the acknowledging of one God Eternall, Infinite, and Omnipotent, may more easily be derived, from the desire men have to know the causes of naturall bodies, and their severall vertues, and operations; than from the feare of what was to befall them in time to come. For he that from any effect hee seeth come to passe, should reason to the next and immediate cause thereof, and from thence to the cause of that cause, and plonge himselfe profoundly in the pursuit of causes; shall at last come to this, that there must be (as even the Heathen Philosophers confessed) one First Mover; that is, a First, and an Eternall cause of all things; which is that which men mean by the name of God: And all this without thought of their fortune; the solicitude whereof, both enclines to fear, and hinders them from the search of the causes of other things; and thereby gives occasion
And suppose
them Incor-
poreall
of feigning of as many Gods, as there be men that feigne them.

And for the matter, or substance of the Invisible Agents,

so fancyed; they could not by naturall cogitation, fall upon any other conceipt, but that it was the same with that of the Soule of man; and that the Soule of man, was of the same substance, with that which appeareth in a Dream, to one that sleepeth; or in a Looking-glasse, to one that is awake; which, men not knowing that such apparitions are nothing else but creatures of the Fancy, think to be reall, and externall Substances; and therefore call them Ghosts; as the Latines called them *Imagines*, and *Umbræ*; and thought them Spirits, that is, thin aëreall bodies; and those Invisible Agents, which they feared, to bee like them; save that they appear, and vanish when they please. But the opinion that such Spirits were Incorporeall, or Immateriall, could never enter into the mind of any man by nature; because, though men may put together words of contradictory signification, as *Spirit*, and *Incorporeall*; yet they can never have the imagination of any thing answering to them: And therefore, men that by their own meditation, arrive to the acknowledgement of one Infinite, Omnipotent, and Eternall God, choose rather to confesse he is Incomprehensible, and above their understanding; than to define his Nature by *Spirit Incorporeall*, and then confesse their definition to be unintelligible: or if they give him such a title, it is not *Dogmatically*, with intention to make the Divine Nature understood; but *Piously*, to honour him with attributes, of significations, as remote as they can from the grossenesse of Bodies Visible.

Then, for the way by which they think these Invisible Agents wrought their effects; that is to say, what immediate causes they used, in bringing things to passe, men that know not what it is that we call *causing*, (that is, almost all men) have no other rule to guesse by, but by observing, and remembring what they have seen to precede the like effect at some other time, or times before, without seeing between the antecedent and subsequent Event, any dependance or connexion at all: And therefore from the like things past, they expect the like things *But know not the way how they effect anything* to come; and hope for good or evill luck, superstitiously, from things that have no part at all in the causing of it: As the Athenians [54] did for their war at *Lepanto*, demand another *Phormio*; The Pompeian faction for their warre in *Afrique*, another *Scipio*;[56] and others have done in divers other occasions since. In like manner they attribute their fortune to a stander by, to a lucky or unlucky place, to words spoken, especially if the name of God be amongst them; as Charming, and Conjuring (the Leiturgy of Witches;) insomuch as to believe, they have power to turn a stone into bread, bread into a man, or any thing, into any thing.

But honour Thirdly, for the worship which naturally men exhib-
them as they ite to Powers invisible, it can be no other, but such
honour men expressions of their reverence, as they would use towards men; Gifts, Petitions, Thanks, Submission of Body, Considerate Addresses, sober Behaviour, premeditated Words, Swearing (that is, assuring one another of their promises,) by invoking them. Beyond that reason suggesteth nothing; but leaves them either to rest there; or for further ceremonies, to rely on those they believe to be wiser than themselves.

And attribute Lastly, concerning how these Invisible Powers declare
to them all to men the things which shall hereafter come to passe,
extraordinary especially concerning their good or evill fortune in
events generall, or good or ill successe in any particular undertaking, men are naturally at a stand; save that using to conjecture of the time to come, by the time past, they are very apt, not onely to take casuall things, after one or two encounters, for Prognostiques of the like encounter ever after, but also to believe the like Prognostiques from other men, of whom they have once conceived a good opinion.

Foure things, And in these foure things, Opinion of Ghosts, Ignor-
Naturall ance of second causes, Devotion towards what men
seeds of fear, and Taking of things Casuall for Prognostiques,
Religion consisteth the Naturall seed of *Religion*; which by reason of the different Fancies, Judgements, and Passions

of severall men, hath grown up into ceremonies so different, that those which are used by one man, are for the most part ridiculous to another.

For these seeds have received culture from two sorts of men. One sort have been they, that have nourished, and ordered them, according to their own invention. The other, have done it, by Gods commandement, and direction: but both sorts have done it, with a purpose to make those men that relyed on them, the more apt to Obedience, Lawes, Peace, Charity, and civill Society. So that the Religion of the former sort, is a part of humane Politiques; and teacheth part of the duty which Earthly Kings require of their Subjects. And the Religion of the later sort is Divine Politiques; and containeth Precepts to those that have yeelded themselves subjects in the Kingdome of God. Of the former sort, were all the founders of Common-wealths, and the Law-givers of the Gentiles: Of the later sort, were *Abraham*, *Moses*, and our *Blessed Saviour*; by whom have been derived unto us the Lawes of the Kingdome of God. *Made different by Culture*

And for that part of Religion, which consisteth in opinions concerning the nature of Powers Invisible, there is almost nothing that has a name, that has not been esteemed amongst the Gentiles, in one [55] place or another, a God, or Divell; or by their Poets feigned to be inanimated, inhabited, or possessed by some Spirit or other. *The absurd opinion of Gentilisme*

The unformed matter of the World, was a God, by the name of *Chaos*.

The Heaven, the Ocean, the Planets, the Fire, the Earth, the Winds, were so many Gods.

Men, Women, a Bird, a Crocodile, a Calf, a Dogge, a Snake, an Onion, a Leeke, Deified.[57] Besides, that they filled almost all places, with spirits called *Dæmons*: the plains, with *Pan*, and *Panises*, or Satyres; the Woods, with Fawnes, and Nymphs; the Sea, with Tritons, and other Nymphs; every River, and Fountayn, with a Ghost of his name, and with Nymphs; every house, with its

Lares, or Familiars; every man, with his *Genius*; Hell, with Ghosts, and spirituall Officers, as *Charon*, *Cerberus*,[58] and the *Furies*; and in the night time, all places with *Larvæ*, *Lemures*, Ghosts of men deceased, and a whole kingdome of Fayries, and Bugbears. They have also ascribed Divinity, and built Temples to meer Accidents, and Qualities; such as are Time, Night, Day, Peace, Concord, Love, Contention, Vertue, Honour, Health, Rust, Fever, and the like; which when they prayed for, or against, they prayed to, as if there were Ghosts of those names hanging over their heads, and letting fall, or withholding that Good, or Evill, for, or against which they prayed. They invoked also their own Wit, by the name of *Muses*; their own Ignorance, by the name of *Fortune*; their own Lust, by the name of *Cupid*; their own Rage, by the name *Furies*; their own privy members by the name of *Priapus*; and attributed their pollutions, to *Incubi*, and *Succubæ*:[59] insomuch as there was nothing, which a Poet could introduce as a person in his Poem, which they did not make either a *God*, or a *Divel*.

The same authors of the Religion of the Gentiles, observing the second ground for Religion, which is mens Ignorance of causes; and thereby their aptnesse to attribute their fortune to causes, on which there was no dependence at all apparent, took occasion to obtrude on their ignorance, in stead of second causes, a kind of second and ministeriall Gods; ascribing the cause of Fœcundity, to *Venus*; the cause of Arts, to *Apollo*; of Subtilty and Craft, to *Mercury*; of Tempests and stormes, to *Æolus*;[60] and of other effects, to other Gods: insomuch as there was amongst the Heathen almost as great variety of Gods, as of businesse.

And to the Worship, which naturally men conceived fit to bee used towards their Gods, namely Oblations, Prayers, Thanks, and the rest formerly named; the same Legislators of the Gentiles have added their Images, both in Picture, and Sculpture; that the more ignorant sort, (that is to say, the most part, or generality

of the people,) thinking the Gods for whose representation they were made, were really included, and as
it were housed within them, might so much the more
stand in feare of them: And endowed them with lands,
and houses, and officers, and revenues, set apart from
all other humane uses; that is, consecrated, and made
holy to those their Idols; as Caverns, Groves, Woods,
Mountains, and whole Ilands; and [56] have attributed
to them, not onely the shapes, some of Men, some of
Beasts, some of Monsters; but also the Faculties, and
Passions of men and beasts; as Sense, Speech, Sex, Lust,
Generation, (and this not onely by mixing one with
another, to propagate the kind of Gods; but also by
mixing with men, and women, to beget mongrill Gods,
and but inmates of Heaven, as *Bacchus*,[61] *Hercules*, and
others;) besides, Anger, Revenge, and other passions of
living creatures, and the actions proceeding from them,
as Fraud, Theft, Adultery, Sodomie, and any vice that
may be taken for an effect of Power, or a cause of Pleasure; and all such Vices, as amongst men are taken to be
against Law, rather than against Honour.

Lastly, to the Prognostiques of time to come; which
are naturally, but Conjectures upon the Experience of
time past; and supernaturally, divine Revelation; the
same authors of the Religion of the Gentiles, partly upon
pretended Experience, partly upon pretended Revelation, have added innumerable other superstitious wayes
of Divination; and made men believe they should find
their fortunes, sometimes in the ambiguous or senslesse
answers of the Priests at *Delphi*, *Delos*, *Ammon*, and
other famous Oracles;[62] which answers, were made
ambiguous by designe, to own the event both wayes; or
absurd by the intoxicating vapour of the place, which
is very frequent in sulphurous Cavernes: Sometimes
in the leaves of the Sibills; of whose Prophecyes (like
those perhaps of *Nostradamus*;[63] for the fragments now
extant seem to be the invention of later times) there
were some books in reputation in the time of the Roman

Republique: Sometimes in the insignificant Speeches
of Mad-men, supposed to be possessed with a divine
Spirit; which Possession they called Enthusiasme; and
these kinds of foretelling events, were accounted The-
omancy, or Prophecy: Sometimes in the aspect of the
Starres at their Nativity; which was called Horoscopy,
and esteemed a part of judiciary Astrology: Sometimes
in their own hopes and feares, called Thumomancy, or
Presage: Sometimes in the Prediction of Witches, that
pretended conference with the dead; which is called
Necromancy, Conjuring, and Witchcraft; and is but jug-
gling and confederate knavery: Sometimes in the Casuall
flight, or feeding of birds; called Augury: Sometimes in
the Entrayles of a sacrificed beast; which was *Aruspi-
cina*: Sometimes in Dreams: Sometimes in Croaking of
Ravens, or chattering of Birds: Sometimes in the Lin-
eaments of the face; which was called Metoposcopy; or
by Palmistry in the lines of the hand; in casuall words,
called *Omina*: Sometimes in Monsters, or unusuall accidents; as Ecclipses, Comets, rare Meteors, Earthquakes,
Inundations, uncouth Births, and the like, which they
called *Portenta*, and *Ostenta*, because they thought
them to portend, or foreshew some great Calamity to
come: Somtimes, in meer Lottery, as Crosse and Pile;[64]
counting holes in a sive; dipping of Verses in *Homer*, and
Virgil;[65] and innumerable other such vaine conceipts. So
easie are men to be drawn to believe any thing, from
such men as have gotten credit with them; and can with
gentlenesse, and dexterity, take hold of their fear, and
ignorance.

The designes   [57] And therefore the first Founders, and Legislators
of the of Common-wealths amongst the Gentiles, whose ends
Authors of were only to keep the people in obedience, and peace,
the Religion have in all places taken care; First, to imprint in their
of the minds a beliefe, that those precepts which they gave
Heathen concerning Religion, might not be thought to proceed
from their own device, but from the dictates of some
God, or other Spirit; or else that they themselves were

of a higher nature than mere mortalls, that their Lawes might the more easily be received: So *Numa Pompilius* pretended to receive the Ceremonies he instituted amongst the Romans, from the Nymph *Egeria*: and the first King and founder of the Kingdome of *Peru*, pretended himselfe and his wife to be the children of the Sunne: and *Mahomet*, to set up his new Religion, pretended to have conferences with the Holy Ghost, in forme of a Dove.[66] Secondly, they have had a care, to make it believed, that the same things were displeasing to the Gods, which were forbidden by the Lawes. Thirdly, to prescribe Ceremonies, Supplications, Sacrifices, and Festivalls, by which they were to believe, the anger of the Gods might be appeased; and that ill success in War, great contagions of Sicknesse, Earthquakes, and each mans private Misery, came from the Anger of the Gods; and their Anger from the Neglect of their Worship, or the forgetting, or mistaking some point of the Ceremonies required. And though amongst the antient Romans, men were not forbidden to deny, that which in the Poets is written of the paines, and pleasures after this life; which divers of great authority, and gravity in that state have in their *Harangues* openly derided; yet that beliefe was alwaies more cherished, than the contrary.

And by these, and such other Institutions, they obtayned in order to their end, (which was the peace of the Commonwealth,) that the common people in their misfortunes, laying the fault on neglect, or errour in their Ceremonies, or on their own disobedience to the lawes, were the lesse apt to mutiny against their Governors. And being entertained with the pomp, and pastime of Festivalls, and publike Games, made in honour of the Gods, needed nothing else but bread, to keep them from discontent, murmuring, and commotion against the State. And therefore the Romans, that had conquered the greatest part of the then known World, made no scruple of tollerating any Religion whatsoever in the City of *Rome* it selfe; unlesse it had somthing in it, that

could not consist with their Civill Government; nor do
we read, that any Religion was there forbidden, but that
of the Jewes; who (being the peculiar Kingdome of God)
thought it unlawfull to acknowledge subjection to any
mortall King or State whatsoever.[67] And thus you see how
the Religion of the Gentiles was a part of their Policy.

The true   But where God himselfe, by supernaturall Revelation,
Religion, and planted Religion; there he also made to himselfe a pecu-
the lawes   liar Kingdome; and gave Lawes, not only of behaviour
of Gods   towards himselfe; but also towards one another; and
kingdome   thereby in the Kingdome of God, the Policy, and lawes
the same   Civill, are a part of Religion; and therefore the [58] distinction of Temporall, and Spirituall Domination, hath
there no place. It is true, that God is King of all the Earth:
Yet may he be King of a peculiar, and chosen Nation.
For there is no more incongruity therein, than that he
that hath the generall command of the whole Army,
should have withall a peculiar Regiment, or Company
of his own. God is King of all the Earth by his Power:
but of his chosen people, he is King by Covenant. But
to speake more largly of the Kingdome of God, both by
Nature, and Covenant, I have in the following discourse
Chap 35   assigned an other place.

The causes   From the propagation of Religion, it is not hard to
of Change in understand the causes of the resolution of the same into
Religion   its first seeds, or principles; which are only an opinion
of a Deity, and Powers invisible, and supernaturall; that
can never be so abolished out of humane nature, but
that new Religions may againe be made to spring out of
them, by the culture of such men, as for such purpose
are in reputation.

For seeing all formed Religion, is founded at first,
upon the faith which a multitude hath in some one
person, whom they believe not only to be a wise man,
and to labour to procure their happiness, but also to
be a holy man, to whom God himselfe vouchsafeth to
declare his will supernaturally; It followeth necessarily,
when they that have the Government of Religion, shall

come to have either the wisedome of those men, their sincerity, or their love suspected; or that they shall be unable to shew any probable token of Divine Revelation; that the Religion which they desire to uphold, must be suspected likewise; and (without the feare of the Civill Sword) contradicted and rejected.

That which taketh away the reputation of Wisedome, in him that formeth a Religion, or addeth to it when it is allready formed, is the enjoyning of a beliefe of contradictories: For both parts of a contradiction cannot possibly be true: and therefore to enjoyne the beleife of them, is an argument of ignorance; which detects the Author in that; and discredits him in all things else he shall propound as from revelation supernaturall: which revelation a man may indeed have of many things above, but of nothing against naturall reason. *Injoyning beleefe of Impossibilities*

That which taketh away the reputation of Sincerity, is the doing, or saying of such things, as appeare to be signes, that what they require other men to believe, is not believed by themselves; all which doings, or sayings are therefore called Scandalous, because they be stumbling blocks, that make men to fall in the way of Religion: as Injustice, Cruelty, Prophanesse, Avarice, and Luxury. For who can believe, that he that doth ordinarily such actions, as proceed from any of these rootes, believeth there is any such Invisible Power to be feared, as he affrighteth other men withall, for lesser faults? *Doing contrary to the Religion they establish*

That which taketh away the reputation of Love, is the being detected of private ends: as when the beliefe they require of others, conduceth or seemeth to conduce to the acquiring of Dominion, Ri[59]ches, Dignity, or secure Pleasure, to themselves onely, or specially. For that which men reap benefit by to themselves, they are thought to do for their own sakes, and not for love of others.

Lastly, the testimony that men can render of divine Calling, can be no other, than the operation of Miracles; or true Prophecy, (which also is a Miracle;) or *Want of the testimony of Miracles*

extraordinary Felicity. And therefore, to those points of
Religion, which have been received from them that did
such Miracles; those that are added by such, as approve
not their Calling by some Miracle, obtain no greater
beliefe, than what the Custome, and Lawes of the places,
in which they be educated, have wrought into them. For
as in naturall things, men of judgement require naturall signes, and arguments; so in supernaturall things,
they require signes supernaturall, (which are Miracles,)
before they consent inwardly, and from their hearts.

All which causes of the weakening of mens faith, do
manifestly appear in the Examples following. First, we
have the Example of the children of Israel; who when
Moses, that had approved his Calling to them by Miracles, and by the happy conduct of them out of *Egypt*,
was absent but 40. dayes, revolted from the worship of
the true God, recommended to them by him; and setting
* Exod.32   up * a Golden Calfe for their God, relapsed into the
1, 2   Idolatry of the Egyptians; from whom they had been so
lately delivered. And again, after *Moses, Aaron, Joshua,*[68]
and that generation which had seen the great works of
* Judges 2   God in Israel, * were dead; another generation arose,
11   and served *Baal*.[69] So that Miracles fayling, Faith also
failed.

* 1 Sam. 8.3   Again, when the sons of *Samuel*,[70] * being constituted
by their father Judges in *Bersabee*, received bribes, and
judged unjustly, the people of Israel refused any more to
have God to be their King, in other manner than he was
King of other people; and therefore cryed out to *Samuel*,
to choose them a King after the manner of the Nations.
So that Justice fayling, Faith also fayled: Insomuch, as
they deposed their God, from reigning over them.

And whereas in the planting of Christian Religion, the
Oracles ceased in all parts of the Roman Empire, and
the number of Christians encreased wonderfully every
day, and in every place, by the preaching of the Apostles, and Evangelists; a great part of that successe, may
reasonably be attributed, to the contempt, into which

the Priests of the Gentiles of that time, had brought themselves, by their uncleannesse, avarice, and jugling between Princes. Also the Religion of the Church of *Rome*, was partly, for the same cause abolished in *England*, and many other parts of Christendome; insomuch, as the fayling of Vertue in the Pastors, maketh Faith faile in the People: and partly from bringing of the Philosophy, and doctrine of *Aristotle* into Religion, by the Schoole-men; from whence there arose so many contradictions, and absurdities, as brought the Clergy into a reputation both of Ignorance, and of Fraudulent intention; and enclined people to revolt from them, either against the will of their own Princes, as in *France*, and *Holland*; or with their will, as in *England*.

[60] Lastly, amongst the points by the Church of *Rome* declared necessary for Salvation, there be so many, manifestly to the advantage of the Pope, and of his spirituall subjects, residing in the territories of other Christian Princes, that were it not for the mutuall emulation of those Princes, they might without warre, or trouble, exclude all forraign Authority, as easily as it has been excluded in *England*. For who is there that does not see, to whose benefit it conduceth, to have it believed, that a King hath not his Authority from Christ, unlesse a Bishop crown him? That a King, if he be a Priest, cannot Marry? That whether a Prince be born in lawfull Marriage, or not, must be judged by Authority from *Rome*? That Subjects may be freed from their Alleageance, if by the Court of *Rome*, the King be judged an Heretique? That a King (as *Chilperique* of *France*) may be deposed by a Pope (as Pope *Zachary*,) for no cause; and his Kingdome given to one of his Subjects?[71] That the Clergy, and Regulars, in what Country soever, shall be exempt from the Jurisdiction of their King, in cases criminall? Or who does not see, to whose profit redound the Fees of private Masses, and Vales of Purgatory; with other signes of private interest, enough to mortifie the most lively Faith, if (as I sayd) the civill Magistrate, and Custome did not

more sustain it, than any opinion they have of the Sanctity, Wisdome, or Probity of their Teachers? So that I may attribute all the changes of Religion in the world, to one and the same cause; and that is, unpleasing Priests; and those not onely amongst Catholiques, but even in that Church that hath presumed most of Reformation.

CHAP. XIII

Of the NATURALL CONDITION *of Mankind, as concerning their Felicity, and Misery*

Men by Nature hath made men so equall, in the faculties of
nature Equall body, and mind; as that though there bee found one man sometimes manifestly stronger in body, or of quicker mind then another; yet when all is reckoned together, the difference between man, and man, is not so considerable, as that one man can thereupon claim to himselfe any benefit, to which another may not pretend, as well as he. For as to the strength of body, the weakest has strength enough to kill the strongest, either by secret machination, or by confederacy with others, that are in the same danger with himselfe.

And as to the faculties of the mind, (setting aside the arts grounded upon words, and especially that skill of proceeding upon generall, and infallible rules, called Science; which very few have, and but in few things; as being not a native faculty, born with us; nor attained, (as Prudence,) while we look after somewhat els,) I find yet a greater equality amongst men, than that of strength. For Prudence, is but Experience; which equall time, equally bestowes on all men, in [61] those things they equally apply themselves unto. That which may perhaps make such equality incredible, is but a vain conceipt of ones owne wisdome, which almost all men think they have in a greater degree, than the Vulgar; that is, than all men

but themselves, and a few others, whom by Fame, or for
concurring with themselves, they approve. For such is
the nature of men, that howsoever they may acknowledge many others to be more witty, or more eloquent,
or more learned; Yet they will hardly believe there be
many so wise as themselves: For they see their own wit
at hand, and other mens at a distance. But this proveth
rather that men are in that point equall, than unequall.
For there is not ordinarily a greater signe of the equall
distribution of any thing, than that every man is contented with his share.

From this equality of ability, ariseth equality of hope *From Equal-*
in the attaining of our Ends. And therefore if any two *ity proceeds*
men desire the same thing, which neverthelesse they can- *Diffidence*
not both enjoy, they become enemies; and in the way
to their End, (which is principally their owne conservation, and sometimes their delectation only,) endeavour
to destroy, or subdue one an other. And from hence it
comes to passe, that where an Invader hath no more
to feare, than an other mans single power; if one plant,
sow, build, or possesse a convenient Seat, others may
probably be expected to come prepared with forces
united, to dispossesse, and deprive him, not only of the
fruit of his labour, but also of his life, or liberty. And the
Invader again is in the like danger of another.

And from this diffidence of one another, there is no *From Diffi-*
way for any man to secure himselfe, so reasonable, as *dence Warre*
Anticipation; that is, by force, or wiles, to master the
persons of all men he can, so long, till he see no other
power great enough to endanger him: And this is no
more than his own conservation requireth, and is generally allowed. Also because there be some, that taking
pleasure in contemplating their own power in the acts of
conquest, which they pursue farther than their security
requires; if others, that otherwise would be glad to be
at ease within modest bounds, should not by invasion
increase their power, they would not be able, long time,
by standing only on their defence, to subsist. And by

consequence, such augmentation of dominion over men, being necessary to a mans conservation, it ought to be allowed him.

Againe, men have no pleasure, (but on the contrary a great deale of griefe) in keeping company, where there is no power able to over-awe them all. For every man looketh that his companion should value him, at the same rate he sets upon himselfe: And upon all signes of contempt, or undervaluing, naturally endeavours, as far as he dares (which amongst them that have no common power to keep them in quiet, is far enough to make them destroy each other,) to extort a greater value from his contemners, by dommage;[72] and from others, by the example.

So that in the nature of man, we find three principall causes of quarrell. First, Competition; Secondly, Diffidence; Thirdly, Glory.

[62] The first, maketh men invade for Gain; the second, for Safety; and the third, for Reputation. The first use Violence, to make themselves Masters of other mens persons, wives, children, and cattell; the second, to defend them; the third, for trifles, as a word, a smile, a different opinion, and any other signe of undervalue, either direct in their Persons, or by reflexion in their Kindred, their Friends, their Nation, their Profession, or their Name.

Out of Civil States, there is alwayes Warre of every one against every one Hereby it is manifest, that during the time men live without a common Power to keep them all in awe, they are in that condition which is called Warre; and such a warre, as is of every man, against every man. For WARRE, consisteth not in Battell onely, or the act of fighting; but in a tract of time, wherein the Will to contend by Battell is sufficiently known: and therefore the notion of *Time*, is to be considered in the nature of Warre; as it is in the nature of Weather. For as the nature of Foule weather, lyeth not in a showre or two of rain; but in an inclination thereto of many dayes together: So the nature of War, consisteth not in actuall fighting;

but in the known disposition thereto, during all the time
there is no assurance to the contrary. All other time is
PEACE.

Whatsoever therefore is consequent to a time of Warre, *The Incom-*
where every man is Enemy to every man; the same is *modites of*
consequent to the time, wherein men live without other *such a War*
security, than what their own strength, and their own
invention shall furnish them withall. In such condition,
there is no place for Industry; because the fruit thereof
is uncertain: and consequently no Culture of the Earth;
no Navigation, nor use of the commodities that may be
imported by Sea; no commodious Building; no Instruments of moving, and removing such things as require
much force; no Knowledge of the face of the Earth; no
account of Time; no Arts; no Letters; no Society; and
which is worst of all, continuall feare, and danger of
violent death; And the life of man, solitary, poore, nasty,
brutish, and short.[73]

It may seem strange to some man, that has not well
weighed these things; that Nature should thus disso-
ciate, and render men apt to invade, and destroy one
another: and he may therefore, not trusting to this
Inference, made from the Passions, desire perhaps to
have the same confirmed by Experience. Let him therefore consider with himselfe, when taking a journey,
he armes himselfe, and seeks to go well accompanied;
when going to sleep, he locks his dores; when even in his
house he locks his chests; and this when he knows there
bee Lawes, and publike Officers, armed, to revenge all
injuries shall bee done him; what opinion he has of his
fellow subjects, when he rides armed; of his fellow Citizens, when he locks his dores; and of his children, and
servants, when he locks his chests. Does he not there
as much accuse mankind by his actions, as I do by my
words? But neither of us accuse mans nature in it. The
Desires, and other Passions of man, are in themselves no
Sin. No more are the Actions, that proceed from those
Passions, till they know a Law that forbids them: which

till Lawes be made they cannot know: nor can any Law be made, till they have agreed upon the Person that shall make it.

[63] It may peradventure be thought, there was never such a time, nor condition of warre as this; and I believe it was never generally so, over all the world: but there are many places, where they live so now. For the savage people in many places of *America*, except the government of small Families, the concord whereof dependeth on naturall lust, have no government at all; and live at this day in that brutish manner, as I said before. Howsoever, it may be perceived what manner of life there would be, where there were no common Power to feare; by the manner of life, which men that have formerly lived under a peacefull government, use to degenerate into, in a civill Warre.

But though there had never been any time, wherein particular men were in a condition of warre one against another; yet in all times, Kings, and Persons of Soveraigne authority, because of their Independency, are in continuall jealousies, and in the state and posture of Gladiators; having their weapons pointing, and their eyes fixed on one another; that is, their Forts, Garrisons, and Guns upon the Frontiers of their Kingdomes; and continuall Spyes upon their neighbours; which is a posture of War. But because they uphold thereby, the Industry of their Subjects; there does not follow from it, that misery, which accompanies the Liberty of particular men.

In such a Warre, nothing is Unjust To this warre of every man against every man, this also is consequent; that nothing can be Unjust. The notions of Right and Wrong, Justice and Injustice have there no place. Where there is no common Power, there is no Law: where no Law, no Injustice. Force, and Fraud, are in warre the two Cardinall vertues. Justice, and Injustice are none of the Faculties neither of the Body, nor Mind. If they were, they might be in a man that were alone in the world, as well as his Senses, and Passions. They are

Qualities, that relate to men in Society, not in Solitude. It is consequent also to the same condition, that there be no Propriety, no Dominion, no *Mine* and *Thine* distinct; but onely that to be every mans, that he can get; and for so long, as he can keep it. And thus much for the ill condition, which man by meer Nature is actually placed in; though with a possiblity to come out of it, consisting partly in the Passions, partly in his Reason.

The Passions that encline men to Peace, are Feare of Death; Desire of such things as are necessary to commodious living; and a Hope by their Industry to obtain them. And Reason suggesteth convenient Articles of Peace, upon which men may be drawn to agreement. These Articles, are they, which otherwise are called the Lawes of Nature: whereof I shall speak more particularly, in the two following Chapters. [64]

The Passions that incline men to Peace

CHAP. XIV

Of the first and second NATURALL LAWES, *and of* CONTRACTS

The RIGHT OF NATURE, which Writers commonly call *Jus Naturale*, is the Liberty each man hath, to use his own power, as he will himselfe, for the preservation of his own Nature; that is to say, of his own Life; and consequently, of doing any thing, which in his own Judgement, and Reason, hee shall conceive to be the aptest means thereunto.

Right of Nature what

By LIBERTY, is understood, according to the proper signification of the word, the absence of externall Impediments: which Impediments, may oft take away part of a mans power to do what hee would; but cannot hinder him from using the power left him, according as his judgement, and reason shall dictate to him.

Liberty what

A LAW OF NATURE, (*Lex Naturalis*,) is a Precept, or

A Law of Nature what

generall Rule, found out by Reason, by which a man is forbidden to do, that, which is destructive of his life, or taketh away the means of preserving the same; and to omit, that, by which he thinketh it may be best preserved. For though they that speak of this subject, use to confound *Jus*, and *Lex*, *Right* and *Law*; yet they ought *Difference* to be distinguished; because RIGHT, consisteth in liberty *of Right and* to do, or to forbeare; Whereas LAW, determineth, and *Law* bindeth to one of them: so that Law, and Right, differ as much, as Obligation, and Liberty; which in one and the same matter are inconsistent.

Naturally   And because the condition of Man, (as hath been *every man* declared in the precedent Chapter) is a condition of *has Right to* Warre of every one against every one; in which case *every thing* every one is governed by his own Reason; and there is nothing he can make use of, that may not be a help unto him, in preserving his life against his enemyes; It followeth, that in such a condition, every man has a Right to every thing; even to one anothers body. And therefore, as long as this naturall Right of every man to every thing endureth, there can be no security to any man, (how strong or wise soever he be,) of living out the time, which Nature ordinarily alloweth men to live. And consequently it is a precept, or generall rule of Reason, *The Funda-* *That every man, ought to endeavour Peace, as farre as* *mentall Law* *he has hope of obtaining it; and when he cannot obtain* *of Nature* *it, that he may seek, and use, all helps, and advantages* *of Warre.* The first branch of which Rule, containeth the first, and Fundamentall Law of Nature; which is, *to seek Peace, and follow it.* The Second, the summe of the Right of Nature; which is, *By all means we can, to* *defend our selves.*

The second   From this Fundamentall Law of Nature, by which *Law of* men are commanded to endeavour Peace, is derived *Nature* this second Law; *That a man be willing, when others* *are so too, as farre-forth, as for Peace, and* [65] *defence* *of himselfe he shall think it necessary, to lay down this* *right to all things; and be contented with so much liberty against other men, as he would allow other men against himselfe.* For as long as every man holdeth this Right, of doing any thing he liketh; so long are all men in the condition of Warre. But if other men will not lay down their Right, as well as he; then there is no Reason for any one, to devest himselfe of his: For that were to expose himselfe to Prey, (which no man is bound to) rather than to dispose himselfe to Peace. This is that Law of the Gospell; *Whatsoever you require that others should do to you, that do ye to them.* And that Law of all men, *Quod tibi fieri non vis, alteri ne feceris.*[74]

To *lay downe* a mans *Right* to any thing, is to *devest* himselfe of the *Liberty*, of hindring another of the benefit of his own Right to the same. For he that renounceth, or passeth away his Right, giveth not to any other man a Right which he had not before; because there is nothing to which every man had not Right by Nature: but onely standeth out of his way, that he may enjoy his own originall Right, without hindrance from him; not without hindrance from another. So that the effect which redoundeth to one man, by another mans defect of Right, is but so much diminution of impediments to the use of his own Right originall. *What it is to lay down a Right*

Right is layd aside, either by simply Renouncing it; or by Transferring it to another. By *Simply* RENOUNCING; when he cares not to whom the benefit thereof redoundeth. By TRANSFERRING; when he intendeth the benefit thereof to some certain person, or persons. And when a man hath in either manner abandoned, or granted away his Right; then is he said to be OBLIGED, or BOUND, not to hinder those, to whom such Right is granted, or abandoned, from the benefit of it: and that he *Ought*, and it is his DUTY, not to make voyd that voluntary act of his own: and that such hindrance is INJUSTICE, and INJURY, as being *Sine Jure*; the Right being before renounced, or transferred. So that *Injury*, or *Injustice*, in the controversies of the world, is somewhat like to that, which in the disputations of Scholers is called *Absurdity*. *Renouncing a Right what it is* *Transferring Right what* *Obligation* *Duty* *Injustice*

For as it is there called an Absurdity, to contradict what one maintained in the Beginning: so in the world, it is called Injustice, and Injury, voluntarily to undo that, which from the beginning he had voluntarily done. The way by which a man either simply Renounceth, or Transferreth his Right, is a Declaration, or Signification, by some voluntary and sufficient signe, or signes, that he doth so Renounce, or Transferre; or hath so Renounced, or Transferred the same, to him that accepteth it. And these Signes are either Words onely, or Actions onely; or (as it happeneth most often) both Words, and Actions. And the same are the BONDS, by which men are bound, and obliged: Bonds, that have their strength, not from their own Nature, (for nothing is more easily broken then a mans word,) but from Feare of some evill consequence upon the rupture.

Not all Rights are alienable   Whensoever a man Transferreth his Right, or Renounceth it; it is either in consideration of some Right reciprocally transferred to [66] himselfe; or for some other good he hopeth for thereby. For it is a voluntary act: and of the voluntary acts of every man, the object is some *Good to himselfe*. And therefore there be some Rights, which no man can be understood by any words, or other signes, to have abandoned, or transferred. As first a man cannot lay down the right of resisting them, that assault him by force, to take away his life; because he cannot be understood to ayme thereby, at any Good to himselfe. The same may be sayd of Wounds, and Chayns, and Imprisonment; both because there is no benefit consequent to such patience; as there is to the patience of suffering another to be wounded, or imprisoned: as also because a man cannot tell, when he seeth men proceed against him by violence, whether they intend his death or not. And lastly the motive, and end for which this renouncing, and transferring of Right is introduced, is nothing else but the security of a mans person, in his life, and in the means of so preserving life, as not to be weary of it. And therefore if a man by words, or other

signes, seem to despoyle himselfe of the End, for which
those signes were intended; he is not to be understood
as if he meant it, or that it was his will; but that he
was ignorant of how such words and actions were to be
interpreted.

The mutuall transferring of Right, is that which men *Contract*
call CONTRACT.   *what*

There is difference, between transferring of Right to
the Thing; and transferring, or tradition, that is, delivery of the Thing it selfe. For the Thing may be delivered
together with the Translation of the Right; as in buying
and selling with ready mony; or exchange of goods, or
lands: and it may be delivered some time after.

Again, one of the Contractors, may deliver the Thing
contracted for on his part, and leave the other to perform his part at some determinate time after, and in the
mean time be trusted; and then the Contract on his part,
is called PACT, or COVENANT: Or both parts may con- *Covenant*
tract now, to performe hereafter: in which cases, he that *what*
is to performe in time to come, being trusted, his performance is called *Keeping of Promise*, or Faith; and the
fayling of performance (if it be voluntary) *Violation of
Faith*.

When the transferring of Right, is not mutuall; but
one of the parties transferreth, in hope to gain thereby
friendship, or service from another, or from his friends;
or in hope to gain the reputation of Charity, or Magnanimity; or to deliver his mind from the pain of
compassion; or in hope of reward in heaven; This is not
Contract, but GIFT, FREE-GIFT, GRACE: which words *Free-gift*
signifie one and the same thing.

Signes of Contract, are either *Expresse*, or *by Infer-* *Signes of*
ence. Expresse, are words spoken with understanding *Contract*
of what they signifie: And such words are either of the *Expresse*
time *Present*, or *Past*; as, *I Give, I Grant, I have Given, I
have Granted, I will that this be yours*: Or of the future;
as, *I will Give, I will Grant*: which words of the future,
are called PROMISE.

Signes of   Signes by Inference, are sometimes the consequence
Contract by of Words; [67] sometimes the consequence of Silence;
Inference   sometimes the consequence of Actions; somtimes the
consequence of Forbearing an Action: and generally a
sign by Inference, of any Contract, is whatsoever sufficiently argues the will of the Contractor.

Free gift   Words alone, if they be of the time to come, and
passeth by   contain a bare promise, are an insufficient signe of a
words of   Free-gift and therefore not obligatory. For if they be of
the Present the time to Come, as, *To morrow I will Give*, they are
or Past   a signe I have not given yet, and consequently that my
right is not transferred, but remaineth till I transferre it
by some other Act. But if the words be of the time Present, or Past, as, *I have given, or do give to be delivered
to morrow*, then is my to morrows Right given away to
day; and that by the vertue of the words, though there
were no other argument of my will. And there is a great
difference in the signification of these words, *Volo hoc
tuum esse cras*, and *Cras dabo*; that is, between *I will
that this be thine to morrow*, and, *I will give it thee to
morrow*: For the word *I will*, in the former manner of
speech, signifies an act of the will Present; but in the
later, it signifies a promise of an act of the will to Come:
and therefore the former words, being of the Present,
transferre a future right; the later, that be of the Future,
transferre nothing. But if there be other signes of the
Will to transferre a Right, besides Words; then, though
the gift be Free, yet may the Right be understood to
passe by words of the future: as if a man propound a
Prize to him that comes first to the end of a race, The
gift is Free; and though the words be of the Future, yet
the Right passeth: for if he would not have his words so
Signes of   be understood, he should not have let them runne.
Contract are   In Contracts, the right passeth, not onely where the
words both   words are of the time Present, or Past; but also where
of the Past, they are of the Future: because all Contract is mutuall
Present, and translation, or change of Right; and therefore he that
Future   promiseth onely, because he hath already received the

benefit for which he promiseth, is to be understood as if
he intended the Right should passe: for unlesse he had
been content to have his words so understood, the other
would not have performed his part first. And for that
cause, in buying, and selling, and other acts of Contract,
a Promise is equivalent to a Covenant; and therefore
obligatory.

He that performeth first in the case of a Contract, is *Merit what*
said to MERIT that which he is to receive by the performance of the other; and he hath it as *Due*. Also when
a Prize is propounded to many, which is to be given to
him onely that winneth; or mony is thrown amongst
many, to be enjoyed by them that catch it; though this
be a Free gift; yet so to Win, or so to Catch, is to *Merit*,
and to have it as DUE. For the Right is transferred in
the Propounding of the Prize, and in throwing down the
mony; though it be not determined to whom, but by the
Event of the contention. But there is between these two
sorts of Merit, this difference, that In Contract, I Merit
by vertue of my own power, and the Contractors need;
but in this case of Free gift, I am enabled to Merit onely
by the benignity of the Giver: In Contract, I merit at the
Contractors hand that hee [68] should depart with his
right; In this case of Gift, I Merit not that the giver should
part with his right; but that when he has parted with it,
it should be mine, rather than anothers. And this I think
to be the meaning of that distinction of the Schooles,
between *Meritum congrui*, and *Meritum condigni*.[75] For
God Almighty, having promised Paradise to those men
(hoodwinkt with carnall desires,) that can walk through
this world according to the Precepts, and Limits prescribed by him; they say, he that shall so walk, shall
Merit Paradise *Ex congruo*. But because no man can
demand a right to it, by his own Righteousnesse, or any
other power in himselfe, but by the Free Grace of God
onely; they say, no man can Merit Paradise *ex condigno*.
This I say, I think is the meaning of that distinction; but
because Disputers do not agree upon the signification

of their own termes of Art, longer than it serves their turn; I will not affirme any thing of their meaning: onely this I say; when a gift is given indefinitely, as a prize to be contended for, he that winneth Meriteth, and may claime the Prize as Due.

Covenants of Mutuall trust, when Invalid If a Covenant be made, wherein neither of the parties performe presently, but trust one another; in the condition of meer Nature, (which is a condition of Warre of every man against every man,) upon any reasonable suspition, it is Voyd: But if there be a common Power set over them both, with right and force sufficient to compell performance; it is not Voyd. For he that performeth first, has no assurance the other will performe after; because the bonds of words are too weak to bridle mens ambition, avarice, anger, and other Passions, without the feare of some coercieve Power; which in the condition of meer Nature, where all men are equall, and judges of the justnesse of their own fears, cannot possibly be supposed. And therfore he which performeth first, does but betray himselfe to his enemy; contrary to the Right (he can never abandon) of defending his life, and means of living.

But in a civill estate, where there is a Power set up to constrain those that would otherwise violate their faith, that feare is no more reasonable; and for that cause, he which by the Covenant is to perform first, is obliged so to do.

The cause of feare, which maketh such a Covenant invalid, must be always something arising after the Covenant made; as some new fact, or other signe of the Will not to performe: else it cannot make the Covenant voyd. For that which could not hinder a man from promising, ought not to be admitted as a hindrance of performing.

Right to the End, Containeth Right to the Means He that transferreth any Right, transferreth the Means of enjoying it, as farre as lyeth in his power. As he that selleth Land, is understood to transferre the Herbage,[76] and whatsoever growes upon it; Nor can he that sells a

Mill turn away the Stream that drives it. And they that give to a man the Right of government in Soveraignty, are understood to give him the right of levying mony to maintain Souldiers; and of appointing Magistrates for the administration of Justice.

To make Covenant with bruit Beasts, is impossible; *No Covenant* because not understanding our speech, they understand *with Beasts* not, nor accept of any [69] translation of Right; nor can translate any Right to another: and without mutuall acceptation, there is no Covenant.

To make Covenant with God, is impossible, but by *Nor with* Mediation of such as God speaketh to, either by Reve- *God without* lation supernaturall, or by his Lieutenants that govern *speciall* under him, and in his Name: For otherwise we know *Revelation* not whether our Covenants be accepted, or not. And therefore they that Vow any thing contrary to any law of Nature, Vow in vain; as being a thing unjust to pay such Vow. And if it be a thing commanded by the Law of Nature, it is not the Vow, but the Law that binds them.

The matter, or subject of a Covenant, is alwayes some- *No Coven-* thing that falleth under deliberation; (For to Covenant, *ant, but of* is an act of the Will; that is to say an act, and the last act, *Possible and* of deliberation;) and is therefore alwayes understood to *Future* be something to come; and which is judged Possible for him that Covenanteth, to performe.

And therefore, to promise that which is known to be Impossible, is no Covenant. But if that prove impossible afterwards, which before was thought possible, the Covenant is valid, and bindeth, (though not to the thing it selfe,) yet to the value; or, if that also be impossible, to the unfeigned endeavour of performing as much as is possible: for to more no man can be obliged.

Men are freed of their Covenants two wayes; by Per- *Covenants* forming; or by being Forgiven. For Performance, is the *how made* naturall end of obligation; and Forgivenesse, the restitu- *voyd* tion of liberty; as being a retransferring of that Right, in which the obligation consisted.

Covenants   Covenants entred into by fear, in the condition of meer
extorted by   Nature, are obligatory. For example, if I Covenant to
feare are   pay a ransome, or service for my life, to an enemy; I am
valide   bound by it. For it is a Contract, wherein one receiveth
the benefit of life; the other is to receive mony, or service
for it; and consequently, where no other Law (as in the
condition, of meer Nature) forbiddeth the performance,
the Covenant is valid. Therefore Prisoners of warre, if
trusted with the payment of their Ransome, are obliged
to pay it: And if a weaker Prince, make a disadvantageous peace with a stronger, for feare; he is bound to
keep it; unlesse (as hath been sayd before) there ariseth
some new, and just cause of feare, to renew the war. And
even in Common-wealths, if I be forced to redeem my
selfe from a Theefe by promising him mony, I am bound
to pay it, till the Civill Law discharge me. For whatsoever I may lawfully do without Obligation, the same I
may lawfully Covenant to do through feare: and what I
lawfully Covenant, I cannot lawfully break.

The former   A former Covenant, makes voyd a later. For a man
Covenant to   that hath passed away his Right to one man to day, hath
one, makes   it not to passe to morrow to another: and therefore the
voyd the later later promise passeth no Right, but is null.
to another

A Covenant not to defend my selfe from force, by
force, is alwayes voyd. For (as I have shewed before) no
A mans Cov-   man can transferre, or lay down his Right to save him-
enant not to selfe from Death, Wounds, and Imprisonment, (the
defend him-   avoyding whereof is the onely End of laying [70] down
selfe, is voyd any Right,) and therefore the promise of not resisting
force, in no Covenant transferreth any right; nor is
obliging. For though a man may Covenant thus, *Unlesse
I do so, or so, kill me*; he cannot Covenant thus,
*Unlesse I do so, or so, I will not resist you, when you
come to kill me.* For man by nature chooseth the lesser
evill, which is danger of death in resisting; rather than
the greater, which is certain and present death in not
resisting. And this is granted to be true by all men, in
that they lead Criminals to Execution, and Prison, with

armed men, notwithstanding that such Criminals have consented to the Law, by which they are condemned.

A Covenant to accuse ones selfe, without assurance of pardon, is likewise invalid. For in the condition of Nature, where every man is Judge, there is no place for Accusation: and in the Civill State, the Accusation is followed with Punishment; which being Force, a man is not obliged not to resist. The same is also true, of the Accusation of those, by whose Condemnation a man falls into misery; as of a Father, Wife, or Benefactor. For the Testimony of such an Accuser, if it be not willingly given, is præsumed to be corrupted by Nature; and therefore not to be received: and where a mans Testimony is not to be credited, he is not bound to give it. Also Accusations upon Torture, are not to be reputed as Testimonies. For Torture is to be used but as means of conjecture, and light, in the further examination, and search of truth: and what is in that case confessed, tendeth to the ease of him that is Tortured; not to the informing of the Torturers: and therefore ought not to have the credit of a sufficient Testimony: for whether he deliver himselfe by true, or false Accusation, he does it by the Right of preserving his own life. *No man obliged to accuse himself*

The force of Words, being (as I have formerly noted) too weak to hold men to the performance of their Covenants; there are in mans nature, but two imaginable helps to strengthen it. And those are either a Feare of the consequence of breaking their word; or a Glory, or Pride in appearing not to need to breake it. This later is a Generosity too rarely found to be presumed on, especially in the pursuers of Wealth, Command, or sensuall Pleasure; which are the greatest part of Mankind. The Passion to be reckoned upon, is Fear; whereof there be two very generall Objects: one, The Power of Spirits Invisible; the other, The Power of those men they shall therein Offend. Of these two, though the former be the greater Power, yet the feare of the later is commonly the greater Feare. The Feare of the former is in every man, *The End of an Oath* his own Religion: which hath place in the nature of man before Civill Society. The later hath not so; at least not place enough, to keep men to their promises; because in the condition of meer Nature, the inequality of Power is not discerned, but by the event of Battell. So that before the time of Civill Society, or in the interruption thereof by Warre, there is nothing can strengthen a Covenant of Peace agreed on, against the temptations of Avarice, Ambition, Lust, or other strong desire, but the feare of that Invisible Power, which they every one Worship as God; and Feare as a Revenger of their perfidy. All therefore that can be done [71] between two men not subject to Civill Power, is to put one another to swear by the God he feareth: Which *Swearing*, or OATH, is a *Forme of Speech, added to a Promise; by which he that promiseth, signifieth, that unlesse he performe, he renounceth the mercy of his God, or calleth to him for vengeance on himselfe.* Such was the Heathen Forme, *Let* Jupiter *kill me else, as I kill this Beast.*[77] So is our Forme, *I shall do thus, and thus, so help me God.* And this, with the Rites and Ceremonies, which every one useth in his own Religion, that the feare of breaking faith might be the greater.

The forme of an Oath

By this it appears, that an Oath taken according to any other Forme, or Rite, then his, that sweareth, is in vain; and no Oath: And that there is no Swearing by any thing which the Swearer thinks not God. For though men have sometimes used to swear by their Kings, for feare, or flattery; yet they would have it thereby understood, they attributed to them Divine honour. And that Swearing unnecessarily by God, is but prophaning of his name: and Swearing by other things, as men do in common discourse, is not Swearing, but an impious Custome, gotten by too much vehemence of talking.

No Oath, but by God

It appears also, that the Oath addes nothing to the Obligation. For a Covenant, if lawfull, binds in the sight of God, without the Oath, as much as with it: if unlawfull, bindeth not at all; though it be confirmed with an Oath.

An Oath addes nothing to the Obligation

Of other Lawes of Nature

From that law of Nature, by which we are obliged to transferre to another, such Rights, as being retained, hinder the peace of Mankind, there followeth a Third; which is this, *That men performe their Covenants made*: without which, Covenants are in vain, and but Empty words; and the Right of all men to all things remaining, wee are still in the condition of Warre. *The third Law of Nature, Justice*

And in this law of Nature, consisteth the Fountain and Originall of JUSTICE. For where no Covenant hath preceded, there hath no Right been transferred, and every man has right to every thing; and consequently, no action can be Unjust. But when a Covenant is made, then to break it is *Unjust*: And the definition of INJUSTICE, is no other than *the not Performance of Covenant*. And whatsoever is not Unjust, is *Just*. *Justice and Injustice what*

But because Covenants of mutuall trust, where there is a feare of not performance on either part, (as hath been said in the former Chapter,) are invalid; though the Originall of Justice be the making of Covenants; yet Injustice actually there can be none, till the cause of such feare be taken away; which while men are in the naturall condition of Warre, cannot be done. Therefore before the names of Just, and Unjust can have place, there must be some coërcive Power, to compell men equally to the performance of their Covenants, by the terrour of some punishment, greater than the benefit they expect [72] by the breach of their Covenant; and to make good that Propriety, which by mutuall Contract men acquire, in recompence of the universall Right they abandon: and such power there is none before the erection of a Common-wealth. And this is also to be gathered out of the ordinary definition of Justice in the Schooles: For they say, that *Justice is the constant Will of giving to* *Justice and Propriety begin with the Constitution of Common-wealth every man his own.*[78] And therefore where there is no *Own*, that is, no Propriety, there is no Injustice; and where there is no coërceive Power erected, that is, where there is no Common-wealth, there is no Propriety; all men having Right to all things: Therefore where there is no Common-wealth, there nothing is Unjust. So that the nature of Justice, consisteth in keeping of valid Covenants: but the Validity of Covenants begins not but with the Constitution of a Civill Power, sufficient to compell men to keep them: And then it is also that Propriety begins.

Justice not   The Foole hath sayd in his heart, there is no such
Contrary to   thing as Justice;[79] and sometimes also with his tongue;
Reason   seriously alleaging, that every mans conservation, and contentment, being committed to his own care, there could be no reason, why every man might not do what he thought conduced thereunto: and therefore also to make, or not make; keep, or not keep Covenants, was not against Reason, when it conduced to ones benefit. He does not therein deny, that there be Covenants; and that they are sometimes broken, sometimes kept; and that such breach of them may be called Injustice, and the observance of them Justice: but he questioneth, whether Injustice, taking away the feare of God, (for the same Foole hath said in his heart there is no God,) may not sometimes stand with that Reason, which dictateth to every man his own good; and particularly then, when it conduceth to such a benefit, as shall put a man in a condition, to neglect not onely the dispraise, and revilings, but also the power of other men. The Kingdome of God is gotten by violence: but what if it could be gotten by unjust violence? were it against Reason so to get it, when it is impossible to receive hurt by it? and if it be not against Reason, it is not against Justice: or else Justice is not to be approved for good. From such reasoning as this, Succesfull wickednesse hath obtained the name of Vertue: and some that in all other things have disallowed the violation of Faith; yet have allowed it,

when it is for the getting of a Kingdome. And the Heathen that believed, that *Saturn* was deposed by his son *Jupiter*, believed neverthelesse the same *Jupiter* to be the avenger of Injustice:[80] Somewhat like to a piece of Law in *Cokes* Commentaries on *Litleton*; where he sayes, If the right Heire of the Crown be attainted of Treason; yet the Crown shall descend to him, and *eo instante* the Atteynder be voyd:[81] From which instances a man will be very prone to inferre; that when the Heire apparent of a Kingdome, shall kill him that is in possession, though his father; you may call it Injustice, or by what other name you will; yet it can never be against Reason, seeing all the voluntary actions of men tend to the benefit of themselves; and those actions are most Reasonable, that conduce most to their [73] ends. This specious reasoning is neverthelesse false.

For the question is not of promises mutuall, where there is no security of performance on either side; as when there is no Civil Power erected over the parties promising; for such promises are no Covenants: But either where one of the parties has performed already; or where there is a Power to make him performe; there is the question whether it be against reason, that is, against the benefit of the other to performe, or not. And I say it is not against reason. For the manifestation whereof, we are to consider; First, that when a man doth a thing, which notwithstanding any thing can be foreseen, and reckoned on, tendeth to his own destruction, howsoever some accident which he could not expect, arriving may turne it to his benefit; yet such events do not make it reasonably or wisely done. Secondly, that in a condition of Warre, wherein every man to every man, for want of a common Power to keep them all in awe, is an Enemy, there is no man can hope by his own strength, or wit, to defend himselfe from destruction, without the help of Confederates; where every one expects the same defence by the Confederation, that any one else does: and therefore he which

declares he thinks it reason to deceive those that help
him, can in reason expect no other means of safety,
than what can be had from his own single Power. He
therefore that breaketh his Covenant, and consequently
declareth that he thinks he may with reason do so, cannot be received into any Society, that unite themselves
for Peace and Defence, but by the errour of them that
receive him; nor when he is received, be retayned in it,
without seeing the danger of their errour; which errours
a man cannot reasonably reckon upon as the means
of his security: and therefore if he be left, or cast out
of Society, he perisheth; and if he live in Society, it is by
the errours of other men, which he could not foresee,
nor reckon upon; and consequently against the reason
of his preservation; and so, as all men that contribute
not to his destruction, forbear him onely out of ignorance of what is good for themselves.

As for the Instance of gaining the secure and perpetuall felicity of Heaven, by any way; it is frivolous: there
being but one way imaginable; and that is not breaking,
but keeping of Covenant.

And for the other Instance of attaining Soveraignty
by Rebellion; it is manifest, that though the event follow, yet because it cannot reasonably be expected, but
rather the contrary; and because by gaining it so, others
are taught to gain the same in like manner, the attempt
thereof is against reason. Justice therefore, that is to say,
Keeping of Covenant, is a Rule of Reason, by which we
are forbidden to do any thing destructive to our life; and
consequently a Law of Nature.

There be some that proceed further; and will not
have the Law of Nature, to be those Rules which conduce to the preservation of mans life on earth; but to
the attaining of an eternall felicity after death; to which
they think the breach of Covenant may conduce; and
consequently be just and reasonable; (such are they that
think it a work of [74] merit to kill, or depose, or rebell
against, the Soveraigne Power constituted over them

by their own consent.) But because there is no naturall knowledge of mans estate after death; much lesse of the reward that is then to be given to breach of Faith; but onely a beliefe grounded upon other mens saying, that they know it supernaturally, or that they know those, that knew them, that knew others, that knew it supernaturally; Breach of Faith cannot be called a Precept of Reason, or Nature.

Others, that allow for a Law of Nature, the keeping of Faith, do neverthelesse make exception of certain persons; as Heretiques, and such as use not to performe their Covenant to others: And this also is against reason. For if any fault of a man, be sufficient to discharge our Covenant made; the same ought in reason to have been sufficient to have hindred the making of it. *Covenants not discharged by the Vice of the Person to whom they are made*

The names of Just, and Injust, when they are attributed to Men, signifie one thing; and when they are attributed to Actions, another. When they are attributed to Men, they signifie Conformity, or Inconformity of Manners, to Reason. But when they are attributed to Actions, they signifie the Conformity, or Inconformity to Reason, not of Manners, or manner of life, but of particular Actions. A Just man therefore, is he that taketh all the care he can, that his Actions may be all Just: and an Unjust man, is he that neglecteth it. And such men are more often in our Language stiled by the names of Righteous, and Unrighteous; then Just, and Unjust; though the meaning be the same. Therefore a Righteous man, does not lose that Title, by one, or a few unjust Actions, that proceed from sudden Passion, or mistake of Things, or Persons: nor does an Unrighteous man, lose his character, for such Actions, as he does, or forbeares to do, for feare: because his Will is not framed by the Justice, but by the apparant benefit of what he is to do. That which gives to humane Actions the relish of Justice, is a certain Noblenesse or Gallantnesse of courage, (rarely found,) by which a man scorns to be beholding for the contentment of his life, to fraud, or breach of promise. This *Justice of Men, & Justice of Actions what*

Justice of the Manners, is that which is meant, where Justice is called a Vertue; and Injustice a Vice.

But the Justice of Actions denominates men, not Just, but *Guiltlesse*: and the Injustice of the same, (which is also called Injury,) gives them but the name of *Guilty*.

Justice of Manners, and Justice of Actions Again, the Injustice of Manners, is the disposition, or aptitude to do Injurie; and is Injustice before it proceed to Act; and without supposing any individuall person injured. But the Injustice of an Action, (that is to say Injury,) supposeth an individuall person Injured; namely him, to whom the Covenant was made: And therefore many times the injury is received by one man, when the dammage redoundeth to another. As when the Master commandeth his servant to give mony to a stranger; if it be not done, the Injury is done to the Master, whom he had before Covenanted to obey; but the dammage redoundeth to the stranger, to whom he had no Obligation; and therefore could not Injure him. And so also in Common-[75]wealths, private men may remit to one another their debts; but not robberies or other violences, whereby they are endammaged; because the detaining of Debt, is an Injury to themselves; but Robbery and Violence, are Injuries to the Person of the Commonwealth.

Nothing done to a man, by his own consent can be Injury Whatsoever is done to a man, conformable to his own Will signified to the doer, is no Injury to him. For if he that doeth it, hath not passed away his originall right to do what he please, by some Antecedent Covenant, there is no breach of Covenant; and therefore no Injury done him. And if he have; then his Will to have it done being signified, is a release of that Covenant: and so again there is no Injury done him.

Justice Commutative, and Distributive Justice of Actions, is by Writers divided into *Commutative*, and *Distributive*: and the former they say consisteth in proportion Arithmeticall; the later in proportion Geometricall. Commutative therefore, they place in the equality of value of the things contracted for; And Distributive,[82] in the distribution of equall benefit, to men of equall merit. As if it were Injustice to sell dearer than we buy; or to give more to a man than he merits. The value of all things contracted for, is measured by the Appetite of the Contractors: and therefore the just value, is that which they be contented to give. And Merit (besides that which is by Covenant, where the performance on one part, meriteth the performance of the other part, and falls under Justice Commutative, not Distributive,) is not due by Justice; but is rewarded of Grace onely. And therefore this distinction, in the sense wherein it useth to be expounded, is not right. To speak properly, Commutative Justice, is the Justice of a Contractor; that is, a Performance of Covenant, in Buying, and Selling; Hiring, and Letting to Hire; Lending, and Borrowing; Exchanging, Bartering, and other acts of Contract.

And Distributive Justice, the Justice of an Arbitrator; that is to say, the act of defining what is Just. Wherein, (being trusted by them that make him Arbitrator,) if he performe his Trust, he is said to distribute to every man his own: and this is indeed Just Distribution, and may be called (though improperly) Distributive Justice; but more properly Equity; which also is a Law of Nature, as shall be shewn in due place.

As Justice dependeth on Antecedent Covenant; so does GRATITUDE depend on Antecedent Grace; that is to say, Antecedent Free-gift: and is the fourth Law of Nature; which may be conceived in this Forme, *That a man which receiveth Benefit from another of meer Grace, Endeavour that he which giveth it, have no reasonable cause to repent him of his good will.* For no man giveth, but with intention of Good to himselfe; because Gift is Voluntary; and of all Voluntary Acts, the Object is to every man his own Good; of which if men see they shall be frustrated, there will be no beginning of benevolence, or trust; nor consequently of mutuall help; nor of reconciliation of one man to another; and therefore they are to remain still in the condition of *War*; which is contrary to the first and Fundamentall Law of Nature,

The fourth Law of Nature, Gratitude

which commandeth men to *Seek Peace*. The breach of
this Law, [76] is called *Ingratitude*; and hath the same
relation to Grace, that Injustice hath to Obligation by
Covenant.

The fifth,   A fifth Law of Nature, is COMPLEASANCE; that is to
Mutuall say, *That every man strive to accommodate himselfe to*
accommo- *the rest*. For the understanding whereof, we may con-
dation, sider, that there is in mens aptnesse to Society, a diversity
or Com- of Nature, rising from their diversity of Affections; not
pleasance unlike to that we see in stones brought together for
building of an Ædifice. For as that stone which by the
asperity, and irregularity of Figure, takes more room
from others, than it selfe fills; and for the hardnesse,
cannot be easily made plain, and thereby hindereth the
building, is by the builders cast away as unprofitable,
and troublesome: so also, a man that by asperity of
Nature, will strive to retain those things which to himselfe are superfluous, and to others necessary; and for
the stubbornness of his Passions, cannot be corrected, is
to be left, or cast out of Society, as combersome thereunto. For seeing every man, not onely by Right, but also
by necessity of Nature, is supposed to endeavour all he
can, to obtain that which is necessary for his conservation; He that shall oppose himselfe against it, for things
superfluous, is guilty of the warre that thereupon is to
follow; and therefore doth that, which is contrary to
the fundamentall Law of Nature, which commandeth
to seek Peace. The observers of this Law, may be called
SOCIABLE, (the Latines call them *Commodi*;) The contrary, *Stubborn, Insociable, Froward, Intractable.*

The sixth,   A sixth Law of Nature, is this, *That upon caution of*
Facility to *the Future time, a man ought to pardon the offences*
Pardon *past of them that repenting, desire it*. For PARDON, is
nothing but granting of Peace; which though granted to
them that persevere in their hostility, be not Peace, but
Feare; yet not granted to them that give caution of the
Future time, is signe of an aversion to Peace; and there-
fore contrary to the Law of Nature.

A seventh is, *That in Revenges,* (that is, retribution of Evil for Evil,) *Men look not at the greatnesse of the evill past, but the greatnesse of the good to follow.* Whereby we are forbidden to inflict punishment with any other designe, than for correction of the offender, or direction of others. For this Law is consequent to the next before it, that commandeth Pardon, upon security of the Future time. Besides, Revenge without respect to the Example, and profit to come, is a triumph, or glorying in the hurt of another, tending to no end; (for the End is alwayes somewhat to Come;) and glorying to no end, is vain-glory, and contrary to reason; and to hurt without reason, tendeth to the introduction of Warre; which is against the Law of Nature; and is commonly stiled by the name of *Cruelty.* *[The seventh, that in Revenges, men respect onely the future good]*

And because all signes of hatred, or contempt, provoke to fight; insomuch as most men choose rather to hazard their life, than not to be revenged; we may in the eighth place, for a Law of Nature, set down this Precept, *That no man by deed, word, countenance, or gesture, declare Hatred, or Contempt of another.* The breach of which Law, is commonly called *Contumely.* *[The eighth, against Contumely]*

The question who is the better man, has no place in the condition of meer Nature; where, (as has been shewn before,) all men are equall. [77] The inequallity that now is, has bin introduced by the Lawes civill. I know that *Aristotle* in the first booke of his Politiques, for a foundation of his doctrine,[83] maketh men by Nature, some more worthy to Command, meaning the wiser sort (such as he thought himselfe to be for his Philosophy;) others to Serve, (meaning those that had strong bodies, but were not Philosophers as he;) as if Master and Servant were not introduced by consent of men, but by difference of Wit: which is not only against reason; but also against experience. For there are very few so foolish, that had not rather governe themselves, than be governed by others: Nor when the wise in their own conceit, contend by force, with them who distrust their *[The ninth, against Pride]* owne wisdome, do they alwaies, or often, or almost at any time, get the Victory. If Nature therefore have made men equall, that equalitie is to be acknowledged: or if Nature have made men unequall; yet because men that think themselves equall, will not enter into conditions of Peace, but upon Equall termes, such equalitie must be admitted. And therefore for the ninth law of Nature, I put this, *That every man acknowledge other for his Equall by Nature*. The breach of this Precept is *Pride*.

The tenth,   On this law, dependeth another, *That at the entrance
against into conditions of Peace, no man require to reserve to
Arrogance himselfe any Right, which he is not content should be reserved to every one of the rest*. As it is necessary for all men that seek peace, to lay down certaine Rights of Nature; that is to say, not to have libertie to do all they list: so is it necessarie for mans life, to retaine some; as right to governe their owne bodies; enjoy aire, water, motion, waies to go from place to place; and all things else without which a man cannot live, or not live well. If in this case, at the making of Peace, men require for themselves, that which they would not have to be granted to others, they do contrary to the precedent law, that commandeth the acknowledgment of naturall equalitie, and therefore also against the law of Nature. The observers of this law, are those we call *Modest*, and the breakers *Arrogant* men. The Greeks call the violation of this law πλεονεξία; that is, a desire of more than their share.[84]

The eleventh   Also if *a man be trusted to judge between man and
Equity man*, it is a precept of the Law of Nature, *that he deale Equally between them*. For without that, the Controversies of men cannot be determined but by Warre. He therefore that is partiall in judgment, doth what in him lies, to deterre men from the use of Judges, and Arbitrators; and consequently, (against the fundamentall Lawe of Nature) is the cause of Warre.

The observance of this law, from the equall distribution to each man, of that which in reason belongeth to him, is called EQUITY, and (as I have sayd before) distributive Justice: the violation, *Acception of persons*, προσωποληψία.[85]

And from this followeth another law, *That such things as cannot be divided, be enjoyed in Common, if it can be; and if the quantity of the thing permit, without Stint; otherwise Proportionably to the number of them that have Right.* For otherwise the distribution is Unequall, and contrary to Equitie.

The twelfth, Equall use of things Common

[78] But some things there be, that can neither be divided, nor enjoyed in common. Then, The Law of Nature, which prescribeth Equity, requireth, *That the Entire Right; or else, (making the use alternate,) the First Possession, be determined by Lot.* For equall distribution, is of the Law of Nature; and other means of equall distribution cannot be imagined.

The thirteenth, of Lot

Of *Lots* there be two sorts, *Arbitrary*, and *Naturall*. Arbitrary, is that which is agreed on by the Competitors: Naturall, is either *Primogeniture*, (which the Greek calls Κληρονομία, which signifies, *Given by Lot*;) or *First Seisure*.

The fourteenth, of Primogeniture, and First seising

And therefore those things which cannot be enjoyed in common, nor divided, ought to be adjudged to the First Possessor; and in some cases to the First-Borne, as acquired by Lot.

It is also a Law of Nature, *That all men that mediate Peace, be allowed safe Conduct.* For the Law that commandeth Peace, as the *End*, commandeth Intercession, as the *Means*; and to Intercession the Means is safe Conduct.

The fifteenth, of Mediators

And because, though men be never so willing to observe these Lawes, there may neverthelesse arise questions concerning a mans action; First, whether it were done, or not done; Secondly (if done) whether against the Law, or not against the Law; the former whereof, is called a question *Of Fact*; the later a question *Of Right*; therefore unlesse the parties to the question, Covenant mutually to stand to the sentence of another, they are as

The sixteenth, of Submission to Arbitrement

farre from Peace as ever. This other, to whose Sentence they submit, is called an ARBITRATOR. And therefore it is of the Law of Nature, *That they that are at controversie, submit their Right to the judgement of an Arbitrator.*

The seven-
teenth, No
man is his
own Judge
And seeing every man is presumed to do all things in order to his own benefit, no man is a fit Arbitrator in his own cause: and if he were never so fit; yet Equity allowing to each party equall benefit, if one be admitted to be Judge, the other is to be admitted also; & so the controversie, that is, the cause of War, remains, against the Law of Nature.

The eight-
eenth, no
man to be
Judge, that
has in him a
natural cause
of Partiality
For the same reason no man in any Cause ought to be received for Arbitrator, to whom greater profit, or honour, or pleasure apparently ariseth out of the victory of one party, than of the other: for hee hath taken (though an unavoydable bribe, yet) a bribe; and no man can be obliged to trust him. And thus also the controversie, and the condition of War remaineth, contrary to the Law of Nature.

The nine-
teenth, of
Witnesses
And in a controversie of *Fact*, the Judge being to give no more credit to one, than to the other, (if there be no other Arguments) must give credit to a third; or to a third and fourth; or more: For else the question is undecided, and left to force, contrary to the Law of Nature.

These are the Lawes of Nature, dictating Peace, for a means of the conservation of men in multitudes; and which onely concern the doctrine of Civill Society. There be other things tending to the destruction of particular men; as Drunkenness, and all other parts of Intemperance; which may therefore also be reckoned amongst those things which the Law of Nature hath forbidden; but are not neces[79]sary to be mentioned, nor are pertinent enough to this place.

A Rule, by
which the
Laws of
Nature may
easily be
examined
And though this may seem too subtile a deduction of the Lawes of Nature, to be taken notice of by all men; whereof the most part are too busie in getting food, and the rest too negligent to understand; yet to leave all men unexcusable, they have been contracted into one easie

sum, intelligible, even to the meanest capacity; and that is, *Do not that to another, which thou wouldest not have done to thy selfe*; which sheweth him, that he has no more to do in learning the Lawes of Nature, but, when weighing the actions of other men with his own, they seem too heavy, to put them into the other part of the ballance, and his own into their place, that his own passions, and selfe-love, may adde nothing to the weight; and then there is none of these Lawes of Nature that will not appear unto him very reasonable.

The Lawes of Nature oblige *in foro interno*; that is to say, they bind to a desire they should take place: but *in foro externo*;[86] that is, to the putting them in act, not alwayes. For he that should be modest, and tractable, and performe all he promises, in such time, and place, where no man els should do so, should but make himselfe a prey to others, and procure his own certain ruine, contrary to the ground of all Lawes of Nature, which tend to Natures preservation. And again, he that having sufficient Security, that others shall observe the same Lawes towards him, observes them not himselfe, seeketh not Peace, but War; & consequently the destruction of his Nature by Violence. *The Lawes of Nature oblige in Conscience alwayes, but in Effect then onely when there is Security*

And whatsoever Lawes bind *in foro interno*, may be broken, not onely by a fact contrary to the Law but also by a fact according to it, in case a man think it contrary. For though his Action in this case, be according to the Law; yet his Purpose was against the Law; which where the Obligation is *in foro interno*, is a breach.

The Lawes of Nature are Immutable and Eternall; For Injustice, Ingratitude, Arrogance, Pride, Iniquity, Accception of persons, and the rest, can never be made lawfull. For it can never be that Warre shall preserve life, and Peace destroy it. *The Laws of Nature are Eternal;*

The same Lawes, because they oblige onely to a desire, and endeavour, I mean an unfeigned and constant endeavour, are easie to be observed. For in that they require nothing but endeavour; he that endeavoureth *And yet Easie*

their performance, fulfilleth them; and he that fulfilleth
the Law, is Just.

*The Science
of these
Lawes, is the
true Morall
Philosophy*   And the Science of them, is the true and onely Moral
Philosophy. For Morall Philosophy is nothing else but
the Science of what is *Good*, and *Evill*, in the conversation, and Society of mankind. *Good*, and *Evill*, are
names that signifie our Appetites, and Aversions; which
in different tempers, customes, and doctrines of men, are
different: And divers men, differ not onely in their Judgement, on the senses of what is pleasant, and unpleasant
to the tast, smell, hearing, touch, and sight; but also of
what is conformable, or disagreeable to Reason, in the
actions of common life. Nay, the same man, in divers
times, differs from himselfe; and one time praiseth, that
is, calleth Good, what another time he dispraiseth, and
calleth Evil: [80] From whence arise Disputes, Controversies, and at last War. And therefore so long a man is
in the condition of meer Nature, (which is a condition
of War,) as private Appetite is the measure of Good, and
Evill: and consequently all men agree on this, that Peace
is Good, and therefore also the way, or means of Peace,
which (as I have shewed before) are *Justice*, *Gratitude*,
Modesty, *Equity*, *Mercy*, & the rest of the Laws of
Nature, are good; that is to say, *Morall Vertues*; and
their contrarie *Vices*, Evill. Now the science of Vertue
and Vice, is Morall Philosophie; and therfore the true
Doctrine of the Lawes of Nature, is the true Morall Philosophie. But the Writers of Morall Philosophie, though
they acknowledge the same Vertues and Vices; Yet not
seeing wherein consisted their Goodnesse; nor that they
come to be praised, as the meanes of peaceable, sociable, and comfortable living; place them in a mediocrity
of passions: as if not the Cause, but the Degree of dar-
ing, made Fortitude; or not the Cause, but the Quantity
of a gift, made Liberality.

These dictates of Reason, men use to call by the name
of Lawes; but improperly: for they are but Conclusions, or Theoremes concerning what conduceth to the

conservation and defence of themselves; wheras Law, properly is the word of him, that by right hath command over others. But yet if we consider the same Theoremes, as delivered in the word of God, that by right commandeth all things; then are they properly called Lawes.

CHAP. XVI

Of PERSONS, AUTHORS, and things Personated

A PERSON, is he, *whose words or actions are considered, either as his own, or as representing the words or actions of an other man, or of any other thing to whom they are attributed, whether Truly or by Fiction.*

When they are considered as his owne, then is he called a *Naturall Person*: And when they are considered as representing the words and actions of an other, then is he a *Feigned* or *Artificiall person*.

The word Person is latine: insteed whereof the Greeks have πρόσωπον, which signifies the *Face*, as *Persona* in latine signifies the *disguise*, or *outward appearance* of a man, counterfeited on the Stage; and somtimes more particularly that part of it, which disguiseth the face, as a Mask or Visard: And from the Stage, hath been translated to any Representer of speech and action, as well in Tribunalls, as Theaters. So that a *Person*, is the same that an *Actor* is, both on the Stage and in common Conversation; and to *Personate*, is to *Act*, or *Represent* himselfe, or an other; and he that acteth another, is said to beare his Person, or act in his name; (in which sence *Cicero* useth it where he saies, *Unus sustineo tres Personas; Mei, Adversarii, & Judicis*, I beare three Persons; my own, my Adversaries, and the Judges;)[87] and is cal[81]led in diverse occasions, diversly; as a *Representer*, or *Representative*, a *Lieutenant*, a *Vicar*, an *Attorney*, a *Deputy*, a *Procurator*, an *Actor*, and the like.

A Person what

Person Naturall, and Artificiall

The word Person, whence

Of Persons Artificiall, some have their words and actions *Owned* by those whom they represent. And then *Actor,* the Person is the *Actor*; and he that owneth his words and *Author,* actions, is the AUTHOR: In which case the Actor acteth by Authority. For that which in speaking of goods and possessions, is called an *Owner,* and in latine *Dominus,* in Greeke κύριος; speaking of Actions, is called Author. And as the Right of possession, is called Dominion; so *Authority* the Right of doing any Action, is called AUTHORITY. So that by Authority, is alwayes understood a Right of doing any act: and *done by Authority,* done by Commission, or Licence from him whose right it is.

Covenants From hence it followeth, that when the Actor maketh *by Author-* a Covenant by Authority, he bindeth thereby the Author, *ity, bind the* no lesse than if he had made it himselfe; and no lesse *Author* subjecteth him to all the consequences of the same. And therfore all that hath been said formerly, (*Chap.* 14.) of the nature of Covenants between man and man in their naturall capacity, is true also when they are made by their Actors, Representers, or Procurators, that have authority from them, so far-forth as is in their Commission, but no farther.

And therefore he that maketh a Covenant with the Actor, or Representer, not knowing the Authority he hath, doth it at his own perill. For no man is obliged by a Covenant, whereof he is not Author; nor consequently by a Covenant made against, or beside the Authority he gave.

But not the When the Actor doth any thing against the Law of *Actor* Nature by command of the Author, if he be obliged by former Covenant to obey him, not he, but the Author breaketh the Law of Nature: for though the Action be against the Law of Nature; yet it is not his: but contrarily; to refuse to do it, is against the Law of Nature, that forbiddeth breach of Covenant.

The Author- And he that maketh a Covenant with the Author, by *ity is to be* mediation of the Actor, not knowing what Authority he *shewne* hath, but onely takes his word; in case such Authority be not made manifest unto him upon demand, is no longer obliged: For the Covenant made with the Author, is not valid, without his Counter-assurance. But if he that so Covenanteth, knew before hand he was to expect no other assurance, than the Actors word; then is the Covenant valid; because the Actor in this case maketh himselfe the Author. And therefore, as when the Authority is evident, the Covenant obligeth the Author, not the Actor; so when the Authority is feigned, it obligeth the Actor onely; there being no Author but himselfe.

There are few things, that are uncapable of being represented by Fiction. Inanimate things, as a Church, an Hospital, a Bridge, may be Personated by a Rector, Master, or Overseer. But things Inanimate, cannot be Authors, nor therefore give Authority to their Actors: Yet the Actors may have Authority to procure their mainte[82]nance, given them by those that are Owners, or Governours of those things. And therefore, such things cannot be Personated, before there be some state of Civill Government. *Things personated, Inanimate*

Likewise Children, Fooles, and Mad-men that have no use of Reason, may be Personated by Guardians, or Curators; but can be no Authors (during that time) of any action done by them, longer then (when they shall recover the use of Reason) they shall judge the same reasonable. Yet during the Folly, he that hath right of governing them, may give Authority to the Guardian. But this again has no place but in a State Civill, because before such estate, there is no Dominion of Persons. *Irrational;*

An Idol, or meer Figment of the brain, may be Personated; as were the Gods of the Heathen; which by such Officers as the State appointed, were Personated, and held Possessions, and other Goods, and Rights, which men from time to time dedicated, and consecrated unto them. But idols cannot be Authors: for an Idol is nothing. The Authority proceeded from the State: and therefore before introduction of Civill Government, the Gods of the Heathen could not be Personated. *False Gods;*

The true God The true God may be Personated. As he was; first, by *Moses*; who governed the Israelites, (that were not his, but Gods people,) not in his own name, with *Hoc dicit Moses*; but in Gods Name, with *Hoc dicit Dominus*.[88] Secondly, by the Son of man, his own Son, our Blessed Saviour *Jesus Christ*, that came to reduce the Jewes, and induce all Nations into the Kingdome of his Father; not as of himselfe, but as sent from his Father. And thirdly, by the Holy Ghost, or Comforter, speaking, and working in the Apostles: which Holy Ghost, was a Comforter that came not of himselfe; but was sent, and proceeded from them both.

A Multitude A Multitude of men, are made *One* Person, when they
of men, how are by one man, or one Person, Represented; so that it
one Person be done with the consent of every one of that Multitude in particular. For it is the *Unity* of the Representer, not the *Unity* of the Represented, that maketh the Person *One*. And it is the Representer that beareth the Person, and but one Person: And *Unity*, cannot otherwise be understood in Multitude.

Every one is And because the Multitude naturally is not *One*, but
Author *Many*; they cannot be understood for one; but many Authors, of every thing their Representative saith, or doth in their name; Every man giving their common Representer, Authority from himself in particular; and owning all the actions the Representer doth, in case they give him Authority without stint: Otherwise, when they limit him in what, and how farre he shall represent them, none of them owneth more, than they gave him commission to Act.

An Actor And if the Representative consist of many men, the
may be Many voyce of the greater number, must be considered as
men made the voyce of them all. For if the lesser number pronounce
One by (for example) in the Affirmative, and the greater in the
Plurality of Negative, there will be Negatives more than [83]
Voyces to destroy the Affirmatives; and thereby the excesse of Negatives, standing uncontradicted, are the onely voyce the Representative hath.

And a Representative of even number, especially when *Representa-* the number is not great, whereby the contradictory *tives, when* voyces are oftentimes equall, is therefore oftentimes *the number is* mute, and uncapable of Action. Yet in some cases con- *even, unprof-* tradictory voyces equall in number, may determine a *itable* question; as in condemning, or absolving, equality of votes, even in that they condemne not, do absolve; but not on the contrary condemne, in that they absolve not. For when a Cause is heard; not to condemne, is to absolve: but on the contrary, to say that not absolving, is condemning, is not true. The like it is in a deliberation of executing presently, or deferring till another time: For when the voyces are equall, the not decreeing Execution, is a decree of Dilation.

Or if the number be odde, as three, or more, (men, or *Negative* assemblies;) whereof every one has by a Negative Voice, *voyce* authority to take away the effect of all the Affirmative Voices of the rest, This number is no Representative; because by the diversity of Opinions, and Interests of men, it becomes oftentimes, and in cases of the greatest consequence, a mute Person, and unapt, as for many things else, so for the government of a Multitude, especially in time of Warre.

Of Authors there be two sorts. The first simply so called; which I have before defined to be him, that owneth the Action of another simply. The second is he, that owneth an Action, or Covenant of another conditionally; that is to say, he undertaketh to do it, if the other doth it not, at, or before a certain time. And these Authors conditionall, are generally called SURETYES, in Latine *Fidejussores*, and *Sponsores*; and particularly for Debt, *Prædes*; and for Appearance before a Judge, or Magistrate, *Vades*. [85]

PART TWO
OF COMMON-WEALTH

CHAP. XVII

Of the Causes, Generation, and Definition of a COMMON-WEALTH

The End of The finall Cause, End, or Designe of men, (who nat-
Common- urally love Liberty, and Dominion over others,) in the
wealth, introduction of that restraint upon themselves, (in which
particular wee see them live in Common-wealths,) is the foresight
Security: of their own preservation, and of a more contented life
thereby; that is to say, of getting themselves out from
that miserable condition of Warre, which is necessarily
Chap. 13 consequent (as hath been shewn) to the naturall Passions of men, when there is no visible Power to keep
them in awe, and tye them by feare of punishment to
the performance of their Covenants, and observation of
those Lawes of Nature set down in the fourteenth and
fifteenth Chapters.

Which is not For the Lawes of Nature (as *Justice, Equity, Mod-*
to be had *esty, Mercy,* and (in summe) *doing to others, as wee*
from the Law *would be done to,*) of themselves, without the terrour
of Nature: of some Power, to cause them to be observed, are contrary to our naturall Passions, that carry us to Partiality,
Pride, Revenge, and the like. And Covenants, without
the Sword, are but Words, and of no strength to secure
a man at all. Therefore notwithstanding the Lawes of
Nature, (which every one hath then kept, when he has
the will to keep them, when he can do it safely,) if there

be no Power erected, or not great enough for our security; every man will, and may lawfully rely on his own strength and art, for caution against all other men. And in all places, where men have lived by small Families, to robbe and spoyle one another, has been a Trade, and so farre from being reputed against the Law of Nature, that the greater spoyles they gained, the greater was their honour; and men observed no other Lawes therein, but the Lawes of Honour; that is, to abstain from cruelty, leaving to men their lives, and instruments of husbandry. And as small Familyes did then; so now do Cities and Kingdomes which are but greater Families (for their own security) enlarge their Dominions, upon all pretences of danger, and fear of Invasion, or assistance that may be given to Invaders, endeavour as much as they can, to subdue, or weaken their neighbours, by open force, and secret arts, for want of other Caution, justly; and are remembred for it in after ages with honour.

Nor is it the joyning together of a small number of men, that gives them this security; because in small numbers, small additions [86] on the one side or the other, make the advantage of strength so great, as is sufficient to carry the Victory; and therefore gives encouragement to an Invasion. The Multitude sufficient to confide in for our Security, is not determined by any certain number, but by comparison with the Enemy we feare; and is then sufficient, when the odds of the Enemy is not of so visible and conspicuous moment, to determine the event of warre, as to move him to attempt. *Nor from the conjunction of a few men or familyes:*

And be there never so great a Multitude; yet if their actions be directed according to their particular judgements, and particular appetites, they can expect thereby no defence, nor protection, neither against a Common enemy, nor against the injuries of one another. For being distracted in opinions concerning the best use and application of their strength, they do not help, but hinder one another; and reduce their strength by mutuall opposition to nothing: whereby they are easily, not onely subdued *Nor from a great Multitude, unlesse directed by one judgement:*

by a very few that agree together; but also when there is no common enemy, they make warre upon each other, for their particular interests. For if we could suppose a great Multitude of men to consent in the observation of Justice, and other Lawes of Nature, without a common Power to keep them all in awe; we might as well suppose all Man-kind to do the same; and then there neither would be, nor need to be any Civill Government, or Common-wealth at all; because there would be Peace without subjection.

And that Nor is it enough for the security, which men desire
continually should last all the time of their life, that they be governed, and directed by one judgement, for a limited time; as in one Battell, or one Warre. For though they obtain a Victory by their unanimous endeavour against a forraign enemy; yet afterwards, when either they have no common enemy, or he that by one part is held for an enemy, is by another part held for a friend, they must needs by the difference of their interests dissolve, and fall again into a Warre amongst themselves.

Why certain It is true, that certain living creatures, as Bees, and
creatures Ants, live sociably one with another, (which are therefore
without by *Aristotle* numbred amongst Politicall creatures;)[1]
reason, or and yet have no other direction, than their particular
speech, do judgements and appetites; nor speech, whereby one of
neverthelesse them can signifie to another, what he thinks expedient
live in Soci- for the common benefit: and therefore some man may
ety, without perhaps desire to know, why Man-kind cannot do the
any coërcive same. To which I answer,
Power First, that men are continually in competition for Honour and Dignity, which these creatures are not; and consequently amongst men there ariseth on that ground, Envy and Hatred, and finally Warre; but amongst these not so.

Secondly, that amongst these creatures, the Common good differeth not from the Private; and being by nature enclined to their private, they procure thereby the common benefit. But man, whose Joy consisteth in comparing himselfe with other men, can relish nothing but what is eminent.

Thirdly, that these creatures, having not (as man) the use of reason, do not see, nor think they see any fault, in the administration of [87] their common businesse: whereas amongst men, there are very many, that thinke themselves wiser, and abler to govern the Publique, better than the rest; and these strive to reforme and innovate, one this way, another that way; and thereby bring it into Distraction and Civill warre.

Fourthly, that these creatures, though they have some use of voice, in making knowne to one another their desires, and other affections; yet they want that art of words, by which some men can represent to others, that which is Good, in the likenesse of Evill; and Evill, in the likenesse of Good; and augment, or diminish the apparent greatnesse of Good and Evill; discontenting men, and troubling their Peace at their pleasure.

Fiftly, irrationall creatures cannot distinguish betweene *Injury*, and *Dammage*; and therefore as long as they be at ease, they are not offended with their fellowes: whereas Man is then most troublesome, when he is most at ease: for then it is that he loves to shew his Wisdome, and controule the Actions of them that governe the Common-wealth.

Lastly, the agreement of these creatures is Naturall; that of men, is by Covenant only, which is Artificiall: and therefore it is no wonder if there be somwhat else required (besides Covenant) to make their Agreement constant and lasting; which is a Common Power, to keep them in awe, and to direct their actions to the Common Benefit.

The only way to erect such a Common Power, as may be able to defend them from the invasion of Forraigners, and the injuries of one another, and thereby to secure them in such sort, as that by their owne industrie, and by the fruites of the Earth, they may nourish themselves and live contentedly; is, to conferre all their power and *The Generation of a Common-wealth* strength upon one Man, or upon one Assembly of men, that may reduce all their Wills, by plurality of voices, unto one Will: which is as much as to say, to appoint one man, or Assembly of men, to beare their Person; and every one to owne, and acknowledge himselfe to be Author of whatsoever he that so beareth their Person, shall Act, or cause to be Acted, in those things which concerne the Common Peace and Safetie; and therein to submit their Wills, every one to his Will, and their Judgements, to his Judgment. This is more than Consent, or Concord; it is a reall Unitie of them all, in one and the same Person, made by Covenant of every man with every man, in such manner, as if every man should say to every man, *I Authorise and give up my Right of Governing my selfe, to this Man, or to this Assembly of men, on this condition, that thou give up thy Right to him, and Authorise all his Actions in like manner.* This done, the Multitude so united in one Person, is called a COMMON-WEALTH, in latine CIVITAS. This is the Generation of that great LEVIATHAN, or rather (to speake more reverently) of that *Mortall God*, to which wee owe under the *Immortall God*, our peace and defence. For by this Authoritie, given him by every particular man in the Common-Wealth, he hath the use of so much Power and Strength [88] conferred on him, that by terror thereof, he is inabled to forme the wills of them all, to Peace at home, and mutuall ayd against their enemies abroad. And in him consisteth the *The Defini-* Essence of the Common-wealth; which (to define it,) is *tion of a* *One Person, of whose Acts a great Multitude, by mutu-* *Common-* *all Covenants one with another, have made themselves* *wealth* *every one the Author, to the end he may use the strength* *and means of them all, as he shall think expedient, for* *their Peace and Common Defence.*

Soveraigne,   And he that carryeth this Person, is called SOVER-
and Subject, AIGNE, and said to have *Soveraigne Power*; and every
what one besides, his SUBJECT.

The attaining to this Soveraigne Power, is by two

wayes. One, by Naturall force; as when a man maketh
his children, to submit themselves, and their children to
his government, as being able to destroy them if they
refuse; or by Warre subdueth his enemies to his will,
giving them their lives on that condition. The other, is
when men agree amongst themselves, to submit to some
Man, or Assembly of men, voluntarily, on confidence to
be protected by him against all others. This later, may be
called a Politicall Common-wealth, or Common-wealth
by *Institution*; and the former, a Common-wealth by
Acquisition. And first, I shall speak of a Common-wealth
by Institution.

CHAP. XVIII

Of the RIGHTS of Soveraignes by Institution

A *Common-wealth* is said to be *Instituted*, when a *Mul-*
titude of men do Agree, and *Covenant, every one, with*
every one, that to whatsoever *Man*, or *Assembly of Men*,
shall be given by the major part, the *Right* to *Present* the
Person of them all, (that is to say, to be their *Repre-*
sentative;) every one, as well he that *Voted for it*, as he
that *Voted against it*, shall *Authorise* all the Actions and
Judgements, of that Man, or Assembly of men, in the
same manner, as if they were his own, to the end, to live
peaceably amongst themselves, and be protected against
other men.

    From this Institution of a Common-wealth are derived
all the *Rights*, and *Facultyes* of him, or them, on whom
the Soveraigne Power is conferred by the consent of the
People assembled.

    First, because they Covenant, it is to be understood,
they are not obliged by former Covenant to any thing
repugnant hereunto. And Consequently they that have
already Instituted a Common-wealth, being thereby

*The act of
Instituting a
Common-
wealth, what*

*The Conse-
quences to
such Institu-
tion, are
1. The Sub-
jects cannot
change the
forme of
government*

bound by Covenant, to own the Actions, and Judge-ments of one, cannot lawfully make a new Covenant, amongst themselves, to be obedient to any other, in any thing whatsoever, without his permission. And therefore, they that are subjects to a Monarch, cannot without his leave cast off Monarchy, and return to the confusion of a disunited Multitude; nor transferre their Person from him that beareth it, to another Man, or other Assembly of men: for they [89] are bound, every man to every man, to Own, and be reputed Author of all, that he that already is their Soveraigne, shall do, and judge fit to be done: so that any one man dissenting, all the rest should break their Covenant made to that man, which is injustice: and they have also every man given the Soveraignty to him that beareth their Person; and therefore if they depose him, they take from him that which is his own, and so again it is injustice. Besides, if he that attempteth to depose his Soveraign, be killed, or punished by him for such attempt, he is author of his own punishment, as being by the Institution, Author of all his Soveraign shall do: And because it is injustice for a man to do any thing, for which he may be pun-ished by his own authority, he is also upon that title, unjust. And whereas some men have pretended for their disobedience to their Soveraign, a new Covenant, made, not with men, but with God; this also is unjust: for there is no Covenant with God, but by mediation of some body that representeth Gods Person; which none doth but Gods Lieutenant, who hath the Soveraignty under God. But this pretence of Covenant with God, is so evi-dent a lye, even in the pretenders own consciences, that it is not onely an act of an unjust, but also of a vile, and unmanly disposition.

2. Soveraigne
Power cannot
be forfeited
Secondly, Because the Right of bearing the Person of them all, is given to him they make Soveraigne, by Cov-enant onely of one to another, and not of him to any of them; there can happen no breach of Covenant on the part of the Soveraigne; and consequently none of

his Subjects, by any pretence of forfeiture, can be freed
from his Subjection. That he which is made Soveraigne
maketh no Covenant with his Subjects beforehand, is
manifest; because either he must make it with the whole
multitude, as one party to the Covenant; or he must
make a severall Covenant with every man. With the
whole, as one party, it is impossible; because as yet they
are not one Person: and if he make so many severall
Covenants as there be men, those Covenants after he
hath the Soveraignty are voyd, because what act soever
can be pretended by any one of them for breach thereof,
is the act both of himselfe, and of all the rest, because
done in the Person, and by the Right of every one of
them in particular. Besides, if any one, or more of them,
pretend a breach of the Covenant made by the Soveraigne at his Institution; and others, or one other of his
Subjects, or himselfe alone, pretend there was no such
breach, there is in this case, no Judge to decide the controversie: it returns therefore to the Sword again; and
every man recovereth the right of Protecting himselfe by
his own strength, contrary to the designe they had in the
Institution. It is therefore in vain to grant Soveraignty
by way of precedent Covenant. The opinion that any
Monarch receiveth his Power by Covenant, that is to
say on Condition, proceedeth from want of understanding this easie truth, that Covenants being but words,
and breath, have no force to oblige, contain, constrain,
or protect any man, but what it has from the publique
Sword; that is, from the untyed hands of that Man, or
Assembly of men that hath the Soveraignty, and whose
actions are avouched by them [90] all, and performed
by the strength of them all, in him united. But when
an Assembly of men is made Soveraigne; then no man
imagineth any such Covenant to have past in the Institution; for no man is so dull as to say, for example, the
People of *Rome*, made a Covenant with the Romans, to
hold the Soveraignty on such or such conditions; which
not performed, the Romans might lawfully depose the

Roman People. That men see not the reason to be alike in a Monarchy, and in a Popular Government, proceedeth from the ambition of some, that are kinder to the government of an Assembly, whereof they may hope to participate, than of Monarchy, which they despair to enjoy.

3. No man can without injustice protest against the Institution of the Soveraigne declared by the major part Thirdly, because the major part hath by consenting voices declared a Soveraigne; he that dissented must now consent with the rest; that is, be contented to avow all the actions he shall do, or else justly be destroyed by the rest. For if he voluntarily entered into the Congregation of them that were assembled, he sufficiently declared thereby his will (and therefore tacitely covenanted) to stand to what the major part should ordayne: and therefore if he refuse to stand thereto, or make Protestation against any of their Decrees, he does contrary to his Covenant, and therfore unjustly. And whether he be of the Congregation, or not; and whether his consent be asked, or not, he must either submit to their decrees, or be left in the condition of warre he was in before; wherein he might without injustice be destroyed by any man whatsoever.

4. The Soveraigns Actions cannot be justly accused by the Subject Fourthly, because every Subject is by this Institution Author of all the Actions, and Judgments of the Soveraigne Instituted; it followes, that whatsoever he doth, it can be no injury to any of his Subjects; nor ought he to be by any of them accused of Injustice. For he that doth any thing by authority from another, doth therein no injury to him by whose authority he acteth: But by this Institution of a Common-wealth, every particular man is Author of all the Soveraigne doth; and consequently he that complaineth of injury from his Soveraigne, complaineth of that whereof he himselfe is Author; and therefore ought not to accuse any man but himselfe; no nor himselfe of injury; because to do injury to ones selfe, is impossible. It is true that they that have Soveraigne power, may commit Iniquity; but not Injustice, or Injury in the proper signification.

Fiftly, and consequently to that which was sayd last, no man that hath Soveraigne power can justly be put to death, or otherwise in any manner by his Subjects punished. For seeing every Subject is Author of the actions of his Soveraigne; he punisheth another, for the actions committed by himselfe.

And because the End of this Institution, is the Peace and Defence of them all; and whosoever has right to the End, has right to the Means; it belongeth of Right, to whatsoever Man, or Assembly that hath the Soveraignty, to be Judge both of the meanes of Peace and Defence; and also of the hindrances, and disturbances of the same; and to do whatsoever he shall think necessary to be done, both before hand, for the preserving of Peace and Security, by prevention of Discord at home, and [91] Hostility from abroad; and, when Peace and Security are lost, for the recovery of the same. And therefore,

Sixtly, it is annexed to the Soveraignty, to be Judge of what Opinions and Doctrines are averse, and what conducing to Peace; and consequently, on what occasions, how farre, and what, men are to be trusted withall, in speaking to Multitudes of people; and who shall examine the Doctrines of all bookes before they be published. For the Actions of men proceed from their Opinions; and in the wel governing of Opinions, consisteth the well governing of mens Actions, in order to their Peace, and Concord. And though in matter of Doctrine, nothing ought to be regarded but the Truth; yet this is not repugnant to regulating of the same by Peace. For Doctrine repugnant to Peace, can no more be True, than Peace and Concord can be against the Law of Nature. It is true, that in a Common-wealth, where by the negligence, or unskilfullnesse of Governours, and Teachers, false Doctrines are by time generally received; the contrary Truths may be generally offensive: Yet the most sudden, and rough busling in of a new Truth, that can be, does never breake the Peace, but only somtimes

5. What soever the Soveraigne doth, is unpunishable by the Subject

6. The Soveraigne is judge of what is necessary for the Peace and Defence of his Subjects

And Judge of what Doctrines are fit to be taught them

awake the Warre. For those men that are so remissely governed, that they dare take up Armes, to defend, or introduce an Opinion, are still in Warre; and their condition not Peace, but only a Cessation of Armes for feare of one another; and they live as it were, in the procincts of battaile continually. It belongeth therefore to him that hath the Soveraign Power, to be Judge, or constitute all Judges of Opinions and Doctrines, as a thing necessary to Peace, thereby to prevent Discord and Civill Warre.

7. The Right of making Rules, whereby the Subjects may every man know what is so his owne, as no other Subject can without injustice take it from him
Seventhly, is annexed to the Soveraigntie, the whole power of prescribing the Rules, whereby every man may know, what Goods he may enjoy, and what Actions he may doe, without being molested by any of his fellow Subjects: And this is it men call *Propriety*. For before constitution of Soveraign Power (as hath already been shewn) all men had right to all things; which necessarily causeth Warre: and therefore this Proprietie, being necessary to Peace, and depending on Soveraign Power, is the Act of that Power, in order to the publique peace. These Rules of Propriety (or *Meum* and *Tuum*)[2] and of *Good, Evill, Lawfull,* and *Unlawfull* in the actions of Subjects, are the Civill Lawes, that is to say, the Lawes of each Common-wealth in particular; though the name of Civill Law be now restrained to the antient Civill Lawes of the City of *Rome*; which being the head of a great part of the World, her Lawes at that time were in these parts the Civill Law.

8. To him also belongeth the Right of all Judicature and decision of Controversies:
Eightly, is annexed to the Soveraigntie, the Right of Judicature; that is to say, of hearing and deciding all Controversies, which may arise concerning Law, either Civill, or Naturall, or concerning Fact. For without the decision of Controversies, there is no protection of one Subject, against the injuries of another; the Lawes concerning *Meum* and *Tuum* are in vaine; and to every man remaineth, from the naturall and necessary appetite of his own conservation, the right of protecting himselfe by his private strength, which is the condition

[92] of Warre; and contrary to the end for which every Common-wealth is instituted.

Ninthly, is annexed to the Soveraignty, the Right of making Warre, and Peace with other Nations, and Common-wealths; that is to say, of Judging when it is for the publique good, and how great forces are to be assembled, armed, and payd for that end; and to levy mony upon the Subjects, to defray the expenses thereof. For the Power by which the people are to be defended, consisteth in their Armies; and the strength of an Army, in the union of their strength under one Command; which Command the Soveraign Instituted, therefore hath; because the command of the *Militia*, without other Institution, maketh him that hath it Soveraign. And therefore whosoever is made Generall of an Army, he that hath the Soveraign Power is alwayes Generalissimo. *9. And of making War, and Peace, as he shall think best:*

Tenthly, is annexed to the Soveraignty, the choosing of all Counsellours, Ministers, Magistrates, and Officers, both in Peace, and War. For seeing the Soveraign is charged with the End, which is the common Peace and Defence; he is understood to have Power to use such Means, as he shall think most fit for his discharge. *10. And of choosing all Counsellours, and Ministers, both of Peace, and Warre:*

Eleventhly, to the Soveraign is committed the Power of Rewarding with riches, or honour; and of Punishing with corporall, or pecuniary punishment, or with ignominy every Subject according to the Law he hath formerly made; or if there be no Law made, according as he shall judge most to conduce to the encouraging of men to serve the Common-wealth, or deterring of them from doing dis-service to the same. *11. And of Rewarding, and Punishing, and that (where no former Law hath determined the measure of it) arbitrary:*

Lastly, considering what values men are naturally apt to set upon themselves; what respect they look for from others; and how little they value other men; from whence continually arise amongst them, Emulation, Quarrells, Factions, and at last Warre, to the destroying of one another, and diminution of their strength against a Common Enemy; It is necessary that there be Lawes *12. And of Honour and Order* of Honour, and a publique rate of the worth of such men as have deserved, or are able to deserve well of the Common-wealth; and that there be force in the hands of some or other, to put those Lawes in execution. But it hath already been shewn, that not onely the whole *Militia*, or forces of the Common-wealth; but also the Judicature of all Controversies, is annexed to the Soveraignty. To the Soveraign therefore it belongeth also to give titles of Honour; and to appoint what Order of place, and dignity, each man shall hold; and what signes of respect, in publique or private meetings, they shall give to one another.

These Rights   These are the Rights, which make the Essence of Sov-
are indivisible eraignty; and which are the markes, whereby a man may discern in what Man, or Assembly of men, the Soveraign Power is placed, and resideth. For these are incommunicable, and inseparable. The Power to coyn Mony; to dispose of the estate and persons of Infant heires; to have præemption in Markets; and all other Statute Præ-rogatives, may be transferred by the Soveraign; and yet the Power to protect his Subjects be retained. But if he transferre the *Militia*, he retains the Ju[93]dicature in vain, for want of execution of the Lawes: Or if he grant away the Power of raising Mony; the *Militia* is in vain: or if he give away the government of Doctrines, men will be frighted into rebellion with the feare of Spirits. And so if we consider any one of the said Rights, we shall presently see, that the holding of all the rest, will produce no effect, in the conservation of Peace and Justice, the end for which all Common-wealths are Instituted. And this division is it, whereof it is said, *a Kingdome divided in it selfe cannot stand*:[3] For unlesse this division precede, division into opposite Armies can never happen. If there had not first been an opinion received of the greatest part of *England*, that these Powers were divided between the King, and the Lords, and the House of Commons, the people had never been divided, and fallen into this Civill Warre; first between those that

disagreed in Politiques; and after between the Dissenters about the liberty of Religion; which have so instructed men in this point of Soveraign Right, that there be few now (in *England*,) that do not see, that these Rights are inseparable, and will be so generally acknowledged, at the next return of Peace; and so continue, till their miseries are forgotten; and no longer, except the vulgar be better taught than they have hetherto been.

And because they are essentiall and inseparable Rights, it follows necessarily, that in whatsoever, words any of them seem to be granted away, yet if the Soveraign Power it selfe be not in direct termes renounced, and the name of Soveraign no more given by the Grantees to him that Grants them, the Grant is voyd: for when he has granted all he can, if we grant back the Soveraignty, all is restored, as inseparably annexed thereunto. *And can by no Grant passe away without direct renouncing of the Soveraign Power*

This great Authority being Indivisible, and inseparably annexed to the Soveraignty, there is little ground for the opinion of them, that say of Soveraign Kings, though they be *singulis majores*, of greater Power than every one of their Subjects, yet they be *Universis minores*, of lesse power than them all together. For if by *all together*, they mean not the collective body as one person, then *all together*, and *every one*, signifie the same; and the speech is absurd. But if by *all together*, they understand them as one Person (which person the Soveraign bears,) then the power of all together, is the same with the Soveraigns power; and so again the speech is absurd: which absurdity they see well enough, when the Soveraignty is in an Assembly of the people; but in a Monarch they see it not; and yet the power of Soveraignty is the same in whomsoever it be placed. *The Power and Honour of Subjects vanisheth in the presence of the Power Soveraign*

And as the Power, so also the Honour of the Soveraign, ought to be greater, than that of any, or all the Subjects. For in the Soveraignty is the fountain of Honour. The dignities of Lord, Earle, Duke, and Prince are his Creatures. As in the presence of the Master, the Servants are equall, and without any honour at all; So are the Subjects, in the presence of the Soveraign. And though they shine some more, some lesse, when they are out of his sight; yet in his presence, they shine no more than the Starres in presence of the Sun.

*Soveraigne
Power not
so hurtfull
as the want
of it, and the
hurt proceeds
for the great-
est part from
not submit-
ting readily,
to a lesse*
[94] But a man may here object, that the Condition of Subjects is very miserable; as being obnoxious to the lusts, and other irregular passions of him, or them that have so unlimited a Power in their hands. And commonly they that live under a Monarch, think it the fault of Monarchy; and they that live under the government of Democracy, or other Soveraign Assembly, attribute all the inconvenience to that forme of Common-wealth; whereas the Power in all formes, if they be perfect enough to protect them, is the same; not considering that the estate of Man can never be without some incommodity or other; and that the greatest, that in any forme of Government can possibly happen to the people in generall, is scarce sensible, in respect of the miseries, and horrible calamities, that accompany a Civill Warre; or that dissolute condition of masterlesse men, without subjection to Lawes, and a coërcive Power to tye their hands from rapine, and revenge: nor considering that the greatest pressure of Soveraign Governours, proceedeth not from any delight, or profit they can expect in the dammage, or weakening of their Subjects, in whose vigor, consisteth their own strength and glory; but in the restiveness of themselves, that unwillingly contributing to their own defence, make it necessary for their Governours to draw from them what they can in time of Peace, that they may have means on any emergent occasion, or sudden need, to resist, or take advantage on their Enemies. For all men are by nature provided of notable multiplying glasses, (that is their Passions and Self-love,) through which, every little payment appeareth a great grievance; but are destitute of those prospective glasses,[4] (namely Morall and Civill Science,) to see a farre off the miseries that hang over them, and cannot without such payments be avoyded.

Of the severall Kinds of Common-wealth by Institution, and of Succession to the Soveraigne Power

The difference of Common-wealths, consisteth in the difference of the Soveraign, or the Person representative of all and every one of the Multitude. And because the Soveraignty is either in one Man, or in an Assembly of more than one; and into that Assembly either Every man hath right to enter, or not every one, but Certain men distinguished from the rest; it is manifest, there can be but Three kinds of Common-wealth. For the Representative must needs be One man, or More: and if more, then it is the Assembly of All, or but of a Part. When the Representative is One man, then is the Common-wealth a MONARCHY: when an Assembly of All that will come together, then it is a DEMOCRACY, or Popular Common-wealth: when an Assembly of a Part onely, then it is called an ARISTOCRACY. Other kind of Common-wealth there can be none: for either One, or More, or All, must have the Soveraign Power (which I have shewn to be indivisible) entire. *The different Formes of Common-wealths but three*

[95] There be other names of Government, in the Histories, and books of Policy; as *Tyranny*, and *Oligarchy*: But they are not the names of other Formes of Government, but of the same Formes misliked.[5] For they that are discontented under *Monarchy*, call it *Tyranny*; and they that are displeased with *Aristocracy*, called it *Oligarchy*: So also, they which find themselves grieved under a *Democracy*, call it *Anarchy*, (which signifies want of Government;) and yet I think no man believes, that want of Government, is any new kind of Government: nor by the same reason ought they to believe, that the Government is of one kind, when they like it, and another, when they mislike it, or are oppressed by the Governours. *Tyranny and Oligarchy, but different names of Monarchy, and Aristocracy*

Subordinate Representatives dangerous

It is manifest, that men who are in absolute liberty, may, if they please, give Authority to One man, to represent them every one; as well as give such Authority to any Assembly of men whatsoever; and consequently may subject themselves, if they think good, to a Monarch, as absolutely, as to any other Representative. Therefore, where there is already erected a Soveraign Power, there can be no other Representative of the same people, but onely to certain particular ends, by the Soveraign limited. For that were to erect two Soveraigns; and every man to have his person represented by two Actors, that by opposing one another, must needs divide that Power, which (if men will live in Peace) is indivisible; and thereby reduce the Multitude into the condition of Warre, contrary to the end for which all Soveraignty is instituted. And therefore as it is absurd, to think that a Soveraign Assembly, inviting the People of their Dominion, to send up their Deputies, with power to make known their Advise, or Desires, should therefore hold such Deputies, rather than themselves, for the absolute Representative of the people: so it is absurd also, to think the same in a Monarchy. And I know not how this so manifest a truth, should of late be so little observed; that in a Monarchy, he that had the Soveraignty from a descent of 600 years, was alone called Soveraign, had the title of Majesty from every one of his Subjects, and was unquestionably taken by them for their King; was notwithstanding never considered as their Representative; that name without contradiction passing for the title of those men, which at his command were sent up by the people to carry their Petitions, and give him (if he permitted it) their advise. Which may serve as an admonition, for those that are the true, and absolute Representative of a People, to instruct men in the nature of that Office, and to take heed how they admit of any other generall Representation upon any occasion whatsoever, if they mean to discharge the truth committed to them.

The difference between these three kindes of Common-wealth, consisteth not in the difference of Power; but in the difference of Convenience, or Aptitude to produce the Peace, and Security of the people; for which end they were instituted. And to compare Monarchy with the other two, we may observe; First, that whosoever beareth the Person of the people, or is one of that Assembly that bears it, beareth also his own naturall Person. And though he be carefull in [96] his politique Person to procure the common interest; yet he is more, or no lesse carefull to procure the private good of himselfe, his family, kindred and friends; and for the most part, if the publique interest chance to crosse the private, he preferrs the private: for the Passions of men, are commonly more potent than their Reason. From whence it follows, that where the publique and private interest are most closely united, there is the publique most advanced. Now in Monarchy, the private interest is the same with the publique. The riches, power, and honour of a Monarch arise onely from the riches, strength and reputation of his Subjects. For no King can be rich, nor glorious, nor secure; whose Subjects are either poore, or contemptible, or too weak through want, or dissention, to maintain a war against their enemies: Whereas in a Democracy, or Aristocracy, the publique prosperity conferres not so much to the private fortune of one that is corrupt, or ambitious, as doth many times a perfidious advice, a treacherous action, or a Civill warre.

Secondly, that a Monarch receiveth counsell of whom, when, and where he pleaseth; and consequently may heare the opinion of men versed in the matter about which he deliberates, of what rank or quality soever, and as long before the time of action, and with as much secrecy, as he will. But when a Soveraigne Assembly has need of Counsell, none are admitted but such as have a Right thereto from the beginning; which for the most part are of those who have beene versed more in the

Comparison of Monarchy, with Soveraign Assemblyes

acquisition of Wealth than of Knowledge; and are to give their advice in long discourses, which may, and do commonly excite men to action, but not governe them in it. For the *Understanding* is by the flame of the Passions, never enlightned, but dazled: Nor is there any place, or time, wherein an Assemblie can receive Counsell with secrecie, because of their owne Multitude.

Thirdly, that the Resolutions of a Monarch, are subject to no other Inconstancy, than that of Humane Nature; but in Assemblies, besides that of Nature, there ariseth an Inconstancy from the Number. For the absence of a few, that would have the Resolution once taken, continue firme, (which may happen by security, negligence, or private impediments,) or the diligent appearance of a few of the contrary opinion, undoes to day, all that was concluded yesterday.

Fourthly, that a Monarch cannot disagree with himselfe, out of envy, or interest; but an Assembly may; and that to such a height, as may produce a Civill Warre.

Fifthly, that in Monarchy there is this inconvenience; that any Subject, by the power of one man, for the enriching of a favourite or flatterer, may be deprived of all he possesseth; which I confesse is a great and inevitable inconvenience. But the same may as well happen, where the Soveraigne Power is in an Assembly: For their power is the same; and they are as subject to evill Counsell, and to be seduced by Orators, as a Monarch by Flatterers; and becoming one an others Flatterers, serve one anothers Covetousnesse and Ambition by turnes. And whereas the Favorites of Monarchs, are few, and they have none els to advance but their owne Kindred; the Favorites of an Assembly, [97] are many; and the Kindred much more numerous, than of any Monarch. Besides, there is no Favourite of a Monarch, which cannot as well succour his friends, as hurt his enemies: But Orators, that is to say, Favourites of Soveraigne Assemblies, though they have great power to hurt, have little to save. For to accuse, requires lesse Eloquence (such is mans Nature) than to excuse; and condemnation, than absolution more resembles Justice.

Sixtly, that it is an inconvenience in Monarchie, that the Soveraigntie may descend upon an Infant, or one that cannot discerne between Good and Evill: and consisteth in this, that the use of his Power, must be in the hand of another Man, or of some Assembly of men, which are to governe by his right, and in his name; as Curators, and Protectors of his Person, and Authority. But to say there is inconvenience, in putting the use of the Soveraign Power, into the hand of a Man, or an Assembly of men; is to say that all Government is more Inconvenient, than Confusion, and Civill Warre. And therefore all the danger that can be pretended, must arise from the Contention of those, that for an office of so great honour, and profit, may become Competitors. To make it appear, that this inconvenience, proceedeth not from that forme of Government we call Monarchy, we are to consider, that the precedent Monarch, hath appointed who shall have the Tuition of his Infant Successor, either expressely by Testament, or tacitly, by not controlling the Custome in that case received: And then such inconvenience (if it happen) is to be attributed, not to the Monarchy, but to the Ambition, and Injustice of the Subjects; which in all kinds of Government, where the people are not well instructed in their Duty, and the Rights of Soveraignty, is the same. Or else the precedent Monarch, hath not at all taken order for such Tuition; And then the Law of Nature hath provided this sufficient rule, That the Tuition shall be in him, that hath by Nature most interest in the preservation of the Authority of the Infant, and to whom least benefit can accrue by his death, or diminution. For seeing every man by nature seeketh his own benefit, and promotion; to put an Infant into the power of those, that can promote themselves by his destruction, or dammage, is not Tuition, but Trechery. So that sufficient provision being taken, against all just quarrell, about the Government under a

Child, if any contention arise to the disturbance of the publique Peace, it is not to be attributed to the forme of Monarchy, but to the ambition of Subjects, and ignorance of their Duty. On the other side, there is no great Common-wealth, the Soveraignty whereof is in a great Assembly, which is not, as to consultations of Peace, and Warre, and making of Lawes, in the same condition, as if the Government were in a Child. For as a Child wants the judgement to dissent from counsell given him, and is thereby necessitated to take the advise of them, or him, to whom he is committed: So an Assembly wanteth the liberty, to dissent from the counsell of the major part, be it good, or bad. And as a Child has need of a Tutor, or Protector, to preserve his Person, and Authority: So also (in great Common-wealths,) the Soveraign Assembly, in all great dangers and [98] troubles, have need of *Custodes libertatis*; that is of Dictators, or Protectors of their Authoritie; which are as much as Temporary Monarchs; to whom for a time, they may commit the entire exercise of their Power; and have (at the end of that time) been oftner deprived thereof, than Infant Kings, by their Protectors, Regents, or any other Tutors.

Though the Kinds of Soveraigntie be, as I have now shewn, but three; that is to say, Monarchie, where One Man has it; or Democracie, where the generall Assembly of Subjects hath it; or Aristocracie, where it is in an Assembly of certain persons nominated, or otherwise distinguished from the rest: Yet he that shall consider the particular Common-wealthes that have been, and are in the world, will not perhaps easily reduce them to three, and may thereby be inclined to think there be other Formes, arising from these mingled together. As for example, Elective Kingdomes; where Kings have the Soveraigne Power put into their hands for a time; or Kingdomes, wherein the King hath a power limited: which Governments, are nevertheless by most Writers called Monarchie. Likewise if a Popular, or Aristocraticall Common-wealth, subdue an Enemies

Countrie, and govern the same, by a President, Procurator, or other Magistrate; this may seeme perhaps
at first sight, to be a Democraticall, or Aristocraticall
Government. But it is not so. For Elective Kings, are
not Soveraignes, but Ministers of the Soveraigne; nor
limited Kings Soveraignes, but Ministers of them that
have the Soveraigne Power: Nor are those Provinces
which are in subjection to a Democracie, or Aristocracie
of another Common-wealth, Democratically, or Aristo-
cratically governed, but Monarchically.

And first, concerning an Elective King, whose power
is limited to his life, as it is in many places of Christendome at this day; or to certaine Yeares or Moneths, as
the Dictators power amongst the Romans; If he have
Right to appoint his Successor, he is no more Elective
but Hereditary. But if he have no Power to elect his
Successor, then there is some other Man, or Assembly
known, which after his decease may elect a new, or else
the Common-wealth dieth, and dissolveth with him, and
returneth to the condition of Warre. If it be known who
have the power to give the Soveraigntie after his death, it
is known also that the Soveraigntie was in them before:
For none have right to give that which they have not
right to possesse, and keep to themselves, if they think
good. But if there be none that can give the Soveraigntie,
after the decease of him that was first elected; then has
he power, nay he is obliged by the Law of Nature, to
provide, by establishing his Successor, to keep those that
had trusted him with the Government, from relapsing
into the miserable condition of Civill warre. And consequently he was, when elected, a Soveraign absolute.

Secondly, that King whose power is limited, is not
superiour to him, or them that have the power to limit
it; and he that is not superiour, is not supreme; that is
to say not Soveraign. The Soveraignty therefore was
alwaies in that Assembly which had the Right to Li[99]
mit him; and by consequence the government not Monarchy, but either Democracy, or Aristocracy; as of old

time in *Sparta*; where the Kings had a priviledge to lead their Armies; but the Soveraignty was in the *Ephori*.[6]

Thirdly, whereas heretofore the Roman People, governed the land of *Judea* (for example) by a President; yet was not *Judea* therefore a Democracy; because they were not governed by any Assembly, into which, any of them, had right to enter; nor by an Aristocracy; because they were not governed by any Assembly, into which, any man could enter by their Election: but they were governed by one Person, which though as to the people of *Rome* was an Assembly of the people, or Democracy; yet as to people of *Judea*, which had no right at all of participating in the government, was a Monarch. For though where the people are governed by an Assembly, chosen by themselves out of their own number, the government is called a Democracy, or Aristocracy; yet when they are governed by an Assembly, not of their own choosing, 'tis a Monarchy; not of *One* man, over another man; but of one people, over another people.

Of the Right   Of all these Formes of Government, the matter being
of Succession mortall, so that not onely Monarchs, but also whole Assemblies dy, it is necessary for the conservation of the peace of men, that as there was order taken for an Artificiall Man, so there be order also taken, for an Artificiall Eternity of life; without which, men that are governed by an Assembly, should return into the condition of Warre in every age; and they that are governed by One man, assoon as their Governour dyeth. This Artificiall Eternity, is that which men call the Right of *Succession*.

There is no perfect forme of Government, where the disposing of the Succession is not in the present Soveraign. For if it be in any other particular Man, or private Assembly, it is in a person subject, and may be assumed by the Soveraign at his pleasure; and consequently the Right is in himselfe. And if it be in no particular man, but left to a new choyce; then is the Common-wealth dissolved; and the Right is in him that can get it; contrary to the intention of them that did Institute the

Common-wealth, for their perpetuall, and not temporary security.

In a Democracy, the whole Assembly cannot faile, unlesse the Multitude that are to be governed faile. And therefore questions of the right of Succession, have in that forme of Government no place at all.

In an Aristocracy, when any of the Assembly dyeth, the election of another into his room belongeth to the Assembly, as the Soveraign, to whom belongeth the choosing of all Counsellours, and Officers. For that which the Representative doth, as Actor, every one of the Subjects doth, as Author. And though the Soveraign Assembly, may give Power to others, to elect new men, for supply of their Court; yet it is still by their Authority, that the Election is made; and by the same it may (when the publique shall require it) be recalled.

[100] The greatest difficultie about the right of Succession, is in Monarchy: And the difficulty ariseth from this, that at first sight, it is not manifest who is to appoint the Successor; nor many times, who it is whom he hath appointed. For in both these cases, there is required a more exact ratiocination, than every man is accustomed to use. As to the question, who shall appoint the Successor, of a Monarch that hath the Soveraign Authority; that is to say, who shall determine of the right of Inheritance, (for Elective Kings and Princes have not the Soveraign Power in propriety, but in use only,) we are to consider, that either he that is in possession, has right to dispose of the Succession, or else that right is again in the dissolved Multitude. For the death of him that hath the Soveraign power in propriety, leaves the Multitude without any Soveraign at all; that is, without any Representative in whom they should be united, and be capable of doing any one action at all: And therefore they are incapable of Election of any new Monarch; every man having equall right to submit himselfe to such as he thinks best able to protect him; or if he can, protect himselfe by his owne sword; which is a returne to

The present Monarch hath Right to dispose of the Succession

Confusion, and to the condition of a War of every man against every man, contrary to the end for which Monarchy had its first Institution. Therefore it is manifest, that by the Institution of Monarchy, the disposing of the Successor, is alwaies left to the Judgment and Will of the present Possessor.

And for the question (which may arise sometimes) who it is that the Monarch in possession, hath designed to the succession and inheritance of his power; it is determined by his expresse Words, and Testament; or by other tacite signes sufficient.

Succession passeth by expresse Words; By expresse Words, or Testament, when it is declared by him in his life time, *viva voce*, or by Writing; as the first Emperours of *Rome* declared who should be their Heires. For the word Heire does not of it selfe imply the Children, or nearest Kindred of a man; but whomsoever a man shall any way declare, he would have to succeed him in his Estate. If therefore a Monarch declare expresly, that such a man shall be his Heire, either by Word or Writing, then is that man immediatly after the decease of his Predecessor, Invested in the right of being Monarch.

Or, by not controlling a Custome; But where Testament, and expresse Words are wanting, other naturall signes of the Will are to be followed: whereof the one is Custome. And therefore where the Custome is, that the next of Kindred absolutely succeedeth, there also the next of Kindred hath right to the Succession; for that, if the will of him that was in posession had been otherwise, he might easily have declared the same in his life time. And likewise where the Custome is, that the next of the Male Kindred succeedeth, there also the right of Succession is in the next of the Kindred Male, for the same reason. And so it is if the Custome were to advance the Female. For whatsoever Custome a man may by a word controule, and does not, it is a naturall signe he would have that Custome stand.

Or, by presumption of naturall affection But where neither Custome, nor Testament hath preceded, there it [101] is to be understood, First, that a

Monarchs will is, that the government remain Monarchicall; because he hath approved that government in
himselfe. Secondly, that a Child of his own, Male, or
Female, be preferred before any other; because men are
presumed to be more enclined by nature, to advance
their own children, than the children of other men; and
of their own, rather a Male than a Female; because men,
are naturally fitter than women, for actions of labour
and danger. Thirdly, where his own Issue faileth, rather
a Brother than a stranger; and so still the neerer in
bloud, rather than the more remote, because it is alwayes
presumed that the neerer of kin, is the neerer in affection; and 'tis evident that a man receives alwayes, by
reflexion, the most honour from the greatnesse of his
neerest kindred.

But if it be lawfull for a Monarch to dispose of the
Succession by words of Contract, or Testament, men
may perhaps object a great inconvenience: for he may
sell, or give his Right of governing to a stranger; which,
because strangers (that is, men not used to live under
the same government, nor speaking the same language) do commonly undervalue one another, may
turn to the oppression of his Subjects; which is indeed
a great inconvenience: but it proceedeth not necessarily from the subjection to a strangers government, but
from the unskilfulnesse of the Governours, ignorant of
the true rules of Politiques. And therefore the Romans
when they had subdued many Nations, to make their
Government digestible, were wont to take away that
grievance, as much as they thought necessary, by giving
sometimes to whole Nations, and sometimes to Principall men of every Nation they conquered, not onely
the Privileges, but also the Name of Romans; and took
many of them into the Senate, and Offices of charge,
even in the Roman City. And this was it our most wise
King, King *James*, aymed at, in endeavouring the Union
of his two Realms of *England* and *Scotland*.[7] Which if
he could have obtained, had in all likelihood prevented

*To dispose of
the Succes-
sion, though
to a King
of another
Nation, not
unlawfull*

the Civill warres, which make both those Kingdomes, at this present, miserable. It is not therefore any injury to the people, for a Monarch to dispose of the Succession by Will; though by the fault of many Princes, it hath been sometimes found inconvenient. Of the lawfulnesse of it, this also is an argument, that whatsoever inconvenience can arrive by giving a Kingdome to a stranger, may arrive also by so marrying with strangers, as the Right of Succession may descend upon them: yet this by all men is accounted lawfull.

CHAP. XX

Of Dominion PATERNALL, *and* DESPOTICALL

A Common-wealth by Acquisition   A *Common-wealth by Acquisition*, is that, where the Soveraign Power is acquired by Force; And it is acquired by force, when men singly, or many together by plurality of voyces, for fear of death, or bonds, do authorise all the [102] actions of that Man, or Assembly, that hath their lives and liberty in his Power.

Wherein different from a Common wealth by Institution   And this kind of Dominion, or Soveraignty, differeth from Soveraignty by Institution, onely in this, That men who choose their Soveraign, do it for fear of one another, and not of him whom they Institute: But in this case, they subject themselves, to him they are afraid of. In both cases they do it for fear: which is to be noted by them, that hold all such Covenants, as proceed from fear of death, or violence, voyd: which if it were true, no man, in any kind of Common-wealth, could be obliged to Obedience. It is true, that in a Common-wealth once Instituted, or acquired, Promises proceeding from fear of death, or violence, are no Covenants, nor obliging, when the thing promised is contrary to the Lawes; But the reason is not, because it was made upon fear, but because he that promiseth, hath no right in the thing promised.

Also, when he may lawfully performe, and doth not, it is not the Invalidity of the Covenant, that absolveth him, but the Sentence of the Soveraign. Otherwise, whensoever a man lawfully promiseth, he unlawfully breaketh: But when the Soveraign, who is the Actor, acquitteth him, then he is acquitted by him that exorted the promise, as by the Author of such absolution.

But the Rights, and Consequences of Soveraignty, are the same in both. His Power cannot, without his consent, be Transferred to another: He cannot Forfeit it: He cannot be Accused by any of his Subjects, of Injury: He cannot be Punished by them: He is Judge of what is necessary for Peace; and Judge of Doctrines: He is Sole Legislator; and Supreme Judge of Controversies; and of the Times, and Occasions of Warre, and Peace: to him it belongeth to choose Magistrates, Counsellours, Commanders, and all other Officers, and Ministers; and to determine of Rewards, and Punishments, Honour, and Order. The reasons whereof, are the same which are alledged in the precedent Chapter, for the same Rights, and Consequences of Soveraignty by Institution. *The Rights of Soveraignty the same in both*

Dominion is acquired two wayes; By Generation, and by Conquest. The right of Dominion by Generation, is that, which the Parent hath over his Children; and is called PATERNALL. And is not so derived from the Generation, as if therefore the Parent had Dominion over his Child because he begat him; but from the Childs Consent, either expresse, or by other sufficient arguments declared. For as to the Generation, God hath ordained to man a helper; and there be always two that are equally Parents: the Dominion therefore over the Child, should belong equally to both; and he be equally subject to both, which is impossible; for no man can obey two Masters. And whereas some have attributed the Dominion to the Man onely, as being of the more excellent Sex; they misreckon in it. For there is not always that difference of strength, or prudence between the man and the woman, as that the right can be determined without War. *Dominion Paternall how attained*

Not by Generation, but by Contract;

In Common-wealths, this controversie is decided by the Civill Law: and for the most part, (but not alwayes) the sentence is in favour of the Father; because for the most part Common-wealths have [103] been erected by the Fathers, not by the Mothers of families. But the question lyeth now in the state of meer Nature; where there are supposed no lawes of Matrimony; no lawes for the Education of Children; but the Law of Nature, and the naturall inclination of the Sexes, one to another, and to their children. In this condition of meer Nature, either the Parents between themselves dispose of the dominion over the Child by Contract; or do not dispose thereof at all. If they dispose thereof, the right passeth according to the Contract. We find in History that the *Amazons* Contracted with the Men of the neighbouring Countries, to whom they had recourse for issue, that the issue Male should be sent back, but the Female remain with themselves: so that the dominion of the Females was in the Mother.[8]

Or Educa- If there be no Contract, the Dominion is in the Mother. *tion;* For in the condition of meer Nature, where there are no Matrimoniall lawes, it cannot be known who is the Father, unlesse it be declared by the Mother: and therefore the right of Dominion over the Child dependeth on her will, and is consequently hers. Again, seeing the Infant is first in the power of the Mother, so as she may either nourish, or expose it; if she nourish it, it oweth its life to the Mother; and is therefore obliged to obey her, rather than any other; and by consequence the Dominion over it is hers. But if she expose it, and another find, and nourish it, the Dominion is in him that nourisheth it. For it ought to obey him by whom it is preserved; because preservation of life being the end, for which one *Or Precedent* man becomes subject to another, every man is supposed *subjection* to promise obedience, to him, in whose power it is to *of one of the* save, or destroy him.

Parents to If the Mother be the Fathers subject, the Child, is in *the other* the Fathers power: and if the Father be the Mothers subject, (as when a Soveraign Queen marrieth one of her subjects,) the Child is subject to the Mother; because the Father also is her subject.

If a man and a woman, Monarches of two sever-all Kingdomes, have a Child, and contract concerning who shall have the Dominion of him, the Right of the Dominion passeth by the Contract. If they contract not, the Dominion followeth the Dominion of the place of his residence. For the Soveraign of each Country hath Dominion over all that reside therein.

He that hath the Dominion over the Child, hath Dominion also over the Children of the Child; and over their Childrens Children. For he that hath Dominion over the person of a man, hath Dominion over all that is his; without which, Dominion were but a Title, without the effect.

The Right of Succession to Paternall Dominion, proceedeth in the same manner, as doth the Right of Succession to Monarchy; of which I have already sufficiently spoken in the precedent chapter. *The Right of Succession followeth the Rules of the Right of Possession*

Dominion acquired by Conquest, or Victory in war, is that which some Writers call DESPOTICALL, from Δεσπότης, which signifieth a *Lord*, or *Master*; and is the Dominion of the Master over his Servant. And this Dominion is then acquired to the Victor, when the [104] Vanquished, to avoyd the present stroke of death, covenanteth either in expresse words, or by other sufficient signes of the Will, that so long as his life, and the liberty of his body is allowed him, the Victor shall have the use thereof, at his pleasure. And after such Covenant made, the Vanquished is a SERVANT, and not before: for by the word *Servant* (whether it be derived from *Servire*, to Serve, or from *Servare*, to Save, which I leave to Grammarians to dispute) is not meant a Captive, which is kept in prison, or bonds, till the owner of him that took him, or bought him of one that did, shall consider what to do with him: (for such men, (commonly called Slaves,) have no obligation at all; but may break their *Despoticall Dominion how attained*

bonds, or the prison; and kill, or carry away captive
their Master, justly:) but one, that being taken, hath corporall liberty allowed him; and upon promise not to run
away, nor to do violence to his Master, is trusted by him.

Not by the   It is not therefore the Victory, that giveth the right of
Victory, but Dominion over the Vanquished, but his own Covenant.
by the Con-   Nor is he obliged because he is Conquered; that is to
sent of the   say, beaten, and taken, or put to flight; but because he
Vanquished   commeth in, and submitteth to the Victor; Nor is the
Victor obliged by an enemies rendring himselfe, (without promise of life,) to spare him for this his yeelding to
discretion; which obliges not the Victor longer, than in
his own discretion hee shall think fit.

And that which men do, when they demand (as it is
now called) *Quarter*, (which the Greeks called Ζωγρία,
taking alive,) is to evade the present fury of the Victor, by
Submission, and to compound for their life, with Ransome, or Service: and therefore he that hath Quarter,
hath not his life given, but deferred till farther deliberation; For it is not an yeelding on condition of life, but
to discretion. And then onely is his life in security, and
his service due, when the Victor hath trusted him with
his corporall liberty. For Slaves that work in Prisons,
or Fetters, do it not of duty, but to avoyd the cruelty of
their task-masters.

The Master of the Servant, is Master also of all he
hath; and may exact the use thereof; that is to say, of
his goods, of his labour, of his servants, and of his children, as often as he shall think fit. For he holdeth his
life of his Master, by the covenant of obedience; that
is, of owning, and authorising whatsoever the Master
shall do. And in case the Master, if he refuse, kill him,
or cast him into bonds, or otherwise punish him for his
disobedience, he is himselfe the author of the same; and
cannot accuse him of injury.

In summe the Rights and Consequences of both *Paternall* and *Despoticall* Dominion, are the very same with
those of a Soveraign by Institution; and for the same

reasons: which reasons are set down in the precedent chapter. So that for a man that is Monarch of divers Nations, whereof he hath, in one the Soveraignty by Institution of the people assembled, and in another by Conquest, that is by the Submission of each particular, to avoyd death or bonds; to demand of one Nation more than of the other, from the title of Conquest, as being a Conquered Nation, is an act of ignorance of the Rights of [105] Soveraignty. For the Soveraign is absolute over both alike; or else there is no Soveraignty at all; and so every man may Lawfully protect himselfe, if he can, with his own sword, which is the condition of war.

By this it appears, that a great Family if it be not part of some Common-wealth, is of it self, as to the Rights of Soveraignty, a little Monarchy; whether that Family consist of a man and his children; or of a man and his servants; or of a man, and his children, and servants together: wherein the Father or Master is the Soveraign. But yet a Family is not properly a Common-wealth; unlesse it be of that power by its own number, or by other opportunities, as not to be subdued without the hazard of war. For where a number of men are manifestly too weak to defend themselves united, every one may use his own reason in time of danger, to save his own life, either by flight, or by submission to the enemy, as hee shall think best; in the same manner as a very small company of souldiers, surprised by an army, may cast down their armes, and demand quarter, or run away, rather than be put to the sword. And thus much shall suffice; concerning what I find by speculation, and deduction, of Soveraign Rights, from the nature, need, and designes of men, in erecting of Common-wealths, and putting themselves under Monarchs, or Assemblies, entrusted with power enough for their protection. *Difference between a Family and a Kingdom*

The Rights of Monarchy from Scripture

Let us now consider what the Scripture teacheth in the same point. To *Moses*, the children of *Israel* say thus. **Speak thou to us, and we will heare thee; but let not God speak to us, lest we dye.* This is absolute obedience

* *Exod.* 20.
19

to *Moses*. Concerning the Right of Kings, God himself by the mouth of *Samuel*, saith, **This shall be the
Right of the King you will have to reigne over you.* He
shall take your sons, and set them to drive his Chariots,
and to be his horsemen, and to run before his chariots; and gather in his harvest; and to make his engines
of War, and Instruments of his chariots; and shall take
your daughters to make perfumes, to be his Cookes, and
Bakers. He shall take your fields, your vine-yards, and
your olive-yards, and give them to his servants. He shall
take the tyth of your corne and wine, and give it to the
men of his chamber, and to his other servants. He shall
take your man-servants, and your maid-servants, and
the choice of your youth, and employ them in his businesse. He shall take the tyth of your flocks; and you shall
be his servants.* This is absolute power, and summed
up in the last words, *you shall be his servants.* Againe,
when the people heard what power their King was to
have, yet they consented thereto, and say thus, **We will
be as all other nations, and our King shall judge our
causes, and goe before us, to conduct our wars.* Here is
confirmed the Right that Soveraigns have, both to the
Militia, and to all *Judicature*; in which is conteined as
absolute power, as one man can possibly transferre to
another. Again, the prayer of King *Salomon*[9] to God,
was this. **Give to thy servant understanding, to judge
thy people, and to discerne between Good and Evill.*
It belongeth therefore to the Soveraigne to bee [106]
Judge, and to præscribe the Rules of *discerning Good
and Evill*: which Rules are Lawes; and therefore in him
is the Legislative Power. *Saul* sought the life of *David*;[10]
yet when it was in his power to slay *Saul*, and his Servants would have done it, *David* forbad them, saying,
**God forbid I should do such an act against my Lord,
the anoynted of God.* For obedience of servants St. *Paul*[11]
saith, **Servants obey your masters in All things*; and,
*Children obey your Parents in All things. There is simple obedience in those that are subject to Paternall, or

* 1 *Sam.* 8.
11, 12, &c.

* *Verse* 19.
&c.

* 1 *Kings* 3.
9

* 1 *Sam.* 24.9

* *Coll.* 3.20

* *Verse* 22

Despoticall Dominion. Again, *The Scribes and Phari-*   * Math.23.
sees sit in Moses chayre, and therefore All that they shall   2, 3
bid you observe, that observe and do. There again is
simple obedience. And St *Paul,* *Warn them that they*   * Tit.3.2
subject themselves to Princes, and to those that are in
Authority, & obey them. This obedience is also simple.
Lastly, our Saviour himselfe acknowledges, that men
ought to pay such taxes as are by Kings imposed, where
he sayes, *Give to Cæsar that which is Cæsars;*[12] and payed
such taxes himselfe. And that the Kings word, is sufficient
to take any thing from any Subject, when there is need;
and that the King is Judge of that need: For he himselfe,
as King of the Jewes, commanded his Disciples to take
the Asse, and Asses Colt to carry him into *Jerusalem,*
saying, *Go into the Village over against you, and you*   * Mat.21.
shall find a shee Asse tyed, and her Colt with her, unty   2, 3
them, and bring them to me. And if any man ask you,
what you mean by it, Say the Lord hath need of them:
And they will let them go. They will not ask whether his
necessity be a sufficient title; nor whether he be judge of
that necessity; but acquiesce in the will of the Lord.

    To these places may be added also that of *Genesis,*
You shall be as Gods, knowing Good and Evill. And   * Gen.3.5
verse 11. *Who told thee that thou wast naked? hast thou*
eaten of the tree, of which I commanded thee thou shoul-
dest not eat? For the Cognisance of Judicature of *Good*
and *Evill,* being forbidden by the name of the fruit of the
tree of Knowledge, as a triall of *Adams* obedience; The
Divel to enflame the Ambition of the woman, to whom
that fruit already seemed beautifull, told her that by tasting it, they should be as Gods, knowing *Good* and *Evill.*
Whereupon having both eaten, they did indeed take
upon them Gods office, which is Judicature of Good and
Evill; but acquired no new ability to distinguish between
them aright. And whereas it is sayd, that having eaten,
they saw they were naked; no man hath so interpreted
that place, as if they had been formerly blind, and saw
not their own skins: the meaning is plain, that it was

then they first judged their nakednesse (wherein it was Gods will to create them) to be uncomely; and by being ashamed, did tacitely censure God himselfe. And thereupon God saith, *Hast thou eaten, &c.* as if he should say, doest thou that owest me obedience, take upon thee to judge of my Commandements? Whereby it is cleerly, (though Allegorically,) signified, that the Commands of them that have the right to command, are not by their Subjects to be censured, nor disputed.

Soveraign Power ought in all Common-wealths to be absolute

So that it appeareth plainly, to my understanding, both from Reason, and Scripture, that the Soveraign Power, whether placed in One [107] Man, as in Monarchy, or in one Assembly of men, as in Popular, and Aristocraticall Common-wealths, is as great, as possibly men can be imagined to make it. And though of so unlimited a Power, men may fancy many evill consequences, yet the consequences of the want of it, which is perpetuall warre of every man against his neighbour, are much worse. The condition of man in this life shall never be without Inconveniences; but there happeneth in no Common-wealth any great Inconvenience, but what proceeds from the Subjects disobedience, and breach of those Covenants, from which the Common-wealth hath its being. And whosoever thinking Soveraign Power too great, will seek to make it lesse; must subject himselfe, to the Power, that can limit it; that is to say, to a greater.

The greatest objection is, that of the Practise; when men ask, where, and when, such Power has by Subjects been acknowledged. But one may ask them again, when, or where has there been a Kingdome long free from Sedition and Civill Warre. In those Nations, whose Common-wealths have been long-lived, and not been destroyed, but by forraign warre, the Subjects never did dispute of the Soveraign Power. But howsoever, an argument from the Practise of men, that have not sifted to the bottom, and with exact reason weighed the causes, and nature of Common-wealths, and suffer daily those miseries, that proceed from the ignorance thereof, is invalid. For though in all places of the world, men should lay the foundation of their houses on the sand, it could not thence be inferred, that so it ought to be. The skill of making, and maintaining Common-wealths, consisteth in certain Rules, as doth Arithmetique and Geometry; not (as Tennis-play) on Practise onely: which Rules, neither poor men have the leisure, nor men that have had the leisure, have hitherto had the curiosity, or the method to find out.

CHAP. XXI

Of the LIBERTY *of Subjects*

LIBERTY, or FREEDOME, signifieth (properly) the absence of Opposition; (by Opposition, I mean externall Impediments of motion;) and may be applyed no lesse to Irrationall, and Inanimate creatures, than to Rationall. For whatsoever is so tyed, or environed, as it cannot move, but within a certain space, which space is determined by the opposition of some externall body, we say it hath not Liberty to go further. And so of all living creatures, whilest they are imprisoned, or restrained, with walls, or chayns; and of the water whilest it is kept in by banks, or vessels, that otherwise would spread it selfe into a larger space, we use to say, they are not at Liberty, to move in such manner, as without those externall impediments they would. But when the impediment of motion, is in the constitution of the thing it selfe, we use not to say, it wants the Liberty; but the Power to move; as when a stone lyeth still, or a man is fastned to his bed by sicknesse. *Liberty what*

[108] And according to this proper, and generally received meaning of the word, *A* FREE-MAN, *is he, that in those things, which by his strength and wit he is able to do, is not hindred to doe what he has a will to.* But *What it is to be free*

when the words *Free*, and *Liberty*, are applyed to any thing but *Bodies*, they are abused; for that which is not subject to Motion, is not subject to Impediment: And therefore, when 'tis said (for example) The way is free, no liberty of the way is signified, but of those that walk in it without stop. And when we say a Guift is free, there is not meant any liberty of the Guift, but of the Giver, that was not bound by any law, or Covenant to give it. So when we *speak freely*, it is not the liberty of voice, or pronunciation, but of the man, whom no law hath obliged to speak otherwise then he did. Lastly, from the use of the word *Freewill*, no liberty can be inferred to the will, desire, or inclination, but the liberty of the man; which consisteth in this, that he finds no stop, in doing what he has the will, desire, or inclination to doe.

Feare and Liberty consistent   Feare and Liberty are consistent; as when a man throweth his goods into the Sea for *feare* the ship should sink, he doth it neverthelesse very willingly, and may refuse to doe it if he will: It is therefore the action, of one that was *free*: so a man sometimes pays his debt, only for *feare* of Imprisonment, which because no body hindred him from detaining, was the action of a man at *liberty*. And generally all actions which men doe in Common-wealths, for *feare* of the law, or actions, which the doers had *liberty* to omit.

Liberty and Necessity Consistent   *Liberty* and *Necessity* are Consistent: As in the water, that hath not only *liberty*, but a *necessity* of descending by the Channel: so likewise in the Actions which men voluntarily doe; which (because they proceed from their will) proceed from *liberty*; and yet because every act of mans will, and every desire, and inclination proceedeth from some cause, and that from another cause, which causes in a continuall chaine (whose first link is the hand of God the first of all causes) proceed from *necessity*. So that to him that could see the connexion of those causes, the *necessity* of all mens voluntary actions, would appeare manifest. And therefore God, that seeth, and disposeth all things, seeth also that the *liberty* of man in doing what he will, is accompanied with the *necessity* of doing that which God will, & no more, nor lesse. For though men may do many things, which God does not command, nor is therefore Author of them; yet they can have no passion, nor appetite to any thing, of which appetite Gods will is not the cause. And did not his will assure the *necessity* of mans will, and consequently of all that on mans will dependeth, the *liberty* of men would be a contradiction, and impediment to the omnipotence and *liberty* of God. And this shall suffice, (as to the matter in hand) of that naturall *liberty*, which only is properly called *liberty*.

But as men, for the atteyning of peace, and conservation of themselves thereby, have made an Artificiall Man, which we call a Common-wealth; so also have they made Artificiall Chains, called *Civill Lawes*, which they themselves, by mutuall covenants, have [109] fastned at one end, to the lips of that Man, or Assembly, to whom they have given the Soveraigne Power; and at the other end to their own Ears. These Bonds in their own nature but weak, may neverthelesse be made to hold, by the danger, though not by the difficulty of breaking them. *Artificiall bonds, or Covenants*

In relation to these Bonds only it is, that I am to speak now, of the *Liberty* of *Subjects*. For seeing there is no Common-wealth in the world, wherein there be Rules enough set down, for the regulating of all the actions, and words of men, (as being a thing impossible:) it followeth necessarily, that in all kinds of actions, by the laws prætermitted, men have the Liberty, of doing what their own reasons shall suggest, for the most profitable to themselves. For if wee take Liberty in the proper sense, for corporall Liberty; that is to say, freedome from chains, and prison, it were very absurd for men to clamor as they doe, for the Liberty they so manifestly enjoy. Againe, if we take Liberty, for an exemption from Lawes, it is no lesse absurd, for men to demand as they doe, that Liberty, by which all other men may be masters of their lives. And yet as absurd as it is, this is it they *Liberty of Subjects consisteth in Liberty from covenants* demand; not knowing that the Lawes are of no power to protect them, without a Sword in the hands of a man, or men, to cause those laws to be put in execution. The Liberty of a Subject, lyeth therefore only in those things, which in regulating their actions, the Soveraign hath prætermitted: such as is the Liberty to buy, and sell, and otherwise contract with one another; to choose their own aboad, their own diet, their own trade of life, and institute their children as they themselves think fit; & the like.

Liberty of the   Neverthelesse we are not to understand, that by
Subject con-   such Liberty, the Soveraign Power of life, and death,
sistent with   is either abolished, or limited. For it has been already
the unlimited shewn, that nothing the Soveraign Representative can
power of the   doe to a Subject, on what pretence soever, can prop-
Soveraign   erly be called Injustice, or Injury; because every Subject
is Author of every act the Soveraign doth; so that he never wanteth Right to any thing, otherwise, than as he himself is the Subject of God, and bound thereby to observe the laws of Nature. And therefore it may, and doth often happen in Common-wealths, that a Subject may be put to death, by the command of the Soveraign Power; and yet neither doe the other wrong: As when *Jeptha* caused his daughter to be sacrificed:[13] In which, and the like cases, he that so dieth, had Liberty to doe the action, for which he is neverthelesse, without Injury put to death. And the same holdeth also in a Soveraign Prince, that putteth to death an Innocent Subject. For though the action be against the law of Nature, as being contrary to Equitie, (as was the killing of *Uriah*, by *David*;)[14] yet it was not an Injurie to *Uriah*; but to *God*. Not to *Uriah*, because the right to doe what he pleased, was given him by *Uriah* himself: And yet to *God*, because *David* was *Gods* Subject; and prohibited all Iniquitie by the law of Nature. Which distinction, *David* himself, when he repented the fact, evidently confirmed, saying, *To thee only have I sinned*.[15] In the same manner, the people of *Athens*, when they bani[110]shed

the most potent of their Common-wealth for ten years, thought they committed no Injustice; and yet they never questioned what crime he had done; but what hurt he would doe: Nay they commanded the banishment of they knew not whom; and every Citizen bringing his Oystershell into the market place, written with the name of him he desired should be banished, without actuall accusing him, sometimes banished an *Aristides*, for his reputation of Justice; And sometimes a scurrilous Jester, as *Hyperbolus*, to make a Jest of it.[16] And yet a man cannot say, the Soveraign People of *Athens* wanted right to banish them; or an *Athenian* the Libertie to Jest, or to be Just.

The Libertie, whereof there is so frequent, and honourable mention, in the Histories, and Philosophy of the Antient Greeks, and Romans, and in the writings, and discourse of those that from them have received all their learning in the Politiques, is not the Libertie of Particular men; but the Libertie of the Common-wealth: which is the same with that, which every man then should have, if there were no Civil Laws, nor Common-wealth at all. And the effects of it also be the same. For as amongst masterlesse men, there is perpetuall war, of every man against his neighbour; no inheritance, to transmit to the Son, nor to expect from the Father; no propriety of Goods, or Lands; no security; but a full and absolute Libertie in every Particular man: So in States, and Common-wealths not dependent on one another, every Common-wealth, (not every man) has an absolute Libertie, to doe what it shall judge (that is to say, what that Man, or Assemblie that representeth it, shall judge) most conducing to their benefit. But withall, they live in the condition of a perpetuall war, and upon the confines of battel, with their frontiers armed, and canons planted against their neighbours round about. The *Athenians*, and *Romanes* were free; that is, free Common-wealths: not that any particular men had the Libertie to resist their own Representative; but that their Representative

The Liberty which writers praise, is the Liberty of Soveraigns; not of Private men

had the Libertie to resist, or invade other people. There is written on the Turrets of the city of *Luca* in great characters at this day, the word *LIBERTAS*; yet no man can thence inferre, that a particular man has more Libertie, or Immunitie from the service of the Commonwealth there, than in *Constantinople*. Whether a Common-wealth be Monarchicall, or Popular, the Freedome is still the same.

But it is an easy thing, for men to be deceived, by the specious name of Libertie; and for want of Judgement to distinguish, mistake that for their Private Inheritance, and Birth right, which is the right of the Publique only. And when the same errour is confirmed by the authority of men in reputation for their writings in this subject, it is no wonder if it produce sedition, and change of Government. In these westerne parts of the world, we are made to receive our opinions concerning the Institution, and Rights of Common-wealths, from *Aristotle*, *Cicero*, and other men, Greeks and Romanes, that living under Popular States, derived those Rights, not from the Principles of Nature, but transcribed them into their books, out of [111] the Practice of their own Common-wealths, which were Popular; as the Grammarians describe the Rules of Language, out of the Practise of the time; or the Rules of Poetry, out of the Poems of *Homer* and *Virgil*. And because the Athenians were taught, (to keep them from desire of changing their Government,) that they were Freemen, and all that lived under Monarchy were slaves; therefore *Aristotle* puts it down in his *Politiques*, (*lib.6.cap.*2) *In democracy,* Liberty *is to be supposed: for 'tis commonly held, that no man is* Free *in any other Government.* And as *Aristotle*; so *Cicero*, and other Writers have grounded their Civill doctrine, on the opinions of the Romans, who were taught to hate Monarchy, at first, by them that having deposed their Soveraign, shared amongst them the Soveraignty of *Rome*; and afterwards by their Successors. And by reading of these Greek, and Latine Authors, men from their childhood have gotten a habit (under a false shew of Liberty,) of favouring tumults, and of licentious controlling the actions of their Soveraigns; and again of controlling those controllers, with the effusion of so much blood; as I think I may truly say, there was never any thing so deerly bought, as these Western parts bought the learning of the Greek and Latine tongues.

To come now to the particulars of the true Liberty of a Subject; that is to say, what are the things, which though commanded by the Soveraign, he may neverthelesse, without Injustice, refuse to do; we are to consider, what Rights we passe away, when we make a Common-wealth; or (which is all one,) what Liberty we deny our selves, by owning all the Actions (without exception) of the Man, or Assembly we make our Soveraign. For in the act of our *Submission*, consisteth both our *Obligation*, and our *Liberty*; which must therefore be inferred by arguments taken from thence; there being no Obligation on any man, which ariseth not from some Act of his own; for all men equally, are by Nature Free. And because such arguments, must either be drawn from the expresse words, *I Authorise all his Actions*, or from the Intention of him that submitteth himselfe to his Power, (which Intention is to be understood by the End for which he so submitteth;) The Obligation, and Liberty of the Subject, is to be derived, either from those Words, (or others equivalent;) or else from the End of the Institution of Soveraignty; namely, the Peace of the Subjects within themselves, and their Defence against a common Enemy.

First therefore, seeing Soveraignty by Institution, is by Covenant of every one to every one; and Soveraignty by Acquisition, by Covenants of the Vanquished to the Victor, or Child to the Parent; It is manifest, that every Subject has Liberty in all those things, the right whereof cannot by Covenant be transferred. I have shewn before in the 14. Chapter, that Covenants, not to defend a mans own body, are voyd. Therefore,

Liberty of Subjects how to be measured

Subjects have Liberty to defend their own bodies, even against them that lawfully invade them;

Are not   If the Soveraign command a man (though justly con-
bound to demned,) to kill, wound, or mayme himselfe; or not to
hurt them- resist those that assault him; or to abstain from the use
selves; of food, ayre, medicine, or any other [112] thing, without which he cannot live; yet hath that man the Liberty
to disobey.

If a man be interrogated by the Soveraign, or his
Authority, concerning a crime done by himselfe, he is
not bound (without assurance of Pardon) to confesse it;
because no man (as I have shewn in the same Chapter)
can be obliged by Covenant to accuse himselfe.

Again, the Consent of a Subject to Soveraign Power,
is contained in these words, *I Authorise, or take upon
me, all his actions*; in which there is no restriction at all,
of his own former naturall Liberty: For by allowing him
to *kill me*, I am not bound to kill my selfe when he commands me. 'Tis one thing to say, *Kill me, or my fellow,
if you please*; another thing to say, *I will kill my selfe, or
my fellow*. It followeth therefore, that

No man is bound by the words themselves, either to
kill himselfe, or any other man; And consequently, that
the Obligation a man may sometimes have, upon the
Command of the Soveraign to execute any dangerous,
or dishonourable Office, dependeth not on the Words
of our Submission; but on the Intention; which is to
be understood by the End thereof. When therefore our
refusall to obey, frustrates the End for which the Soveraignty was ordained; then there is no Liberty to refuse:
otherwise there is.

Nor to   Upon this ground, a man that is commanded as a
warfare, Souldier to fight against the enemy, though his Sov-
unlesse they eraign have Right enough to punish his refusall with
voluntarily death, may neverthelesse in many cases refuse, without
undertake it Injustice; as when he substituteth a sufficient Souldier
in his place: for in this case he deserteth not the service
of the Common-wealth. And there is allowance to be
made for naturall timorousness, not onely to women,
(of whom no such dangerous duty is expected,) but also

to men of feminine courage. When Armies fight, there is on one side, or both, a running away; yet when they do it not out of trechery, but fear, they are not esteemed to do it unjustly, but dishonourably. For the same reason, to avoyd battell, is not Injustice, but Cowardise. But he that inrowleth himselfe a Souldier, or taketh imprest mony, taketh away the excuse of a timorous nature; and is obliged, not onely to go to the battell, but also not to run from it, without his Captaines leave. And when the Defence of the Common-wealth, requireth at once the help of all that are able to bear Arms, every one is obliged; because otherwise the Institution of the Common-wealth, which they have not the purpose, or courage to preserve, was in vain.

To resist the Sword of the Common-wealth, in defence of another man, guilty, or innocent, no man hath Liberty; because such Liberty, takes away from the Soveraign, the means of Protecting us; and is therefore destructive of the very essence of Government. But in case a great many men together, have already resisted the Soveraign Power unjustly, or committed some Capitall crime, for which every one of them expecteth death, whether have they not the Liberty then to joyn together, and assist, and defend one another? Certainly they have: For they but defend their lives, which the Guil[113]ty man may as well do, as the Innocent. There was indeed injustice in the first breach of their duty; Their bearing of Arms subsequent to it, though it be to maintain what they have done, is no new unjust act. And if it be onely to defend their persons, it is not unjust at all. But the offer of Pardon taketh from them, to whom it is offered, the plea of self-defence, and maketh their perseverance in assisting, or defending the rest, unlawfull.

As for other Lyberties, they depend on the silence of the Law. In cases where the Soveraign has prescribed no rule, there the Subject hath the liberty to do, or forbeare, according to his own discretion. And therefore such Liberty is in some places more, and in some lesse; *The Greatest Liberty of Subjects, dependeth on the silence of the Law* and in some times more, in other times lesse, according as they that have the Soveraignty shall think most convenient. As for Example, there was a time, when in *England* a man might enter in to his own Land, (and dispossesse such as wrongfully possessed it) by force. But in after-times, that Liberty of Forcible entry, was taken away by a Statute made (by the King) in Parliament.[17] And in some places of the world, men have the Liberty of many wives: in other places, such Liberty is not allowed.

If a Subject have a controversie with his Soveraigne, of Debt, or of right of possession of lands or goods, or concerning any service required at his hands, or concerning any penalty corporall, or pecuniary, grounded on a precedent Law; He hath the same Liberty to sue for his right, as if it were against a Subject; and before such Judges, as are appointed by the Soveraign. For seeing the Soveraign demandeth by force of a former Law, and not by vertue of his Power; he declareth thereby, that he requireth no more, than shall appear to be due by that Law. The sute therefore is not contrary to the will of the Soveraign; and consequently the Subject hath the Liberty to demand the hearing of his Cause; and sentence, according to that Law. But if he demand, or take any thing by pretence of his Power; there lyeth, in that case, no action of Law: for all that is done by him in Vertue of his Power, is done by the Authority of every subject, and consequently, he that brings an action against the Soveraign, brings it against himselfe.

If a Monarch, or Soveraign Assembly, grant a Liberty to all, or any of his Subjects; which Grant standing, he is disabled to provide for their safety, the Grant is voyd; unlesse he directly renounce, or transferre the Soveraignty to another. For in that he might openly, (if it had been his will,) and in plain termes, have renounced, or transferred it, and did not; it is to be understood it was not his will; but that the Grant proceeded from ignorance of the repugnancy between such a Liberty and the Soveraign Power; and therefore the Soveraignty is still retayned; and consequently all those Powers, which are necessary to the exercising thereof; such as are the Power of Warre, and Peace, of Judicature, of appointing Officers, and Councellours, of levying Mony, and the rest named in the 18th Chapter.

[114] The Obligation of Subjects to the Soveraign, is understood to last as long, and no longer, than the power lasteth, by which he is able to protect them. For the right men have by Nature to protect themselves, when none else can protect them, can by no Covenant be relinquished. The Soveraignty is the Soule of the Common-wealth; which once departed from the Body, the members doe no more receive their motion from it. The end of Obedience is Protection; which, wheresoever a man seeth it, either in his own, or in anothers sword, Nature applyeth his obedience to it, and his endeavour to maintaine it. And though Soveraignty, in the intention of them that make it, be immortall; yet is it in its own nature, not only subject to violent death, by forreign war; but also through the ignorance, and passions of men, it hath in it, from the very institution, many seeds of a naturall mortality, by Intestine Discord. *In what Cases Subjects are absolved of their obedi-ence to their Soveraign*

If a Subject be taken prisoner in war; or his person, or his means of life be within the Guards of the enemy, and hath his life and corporall Libertie given him, on condition to be Subject to the Victor, he hath Libertie to accept the condition; and having accepted it, is the subject of him that took him; because he had no other way to preserve himself. The case is the same, if he be deteined on the same termes, in a forreign country. But if a man be held in prison, or bonds, or is not trusted with the libertie of his bodie; he cannot be understood to be bound by Covenant to subjection; and therefore may, if he can, make his escape by any means whatsoever. *In case of Captivity*

If a Monarch shall relinquish the Soveraignty, both for himself, and his heires; His Subjects returne to the absolute Libertie of Nature; because, though Nature *In case the Soveraign cast off the government from himself and his Heyrs*

may declare who are his Sons, and who are the nerest of
his Kin; yet it dependeth on his own will, (as hath been
said in the precedent chapter,) who shall be his Heyr. If
therefore he will have no Heyre, there is no Soveraignty,
nor Subjection. The case is the same, if he dye without
known Kindred, and without declaration of his Heyre.
For then there can no Heire be known, and consequently
no Subjection be due.

In case of   If the Soveraign Banish his Subject; during the Banish-
Banishment ment, he is not Subject. But he that is sent on a message,
or hath leave to travell, is still Subject; but it is, by Contract between Soveraigns, not by vertue of the covenant
of Subjection. For whosoever entreth into anothers
dominion, is Subject to all the Laws thereof; unlesse he
have a privilege by the amity of the Soveraigns, or by
speciall licence.

In case the   If a Monarch subdued by war, render himself Subject
Soveraign   to the Victor; his Subjects are delivered from their former
render   obligation, and become obliged to the Victor. But if he be
himself   held prisoner, or have not the liberty of his own Body; he
Subject to   is not understood to have given away the Right of Sov-
another   eraigntie; and therefore his Subjects are obliged to yield
obedience to the Magistrates formerly placed, governing
not in their own name, but in his. For, his Right remaining, the question is only of the Administration; that is
to say, of the Magi[115]strates and Officers; which, if
he have not means to name, he is supposed to approve
those, which he himself had formerly appointed.

CHAP. XXII

Of SYSTEMES *Subject, Politicall, and Private*

The divers
sorts of   Having spoken of the Generation, Forme, and Power of
Systemes of a Common-wealth, I am in order to speak next of the
People   parts thereof. And first of Systemes, which resemble the

similar parts, or Muscles of a Body naturall. By Systemes; I understand any numbers of men joyned in one
Interest, or one Businesse. Of which, some are *Regular*,
and some *Irregular*. *Regular* are those, where one Man,
or Assembly of men, is constituted Representative of the
whole number. All other are *Irregular*.

Of Regular, some are *Absolute*, and *Independent*,
subject to none but their own Representative: such are
only Common-wealths; Of which I have spoken already
in the 5. last precedent chapters. Others are Dependent;
that is to say, Subordinate to some Soveraign Power, to
which every one, as also their Representative is *Subject*.

Of Systemes subordinate, some are *Politicall*, and some
Private. *Politicall* (otherwise Called *Bodies Politique*, and
Persons in Law,) are those, which are made by author-
ity from the Soveraign Power of the Common-wealth.
Private, are those, which are constituted by Subjects
amongst themselves, or by authoritie from a stranger.
For no authority derived from forraign power, within
the Dominion of another, is Publique there, but Private.

And of Private Systemes, some are *Lawfull*; some
Unlawfull: *Lawfull*, are those which are allowed by the
Common-wealth: all other are *Unlawfull*. *Irregular* Systemes, are those which having no Representative, consist
only in concourse of People; which if not forbidden by
the Common-wealth, nor made on evill designe, (such as
are conflux of People to markets, or shews, or any other
harmelesse end,) are Lawfull. But when the Intention is
evill, or (if the number be considerable) unknown, they
are Unlawfull.

In Bodies Politique, the power of the Representative is
alwaies Limited: And that which prescribeth the Limits
thereof, is the Power Soveraign. For Power Unlimited, is
absolute Soveraignty. And the Soveraign, in every Commonwealth, is the absolute Representative of all the
subjects; and therefore no other, can be Representative
of any part of them, but so far forth, as he shall give
leave: And to give leave to a Body Politique of Subjects,

In all Bodies Politique the power of the Representative is Limited to have an absolute Representative to all intents and purposes, were to abandon the government of so much of the Commonwealth, and to divide the Dominion, contrary to their Peace and Defence, which the Soveraign cannot be understood to doe, by any Grant, that does not [116] plainly, and directly discharge them of their subjection. For consequences of words, are not the signes of his will, when other consequences are signes of the contrary; but rather signes of errour, and misreckonning; to which all mankind is too prone.

The bounds of that Power, which is given to the Representative of a Bodie Politique, are to be taken notice of, from two things. One is their Writt, or Letters from the Soveraign: the other is the Law of the Common-wealth.

By Letters Patents: For though in the Institution or Acquisition of a Common-wealth, which is independent, there needs no Writing, because the Power of the Representative has there no other bounds, but such as are set out by the unwritten Law of Nature; yet in subordinate bodies, there are such diversities of Limitation necessary, concerning their businesses, times, and places, as can neither be remembred without Letters, nor taken notice of, unlesse such Letters be Patent, that they may be read to them, and withall sealed, or testified, with the Seales, or other permanent signes of the Authority Soveraign.

And the Lawes And because such Limitation is not alwaies easie, or perhaps possible to be described in writing; the ordinary Lawes, common to all Subjects, must determine, what the Representative may lawfully do, in all Cases, where the Letters themselves are silent. And therefore

When the Representative is one man, his unwarranted Acts are his own onely In a Body Politique, if the Representative be one man, whatsoever he does in the Person of the Body, which is not warranted in his Letters, nor by the Lawes, is his own act, and not the act of the Body, nor of any other Member thereof besides himselfe: Because further than his Letters, or the Lawes limit, he representeth no mans person, but his own. But what he does according to these, is the act of every one: For of the Act of the

Soveraign every one is Author, because he is their Representative unlimited; and the act of him that recedes not from the Letters of the Soveraign, is the act of the Soveraign, and therefore every member of the Body is Author of it.

But if the Representative be an Assembly; whatsoever that Assembly shall Decree, not warranted by their Letters, or the Lawes, is the act of the Assembly, or Body Politique, and the act of every one by whose Vote the Decree was made; but not the act of any man that being present Voted to the contrary; nor of any man absent, unlesse he Voted it by procuration. It is the act of the Assembly, because Voted by the major part; and if it be a crime, the Assembly may be punished, as farre-forth as it is capable, as by dissolution, or forfeiture of their Letters, (which is to such artificiall, and fictitious Bodies, capitall,) or (if the Assembly have a Common stock, wherein none of the Innocent Members have propriety,) by pecuniary Mulct. For from corporall penalties Nature hath exempted all Bodies Politique. But they that gave not their Vote, are therefore Innocent, because the Assembly cannot Represent any man in things unwarranted by their Letters, and consequently are not involved in their Votes. *When it is an Assembly, it is the act of them that assented onely*

If the person of the Body Politique being in one man, borrow mony of a stranger, that is, of one that is not of the same Body, (for no Letters need limit borrowing, seeing it is left to mens own incli[117]nations to limit lending) the debt is the Representatives. For if he should have Authority from his Letters, to make the members pay what he borroweth, he should have by consequence the Soveraignty of them; and therefore the grant were either voyd, as proceeding from Errour, commonly incident to humane Nature, and an unsufficient signe of the will of the Granter; or if it be avowed by him, then is the Representer Soveraign, and falleth not under the present question, which is onely of Bodies subordinate. No member therefore is obliged to pay the debt so borrowed, but *When the Representative is one man, if he borrow mony, or owe it, by Contract; he is lyable onely, the members not* the Representative himselfe: because he that lendeth it, being a stranger to the Letters, and to the qualification of the Body, understandeth those onely for his debtors, that are engaged; and seeing the Representer can ingage himselfe, and none else, has him onely for Debtor; who must therefore pay him, out of the common stock (if there be any,) or (if there be none) out of his own estate.

If he come into debt by Contract, or Mulct, the case is the same.

When it is But when the Representative is an Assembly, and the
an Assembly, debt to a stranger; all they, and onely they are respon-
they onely sible for the debt, that gave their votes to the borrowing
are liable that of it, or to the Contract that made it due, or to the fact
have assented for which the Mulct was imposed; because every one of those in voting did engage himselfe for the payment: For he that is author of the borrowing, is obliged to the payment, even of the whole debt, though when payd by any one, he be discharged.

If the debt be But if the debt be to one of the Assembly, the Assem-
to one of the bly onely is obliged to the payment, out of their common
Assembly, the stock (if they have any:) For having liberty of Vote, if he
Body onely is Vote the Mony shall be borrowed, he Votes it shall be
obliged payd; If he Vote it shall not be borrowed, or be absent, yet because in lending, he voteth the borrowing, he contradicteth his former Vote, and is obliged by the later, and becomes both borrower and lender, and consequently cannot demand payment from any particular man, but from the common Treasure onely; which
Protestation fayling he hath no remedy, nor complaint, but against
against the himselfe, that being privy to the acts of the Assembly,
Decrees and to their means to pay, and not being enforced, did
of Bodies neverthelesse through his own folly lend his mony.
Politique It is manifest by this, that in Bodies Politique subor-
sometimes dinate, and subject to a Soveraign Power, it is sometimes
lawful; not onely lawfull, but expedient, for a particular man
but against to make open protestation against the decrees of the
Soveraign Representative Assembly, and cause their dissent to be
Power never Registred, or to take witnesse of it; because otherwise

they may be obliged to pay debts contracted, and be responsible for crimes committed by other men: But in a Soveraign Assembly, that liberty is taken away, both because he that protesteth there, denies their Soveraignty; and also because whatsoever is commanded by the Soveraign Power, is as to the Subject (though not so alwayes in the sight of God) justified by the Command; for of such command every Subject is the Author.

The variety of Bodies Politique, is almost infinite: for they are not onely distinguished by the severall affaires, for which they are [118] constituted, wherein there is an unspeakable diversitie; but also by the times, places, and numbers, subject to many limitations. And as to their affaires, some are ordained for Government; As first, the Government of a Province may be committed to an Assembly of men, wherein all resolutions shall depend on the Votes of the major part; and then this Assembly is a Body Politique, and their power limited by Commission. This word Province signifies a charge, or care of businesse, which he whose businesse it is, committeth to another man, to be administred for, and under him; and therefore when in one Common-wealth there be divers Countries, that have their Lawes distinct one from another, or are farre distant in place, the Administration of the Government being committed to divers persons, those Countries where the Soveraign is not resident, but governs by Commission, are called Provinces. But of the government of a Province, by an Assembly residing in the Province it selfe, there be few examples. The Romans who had the Soveraignty of many Provinces; yet governed them alwaies by Presidents, and Prætors; and not by Assemblies, as they governed the City of *Rome*, and Territories adjacent. In like manner, when there were Colonies sent from *England*, to Plant *Virginia*, and *Sommer-Ilands*;[18] though the government of them here, were committed to Assemblies in *London*, yet did those Assemblies never commit the Government under them to any Assembly there; but did to each

Bodies Politique for Government of a Province, Colony, or Town

Plantation send one Governour; For though every man, where he can be present by Nature, desires to participate of government; yet where they cannot be present, they are by Nature also enclined, to commit the Government of their common Interest rather to a Monarchicall, then a Popular form of Government: which is also evident in those men that have great private estates; who when they are unwilling to take the paines of administring the businesse that belongs to them, choose rather to trust one Servant, than an Assembly either of their friends or servants. But howsoever it be in fact, yet we may suppose the Government of a Province, or Colony committed to an Assembly: and when it is, that which in this place I have to say, is this; that whatsoever debt is by that Assembly contracted; or whatsoever unlawfull Act is decreed, is the Act onely of those that assented, and not of any that dissented, or were absent, for the reasons before alledged. Also that an Assembly residing out of the bounds of that Colony whereof they have the government, cannot execute any power over the persons, or goods of any of the Colonie, to seize on them for debt, or other duty, in any place without the Colony it selfe, as having no Jurisdiction, nor Authoritie elsewhere, but are left to the remedie, which the Law of the place alloweth them. And though the Assembly have right, to impose a Mulct upon any of their members, that shall break the Lawes they make; yet out of the Colonie it selfe, they have no right to execute the same. And that which is said here, of the Rights of an Assembly, for the government of a Province, or a Colony, is appliable also to an Assembly for the Government of a Town, an University, or a College, or a Church, or for any other Government over the persons of men.

[119] And generally, in all Bodies Politique, if any particular member conceive himself Injuried by the Body it self, the Cognisance of his cause belongeth to the Soveraign, and those the Soveraign hath ordained for Judges in such causes, or shall ordaine for that particular cause;

and not to the Body it self. For the whole Body is in this case his fellow subject, which in a Soveraign Assembly, is otherwise: for there, if the Soveraign be not Judge, though in his own cause, there can be no Judge at all.

In a Bodie Politique, for the well ordering of forraigne Traffique, the most commodious Representative is an Assembly of all the members; that is to say, such a one, as every one that adventureth his mony, may be present at all the Deliberations, and Resolutions of the Body, if they will themselves. For proof whereof, we are to consider the end, for which men that are Merchants, and may buy and sell, export, and import their Merchandise, according to their own discretions, doe neverthelesse bind themselves up in one Corporation. It is true, there be few Merchants, that with the Merchandise they buy at home, can fraight a Ship, to export it; or with that they buy abroad, to bring it home; and have therefore need to joyn together in one Society; where every man may either participate of the gaine, according to the proportion of his adventure; or take his own, and sell what he transports, or imports, at such prices as he thinks fit. But this is no Body Politique, there being no Common Representative to oblige them to any other Law, than that which is common to all other subjects. The End of their Incorporating, is to make their gaine the greater; which is done two wayes; by sole buying, and sole selling, both at home, and abroad. So that to grant to a Company of Merchants to be a Corporation, or Body Politique, is to grant them a double Monopoly, whereof one is to be sole buyers; another to be sole sellers. For when there is a Company incorporate for any particular forraign Country, they only export the Commodities vendible in that Country; which is sole buying at home, and sole selling abroad. For at home there is but one buyer, and abroad but one that selleth: both which is gainfull to the Merchant, because thereby they buy at home at lower, and sell abroad at higher rates: And abroad there is but one buyer of forraign Merchandise,

Bodies Politique for ordering of Trade

and but one that sels them at home; both which againe are gainfull to the adventurers.

Of this double Monopoly one part is disadvantageous to the people at home, the other to forraigners. For at home by their sole exportation they set what price they please on the husbandry, and handy-works of the people; and by the sole importation, what price they please on all forraign commodities the people have need of; both which are ill for the people. On the contrary, by the sole selling of the native commodities abroad, and sole buying the forraign commodities upon the place, they raise the price of those, and abate the price of these, to the disadvantage of the forraigner: For where but one selleth, the Merchandise is the dearer; and where [120] but one buyeth the cheaper: Such Corporations therefore are no other then Monopolies; though they would be very profitable for a Common-wealth, if being bound up into one body in forraigne Markets they were at liberty at home, every man to buy, and sell at what price he could.

The end then of these Bodies of Merchants, being not a Common benefit to the whole Body, (which have in this case no common stock, but what is deducted out of the particular adventures, for building, buying, victualling and manning of Ships,) but the particular gaine of every adventurer, it is reason that every one be acquainted with the employment of his own; that is, that every one be of the Assembly, that shall have the power to order the same; and be acquainted with their accounts. And therefore the Representative of such a Body must be an Assembly, where every member of the Body may be present at the consultations, if he will.

If a Body Politique of Merchants, contract a debt to a stranger by the act of their Representative Assembly, every Member is lyable by himself for the whole. For a stranger can take no notice of their private Lawes, but considereth them as so many particular men, obliged every one to the whole payment, till payment made by

one dischargeth all the rest: But if the debt be to one
of the Company, the creditor is debter for the whole to
himself, and cannot therefore demand his debt, but only
from the common stock, if there be any.

If the Common-wealth impose a Tax upon the Body,
it is understood to be layd upon every Member proportionably to his particular adventure in the Company.
For there is in this case no other common stock, but
what is made of their particular adventures.

If a Mulct be layd upon the Body for some unlawfull act, they only are lyable by whose votes the act was
decreed, or by whose assistance it was executed; for in
none of the rest is there any other crime but being of the
Body; which if a crime, (because the Body was ordeyned
by the authority of the Common-wealth,) is not his.

If one of the Members be indebted to the Body, he may
be sued by the Body; but his goods cannot be taken, nor
his person imprisoned by the authority of the Body; but
only by Authority of the Common-wealth: for if they
can doe it by their own Authority, they can by their own
Authority give judgement that the debt is due, which is
as much as to be Judge in their own Cause.

These Bodies made for the government of Men, or of *A Bodie*
Traffique, be either perpetuall, or for a time prescribed *Politique for*
by writing. But there be Bodies also whose times are *Counsel to be*
limited, and that only by the nature of their business. For *given to the*
example, if a Soveraign Monarch, or a Soveraign Assem- *Soveraign*
bly, shall think fit to give command to the towns, and
other severall parts of their territory, to send to him their
Deputies, to enforme him of the condition, and necessities of the Subjects, or to advise with him for the making
of good Lawes, or [121] for any other cause, as with one
Person representing the whole Country, such Deputies,
having a place and time of meeting assigned them, are
there, and at that time, a Body Politique, representing
every Subject of that Dominion; but it is onely for such
matters as shall be propounded unto them by that Man,
or Assembly, that by the Soveraign Authority sent for

them; and when it shall be declared that nothing more shall be propounded, nor debated by them, the Body is dissolved. For if they were the absolute Representative of the people, then were it the Soveraign Assembly; and so there would be two Soveraign Assemblies, or two Soveraigns, over the same people; which cannot consist with their Peace. And therefore where there is once a Soveraignty, there can be no absolute Representation of the people, but by it. And for the limits of how farre such a Body shall represent the whole People, they are set forth in the Writing by which they were sent for. For the People cannot choose their Deputies to other intent, than is in the Writing directed to them from their Soveraign expressed.

A Regular Private Body, Lawfull, as a Family Private Bodies Regular, and Lawfull, are those that are constituted without Letters, or other written Authority, saving the Lawes common to all other Subjects. And because they be united in one Person Representative, they are held for Regular; such as are all Families, in which the Father, or Master ordereth the whole Family. For he obligeth his Children, and Servants, as farre as the Law permitteth, though not further, because none of them are bound to obedience in those actions, which the Law hath forbidden to be done. In all other actions, during the time they are under domestique government, they are subject to their Fathers, and Masters, as to their immediate Soveraigns. For the Father, and Master being before the Institution of Common-wealth, absolute Soveraigns in their own Families, they lose afterward no more of their Authority, than the Law of the Common-wealth taketh from them.

Private Bodies Regular, but Unlawfull Private Bodies Regular, but Unlawfull, are those that unite themselves into one person Representative, without any publique Authority at all; such as are the Corporations of Beggars, Theeves and Gipsies, the better to order their trade of begging, and stealing; and the Corporations of men, that by Authority from any forraign Person, unite themselves in anothers Dominion,

for the easier propagation of Doctrines, and for making
a party, against the Power of the Common-wealth.

Irregular Systemes, in their nature, but Leagues, or *Systemes*
sometimes meer concourse of people, without union *Irregular,*
to any particular designe, not by obligation[19] of one *such as*
to another, but proceeding onely from a similitude of *are Private*
wills and inclinations, become Lawfull, or Unlawfull, *Leagues*
according to the lawfulnesse, or unlawfulnesse of every
particular mans designe therein: And his designe is to be
understood by the occasion.

The Leagues of Subjects, (because Leagues are commonly made for mutuall defence,) are in a Common-wealth
(which is no more than a League of all the Subjects
together) for the most part unnecessary, and savour
of unlawfull designe; and are for that cause Un[122]-
lawfull, and go commonly by the name of Factions, or
Conspiracies. For a League being a connexion of men
by Covenants, if there be no power given to any one
Man, or Assembly (as in the condition of meer Nature)
to compell them to performance, is so long onely valid,
as there ariseth no just cause of distrust: and therefore
Leagues between Common-wealths, over whom there is
no humane Power established, to keep them all in awe,
are not onely lawfull, but also profitable for the time
they last. But Leagues of the Subjects of one and the same
Common-wealth, where every one may obtain his right
by means of the Soveraign Power, are unnecessary to the
maintaining of Peace and Justice, and (in case the designe
of them be evill, or Unknown to the Common-wealth)
unlawfull. For all uniting of strength by private men, is,
if for evill intent, unjust; if for intent unknown, dangerous to the Publique, and unjustly concealed.

If the Soveraign Power be in a great Assembly, and a *Secret Cabals*
number of men, part of the Assembly, without author-
ity, consult a part, to contrive the guidance of the rest;
This is a Faction, or Conspiracy unlawfull, as being a
fraudulent seducing of the Assembly for their particular interest. But if he, whose private interest is to be

debated, and judged in the Assembly, make as many
friends as he can; in him it is no Injustice; because in this
case he is no part of the Assembly. And though he hire
such friends with mony, (unlesse there be an expresse
Law against it,) yet it is not Injustice. For sometimes,
(as mens manners are,) Justice cannot be had without
mony; and every man may think his own cause just, till
it be heard, and judged.

Feuds of private Families   In all Common-wealths, if a private man entertain
more servants, than the government of his estate, and
lawfull employment he has for them requires, it is Faction, and unlawfull. For having the protection of the
Common-wealth, he needeth not the defence of private
force. And whereas in Nations not throughly civilized,
severall numerous Families have lived in continuall hostility, and invaded one another with private force; yet it
is evident enough, that they have done unjustly; or else
that they had no Common-wealth.

Factions for Government   And as Factions for Kindred, so also Factions for Government of Religion, as of Papists, Protestants, &c. or of
State, as Patricians, and Plebeians of old time in *Rome*,
and of Aristocraticalls and Democraticalls of old time in
Greece, are unjust, as being contrary to the peace and
safety of the people, and a taking of the Sword out of
the hand of the Soveraign.

Concourse of people, is an Irregular Systeme, the lawfulnesse, or unlawfulnesse, whereof dependeth on the
occasion, and on the number of them that are assembled.
If the occasion be lawfull, and manifest, the Concourse
is lawfull; as the usuall meeting of men at Church, or at
a publique Shew, in usuall numbers: for if the numbers
be extraordinarily great, the occasion is not evident;
and consequently he that cannot render a particular and
good account of his being amongst them, is to be judged
conscious of an unlawfull, and tumultuous designe. It
may be lawfull for a thousand men, to joyn in a Petition to be delivered to a Judge, or Magistrate; yet if a
thou[123]sand men come to present it, it is a tumultuous

Assembly; because there needs but one or two for that purpose. But in such cases as these, it is not a set number that makes the Assembly Unlawfull, but such a number, as the present Officers are not able to suppresse, and bring to Justice.

When an unusuall number of men, assemble against a man whom they accuse; the Assembly is an Unlawfull tumult; because they may deliver their accusation to the Magistrate by a few, or by one man. Such was the case of St. *Paul* at *Ephesus*; where *Demetrius*,[20] and a great number of other men, brought two of *Pauls* companions before the Magistrate, saying with one Voyce, *Great is Diana of the Ephesians*; which was their way of demanding Justice against them for teaching the people such doctrine, as was against their Religion, and Trade. The occasion here, considering the Lawes of that People, was just; yet was their Assembly Judged Unlawfull, and the Magistrate reprehended them for it, in these words, *If Demetrius and the other work-men can accuse any man, of any thing, there be Pleas, and Deputies, let them accuse one another. And if you have any other thing to demand, your case may be judged in an Assembly Lawfully called. For we are in danger to be accused for this dayes sedition, because, there is no cause by which any man can render any reason of this Concourse of People.* Where he calleth an Assembly, whereof men can give no just account, a Sedition, and such as they could not answer for. And this is all I shall say concerning *Systemes*, and Assemblyes of People, which may be compared (as I said,) to the Similar parts of mans Body; such as be Lawfull, to the Muscles; such as are Unlawfull, to Wens, Biles, and Apostemes, engendred by the unnaturall conflux of evill humours.

* Acts 19. 40

Of the PUBLIQUE MINISTERS of
Soveraign Power

In the last Chapter I have spoken of the Similar parts of a Common-wealth: In this I shall speak of the parts Organicall, which are Publique Ministers.

Publique Minister Who A PUBLIQUE MINISTER, is he, that by the Soveraign, (whether a Monarch, or an Assembly,) is employed in any affaires, with Authority to represent in that employment, the Person of the Common-wealth. And whereas every man, or assembly that hath Soveraignty, representeth two Persons, or (as the more common phrase is) has two Capacities, one Naturall, and another Politique, (as a Monarch, hath the person not onely of the Common-wealth, but also of a man; and a Soveraign Assembly hath the Person not onely of the Common-wealth, but also of the Assembly); they that be servants to them in their naturall Capacity, are not Publique Ministers; but those onely that serve them in the Administration of [124] the Publique businesse. And therefore neither Ushers, nor Sergeants, nor other Officers that waite on the Assembly, for no other purpose, but for the commodity of the men assembled, in an Aristocracy, or Democracy; nor Stewards, Chamberlains, Cofferers, or any other Officers of the houshold of a Monarch, are Publique Ministers in a Monarchy.

Ministers for the generall Administration Of Publique Ministers, some have charge committed to them of a general Administration, either of the whole Dominion, or of a part thereof. Of the whole, as to a Protector, or Regent, may bee committed by the Predecessor of an Infant King, during his minority, the whole Administration of his Kingdome. In which case, every Subject is so far obliged to obedience, as the Ordinances he shall make, and the commands he shall give be in the Kings name, and not inconsistent with his Soveraigne Power. Of a part, or Province; as when either a Monarch, or a Soveraign Assembly, shall give the generall charge thereof to a Governour, Lieutenant, Præfect or Vice-Roy: And in this case also, every one of that Province, is obliged to all he shall doe in the name of the Soveraign, and that not incompatible with the Soveraigns Right. For such Protectors, Vice-Roys, and Governors, have no other right, but what depends on the Soveraigns Will; and no Commission that can be given them, can be interpreted for a Declaration of the will to transferre the Soveraignty, without expresse and perspicuous words to that purpose. And this kind of Publique Ministers resembleth the Nerves, and Tendons that move the severall limbs of a body naturall.

Others have speciall Administration; that is to say, charges of some speciall businesse, either at home, or abroad: As at home, First, for the Oeconomy of a Common-wealth, They that have Authority concerning the *Treasure*, as Tributes, Impositions, Rents, Fines, or whatsoever publique revenue, to collect, receive, issue, or take the Accounts thereof, are Publique Ministers: Ministers, because they serve the Person Representative, and can doe nothing against his Command, nor without his Authority: Publique, because they serve him in his Politicall Capacity. *For speciall Administration, as for Oeconomy*

Secondly, they that have Authority concerning the *Militia*; to have the custody of Armes, Forts, Ports; to Levy, Pay, or Conduct Souldiers; or to provide for any necessary thing for the use of war, either by Land or Sea, are publique Ministers. But a Souldier without Command, though he fight for the Common-wealth, does not therefore represent the Person of it; because there is none to represent it to. For every one that hath command, represents it to them only whom he commandeth.

They also that have authority to teach, or to enable others to teach the people their duty to the Soveraign Power, and instruct them in the knowledge of what is just, and unjust, thereby to render them more apt to *For instruction of the People* live in godlinesse, and in peace amongst themselves, and resist the publique enemy, are Publique Ministers: Ministers, in that they doe it not by their own Authority, but by anothers; and Publique, because they doe it (or should doe it) by [125] no Authority, but that of the Soveraign. The Monarch, or the Soveraign Assembly only hath immediate Authority from God, to teach and instruct the people; and no man but the Soveraign, receiveth his power *Dei gratiâ* simply; that is to say, from the favour of none but God: All other, receive theirs from the favour and providence of God, and their Soveraigns; as in a Monarchy *Dei gratiâ & Regis*; or *Dei providentiâ & voluntate Regis.*[21]

For Judicature   They also to whom Jurisdiction is given, are Publique Ministers. For in their Seats of Justice they represent the person of the Soveraign; and their Sentence, is his Sentence; For (as hath been before declared) all Judicature is essentially annexed to the Soveraignty; and therefore all other Judges are but Ministers of him, or them that have the Soveraign Power. And as Controversies are of two sorts, namely of *Fact*, and of *Law*; so are Judgements, some of Fact, some of Law: And consequently in the same controversie, there may be two Judges, one of Fact, another of Law.

And in both these controversies, there may arise a controversie between the party Judged, and the Judge; which because they be both Subjects to the Soveraign, ought in Equity to be Judged by men agreed on by consent of both; for no man can be Judge in his own cause. But the Soveraign is already agreed on for Judge by them both, and is therefore either to heare the Cause, and determine it himself, or appoint for Judge such as they shall both agree on. And this agreement is then understood to be made between them divers wayes; as first, if the Defendant be allowed to except against such of his Judges, whose interest maketh him suspect them, (for as to the Complaynant he hath already chosen his own Judge,) those which he excepteth not against, are

Judges he himself agrees on. Secondly, if he appeale to any other Judge, he can appeale no further; for his appeale is his choice. Thirdly, if he appeale to the Soveraign himself, and he by himself, or by Delegates which the parties shall agree on, give Sentence; that Sentence is finall: for the Defendant is Judged by his own Judges, that is to say, by himself.

These properties of just and rationall Judicature considered, I cannot forbeare to observe the excellent constitution of the Courts of Justice, established both for Common, and also for Publique Pleas in *England*. By Common Pleas, I meane those, where both the Complaynant and Defendant are Subjects: and by Publique, (which are also called Pleas of the Crown) those, where the Complaynant is the Sovereign. For whereas there were two orders of men, whereof one was Lords, the other Commons; The Lords had this Priviledge, to have for Judges in all Capitall crimes, none but Lords; and of them, as many as would be present; which being ever acknowledged as a Priviledge of favour, their Judges were none but such as they had themselves desired. And in all controversies, every Subject (as also in civill controversies the Lords) had for Judges, men of the Country where the matter in controversie lay; against which he might make his exceptions, till at last Twelve [126] men without exception being agreed on, they were Judged by those twelve. So that having his own Judges, there could be nothing alledged by the party, why the sentence should not be finall. These publique persons, with Authority from the Sovereign Power, either to Instruct, or Judge the people, are such members of the Common-wealth, as may fitly be compared to the organs of Voice in a Body naturall.

Publique Ministers are also all those, that have Authority *For Execution* from the Sovereign, to procure the Execution of Judgements given; to publish the Soveraigns Commands; to suppresse Tumults; to apprehend, and imprison Malefactors; and other acts tending to the conservation of the

Peace. For every act they doe by such Authority, is the act of the Common-wealth; and their service, answerable to that of the Hands, in a Bodie naturall.

Publique Ministers abroad, are those that represent the Person of their own Soveraign, to forraign States. Such are Ambassadors, Messengers, Agents, and Heralds, sent by publique Authoritie, and on publique Businesse.

But such as are sent by Authoritie only of some private partie of a troubled State, though they be received, are neither Publique, nor Private Ministers of the Common-wealth; because none of their actions have the Common-wealth for Author. Likewise, an Ambassador sent from a Prince, to congratulate, condole, or to assist at a solemnity, though the Authority be Publique; yet because the businesse is Private, and belonging to him in his naturall capacity; is a Private person. Also if a man be sent into another Country, secretly to explore their counsels, and strength; though both the Authority, and the Businesse be Publique; yet because there is none to take notice of any Person in him, but his own; he is but a Private Minister; but yet a Minister of the Common-wealth; and may be compared to an Eye in the Body naturall. And those that are appointed to receive the Petitions or other informations of the People, and are as it were the publique Eare, are Publique Ministers, and represent their Soveraign in that office.

Counsellers without other employment then to Advise are not Publique Ministers Neither a Counsellor (nor a Councell of State, if we consider it with no Authority of Judicature or Command, but only of giving Advice to the Soveraign when it is required,) or of offering it when it is not required, is a Publique Person. For the Advice is addressed to the Soveraign only, whose person cannot in his own presence, be represented to him, by another. But a Body of Counsellors, are never without some other Authority, either of Judicature, or of immediate Administration: As in a Monarchy, they represent the Monarch, in delivering his Commands to the Publique Ministers:

In a Democracy, the Councell, or Senate propounds the Result of their deliberations to the people, as a Councell; but when they appoint Judges, or heare Causes, or give Audience to Ambassadors, it is in the quality of a Minister of the People: And in an Aristocracy the Councell of State is the Soveraign Assembly it self; and gives counsell to none but themselves. [127]

CHAP. XXIV

Of the NUTRITION, *and* PROCREATION *of a Common-wealth*

The NUTRITION of a Common-wealth consisteth, in the Plenty, and *Distribution* of *Materials* conducing to Life: In *Concoction*, or *Preparation*; and (when concocted) in the *Conveyance* of it, by convenient conduits, to the Publique use.

The Nourishment of a Common-wealth consisteth in the Commodities of Sea and Land:

As for the Plenty of Matter, it is a thing limited by Nature, to those commodities, which from (the two breasts of our common Mother) Land, and Sea, God usually either freely giveth, or for labour selleth to man-kind.

For the Matter of this Nutriment, consisting in Animals, Vegetals, and Minerals, God hath freely layd them before us, in or neer to the face of the Earth; so as there needeth no more but the labour, and industry of receiving them. Insomuch as Plenty dependeth (next to Gods favour) meerly on the labour and industry of men.

This Matter, commonly called Commodities, is partly *Native*, and partly *Forraign*: *Native*, that which is to be had within the Territory of the Common-wealth: *Forraign*, that which is imported from without. And because there is no Territory under the Dominion of one Common-wealth, (except it be of very vast extent,) that

produceth all things needfull for the maintenance, and
motion of the whole Body; and few that produce not
something more than necessary; the superfluous commodities to be had within, become no more superfluous,
but supply these wants at home, by importation of that
which may be had abroad, either by Exchange, or by
just Warre, or by Labour: for a mans Labour also, is
a commodity exchangeable for benefit, as well as any
other thing: And there have been Common-wealths that
having no more Territory, than hath served them for
habitation, have neverthelesse, not onely maintained,
but also encreased their Power, partly by the labour of
trading from one place to another, and partly by selling
the Manifactures, whereof the Materials were brought
in from other places.

And the right   The Distribution of the Materials of this Nourish-
Distribution ment, is the constitution of *Mine*, and *Thine*, and *His*;
of them that is to say, in one word *Propriety*; and belongeth in
all kinds of Common-wealth to the Soveraign Power.
For where there is no Common-wealth, there is (as hath
been already shewn) a perpetuall warre of every man
against his neighbour; And therefore every thing is his
that getteth it, and keepeth it by force; which is neither
Propriety nor *Community*; but *Uncertainty*. Which is
so evident, that even *Cicero*, (a passionate defender of
Liberty,) in a publique pleading, attributeth all Propriety to the Law Civil, *Let the Civill Law*, saith he, *be
once abandoned, or but negligently guarded, (not to say
oppressed,) and there is nothing,* [128] *that any man
can be sure to receive from his Ancestor, or leave to his
Children.* And again; *Take away the Civill Law, and no
man knows what is his own, and what another mans.*[22]
Seeing therefore the Introduction of *Propriety* is an
effect of Common-wealth; which can do nothing but by
the Person that Represents it, it is the act onely of the
Soveraign; and consisteth in the Lawes, which none can
make that have not the Soveraign Power. And this they
well knew of old, who called that Νόμος, (that is to say,

Distribution,) which we call Law; and defined Justice, by *distributing* to every man *his own*.

In this Distribution, the First Law, is for Division of the Land it selfe: wherein the Soveraign assigneth to every man a portion, according as he, and not according as any Subject, or any number of them, shall judge agreeable to Equity, and the Common Good. The Children of Israel, were a Common-wealth in the Wildernesse; but wanted the commodities of the Earth, till they were masters of the Land of Promise; which afterward was divided amongst them, not by their own discretion, but by the discretion of *Eleazar* the Priest,[23] and *Joshua* their Generall: who when there were twelve Tribes, making them thirteen by subdivision of the Tribe of *Joseph*; made neverthelesse but twelve portions of the Land; and ordained for the Tribe of *Levi*[24] no land; but assigned them the Tenth part of the whole fruits; which division was therefore Arbitrary. And though a People comming into possession of a Land by warre, do not alwaies exterminate the antient Inhabitants, (as did the Jewes,) but leave to many, or most, or all of them their Estates;[25] yet it is manifest they hold them afterwards, as of the Victors distribution; as the people of *England* held all theirs of *William* the *Conquerour*.[26]

From whence we may collect, that the Propriety which a subject hath in his lands, consisteth in a right to exclude all other subjects from the use of them; and not to exclude their Soveraign, be it an Assembly, or a Monarch. For seeing the Soveraign, that is to say, the Common-wealth (whose Person he representeth,) is understood to do nothing but in order to the common Peace and Security, this Distribution of lands, is to be understood as done in order to the same: And consequently, whatsoever Distribution he shall make in prejudice thereof, is contrary to the will of every subject, that committed his Peace, and safety to his discretion, and conscience; and therefore by the will of every one of them, is to be reputed voyd. It is true, that a Soveraign

All private Estates of land proceed originally from the Arbitrary Distribution of the Soveraign

Propriety of a Subject excludes not the Dominion of the Soveraign, but onely of another Subject

Monarch, or the greater part of a Soveraign Assembly,
may ordain the doing of many things in pursuit of their
Passions, contrary to their own consciences, which is
a breach of trust, and of the Law of Nature; but this
is not enough to authorise any subject, either to make
warre upon, or so much as to accuse of Injustice, or any
way to speak evill of their Soveraign; because they have
authorised all his actions, and in bestowing the Soveraign Power, made them their own. But in what cases
the Commands of Soveraigns are contrary to Equity,
and the Law of Nature, is to be considered hereafter in
another place.

The Publique   In the Distribution of land, the Common-wealth it
is not to be   selfe, may be [129] conceived to have a portion, and
dieted   possesse, and improve the same by their Representative; and that such portion may be made sufficient, to
susteine the whole expence to the common Peace, and
defence necessarily required: Which were very true, if
there could be any Representative conceived free from
humane passions, and infirmities. But the nature of men
being as it is, the setting forth of Publique Land, or of any
certaine Revenue for the Common-wealth, is in vaine;
and tendeth to the dissolution of Government, and to
the condition of meere Nature, and War, assoon as ever
the Soveraign Power falleth into the hands of a Monarch, or of an Assembly, that are either too negligent of
mony, or too hazardous in engaging the publique stock,
into a long, or costly war. Common-wealths can endure
no Diet: For seeing their expence is not limited by their
own appetite, but by externall Accidents, and the appetites of their neighbours, the Publique Riches cannot be
limited by other limits, than those which the emergent
occasions shall require. And whereas in *England*, there
were by the Conquerour, divers Lands reserved to his
own use, (besides Forrests, and Chases, either for his
recreation, or for preservation of Woods,) and divers
services reserved on the Land he gave his Subjects; yet
it seems they were not reserved for his Maintenance in

his Publique, but in his Naturall capacity: For he, and his Successors did for all that, lay Arbitrary Taxes on all Subjects Land, when they judged it necessary. Or if those publique Lands, and Services, were ordained as a sufficient maintenance of the Common-wealth, it was contrary to the scope of the Institution; being (as it appeared by those ensuing Taxes) insufficient, and (as it appeares by the late small Revenue of the Crown) Subject to Alienation, and Diminution. It is therefore in vaine, to assign a portion to the Common-wealth; which may sell, or give it away; and does sell, and give it away when tis done by their Representative.

As the Distribution of Lands at home; so also to assigne in what places, and for what commodities, the Subject shall traffique abroad, belongeth to the Soveraign. For if it did belong to private persons to use their own discretion therein, some of them would bee drawn for gaine, both to furnish the enemy with means to hurt the Common-wealth, and hurt it themselves, by importing such things, as pleasing mens appetites, be neverthelesse noxious, or at least unprofitable to them. And therefore it belongeth to the Common-wealth, (that is, to the Soveraign only,) to approve, or disapprove both of the places, and matter of forraign Traffique. *The Places and matter of Traffique depend, as their Distribution, on the Soveraign*

Further, seeing it is not enough to the Sustentation of a Common-wealth, that every man have a propriety in a portion of Land, or in some few commodities, or a naturall property in some usefull art, and there is no art in the world, but is necessary either for the being, or well being almost of every particular man; it is necessary, that men distribute that which they can spare, and transferre their propriety therein, mutually one to another, by exchange, and mutuall contract. And therefore it belongeth to the Common-wealth, [130] (that is to say, to the Soveraign,) to appoint in what manner, all kinds of contract between Subjects, (as buying, selling, exchanging, borrowing, lending, letting, and taking to hire,) are to bee made; and by what words, and signes *The Laws of transferring propriety belong also to the Soveraign* they shall be understood for valid. And for the Matter, and Distribution of the Nourishment, to the severall Members of the Common-wealth, thus much (considering the modell of the whole worke) is sufficient.

Mony the Bloud of a Common-wealth

By Concoction, I understand the reducing of all commodities, which are not presently consumed, but reserved for Nourishment in time to come, to some thing of equall value, and withall so portable, as not to hinder the motion of men from place to place; to the end a man may have in what place soever, such Nourishment as the place affordeth. And this is nothing else but Gold, and Silver, and Mony. For Gold and Silver, being (as it happens) almost in all Countries of the world highly valued, is a commodious measure of the value of all things else between Nations; and Mony (of what matter soever coyned by the Soveraign of a Common-wealth,) is a sufficient measure of the value of all things else, between the Subjects of that Common-wealth. By the means of which measures, all commodities, Moveable, and Immoveable, are made to accompany a man, to all places of his resort, within and without the place of his ordinary residence; and the same passeth from Man to Man, within the Common-wealth; and goes round about, Nourishing (as it passeth) every part thereof; In so much as this Concoction, is as it were the Sanguification of the Common-wealth: For naturall Bloud is in like manner made of the fruits of the Earth; and circulating, nourisheth by the way, every Member of the Body of Man.

And because Silver and Gold, have their value from the matter it self; they have first this priviledge, that the value of them cannot be altered by the power of one, nor of a few Common-wealths; as being a common measure of the commodities of all places. But base Mony, may easily be enhansed, or abased. Secondly, they have the priviledge to make Common-wealths move, and stretch out their armes, when need is, into forraign Countries; and supply, not only private Subjects that travell, but also whole Armies with Provision. But that Coyne, which is not considerable for the Matter, but for the Stamp of the place, being unable to endure change of ayr, hath its effect at home only; where also it is subject to the change of Laws, and thereby to have the value diminished, to the prejudice many times of those that have it.

The Conduits, and Wayes by which it is conveyed to the Publique use, are of two sorts; One, that Conveyeth it to the Publique Coffers; The other, that Issueth the same out againe for publique payments. Of the first sort, are Collectors, Receivers, and Treasurers; of the second are the Treasurers againe, and the Officers appointed for payment of severall publique or private Ministers. And in this also, the Artificiall Man maintains his resemblance with the Naturall; whose Veins receiving the Bloud from the severall [131] Parts of the Body, carry it to the Heart; where being made Vitall, the Heart by the Arteries sends it out again, to enliven, and enable for motion all the Members of the same. *The Conduits and Way of mony to the Publique use*

The Procreation, or Children of a Common-wealth, are those we call *Plantations*, or *Colonies*; which are numbers of men sent out from the Common-wealth, under a Conductor, or Governour, to inhabit a Forraign Country, either formerly voyd of Inhabitants, or made voyd then, by warre. And when a Colony is setled, they are either a Common-wealth of themselves, discharged of their subjection to their Soveraign that sent them, (as hath been done by many Common-wealths of antient time,) in which case the Common-wealth from which they went was called their Metropolis, or Mother, and requires no more of them, then Fathers require of the Children, whom they emancipate, and make free from their domestique government, which is Honour, and Friendship; or else they remain united to their Metropolis, as were the Colonies of the people of *Rome*; and then they are no Common-wealths themselves, but Provinces, and parts of the Common-wealth that sent them. So that the Right of Colonies (saving Honour, *The Children of a Commonwealth Colonies* and League with their Metropolis,) dependeth wholly on their Licence, or Letters, by which their Soveraign authorised them to Plant.

CHAP. XXV

Of COUNSELL

Counsell what How fallacious it is to judge of the nature of things, by the ordinary and inconstant use of words, appeareth in nothing more, than in the confusion of Counsels, and Commands, arising from the Imperative manner of speaking in them both, and in many other occasions besides. For the words *Doe this*, are the words not onely of him that Commandeth; but also of him that giveth Counsell; and of him that Exhorteth; and yet there are but few, that see not, that these are very different things; or that cannot distinguish between them, when they perceive who it is that speaketh, and to whom the Speech is directed, and upon what occasion. But finding those phrases in mens writings, and being not able, or not willing to enter into a consideration of the circumstances, they mistake sometimes the Precepts of Counsellours, for the Precepts of them that Command; and sometimes the contrary; according as it best agreeth with the conclusions they would inferre, or the actions they approve. To avoyd which mistakes, and render to those termes of Commanding, Counselling, and Exhorting, their proper and distinct significations, I define them thus.

Differences between Command, and Counsell COMMAND is, where a man saith, *Doe this*, or *Doe not this*, without expecting other reason than the Will of him that sayes it. From this it followeth manifestly, that he that Commandeth, pretendeth thereby his own Benefit: For the reason of his Command is his own [132] Will onely, and the proper object of every mans Will, is some Good to himselfe.

COUNSELL, is where a man saith, *Doe*, or *Doe not this*, and deduceth his reasons from the benefit that arriveth by it to him to whom he saith it. And from this it is evident, that he that giveth Counsell, pretendeth onely (whatsoever he intendeth) the good of him, to whom he giveth it.

Therefore between Counsell and Command, one great difference is, that Command is directed to a mans own benefit; and Counsell to the benefit of another man. And from this ariseth another difference, that a man may be obliged to do what he is Commanded; as when he hath covenanted to obey: But he cannot be obliged to do as he is Counselled, because the hurt of not following it, is his own; or if he should covenant to follow it, then is the Counsell turned into the nature of a Command. A third difference between them is, that no man can pretend a right to be of another mans Counsell; because he is not to pretend benefit by it to himselfe: but to demand right to Counsell another, argues a will to know his designes, or to gain some other Good to himselfe; which (as I said before) is of every mans will the proper object.

This also is incident to the nature of Counsell; that whatsoever it be, he that asketh it, cannot in equity accuse, or punish it: For to ask Counsell of another, is to permit him to give such Counsell as he shall think best; And consequently, he that giveth counsell to his Soveraign, (whether a Monarch, or an Assembly) when he asketh it, cannot in equity be punished for it, whether the same be conformable to the opinion of the most, or not, so it be to the Proposition in debate. For if the sense of the Assembly can be taken notice of, before the Debate be ended, they should neither ask, nor take any further Counsell; For the Sense of the Assembly, is the Resolution of the Debate, and End of all Deliberation. And generally he that demandeth Counsell, is Author of it; and therefore cannot punish it; and what the Soveraign cannot, no man else can. But if one Subject giveth Counsell to another, to do any thing contrary to the

Lawes, whether that Counsell proceed from evill intention, or from ignorance onely, it is punishable by the
Common-wealth; because ignorance of the Law, is no
good excuse, where every man is bound to take notice
of the Lawes to which he is subject.

Exhortation   EXHORTATION, and DEHORTATION, is Counsell,
and Dehort-   accompanied with signes in him that giveth it, of vehe-
ation what   ment desire to have it followed; or to say it more briefly,
Counsell vehemently pressed. For he that Exhorteth,
doth not deduce the consequences of what he adviseth
to be done, and tye himselfe therein to the rigour of
true reasoning; but encourages him he Counselleth, to
Action: As he that Dehorteth, deterreth him from it.
And therefore they have in their speeches, a regard to
the common Passions, and opinions of men, in deducing
their reasons; and make use of Similitudes, Metaphors,
Examples, and other tooles of Oratory, to perswade
their Hearers of the Utility, Honour, or Justice of following their advise.

[133] From whence may be inferred, First, that Exhortation and Dehortation, is directed to the Good of him
that giveth the Counsell, not of him that asketh it, which
is contrary to the duty of a Counsellour; who (by the
definition of Counsell) ought to regard, not his own
benefit, but his whom he adviseth. And that he directeth
his Counsell to his own benefit, is manifest enough, by
the long and vehement urging, or by the artificiall giving
thereof; which being not required of him, and consequently proceeding from his own occasions, is directed
principally to his own benefit, and but accidentarily to
the good of him that is Counselled, or not at all.

Secondly, that the use of Exhortation and Dehortation lyeth onely, where a man is to speak to a Multitude;
because when the Speech is addressed to one, he may
interrupt him, and examine his reasons more rigorously,
than can be done in a Multitude; which are too many to
enter into Dispute, and Dialogue with him that speaketh
indifferently to them all at once.

Thirdly, that they that Exhort and Dehort, where they are required to give Counsell, are corrupt Counsellours, and as it were bribed by their own interest. For though the Counsell they give be never so good; yet he that gives it, is no more a good Counsellour, than he that giveth a Just Sentence for a reward, is a Just Judge. But where a man may lawfully Command, as a Father in his Family, or a Leader in an Army, his Exhortations and Dehortations, are not onely lawfull, but also necessary, and laudable: But then they are no more Counsells, but Commands; which when they are for Execution of soure labour; sometimes necessity, and alwayes humanity requireth to be sweetned in the delivery, by encouragement, and in the tune and phrase of Counsell, rather then in harsher language of Command.

Examples of the difference between Command and Counsell, we may take from the formes of Speech that expresse them in Holy Scripture.[27] *Have no other Gods but me*; *Make to thy selfe no graven Image*; *Take not Gods name in vain*; *Sanctifie the Sabbath*; *Honour thy Parents*; *Kill not*; *Steale not*, &c. are Commands; because the reason for which we are to obey them, is drawn from the will of God our King, whom we are obliged to obey. But these words,[28] *Sell all thou hast; give it to the poore; and follow me*, are Counsell; because the reason for which we are to do so, is drawn from our own benefit; which is this, that we shall have *Treasure in heaven*. These words,[29] *Go into the Village over against you, and you shall find an Asse tyed, and her Colt; loose her, and bring her to me*, are a Command: for the reason of their fact is drawn from the will of their Master: but these words,[30] *Repent, and be Baptized in the Name of Jesus*, are Counsell; because the reason why we should so do, tendeth not to any benefit of God Almighty, who shall still be King in what manner soever we rebell; but of our selves, who have no other means of avoyding the punishment hanging over us for our sins. *Differences of fit and unfit Counsellours*

As the difference of Counsell from Command, hath

been now deduced from the nature of Counsell, consisting in a deducing of the [134] benefit, or hurt that may arise to him that is to be Counselled, by the necessary or probable consequences of the action he propoundeth; so may also the differences between *apt*, and *inept* Counsellours be derived from the same. For Experience, being but Memory of the consequences of like actions formerly observed, and Counsell but the Speech whereby that experience is made known to another; the Vertues, and Defects of Counsell, are the same with the Vertues, and Defects Intellectuall: And to the Person of a Common-wealth, his Counsellours serve him in the place of Memory, and Mentall Discourse. But with this resemblance of the Common-wealth, to a naturall man, there is one dissimilitude joyned, of great importance; which is, that a naturall man receiveth his experience, from the naturall objects of sense, which work upon him without passion, or interest of their own; whereas they that give Counsell to the Representative person of a Common-wealth, may have, and have often their particular ends, and passions, that render their Counsells always suspected, and many times unfaithfull. And therefore we may set down for the first condition of a good Counsellour, *That his Ends, and Interest, be not inconsistent with the Ends and Interest of him he Counselleth.*

Secondly, Because the office of a Counsellour, when an action comes into deliberation, is to make manifest the consequences of it, in such manner, as he that is Counselled may be truly and evidently informed; he ought to propound his advise, in such forme of speech, as may make the truth most evidently appear; that is to say, with as firme ratiocination, as significant and proper language, and as briefly, as the evidence will permit. And therefore *rash, and unevident Inferences*; (such as are fetched onely from Examples, or authority of Books, and are not arguments of what is good, or evill, but witnesses of fact, or of opinion,) *obscure, confused, and ambiguous Expressions, also all metaphoricall Speeches, tending to the stirring up of Passion,* (because such reasoning, and such expressions, are usefull onely to deceive, or to lead him we Counsell towards other ends than his own) *are repugnant to the Office of a Counsellour.*

Thirdly, Because the Ability of Counselling proceedeth from Experience, and long study; and no man is presumed to have experience in all those things that to the Administration of a great Common-wealth are necessary to be known, *No man is presumed to be a good Counsellour, but in such Businesse, as he hath not onely been much versed in, but hath also much meditated on, and considered.* For seeing the businesse of a Common-wealth is this, to preserve the people in Peace at home, and defend them against forraign Invasion, we shall find, it requires great knowledge of the disposition of Man-kind, of the Rights of Government, and of the nature of Equity, Law, Justice, and Honour, not to be attained without study; And of the Strength, Commodities, Places, both of their own Country, and their Neighbours; as also of the inclinations, and designes of all Nations that may any way annoy them. And this is not attained to, without much experience. Of which things, not onely the whole summe, [135] but every one of the particulars requires the age, and observation of a man in years, and of more than ordinary study. The wit required for Counsel, as I have said before (Chap. 8.) is Judgement. And the differences of men in that point come from different education, of some to one kind of study, or businesse, and of others to another. When for the doing of any thing, there be Infallible rules, (as in Engines, and Edifices, the rules of Geometry,) all the experience of the world cannot equall his Counsell, that has learnt, or found out the Rule. And when there is no such Rule, he that hath most experience in that particular kind of businesse, has therein the best Judgement, and is the best Counsellour.

Fourthly, to be able to give Counsell to a Common-wealth, in a businesse that hath reference to another Common-wealth, *It is necessary to be acquainted with the Intelligences, and Letters* that come from thence, *and with all the records of Treaties, and other transactions of State* between them; which none can doe, but such as the Representative shall think fit. By which we may see, that they who are not called to Counsell, can have no good Counsell in such cases to obtrude.

Fifthly, Supposing the number of Counsellors equall, a man is better Counselled by hearing them apart, then in an Assembly; and that for many causes. First, in hearing them apart, you have the advice of every man; but in an Assembly many of them deliver their advise with *I*, or *No*, or with their hands, or feet, not moved by their own sense, but by the eloquence of another, or for feare of displeasing some that have spoken, or the whole Assembly, by contradiction; or for feare of appearing duller in apprehension, than those that have applauded the contrary opinion. Secondly, in an Assembly of many, there cannot choose but be some whose interests are contrary to that of the Publique; and these their Interests make passionate, and Passion eloquent, and Eloquence drawes others into the same advice. For the Passions of men, which asunder are moderate, as the heat of one brand; in Assembly are like many brands, that enflame one another, (especially when they blow one another with Orations) to the setting of the Common-wealth on fire, under pretence of Counselling it. Thirdly, in hearing every man apart, one may examine (when there is need) the truth, or probability of his reasons, and of the grounds of the advise he gives, by frequent interruptions, and objections; which cannot be done in an Assembly, where (in every difficult question) a man is rather astonied, and dazled with the variety of discourse upon it, than informed of the course he ought to take. Besides, there cannot be an Assembly of many, called together for advice, wherein there be not some, that have the ambition to be thought eloquent, and also learned in the Politiques; and give not their advice with care of the businesse propounded, but of the applause of their motly orations, made of the divers colored threds, or shreds of Authors; which is an Impertinence at least, that takes away the time of serious Consultation, and in the secret way of Counselling apart, is easily a[136]-voided. Fourthly, in Deliberations that ought to be kept secret, (whereof there be many occasions in Publique Businesse,) the Counsells of many, and especially in Assemblies, are dangerous; And therefore great Assemblies are necessitated to commit such affaires to lesser numbers, and of such persons as are most versed, and in whose fidelity they have most confidence.

To conclude, who is there that so far approves the taking of Counsell from a great Assembly of Counsellours, that wisheth for, or would accept of their pains, when there is a question of marrying his Children, disposing of his Lands, governing his Household, or managing his private Estate, especially if there be amongst them such as wish not his prosperity? A man that doth his businesse by the help of many and prudent Counsellours, with every one consulting apart in his proper element, does it best, as he that useth able Seconds at Tennis play, placed in their proper stations. He does next best, that useth his own Judgement only; as he that has no Second at all. But he that is carried up and down to his businesse in a framed Counsell, which cannot move but by the plurality of consenting opinions, the execution whereof is commonly (out of envy, or interest) retarded by the part dissenting, does it worst of all, and like one that is carried to the ball, though by good Players, yet in a Wheele-barrough,[31] or other frame, heavy of it self, and retarded also by the inconcurrent judgements, and endeavours of them that drive it; and so much the more, as they be more that set their hands to it; and most of all, when there is one, or more amongst them, that desire to have him lose. And though it be true, that many eys see more then one; yet it is not to be understood of many Counsellours; but then only, when the finall Resolution is in one man. Otherwise, because many eyes see the same thing in divers lines, and are apt to look asquint towards their private benefit; they that desire not to misse their marke, though they look about with two eyes, yet they never ayme but with one; And therefore no great Popular Common-wealth was ever kept up; but either by a forraign Enemy that united them; or by the reputation of some one eminent Man amongst them; or by the secret Counsell of a few; or by the mutuall feare of equall factions; and not by the open Consultations of the Assembly. And as for very little Common-wealths, be they Popular, or Monarchicall, there is no humane wisdome can uphold them, longer then the Jealousy lasteth of their potent Neighbours.

CHAP. XXVI

Of Civill Lawes

Civill Law By Civill Lawes, I understand the Lawes, that men are
what therefore bound to observe, because they are Members, not of this, or that Common-wealth in particular, but of a Common-wealth. For the knowledge of particular Lawes [137] belongeth to them, that professe the study of the Lawes of their severall Countries; but the knowledge of Civill Law in generall, to any man. The antient Law of *Rome* was called their *Civil Law*, from the word *Civitas*, which signifies a Common-wealth: And those Countries, which having been under the Roman Empire, and governed by that Law, retaine still such part thereof as they think fit, call that part the Civill Law, to distinguish it from the rest of their own Civill Lawes. But that is not it I intend to speak of here; my designe being not to shew what is Law here, and there; but what is Law;

as *Plato*,[32] *Aristotle*, *Cicero*, and divers others have done, without taking upon them the profession of the study of the Law.

And first it is manifest, that Law in generall, is not Counsell, but Command; nor a Command of any man to any man; but only of him, whose Command is addressed to one formerly obliged to obey him. And as for Civill Law, it addeth only the name of the person Commanding, which is *Persona Civitatis*, the Person of the Common-wealth.

Which considered, I define Civill Law in this manner. CIVILL LAW, *Is to every Subject, those Rules, which the Common-wealth hath Commanded him, by Word, Writing, or other sufficient Sign of the Will, to make use of, for the Distinction of Right, and Wrong; that is to say, of what is contrary, and what is not contrary to the Rule.*

In which definition, there is nothing that is not at first sight evident. For every man seeth, that some Lawes are addressed to all the Subjects in generall; some to particular Provinces; some to particular Vocations; and some to particular Men; and are therefore Lawes, to every of those to whom the Command is directed; and to none else. As also, that Lawes are the Rules of Just, and Unjust; nothing being reputed Unjust, that is not contrary to some Law. Likewise, that none can make Lawes but the Common-wealth; because our Subjection is to the Common-wealth only: and that Commands, are to be signified by sufficient Signs; because a man knows not otherwise how to obey them. And therefore, whatsoever can from this definition by necessary consequence be deduced, ought to be acknowledged for truth. Now I deduce from it this that followeth.

1. The Legislator in all Common-wealths, is only the Soveraign, be he one Man, as in a Monarchy, or one Assembly of men, as in a Democracy, or Aristocracy. For the Legislator, is he that maketh the Law. And the Common-wealth only, præscribes, and commandeth *The Soveraign is Legislator:*

the observation of those rules, which we call Law: Therefore the Common-wealth is the Legislator. But the
Common-wealth is no Person, nor has capacity to
doe any thing, but by the Representative, (that is, the
Soveraign;) and therefore the Soveraign is the sole Legislator. For the same reason, none can abrogate a Law
made, but the Soveraign; because a Law is not abrogated, but by another Law, that forbiddeth it to be put
in execution.

And not   2. The Soveraign of a Common-wealth, be it an Assem-
Subject to   bly, or one Man, is not Subject to the Civill Lawes. For
Civill Law   having power to [138] make, and repeale Lawes, he may
when he pleaseth, free himselfe from that subjection, by
repealing those Lawes that trouble him, and making
of new; and consequently he was free before. For he is
free, that can be free when he will: Nor is it possible
for any person to be bound to himselfe; because he that
can bind, can release; and therefore he that is bound to
himselfe onely, is not bound.

Use, a Law   3. When long Use obtaineth the authority of a Law,
not by vertue it is not the Length of Time that maketh the Authority,
of Time,   but the Will of the Soveraign signified by his silence, (for
but of the   Silence is sometimes an argument of Consent;) and it is
Soveraigns   no longer Law, then the Soveraign shall be silent therein.
consent   And therefore if the Soveraign shall have a question of
Right grounded, not upon his present Will, but upon the
Lawes formerly made; the Length of Time shal bring no
prejudice to his Right; but the question shal be judged
by Equity. For many unjust Actions, and unjust Sentences, go uncontrolled a longer time, than any man can
remember. And our Lawyers account no Customes Law,
but such as are reasonable, and that evill Customes are
to be abolished: But the Judgement of what is reason-
The Law of   able, and of what is to be abolished, belongeth to him
Nature, and   that maketh the Law, which is the Soveraign Assembly,
the Civill   or Monarch.
Law contain   4. The Law of Nature, and the Civill Law, contain
each other   each other, and are of equall extent. For the Lawes of

Nature, which consist in Equity, Justice, Gratitude, and other morall Vertues on these depending, in the condition of meer Nature (as I have said before in the end of the 15th Chapter,) are not properly Lawes, but qualities that dispose men to peace, and to obedience. When a Common-wealth is once settled, then are they actually Lawes, and not before; as being then the commands of the Common-wealth; and therefore also Civill Lawes: For it is the Soveraign Power that obliges men to obey them. For in the differences of private men, to declare, what is Equity, what is Justice, and what is morall Vertue, and to make them binding, there is need of the Ordinances of Soveraign Power, and Punishments to be ordained for such as shall break them; which Ordinances are therefore part of the Civill Law. The Law of Nature therefore is a part of the Civill Law in all Common-wealths of the world. Reciprocally also, the Civill Law is a part of the Dictates of Nature. For Justice, that is to say, Performance of Covenant, and giving to every man his own, is a Dictate of the Law of Nature. But every subject in a Common-wealth, hath covenanted to obey the Civill Law, (either one with another, as when they assemble to make a common Representative, or with the Representative it selfe one by one, when subdued by the Sword they promise obedience, that they may receive life;) And therefore Obedience to the Civill Law is part also of the Law of Nature. Civill, and Naturall Law are not different kinds, but different parts of Law; whereof one part being written, is called Civill, the other unwritten, Naturall. But the Right of Nature, that is, the naturall Liberty of man, may by the Civill Law be abridged, and restrained: nay, the end of making Lawes, is no other, but such Restraint; without the which there cannot possibly be any Peace. And Law was brought into the world for nothing else, [139] but to limit the naturall liberty of particular men, in such manner, as they might not hurt, but assist one another, and joyn together against a common Enemy.

Provinciall   5. If the Soveraign of one Common-wealth, subdue a
Lawes are People that have lived under other written Lawes, and
not made by afterwards govern them by the same Lawes, by which
Custome, they were governed before; yet those Lawes are the
but by the Civill Lawes of the Victor, and not of the Vanquished
Soveraign Common-wealth. For the Legislator is he, not by whose
Power authority the Lawes were first made, but by whose
authority they now continue to be Lawes. And therefore
where there be divers Provinces, within the Dominion
of a Common-wealth, and in those Provinces diversity
of Lawes, which commonly are called the Customes of
each severall Province, we are not to understand that
such Customes have their force, onely from Length
of Time; but that they were antiently Lawes written,
or otherwise made known, for the Constitutions, and
Statutes of their Soveraigns; and are now Lawes, not by
vertue of the Præscription of time, but by the Constitutions of their present Soveraigns. But if an unwritten
Law, in all the Provinces of a Dominion, shall be generally observed, and no iniquity appear in the use thereof;
that Law can be no other but a Law of Nature, equally
obliging all man-kind.

Some foolish   6. Seeing then all Lawes, written, and unwritten,
opinions have their Authority, and force, from the Will of the
of Lawyers Common-wealth; that is to say, from the Will of the
concerning Representative; which in a Monarchy is the Monarch,
the making of and in other Common-wealths the Soveraign Assembly;
Lawes a man may wonder from whence proceed such opinions,
as are found in the Books of Lawyers of eminence in
severall Common-wealths, directly, or by consequence
making the Legislative Power depend on private men, or
subordinate Judges. As for example, *That the Common
Law, hath no Controuler but the Parlament*; which is
true onely where a Parlament has the Soveraign Power,
and cannot be assembled, nor dissolved, but by their
own discretion. For if there be a right in any else to
dissolve them, there is a right also to controule them,
and consequently to controule their controulings. And

if there be no such right, then the Controuler of Lawes is not *Parlamentum*, but *Rex in Parlamento*. And where a Parlament is Soveraign, if it should assemble never so many, or so wise men, from the Countries subject to them, for whatsoever cause; yet there is no man will believe, that such an Assembly hath thereby acquired to themselves a Legislative Power. *Item*, that the two arms of a Common-wealth, are *Force, and Justice; the first whereof is in the King; the other deposited in the hands of the Parlament*. As if a Common-wealth could consist, where the Force were in any hand, which Justice had not the Authority to command and govern.

7. That Law can never be against Reason, our Lawyers are agreed; and that not the Letter, (that is, every construction of it,) but that which is according to the Intention of the Legislator, is the Law. And it is true: but the doubt is, of whose Reason it is, that shall be received for Law. It is not meant of any private Reason; for [140] then there would be as much contradiction in the Lawes, as there is in the Schooles; nor yet, (as Sr. *Ed. Coke* makes it,) an *Artificiall perfection of Reason, gotten by long study, observation, and experience*, (as his was.) For it is possible long study may encrease, and confirm erroneous Sentences: and where men build on false grounds, the more they build, the greater is the ruine: and of those that study, and observe with equall time, and diligence, the reasons and resolutions are, and must remain discordant: and therefore it is not that *Juris prudentia*, or wisedome of subordinate Judges; but the Reason of this our Artificiall Man the Common-wealth, and his Command, that maketh Law: And the Common-wealth being in their Representative but one Person, there cannot easily arise any contradiction in the Lawes; and when there doth, the same Reason is able, by interpretation, or alteration, to take it away. In all Courts of Justice, the Soveraign (which is the Person of the Common-wealth,) is he that Judgeth: The subordinate Judge, ought to have regard to the

Sir Edw.
Coke, *upon*
Littleton,
Lib. 2. *Ch.* 6.
fol. 97.*b*

reason, which moved his Soveraign to make such Law, that his Sentence may be according thereunto; which then is his Soveraigns Sentence; otherwise it is his own, and an unjust one.

Law made,
if not also
made known,
is no Law

8. From this, that the Law is a Command, and a Command consisteth in declaration, or manifestation of the will of him that commandeth, by voyce, writing, or some other sufficient argument of the same, we may understand, that the Command of the Common-wealth, is Law onely to those, that have means to take notice of it. Over naturall fooles, children, or mad-men there is no Law, no more than over brute beasts; nor are they capable of the title of just, or unjust; because they had never power to make any covenant, or to understand the consequences thereof; and consequently never took upon them to authorise the actions of any Soveraign, as they must do that make to themselves a Common-wealth. And as those from whom Nature, or Accident hath taken away the notice of all Lawes in generall; so also every man, from whom any accident, not proceeding from his own default, hath taken away the means to take notice of any particular Law, is excused, if he observe it not; And to speak properly, that Law is no Law to him. It is therefore necessary, to consider in this place, what arguments, and signes be sufficient for the knowledge of what is the Law; that is to say, what is the will of the Soveraign, as well in Monarchies, as in other formes of government.

Unwritten
Lawes are
all of them
Lawes of
Nature

And first, if it be a Law that obliges all the Subjects without exception, and is not written, nor otherwise published in such places as they may take notice thereof, it is a Law of Nature. For whatsoever men are to take knowledge of for Law, not upon other mens words, but every one from his own reason, must be such as is agreeable to the reason of all men; which no Law can be, but the Law of Nature. The Lawes of Nature therefore need not any publishing, nor Proclamation; as being contained in this one Sentence, approved by all the world,

*Do not that to another, which thou thinkest unreason-
able to be done by another to thy selfe.*

[141] Secondly, if it be a Law that obliges only some
condition of men, or one particular man, and be not
written, nor published by word, then also it is a Law
of Nature; and known by the same arguments, and
signs, that distinguish those in such a condition, from
other Subjects. For whatsoever Law is not written, or
some way published by him that makes it Law, can be
known no way, but by the reason of him that is to obey
it; and is therefore also a Law not only Civill, but Naturall. For Example, if the Soveraign employ a Publique
Minister, without written Instructions what to doe; he
is obliged to take for Instructions the Dictates of Reason; As if he make a Judge, The Judge is to take notice,
that his Sentence ought to be according to the reason
of his Soveraign, which being alwaies understood to be
Equity, he is bound to it by the Law of Nature: Or if
an Ambassador, he is (in all things not conteined in his
written Instructions) to take for Instruction that which
Reason dictates to be most conducing to his Soveraigns
interest; and so of all other Ministers of the Soveraignty,
publique and private. All which Instructions of naturall
Reason may be comprehended under one name of *Fidelity*; which is a branch of naturall Justice.

The Law of Nature excepted, it belongeth to the
essence of all other Lawes, to be made known, to every
man that shall be obliged to obey them, either by word,
or writing, or some other act, known to proceed from
the Soveraign Authority. For the will of another, cannot be understood, but by his own word, or act, or by
conjecture taken from his scope and purpose; which in
the person of the Common-wealth, is to be supposed
alwaies consonant to Equity and Reason. And in antient
time, before letters were in common use, the Lawes were
many times put into verse; that the rude people taking
pleasure in singing, or reciting them, might the more
easily reteine them in memory. And for the same reason

Solomon adviseth a man, to bind the ten Commande-
Prov. 7. 3 ments * upon his ten fingers. And for the Law which
Moses gave to the people of *Israel* at the renewing of the
Deut. 11. 19 Covenant, * he biddeth them to teach it their Children,
by discoursing of it both at home, and upon the way;
at going to bed, and at rising from bed; and to write
Deut. 31. 12 it upon the posts, and dores of their houses; and * to
assemble the people, man, woman, and child, to heare
it read.

Nothing is   Nor is it enough the Law be written, and published;
Law where but also that there be manifest signs, that it proceedeth
the Legisla- from the will of the Soveraign. For private men, when
tor cannot be they have, or think they have force enough to secure
known   their unjust designes, and convoy them safely to their
ambitious ends, may publish for Lawes what they
please, without, or against the Legislative Authority.
There is therefore requisite, not only a Declaration of
the Law, but also sufficient signes of the Author, and
Authority. The Author, or Legislator is supposed in
every Common-wealth to be evident, because he is the
Soveraign, who having been Constituted by the consent
of every one, is supposed by every one to be sufficiently
known. And though the ignorance, and security of men
be such, for the most part, as that when [142] the memory of the first Constitution of their Common-wealth is
worn out, they doe not consider, by whose power they
use to be defended against their enemies, and to have
their industry protected, and to be righted when injury
is done them; yet because no man that considers, can
make question of it, no excuse can be derived from the
ignorance of where the Soveraignty is placed. And it
is a Dictate of Naturall Reason, and consequently an
evident Law of Nature, that no man ought to weaken
that power, the protection whereof he hath himself
demanded, or wittingly received against others. Therefore of who is Soveraign, no man, but by his own fault,
(whatsoever evill men suggest,) can make any doubt.
The difficulty consisteth in the evidence of the Authority

derived from him; The removing whereof, dependeth
on the knowledge of the publique Registers, publique
Counsels, publique Ministers, and publique Seales; by
which all Lawes are sufficiently verified; Verifyed, I say, *Difference*
not Authorised: for the Verification, is but the Testi- *between*
mony and Record; not the Authority of the Law; which *Verifying and*
consisteth in the Command of the Soveraign only. *Authorising*

If therefore a man have a question of Injury, depend- *The Law*
ing on the Law of Nature; that is to say, on common *Verifyed by*
Equity; the Sentence of the Judge, that by Commis- *the subordin-*
sion hath Authority to take cognisance of such causes, *ate Judge*
is a sufficient Verification of the Law of Nature in that
individuall case. For though the advice of one that professeth the study of the Law, be usefull for the avoyding
of contention; yet it is but advice: tis the Judge must tell
men what is Law, upon the hearing of the Controversy.

But when the question is of injury, or crime, upon a *By the*
written Law; every man by recourse to the Registers, *Publique*
by himself, or others, may (if he will) be sufficiently *Registers*
enformed, before he doe such injury, or commit the
crime, whither it be an injury, or not: Nay he ought to
doe so: For when a man doubts whether the act he goeth
about, be just, or injust; and may informe himself, if
he will; the doing is unlawfull. In like manner, he that
supposeth himself injured, in a case determined by the
written Law, which he may by himself, or others see
and consider; if he complaine before he consults with
the Law, he does unjustly, and bewrayeth a disposition *By Letters*
rather to vex other men, than to demand his own right. *Patent, and*

If the question be of Obedience to a publique Offi- *Publique*
cer; To have seen his Commission, with the Publique *Seale*
Seale, and heard it read; or to have had the means to be
informed of it, if a man would, is a sufficient Verification *The Inter-*
of his Authority. For every man is obliged to doe his best *pretation*
endeavour, to informe himself of all written Lawes, that *of the Law*
may concerne his own future actions. *dependeth on*

The Legislator known; and the Lawes, either by writ- *the Soveraign*
ing, or by the light of Nature, sufficiently published; *Power*

there wanteth yet another very materiall circumstance to make them obligatory. For it is not the Letter, but the Intendment, or Meaning; that is to say, the authentique Interpretation of the Law (which is the sense of the Legislator,) in which the nature of the Law consisteth; And therefore [143] the Interpretation of all Lawes dependeth on the Authority Soveraign; and the Interpreters can be none but those, which the Soveraign, (to whom only the Subject oweth obedience) shall appoint. For else, by the craft of an Interpreter, the Law may be made to beare a sense, contrary to that of the Soveraign; by which means the Interpreter becomes the Legislator.

All Lawes need Interpretation   All Laws, written, and unwritten, have need of Interpretation. The unwritten Law of Nature, though it be easy to such, as without partiality, and passion, make use of their naturall reason, and therefore leaves the violaters thereof without excuse; yet considering there be very few, perhaps none, that in some cases are not blinded by self love, or some other passion, it is now become of all Laws the most obscure; and has consequently the greatest need of able Interpreters. The written Laws, if they be short, are easily mis-interpreted, from the divers significations of a word, or two: if long, they be more obscure by the diverse significations of many words: in so much as no written Law, delivered in few, or many words, can be well understood, without a perfect understanding of the finall causes, for which the Law was made; the knowledge of which finall causes is in the Legislator. To him therefore there can not be any knot in the Law, insoluble; either by finding out the ends, to undoe it by; or else by making what ends he will, (as *Alexander* did with his sword in the Gordian knot,)[33] by the Legislative power; which no other Interpreter can doe.

The Authenticall Interpretation of Law is not that of writers   The Intepretation of the Lawes of Nature, in a Common-wealth, dependeth not on the books of Morall Philosophy. The Authority of writers, without the Authority of the Common-wealth, maketh not their opinions Law, be they never so true. That which I have written in this Treatise, concerning the Morall Vertues, and of their necessity, for the procuring, and maintaining peace, though it bee evident Truth, is not therefore presently Law; but because in all Common-wealths in the world, it is part of the Civill Law: For though it be naturally reasonable; yet it is by the Soveraigne Power that it is Law: Otherwise, it were a great errour, to call the Lawes of Nature unwritten Law; whereof wee see so many volumes published, and in them so many contradictions of one another, and of themselves.

The Interpretation of the Law of Nature, is the Sentence of the Judge constituted by the Soveraign Authority, to heare and determine such controversies, as depend thereon; and consisteth in the application of the Law to the present case. For in the act of Judicature, the Judge doth no more but consider, whither the demand of the party, be consonant to naturall reason, and Equity; and the Sentence he giveth, is therefore the Interpretation of the Law of Nature; which Interpretation is Authentique; not because it is his private Sentence; but because he giveth it by Authority of the Soveraign, whereby it becomes the Soveraigns Sentence; which is Law for that time, to the parties pleading. *The Interpreter of the Law is the Judge giving sentence vivâ voce in every particular case*

[144] But because there is no Judge Subordinate, nor Soveraign, but may erre in a Judgement of Equity; if afterward in another like case he find it more consonant to Equity to give a contrary Sentence, he is obliged to doe it. No mans error becomes his own Law; nor obliges him to persist in it. Neither (for the same reason) becomes it a Law to other Judges, though sworn to follow it. For though a wrong Sentence given by authority of the Soveraign, if he know and allow it, in such Lawes as are mutable, be a constitution of a new Law, in cases, in which every little circumstance is the same; yet in Lawes immutable, such as are the Lawes of Nature, they are no Lawes to the same, or other Judges, in the like cases for ever after. Princes succeed one another; and one Judge passeth, another commeth; nay, Heaven and *The Sentence of a Judge, does not bind him, or another Judge to give like Sentence in like Cases ever after*

Earth shall passe; but not one title of the Law of Nature shall passe; for it is the Eternall Law of God.[34] Therefore all the Sentences of precedent Judges that have ever been, cannot all together make a Law contrary to naturall Equity: Nor any Examples of former Judges, can warrant an unreasonable Sentence, or discharge the present Judge of the trouble of studying what is Equity (in the case he is to Judge,) from the principles of his own naturall reason. For example sake, 'Tis against the Law of Nature, *To punish the Innocent*; and Innocent is he that acquitteth himselfe Judicially, and is acknowledged for Innocent by the Judge. Put the case now, that a man is accused of a capitall crime, and seeing the power and malice of some enemy, and the frequent corruption and partiality of Judges, runneth away for feare of the event, and afterwards is taken, and brought to a legall triall, and maketh it sufficiently appear, he was not guilty of the crime, and being thereof acquitted, is neverthelesse condemned to lose his goods; this is a manifest condemnation of the Innocent. I say therefore, that there is no place in the world, where this can be an interpretation of a Law of Nature, or be made a Law by the Sentences of precedent Judges, that had done the same. For he that judged it first, judged unjustly; and no Injustice can be a pattern of Judgement to succeeding Judges. A written Law may forbid innocent men to fly, and they may be punished for flying: But that flying for feare of injury, should be taken for presumption of guilt, after a man is already absolved of the crime Judicially, is contrary to the nature of a Presumption, which hath no place after Judgement given. Yet this is set down by a great Lawyer for the common Law of *England*.[35] *If a man* (saith he) *that is Innocent, be accused of Felony, and for feare flyeth for the same; albeit he judicially acquitteth himselfe of the Felony; yet if it be found that he fled for the Felony, he shall notwithstanding his Innocency, Forfeit all his goods, chattells, debts, and duties. For as to the Forfeiture of them, the Law will admit no proofe against the Presumption in Law, grounded upon his flight.* Here you see, *An Innocent man, Judicially acquitted, notwithstanding his Innocency,* (when no written Law forbad him to fly) after his acquitall, *upon a Presumption in Law,* condemned to lose all the goods he hath. If the Law ground upon his flight a Presumption of the fact, (which was Capitall,) the Sen[145]tence ought to have been Capitall: if the Presumption were not of the Fact, for what then ought he to lose his goods? This therefore is no Law of *England*; nor is the condemnation grounded upon a Presumption of Law, but upon the Presumption of the Judges. It is also against Law, to say that no Proofe shall be admitted against a Presumption of Law. For all Judges, Soveraign and subordinate, if they refuse to heare Proofe, refuse to do Justice: for though the Sentence be Just, yet the Judges that condemn without hearing the Proofes offered, are Unjust Judges; and their Presumption is but Prejudice; which no man ought to bring with him to the Seat of Justice, whatsoever precedent judgements, or examples he shall pretend to follow. There be other things of this nature, wherein mens Judgements have been perverted, by trusting to Precedents: but this is enough to shew, that though the Sentence of the Judge, be a Law to the party pleading, yet it is no Law to any Judge, that shall succeed him in that Office.

In like manner, when question is of the Meaning of written Lawes, he is not the Interpreter of them, that writeth a Commentary upon them. For Commentaries are commonly more subject to cavill, than the Text; and therefore need other Commentaries; and so there will be no end of such Interpretation. And therefore unlesse there be an Interpreter authorised by the Soveraign, from which the subordinate Judges are not to recede, the Interpreter can be no other than the ordinary Judges, in the same manner, as they are in cases of the unwritten Law; and their Sentences are to be taken by them that plead, for Lawes in that particular case; but not to bind other Judges, in like cases to give like judgements. For a Judge may erre in the Interpretation even of written Lawes; but no errour of a subordinate Judge, can change the Law, which is the generall Sentence of the Soveraigne.

The difference between the Letter and Sentence of the Law

In written Lawes, men use to make a difference between the Letter, and the Sentence of the Law: And when by the Letter, is meant whatsoever can be gathered from the bare words, 'tis well distinguished. For the significations of almost all words, are either in themselves, or in the metaphoricall use of them, ambiguous; and may be drawn in argument, to make many senses; but there is onely one sense of the Law. But if by the Letter, be meant the literall sense, then the Letter, and the Sentence or intention of the Law, is all one. For the literall sense is that, which the Legislator intended, should by the letter of the Law be signified. Now the Intention of the Legislator is alwayes supposed to be Equity: For it were a great contumely for a Judge to think otherwise of the Soveraigne. He ought therefore, if the Word of the Law doe not fully authorise a reasonable Sentence, to supply it with the Law of Nature; or if the case be difficult, to respit Judgement till he have received more ample authority. For Example, a written Law ordaineth, that he which is thrust out of his house by force, shall be restored by force: It happens that a man by negligence leaves his house empty, and returning is kept out by force, in which case there is no speciall Law ordained. It is evi[146]dent, that this case is contained in the same Law: for else there is no remedy for him at all; which is to be supposed against the Intention of the Legislator. Again, the word of the Law, commandeth to Judge according to the Evidence: A man is accused falsly of a fact, which the Judge saw himself done by another; and not by him that is accused. In this case neither shall the Letter of the Law be followed to the condemnation of the Innocent, nor shall the Judge give Sentence against the evidence of the Witnesses; because the Letter of the

Law is to the contrary: but procure of the Soveraign that another be made Judge, and himself Witnesse. So that the incommodity that follows the bare words of a written Law, may lead him to the Intention of the Law, whereby to interpret the same the better; though no Incommodity can warrant a Sentence against the Law. For every Judge of Right, and Wrong, is not Judge of what is Commodious, or Incommodious to the Common-wealth.

The abilities required in a good Interpreter of the Law, that is to say, in a good Judge, are not the same with those of an Advocate; namely the study of the Lawes. For a Judge, as he ought to take notice of the Fact, from none but the Witnesses; so also he ought to take notice of the Law, from nothing but the Statutes, and Constitutions of the Soveraign, alledged in the pleading, or declared to him by some that have authority from the Soveraign Power to declare them; and need not take care before-hand, what hee shall Judge; for it shall bee given him what hee shall say concerning the Fact, by Witnesses; and what hee shall say in point of Law, from those that shall in their pleadings shew it, and by authority interpret it upon the place. The Lords of Parlament in *England* were Judges, and most difficult causes have been heard and determined by them; yet few of them were much versed in the study of the Lawes, and fewer had made profession of them: and though they consulted with Lawyers, that were appointed to be present there for that purpose; yet they alone had the authority of giving Sentence. In like manner, in the ordinary trialls of Right, Twelve men of the common People, are the Judges, and give Sentence, not onely of the Fact, but of the Right; and pronounce simply for the Complaynant, or for the Defendant; that is to say, are Judges not onely of the Fact, but also of the Right: and in a question of crime, not onely determine whether done, or not done; but also whether it be *Murder*, *Homicide*, *Felony*, *Assault*, and the like, which are determinations of Law: but because they are not supposed to know the Law of

The abilities required in a Judge

themselves, there is one that hath Authority to enforme them of it, in the particular case they are to Judge of. But yet if they judge not according to that he tells them, they are not subject thereby to any penalty; unlesse it be made appear, they did it against their consciences, or had been corrupted by reward.

The things that make a good Judge, or good Interpreter of the Lawes, are, first, *A right understanding* of that principall Law of Nature called *Equity*; which depending not on the reading of other mens Writings, but on the goodnesse of a mans own naturall [147] Reason, and Meditation, is presumed to be in those most, that have had most leisure, and had the most inclination to meditate thereon. Secondly, *Contempt of unnecessary Riches*, and Preferments. Thirdly, *To be able in judgement to devest himselfe of all feare, anger, hatred, love*, and *compassion*. Fourthly, and lastly, *Patience to heare; diligent attention in hearing; and memory to retain, digest and apply what he hath heard.*

Divisions of Law   The difference and division of the Lawes, has been made in divers manners, according to the different methods, of those men that have written of them. For it is a thing that dependeth not on Nature, but on the scope of the Writer; and is subservient to every mans proper method. In the Institutions of *Justinian*, we find seven sorts of Civill Lawes.[36] 1. The *Edicts, Constitutions*, and *Epistles of the Prince*, that is, of the Emperour; because the whole power of the people was in him. Like these, are the Proclamations of the Kings of *England*.

2. *The Decrees of the whole people of Rome* (comprehending the Senate,) when they were put to the Question by the *Senate*. These were Lawes, at first, by the vertue of the Soveraign Power residing in the people; and such of them as by the Emperours were not abrogated, remained Lawes by the Authority Imperiall. For all Lawes that bind, are understood to be Lawes by his authority that has power to repeale them. Somewhat like to these Lawes, are the Acts of Parliament in *England*.

3. *The Decrees of the Common people* (excluding the Senate,) when they were put to the question by the *Tribune* of the people. For such of them as were not abrogated by the Emperours, remained Lawes by the Authority Imperiall. Like to these, were the Orders of the House of Commons in *England*.

4. *Senatûs consulta*, the *Orders of the Senate*; because when the people of *Rome* grew so numerous, as it was inconvenient to assemble them; it was thought fit by the Emperour, that men should Consult the Senate, in stead of the people: And these have some resemblance with the Acts of Counsell.

5. *The Edicts of Prætors*, and (in some Cases) of the *Ædiles*: such as are the Chiefe Justices in the Courts of *England*.

6. *Responsa Prudentum*; which were the Sentences, and Opinions of those Lawyers, to whom the Emperour gave Authority to interpret the Law, and to give answer to such as in matter of Law demanded their advice; which Answers, the Judges in giving Judgement were obliged by the Constitutions of the Emperour to observe: And should be like the Reports of Cases Judged, if other Judges be by the Law of *England* bound to observe them. For the Judges of the Common Law of *England*, are not properly Judges, but *Juris Consulti*; of whom the Judges, who are either the Lords, or Twelve men of the Country, are in point of Law to ask advice.

7. Also, *Unwritten Customes*, (which in their own nature are an imitation of Law,) by the tacite consent of the Emperour, in case they be not contrary to the Law of Nature, are very Lawes.

Another division of Lawes, is into *Naturall* and *Positive*. *Natu*[148]*rall* are those which have been Lawes from all Eternity; and are called not onely *Naturall*, but also *Morall* Lawes; consisting in the Morall Vertues, as Justice, Equity, and all habits of the mind that conduce to Peace, and Charity; of which I have already spoken in the fourteenth and fifteenth Chapters.

Positive, are those which have not been from Eternity; but have been made Lawes by the Will of those that have had the Soveraign Power over others; and are either written, or made known to men, by some other argument of the Will of their Legislator.

Again, of Positive Lawes some are *Humane*, some *Divine*: And of Humane positive lawes, some are *Distributive*, some *Penal*. *Distributive* are those that determine the Rights of the Subjects, declaring to every man what it is, by which he acquireth and holdeth a propriety in lands, or goods, and a right or liberty of action: and these speak to all the Subjects. *Penal* are those, which declare, what Penalty shall be inflicted on those that violate the Law; and speak to the Ministers and Officers ordained for execution. For though every one ought to be informed of the Punishments ordained beforehand for their transgression; neverthelesse the Command is not addressed to the Delinquent, (who cannot be supposed will faithfully punish himselfe,) but to publique Ministers appointed to see the Penalty executed. And these Penal Lawes are for the most part written together with the Lawes Distributive; and are sometimes called Judgements. For all Lawes are generall Judgements, or Sentences of the Legislator; as also every particular Judgement, is a Law to him, whose case is Judged.

Divine Positive Lawes (for Naturall Lawes being Eternall, and Universall, are all Divine,) are those, which being the Commandements of God, (not from all Eternity, nor universally addressed to all men, but onely to a certain people, or to certain persons,) are declared for such, by those whom God hath authorised to declare them. But this Authority of man to declare what be these Positive Lawes of God, how can it be known? God may command a man by a supernaturall way, to deliver Lawes to other men. But because it is of the essence of Law, that he who is to be obliged, be assured of the Authority of him that declareth it, which we cannot naturally take notice to be from God, *How can a man without supernaturall Revelation be assured of the Revelation received by the declarer?* and *how can he be bound to obey them?* For the first question, how a man can be assured of the Revelation of another, without a Revelation particularly to himselfe, it is evidently impossible: For though a man may be induced to believe such Revelation, from the Miracles they see him doe, or from seeing the Extraordinary sanctity of his life, or from seeing the Extraordinary wisedome, or Extraordinary felicity of his Actions, all which are marks of God's extraordinary favour; yet they are not assured evidences of speciall Revelation. Miracles are Marvellous workes: but that which is marvellous to one, may not be so to another. Sanctity may be feigned; and the visible felicities of this world, are most often the work of God by Naturall, [149] and ordinary causes. And therefore no man can infallibly know by naturall reason, that another has had a supernaturall revelation of Gods will; but only a beliefe; every one (as the signs thereof shall appear greater, or lesser) a firmer, or a weaker belief.

But for the second, how he can be bound to obey them; it is not so hard. For if the Law declared, be not against the Law of Nature (which is undoubtedly Gods Law) and he undertake to obey it, he is bound by his own act; bound I say to obey it, but not bound to believe it: for mens beliefe, and interiour cogitations, are not subject to the commands, but only to the operation of God, ordinary, or extraordinary. Faith of Supernaturall Law, is not a fulfilling, but only an assenting to the same; and not a duty that we exhibit to God, but a gift which God freely giveth to whom he pleaseth; as also Unbelief is not a breach of any of his Lawes; but a rejection of them all, except the Laws Naturall. But this that I say, will be made yet cleerer, by the Examples, and Testimonies concerning this point in holy Scripture. The Covenant God made with *Abraham* (in a Supernaturall manner) was thus, *This is the Covenant which thou* Gen. 17.10

shalt observe between Me and Thee and thy Seed after thee. Abrahams Seed had not this revelation, nor were yet in being; yet they are a party to the Covenant, and bound to obey what *Abraham* should declare to them for Gods Law; which they could not be, but in vertue of the obedience they owed to their Parents; who (if they be Subject to no other earthly power, as here in the case of *Abraham*) have Soveraign power over their children, and servants. Againe, where God saith to *Abraham*,[37] *In thee shall all Nations of the earth be blessed: For I know thou wilt command thy children, and thy house after thee to keep the way of the Lord, and to observe Right-eousnesse and Judgement,* it is manifest, the obedience of his Family, who had no Revelation, depended on their former obligation to obey their Soveraign. At Mount *Sinai Moses* only went up to God;[38] the people were for-bidden to approach on paine of death; yet were they bound to obey all that *Moses* declared to them for Gods Law. Upon what ground, but on this submission of their own, *Speak thou to us, and we will heare thee; but let not God speak to us, lest we dye?* By which two places it sufficiently appeareth, that in a Common-wealth, a subject that has no certain and assured Revelation par-ticularly to himself concerning the Will of God, is to obey for such, the Command of the Common-wealth: for if men were at liberty, to take for Gods Comman-dements, their own dreams, and fancies, or the dreams and fancies of private men; scarce two men would agree upon what is Gods Commandement; and yet in respect of them, every man would despise the Commandements of the Common-wealth. I conclude therefore, that in all things not contrary to the Morall Law, (that is to say, to the Law of Nature,) all Subjects are bound to obey that for divine Law, which is declared to be so, by the Lawes of the Common-wealth. Which also is evident to any mans reason; for whatsoever is not against the Law of Nature, may be made Law in the name of them [150] that have the Soveraign power; and there is no reason

men should be the lesse obliged by it, when tis propounded in the name of God. Besides, there is no place
in the world where men are permitted to pretend other
Commandements of God, than are declared for such
by the Common-wealth. Christian States punish those
that revolt from Christian Religion, and all other States,
those that set up any Religion by them forbidden. For
in whatsoever is not regulated by the Common-wealth,
tis Equity (which is the Law of Nature, and therefore an
eternall Law of God) that every man equally enjoy his
liberty.

There is also another distinction of Laws, into *Funda-* *Another*
mentall, and *not Fundamentall*: but I could never see in *division of*
any Author, what a Fundamentall Law signifieth. Never- *Lawes*
thelesse one may very reasonably distinguish Laws in
that manner.

For a Fundamentall Law in every Common-wealth *A Funda-*
is that, which being taken away, the Common-wealth *mentall Law*
faileth, and is utterly dissolved; as a building whose *what*
Foundation is destroyed. And therefore a Fundamentall Law is that, by which Subjects are bound to uphold
whatsoever power is given to the Soveraign, whether a
Monarch, or a Soveraign Assembly, without which the
Common-wealth cannot stand; such as is the power of
War and Peace, of Judicature, of Election of Officers,
and of doing whatsoever he shall think necessary for
the Publique good. Not Fundamentall is that the abro-
gating whereof, draweth not with it the dissolution of
the Common-Wealth; such as are the Lawes concerning
Controversies between subject and subject. Thus much
of the Division of Lawes.

I find the words *Lex Civilis*, and *Jus Civile*, that is to *Difference*
say, *Law* and *Right Civil*, promiscuously used for the *between Law*
same thing, even in the most learned Authors; which *and Right*
neverthelesse ought not to be so. For *Right* is *Liberty*,
namely that Liberty which the Civil Law leaves us: But
Civill Law is an *Obligation*; and takes from us the Liberty which the Law of Nature gave us. Nature gave

a Right to every man to secure himselfe by his own strength, and to invade a suspected neighbour, by way of prevention; but the Civill Law takes away that Liberty, in all cases where the protection of the Law may be safely stayd for. Insomuch as *Lex* and *Jus*, are as different as *Obligation* and *Liberty*.

And between a Law and a Charter

Likewise *Lawes* and *Charters* are taken promiscuously for the same thing. Yet Charters are Donations of the Soveraign; and not Lawes, but exemptions from the Law. The phrase of a Law is *Jubeo, Injungo, I Command,* and *Enjoyn*: the phrase of a Charter is *Dedi, Concessi, I have Given, I have Granted*: but what is given or granted, to a man, is not forced upon him, by a Law. A Law may be made to bind All the Subjects of a Common-wealth: a Liberty, or Charter is only to One man, or some One part of the people. For to say all the people of a Common-wealth, have Liberty in any case whatsoever; is to say, that in such case, there hath been no Law made; or else having been made, is now abrogated. [151]

CHAP. XXVII

Of CRIMES, EXCUSES, *and* EXTENUATIONS

Sinne what

A *Sinne*, is not onely a Transgression of a Law, but also any Contempt of the Legislator. For such Contempt, is a breach of all his Lawes at once. And therefore may consist, not onely in the *Commission* of a Fact, or in the Speaking of Words by the Lawes forbidden, or in the *Omission* of what the Law commandeth, but also in the *Intention*, or purpose to transgresse. For the purpose to breake the Law, is some degree of Contempt of him, to whom it belongeth to see it executed. To be delighted in the Imagination onely, of being possessed of another mans goods, servants, or wife, without any intention to

take them from him by force, or fraud, is no breach of
the Law, that sayth, *Thou shalt not covet*:[39] nor is the
pleasure a man may have in imagining, or dreaming of
the death of him, from whose life he expecteth nothing
but dammage, and displeasure, a Sinne; but the resolving to put some Act in execution, that tendeth thereto.
For to be pleased in the fiction of that, which would
please a man if it were reall, is a Passion so adhærent to
the Nature both of a man, and every other living creature, as to make it a Sinne, were to make Sinne of being
a man. The consideration of this, has made me think
them too severe, both to themselves, and others, that
maintain, that the First motions of the mind, (though
checked with the fear of God) be Sinnes. But I confesse
it is safer to erre on that hand, than on the other.

A CRIME, is a sinne, consisting in the Committing (by **A Crime**
Deed, or Word) of that which the Law forbiddeth, or **what**
the Omission of what it hath commanded. So that every
Crime is a sinne; but not every sinne a Crime. To intend
to steale, or kill, is a sinne, though it never appeare in
Word, or Fact: for God that seeth the thoughts of man,
can lay it to his charge: but till it appear by something
done, or said, by which the intention may be argued by
a humane Judge, it hath not the name of Crime: which
distinction the Greeks observed, in the word ἁμάρτημα,
and ἔγκλημα, or αἰτία; wherof the former, (which is
translated *Sinne*,) signifieth any swarving from the Law
whatsoever; but the two later, (which are translated
Crime,) signifie that sinne onely, whereof one man may
accuse another. But of Intentions, which never appear
by any outward act, there is no place for humane accusation. In like manner the Latines by *Peccatum*, which is
Sinne, signifie all manner of deviation from the Law; but
by *Crimen*, (which word they derive from *Cerno*, which
signifies to perceive,) they mean onely such sinnes, as **Where no**
may be made appear before a Judge; and therfore are **Civill Law**
not meer Intentions. **is, there is**

From this relation of Sinne to the Law, and of Crime **no Crime** to the Civill Law, may be inferred, First, that where Law ceaseth, Sinne cea[152]seth. But because the Law of Nature is eternall, Violation of Covenants, Ingratitude, Arrogance, and all Facts contrary to any Morall vertue, can never cease to be Sinne. Secondly, that the Civill Law ceasing, Crimes cease: for there being no other Law remaining, but that of Nature, there is no place for Accusation; every man being his own Judge, and accused onely by his own Conscience, and cleared by the Uprightnesse of his own Intention. When therefore his Intention is Right, his fact is no Sinne: if otherwise, his fact is Sinne; but not Crime. Thirdly, That when the Soveraign Power ceaseth, Crime also ceaseth: for where there is no such Power, there is no protection to be had from the Law; and therefore every one may protect himself by his own power: for no man in the Institution of Soveraign Power can be supposed to give away the Right of preserving his own body; for the safety whereof all Soveraignty was ordained. But this is to be understood onely of those, that have not themselves contributed to the taking away of the Power that protected them: for that was a Crime from the beginning.

Ignorance of the Law of Nature excuseth no man The source of every Crime, is some defect of the Understanding; or some errour in Reasoning; or some sudden force of the Passions. Defect in the Understanding, is *Ignorance*; in Reasoning, *Erroneous Opinion*. Again, Ignorance is of three sorts; of the *Law*, and of the *Soveraign*, and of the *Penalty*. Ignorance of the Law of Nature Excuseth no man; because every man that hath attained to the use of Reason, is supposed to know, he ought not to do to another, what he would not have done to himselfe. Therefore into what place soever a man shall come, if he do any thing contrary to that Law, it is a Crime. If a man come from the *Indies* hither, and perswade men here to receive a new Religion, or teach them any thing that tendeth to disobedience of the Lawes of this Country, though he be never so well perswaded of the truth of what he teacheth, he commits a Crime, and may be justly punished for the same, not onely because his doctrine is false, but also because he does that which he would not approve in another, namely, that comming from hence, he should endeavour to alter the Religion there. But ignorance of the Civill Law, shall Excuse a man in a strange Country, till it be declared to him; because, till then no Civill Law is binding.

In the like manner, if the Civill Law of a mans own Country, be not so sufficiently declared, as he may know it if he will; nor the Action against the Law of Nature; the Ignorance is a good Excuse: In other cases Ignorance of the Civill Law, Excuseth not. *Ignorance of the Civill Law excuseth sometimes*

Ignorance of the Soveraign Power, in the place of a mans ordinary residence, Excuseth him not; because he ought to take notice of the Power, by which he hath been protected there. *Ignorance of the Soveraign excuseth not*

Ignorance of the Penalty, where the Law is declared, Excuseth no man: For in breaking the Law, which without a fear of penalty to follow, were not a Law, but vain words, he undergoeth the penalty, though he know not what it is; because, whosoever voluntarily doth any action, accepteth all the known consequence of it; but Punishment is a known consequence of the violation of the Lawes, in every [153] Common-wealth; which punishment, if it be determined already by the Law, he is subject to that; if not, then is he subject to Arbitrary punishment. For it is reason, that he which does Injury, without other limitation than that of his own Will, should suffer punishment without other limitation, than that of his Will whose Law is thereby violated. *Ignorance of the Penalty excuseth not*

But when a penalty, is either annexed to the Crime in the Law it selfe, or hath been usually inflicted in the like cases; there the Delinquent is Excused from a greater penalty. For the punishment foreknown, if not great enough to deterre men from the action, is an invitement to it: because when men compare the benefit of their Injustice, with the harm of their punishment, by *Punishments declared before the Fact, excuse from greater punishments after it* necessity of Nature they choose that which appeareth best for themselves: and therefore when they are punished more than the Law had formerly determined, or more than others were punished for the same Crime; it is the Law that tempted, and deceiveth them.

Nothing can No Law, made after a Fact done, can make it a Crime: *be made a* because if the Fact be against the Law of Nature, the *Crime by a* Law was before the Fact; and a Positive Law cannot be *Law made* taken notice of, before it be made; and therefore can- *after the Fact* not be Obligatory. But when the Law that forbiddeth a Fact, is made before the Fact be done; yet he that doth the Fact, is lyable to the Penalty ordained after, in case no lesser Penalty were made known before, neither by Writing, nor by Example, for the reason immediatly before alledged.

False From defect in Reasoning, (that is to say, from Errour,) *Principles of* men are prone to violate the Lawes, three wayes. First, *Right and* by Presumption of false Principles: as when men from *Wrong causes* having observed how in all places, and in all ages, unjust *of Crime* Actions have been authorised, by the force, and victor- ies of those who have committed them; and that potent men, breaking through the Cob-web Lawes of their Country, the weaker sort, and those that have failed in their Enterprises, have been esteemed the onely Crim- inals; have thereupon taken for Principles, and grounds of their Reasoning, *That Justice is but a vain word: That whatsoever a man can get by his own Industry, and hazard, is his own: That the Practice of all Nations can- not be unjust: That Examples of former times are good Arguments of doing the like again*; and many more of that kind: Which being granted, no Act in it selfe can be a Crime, but must be made so (not by the Law, but) by the successe of them that commit it; and the same Fact be vertuous, or vicious, as Fortune pleaseth; so that what *Marius* makes a Crime, *Sylla* shall make meritori- ous,[40] and *Cæsar* (the same Lawes standing) turn again into a Crime, to the perpetuall disturbance of the Peace of the Common-wealth.

Secondly, by false Teachers, that either misinterpret *False*
the Law of Nature, making it thereby repugnant to the *Teachers mis-*
Law Civill; or by teaching for Lawes, such Doctrines of *interpreting*
their own, or Traditions of former times, as are inconsist- *the Law of*
ent with the duty of a Subject. *Nature,*

Thirdly, by Erroneous Inferences from True Principles; *And false*
which happens commonly to men that are hasty, and *Inferences*
præcipitate in conclu[154]ding, and resolving what to *from true*
do; such as are they, that have both a great opinion of *Principles,*
their own understanding, and believe that things of this *by Teachers*
nature require not time and study, but onely common
experience, and a good naturall wit; whereof no man
thinks himselfe unprovided: whereas the knowledge, of
Right and Wrong, which is no lesse difficult, there is
no man will pretend to, without great and long study.
And of those defects in Reasoning, there is none that
can Excuse (though some of them may Extenuate) a
Crime, in any man, that pretendeth to the administration of his own private businesse; much lesse in them
that undertake a publique charge; because they pretend to the Reason, upon the want whereof they would
ground their Excuse.

Of the Passions that most frequently are the causes *By their*
of Crime, one, is Vain-glory, or a foolish over-rating of *Passions;*
their own worth; as if difference of worth, were an effect
of their wit, or riches, or bloud, or some other naturall
quality, not depending on the Will of those that have the
Soveraign Authority. From whence proceedeth a Presumption that the punishments ordained by the Lawes,
and extended generally to all Subjects, ought not to be
inflicted on them, with the same rigour they are inflicted
on poore, obscure, and simple men, comprehended
under the name of the *Vulgar.*

Therefore it happeneth commonly, that such as value *Presumption*
themselves by the greatnesse of their wealth, adventure *of Riches,*
on Crimes, upon hope of escaping punishment, by corrupting publique Justice, or obtaining Pardon by Mony,
or other rewards.

And Friends;   And that such as have multitude of Potent Kindred; and popular men, that have gained reputation amongst the Multitude, take courage to violate the Lawes, from a hope of oppressing the Power, to whom it belongeth to put them in execution.

Wisedome   And that such as have a great, and false opinion of their own Wisedome, take upon them to reprehend the actions, and call in question the Authority of them that govern, and so to unsettle the Lawes with their publique discourse, as that nothing shall be a Crime, but what their own designes require should be so. It happeneth also to the same men, to be prone to all such Crimes, as consist in Craft, and in deceiving of their Neighbours; because they think their designes are too subtile to be perceived. These I say are effects of a false presumption of their own Wisdome. For of them that are the first movers in the disturbance of Common-wealth, (which can never happen without a Civill Warre,) very few are left alive long enough, to see their new Designes established: so that the benefit of their Crimes, redoundeth to Posterity, and such as would least have wished it: which argues they were not so wise, as they thought they were. And those that deceive upon hope of not being observed, do commonly deceive themselves, (the darknesse in which they believe they lye hidden, being nothing else but their own blindnesse;) and are no wiser than Children, that think all hid, by hiding their own eyes.

And generally all vain-glorious men, (unlesse they be withall [155] timorous,) are subject to Anger; as being more prone than others to interpret for contempt, the ordinary liberty of conversation: And there are few Crimes that may not be produced by Anger.

Hatred, Lust,   As for the Passions, of Hate, Lust, Ambition, and
Ambition,   Covetousnesse, what Crimes they are apt to produce, is
Covetous-   so obvious to every mans experience and understanding,
nesse, causes   as there needeth nothing to be said of them, saving that
of Crime   they are infirmities, so annexed to the nature, both of man, and all other living creatures, as that their effects

cannot be hindred, but by extraordinary use of Reason, or a constant severity in punishing them. For in those things men hate, they find a continuall, and unavoydable molestation; whereby either a mans patience must be everlasting, or he must be eased by removing the power of that which molesteth him: The former is difficult; the later is many times impossible, without some violation of the Law. Ambition, and Covetousnesse are Passions also that are perpetually incumbent, and pressing; whereas Reason is not perpetually present, to resist them: and therefore whensoever the hope of impunity appears, their effects proceed. And for Lust, what it wants in the lasting, it hath in the vehemence, which sufficeth to weigh down the apprehension of all easie, or uncertain punishments.

Of all Passions, that which enclineth men least to break the Lawes, is Fear. Nay, (excepting some generous natures,) it is the onely thing, (when there is apparence of profit, or pleasure by breaking the Lawes,) that makes men keep them. And yet in many cases a Crime may be committed through Feare. *Fear sometimes cause of Crime, as when the danger is neither present, nor corporeall*

For not every Fear justifies the Action it produceth, but the fear onely of corporeall hurt, which we call *Bodily Fear*, and from which a man cannot see how to be delivered, but by the action. A man is assaulted, fears present death, from which he sees not how to escape, but by wounding him that assaulteth him; If he wound him to death, this is no Crime; because no man is supposed at the making of a Common-wealth, to have abandoned the defence of his life, or limbes, where the Law cannot arrive time enough to his assistance. But to kill a man, because from his actions, or his threatnings, I may argue he will kill me when he can, (seeing I have time, and means to demand protection, from the Soveraign Power,) is a Crime. Again, a man receives words of disgrace, or some little injuries (for which they that made the Lawes, had assigned no punishment, nor thought it worthy of a man that hath the use of Reason, to take notice of,) and is afraid, unlesse he revenge it, he shall fall into contempt, and consequently be obnoxious to the like injuries from others; and to avoyd this, breaks the Law, and protects himselfe for the future, by the terrour of his private revenge. This is a Crime: For the hurt is not Corporeall, but Phantasticall, and (though in this corner of the world, made sensible by a custome not many years since begun, amongst young and vain men,) so light, as a gallant man, and one that is assured of his own courage, cannot take notice of. Also a man may stand in fear of Spirits, either through his own superstition, or through too much credit given to other men, that tell him of strange [156] Dreams and Visions; and thereby be made believe they will hurt him, for doing, or omitting divers things, which neverthelesse, to do, or omit, is contrary to the Lawes; And that which is so done, or omitted, is not to be Excused by this fear; but is a Crime. For (as I have shewn before in the second Chapter) Dreams be naturally but the fancies remaining in sleep, after the impressions our Senses had formerly received waking; and when men are by any accident unassured they have slept, seem to be reall Visions; and therefore he that presumes to break the Law upon his own, or anothers Dream, or pretended Vision, or upon other Fancy of the power of Invisible Spirits, than is permitted by the Common-wealth, leaveth the Law of Nature, which is a certain offence, and followeth the imagery of his own, or another private mans brain, which he can never know whether it signifieth any thing, or nothing, nor whether he that tells his Dream, say true, or lye; which if every private man should have leave to do, (as they must by the Law of Nature, if any one have it) there could no Law be made to hold, and so all Common-wealth would be dissolved.

Crimes not equall   From these different sources of Crimes, it appeares already, that all Crimes are not (as the Stoicks of old time maintained) of the same allay.[41] There is place, not only for EXCUSE, by which that which seemed a Crime, is proved to be none at all; but also for EXTENUATION, by which the Crime, that seemed great, is made lesse. For though all Crimes doe equally deserve the name of Injustice, as all deviation from a strait line is equally crookednesse, which the Stoicks rightly observed; yet it does not follow that all Crimes are equally unjust, no more than that all crooked lines are equally crooked; which the Stoicks not observing, held it as great a Crime, to kill a Hen, against the Law, as to kill ones Father.

That which totally Excuseth a Fact, and takes away *Totall* from it the nature of a Crime, can be none but that, *Excuses* which at the same time, taketh away the obligation of the Law. For the fact committed once against the Law, if he that committed it be obliged to the Law, can be no other than a Crime.

The want of means to know the Law, totally Excuseth: For the Law whereof a man has no means to enforme himself, is not obligatory. But the want of diligence to enquire, shall not be considered as a want of means; Nor shall any man, that pretendeth to reason enough for the Government of his own affairs, be supposed to want means to know the Lawes of Nature; because they are known by the reason he pretends to: only Children, and Madmen are Excused from offences against the Law Naturall.

Where a man is captive, or in the power of the enemy, (and he is then in the power of the enemy, when his person, or his means of living, is so,) if it be without his own fault, the Obligation of the Law ceaseth; because he must obey the enemy, or dye; and consequently such obedience is no Crime: for no man is obliged (when the protection of the Law faileth,) not to protect himself, by the best means he can.

[157] If a man by the terrour of present death, be compelled to doe a fact against the Law, he is totally Excused; because no Law can oblige a man to abandon his own preservation. And supposing such a Law were obligatory; yet a man would reason thus, *If I doe it not,*

I die presently; if I doe it, I die afterwards; therefore by doing it, there is time of life gained; Nature therefore compells him to the fact.

When a man is destitute of food, or other thing necessary for his life, and cannot preserve himselfe any other way, but by some fact against the Law; as if in a great famine he take the food by force, or stealth, which he cannot obtaine for mony nor charity; or in defence of his life, snatch away another mans Sword, he is totally Excused,[42] for the reason next before alledged.

Excuses   Again, Facts done against the Law, by the author-
against the ity of another, are by that authority Excused against
Author   the Author; because no man ought to accuse his own fact in another, that is but his instrument: but it is not Excused against a third person thereby injured; because in the violation of the Law, both the Author, and Actor are Criminalls. From hence it followeth that when that Man, or Assembly, that hath the Soveraign Power, commandeth a man to do that which is contrary to a former Law, the doing of it is totally Excused: For he ought not to condemn it himselfe, because he is the Author; and what cannot justly be condemned by the Soveraign, cannot justly be punished by any other. Besides, when the Soveraign commandeth any thing to be done against his own former Law, the Command, as to that particular fact, is an abrogation of the Law.

If that Man, or Assembly, that hath the Soveraign Power, disclaime any Right essentiall to the Soveraignty, whereby there accrueth to the Subject, any liberty inconsistent with the Soveraign Power, that is to say, with the very being of a Common-wealth, if the Subject shall refuse to obey the Command in any thing, contrary to the liberty granted, this is neverthelesse a Sinne, and contrary to the duty of the Subject: for he ought to take notice of what is inconsistent with the Soveraignty, because it was erected by his own consent, and for his own defence; and that such liberty as is inconsistent with it, was granted through ignorance of the evill consequence thereof. But if he not onely disobey, but also resist a publique Minister in the execution of it, then it is a Crime; because he might have been righted, (without any breach of the Peace,) upon complaint.

The Degrees of Crime are taken on divers Scales, and measured, First, by the malignity of the Source, or Cause: Secondly, by the contagion of the Example: Thirdly, by the mischiefe of the Effect; and Fourthly, by the concurrence of Times, Places, and Persons.

The same Fact done against the Law, if it proceed from Presumption of strength, riches, or friends to resist those that are to execute the Law, is a greater Crime, than if it proceed from hope of not being discovered, or of escape by flight: For Presumption of impu[158]nity by force, is a Root, from whence springeth, at all times, and upon all temptations, a contempt of all Lawes; whereas in the later case, the apprehension of danger, that makes a man fly, renders him more obedient for the future. A Crime which we know to be so, is greater than the same Crime proceeding from a false perswasion that it is lawfull: For he that committeth it against his own conscience, presumeth on his force, or other power, which encourages him to commit the same again: but he that doth it by errour, after the errour shewn him, is conformable to the Law. *Presumption of Power, aggravateth*

Hee, whose errour proceeds from the authority of a Teacher, or an Interpreter of the Law publiquely authorised, is not so faulty, as he whose errour proceedeth from a peremptory pursute of his own principles, and reasoning: For what is taught by one that teacheth by publique Authority, the Common-wealth teacheth, and hath a resemblance of Law, till the same Authority controuleth it; and in all Crimes that contain not in them a denyall of the Soveraign Power, nor are against an evident Law, Excuseth totally: whereas he that groundeth his actions, on his private Judgement, ought according to the rectitude, or errour thereof, to stand, or fall. *Evill Teachers, Extenuate*

Examples of Impunity, Extenuate The same Fact, if it have been constantly punished in other men, is a greater Crime, than if there have been many precedent Examples of impunity. For those Examples, are so many hopes of Impunity, given by the Soveraign himselfe: And because he which furnishes a man with such a hope, and presumption of mercy, as encourageth him to offend, hath his part in the offence; he cannot reasonably charge the offender with the whole.

Præmeditation, Aggravateth A Crime arising from a sudden Passion, is not so great, as when the same ariseth from long meditation: For in the former case there is a place for Extenuation, in the common infirmity of humane nature: but he that doth it with præmeditation, has used circumspection, and cast his eye, on the Law, on the punishment, and on the consequence thereof to humane society; all which in committing the Crime, hee hath contemned, and postposed to his own appetite. But there is no suddennesse of Passion sufficient for a totall Excuse: For all the time between the first knowing of the Law, and the Commission of the Fact, shall be taken for a time of deliberation; because he ought by meditation of the Law, to rectifie the irregularity of his Passions.

Where the Law is publiquely, and with assiduity, before all the people read, and interpreted; a fact done against it, is a greater Crime, than where men are left without such instruction, to enquire of it with difficulty, uncertainty, and interruption of their Callings, and be informed by private men: for in this case, part of the fault is discharged upon common infirmity; but in the former, there is apparent negligence, which is not without some contempt of the Soveraign Power.

Tacite approbation of the Soveraign, Extenuates Those facts which the Law expresly condemneth, but the Law-maker by other manifest signes of his will tacitly approveth, are lesse Crimes, than the same facts, condemned both by the Law, and Law-maker. For seeing the will of the Law-maker is a Law, there appear [159] in this case two contradictory Lawes; which would totally Excuse, if men were bound to take notice of the Soveraigns approbation, by other arguments, than are expressed by his command. But because there are punishments consequent, not onely to the transgression of his Law, but also to the observing of it, he is in part a cause of the transgression, and therefore cannot reasonably impute the whole Crime to the Delinquent. For example, the Law condemneth Duells; the punishment is made capitall: On the contrary part, he that refuseth Duell, is subject to contempt and scorne, without remedy; and sometimes by the Soveraign himselfe thought unworthy to have any charge, or preferment in Warre: If thereupon he accept Duell, considering all men lawfully endeavour to obtain the good opinion of them that have the Soveraign Power, he ought not in reason to be rigorously punished; seeing part of the fault may be discharged on the punisher: which I say, not as wishing liberty of private revenges, or any other kind of disobedience; but a care in Governours, not to countenance any thing obliquely, which directly they forbid. The examples of Princes, to those that see them, are, and ever have been, more potent to govern their actions, than the Lawes themselves. And though it be our duty to do, not what they do, but what they say; yet will that duty never be performed, till it please God to give men an extraordinary, and supernaturall grace to follow that Precept.

Again, if we compare Crimes by the mischiefe of their Effects, First, the same fact, when it redounds to the dammage of many, is greater, than when it redounds to the hurt of few. And therefore, when a fact hurteth, not onely in the present, but also, (by example) in the future, it is a greater Crime, than if it hurt onely in the present: for the former, is a fertile Crime, and multiplyes to the hurt of many; the later is barren. To maintain doctrines contrary to the Religion established in the Common-wealth, is a greater fault, in an authorised Preacher, than in a private person: So also is it, to live

Comparison of Crimes from their Effects

prophanely, incontinently, or do any irreligious act what-soever. Likewise in a Professor of the Law, to maintain any point, or do any act, that tendeth to the weak-ning of the Soveraign Power, is a greater Crime, than in another man: Also in a man that hath such reputation for wisedome, as that his counsells are followed, or his actions imitated by many, his fact against the Law, is a greater Crime, than the same fact in another: For such men not onely commit Crime, but teach it for Law to all other men. And generally all Crimes are the greater, by the scandall they give; that is to say, by becomming stumbling-blocks to the weak, that look not so much upon the way they go in, as upon the light that other men carry before them.

Læsa Majestas   Also Facts of hostility against the present state of the Common-wealth, are greater Crimes, than the same acts done to private men: For the dammage extends it selfe to all: Such are the betraying of the strengths, or revealing of the secrets of the Common-wealth to an Enemy; also all attempts upon the Representative of the Common-wealth, be it a Monarch, or an Assembly; and all endeavours by [160] word, or deed to diminish the Authority of the same, either in the present time, or in succession: which Crimes the Latines understand by *Crimina læsæ Majestatis*, and consist in designe, or act, contrary to a Fundamentall Law.[43]

Bribery and False testimony   Likewise those Crimes, which render Judgements of no effect, are greater Crimes, than Injuries done to one, or a few persons; as to receive mony to give False judge-ment, or testimony, is a greater Crime, than otherwise to deceive a man of the like, or a greater summe; because not onely he has wrong, that falls by such judgements; but all Judgements are rendered uselesse, and occasion ministred to force, and private revenges.

Depeculation   Also Robbery, and Depeculation of the Publique treasure, or Revenues, is a greater Crime, than the rob-bing, or defrauding of a Private man; because to robbe the publique, is to robbe many at once.

Also the Counterfeit usurpation of publique Minis- *Counterfeiting*
tery, the Counterfeiting of publique Seales, or publique *Authority*
Coine, than counterfeiting of a private mans person, or
his seale; because the fraud thereof, extendeth to the
dammage of many.

Of facts against the Law, done to private men, the *Crimes*
greater Crime, is that, where the dammage in the com- *against*
mon opinion of men, is most sensible. And therefore *private men*
To kill against the Law, is a greater Crime, than any *compared*
other injury, life preserved.

And to kill with Torment, greater, than simply to kill.

And Mutilation of a limbe, greater, than the spoyling
a man of his goods.

And the spoyling a man of his goods, by Terrour of
death, or wounds, than by clandestine surreption.

And by clandestine Surreption, than by consent fraud-
ulently obtained.

And the violation of chastity by Force, greater, than
by flattery.

And of a woman Married, than of a woman not
married.

For all these things are commonly so valued; though
some men are more, and some lesse sensible of the same
offence. But the Law regardeth not the particular, but
the generall inclination of mankind.

And therefore the offence men take, from contumely,
in words, or gesture, when they produce no other harme,
than the present griefe of him that is reproached, hath
been neglected in the Lawes of the Greeks, Romans,
and other both antient, and moderne Common-wealths;
supposing the true cause of such griefe to consist, not
in the contumely, (which takes no hold upon men conscious of their own vertue,) but in the Pusillanimity of
him that is offended by it.

Also a Crime against a private man, is much aggra-
vated by the person, time, and place. For to kill ones
Parent, is a greater Crime, than to kill another: for the
Parent ought to have the honour of a Soveraign, (though

he have surrendred his Power to the Civill Law,) because he had it originally by Nature. And to Robbe a poore [161] man, is a greater Crime, than to robbe a rich man; because 'tis to the poore a more sensible dammage.

And a Crime committed in the Time, or Place appointed for Devotion, is greater, than if committed at another time or place: for it proceeds from a greater contempt of the Law.

Many other cases of Aggravation, and Extenuation might be added: but by these I have set down, it is obvious to every man, to take the altitude of any other Crime proposed.

Publique | Lastly, because in almost all Crimes there is an Injury *Crimes what* | done, not onely to some Private men, but also to the Common-wealth; the same Crime, when the accusation is in the name of the Common-wealth, is called Publique Crime; and when in the name of a Private man, a Private Crime; And the Pleas according thereunto called Publique, *Judicia Publica*, Pleas of the Crown; or Private Pleas. As in an Accusation of Murder, if the accuser be a Private man, the plea is a Private plea; if the accuser be the Soveraign, the plea is a Publique plea.

CHAP. XXVIII

Of PUNISHMENTS, *and* REWARDS

The def- | A PUNISHMENT, *is an Evill inflicted by publique* *inition of* | *Authority, on him that hath done, or omitted that which* *Punishment* | *is Judged by the same Authority to be a Transgression* *of the Law; to the end that the will of men may thereby the better be disposed to obedience.*

Right to | Before I inferre any thing from this definition, there is *Punish* | a question to be answered, of much importance; which *whence* | is, by what door the Right, or Authority of Punishing in *derived* | any case, came in. For by that which has been said before, no man is supposed bound by Covenant, not to resist violence; and consequently it cannot be intended, that he gave any right to another to lay violent hands upon his person. In the making of a Common-wealth, every man giveth away the right of defending another; but not of defending himselfe. Also he obligeth himselfe, to assist him that hath the Soveraignty, in the Punishing of another; but of himselfe not. But to covenant to assist the Soveraign, in doing hurt to another, ùnlesse he that so covenanteth have a right to doe it himselfe, is not to give him a Right to Punish. It is manifest therefore that the Right which the Common-wealth (that is, he, or they that represent it) hath to Punish, is not grounded on any concession, or gift of the Subjects. But I have also shewed formerly, that before the Institution of Common-wealth, every man had a right to every thing, and to do whatsoever he thought necessary to his own preservation; subduing, hurting, or killing any man in order thereunto. And this is the foundation of that right of Punishing, [162] which is exercised in every Common-wealth. For the Subjects did not give the Soveraign that right; but onely in laying down theirs, strengthned him to use his own, as he should think fit, for the preservation of them all: so that it was not given, but left to him, and to him onely; and (excepting the limits set him by naturall Law) as entire, as in the condition of meer Nature, and of warre of every one against his neighbour.

From the definition of Punishment, I inferre, First, that neither private revenges, nor injuries of private men, can properly be stiled Punishment; because they proceed not from publique Authority. *Private injuries, and revenges no Punishments:*

Secondly, that to be neglected, and unpreferred by the publique favour, is not a Punishment; because no new evill is thereby on any man Inflicted; he is onely left in the estate he was in before. *Nor denyall of preferment:*

Thirdly, that the evill inflicted by publique Authority, without precedent publique condemnation, is not to be *Nor pain inflicted without publique hearing:*

stiled by the name of Punishment; but of an hostile act; because the fact for which a man is Punished, ought first to be Judged by publique Authority, to be a transgression of the Law.

Nor pain
inflicted by
Usurped
power:
Fourthly, that the evill inflicted by usurped power, and Judges without Authority from the Soveraign, is not Punishment; but an act of hostility; because the acts of power usurped, have not for Author, the person condemned; and therefore are not acts of publique Authority.

Nor pain
inflicted
without
respect to the
future good
Fifthly, that all evill which is inflicted without intention, or possibility of disposing the Delinquent, or (by his example) other men, to obey the Lawes, is not Punishment; but an act of hostility; because without such an end, no hurt done is contained under that name.

Naturall
evill conse-
quences, no
Punishments
Sixthly, whereas to certain actions, there be annexed by Nature, divers hurtfull consequences; as when a man in assaulting another, is himselfe slain, or wounded; or when he falleth into sicknesse by the doing of some unlawfull act; such hurt, though in respect of God, who is the author of Nature, it may be said to be inflicted, and therefore a Punishment divine; yet it is not contaned in the name of Punishment in respect of men, because it is not inflicted by the Authority of man.

Hurt inflicted,
if lesse than
the benefit of
transgressing,
is not
Punishment
Seventhly, If the harm inflicted be lesse than the benefit, or contentment that naturally followeth the crime committed, that harm is not within the definition; and is rather the Price, or Redemption, than the Punishment of a Crime: Because it is of the nature of Punishment, to have for end, the disposing of men to obey the Law; which end (if it be lesse than the benefit of the transgression) it attaineth not, but worketh a contrary effect.

Where the
Punishment
is annexed
to the Law, a
greater hurt
is not Punish-
ment, but
Hostility
Eighthly, If a Punishment be determined and prescribed in the Law it selfe, and after the crime committed, there be a greater Punishment inflicted, the excesse is not Punishment, but an act of hostility. For seeing the aym of Punishment is not a revenge, but terrour; and the terrour of a great Punishment unknown, is taken away by

the declaration of a lesse, the unexpected addition is no part of [163] the Punishment. But where there is no Punishment at all determined by the Law, there whatsoever is inflicted, hath the nature of Punishment. For he that goes about the violation of a Law, wherein no penalty is determined, expecteth an indeterminate, that is to say, an arbitrary Punishment.

Ninthly, Harme inflicted for a Fact done before there was a Law that forbad it, is not Punishment, but an act of Hostility: For before the Law, there is no transgression of the Law: But Punishment supposeth a fact judged, to have been a transgression of the Law; Therefore Harme inflicted before the Law made, is not Punishment, but an act of Hostility. *Hurt inflicted for a fact done before the Law, no Punishment*

Tenthly, Hurt inflicted on the Representative of the Common-wealth, is not Punishment, but an act of Hostility: Because it is of the nature of Punishment, to be inflicted by publique Authority, which is the Authority only of the Representative it self. *The Representative of the Common-wealth Unpunishable*

Lastly, Harme inflicted upon one that is a declared enemy, fals not under the name of Punishment: Because seeing they were either never subject to the Law, and therefore cannot transgresse it; or having been subject to it, and professing to be no longer so, by consequence deny they can transgresse it, all the Harmes that can be done them, must be taken as acts of Hostility. But in declared Hostility, all infliction of evill is lawfull. From whence it followeth, that if a subject shall by fact, or word, wittingly, and deliberatly deny the authority of the Representative of the Common-wealth, (whatsoever penalty hath been formerly ordained for Treason,) he may lawfully be made to suffer whatsoever the Representative will: For in denying subjection, he denyes such Punishment as by the Law hath been ordained; and therefore suffers as an enemy of the Common-wealth; that is, according to the will of the Representative. For the Punishments set down in the Law, are to Subjects, not to Enemies; such as are they, that having been by *Hurt to Revolted Subjects is done by right of War, not by way of Punishment* their own act Subjects, deliberately revolting, deny the Soveraign Power.

The first, and most generall distribution of Punishments, is into *Divine*, and *Humane*. Of the former I shall have occasion, to speak, in a more convenient place hereafter.

Humane, are those Punishments that be inflicted by the Commandement of Man; and are either *Corporall*, or *Pecuniary*, or *Ignominy*, or *Imprisonment*, or *Exile*, or mixt of these.

Punishments   *Corporall Punishment* is that, which is inflicted on
Corporall the body directly, and according to the intention of him that inflicteth it: such as are stripes, or wounds, or deprivation of such pleasures of the body, as were before lawfully enjoyed.

Capitall   And of these, some be *Capitall*, some *Lesse* than *Capitall*. Capitall, is the Infliction of Death; and that either simply, or with torment. Lesse than Capitall, are Stripes, Wounds, Chains, and any other corporall Paine, not in its own nature mortall. For if upon the Infliction of a Punishment death follow not in the intention of the Inflicter, the Punishment is not to bee esteemed Capitall, though the harme prove mortall by an accident not to be fore[164]seen; in which case death is not inflicted, but hastened.

Pecuniary Punishment, is that which consisteth not only in the deprivation of a Summe of Mony, but also of Lands, or any other goods which are usually bought and sold for mony. And in case the Law, that ordaineth such a punishment, be made with design to gather mony, from such as shall transgresse the same, it is not properly a Punishment, but the Price of priviledge, and exemption from the Law, which doth not absolutely forbid the fact, but only to those that are not able to pay the mony: except where the Law is Naturall, or part of Religion; for in that case it is not an exemption from the Law, but a transgression of it. As where a Law exacteth a Pecuniary mulct, of them that take the name of God in vaine, the payment of the mulct, is not the price of a dispensation to sweare, but the Punishment of the transgression of a Law undispensable. In like manner if the Law impose a Summe of Mony to be payd, to him that has been Injured; this is but a satisfaction for the hurt done him; and extinguisheth the accusation of the party injured, not the crime of the offender.

Ignominy, is the infliction of such Evill, as is made Dishonorable; or the deprivation of such Good, as is made Honourable by the Common-wealth. For there be some things Honorable by Nature; as the effects of Courage, Magnanimity, Strength, Wisdome, and other abilities of body and mind: Others made Honorable by the Common-wealth; as Badges, Titles, Offices, or any other singular marke of the Soveraigns favour. The former, (though they may faile by nature, or accident,) cannot be taken away by a Law; and therefore the losse of them is not Punishment. But the later, may be taken away by the publique authority that made them Honorable, and are properly Punishments: Such are degrading men condemned, of their Badges, Titles, and Offices; or declaring them uncapable of the like in time to come. *Ignominy*

Imprisonment, is when a man is by publique Authority deprived of liberty; and may happen from two divers ends; whereof one is the safe custody of a man accused; the other is the inflicting of paine on a man condemned. The former is not Punishment; because no man is supposed to be Punisht, before he be Judicially heard, and declared guilty. And therefore whatsoever hurt a man is made to suffer by bonds, or restraint, before his cause be heard, over and above that which is necessary to assure his custody, is against the Law of Nature. But the later is Punishment, because Evill, and inflicted by publique Authority, for somewhat that has by the same Authority been Judged a Transgression of the Law. Under this word Imprisonment, I comprehend all restraint of motion, caused by an externall obstacle, be it a House, which is called by the general name of a Prison; or an *Imprisonment*

Iland, as when men are said to be confined to it; or a
place where men are set to worke, as in old time men
have been condemned to Quarries, and in these times to
Gallies; or be it a Chaine, or any other such impediment.

Exile   *Exile*, (Banishment) is when a man is for a crime,
con[165]demned to depart out of the dominion of the
Common-wealth, or out of a certaine part thereof;
and during a prefixed time, or for ever, not to return
into it: and seemeth not in its own nature, without
other circumstances, to be a Punishment; but rather an
escape, or a publique commandement to avoid Punishment by flight. And *Cicero* sayes, there was never
any such Punishment ordained in the City of *Rome*;
but cals it a refuge of men in danger.[44] For if a man banished, be neverthelesse permitted to enjoy his Goods,
and the Revenue of his Lands, the meer change of ayr
is no Punishment; nor does it tend to that benefit of
the Common-wealth, for which all Punishments are
ordained, (that is to say, to the forming of mens wils
to the observation of the Law;) but many times to the
dammage of the Common-wealth. For a Banished man,
is a lawfull enemy of the Common-wealth that banished
him; as being no more a Member of the same. But if he
be withall deprived of his Lands, or Goods, then the
Punishment lyeth not in the Exile, but is to be reckoned
amongst Punishments Pecuniary.

The   All Punishments of Innocent subjects, be they great or
Punishment little, are against the Law of Nature: For Punishment is
of Innocent only for Transgression of the Law, and therefore there
Subjects is can be no Punishment of the Innocent. It is therefore a
contrary to violation, First, of that Law of Nature, which forbid-
the Law of deth all men, in their Revenges, to look at any thing but
Nature   some future good: For there can arrive no good to the
Common-wealth, by Punishing the Innocent. Secondly,
of that, which forbiddeth Ingratitude: For seeing all Soveraign Power, is originally given by the consent of every
one of the Subjects, to the end they should as long as
they are obedient, be protected thereby; the Punishment

of the Innocent, is a rendring of Evill for Good. And
thirdly, of the Law that commandeth Equity; that is to
say, an equall distribution of Justice; which in Punishing
the Innocent is not observed.

But the Infliction of what evill soever, on an Innocent *But the*
man, that is not a Subject, if it be for the benefit of the *Harme done*
Common-wealth, and without violation of any former *to Innocents*
Covenant, is no breach of the Law of Nature. For all *in War, not*
men that are not Subjects, are either Enemies, or else *so:*
they have ceased from being so, by some precedent covenants. But against Enemies, whom the Common-wealth
judgeth capable to do them hurt, it is lawfull by the
originall Right of Nature to make warre; wherein the
Sword Judgeth not, nor doth the Victor make distinction of Nocent, and Innocent, as to the time past; nor
has other respect of mercy, than as it conduceth to the *Nor that*
good of his own People. And upon this ground it is, *which is done*
that also in Subjects, who deliberatly deny the Author- *to declared*
ity of the Common-wealth established, the vengeance *Rebels*
is lawfully extended, not onely to the Fathers, but also
to the third and fourth generation not yet in being, and
consequently innocent of the fact, for which they are
afflicted: because the nature of this offence, consisteth
in the renouncing of subjection; which is a relapse into
the condition of warre, commonly called Rebellion; and
they that so offend, suffer not as Subjects, [166] but as
Enemies. For *Rebellion*, is but warre renewed.

REWARD, is either of *Gift*, or by *Contract*. When by *Reward, is*
Contract, it is called *Salary*, and *Wages*; which is benefit *either Salary,*
due for service performed, or promised. When of Gift, it *or Grace*
is benefit proceeding from the *grace* of them that bestow
it, to encourage, or enable men to do them service. And
therefore when the Soveraign of a Common-wealth
appointeth a Salary to any publique Office, he that
receiveth it, is bound in Justice to performe his office;
otherwise, he is bound onely in honour, to acknowledgement, and an endeavour of requitall. For though
men have no lawfull remedy, when they be commanded

to quit their private businesse, to serve the publique, without Reward, or Salary; yet they are not bound thereto, by the Law of Nature, nor by the Institution of the Common-wealth, unlesse the service cannot otherwise be done; because it is supposed the Soveraign may make use of all their means, insomuch as the most common Souldier, may demand the wages of his warrefare, as a debt.

Benefits The benefits which a Soveraign bestoweth on a Sub-
bestowed for ject, for fear of some power, and ability he hath to do
fear, are not hurt to the Common-wealth, are not properly Rewards;
Rewards for they are not Salaryes; because there is in this case no contract supposed, every man being obliged already not to do the Common-wealth disservice: nor are they Graces; because they be extorted by fear, which ought not to be incident to the Soveraign Power: but are rather Sacrifices, which the Soveraign (considered in his naturall person, and not in the person of the Common-wealth) makes, for the appeasing the discontent of him he thinks more potent than himselfe; and encourage not to obedience, but on the contrary, to the continuance, and increasing of further extortion.

Salaries And whereas some Salaries are certain, and proceed
Certain and from the publique Treasure; and others uncertain, and
Casuall casuall, proceeding from the execution of the Office for which the Salary is ordained; the later is in some cases hurtfull to the Common-wealth; as in the case of Judicature. For where the benefit of the Judges, and Ministers of a Court of Justice, ariseth for the multitude of Causes that are brought to their cognisance, there must needs follow two Inconveniences: One, is the nourishing of sutes; for the more sutes, the greater benefit: and another that depends on that, which is contention about Jurisdiction; each Court drawing to it selfe, as many Causes as it can. But in offices of Execution there are not those Inconveniences; because their employment cannot be encreased by any endeavour of their own. And thus much shall suffice for the nature of Punishment, and

Reward; which are, as it were, the Nerves and Tendons,
that move the limbes and joynts of a Common-wealth.

Hitherto I have set forth the nature of Man, (whose
Pride and other Passions have compelled him to submit
himselfe to Government;) together with the great power
of his Governour, whom I compared to *Leviathan*, taking that comparison out of the two last verses of the
one and fortieth of *Job*;[45] where God having set forth
the great power of *Leviathan*, calleth him King of the
Proud. *There* [167] *is nothing*, saith he, *on earth, to be
compared with him. He is made so as not to be afraid.
Hee seeth every high thing below him; and is King of
all the children of pride.* But because he is mortall, and
subject to decay, as all other Earthly creatures are; and
because there is that in heaven, (though not on earth)
that he should stand in fear of, and whose Lawes he
ought to obey; I shall in the next following Chapters
speak of his Diseases, and the causes of his Mortality;
and of what Lawes of Nature he is bound to obey.

CHAP. XXIX

Of those things that Weaken, or tend to the DISSOLUTION of a Common-wealth

Though nothing can be immortall, which mortals *Dissolution*
make; yet, if men had the use of reason they pretend *of Common-*
to, their Common-wealths might be secured, at least, *wealths*
from perishing by internall diseases. For by the nature *proceedeth*
of their Institution, they are designed to live, as long as *from their*
Man-kind, or as the Lawes of Nature, or as Justice it *Imperfect*
selfe, which gives them life. Therefore when they come *Institution*
to be dissolved, not by externall violence, but intestine
disorder, the fault is not in men, as they are the *Matter*;
but as they are the *Makers*, and orderers of them. For
men, as they become at last weary of irregular justling,

and hewing one another, and desire with all their hearts, to conforme themselves into one firme and lasting edifice; so for want, both of the art of making fit Lawes, to square their actions by, and also of humility, and patience, to suffer the rude and combersome points of their present greatnesse to be taken off, they cannot without the help of a very able Architect, be compiled, into any other than a crasie building, such as hardly lasting out their own time, must assuredly fall upon the heads of their posterity.

Amongst the *Infirmities* therefore of a Common-wealth, I will reckon in the first place, those that arise from an Imperfect Institution, and resemble the diseases of a naturall body, which proceed from a Defectuous Procreation.

Want of   Of which, this is one, *That a man to obtain a King-*
Absolute *dome, is sometimes content with lesse Power, than to*
power *the Peace, and defence of the Common-wealth is neces-*
sarily required. From whence it commeth to passe, that when the exercise of the Power layd by, is for the publique safety to be resumed, it hath the resemblance of an unjust act; which disposeth great numbers of men (when occasion is presented) to rebell; In the same manner as the bodies of children, gotten by diseased parents, are subject either to untimely death, or to purge the ill quality, derived from their vicious conception, by breaking out into biles and scabbs. And when Kings deny themselves some such necessary Power, it is not alwayes (though sometimes) out of ignorance of what is necessary to the office they undertake; but many [168] times out of a hope to recover the same again at their pleasure: Wherein they reason not well; because such as will hold them to their promises, shall be maintained against them by forraign Common-wealths; who in order to the good of their own Subjects let slip few occasions to *weaken* the estate of their Neighbours. So was *Thomas Becket* Archbishop of *Canterbury*, supported against *Henry* the Second, by the Pope;[46] the subjection of Ecclesiastiques

to the Common-wealth, having been dispensed with by *William the Conquerour* at his reception, when he took an Oath, not to infringe the liberty of the Church. And so were the *Barons*, whose power was by *William Rufus* (to have their help in transferring the Succession from his Elder brother, to himselfe,)[47] encreased to a degree, inconsistent with the Soveraign Power, maintained in their Rebellion against King *John*, by the French.[48]

Nor does this happen in Monarchy onely. For whereas the stile of the antient Roman Common-wealth, was, *The Senate, and People of Rome*; neither Senate, nor People pretended to the whole Power; which first caused the seditions, of *Tiberius Gracchus, Caius Gracchus, Lucius Saturninus*,[49] and others; and afterwards the warres between the Senate and the People, under *Marius* and *Sylla*; and again under *Pompey* and *Cæsar*, to the Extinction of their Democraty, and the setting up of Monarchy.

The people of *Athens* bound themselves but from one onely Action;[50] which was, that no man on pain of death should propound the renewing of the warre for the Island of *Salamis*; And yet thereby, if *Solon* had not caused to be given out he was mad, and afterwards in gesture and habit of a mad-man, and in verse, propounded it to the People that flocked about him, they had had an enemy perpetually in readinesse, even at the gates of their Citie; such dammage, or shifts, are all Common-wealths forced to, that have their Power never so little limited.

In the second place, I observe the *Diseases* of a Common-wealth, that proceed from the poyson of seditious doctrines; whereof one is, *That every private man is Judge of Good and Evill actions*. This is true in the condition of meer Nature, where there are no Civill Lawes; and also under Civill Government, in such cases as are not determined by the Law. But otherwise, it is manifest, that the measure of Good and Evill actions, is the Civill Law; and the Judge the Legislator, who is alwayes

Private Judgement of Good and Evill

Representative of the Common-wealth. From this false doctrine, men are disposed to debate with themselves, and dispute the commands of the Common-wealth; and afterwards to obey, or disobey them, as in their private judgements they shall think fit. Whereby the Common-wealth is distracted and *Weakened*.

Erroneous conscience   Another doctrine repugnant to Civill Society, is, that *whatsoever a man does against his Conscience, is Sinne*; and it dependeth on the presumption of making himself judge of Good and Evill. For a mans Conscience, and his Judgement is the same thing; and as the Judgement, so also the Conscience may be erroneous. Therefore, though [169] he that is subject to no Civill Law, sinneth in all he does against his Conscience, because he has no other rule to follow but his own reason; yet it is not so with him that lives in a Common-wealth; because the Law is the publique Conscience, by which he hath already undertaken to be guided. Otherwise in such diversity, as there is of private Consciences, which are but private opinions, the Common-wealth must needs be distracted, and no man dare to obey the Soveraign Power, farther than it shall seem good in his own eyes.

Pretence of Inspiration   It hath been also commonly taught, *That Faith and Sanctity, are not to be attained by Study and Reason, but by supernaturall Inspiration, or Infusion*. Which granted, I see not why any man should render a reason of his Faith; or why every Christian should not be also a Prophet; or why any man should take the Law of his Country, rather than his own Inspiration, for the rule of his action. And thus wee fall again into the fault of taking upon us to Judge of Good and Evill; or to make Judges of it, such private men as pretend to be supernaturally Inspired, to the Dissolution of all Civill Government. Faith comes by hearing, and hearing by those accidents, which guide us into the presence of them that speak to us; which accidents are all contrived by God Almighty; and yet are not supernaturall, but onely, for the great number of them that concurre to every effect, unobservable. Faith, and Sanctity, are indeed not very frequent; but yet they are not Miracles, but brought to passe by education, discipline, correction, and other naturall wayes, by which God worketh them in his elect, at such time as he thinketh fit. And these three opinions, pernicious to Peace and Government, have in this part of the world, proceeded chiefly from the tongues, and pens of unlearned Divines; who joyning the words of Holy Scripture together, otherwise than is agreeable to reason, do what they can, to make men think, that Sanctity and Naturall Reason, cannot stand together.

A fourth opinion, repugnant to the nature of a Common-wealth, is this, *That he that hath the Soveraign Power, is subject to the Civill Lawes.* It is true, that Soveraigns are all subject to the Lawes of Nature; because such lawes be Divine, and cannot by any man, or Common-wealth be abrogated. But to those Lawes which the Soveraign himselfe, that is, which the Common-wealth maketh, he is not subject. For to be subject to Lawes, is to be subject to the Common-wealth, that is to the Soveraign Representative, that is to himselfe; which is not subjection, but freedome from the Lawes. Which errour, because it setteth the Lawes above the Soveraign, setteth also a Judge above him, and a Power to punish him; which is to make a new Soveraign; and again for the same reason a third, to punish the second; and so continually without end, to the Confusion, and Dissolution of the Common-wealth. *Subjecting the Soveraign Power to Civill Lawes*

A Fifth doctrine, that tendeth to the Dissolution of a Common-wealth, is, *That every private man has an absolute Propriety in his Goods; such, as excludeth the Right of the Soveraign.* Every man has indeed a Propriety that excludes the Right of every other Subject: And he has it onely from the Soveraign Power; without the prote[170]ction whereof, every other man should have equall Right to the same. But if the Right of the Soveraign also be excluded, he cannot performe *Attributing of absolute Propriety to Subjects*

the office they have put him into; which is, to defend
them both from forraign enemies, and from the injuries
of one another; and consequently there is no longer a
Common-wealth.

And if the Propriety of Subjects, exclude not the Right
of the Soveraign Representative to their Goods; much
lesse to their offices of Judicature, or Execution, in
which they Represent the Soveraign himselfe.

Dividing of   There is a Sixth doctrine, plainly, and directly against
the Soveraign the essence of a Common-wealth; and 'tis this, *That the*
Power   *Soveraign Power may be divided.* For what is it to divide the Power of a Common-wealth, but to Dissolve it;
for Powers divided mutually destroy each other. And for
these doctrines, men are chiefly beholding to some of
those, that making profession of the Lawes, endeavour
to make them depend upon their own learning, and not
upon the Legislative Power.

Imitation of   And as False Doctrine, so also often-times the Exam-
Neighbour   ple of different Government in a neighbouring Nation,
Nations   disposeth men to alteration of the forme already setled.
So the people of the Jewes were stirred up to reject God,
and to call upon the Prophet *Samuel*, for a King after
the manner of the Nations:[51] So also the lesser Cities of
Greece, were continually disturbed, with seditions of
the Aristocraticall, and Democraticall factions; one part
of almost every Common-wealth, desiring to imitate the
Lacedæmonians;[52] the other, the Athenians. And I doubt
not, but many men, have been contented to see the late
troubles in *England*, out of an imitation of the Low
Countries; supposing there needed no more to grow
rich, than to change, as they had done, the forme of their
Government. For the constitution of mans nature, is of
it selfe subject to desire novelty: When therefore they
are provoked to the same, by the neighbourhood also of
those that have been enriched by it, it is almost impossible for them, not to be content with those that solicite
them to change; and love the first beginnings, though
they be grieved with the continuance of disorder; like

hot blouds, that having gotten the itch, tear themselves
with their own nayles, till they can endure the smart no
longer.

And as to Rebellion in particular against Monarchy; *Imitation of*
one of the most frequent causes of it, is the Reading of *the Greeks,*
the books of Policy, and Histories of the antient Greeks, *and Romans*
and Romans; from which, young men, and all others
that are unprovided of the Antidote of solid Reason,
receiving a strong, and delightfull impression, of the
great exploits of warre, atchieved by the Conductors of
their Armies, receive withall a pleasing Idea, of all they
have done besides; and imagine their great prosperity,
not to have proceeded from the æmulation of particular men, but from the vertue of their popular forme of
government: Not considering the frequent Seditions,
and Civill warres, produced by the imperfection of their
Policy. From the reading, I say, of such books, men have
undertaken to kill their Kings,[53] because the Greek and
Latine writers, in their books, and [171] discourses of
Policy, make it lawfull, and laudable, for any man so to
do; provided before he do it, he call him Tyrant. For they
say not *Regicide*, that is, killing of a King, but *Tyran-
nicide*, that is, killing of a Tyrant is lawfull. From the
same books, they that live under a Monarch conceive an
opinion, that the Subjects in a Popular Common-wealth
enjoy Liberty; but that in a Monarchy they are all Slaves.
I say, they that live under a Monarchy conceive such
an opinion; not they that live under a Popular Government: for they find no such matter. In summe, I cannot
imagine, how anything can be more prejudiciall to a
Monarchy, than the allowing of such books to be pub-
likely read, without present applying such correctives of
discreet Masters, as are fit to take away their Venime:
Which Venime I will not doubt to compare to the bit-
ing of a mad Dogge, which is a disease the Physicians
call *Hydrophobia*, or *fear of Water*. For as he that is so
bitten, has a continuall torment of thirst, and yet abhor-
reth water; and is in such an estate, as if the poyson

endeavoured to convert him into a Dogge: So when a Monarchy is once bitten to the quick, by those Democraticall writers, that continually snarle at that estate; it wanteth nothing more than a strong Monarch, which neverthelesse out of a certain *Tyrannophobia*, or feare of being strongly governed, when they have him, they abhorre.

As there have been Doctors, that hold there be three Soules in a man; so there be also that think there may be more Soules, (that is, more Soveraigns,) than one, in a Common-wealth; and set up a *Supremacy* against the *Soveraignty*; *Canons* against *Lawes*; and a *Ghostly Authority* against the *Civill*; working on mens minds, with words and distinctions, that of themselves signifie nothing, but bewray (by their obscurity) that there walketh (as some think invisibly) another Kingdome, as it were a Kingdome of Fayries, in the dark. Now seeing it is manifest, that the Civill Power, and the Power of the Common-wealth is the same thing; and that Supremacy, and the Power of making Canons, and granting Faculties, implyeth a Common-wealth; it followeth, that where one is Soveraign, another Supreme; where one can make Lawes, and another make Canons; there must needs be two Common-wealths, of one & the same Subjects; which is a Kingdome divided in it selfe, and cannot stand.[54] For notwithstanding the insignificant distinction of *Temporall*, and *Ghostly*, they are still two Kingdomes, and every Subject is subject to two Masters. For seeing the *Ghostly* Power challengeth the Right to declare what is Sinne it challengeth by consequence to declare what is Law, (Sinne being nothing but the transgression of the Law;) and again, the Civill Power challenging to declare what is Law, every Subject must obey two Masters, who both will have their Commands be observed as Law; which is impossible. Or, if it be but one Kingdome, either the *Civill*, which is the Power of the Common-wealth, must be subordinate to the *Ghostly*, and then there is no Soveraignty but the *Ghostly*;

or the *Ghostly* must be subordinate to the *Temporall*
and then there is no *Supremacy* but the *Temporall*. When
therefore these two Powers oppose one another, the
Common-wealth cannot but be in great [172] danger
of Civill warre, and Dissolution. For the *Civill* Authority being more visible, and standing in the cleerer light
of naturall reason cannot choose but draw to it in all
times a very considerable part of the people: And the
Spirituall, though it stand in the darknesse of Schoole
distinctions, and hard words; yet because the fear of
Darknesse, and Ghosts, is greater than other fears, cannot want a party sufficient to Trouble, and sometimes
to Destroy a Common-wealth. And this is a Disease
which not unfitly may be compared to the Epilepsie,[55] or
Falling-sicknesse (which the Jewes took to be one kind
of possession by Spirits) in the Body Naturall. For as
in this Disease, there is an unnaturall spirit, or wind in
the head that obstructeth the roots of the Nerves, and
moving them violently, taketh away the motion which
naturally they should have from the power of the Soule
in the Brain, and thereby causeth violent, and irregular motions (which men call Convulsions) in the parts;
insomuch as he that is seized therewith, falleth down
sometimes into the water, and sometimes into the fire,
as a man deprived of his senses; so also in the Body Politique, when the Spirituall power, moveth the Members
of a Common-wealth, by the terrour of punishments,
and hope of rewards (which are the Nerves of it,) otherwise than by the Civill Power (which is the Soule of
the Common-wealth) they ought to be moved; and by
strange, and hard words suffocates their understanding,
it must needs thereby Distract the people, and either
Overwhelm the Common-wealth with Oppression, or
cast it into the Fire of a Civill warre.

Sometimes also in the meerly Civill government, there *Mixt*
be more than one Soule: As when the Power of levy- *Government*
ing mony, (which is the Nutritive faculty,) has depended
on a generall Assembly; the Power of conduct and

command, (which is the Motive faculty,) on one man; and the Power of making Lawes, (which is the Rationall faculty,) on the accidentall consent, not onely of those two, but also of a third; This endangereth the Common-wealth, somtimes for want of consent to good Lawes; but most often for want of such Nourishment, as is necessary to Life, and Motion. For although few perceive, that such government, is not government, but division of the Common-wealth into three Factions, and call it mixt Monarchy; yet the truth is, that it is not one independent Common-wealth, but three independent Factions; nor one Representative Person, but three. In the Kingdome of God, there may be three Persons independent, without breach of unity in God that Reigneth; but where men Reigne, that be subject to diversity of opinions, it cannot be so. And therefore if the King bear the person of the People, and the generall Assembly bear also the person of the People, and another Assembly bear the person of a Part of the people, they are not one Person, nor one Soveraign, but three Persons, and three Soveraigns.

To what Disease in the Naturall Body of man, I may exactly compare this irregularity of a Common-wealth, I know not. But I have seen a man, that had another man growing out of his side, with an head, armes, breast, and stomach, of his own: If he had had another [173] man growing out of his other side, the comparison might then have been exact.

Want of Hitherto I have named such Diseases of a Common-
Mony wealth, as are of the greatest, and most present danger. There be other, not so great; which neverthelesse are not unfit to be observed. As first, the difficulty of raising Mony, for the necessary uses of the Common-wealth; especially in the approach of warre. This difficulty ariseth from the opinion, that every Subject hath of a Propriety in his lands and goods, exclusive of the Sovereigns Right to the use of the same. From whence it commeth to passe, that the Sovereign Power, which foreseeth

the necessities and dangers of the Common-wealth,
(finding the passage of mony to the publique Treasure
obstructed, by the tenacity of the people,) whereas it
ought to extend it selfe, to encounter, and prevent such
dangers in their beginnings, contracteth it selfe as long
as it can, and when it cannot longer, struggles with the
people by stratagems of Law, to obtain little summes,
which not sufficing, he is fain at last violently to open
the way for present supply, or Perish; and being put often
to these extremities, at last reduceth the people to their
due temper; or else the Common-wealth must perish.
Insomuch as we may compare this Distemper very aptly
to an Ague; wherein, the fleshy parts being congealed,
or by venomous matter obstructed; the Veins which by
their naturall course empty themselves into the Heart,
are not (as they ought to be) supplyed from the Arteries, whereby there succeedeth at first a cold contraction,
and trembling of the limbes; and afterwards a hot, and
strong endeavour of the Heart, to force a passage for
the Bloud; and before it can do that, contenteth it selfe
with the small refreshments of such things as coole for
a time, till (if Nature be strong enough) it break at last
the contumacy of the parts obstructed, and dissipateth
the venome into sweat; or (if Nature be too weak) the
Patient dyeth.

Again, there is sometimes in a Common-wealth, a *Monopolies*
Disease, which resembleth the Pleurisie; and that is, *and abuses of*
when the Treasure of the Common-wealth, flowing out *Publicans*
of its due course, is gathered together in too much abun-
dance, in one, or a few private men, by Monopolies, or
by Farmes of the Publique Revenues; in the same manner
as the Blood in a Pleurisie, getting into the Membrane
of the breast, breedeth there an Inflammation, accompanied with a Fever, and painfull stitches.

Also, the Popularity of a potent Subject, (unlesse the *Popular men*
Common-wealth have very good caution of his fidel-
ity,) is a dangerous Disease; because the people (which
should receive their motion from the Authority of the

Soveraign,) by the flattery, and by the reputation of an ambitious man, are drawn away from their obedience to the Lawes, to follow a man, of whose vertues, and designes they have no knowledge. And this is commonly of more danger in a Popular Government, than in a Monarchy; because an Army is of so great force, and multitude, as it may easily be made believe, they are the People. By this means it was, that *Julius Cæsar*, who was [174] set up by the People against the Senate, having won to himselfe the affections of his Army, made himselfe Master, both of Senate and People. And this proceeding of popular, and ambitious men, is plain Rebellion; and may be resembled to the effects of Witchcraft.

Excessive greatnesse of a Town, multitude of Corporations   Another infirmity of a Common-wealth, is the immoderate greatnesse of a Town, when it is able to furnish out of its own Circuit, the number, and expence of a great Army: As also the great number of Corporations; which are as it were many lesser Common-wealths in the bowels of a greater, like wormes in the entrayles of a naturall man.

Liberty of disputing against Soveraign Power   To which may be added, the Liberty of Disputing against absolute Power, by pretenders to Politicall Prudence; which though bred for the most part in the Lees of the people; yet animated by False Doctrines, are perpetually medling with the Fundamentall Lawes, to the molestation of the Common-wealth; like the little Wormes, which Physicians call *Ascarides*.

We may further adde, the insatiable appetite, or *Bulimia*, of enlarging Dominion; with the incurable *Wounds* thereby many times received from the enemy; And the *Wens*, of ununited conquests, which are many times a burthen, and with lesse danger lost, than kept; As also the *Lethargy* of Ease, and *Consumption* of Riot and Vain Expence.

Dissolution of the Common-wealth   Lastly, when in a warre (forraign, or intestine,) the enemies get a final Victory; so as (the forces of the Common-wealth keeping the field no longer) there is no farther protection of Subjects in their loyalty; then is the Common-wealth DISSOLVED, and every man at liberty to protect himselfe by such courses as his own discretion shall suggest unto him. For the Soveraign, is the publique Soule, giving Life and Motion to the Common-wealth; which expiring, the Members are governed by it no more, than the Carcasse of a man, by his departed (though Immortall) Soule. For though the Right of a Soveraign Monarch cannot be extinguished by the act of another; yet the Obligation of the members may. For he that wants protection, may seek it anywhere; and when he hath it, is obliged (without fraudulent pretence of having submitted himselfe out of fear,) to protect his Protection as long as he is able. But when the Power of an Assembly is once suppressed, the Right of the same perisheth utterly; because the Assembly it selfe is extinct; and consequently, there is no possibility for the Soveraignty to re-enter. [175]

CHAP. XXX

Of the OFFICE of the Soveraign Representative

The OFFICE of the Soveraign, (be it a Monarch, or an Assembly,) consisteth in the end, for which he was trusted with the Soveraign Power, namely the procuration of *the safety of the people*; to which he is obliged by the Law of Nature, and to render an account thereof to God, the Author of that Law, and to none but him. But by Safety here, is not meant a bare Preservation, but also all other Contentments of life, which every man by lawfull Industry, without danger, or hurt to the Common-wealth, shall acquire to himselfe. *The Procuration of the Good of the People*

And this is intended should be done, not by care applyed to Individualls, further than their protection from injuries, when they shall complain; but by a generall Providence, contained in publique Instruction, both of Doctrine, and Example; and in the making, and *By Instruction & Lawes* executing of good Lawes, to which individuall persons may apply their own cases.

Against the duty of a Soveraign to relinquish any Essentiall Right of Soveraignty: And because, if the essentiall Rights of Soveraignty (specified before in the eighteenth Chapter) be taken away, the Common-wealth is thereby dissolved, and every man returneth into the condition, and calamity of a warre with every other man, (which is the greatest evill that can happen in this life;) it is the Office of the Soveraign, to maintain those Rights entire; and consequently against his duty, First, to transferre to another, or to lay from himselfe any of them. For he that deserteth the Means, deserteth the Ends; and he deserteth the Means, that being the Soveraign, acknowledgeth himselfe subject to the Civill Lawes; and renounceth the Power of Supreme Judicature; or of making Warre, or Peace by his own Authority; or of Judging of the Necessities of the Common-wealth; or of levying Mony, and Souldiers, when, and as much as in his own conscience he shall judge necessary; or of making Officers, and Ministers both of Warre, and Peace; or of appointing Teachers, and examining what Doctrines are conformable, or contrary to the Defence, Peace, and Good of the people. Secondly, it is against his Duty, to let the people be ignorant, or mis-informed of the grounds, and reasons of those his essentiall Rights; because thereby men are easie to be seduced, and drawn to resist him, when the Common-wealth shall require their use and exercise.

Or not to see the people taught the grounds of them

And the grounds of these Rights, have the rather need to be diligently, and truly taught; because they cannot be maintained by any Civill Law, or terrour of legal punishment. For a Civill Law, that shall forbid Rebellion, (and such is all resistance to the essentiall Rights of Soveraignty,) is not (as a Civill Law) any obligation, [176] but by vertue onely of the Law of Nature, that forbiddeth the violation of Faith; which naturall obligation if men know not, they cannot know the Right of any Law the Soveraign maketh. And for the Punishment, they take it but for an act of Hostility; which when they think they have strength enough, they will endeavour by acts of Hostility, to avoyd.

As I have heard some say, that Justice is but a word, without substance; and that whatsoever a man can by force, or art, acquire to himselfe, (not onely in the condition of warre, but also in a Common-wealth,) is his own, which I have already shewed to be false: So there be also that maintain, that there are no grounds, nor Principles of Reason, to sustain those essentiall Rights, which make Soveraignty absolute. For if there were, they would have been found out in some place, or other; whereas we see, there has not hitherto been any Common-wealth, where those Rights have been acknowledged, or challenged. Wherein they argue as ill, as if the Savage people of America, should deny there were any grounds, or Principles of Reason, so to build a house, as to last as long as the materials, because they never yet saw any so well built. Time, and Industry, produce every day new knowledge. And as the art of well building, is derived from Principles of Reason, observed by industrious men, that had long studied the nature of materials, and the divers effects of figure, and proportion, long after mankind began (though poorly) to build: So, long time after men have begun to constitute Common-wealths, imperfect, and apt to relapse into disorder, there may, Principles of Reason be found out, by industrious meditation, to make their constitution (excepting by externall violence) everlasting. And such are those which I have in this discourse set forth: Which whether they come not into the sight of those that have Power to make use of them, or be neglected by them, or not, concerneth my particular interest, at this day, very little. But supposing that these of mine are not such Principles of Reason; yet I am sure they are Principles from Authority of Scripture; as I shall make it appear, when I shall come to speak of the Kingdome of God, (administred by *Moses*,) over the Jewes, his peculiar people by Covenant.

Objection of those that say there are no Principles of Reason for absolute Soveraignty

Objection   But they say again, that though the Principles be right,
from the yet Common people are not of capacity enough to be
Incapacity of made to understand them. I should be glad, that the
the vulgar Rich, and Potent Subjects of a Kingdome, or those that
are accounted the most Learned, were no lesse incapable
than they. But all men know, that the obstructions to
this kind of doctrine, proceed not so much from the difficulty of the matter, as from the interest of them that are
to learn. Potent men, digest hardly any thing that setteth
up a Power to bridle their affections; and Learned men,
any thing that discovereth their errours, and thereby
lesseneth their Authority: whereas the Common-peoples
minds, unlesse they be tainted with dependance on the
Potent, or scribbled over with the opinions of their Doctors, are like clean paper, fit to receive whatsoever by
Publique Authority shall be imprinted in them. Shall
whole Nations be brought to *acquiesce* [177] in the great
Mysteries of Christian Religion, which are above Reason; and millions of men be made believe, that the same
Body may be in innumerable places, at one and the
same time, which is against Reason; and shall not men
be able, by their teaching, and preaching, protected by
the Law, to make that received, which is so consonant to
Reason, that any unprejudicated man, needs no more
to learn it, than to hear it? I conclude therefore, that
in the instruction of the people in the Essentiall Rights
(which are the Naturall, and Fundamentall Lawes) of
Soveraignty, there is no difficulty, (whilest a Soveraign
has his Power entire,) but what proceeds from his
own fault, or the fault of those whom he trusteth in
the administration of the Common-wealth; and consequently, it is his Duty, to cause them so to be instructed;
and not onely his Duty, but his Benefit also, and Secur-
Subjects are ity, against the danger that may arrive to himselfe in his
to be taught, naturall Person, from Rebellion.
not to affect   And (to descend to particulars) the People are to be
change of taught, First, that they ought not to be in love with
Government: any forme of Government they see in their neighbour

Nations, more than with their own, nor (whatsoever present prosperity they behold in Nations that are otherwise governed than they,) to desire change. For the prosperity of a People ruled by an Aristocraticall, or Democraticall assembly, commeth not from Aristocracy, nor from Democracy, but from the Obedience, and Concord of the Subjects: nor do the people flourish in a Monarchy, because one man has the right to rule them, but because they obey him. Take away in any kind of State, the Obedience, (and consequently the Concord of the People,) and they shall not onely not flourish, but in short time be dissolved. And they that go about by disobedience, to doe no more than reforme the Common-wealth, shall find they do thereby destroy it; like the foolish daughters of *Peleus* (in the fable;) which desiring to renew the youth of their decrepit Father, did by the Counsell of *Medea*, cut him in pieces,[56] and boyle him, together with strange herbs, but made not of him a new man. This desire of change, is like the breach of the first of Gods Commandements: For there God sayes, *Non habebis Deos alienos*; Thou shalt not have the Gods of other Nations;[57] and in another place concerning *Kings*, that they are *Gods*.

Secondly, they are to be taught, that they ought not to be led with admiration of the vertue of any of their fellow Subjects, how high soever he stand, nor how conspicuously soever he shine in the Common-wealth; nor of any Assembly, (except the Soveraign Assembly,) so as to deferre to them any obedience, or honour, appropriate to the Soveraign onely, whom (in their particular stations) they represent; nor to receive any influence from them, but such as is conveighed by them from the Soveraign Authority. For that Soveraign, cannot be imagined to love his People as he ought, that is not Jealous of them, but suffers them by the flattery of Popular men, to be seduced from their loyalty, as they have often been, not onely secretly, but openly, so as to proclaime Marriage with them *in facie Ecclesiæ* by Preachers; and

Nor adhere (against the Soveraign) to Popular men:

by publishing the same in the open streets: which [178] may fitly be compared to the violation of the second of the ten Commandements.[58]

Nor to Dispute the Soveraign Power: Thirdly, in consequence to this, they ought to be informed, how great a fault it is, to speak evill of the Soveraign Representative, (whether One man, or an Assembly of men;) or to argue and dispute his Power, or any way to use his Name irreverently, whereby he may be brought into Contempt with his People, and their Obedience (in which the safety of the Common-wealth consisteth) slackened. Which doctrine the third Commandement by resemblance pointeth to.[59]

And to have dayes set apart to learn their Duty: Fourthly, seeing people cannot be taught this, nor when 'tis taught, remember it, nor after one generation past, so much as know in whom the Soveraign Power is placed, without setting a part from their ordinary labour, some certain times, in which they may attend those that are appointed to instruct them; It is necessary that some such times be determined, wherein they may assemble together, and (after prayers and praises given to God, the Soveraign of Soveraigns) hear those their Duties told them, and the Positive Lawes, such as generally concern them all, read and expounded, and be put in mind of the Authority that maketh them Lawes. To this end had the *Jewes* every seventh day, a *Sabbath*, in which the Law was read and expounded; and in the solemnity whereof they were put in mind, that their King was God; that having created the world in six dayes, he rested the seventh day; and by their resting on it from their labour, that that God was their King, which redeemed them from their servile, and painfull labour in *Egypt*, and gave them a time, after they had rejoyced in God, to take joy also in themselves, by lawfull recreation.[60] So that the first Table of the Commandements, is spent all, in setting down the summe of Gods absolute Power; not onely as God, but as King by pact, (in peculiar) of the Jewes; and may therefore give light, to those that have Soveraign Power conferred on them by the consent of men, to see what doctrine they Ought to teach their Subjects.

And because the first instruction of Children, depend- *And to* eth on the care of their Parents; it is necessary that they *Honour their* should be obedient to them,[61] whilest they are under their *Parents* tuition; and not onely so, but that also afterwards (as gratitude requireth,) they acknowledge the benefit of their education, by externall signes of honour. To which end they are to be taught, that originally the Father of every man was also his Soveraign Lord, with power over him of life and death; and that the Fathers of families, when by instituting a Common-wealth, they resigned that absolute Power, yet it was never intended, they should lose the honour due unto them for their education. For to relinquish such right, was not necessary to the Institution of Soveraign Power; nor would there be any reason, why any man should desire to have children, or take the care to nourish, and instruct them, if they were afterwards to have no other benefit from them, than from other men. And this accordeth with the fifth Commandement.

[179] Again, every Soveraign Ought to cause Justice *And to avoyd* to be taught, which (consisting in taking from no man *doing of* what is his) is as much as to say, to cause men to be taught *Injury:* not to deprive their Neighbours, by violence, or fraud, of any thing which by the Soveraign Authority is theirs. Of things held in propriety, those that are dearest to a man are his own life, & limbs; and in the next degree, (in most men,) those that concern conjugall affection; and after them riches and means of living. Therefore the People are to be taught, to abstain from violence to one anothers person, by private revenges; from violation of conjugall honour; and from forcible rapine, and fraudulent surreption of one anothers goods. For which purpose also it is necessary they be shewed the evill consequences of false Judgement, by corruption either of Judges or Witnesses, whereby the distinction of propriety is taken away, and Justice becomes of no effect: all

which things are intimated in the sixth, seventh, eighth, and ninth Commandements.[62]

And to do all this sincerely from the heart Lastly, they are to be taught, that not onely the unjust facts, but the designes and intentions to do them, (though by accident hindred,) are Injustice; which consisteth in the pravity of the will, as well as in the irregularity of the act. And this is the intention of the tenth Commandement,[63] and the summe of the second Table; which is reduced all to this one Commandement of mutuall Charity, *Thou shalt love thy neighbour as thy selfe*:[64] as the summe of the first Table is reduced to *the love of God*; whom they had then newly received as their King.

The use of Universities As for the Means, and Conduits, by which the people may receive this Instruction, wee are to search, by what means so many Opinions, contrary to the peace of Man-kind, upon weak and false Principles, have neverthelesse been so deeply rooted in them. I mean those, which I have in the precedent Chapter specified: as That men shall Judge of what is lawfull and unlawfull, not by the Law it selfe, but by their own Consciences; that is to say, by their own private Judgements: That Subjects sinne in obeying the Commands of the Common-wealth, unlesse they themselves have first judged them to be lawfull: That their Propriety in their riches is such, as to exclude the Dominion, which the Common-wealth hath over the same: That it is lawfull for Subjects to kill such, as they call Tyrants: That the Soveraign Power may be divided, and the like; which come to be instilled into the People by this means. They whom necessity, or covetousnesse keepeth attent on their trades, and labour; and they, on the other side, whom superfluity, or sloth carrieth after their sensuall pleasures, (which two sorts of men take up the greatest part of Man-kind,) being diverted from the deep meditation, which the learning of truth, not onely in the matter of Naturall Justice, but also of all other Sciences necessarily requireth, receive the Notions of their duty, chiefly from Divines in the Pulpit, and partly from such of their Neighbours, or

familiar acquaintance, as having the Faculty of discoursing readily, and plausibly, seem wiser and better learned
in cases of Law, and Conscience, than themselves. And
the Divines, and such others as make shew of Learning,
derive their [180] knowledge from the Universities, and
from the Schooles of Law, or from the Books, which
by men eminent in those Schooles, and Universities
have been published. It is therefore manifest, that the
Instruction of the people, dependeth wholly, on the
right teaching of Youth in the Universities. But are not
(may some man say) the Universities of *England* learned
enough already to do that? or is it you will undertake
to teach the Universities? Hard questions. Yet to the
first, I doubt not to answer; that till towards the later
end of *Henry the eighth*,[65] the Power of the Pope, was
alwayes upheld against the Power of the Common-wealth,
principally by the Universities; and that the doctrines
maintained by so many Preachers, against the Soveraign
Power of the King, and by so many Lawyers, and others,
that had their education there, is a sufficient argument,
that though the Universities were not authors of those
false doctrines, yet they knew not how to plant the true.
For in such a contradiction of Opinions, it is most certain, that they have not been sufficiently instructed; and
'tis no wonder, if they yet retain a relish of that subtile
liquor, wherewith they were first seasoned, against the
Civill Authority. But to the later question, it is not fit,
nor needfull for me to say either I, or No: for any man
that sees what I am doing, may easily perceive what
I think.

The safety of the People, requireth further, from him,
or them that have the Soveraign Power, that Justice be
equally administred to all degrees of People; that is, that
as well the rich, and mighty, as poor and obscure persons, may be righted of the injuries done them; so as the
great, may have no greater hope of impunity, when they
doe violence, dishonour, or any Injury to the meaner
sort, than when one of these, does the like to one of

them: For in this consisteth Equity; to which, as being
a Precept of the Law of Nature, a Soveraign is as much
subject, as any of the meanest of his People. All breaches
of the Law, are offences against the Common-wealth:
but there be some, that are also against private Persons.
Those that concern the Common-wealth onely, may
without breach of Equity be pardoned; for every man
may pardon what is done against himselfe, according
to his own discretion. But an offence against a private
man, cannot in Equity be pardoned, without the consent
of him that is injured; or reasonable satisfaction.

The Inequality of Subjects, proceedeth from the Acts
of Soveraign Power; and therefore has no more place in
the presence of the Soveraign; that is to say, in a Court
of Justice, then the Inequality between Kings, and their
Subjects, in the presence of the King of Kings. The honour of great Persons, is to be valued for their beneficence,
and the aydes they give to men of inferiour rank, or not
at all. And the violences, oppressions, and injuries they
do, are not extenuated, but aggravated by the greatnesse
of their persons; because they have least need to commit
them. The consequences of this partiality towards the
great, proceed in this manner. Impunity maketh Insolence; Insolence Hatred; and Hatred, an Endeavour to
pull down all oppressing and contumelious greatnesse,
though with the ruine of the Common-wealth.

Equall Taxes   [181] To Equall Justice, appertaineth also the Equall
imposition of Taxes; the Equality whereof dependeth
not on the Equality of riches, but on the Equality of the
debt, that every man oweth to the Common-wealth for
his defence. It is not enough, for a man to labour for the
maintenance of his life; but also to fight, (if need be,) for
the securing of his labour. They must either do as the
Jewes did after their return from captivity, in re-edifying
the Temple, build with one hand, and hold the Sword
in the other;⁶⁶ or else they must hire others to fight for
them. For the Impositions, that are layd on the People
by the Soveraign Power, are nothing else but the Wages,

due to them that hold the publique Sword, to defend private men in the exercise of severall Trades, and Callings. Seeing then the benefit that every one receiveth thereby, is the enjoyment of life, which is equally dear to poor, and rich; the debt which a poor man oweth them that defend his life, is the same which a rich man oweth for the defence of his; saving that the rich, who have the service of the poor, may be debtors not onely for their own persons, but for many more. Which considered, the Equality of Imposition, consisteth rather in the Equality of that which is consumed, than of the riches of the persons that consume the same. For what reason is there, that he which laboureth much, and sparing the fruits of his labour, consumeth little, should be more charged, then he that living idlely, getteth little, and spendeth all he gets; seeing the one hath no more protection from the Common-wealth, then the other? But when the Impositions, are layd upon those things which men consume, every man payeth Equally for what he useth: Nor is the Common-wealth defrauded, by the luxurious waste of private men.

And whereas many men, by accident unevitable, become unable to maintain themselves by their labour; they ought not to be left to the Charity of private persons; but to be provided for, (as far-forth as the necessities of Nature require,) by the Lawes of the Common-wealth. For as it is Uncharitablenesse in any man, to neglect the impotent; so it is in the Soveraign of a Common-wealth, to expose them to the hazard of such uncertain Charity. *Publique Charity*

But for such as have strong bodies, the case is otherwise: they are to be forced to work; and to avoyd the excuse of not finding employment, there ought to be such Lawes, as may encourage all manner of Arts; as Navigation, Agriculture, Fishing, and all manner of Manifacture that requires labour. The multitude of poor, and yet strong people still encreasing, they are to be transplanted into Countries not sufficiently inhabited: where neverthelesse, they are not to exterminate those *Prevention of Idlenesse* they find there; but constrain them to inhabit closer together, and not range a great deal of ground, to snatch what they find; but to court each little Plot with art and labour, to give them their sustenance in due season. And when all the world is overchargd with Inhabitants, then the last remedy of all is Warre; which provideth for every man, by Victory, or Death.

Good Lawes
what

To the care of the Soveraign, belongeth the making of Good Lawes. But what is a good Law? By a Good Law, I mean not a [182] Just Law: for no Law can be Unjust. The Law is made by the Soveraign Power, and all that is done by such Power, is warranted, and owned by every one of the people; and that which every man will have so, no man can say is unjust. It is in the Lawes of a Common-wealth, as in the Lawes of Gaming: whatsoever the Gamesters all agree on, is Injustice to none of them. A good Law is that, which is *Needfull*, for the *Good of the People*, and withall *Perspicuous*.

Such as are
Necessary

For the use of Lawes, (which are but Rules Authorised) is not to bind the People from all Voluntary actions; but to direct and keep them in such a motion, as not to hurt themselves by their own impetuous desires, rashnesse, or indiscretion; as Hedges are set, not to stop Travellers, but to keep them in the way. And therefore a Law that is not Needfull, having not the true End of a Law, is not Good. A Law may be conceived to be Good, when it is for the benefit of the Soveraign; though it be not Necessary for the People; but it is not so. For the good of the Soveraign and People, cannot be separated. It is a weak Soveraign, that has weak Subjects; and a weak People, whose Soveraign wanteth Power to rule them at his will. Unnecessary Lawes are not good Lawes; but trapps for Mony: which where the right of Soveraign Power is acknowledged, are superfluous; and where it is not acknowledged, unsufficient to defend the People.

Such as are
Perspicuous

The Perspicuity, consisteth not so much in the words of the Law it selfe, as in a Declaration of the Causes, and Motives, for which it was made. That is it, that shewes

us the meaning of the Legislator; and the meaning of the
Legislator known, the Law is more easily understood
by few, than many words. For all words, are subject to
ambiguity; and therefore multiplication of words in the
body of the Law, is multiplication of ambiguity: Besides
it seems to imply, (by too much diligence,) that whosoever can evade the words, is without the compasse of
the Law. And this is a cause of many unnecessary Pro-
cesses. For when I consider how short were the Lawes of
antient times; and how they grew by degrees still longer;
me thinks I see a contention between the Penners, and
Pleaders of the Law; the former seeking to circumscribe
the later; and the later to evade their circumscriptions;
and that the Pleaders have got the Victory. It belongeth
therefore to the Office of a Legislator, (such as is in all
Common-wealths the Supreme Representative, be it one
Man, or an Assembly,) to make the reason Perspicuous,
why the Law was made; and the Body of the Law it
selfe, as short, but in as proper, and significant termes,
as may be.

It belongeth also to the Office of the Soveraign, to   *Punishments*
make a right application of Punishments, and Rewards.
And seeing the end of punishing is not revenge, and discharge of choler; but correction, either of the offender,
or of others by his example; the severest Punishments
are to be inflicted for those Crimes, that are of most
Danger to the Publique; such as are those which proceed from malice to the Government established; those
that spring from contempt of Justice; those that provoke Indignation in the Multitude; and those, [183]
which unpunished, seem Authorised, as when they
are committed by Sonnes, Servants, or Favorites of
men in Authority: For Indignation carrieth men, not
onely against the Actors, and Authors of Injustice; but
against all Power that is likely to protect them; as in
the case of *Tarquin*; when for the Insolent act of one of
his Sonnes, he was driven out of *Rome*, and the Monarchy it selfe dissolved.[67] But Crimes of Infirmity; such as

are those which proceed from great provocation, from great fear, great need, or from ignorance whether the Fact be a great Crime, or not, there is place many times for Lenity, without prejudice to the Common-wealth; and Lenity when there is such place for it, is required by the Law of Nature. The Punishment of the Leaders, and teachers in a Commotion; not the poore seduced People, when they are punished, can profit the Common-wealth by their example. To be severe to the People, is to punish that ignorance, which may in great part be imputed to the Soveraign, whose fault it was, they were no better instructed.

Rewards   In like manner it belongeth to the Office, and Duty of the Soveraign, to apply his Rewards alwayes so, as there may arise from them benefit to the Common-wealth: wherein consisteth their Use, and End; and is then done, when they that have well served the Common-wealth, are with as little expence of the Common Treasure, as is possible, so well recompenced, as others thereby may be encouraged, both to serve the same as faithfully as they can, and to study the arts by which they may be enabled to do it better. To buy with Mony, or Preferment, from a Popular ambitious Subject, to be quiet, and desist from making ill impressions in the mindes of the People, has nothing of the nature of Reward; (which is ordained not for disservice, but for service past;) nor a signe of Gratitude, but of Fear: nor does it tend to the Benefit, but to the Dammage of the Publique. It is a contention with Ambition, like that of *Hercules* with the Monster *Hydra*, which having many heads, for every one that was vanquished, there grew up three.[68] For in like manner, when the stubbornnesse of one Popular man, is overcome with Reward, there arise many more (by the Example) that do the same Mischiefe, in hope of like Benefit: and as all sorts of Manifacture, so also Malice encreaseth by being vendible. And though sometimes a Civill warre, may be differred, by such wayes as that, yet the danger growes still the greater, and the

Publique ruine more assured. It is therefore against the
Duty of the Soveraign, to whom the Publique Safety is
committed, to Reward those that aspire to greatnesse by
disturbing the Peace of their Country, and not rather to
oppose the beginnings of such men, with a little danger,
than after a longer time with greater.

Another Businesse of the Soveraign, is to choose good *Counsellours*
Counsellours; I mean such, whose advice he is to take in
the Government of the Common-wealth. For this word
Counsell, *Consilium*, corrupted from *Considium*, is a
large signification, and comprehendeth all Assemblies
of men that sit together, not onely to deliberate what
is to be done hereafter, but also to judge of Facts past,
and of Law [184] for the present. I take it here in the
first sense onely: And in this sense, there is no choyce
of Counsell, neither in a Democracy, nor Aristocracy;
because the persons Counselling are members of the
person Counselled. The choyce of Counsellours therefore is proper to Monarchy; In which, the Soveraign
that endeavoureth not to make choyce of those, that in
every kind are the most able, dischargeth not his Office
as he ought to do. The most able Counsellours, are they
that have least hope of benefit by giving evill Counsell,
and most knowledge of those things that conduce to the
Peace, and Defence of the Common-wealth. It is a hard
matter to know who expecteth benefit from publique
troubles; but the signes that guide to a just suspicion,
is the soothing of the people in their unreasonable, or
irremediable grievances, by men whose estates are not
sufficient to discharge their accustomed expences, and
may easily be observed by any one whom it concerns
to know it. But to know, who has most knowledge of
the Publique affaires, is yet harder; and they that know
them, need them a great deale the lesse. For to know,
who knowes the Rules almost of any Art, is a great
degree of the knowledge of the same Art; because no
man can be assured of the truth of anothers Rules, but
he that is first taught to understand them. But the best

signes of Knowledge of any Art, are, much conversing in it, and constant good effects of it. Good Counsell comes not by Lot, nor by Inheritance; and therefore there is no more reason to expect good Advice from the rich, or noble, in matter of State, than in delineating the dimensions of a fortresse; unlesse we shall think there needs no method in the study of the Politiques, (as there does in the study of Geometry,) but onely to be lookers on; which is not so. For the Politiques is the harder study of the two. Whereas in these parts of *Europe*, it hath been taken for a Right of certain persons, to have place in the highest Councell of State by Inheritance; it is derived from the Conquests of the antient Germans; wherein many absolute Lords joyning together to conquer other Nations, would not enter in to the Confederacy, without such Priviledges, as might be marks of difference in time following, between their Posterity, and the Posterity of their Subjects; which Priviledges being inconsistent with the Soveraign Power, by the favour of the Soveraign, they may seem to keep; but contending for them as their Right, they must needs by degrees let them go, and have at last no further honour, than adhæreth naturally to their abilities.

And how able soever be the Counsellours in any affaire, the benefit of their Counsell is greater, when they give every one his Advice, and the reasons of it apart, than when they do it in an Assembly, by way of Orations; and when they have præmeditated, than when they speak on the sudden; both because they have more time, to survey the consequences of action; and are lesse subject to be carried away to contradiction, through Envy, Emulation, or other Passions arising from the difference of opinion.

The best Counsell, in those things that concern not other Nations, but onely the ease, and benefit the Subjects may enjoy, by Lawes [185] that look onely inward, is to be taken from the generall informations, and complaints of the people of each Province, who are best acquainted with their own wants, and ought therefore, when they demand nothing in derogation of the essentiall Rights of Soveraignty, to be diligently taken notice of. For without those Essentiall Rights, (as I have often before said,) the Common-wealth cannot at all subsist.

A Commander of an Army in chiefe, if he be not Popular, shall not be beloved, nor feared as he ought to be by his Army; and consequently cannot performe that office with good successe. He must therefore be Industrious, Valiant, Affable, Liberall and Fortunate, that he may gain an opinion both of sufficiency, and of loving his Souldiers. This is Popularity, and breeds in the Souldiers both desire, and courage, to recommend themselves to his favour; and protects the severity of the Generall, in punishing (when need is) the Mutinous, or negligent Souldiers. But this love of Souldiers, (if caution be not given of the Commanders fidelity,) is a dangerous thing to Soveraign Power; especially when it is in the hands of an Assembly not popular. It belongeth therefore to the safety of the People, both that they be good Conductors, and faithfull Subjects, to whom the Soveraign Commits his Armies. *Commanders*

But when the Soveraign himselfe is Popular; that is, reverenced and beloved of his People, there is no danger at all from the Popularity of a Subject. For Souldiers are never so generally unjust, as to side with their Captain; though they love him, against their Soveraign, when they love not onely his Person, but also his Cause. And therefore those, who by violence have at any time suppressed the Power of their lawfull Soveraign, before they could settle themselves in his place, have been alwayes put to the trouble of contriving their Titles, to save the People from the shame of receiving them. To have a known Right to Soveraign Power, is so popular a quality, as he that has it needs no more, for his own part, to turn the hearts of his Subjects to him, but that they see him able absolutely to govern his own Family: Nor, on the part of his enemies, but a disbanding of their Armies. For the greatest and most active part of Mankind, has never hetherto been well contented with the present.

Concerning the Offices of one Soveraign to another, which are comprehended in that Law, which is commonly called the *Law of Nations*, I need not say any thing in this place; because the Law of Nations, and the Law of Nature, is the same thing. And every Soveraign hath the same Right, in procuring the safety of his People, that any particular man can have, in procuring the safety of his own Body. And the same Law, that dictateth to men that have no Civil Government, what they ought to do, and what to avoyd in regard of one another, dictateth the same to Common-wealths, that is, to the Consciences of Soveraign Princes, and Soveraign Assemblies; there being no Court of Naturall Justice, but in the Conscience onely; where not Man, but God raigneth; whose Lawes, (such of them as oblige all Mankind,) in respect of God, as he is the Author of [186] Nature, are *Naturall*; and in respect of the same God, as he is King of Kings, are *Lawes*. But of the Kingdome of God, as King of Kings, and as King also of a peculiar People, I shall speak in the rest of this discourse.

CHAP. XXXI

Of the KINGDOME OF GOD BY NATURE

The scope of That the condition of meer Nature, that is to say, of
the following absolute Liberty, such as is theirs, that neither are Sov-
Chapters eraigns, nor Subjects, is Anarchy, and the condition of
Warre: That the Præcepts, by which men are guided to
avoyd that condition, are the Lawes of Nature: That
a Common-wealth, without Soveraign Power, is but a
word, without substance, and cannot stand: That Subjects owe to Soveraigns, simple Obedience, in all things,
wherein their obedience is not repugnant to the Lawes

of God, I have sufficiently proved, in that which I have
already written. There wants onely, for the entire knowledge of Civill duty, to know what are those Lawes of
God. For without that, a man knows not, when he is
commanded any thing by the Civill Power, whether it be
contrary to the Law of God, or not: and so, either by too
much civill obedience, offends the Divine Majesty, or
through feare of offending God, transgresses the commandements of the Common-wealth. To avoyd both
these Rocks, it is necessary to know what are the Lawes
Divine. And seeing the knowledge of all Law, dependeth
on the knowledge of the Soveraign Power; I shall say
something in that which followeth, of the KINGDOME
OF GOD.

God is King, let the Earth rejoyce, saith the Psalm-   *Psal. 96. 1*[69]
ist. And again, God is King though the Nations be   *Psal. 98. 1*[70]
angry; and he that sitteth on the Cherubins, though the   *Who are*
earth be moved. Whether men will or not, they must   *subjects in*
be subject alwayes to the Divine Power. By denying the   *the kingdome*
Existence, or Providence of God, men may shake off   *of God*
their Ease, but not their Yoke. But to call this Power
of God, which extendeth it selfe not onely to Man, but
also to Beasts, and Plants, and Bodies inanimate, by
the name of Kingdome, is but a metaphoricall use of
the word. For he onely is properly said to Raigne, that
governs his Subjects, by his Word, and by promise of
Rewards to those that obey it, and by threatning them
with Punishment that obey it not. Subjects therefore in
the Kingdome of God, are not Bodies Inanimate, nor
creatures Irrationall; because they understand no Precepts as his: Nor Atheists; nor they that believe not that
God has any care of the actions of mankind; because
they acknowledge no Word for his, nor have hope of his
rewards, or fear of his threatnings. They therefore that
believe there is a God that governeth the [187] world,
and hath given Præcepts, and propounded Rewards,
and Punishments to Mankind, are Gods Subjects; all the
rest, are to be understood as Enemies.

A Threefold
Word of
God, Reason,
Revelation,
Prophecy
To rule by Words, requires that such Words be manifestly made known; for else they are no Lawes: For to the nature of Lawes belongeth a sufficient, and clear Promulgation, such as may take away the excuse of Ignorance; which in the Lawes of men is but of one onely kind, and that is, Proclamation, or Promulgation by the voyce of man. But God declareth his Lawes three wayes; by the Dictates of *Naturall Reason*, by *Revelation*, and by the *Voyce* of some *man*, to whom by the operation of Miracles, he procureth credit with the rest. From hence there ariseth a triple Word of God, *Rational, Sensible* and *Prophetique*: to which Correspondeth a triple Hearing; *Right Reason, Sense Supernaturall*, and *Faith*. As for Sense Supernaturall, which consisteth in Revelation, or Inspiration, there have not been any Universall Lawes so given, because God speaketh not in that manner, but to particular persons, and to divers men divers things.

A twofold
Kingdome
of God,
Naturall and
Prophetique
From the difference between the other two kinds of Gods Word, *Rationall*, and *Prophetique*, there may be attributed to God, a two-fold Kingdome, *Naturall*, and *Prophetique*: Naturall, wherein he governeth as many of Mankind as acknowledge his Providence, by the naturall Dictates of Right Reason; And Prophetique, wherein having chosen out one peculiar Nation (the Jewes) for his Subjects, he governed them, and none but them, not onely by naturall Reason, but by Positive Lawes, which he gave them by the mouths of his holy Prophets. Of the Naturall Kingdome of God I intend to speak in this Chapter.

The Right
of Gods
Soveraignty
is derived
from his
Omnipotence
The Right of Nature, whereby God reigneth over men, and punisheth those that break his Lawes, is to be derived, not from his Creating them, as if he required obedience, as of Gratitude for his benefits; but from his *Irresistible Power*. I have formerly shewn, how the Soveraign Right ariseth from Pact: To shew how the same Right may arise from Nature, requires no more, but to shew in what case it is never taken away. Seeing all

men by Nature had Right to All things, they had Right
every one to reigne over all the rest. But because this
Right could not be obtained by force, it concerned the
safety of every one, laying by that Right, to set up men
(with Soveraign Authority) by common consent, to rule
and defend them: whereas if there had been any man
of Power Irresistible; there had been no reason, why he
should not by that Power have ruled, and defended both
himselfe, and them, according to his own discretion. To
those therefore whose Power is irresistible, the dominion of all men adhæreth naturally by their excellence
of Power; and consequently it is from that Power, that
the Kingdome over men, and the Right of afflicting men
at his pleasure, belongeth Naturally to God Almighty;
not as Creator, and Gracious; but as Omnipotent. And
though Punishment be due for Sinne onely, because by
that word is understood Affliction for Sinne; yet the
Right of [188] Afflicting, is not alwayes derived from
mens Sinne, but from Gods Power.

This question, *Why Evill men often Prosper, and* *Sinne not the*
Good men suffer Adversity, has been much disputed by *cause of all*
the Antient, and is the same with this of ours, *by what* *Affliction*
Right God dispenseth the Prosperities and Adversities
of this life; and is of that difficulty, as it hath shaken
the faith, not onely of the Vulgar, but of Philosophers,
and which is more, of the Saints, concerning the Divine
Providence. *How Good* (saith *David*) *is the God of* *Psal.* 72.
Israel to those that are Upright in Heart; and yet my feet *ver.* 1, 2, 3[71]
were almost gone, my treadings had well-nigh slipt; for
I was grieved at the Wicked, when I saw the Ungodly in
such Prosperity. And *Job,* how earnestly does he expos-
tulate with God, for the many Afflictions he suffered,
notwithstanding his Righteousnesse? This question in
the case of *Job,* is decided by God himselfe, not by arguments derived from *Job's* Sinne, but his own Power. For
whereas the friends of *Job* drew their arguments from
his Affliction to his Sinne, and he defended himselfe by
the conscience of his Innocence, God himselfe taketh up

the matter, and having justified the Affliction by argu-
Job 38. v. 4 ments drawn from his Power, such as this, *Where wast thou when I layd the foundations of the earth*, and the like, both approved *Job's* Innocence, and reproved the Erroneous doctrine of his friends. Conformable to this doctrine is the sentence of our Saviour, concerning the man that was born Blind, in these words,[72] *Neither hath this man sinned, nor his fathers; but that the works of God might be made manifest in him.* And though it be said,[73] *That Death entred into the world by sinne*, (by which is meant that if *Adam* had never sinned, he had never dyed, that is, never suffered any separation of his soule from his body,) it follows not thence, that God could not justly have Afflicted him, though he had not Sinned, as well as he afflicteth other living creatures, that cannot sinne.

Divine Lawes   Having spoken of the Right of Gods Soveraignty, as grounded onely on Nature; we are to consider next, what are the Divine Lawes, or Dictates of Naturall Reason; which Lawes concern either the naturall Duties of one man to another, or the Honour naturally due to our Divine Soveraign. The first are the same Lawes of Nature, of which I have spoken already in the 14. and 15. Chapters of this Treatise; namely, Equity, Justice, Mercy, Humility, and the rest of the Morall Vertues. It remaineth therefore that we consider, what Præcepts are dictated to men, by their Naturall Reason onely, without other word of God, touching the Honour and Worship of the Divine Majesty.

Honour and   Honour consisteth in the inward thought, and opin-
Worship what ion of the Power, and Goodnesse of another: and therefore to Honour God, is to think as Highly of his Power and Goodnesse, as is possible. And of that opinion, the externall signes appearing in the Words, and Actions of men, are called *Worship*; which is one part of that which the Latines understand by the word *Cultus*: For *Cultus* signifieth properly, and constantly, that labour which a man bestowes on any thing, with a

purpose to make benefit by it. Now those things [189] whereof we make benefit, are either subject to us, and the profit they yeeld, followeth the labour we bestow upon them, as a naturall effect; or they are not subject to us, but answer our labour, according to their own Wills. In the first sense the labour bestowed on the Earth, is called *Culture*; and the education of Children a *Culture* of their mindes. In the second sense, where mens wills are to be wrought to our purpose, not by Force, but by Compleasance, it signifieth as much as Courting, that is, a winning of favour by good offices; as by praises, by acknowledging their Power, and by whatsoever is pleasing to them from whom we look for any benefit. And this is properly *Worship*: in which sense *Publicola*, is understood for a Worshipper of the People; and *Cultus Dei*, for the Worship of God.

From internall Honour, consisting in the opinion of Power and Goodnesse, arise three Passions; *Love*, which hath reference to Goodnesse; and *Hope*, and *Fear*, that relate to Power: And three parts of externall worship; *Praise*, *Magnifying*, and *Blessing*: The subject of Praise, being Goodnesse; the subject of Magnifying, and Blessing, being Power, and the effect thereof Felicity. Praise, and Magnifying are significant both by Words, and Actions: By Words, when we say a man is Good, or Great: By Actions, when we thank him for his Bounty, and obey his Power. The opinion of the Happinesse of another, can onely be expressed by words. *Severall signes of Honour*

There be some signes of Honour, (both in Attributes and Actions,) that be Naturally so; as amongst Attributes, *Good*, *Just*, *Liberall*, and the like; and amongst Actions, *Prayers*, *Thanks*, and *Obedience*. Others are so by Institution, or Custome of men; and in some times and places are Honourable; in others Dishonourable; in others Indifferent: such as are the Gestures in Salutation, Prayer, and Thanksgiving, in different times and places, differently used. The former is *Naturall*; the later *Arbitrary* Worship. *Worship Naturall and Arbitrary*

Worship   And of Arbitrary Worship, there bee two differences:
Commanded For sometimes it is a *Commanded*, sometimes *Vol-*
and Free *untary* Worship: Commanded, when it is such as hee
requireth, who is Worshipped: Free, when it is such as
the Worshipper thinks fit. When it is Commanded, not
the words, or gesture, but the obedience is the Worship.
But when Free, the Worship consists in the opinion of
the beholders: for if to them the words, or actions by
which we intend honour, seem ridiculous, and tending
to contumely; they are no Worship; because no signes
of Honour; and no signes of Honour; because a signe is
not a signe to him that giveth it, but to him to whom it
is made; that is, to the spectator.

Worship   Again, there is a *Publique*, and a *Private* Worship.
Publique and Publique, is the Worship that a Common-wealth per-
Private formeth, as one Person. Private, is that which a Private
person exhibiteth. Publique, in respect of the whole
Common-wealth, is Free; but in respect of Particular
men it is not so. Private, is in secret Free; but in the sight
of the multitude, it is never without some Restraint,
either from the Lawes, or from the Opinion of men;
which is contrary to the nature of Liberty.

The End of   The End of Worship amongst men, is Power. For
Worship where a man [190] seeth another worshipped, he supposeth him powerfull, and is the readier to obey him;
which makes his Power greater. But God has no Ends:
the worship we do him, proceeds from our duty, and
is directed according to our capacity, by those rules of
Honour, that Reason dictateth to be done by the weak
to the more potent men, in hope of benefit, for fear of
dammage, or in thankfulnesse for good already received
from them.

Attributes   That we may know what worship of God is taught us
of Divine by the light of Nature, I will begin with his Attributes.
Honour Where, First, it is manifest, we ought to attribute to him
Existence: For no man can have the will to honour that,
which he thinks not to have any Beeing.

Secondly, that those Philosophers, who sayd the

World, or the Soule of the World was God, spake unwor-
thily of him; and denyed his Existence: For by God, is
understood the cause of the World; and to say the World
is God, is to say there is no cause of it, that is, no God.

Thirdly, to say the World was not Created, but Eternall, (seeing that which is Eternall has no cause,) is to
deny there is a God.

Fourthly, that they who attributing (as they think)
Ease to God, take from him the care of Mankind; take
from him his Honour: for it takes away mens love, and
fear of him; which is the root of Honour.

Fifthly, in those things that signifie Greatnesse, and
Power; to say he is *Finite*, is not to Honour him: For it
is not a signe of the Will to Honour God, to attribute to
him lesse than we can; and Finite, is lesse than we can;
because to Finite, it is easie to adde more.

Therefore to attribute *Figure* to him, is not Honour;
for all Figure is Finite:

Nor to say we conceive, and imagine, or have an
Idea of him, in our mind: for whatsoever we conceive
is Finite:

Nor to attribute to him *Parts*, or *Totality*; which are
the Attributes onely of things Finite:

Nor to say he is in this, or that *Place*: for whatsoever
is in Place, is bounded, and Finite:

Nor that he is *Moved*, or *Resteth*: for both these
Attributes ascribe to him Place:

Nor that there be more Gods than one; because it
implies them all Finite: for there cannot be more than
one Infinite:

Nor to ascribe to him (unlesse Metaphorically, meaning not the Passion, but the Effect) Passions that partake
of Griefe; as *Repentance*, *Anger*, *Mercy*: or of Want; as
Appetite, *Hope*, *Desire*; or of any Passive faculty: For
Passion, is Power limited by somewhat else.

And therefore when we ascribe to God a *Will*, it is not
to be understood, as that of Man, for a *Rationall Appetite*; but as the Power, by which he effecteth every thing.

Likewise when we attribute to him *Sight*, and other acts of Sense; as also *Knowledge*, and *Understanding*; which in us is nothing else, but a tumult of the mind, raised by externall things that presse the organicall parts of mans body: For there is no such thing in God; and being things that depend on naturall causes, cannot be attributed to him.

[191]Hee that will attribute to God, nothing but what is warranted by naturall Reason, must either use such Negative Attributes, as *Infinite*, *Eternall*, *Incomprehensible*; or Superlatives, as *Most High*, *most Great*, and the like; or Indefinite, as *Good*, *Just*, *Holy*, *Creator*; and in such sense, as if he meant not to declare what he is, (for that were to circumscribe him within the limits of our Fancy,) but how much wee admire him, and how ready we would be to obey him; which is a signe of Humility, and of a Will to honour him as much as we can: For there is but one Name to signifie our Conception of his Nature, and that is, I AM: and but one Name of his Relation to us, and that is *God*; in which is contained Father, King, and Lord.

Actions that are signes of Divine Honour   Concerning the actions of Divine Worship, it is a most generall Precept of Reason, that they be signes of the Intention to Honour God; such as are, First, *Prayers*: For not the Carvers, when they made Images, were thought to make them Gods; but the People that *Prayed* to them.

Secondly, *Thanksgiving*; which differeth from Prayer in Divine Worship, no otherwise, than that Prayers precede, and Thanks succeed the benefit; the end both of the one, and the other, being to acknowledge God, for Author of all benefits, as well past, as future.

Thirdly, *Gifts*; that is to say, *Sacrifices*, and *Oblations*, (if they be of the best,) are signes of Honour: for they are Thanksgivings.

Fourthly, *Not to swear by any but God*, is naturally a signe of Honour: for it is a confession that God onely knoweth the heart; and that no mans wit, or strength can protect a man against Gods vengence on the perjured.

Fifthly, it is a part of Rationall Worship, to speak Considerately of God; for it argues a Fear of him, and Fear, is a confession of his Power. Hence followeth, That the name of God is not to be used rashly, and to no purpose; for that is as much, as in Vain: And it is to no purpose, unlesse it be by way of Oath, and by order of the Common-wealth, to make Judgements certain; or between Common-wealths, to avoyd Warre. And that disputing of Gods nature is contrary to his Honour: For it is supposed, that in this naturall Kingdome of God, there is no other way to know any thing, but by naturall Reason; that is, from the Principles of naturall Science; which are so farre from teaching us any thing of Gods nature, as they cannot teach us our own nature, nor the nature of the smallest creature living. And therefore, when men out of the Principles of naturall Reason, dispute of the Attributes of God, they but dishonour him: For in the Attributes which we give to God, we are not to consider the signification of Philosophicall Truth; but the signification of Pious Intention, to do him the greatest Honour we are able. From the want of which consideration, have proceeded the volumes of disputation about the Nature of God, that tend not to his Honour, but to the honour of our own wits, and learning; and are nothing else but inconsiderate, and vain abuses of his Sacred Name.

Sixthly, in *Prayers, Thanksgiving, Offerings* and *Sacrifices*, it is a Dictate of naturall Reason, that they be every one in his kind the [192] best, and most significant of Honour. As for example, that Prayers, and Thanksgiving, be made in Words and Phrases, not sudden, nor light, nor Plebeian; but beautifull, and well composed; For else we do not God as much honour as we can. And therefore the Heathens did absurdly, to worship Images for Gods: But their doing it in Verse, and with Musick, both of Voyce, and Instruments, was reasonable. Also

that the Beasts they offered in sacrifice, and the Gifts
they offered, and their actions in Worshipping, were full
of submission, and commemorative of benefits received,
was according to reason, as proceeding from an intention to honour him.

Seventhly, Reason directeth not onely to worship God
in Secret; but also, and especially, in Publique, and in
the sight of men: For without that, (that which in honour is most acceptable) the procuring others to honour
him, is lost.

Lastly, Obedience to his Lawes (that is, in this case
to the Lawes of Nature,) is the greatest worship of all.
For as Obedience is more acceptable to God than Sacrifice; so also to set light by his Commandements, is the
greatest of all contumelies. And these are the Lawes of
that Divine Worship, which naturall Reason dictateth to
private men.

Publique   But seeing a Common-wealth is but one Person, it
Worship   ought also to exhibite to God but one Worship; which
consisteth in   then it doth, when it commandeth it to be exhibited
Uniformity by Private men, Publiquely. And this is Publique Worship; the property whereof, is to be *Uniforme*: For those
actions that are done differently, by different men, cannot be said to be a Publique Worship. And therefore,
where many sorts of Worship be allowed, proceeding
from the different Religions of Private men, it cannot
be said there is any Publique Worship, nor that the
Common-wealth is of any Religion at all.

All Attributes   And because words (and consequently the Attrib-
depend on   utes of God) have their signification by agreement, and
the Lawes constitution of men; those Attributes are to be held sig-
Civill   nificative of Honour, that men intend shall so be; and
whatsoever may be done by the wills of particular men,
where there is no Law but Reason, may be done by
the will of the Common-wealth, by Lawes Civill. And
because a Common-wealth hath no Will, nor makes no
Lawes, but those that are made by the Will of him, or
them that have the Soveraign Power; it followeth, that

those Attributes which the Soveraign ordaineth, in the
Worship of God, for signes of Honour, ought to be
taken and used for such, by private men in their publique Worship.

But because not all Actions are signes by Constitu- *Not all*
tion; but some are Naturally signes of Honour, others *Actions*
of Contumely, these later (which are those that men
are ashamed to do in the sight of them they reverence)
cannot be made by humane power a part of Divine worship; nor the former (such as are decent, modest, humble
Behaviour) ever be separated from it. But whereas there
be an infinite number of Actions, and Gestures, of an
indifferent nature; such of them as the Common-wealth
shall ordain to be Publiquely and Universally in use, as
signes of Honour, and part of Gods Worship, are to be
taken [193] and used for such by the Subjects. And that
which is said in the Scripture, *It is better to obey God
than men,*[74] hath place in the kingdome of God by Pact,
and not by Nature.

Having thus briefly spoken of the Naturall Kingdome *Naturall*
of God, and his Naturall Lawes, I will adde onely to *Punishments*
this Chapter a short declaration of his Naturall Punishments. There is no action of man in this life, that is not
the beginning of so long a chayn of Consequences, as
no humane Providence, is high enough, to give a man
a prospect to the end. And in this Chayn, there are
linked together both pleasing and unpleasing events;
in such manner, as he that will do any thing for his
pleasure, must engage himselfe to suffer all the pains
annexed to it; and these pains, are the Naturall Punishments of those actions, which are the beginning of
more Harme than Good. And hereby it comes to passe,
that Intemperance, is naturally punished with Diseases;
Rashnesse, with Mischances; Injustice, with the Violence of Enemies; Pride, with Ruine; Cowardise, with
Oppression; Negligent government of Princes, with
Rebellion; and Rebellion, with Slaughter. For seeing
Punishments are consequent to the breach of Lawes;

Naturall Punishments must be naturally consequent to the breach of the Lawes of Nature; and therfore follow them as their naturall, not arbitrary effects.

The Conclu- And thus farre concerning the Constitution, Nature, *sion of the* and Right of Soveraigns; and concerning the Duty of *Second Part* Subjects, derived from the Principles of Naturall Reason. And now, considering how different this Doctrine is, from the Practise of the greatest part of the world, especially of these Western parts, that have received their Morall learning from *Rome*, and *Athens*; and how much depth of Morall Philosophy is required, in them that have the Administration of the Soveraign Power; I am at the point of believing this my labour, as uselesse, as the Common-wealth of *Plato*; For he also is of opinion that it is impossible for the disorders of State, and change of Governments by Civill Warre, ever to be taken away, till Soveraigns be Philosophers.[75] But when I consider again, that the Science of Naturall Justice, is the onely Science necessary for Soveraigns, and their principall Ministers; and that they need not be charged with the Sciences Mathematicall, (as by *Plato* they are,)[76] further, than by good Lawes to encourage men to the study of them; and that neither *Plato*, nor any other Philosopher hitherto, hath put into order, and sufficiently, or probably proved all the Theoremes of Morall doctrine, that men may learn thereby, both how to govern, and how to obey; I recover some hope, that one time or other, this writing of mine, may fall into the hands of a Soveraign, who will consider it himselfe, (for it is short, and I think clear,) without the help of any interested, or envious Interpreter; and by the exercise of entire Soveraignty, in protecting the Publique teaching of it, convert this Truth of Speculation, into the Utility of Practice. [195]

PART THREE
OF A CHRISTIAN COMMON-WEALTH

CHAP. XXXII

Of the Principles of CHRISTIAN POLITIQUES

I have derived the Rights of Soveraigne Power, and the duty of Subjects hitherto, from the Principles of Nature onely; such as Experience has found true, or Consent (concerning the use of words) has made so; that is to say, from the nature of Men, known to us by Experience, and from Definitions (of such words as are Essentiall to all Politicall reasoning) universally agreed on. But in that I am next to handle, which is the Nature and Rights of a CHRISTIAN COMMON-WEALTH, whereof there dependeth much upon Supernaturall Revelations of the Will of God; the ground of my Discourse must be, not only the Naturall Word of God, but also the Propheticall.

The Word of God delivered by Prophets is the main principle of Christian Politiques

Neverthelesse, we are not to renounce our Senses, and Experience; nor (that which is the undoubted Word of God) our naturall Reason. For they are the talents which he hath put into our hands to negotiate, till the coming again of our blessed Saviour; and therefore not to be folded up in the Napkin of an Implicite Faith, but employed in the purchase of Justice, Peace, and true Religion. For though there be many things in Gods Word above Reason; that is to say, which cannot by naturall reason be either demonstrated, or confuted; yet there is nothing contrary to it; but when it seemeth so, the fault is either in our unskilfull Interpretation, or erroneous Ratiocination.

Yet is not naturall Reason to be renounced

Therefore, when any thing therein written is too hard for our examination, wee are bidden to captivate our understanding to the Words; and not to labour in sifting out a Philosophicall truth by Logick, of such mysteries as are not comprehensible, nor fall under any rule of naturall science. For it is with the mysteries of our Religion, as with wholsome pills for the sick, which swallowed whole, have the vertue to cure; but chewed, are for the most part cast up again without effect.

What it is to [196] But by the Captivity of our Understanding,
captivate is not meant a Submission of the Intellectuall faculty,
the Under- to the Opinion of any other man; but of the Will to
standing Obedience, where obedience is due. For Sense, Memory, Understanding, Reason, and Opinion are not in our power to change; but alwaies, and necessarily such, as the things we see, hear, and consider suggest unto us; and therefore are not effects of our Will, but our Will of them. We then Captivate our Understanding and Reason, when we forbear contradiction; when we so speak, as (by lawfull Authority) we are commanded; and when we live accordingly; which in sum, is Trust, and Faith reposed in him that speaketh, though the mind be incapable of any Notion at all from the words spoken.

How God When God speaketh to man, it must be either imme-
speaketh diately; or by mediation of another man, to whom he
to men had formerly spoken by himself immediately. How God speaketh to a man immediately, may be understood by those well enough, to whom he hath so spoken; but how the same should be understood by another, is hard, if not impossible to know. For if a man pretend to me, that God hath spoken to him supernaturally, and immediately, and I make doubt of it, I cannot easily perceive what argument he can produce, to oblige me to beleeve it. It is true, that if he be my Soveraign, he may oblige me to obedience, so, as not by act or word to declare I beleeve him not; but not to think any otherwise then my reason perswades me. But if one that hath not

such authority over me, shall pretend the same, there is nothing that exacteth either beleefe, or obedience.

For to say that God hath spoken to him in the Holy Scripture, is not to say God hath spoken to him immediately, but by mediation of the Prophets, or of the Apostles, or of the Church, in such manner as he speaks to all other Christian men. To say he hath spoken to him in a Dream, is no more than to say he dreamed that God spake to him; which is not of force to win beleef from any man, that knows dreams are for the most part naturall, and may proceed from former thoughts; and such dreams as that, from selfe conceit, and foolish arrogance, and false opinion of a mans own godlinesse, or other vertue, by which he thinks he hath merited the favour of extraordinary Revelation. To say he hath seen a Vision, or heard a Voice, is to say, that he hath dreamed between sleeping and waking: for in such manner a man doth many times naturally take his dream for a vision, as not having well observed his own slumbering. To say he speaks by supernaturall Inspiration, is to say he finds an ardent desire to speak, or some strong opinion of himself, for which he can alledge no naturall and sufficient reason. So that though God Almighty can speak to a man, by Dreams, Visions, Voice, and Inspiration; yet he obliges no man to beleeve he hath so done to him that pretends it; who (being a man), may erre, and (which is more) may lie.

How then can he, to whom God hath never revealed his Wil immediately (saving by the way of natural reason) know when he is to obey, or not to obey his Word, delivered by him, that sayes he is a Prophet? Of 400 Prophets, of whom the K. of *Israel* asked counsel, concerning [197] the warre he made against *Ramoth Gilead,* only *Micaiah* was a true one.[1] The Prophet that was sent to prophecy against the Altar set up by *Jeroboam,*[2] though a true Prophet, and that by two miracles done in his presence appears to be a Prophet sent from God, was yet deceived by another old Prophet, that perswaded him

By what marks Prophets are known
1 Kings 22
1 Kings 13

as from the mouth of God, to eat and drink with him. If one Prophet deceive another, what certainty is there of knowing the will of God, by other way than that of Reason? To which I answer out of the Holy Scripture, that there be two marks, by which together, not asunder, a true Prophet is to be known. One is the doing of miracles; the other is the not teaching any other Religion than that which is already established. Asunder (I say) neither of these is sufficient. *If a Prophet rise amongst you, or a Dreamer of dreams, and shall pretend the doing of a miracle, and the miracle come to passe; if he say, Let us follow strange Gods, which thou hast not known, thou shalt not hearken to him, &c. But that Prophet and Dreamer of dreams shall be put to death, because he hath spoken to you to Revolt from the Lord your God.* In which words two things are to be observed; First, that God wil not have miracles alone serve for arguments, to approve the Prophets calling; but (as it is in the third verse) for an experiment of the constancy of our adherence to himself. For the works of the *Egyptian* Sorcerers, though not so great as those of *Moses*, yet were great miracles.[3] Secondly, that how great soever the miracle be, yet if it tend to stir up revolt against the King, or him that governeth by the Kings authority, he that doth such miracle, is not to be considered otherwise than as sent to make triall of their allegiance. For these words, *revolt from the Lord your God*, are in this place equivalent to *revolt from your King*. For they had made God their King by pact at the foot of Mount *Sinai*; who ruled them by *Moses* only; for he only spake with God, and from time to time declared Gods Commandements to the people. In like manner, after our Saviour Christ had made his Disciples acknowledge him for the *Messiah*, (that is to say, for Gods anointed, whom the nation of the *Jews* daily expected for their King, but refused when he came,) he omitted not to advertise them of the danger of miracles. *There shall arise* (saith he) *false Christs, and false Prophets, and shall doe great wonders*

Deut. 13 *v.* 1, 2, 3, 4, 5

Mat. 24. 24

*and miracles, even to the seducing (if it were possible) of
the very Elect.* By which it appears, that false Prophets
may have the power of miracles; yet are wee not to take
their doctrin for Gods Word. St. *Paul* says further to
the *Galatians,* that *if himself, or an Angell from heaven*   Gal. 1. 8
*preach another Gospel to them, than he had preached,
let him be accursed.* That Gospel was, that Christ was
King; so that all preaching against the power of the King
received, in consequence to these words, is by St. *Paul*
accursed. For his speech is addressed to those, who by
his preaching had already received *Jesus* for the *Christ,*
that is to say, for King of the *Jews.*

And as Miracles, without preaching that Doctrine   *The marks*
which God hath established; so preaching the true Doc-   *of a Prophet*
trine, without the doing of Miracles, is an unsufficient   *in the old*
argument of immediate Revelation. For [198] if a man   *law, Miracles,*
that teacheth not false Doctrine, should pretend to bee   *and Doctrine*
a Prophet without shewing any Miracle, he is never the   *conformable*
more to bee regarded for his pretence, as is evident by   *to the law*
Deut. 18. *v.* 21, 22. *If thou say in thy heart, How shall
we know that the Word* (of the Prophet) *is not that
which the Lord hath spoken. When the Prophet shall
have spoken in the name of the Lord, that which shall
not come to passe, that's the word which the Lord hath
not spoken, but the Prophet has spoken it out of the
pride of his own heart, fear him not.* But a man may here
again ask, When the Prophet hath foretold a thing, how
shal we know whether it will come to passe or not? For
he may foretel it as a thing to arrive after a certain long
time, longer then the time of mans life; or indefinitely,
that it will come to passe one time or other: in which
case this mark of a Prophet is unusefull; and therefore
the miracles that oblige us to beleeve a Prophet, ought
to be confirmed by an immediate, or a not long deferr'd
event. So that it is manifest, that the teaching of the Religion which God hath established, and the shewing of a
present Miracle, joined together, were the only marks
whereby the Scripture would have a true Prophet, that

is to say, immediate Revelation to be acknowledged; neither of them being singly sufficient to oblige any other man to regard what he saith.

Miracles   Seeing therefore Miracles now cease, we have no sign *ceasing,* left, whereby to acknowledge the pretended Revela-*Prophets* tions, or Inspirations of any private man; nor obligation *cease, and* to give ear to any Doctrine, farther than it is conform-*the Scripture* able to the Holy Scriptures, which since the time of our *supplies their* Saviour, supply the place, and sufficiently recompense *place* the want of all other Prophecy; and from which, by wise and learned interpretation, and carefull ratiocination, all rules and precepts necessary to the knowledge of our duty both to God and man, without Enthusiasme, or supernaturall Inspiration, may easily be deduced. And this Scripture is it, out of which I am to take the Principles of my Discourse, concerning the Rights of those that are the Supream Governors on earth, of Christian Common-wealths; and of the duty of Christian Subjects towards their Soveraigns. And to that end, I shall speak in the next Chapter, of the Books, Writers, Scope and Authority of the Bible. [199]

CHAP. XXXIII

Of the Number, Antiquity, Scope, Authority, and Interpreters of the Books of Holy SCRIPTURE

Of the Books By the Books of Holy SCRIPTURE, are understood those, *of Holy* which ought to be the *Canon,* that is to say, the Rules *Scripture* of Christian life. And because all Rules of life, which men are in conscience bound to observe, are Laws; the question of the Scripture, is the question of what is Law throughout all Christendome, both Naturall, and Civill. For though it be not determined in Scripture, what Laws every Christian King shall constitute in his own Dominions; yet it is determined what laws he shall not constitute. Seeing therefore I have already proved, that Soveraigns in their own Dominions are the sole Legislators; those Books only are Canonicall, that is, Law, in every nation, which are established for such by the Soveraign Authority. It is true, that God is the Soveraign of all Soveraigns; and therefore, when he speaks to any Subject, he ought to be obeyed, whatsoever any earthly Potentate command to the contrary. But the question is not of obedience to God, but of *when*, and *what* God hath said; which to Subjects that have no supernaturall revelation, cannot be known, but by that naturall reason, which guided them, for the obtaining of Peace and Justice, to obey the authority of their severall Common-wealths; that is to say, of their lawfull Soveraigns. According to this obligation, I can acknowledge no other Books of the Old Testament, to be Holy Scripture, but those which have been commanded to be acknowledged for such, by the Authority of the Church of *England*. What Books these are, is sufficiently known, without a Catalogue of them here; and they are the same that are acknowledged by St. *Jerome*,[4] who holdeth the rest, namely, the *Wisdome of Solomon, Ecclesiasticus, Judith, Tobias*, the first and the second of *Maccabees*, (though he had seen the first in *Hebrew*) and the third and fourth of *Esdras*, for *Apocrypha*. Of the Canonicall, *Josephus* a learned *Jew*, that wrote in the time of the Emperour *Domitian*, reckoneth *twenty two*, making the number agree with the *Hebrew* Alphabet.[5] St. *Jerome* does the same, though they reckon them in different manner. For *Josephus* numbers *five* Books of *Moses*, *thirteen* of *Prophets*, that writ the History of their own times (which how it agrees with the Prophets writings contained in the Bible wee shall see hereafter), and *four* of *Hymnes* and Morall Precepts. But St. *Jerome* reckons *five* Books of *Moses*, *eight* of *Prophets*, and *nine* of other Holy writ, which he calls of *Hagiographa*. The *Septuagint*, who were 70. learned men of the *Jews*, sent for by *Ptolemy* King of *Egypt*,[6] to translate the *Jewish* law, out of the *Hebrew* into the *Greek*, have [200] left us no other for holy Scripture in the *Greek* tongue, but the same that are received in the Church of *England*.

As for the Books of the New Testament, they are equally acknowledged for Canon by all Christian Churches, and by all Sects of Christians, that admit any Books at all for Canonicall.

Their Antiquity Who were the originall writers of the severall Books of Holy Scripture, has not been made evident by any sufficient testimony of other History, (which is the only proof of matter of fact); nor can be by any arguments of naturall Reason: for Reason serves only to convince the truth (not of fact, but) of consequence. The light therefore that must guide us in this question, must be that which is held out unto us from the Bookes themselves: And this light, though it shew us not the writer of every book, yet it is not unusefull to give us knowledge of the time, wherein they were written.

And first, for the *Pentateuch*, it is not argument enough that they were written by *Moses*, because they are called the five Books of *Moses*; no more than these titles, The Book of *Joshua*, the Book of *Judges*, the Book of *Ruth*, and the Books of the *Kings*, are arguments sufficient to prove, that they were written by *Joshua*, by the *Judges*, by *Ruth*, and by the *Kings*. For in titles of Books, the subject is marked, as often as the writer. The *History of Livy*, denotes the Writer; but the *History of Scanderbeg*, is denominated from the subject.[7] We read *The Pentateuch not written by Moses* in the last Chapter of *Deuteronomie*, *ver.* 6. concerning the sepulcher of *Moses*, *that no man knoweth of his sepulcher to this day*, that is, to the day wherein those words were written. It is therefore manifest, that those words were written after his interrement. For it were a strange interpretation, to say *Moses* spake of his own sepulcher (though by Prophecy), that it was not found to that day, wherein he was yet living. But it may perhaps be alledged, that the last Chapter only, not the whole *Pentateuch*, was written by some other man, but the rest not: Let us therefore consider that which we find in the Book of *Genesis, chap.* 12. *ver.* 6. *And* Abraham *passed through the land to the place of* Sichem, *unto the plain of* Moreh, *and the* Canaanite *was then in the land*; which must needs bee the words of one that wrote when the *Canaanite* was not in the land; and consequently, not of *Moses*, who dyed before he came into it. Likewise *Numbers* 21. *ver.* 14. the Writer citeth another more ancient Book, Entituled, *The Book of the Warres of the Lord*, wherein were registred the Acts of *Moses*, at the Red-sea, and at the brook of *Arnon*. It is therefore sufficiently evident, that the five Books of *Moses* were written after his time, though how long after it be not so manifest.

But though *Moses* did not compile those Books entirely, and in the form we have them; yet he wrote all that which hee is there said to have written: as for example, the Volume of the Law, which is contained, as it seemeth, in the 11 of *Deuteronomie*, and the following Chapters to the 27. which was also commanded to be written on stones, in their entry into the land of *Canaan*. And this did *Moses* himself write, and deliver to the Priests and Elders of *Israel*, to be [201] read every seventh year to all *Israel*, at their assembling in the feast of Tabernacles. And this is that Law which God commanded, that their Kings (when they should have established that form of Government) should take a copy of from the Priests and Levites; and which *Moses* commanded the Priests and Levites to lay in the side of the Arke; and the same which having been lost, was long time after found again by *Hilkiah*, and sent to King *Josias*,[8] who causing it to be read to the People, renewed the Covenant between God and them.

Deut. 31. 9

Deut. 31. 26

2 *King.* 22. 8
& 23. 1, 2, 3
*The Book
of Joshua
written after
his time*

That the Book of *Joshua* was also written long after the time of *Joshua*, may be gathered out of many places of the Book it self. *Joshua* had set up twelve stones in

Josh. 4. 9 the middest of *Jordan*, for a monument of their passage;
of which the Writer saith thus, *They are there unto this*
Josh. 5. 9 *day*; for *unto this day*, is a phrase that signifieth a time
past, beyond the memory of man. In like manner, upon
the saying of the Lord, that he had rolled off from the
people the Reproach of *Egypt*, the Writer saith, *The*
place is called Gilgal *unto this day*; which to have said in
the time of *Joshua* had been improper. So also the name
Josh. 7. 26 of the Valley of *Achor*, from the trouble that *Achan*
raised in the Camp,⁹ the Writer saith, *remaineth unto*
this day; which must needs bee therefore long after the
time of *Joshua*. Arguments of this kind there be many
other; as *Josh.* 8.29. 13.13. 14.14. 15.63.

The Booke of   The same is manifest by like arguments of the Book
Judges and   of *Judges*, chap. 1.21, 26. 6.24. 10.4. 15.19. 17.6.
Ruth written and *Ruth* 1. 1. but especially *Judg.* 18. 30. where
long after the it is said, that Jonathan¹⁰ *and his sonnes were Priests*
Captivity   *to the Tribe* of Dan, *untill the day of the captivity of*
the land.

The like of   That the Books of *Samuel* were also written after his
the Bookes of own time, there are the like arguments, 1 *Sam.* 5. 5. 7.13,
Samuel   15. 27.6. & 30.25. where, after *David* had adjudged
equall part of the spoiles, to them that guarded the
Ammunition, with them that fought, the Writer saith,
2 Sam. 6. 4 *He made it a Statute and an Ordinance to* Israel *to this*
day. Again, when *David* (displeased, that the Lord had
slain *Uzzah*, for putting out his hand to sustain the Ark,)
called the place *Perez-Uzzah*,¹¹ the Writer saith, it is called
so *to this day*: the time therefore of the writing of that
Book, must be long after the time of the fact; that is,
long after the time of *David*.

The Books   As for the two Books of the *Kings*, and the two books
of the Kings, of the *Chronicles*, besides the places which mention
and the such monuments, as the Writer saith, remained till his
Chronicles own days; such as are 1 *Kings* 9.13. 9.21. 10.12. 12.19.
2 *Kings* 2.22. 8.22. 10.27. 14.7. 16.6. 17.23. 17.34.
17.41. 1 *Chron.* 4.41. 5.26. It is argument sufficient
they were written after the captivity in *Babylon*, that

the History of them is continued till that time. For the Facts Registred are alwaies more ancient than the Register; and much more ancient than such Books as make mention of, and quote the Register; as these Books doe in divers places, referring the Reader to the Chronicles of the Kings of *Juda*, to the Chronicles of the Kings of *Israel*, to the Books of the Prophet *Samuel*, of the Prophet *Nathan*, of the Prophet *Ahijah*; to the Vision of *Jehdo*, to the Books of the Prophet *Serveiah*, and of the Prophet *Addo*.[12]

[202] The Books of *Esdras* and *Nehemiah* were written certainly after their return from captivity; because their return, the re-edification of the walls and houses of *Jerusalem*, the renovation of the Covenant, and ordination of their policy are therein contained. *Ezra and Nehemiah*

The History of Queen *Esther* is of the time of the Captivity; and therefore the Writer must have been of the same time, or after it. *Esther*

The Book of *Job* hath no mark in it of the time wherein it was written: and though it appear sufficiently (*Ezekiel* 14.14. and *James* 5.11.) that he was no fained person; yet the Book it self seemeth not to be a History, but a Treatise concerning a question in ancient time much disputed, *why wicked men have often prospered in this world, and good men have been afflicted*; and it is the more probable, because from the beginning, to the third verse of the third chapter, where the complaint of *Job* beginneth, the *Hebrew* is (as St. *Jerome* testifies) in prose; and from thence to the sixt verse of the last chapter in Hexameter Verses; and the rest of that chapter again in prose. So that the dispute is all in verse; and the prose is added, but as a Preface in the beginning, and an Epilogue in the end. But Verse is no usuall stile of such, as either are themselves in great pain, as *Job*; or of such as come to comfort them, as his friends; but in Philosophy, especially morall Philosophy, in ancient time frequent. *Job*

The *Psalmes* were written the most part by *David*, *The Psalter* for the use of the Quire. To these are added some Songs of *Moses*, and other holy men; and some of them after the return from the Captivity, as the 137. and the 126. whereby it is manifest that the Psalter was compiled, and put into the form it now hath, after the return of the *Jews* from *Babylon*.

The Proverbs   The *Proverbs*, being a Collection of wise and godly Sayings, partly of *Solomon*, partly of *Agur* the son of *Jakeh*; and partly of the Mother of King *Lemuel*,[13] cannot probably be thought to have been collected by *Solomon*, rather then by *Agur*, or the Mother of *Lemuel*; and that, though the sentences be theirs, yet the collection or compiling them into this one Book, was the work of some other godly man, that lived after them all.

Ecclesiastes   The Books of *Ecclesiastes* and the *Canticles* have
and the Can-   nothing that was not *Solomons*, except it be the Titles,
ticles   or Inscriptions. For *The Words of the Preacher, the Son of* David, *King in* Jerusalem; and, *The Song of Songs*, which is *Solomon*'s, seem to have been made for distinctions sake, then, when the Books of Scripture were gathered into one body of the Law; to the end, that not the Doctrine only, but the Authors also might be extant.

The Prophets   Of the Prophets, the most ancient, are *Sophoniah*, *Jonas*, *Amos*, *Hosea*, *Isaiah* and *Michaiah*, who lived in the time of *Amaziah*, and *Azariah*, otherwise *Ozias*, Kings of *Judah*.[14] But the Book of *Jonas* is not properly a Register of his Prophecy, (for that is contained in these few words, *Fourty dayes and* Ninivy *shall be destroyed*,)[15] but a History or Narration of his frowardenesse and disputing Gods commandements; so that there is small probability he should be the Author, seeing he is the subject of it. But the Book of *Amos* is his Prophecy.

[203] *Jeremiah*, *Abdias*,[16] *Nahum*, and *Habakkuk* prophecyed in the time of *Josiah*.

Ezekiel, *Daniel*, *Aggeus*, and *Zacharias*, in the Captivity.[17]

When *Joel* and *Malachi* prophecyed,[18] is not evident by their Writings. But considering the Inscriptions, or Titles of their Books, it is manifest enough, that the whole Scripture of the Old Testament, was set forth in the form we have it, after the return of the *Jews* from their Captivity in *Babylon*, and before the time of *Ptolemæus Philadelphus*, that caused it to bee translated into *Greek* by seventy men, which were sent him out of *Judea* for that purpose. And if the Books of *Apocrypha* (which are recommended to us by the Church, though not for Canonicall, yet for profitable Books for our instruction) may in this point be credited, the Scripture was set forth in the form wee have it in, by *Esdras*;[19] as may appear by that which he himself saith, in the second book, chapt. 14. verse 21, 22, &c. where speaking to God, he saith thus, *Thy law is burnt; therefore no man knoweth the things which thou hast done, or the works that are to begin. But if I have found Grace before thee, send down the holy Spirit into me, and I shall write all that hath been done in the world, since the beginning, which were written in thy Law, that men may find thy path, and that they which will live in the later days, may live.* And verse 45. *And it came to passe when the forty dayes were fulfilled, that the Highest spake, saying, The first that thou hast written, publish openly, that the worthy and unworthy may read it; but keep the seventy last, that thou mayst deliver them onely to such as be wise among the people.* And thus much concerning the time of the writing of the Bookes of the Old Testament.

The Writers of the New Testament lived all in lesse then an age after Christs Ascension, and had all of them seen our Saviour, or been his Disciples, except St. *Paul*, and St. *Luke*;[20] and consequently whatsoever was written by them, is as ancient as the time of the Apostles. But the time wherein the Books of the New Testament were received, and acknowledged by the Church to be of their writing, is not altogether so ancient. For, as the Bookes of the Old Testament are derived to us, from no higher time then that of *Esdras*, who by the direction of Gods Spirit retrived them, when they were lost: Those of the

The New Testament

New Testament, of which the copies were not many, nor could easily be all in any one private mans hand, cannot bee derived from a higher time, than that wherein the Governours of the Church collected, approved, and recommended them to us, as the writings of those Apostles and Disciples; under whose names they go. The first enumeration of all the Bookes, both of the Old, and New Testament, is in the Canons of the Apostles, supposed to be collected by *Clement* the first (after St. *Peter*) Bishop of *Rome*.[21] But because that is but supposed, and by many questioned, the Councell of *Laodicea* is the first we know, that recommended the Bible to the then Christian Churches, for the Writings of the Prophets and Apostles: and this Councell was held in the 364. yeer after Christ. At which time, though ambition had so far prevailed on the great Doctors of the Church, as [204] no more to esteem Emperours, though Christian, for the Shepherds of the people, but for Sheep; and Emperours not Christian, for Wolves; and endeavoured to passe their Doctrine, not for Counsell, and Information, as Preachers; but for Laws, as absolute Governours; and thought such frauds as tended to make the people the more obedient to Christian Doctrine, to be pious; yet I am perswaded they did not therefore falsifie the Scriptures, though the copies of the Books of the New Testament, were in the hands only of the Ecclesiasticks; because if they had had an intention so to doe, they would surely have made them more favorable to their power over Christian Princes, and Civill Soveraignty, than they are. I see not therefore any reason to doubt, but that the Old, and New Testament, as we have them now, are the true Registers of those things, which were done and said by the Prophets, and Apostles. And so perhaps are some of those Books which are called Apocrypha, if left out of the Canon, not for inconformity of Doctrine with the rest, but only because they are not found in the Hebrew. For after the conquest of Asia by Alexander the Great, there were few learned Jews, that were not perfect in

the Greek tongue. For the seventy Interpreters that converted the Bible into Greek, were all of them Hebrews;
and we have extant the works of *Philo*[22] and *Josephus*
both Jews, written by them eloquently in Greek. But it
is not the Writer, but the authority of the Church, that
maketh a Book Canonicall. And although these Books
were written by divers men, yet it is manifest the Writers *Their Scope*
were all indued with one and the same Spirit, in that they
conspire to one and the same end, which is the setting
forth of the Rights of the Kingdome of *God*, the *Father*,
Son, and *Holy Ghost*. For the Book of *Genesis*, deriveth
the Genealogy of Gods people, from the creation of the
World, to the going into Egypt: the other four Books
of *Moses*, contain the Election of God for their King,
and the Laws which hee prescribed for their Government: The Books of *Joshua*, *Judges*, *Ruth*, and *Samuel*,
to the time of *Saul*, describe the acts of Gods people, till
the time they cast off Gods yoke, and called for a King,
after the manner of their neighbour nations: The rest of
the History of the Old Testament, derives the succession
of the line of *David*, to the Captivity, out of which line
was to spring the restorer of the Kingdome of God, even
our blessed Saviour *God the Son*, whose coming was
foretold in the Bookes of the Prophets, after whom the
Evangelists writt his life, and actions, and his claim to
the Kingdome, whilst he lived on earth: and lastly, the
Acts, and Epistles of the Apostles, declare the coming
of God, the *Holy Ghost*, and the Authority he left with
them, and their successors, for the direction of the Jews,
and for the invitation of the Gentiles. In summe, the
Histories and the Prophecies of the old Testament, and
the Gospels and Epistles of the New Testament, have
had one and the same scope, to convert men to the obedience of God; 1. in *Moses*, and the Priests; 2. in the
man *Christ*; and 3. in the *Apostles* and the successors to
Apostolicall power. For these three at several times did
represent the person of God: *Moses*, and his successors
the High Priests, and Kings of Judah, in the [205] Old

Testament: *Christ* himself, in the time he lived on earth: and the *Apostles*, and their successors, from the day of Pentecost (when the *Holy Ghost* descended on them) to this day.

The question It is a question much disputed between the divers sects
of the of Christian Religion, *From whence the Scriptures derive*
Authority of *their Authority*; which question is also propounded
the Scriptures sometimes in other terms, as, *How wee know them to*
stated *be the Word of God*, or, *Why we beleeve them to be so*:
And the difficulty of resolving it, ariseth chiefly from the impropernesse of the words wherein the question it self is couched. For it is beleeved on all hands, that the first and originall *Author* of them is God; and consequently the question disputed, is not that. Again, it is manifest, that none can know they are Gods Word, (though all true Christians beleeve it,) but those to whom God himself hath revealed it supernaturally; and therefore the question is not rightly moved, of our *Knowledge* of it. Lastly, when the question is propounded of our *Beleefe*; because some are moved to beleeve for one, and others for other reasons, there can be rendred no one generall answer for them all. The question truly stated is, *By what Authority they are made Law.*

Their As far as they differ not from the Laws of Nature,
Authority there is no doubt, but they are the Law of God, and
and Inter- carry their Authority with them, legible to all men that
pretation have the use of naturall reason: but this is no other Authority, then that of all other Morall Doctrine consonant to Reason; the Dictates whereof are Laws, not *made*, but *Eternall*.

If they be made Law by God himselfe, they are of the nature of written Law, which are Laws to them only to whom God hath so sufficiently published them, as no man can excuse himself, by saying, he knew not they were his.

He therefore, to whom God hath not supernaturally revealed, that they are his, nor that those that published them, were sent by him, is not obliged to obey them, by any Authority, but his, whose Commands have already the force of Laws; that is to say, by any other Authority, then that of the Common-wealth, residing in the Soveraign, who only has the Legislative power. Again, if it be not the Legislative Authority of the Common-wealth, that giveth them the force of Laws, it must bee some other Authority derived from God, either private, or publique: if private, it obliges onely him, to whom in particular God hath been pleased to reveale it. For if every man should be obliged, to take for Gods Law, what particular men, on pretence of private Inspiration, or Revelation, should obtrude upon him, (in such a number of men, that out of pride, and ignorance, take their own Dreams, and extravagant Fancies, and Madnesse, for testimonies of Gods Spirit; or out of ambition, pretend to such Divine testimonies, falsely, and contrary to their own consciences,) it were impossible that any Divine Law should be acknowledged. If publique, it is the Authority of the *Common-wealth*, or of the *Church*. But the Church, if it be one person, is the same thing with a Common-wealth of [206] Christians; called a *Common-wealth*, because it consisteth of men united in one person, their Soveraign; and a *Church*, because it consisteth in Christian men, united in one Christian Soveraign. But if the Church be not one person, then it hath no authority at all; it can neither command, nor doe any action at all; nor is capable of having any power, or right to any thing; nor has any Will, Reason, nor Voice; for all these qualities are personall. Now if the whole number of Christians be not contained in one Common-wealth, they are not one person; nor is there an Universall Church that hath any authority over them; and therefore the Scriptures are not made Laws, by the Universall Church: or if it bee one Common-wealth, then all Christian Monarchs, and States are private persons, and subject to bee judged, deposed, and punished by an Universall Soveraigne of all Christendome. So that the question of the Authority of the Scriptures, is reduced to this, *Whether Christian Kings, and the Soveraigne Assemblies in Christian Common-wealths, be absolute in their own Territories, immediately under God; or subject to one Vicar of Christ, constituted over the Universall Church; to bee judged, condemned, deposed, and put to death, as hee shall think expedient, or necessary for the common good.*

Which question cannot bee resolved, without a more particular consideration of the Kingdome of God; from whence also, wee are to judge of the Authority of Interpreting the Scripture. For, whosoever hath a lawfull power over any Writing, to make it Law, hath the power also to approve, or disapprove the interpretation of the same. [207]

CHAP. XXXIV

Of the Signification of SPIRIT, ANGEL, and INSPIRATION in the Books of Holy Scripture

Body and Spirit how taken in the Scripture Seeing the foundation of all true Ratiocination, is the constant Signification of words; which in the Doctrine following, dependeth not (as in naturall science) on the Will of the Writer, nor (as in common conversation) on vulgar use, but on the sense they carry in the Scripture; It is necessary, before I proceed any further, to determine, out of the Bible, the meaning of such words, as by their ambiguity, may render what I am to inferre upon them, obscure, or disputable. I will begin with the words BODY, and SPIRIT, which in the language of the Schools are termed, *Substances, Corporeall,* and *Incorporeall.*

The Word *Body,* in the most generall acceptation, signifieth that which filleth, or occupyeth some certain room, or imagined place; and dependeth not on the imagination, but is a reall part of that we call the

Universe. For the *Universe*, being the Aggregate of all Bodies, there is no reall part thereof that is not also *Body*; nor any thing properly a *Body*, that is not also part of (that Aggregate of all *Bodies*) the *Universe*. The same also, because Bodies are subject to change, that is to say, to variety of apparence to the sense of living creatures, is called *Substance*, that is to say, *Subject*, to various accidents; as sometimes to be Moved, sometimes to stand Still; and to seem to our senses sometimes Hot, sometimes Cold, sometimes of one Colour, Smel, Tast, or Sound, somtimes of another. And this diversity of Seeming, (produced by the diversity of the operation of bodies, on the organs of our sense) we attribute to alterations of the Bodies that operate, & call them *Accidents* of those Bodies. And according to this acceptation of the word, *Substance* and *Body*, signifie the same thing; and therefore *Substance incorporeall* are words, which when they are joined together, destroy one another, as if a man should say, an *Incorporeall Body.*

But in the sense of common people, not all the Universe is called Body, but only such parts thereof as they can discern by the sense of Feeling, to resist their force, or by the sense of their Eyes, to hinder them from a farther prospect. Therefore in the common language of men, *Aire*, and *aeriall substances*, use not to be taken for *Bodies*, but (as often as men are sensible of their effects) are called *Wind*, or *Breath*, or (because the same are called in the Latine *Spiritus*) *Spirits*; as when they call that aeriall substance, which in the body of any living creature, gives it life and motion, *Vitall* and *Animall spirits*. But for those Idols of the brain, which represent Bodies to us, where they are not, as in a Lookingglasse, in a Dream, or to a [208] Distempered brain waking, they are (as the Apostle saith generally of all Idols)[23] nothing; Nothing at all, I say, there where they seem to bee; and in the brain it self, nothing but tumult, proceeding either from the action of the objects, or from the disorderly agitation of the Organs of our Sense.

And men, that are otherwise imployed, then to search into their causes, know not of themselves, what to call them; and may therefore easily be perswaded, by those whose knowledge they much reverence, some to call them *Bodies*, and think them made of aire compacted by a power supernaturall, because the sight judges them corporeall; and some to call them *Spirits*, because the sense of Touch discerneth nothing in the place where they appear, to resist their fingers: So that the proper signification of *Spirit* in common speech, is either a subtile, fluid, and invisible Body, or a Ghost, or other Idol or Phantasme of the Imagination. But for metaphoricall significations, there be many: for sometimes it is taken for Disposition or Inclination of the mind; as when for the disposition to controwl the sayings of other men, we say, *a spirit of contradiction*; For *a disposition to uncleannesse, an unclean spirit*; for *perversenesse, a froward spirit*; for *sullennesse, a dumb spirit*, and for *inclination to godlinesse, and Gods service, the Spirit of God*: sometimes for any eminent ability, or extraordinary passion, or disease of the mind, as when *great wisdome* is called the *spirit of wisdome*; and *mad men* are said to be *possessed with a spirit*.

Other signification of *Spirit* I find no where any; and where none of these can satisfie the sense of that word in Scripture, the place falleth not under humane Understanding; and our Faith therein consisteth not in our Opinion, but in our Submission; as in all places where God is said to be a *Spirit*; or where by the *Spirit of God*, is meant God himself. For the nature of God is incomprehensible; that is to say, we understand nothing of *what he is*, but only *that he is*; and therefore the Attributes we give him, are not to tell one another, *what he is*, nor to signifie our opinion of his Nature, but our desire to honor him with such names as we conceive most honorable amongst our selves.

Gen. 1.2. *The Spirit of God moved upon the face of the Waters*. Here if by the *Spirit of God* be meant God

The Spirit of God taken in the Scripture sometimes for a Wind, or Breath

himself, then is *Motion* attributed to God, and consequently *Place*, which are intelligible only of Bodies, and not of substances incorporeall; and so the place is above our understanding, that can conceive nothing moved that changes not place, or that has not dimension; and whatsoever has dimension, is Body. But the meaning of those words is best understood by the like place, *Gen.*8.1. Where when the earth was covered with Waters, as in the beginning, God intending to abate them, and again to discover the dry land, useth the like words, *I will bring my Spirit upon the Earth, and the waters shall be diminished*: in which place by *Spirit* is understood a Wind, (that is an Aire or *Spirit moved*,) which might be called (as in the former place) the *Spirit of God*, because it was Gods work.

[209] *Gen.* 41.38. *Pharaoh* calleth the *Wisdome* of *Joseph*, the *Spirit of God*. For *Joseph* having advised him to look out a wise and discreet man, and to set him over the land of Egypt, he saith thus, *Can we find such a man as this is, in whom is the Spirit of God?* And *Exod.* 28.3. *Thou shalt speak* (saith God) *to all that are wise hearted, whom I have filled with the Spirit of Wisdome, to make Aaron Garments, to consecrate him.* Where extraordinary Understanding, though but in making Garments, as being the *Gift* of God, is called the *Spirit* of God. The same is found again, *Exod.* 31. 3, 4, 5, 6. and 35.31. And *Isaiah* 11. 2, 3. where the Prophet speaking of the Messiah, saith, *The Spirit of the Lord shall abide upon him, the Spirit of wisdome and understanding, the Spirit of counsell, and fortitude; and the Spirit of the fear of the Lord.* Where manifestly is meant, not so many Ghosts, but so many eminent *graces* that God would give him. *Secondly, for extraordinary gifts of the Understanding*

In the Book of *Judges*, an extraordinary Zeal, and Courage in the defence of Gods people, is called the *Spirit* of God; as when it excited Othoniel, Gideon, Jephtha, and Samson to deliver them from servitude, *Judg.* 3.10. 6.34. 11.29. 13.25. 14.6,19.[24] And of *Saul*, upon the *Thirdly, for extraordinary Affections* newes of the insolence of the Ammonites towards the men of Jabesh Gilead, it is said (1 *Sam.*11.6.) that *The Spirit of God came upon Saul, and his Anger* (or, as it is in the Latine, *his Fury*) *was kindled greatly.* Where it is not probable was meant a Ghost, but an extraordinary *Zeal* to punish the cruelty of the Ammonites. In like manner by the *Spirit* of God, that came upon Saul, when hee was amongst the Prophets that praised God in Songs, and Musick (1 *Sam.*19.20.) is to be understood, not a Ghost, but an unexpected and sudden *zeal* to join with them in their devotion.

Fourthly, for the gift of Prediction by Dreams and Visions   The false Prophet *Zedekiah*,[25] saith to *Micaiah* (1 *Kings* 22.24.) *Which way went the Spirit of the Lord from me to speak to thee?* Which cannot be understood of a Ghost; for *Micaiah* declared before the Kings of Israel and Judah, the event of the battle, as from a *Vision*, and not as from a *Spirit*, speaking in him.

In the same manner it appeareth, in the Books of the Prophets, that though they spake by the *Spirit* of God, that is to say, by a speciall grace of Prediction; yet their knowledge of the future, was not by a Ghost within them, but by some supernaturall *Dream* or *Vision.*

Fiftly, for Life   *Gen.* 2.7. It is said, *God made man of the dust of the Earth, and breathed into his nostrills* (spiraculum vitæ) *the breath of life, and man was made a living soul.* There the *breath of life* inspired by God, signifies no more, but that God gave him life; And (*Job* 27.3.) *as long as the Spirit of God is in my nostrils*; is no more then to say, *as long as I live.* So in *Ezek.* 1.20. *the Spirit of life was in the wheels*, is equivalent to, *the wheels were alive.* And (*Ezek.* 2.30.)[26] *the Spirit entred into me, and set me on my feet*, that is, I *recovered my vitall strength*; not that any Ghost, or incorporeall substance entred into, and possessed his body.

Sixtly, for a subordination to authority   In the 11 chap. of *Numbers.* verse 17. I *will take* (saith God) *of the Spirit, which is upon thee, and will put it upon them, and they shall bear* [210] *the burthen of the people with thee*; that is, upon the seventy Elders:

whereupon two of the seventy are said to prophecy in the campe; of whom some complained, and Joshua desired Moses to forbid them; which Moses would not doe. Whereby it appears; that Joshua knew not they had received authority so to do, and prophecyed according to the mind of Moses, that is to say, by a *Spirit*, or *Authority* subordinate to his own.

In the like sense we read (*Deut.* 34.9.) that *Joshua was full of the Spirit of wisdome, because Moses had laid his hands upon him*: that is, because he was *ordained* by Moses, to prosecute the work hee had himselfe begun, (namely, the bringing of Gods people into the promised land), but prevented by death, could not finish.

In the like sense it is said, (*Rom.* 8.9.) *If any man have not the Spirit of Christ, he is none of his*: not meaning thereby the *Ghost* of Christ, but a *submission* to his Doctrine. As also (1 *John* 4.2.) *Hereby you shall know the Spirit of God; Every spirit that confesseth that Jesus Christ is come in the flesh, is of God*; by which is meant the Spirit of unfained Christianity, or *submission* to that main Article of Christian faith, that Jesus is the Christ; which cannot be interpreted of a Ghost.

Likewise these words (*Luke* 4.1.) *And Jesus full of the Holy Ghost* (that is, as it is exprest, *Mat.* 4.1. and *Mar.* 1. 12. *of the Holy Spirit,*) may be understood, for *Zeal* to doe the work for which hee was sent by God the Father: but to interpret it of a Ghost, is to say, that God himselfe (for so our Saviour was,) was filled with God; which is very unproper, and unsignificant. How we came to translate *Spirits*, by the word *Ghosts*, which signifieth nothing, neither in heaven, nor earth, but the Imaginary inhabitants of mans brain, I examine not: but this I say, the word *Spirit* in the text signifieth no such thing; but either properly a reall *substance*, or Metaphorically, some extraordinary *ability* or *affection* of the Mind, or of the Body.

The Disciples of Christ, seeing him walking upon the sea, (*Mat.* 14.26. and *Marke* 6.49.) supposed him to be

Seventhly, for Aeriall Bodies

a *Spirit*, meaning thereby an Aeriall *Body*, and not a Phantasme: for it is said, they all saw him; which cannot be understood of the delusions of the brain, (which are not common to many at once, as visible Bodies are; but singular, because of the differences of Fancies), but of Bodies only. In like manner, where he was taken for a *Spirit*, by the same Apostles (*Luke* 24. 3, 7.): So also (*Acts* 12.15.) when St. *Peter* was delivered out of Prison, it would not be beleeved; but when the Maid said he was at the dore, they said it was his *Angel*; by which must be meant a corporeall substance, or we must say, the Disciples themselves did follow the common opinion of both Jews and Gentiles, that some such apparitions were not Imaginary, but Reall; and such as needed not the fancy of man for their Existence: These the Jews called *Spirits*, and *Angels*, Good or Bad; as the Greeks called the same by the name of *Dæmons*. And some such apparitions may be [211] reall, and substantiall; that is to say, subtile Bodies, which God can form by the same power, by which he formed all things, and make use of, as of Ministers, and Messengers (that is to say, Angels) to declare his will, and execute the same when he pleaseth, in extraordinary and supernaturall manner. But when hee hath so formed them they are Substances, endued with dimensions, and take up roome, and can be moved from place to place, which is peculiar to Bodies; and therefore are not Ghosts *incorporeall*, that is to say, Ghosts that are in *no place*; that is to say, that are *no where*; that is to say, that seeming to be *somewhat*, are *nothing*. But if Corporeall be taken in the most vulgar manner, for such Substances as are perceptible by our externall Senses; then is Substance Incorporeall, a thing not Imaginary, but Reall; namely, a thin Substance Invisible, but that hath the same dimensions that are in grosser Bodies.

Angel what   By the name of ANGEL, is signified generally, a *Messenger*; and most often, a *Messenger of God*: And by a Messenger of God, is signified, any thing that makes known his extraordinary Presence; that is to say, the extraordinary manifestation of his power, especially by a Dream, or Vision.

Concerning the creation of *Angels*, there is nothing delivered in the Scriptures. That they are Spirits, is often repeated: but by the name of Spirit, is signified both in Scripture, and vulgarly, both amongst Jews, and Gentiles, sometimes thin Bodies; as the Aire, the Wind, the Spirits Vitall, and Animall, of living creatures; and sometimes the Images that rise in the fancy in Dreams, and Visions; which are not reall Substances, nor last any longer then the Dream, or Vision they appear in; which Apparitions, though no reall Substances, but accidents of the brain; yet when God raiseth them supernaturally, to signifie his Will, they are not unproperly termed Gods Messengers, that is to say, his *Angels*.

And as the Gentiles did vulgarly conceive the Imagery of the brain, for things really subsistent without them, and not dependent on the fancy; and out of them framed their opinions of *Dæmons*, Good and Evill; which because they seemed to subsist really, they called *Substances*; and because they could not feel them with their hands, *Incorporeall*: so also the Jews upon the same ground, without any thing in the Old Testament that constrained them thereunto, had generally an opinion, (except the sect of the *Sadduces*,) that those apparitions (which it pleased God sometimes to produce in the fancie of men, for his own service, and therefore called them his *Angels*) were substances, not dependent on the fancy, but permanent creatures of God; whereof those which they thought were good to them, they esteemed the *Angels of God*, and those they thought would hurt them, they called *Evill Angels*, or Evill Spirits; such as was the Spirit of Python,[27] and the Spirits of Mad-men, of Lunatiques, and Epileptiques: For they esteemed such as were troubled with such diseases, *Dæmoniaques*.

But if we consider the places of the Old Testament where Angels are mentioned, we shall find, that in most of them, there can nothing [212] else be understood by the word *Angel*, but some image raised (supernaturally) in the fancy, to signifie the presence of God in the execution of some supernaturall work; and therefore in the rest, where their nature is not exprest, it may be understood in the same manner.

For we read *Gen.* 16. that the same apparition is called, not onely an *Angel*, but *God*; where that which (verse 7.) is called the *Angel* of the Lord, in the tenth verse, saith to Agar,[28] *I will multiply thy seed exceedingly*; that is, speaketh in the person of God. Neither was this apparition a Fancy figured, but a Voice. By which it is manifest, that *Angel* signifieth there, nothing but *God* himself, that caused Agar supernaturally to apprehend a voice from heaven; or rather, nothing else but a Voice supernaturall, testifying Gods speciall presence there. Why therefore may not the Angels that appeared to Lot, and are called *Gen.* 19. 13. *Men*;[29] and to whom, though they were two, Lot speaketh (ver. 18.) as but one, and that one, as God, (for the words are, *Lot said unto them, Oh not so my Lord*) be understood of images of men, supernaturally formed in the Fancy; as well as before by Angel was understood a fancyed Voice? When the Angel called to Abraham out of heaven, to stay his hand (*Gen.* 22.11.) from slaying Isaac,[30] there was no Apparition, but a Voice; which neverthelesse was called properly enough a Messenger, or *Angel* of God, because it declared Gods will supernaturally, and saves the labour of supposing any permanent Ghosts. The Angels which Jacob saw on the Ladder of Heaven[31] (*Gen.* 28.12.) were a Vision of his sleep; therefore onely Fancy, and a Dream; yet being supernaturall, and signs of Gods speciall presence, those apparitions are not improperly called *Angels*. The same is to be understood (*Gen.* 31.11.) where Jacob saith thus, *The Angel of the Lord appeared to mee in my sleep*. For an apparition made to a man in his sleep, is that which all men call a Dreame, whether such Dreame be naturall, or supernaturall: and that which there Jacob calleth an *Angel*, was God himselfe; for the same Angel saith (verse 13.) *I am the God of Bethel.*

Also (*Exod.* 14.9.) the Angel that went before the Army of Israel to the Red Sea, and then came behind it, is (verse 19.) the Lord himself; and he appeared not in the form of a beautifull man, but in form (by day) of a *pillar of cloud*, and (by night) in form of a *pillar of fire*; and yet this Pillar was all the apparition, and *Angel* promised to Moses (*Exod.* 14.9.) for the Armies guide:[32] For this cloudy pillar, is said, to have descended, and stood at the dore of the Tabernacle, and to have talked with Moses.

There you see Motion, and Speech, which are commonly attributed to Angels, attributed to a Cloud, because the Cloud served as a sign of Gods presence; and was no lesse an Angel, then if it had had the form of a Man, or Child of never so great beauty; or Wings, as usually they are painted, for the false instruction of common people. For it is not the shape; but their use, that makes them Angels. But their use is to be significations of Gods presence in super[213]naturall operations; As when Moses (*Exod.* 33.14.) had desired God to goe along with the Campe, (as he had done alwaies before the making of the Golden Calfe,) God did not answer, *I will goe*, nor *I will send an Angell in my stead*; but thus, *my presence shall goe with thee.*

To mention all the places of the Old Testament where the name of Angel is found, would be too long. Therefore to comprehend them all at once, I say, there is no text in that part of the Old Testament, which the Church of England holdeth for Canonicall; from which we can conclude, there is, or hath been created, any permanent thing (understood by the name of *Spirit* or *Angel*,) that hath not quantity; and that may not be, by the understanding divided; that is to say, considered by parts; so as one part may bee in one place, and the next part in the next place to it; and, in summe, which is not (taking Body for that, which is some what, or some where)

Corporeall; but in every place, the sense will bear the interpretation of Angel, for Messenger; as John Baptist is called an Angel,[33] and Christ the Angel of the Covenant; and as (according to the same Analogy) the Dove, and the Fiery Tongues, in that they were signes of Gods speciall presence, might also be called Angels. Though we find in Daniel two names of Angels, *Gabriel*, and Michael;[34] yet it is cleer out of the text it selfe, (*Dan.* 12.1.) that by *Michael* is meant *Christ*, not as an Angel, but as a Prince: and that *Gabriel* (as the like apparitions made to other holy men in their sleep) was nothing but a supernaturall phantasme, by which it seemed to *Daniel*, in his dream, that two Saints being in talke, one of them said to the other, *Gabriel, let us make this man understand his Vision*: For God needeth not, to distinguish his Celestiall servants by names, which are usefull onely to the short memories of Mortalls. Nor in the New Testament is there any place, out of which it can be proved, that Angels (except when they are put for such men, as God hath made the Messengers, and Ministers of his word, or works) are things permanent, and withall incorporeall. That they are permanent, may bee gathered from the words of our Saviour himselfe, (*Mat.* 25.41.) where he saith, it shall be said to the wicked in the last day, *Go ye cursed into everlasting fire prepared for the Devil and his Angels*: which place is manifest for the permanence of Evill Angels, (unlesse wee might think the name of Devill and his Angels may be understood of the Churches Adversaries and their Ministers;) but then it is repugnant to their Immateriality; because Everlasting fire is no punishment to impatible[35] substances, such as are all things Incorporeall. Angels therefore are not thence proved to be Incorporeall. In like manner where St. Paul sayes (1 *Cor.* 6.3.) *Know ye not that wee shall judge the Angels?* And (2 *Pet.* 2.4.) *For if God spared not the Angels that sinned, but cast them down into hell.* And (*Jude* 1, 6.) *And the Angels that kept not their first estate, but left their owne habitation, hee hath reserved in everlasting chaines under darknesse unto the Judgment of the last day*; though it prove the Permanence of Angelicall nature, it confirmeth also their Materiality. And (*Mat.* 22.30.) *In the resurrection men* [214] *doe neither marry, nor give in marriage, but are as the Angels of God in heaven*: but in the resurrection men shall be Permanent, and not Incorporeall; so therefore also are the Angels.

There be divers other places out of which may be drawn the like conclusion. To men that understand the signification of these words, *Substance*, and *Incorporeall*; as *Incorporeall* is taken not for subtile body, but for *not Body*, they imply a contradiction: insomuch as to say, an Angel, or Spirit is (in that sense) an Incorporeall Substance, is to say in effect, there is no Angel nor Spirit at all. Considering therefore the signification of the word Angel in the Old Testament, and the nature of Dreams and Visions that happen to men by the ordinary way of Nature; I was enclined to this opinion, that Angels were nothing but supernaturall apparitions of the Fancy, raised by the speciall and extraordinary operation of God, thereby to make his presence and commandements known to mankind, and chiefly to his own people. But the many places of the New Testament, and our Saviours own words, and in such texts, wherein is no suspicion of corruption of the Scripture, have extorted from my feeble Reason, an acknowledgment, and beleef, that there be also Angels substantiall, and permanent. But to beleeve they be in no place, that is to say, no where, that is to say, nothing, as they (though indirectly) say, that will have them Incorporeall, cannot by Scripture bee evinced.

On the signification of the word *Spirit*, dependeth that *Inspiration* of the word INSPIRATION; which must either be taken *what* properly; and then it is nothing but the blowing into a man some thin and subtile aire, or wind, in such manner as a man filleth a bladder with his breath; or if Spirits be not corporeall, but have their existence only in the fancy, it is nothing but the blowing in of a Phantasme; which is improper to say, and impossible; for Phantasmes are not, but only seem to be somewhat. That word therefore is used in the Scripture metaphorically onely: As (*Gen.* 2.7.) where it is said, that God *inspired* into man the breath of life, no more is meant, then that God gave unto him vitall motion. For we are not to think that God made first a living breath, and then blew it into Adam after he was made, whether that breath were reall, or seeming; but only as it is (*Acts* 17.25.) *that he gave him life, and breath*; that is, made him a living creature. And where it is said (*2 Tim.* 3.16.) *all Scripture is given by Inspiration from God*, speaking there of the Scripture of the Old Testament, it is an easie metaphor, to signifie, that God enclined the spirit or mind of those Writers, to write that which should be usefull, in teaching, reproving, correcting, and instructing men in the way of righteous living. But where St. Peter (*2 Pet.* 1.21.) saith, that *Prophecy came not in old time by the will of man, but the holy men of God spake as they were moved by the Holy Spirit*, by the Holy Spirit, is meant the voice of God in a Dream, or Vision supernaturall, which is not *Inspiration*: Nor when our Saviour breathing on his Disciples, said, *Receive the Holy Spirit*, was that Breath the Spirit, but a sign of the spirituall graces he gave unto them. And though it be [215] said of many, and of our Saviour himself, that he was full of the Holy *Spirit*; yet that Fulnesse is not to be understood for *Infusion* of the substance of God, but for accumulation of his gifts, such as are the gift of sanctity of life, of tongues, and the like, whether attained supernaturally, or by study and industry; for in all cases they are the gifts of God. So likewise where God sayes (*Joel* 2.28.) *I will powre out my Spirit upon all flesh, and your Sons and your Daughters shall prophecy, your Old men shall dream Dreams, and your Young men shall see Visions*, wee are not to understand it in the proper sense, as if his *Spirit* were like water, subject to effusion, or infusion; but as if God had promised to give them Propheticall Dreams, and Visions. For the proper use of the word *infused*, in speaking of the graces of God, is an abuse of it; for those graces are Vertues, not Bodies to be carryed hither and thither, and to be powred into men, as into barrels.

In the same manner, to take *Inspiration* in the proper sense, or to say that Good *Spirits* entred into men to make them prophecy, or Evill *Spirits* into those that became Phrenetique, Lunatique, or Epileptique, is not to take the word in the sense of the Scripture; for the Spirit there is taken for the power of God, working by causes to us unknown. As also (*Acts* 2. 2.) the wind, that is there said to fill the house wherein the Apostles were assembled on the day of Pentecost, is not to be understood for the Holy *Spirit*, which is the Deity it self; but for an Externall sign of Gods speciall working on their hearts, to effect in them the internall graces, and holy vertues hee thought requisite for the performance of their Apostleship. [216]

CHAP. XXXV

Of the Signification in Scripture of KINGDOME OF GOD, of HOLY, SACRED, and SACRAMENT

The *Kingdome of God* in the Writings of Divines, and specially in Sermons, and Treatises of Devotion, is taken most commonly for Eternall Felicity, after this life, in the Highest Heaven, which they also call the Kingdome of Glory; and sometimes for (the earnest of that felicity) Sanctification, which they terme the Kingdome of Grace; but never for the Monarchy, that is to say, the Soveraign Power of God over any Subjects acquired by their own consent, which is the proper signification of Kingdome. *The Kingdom of God taken by Divines Metaphorically, but in the Scriptures properly*

To the contrary, I find the KINGDOME OF GOD, to signifie in most places of Scripture, a *Kingdome properly so named*, constituted by the Votes of the People of Israel in peculiar manner; wherein they chose God for their King by Covenant made with him, upon Gods promising them the possession of the land of Canaan; and but seldom metaphorically; and then it is taken for *Dominion over sinne*; (and only in the New Testament;) because such a Dominion as that, every Subject shall have in the Kingdome of God, and without prejudice to the Soveraign.

From the very Creation, God not only reigned over all men *naturally* by his might; but also had *peculiar* Subjects, whom he commanded by a Voice, as one man speaketh to another. In which manner he *reigned* over Adam, and gave him commandement to abstaine from the tree of cognizance of Good and Evill;[36] which when he obeyed not, but tasting thereof, took upon him to be as God, judging between Good and Evill, not by his Creators commandement, but by his own sense, his punishment was a privation of the estate of Eternall life, wherein God had at first created him: And afterwards God punished his posterity, for their vices, all but eight persons, with an universall deluge;[37] And in these eight did consist the then *Kingdom of God*.

The originall of the King- dome of God   After this, it pleased God to speak to Abraham, and (*Gen.* 17.7, 8.) to make a Covenant with him in these words, *I will establish my Covenant between me, and thee, and thy seed after thee in their generations, for an everlasting Covenant, to be a God to thee, and to thy seed after thee; And I will give unto thee, and to thy seed after thee, the land wherein thou art a stranger, all the land of Canaan for an everlasting possession.* In this Covenant *Abraham promiseth for himselfe and his posterity to obey as God, the Lord that spake to him: and God on his part promiseth to Abraham the land of Canaan for an everlasting possession.* [217] And for a memoriall, and a token of this Covenant, he ordaineth

(verse 11.) the *Sacrament of Circumcision*. This is it
which is called the *Old Covenant*, or *Testament*; and
containeth a Contract between God and Abraham; by
which Abraham obligeth himself, and his posterity, in
a peculiar manner to be subject to Gods positive Law;
for to the Law Morall he was obliged before, as by an
Oath of Allegiance. And though the name of *King* be
not yet given to God, nor of *Kingdome* to Abraham and
his seed; yet the thing is the same; namely, an Institution
by pact, of Gods peculiar Soveraignty over the seed of
Abraham; which in the renewing of the same Covenant
by Moses, at Mount Sinai, is expressely called a peculiar
Kingdome of God over the Jews: and it is of Abraham
(not of Moses) St. Paul saith (*Rom.* 4.11.) that he is the
Father of the Faithfull; that is, of those that are loyall,
and doe not violate their Allegiance sworn to God, then
by Circumcision, and afterwards in the *New Covenant*
by Baptisme.

This Covenant, at the Foot of Mount Sinai, was
renewed by Moses (*Exod.* 19.5.) where the Lord commandeth Moses to speak to the people in this manner,
*If you will obey my voice indeed, and keep my Coven-
ant, then yee shall be a peculiar people to me, for all the
Earth is mine; And yee shall be unto me a Sacerdotall
Kingdome, and an holy Nation.* For a *Peculiar people*,
the vulgar Latine hath, *Peculium de cunctis populis*: the
English Translation made in the beginning of the Reign
of King James, hath, a *Peculiar treasure unto me above
all Nations*; and the Geneva French, *the most precious
Jewel of all Nations.* But the truest Translation is the
first, because it is confirmed by St. Paul himself (*Tit.*
2.14.) where he saith, alluding to that place, that our
blessed Saviour *gave himself for us, that he might purifie us to himself, a peculiar* (that is, an extraordinary)
people: for the word is in the Greek περιούσιος, which
is opposed commonly to the word ἐπιούσιος: and as
this signifieth *ordinary, quotidian*, or (as in the Lords
Prayer)[38] *of daily use*; so the other signifieth that which

That the
Kingdome of
God is prop-
erly his Civill
Soveraignty
over a pecu-
liar people by
pact

is *overplus*, and *stored up*, and *enjoyed in a speciall manner*; which the Latines call *Peculium*: and this meaning of the place is confirmed by the reason God rendereth of it, which followeth immediately, in that he addeth, *For all the Earth is mine*, as if he should say, *All the Nations of the world are mine*; but it is not so that you are mine, but in a *speciall manner*: For they are all mine, by reason of my Power; but you shall be mine, by your own Consent, and Covenant; which is an addition to his ordinary title, to all nations.

The same is again confirmed in expresse words in the same text, *Yee shall be to me a Sacerdotall Kingdome, and an holy Nation.* The Vulgar Latine hath it, *Regnum Sacerdotale*, to which agreeth the Translation of that place (1 *Pet.* 2.9.) *Sacerdotium Regale, a Regal Priesthood*; as also the Institution it self, by which no man might enter into the *Sanctum Sanctorum*,[39] that is to say, no man might enquire Gods will immediately of God himselfe, but onely the High Priest. The English Translation before mentioned, following that of Geneva, has, *a Kingdom of Priests*; which is either meant of the [218] succession of one High Priest after another, or else it accordeth not with St. Peter, nor with the exercise of the High priesthood: For there was never any but the High priest onely, that was to informe the People of Gods Will; nor any Convocation of Priests ever allowed to enter into the *Sanctum Sanctorum*.

Again, the title of a *Holy Nation* confirmes the same: For *Holy* signifies, that which is Gods by speciall, not by generall Right. All the Earth (as is said in the text) is Gods; but all the Earth is not called *Holy*, but that onely which is set apart for his especiall service, as was the Nation of the Jews. It is therefore manifest enough by this one place, that by the *Kingdome of God*, is properly meant a Common-wealth, instituted (by the consent of those which were to be subject thereto) for their Civill Government, and the regulating of their behaviour, not onely towards God their King, but also towards one another in point of justice, and towards other Nations both in peace and warre; which properly was a Kingdome, wherein God was King, and the High priest was to be (after the death of Moses) his sole Viceroy, or Lieutenant.

But there be many other places that clearly prove the same. As first (1 *Sam.* 8.7.) when the Elders of Israel (grieved with the corruption of the Sons of Samuel) demanded a King, Samuel displeased therewith, prayed unto the Lord; and the Lord answering said unto him, *Hearken unto the voice of the People, for they have not rejected thee, but they have rejected me, that I should not reign over them.* Out of which it is evident, that God himself was then their King; and Samuel did not command the people, but only delivered to them that which God from time to time appointed him.

Again, (1 *Sam.* 12.12.) where Samuel saith to the People, *When yee saw that Nahash King of the Children of Ammon came against you, ye said unto me, Nay, but a King shall reign over us, when the Lord your God was your King*: It is manifest that God was their King, and governed the Civill State of their Common-wealth.

And after the Israelites had rejected God, the Prophets did foretell his restitution; as (*Isaiah* 24.23.) *Then the Moon shall be confounded, and the Sun ashamed when the Lord of Hosts shall reign in Mount Zion, and in Jerusalem*; where he speaketh expressely of his Reign in Zion, and Jerusalem; that is, on Earth. And (*Micah* 4.7.) *And the Lord shall reign over them in Mount Zion*: This Mount Zion is in Jerusalem upon the Earth. And (*Ezek.* 20.33.) *As I live, saith the Lord God, surely with a mighty hand, and a stretched out arme, and with fury powred out, I wil rule over you; and* (verse 37.) *I will cause you to passe under the rod, and I will bring you into the bond of the Covenant*; that is, I will reign over you, and make you to stand to that Covenant which you made with me by Moses, and brake in your rebellion against me in the days of Samuel, and in your election of another King.

And in the New Testament, the Angel Gabriel saith of our Saviour (*Luke* 1.32, 33.) *He shall be great, and be called the Son of the most High, and the Lord shall give him the throne of his Father* [219] *David; and he shall reign over the house of Jacob for ever; and of his Kingdome there shall be no end.* This is also a Kingdome upon Earth; for the claim whereof, as an enemy to Cæsar, he was put to death; the title of his crosse, was, *Jesus of Nazareth, King of the Jews*; hee was crowned in scorn with a crown of Thornes;[40] and for the proclaiming of him, it is said of the Disciples (*Acts* 17.7.) *That they did all of them contrary to the decrees of Cæsar, saying there was another King, one Jesus.* The Kingdome therefore of God, is a reall, not a metaphoricall Kingdome; and so taken, not onely in the Old Testament, but the New; when we say, *For thine is the Kingdome, the Power, and Glory*,[41] it is to be understood of Gods Kingdome, by force of our Covenant, not by the Right of Gods Power; for such a Kingdome God alwaies hath; so that it were superfluous to say in our prayer, *Thy Kingdome come*, unlesse it be meant of the Restauration of that Kingdome of God by Christ, which by revolt of the Israelites had been interrupted in the election of Saul. Nor had it been proper to say, *The Kingdome of Heaven is at hand*; or to pray, *Thy Kingdome come*, if it had still continued.

There be so many other places that confirm this interpretation, that it were a wonder there is no greater notice taken of it, but that it gives too much light to Christian Kings to see their right of Ecclesiasticall Government. This they have observed, that in stead of a *Sacerdotall Kingdome*, translate, *a Kingdome of Priests*: for they may as well translate a *Royall Priesthood*, (as it is in St. Peter) into a *Priesthood of Kings*. And whereas, for a *peculiar people*, they put a *pretious jewel*, or *treasure*, a man might as well call the speciall Regiment, or

Company of a Generall, the Generalls pretious Jewel, or his Treasure.

In short, the Kingdome of God is a Civill Kingdome; which consisted, first in the obligation of the people of Israel to those Laws, which Moses should bring unto them from Mount Sinai; and which afterwards the High Priest for the time being, should deliver to them from before the *Cherubins* in the *Sanctum Sanctorum*;[42] and which Kingdome having been cast off, in the election of Saul, the Prophets foretold, should be restored by Christ; and the Restauration whereof we daily pray for, when we say in the Lords Prayer, *Thy Kingdome come*; and the Right whereof we acknowledge, when we adde, *For thine is the Kingdome, the Power, and Glory, for ever and ever, Amen*; and the Proclaiming whereof, was the Preaching of the Apostles; and to which men are prepared, by the Teachers of the Gospel; to embrace which Gospel, (that is to say, to promise obedience to Gods government) is, to bee in the *Kingdome of Grace*, because God hath *gratis* given to such the power to bee the Subjects (that is, Children) of God hereafter, when Christ shall come in Majesty to judge the world, and actually to govern his owne people, which is called *the Kingdome of Glory.* If the Kingdome of God (called also the Kingdome of Heaven, from the gloriousnesse, and admirable height of that throne) were not a Kingdome which God by his Lieutenants, or Vicars, who [220] deliver his Commandements to the people, did exercise on Earth; there would not have been so much contention, and warre, about who it is, by whom God speaketh to us; neither would many Priests have troubled themselves with Spirituall Jurisdiction, nor any King have denied it them.

Out of this literall interpretation of the *Kingdome of God*, ariseth also the true interpretation of the word HOLY. For it is a word, which in Gods Kingdome answereth to that, which men in their Kingdomes use to call *Publique*, or the *Kings*.

Holy what

The King of any Countrey is the *Publique* Person, or Representative of all his own Subjects. And God the King of Israel was the *Holy one* of Israel. The Nation which is subject to one earthly Soveraign, is the Nation of that Soveraign, that is, of the Publique Person. So the Jews, who were Gods Nation, were called (*Exod.* 19.6.) *a Holy Nation*. For by *Holy*, is alwaies understood, either God himselfe, or that which is Gods in propriety; as by Publique is alwaies meant, either the Person of the Common-wealth it self, or something that is so the Common-wealths, as no private person can claim any propriety therein.

Therefore the Sabbath (Gods day) is a *Holy day*; the Temple, (Gods house) *a Holy house*; Sacrifices, Tithes, and Offerings (Gods tribute) *Holy duties*; Priests, Prophets, and anointed Kings, under Christ (Gods Ministers) *Holy men*; the Cœlestiall ministring Spirits (Gods Messengers) *Holy Angels*; and the like: and wheresoever the word Holy is taken properly, there is still something signified of Propriety, gotten by consent. In saying *Hallowed be thy name*, we do but pray to God for grace to keep the first Commandement, of *having no other Gods but him*. Mankind is Gods Nation in propriety: but the Jews only were a *Holy Nation*. Why, but because they became his Propriety by covenant?

And the word *Profane*, is usually taken in the Scripture for the same with *Common*; and consequently their contraries, *Holy*, and *Proper*, in the Kingdome of God must be the same also. But figuratively, those men also are called *Holy*, that led such godly lives, as if they had forsaken all worldly designs, and wholly devoted, and given themselves to God. In the proper sense, that which is made *Holy* by Gods appropriating or separating it to his own use, is said to be *sanctified* by God, as the Seventh day in the fourth Commandement; and as the Elect in the New Testament were said to bee *sanctified*, when they were endued with the Spirit of godlinesse. And that which is made *Holy* by the dedication of men, and given

Sacred what

to God, so as to be used onely in his publique service, is called also SACRED, and said to be consecrated, as Temples, and other Houses of Publique Prayer, and their Utensils, Priests, and Ministers, Victimes, Offerings, and the externall matter of Sacraments.

Of *Holinesse* there be degrees: for of those things that are set apart for the service of God, there may bee some set apart again, for a neerer and more especial service. The whole Nation of the Israelites were a people Holy to God; yet the tribe of Levi was amongst the [221] Israelites a Holy tribe; and amongst the Levites, the Priests were yet more Holy; and amongst the Priests, the High Priest was the most Holy. So the Land of Judea was the Holy Land; but the Holy City wherein God was to be worshipped, was more Holy; and again, the Temple more Holy than the City; and the *Sanctum Sanctorum* more Holy than the rest of the Temple. *Degrees of Sanctity*

A SACRAMENT, is a separation of some visible thing from common use; and a consecration of it to Gods service, for a sign, either of our admission into the Kingdome of God, to be of the number of his peculiar people, or for a Commemoration of the same. In the Old Testament, the sign of Admission was *Circumcision*; in the New Testament, *Baptisme*. The Commemoration of it in the Old Testament, was the *Eating* (at a certaine time, which was Anniversary) of the *Paschall Lamb*; by which they were put in mind of the night wherein they were delivered out of their bondage in Egypt; and in the New Testament, the celebrating of the *Lords Supper*; by which, we are put in mind, of our deliverance from the bondage of sin, by our Blessed Saviours death upon the crosse. The Sacraments of *Admission*, are but once to be used, because there needs but one *Admission*; but because we have need of being often put in mind of our deliverance, and of our Alleageance, the Sacraments of *Commemoration* have need to be reiterated. And these are the principall Sacraments, and as it were the solemne oathes we make of our Alleageance. There be also other *Sacrament*

Consecrations, that may be called Sacraments, as the word implyeth onely Consecration to Gods service; but as it implies an oath, or promise of Alleageance to God, there were no other in the Old Testament, but *Circumcision*, and the *Passeover*; nor are there any other in the New Testament, but *Baptisme*, and the *Lords Supper.* [222]

CHAP. XXXVI

Of the WORD OF GOD, *and of* PROPHETS

Word what When there is mention of the *Word of God*, or of *Man*, it doth not signifie a part of Speech, such as Grammarians call a Nown, or a Verb, or any simple voice, without a contexture with other words to make it significative; but a perfect Speech or Discourse, whereby the speaker *affirmeth, denieth, commandeth, promiseth, threatneth, wisheth,* or *interrogateth.* In which sense it is not *Vocabulum*, that signifies a *Word*; but *Sermo*, (in Greek λόγος) that is, some *Speech*, *Discourse*, or *Saying.*

The words Again, if we say the *Word* of *God*, or of *Man*, it may
spoken by bee understood sometimes of the Speaker, (as the words
God, and that God hath spoken, or that a Man hath spoken): In
concerning which sense, when we say, the Gospel of St. Matthew,
God, both we understand St. Matthew to be the Writer of it: and
are called sometimes of the Subject:[43] In which sense, when we
Gods Word read in the Bible, *The words of the days of the Kings of*
in Scripture *Israel, or Judah,* 'tis meant, that the acts that were done in those days, were the Subject of those Words; And in the Greek, which (in the Scripture) retaineth many Hebraismes, by the Word of God is oftentimes meant, not that which is spoken by God, but concerning God, and his government; that is to say, the Doctrine of Religion: Insomuch, as it is all one, to say λόγος θεοῦ, and

Theologia; which is, that Doctrine which wee usually call *Divinity*, as is manifest by the places following [*Acts* 13. 46.] *Then Paul and Barnabas waxed bold, and said, It was necessary that the Word of God should first have been spoken to you, but seeing you put it from you, and judge your selves unworthy of everlasting life, loe, we turn to the Gentiles.* That which is here called the Word of God, was the Doctrine of Christian Religion; as it appears evidently by that which goes before. And [*Acts* 5. 20.] where it is said to the Apostles by an Angel, *Go stand and speak in the Temple, all the Words of this life*; by the Words of this life, is meant, the Doctrine of the Gospel; as is evident by what they did in the Temple, and is expressed in the last verse of the same Chap. *Daily in the Temple, and in every house they ceased not to teach and preach Christ Jesus*: In which place it is manifest, that Jesus Christ was the subject of this *Word of life*; or (which is all one) the subject of the *Words of this life eternall*, that our Saviour offered them. So [*Acts* 15. 7.] the Word of God, is called *the Word of the Gospel*, because it containeth the Doctrine of the Kingdome of Christ; and the same Word [*Rom.* 10. 8, 9.] is called *the Word of Faith*; that is, as is there expressed, the Doctrine of Christ come, and raised from the dead. [223] Also [*Mat.* 13. 19.] *When any one heareth the Word of the Kingdome*; that is, the Doctrine of the Kingdome taught by Christ. Again, the same Word, is said [*Acts* 12. 24.] *to grow and to be multiplied*; which to understand of the Evangelicall Doctrine is easie, but of the Voice, or Speech of God, hard and strange. In the same sense the *Doctrine of Devils*, signifieth not the Words of any Devill, but the Doctrine of Heathen men concerning *Dæmons*, and those Phantasms which they worshipped as Gods. *i Tim.* 4. 1

Considering these two significations of the WORD OF GOD, as it is taken in Scripture, it is manifest in this later sense (where it is taken for the Doctrine of the Christian Religion,) that the whole Scripture is the Word of God: but in the former sense not so. For example, though these words, *I am the Lord thy God, &c.* to the end of the Ten Commandements, were spoken by God to Moses; yet the Preface, *God spake these words and said*, is to be understood for the Words of him that wrote the holy History.[44] The *Word of God*, as it is taken for that which he hath spoken, is understood sometimes *Properly*, sometimes *Metaphorically*. *Properly*, as the words, he hath spoken to his Prophets: *Metaphorically*, for his Wisdome, Power, and eternall Decree, in making the world; in which sense, those *Fiats, Let there be light, Let there be a firmament, Let us make man, &c.* [*Gen.* 1.] are the Word of God. And in the same sense it is said [*John* 1. 3.] *All things were made by it, and without it was nothing made that was made*: And [*Heb.* 1. 3.] *He upholdeth all things by the word of his Power*; that is, by the Power of his Word; that is, by his Power: and [*Heb.* 11. 3.] *The worlds were framed by the Word of God*; and many other places to the same sense: As also amongst the Latines, the name of *Fate*, which signifieth properly *The word spoken*, is taken in the same sense.

Secondly, for the effect of his Word; that is to say, for the thing it self, which by his Word is Affirmed, Commanded, Threatned, or Promised; as [*Psalm* 105.19.] where Joseph is said to have been kept in prison, *till his Word was come*; that is, till that was come to passe which he had [*Gen.* 40.13.] foretold to Pharaohs Butler, concerning his being restored to his office: for there by *his word was come*, is meant, the thing it self was come to passe. So also [1 *King.* 18.36.] Elijah saith to God,[45] *I have done all these thy Words*, in stead of *I have done all these things at thy Word*, or commandement: and [*Jer.* 17.15.] *Where is the Word of the Lord*, is put for, *Where is the Evill he threatened*: And [*Ezek.* 12.28.] *There shall none of my Words be prolonged any more*: by *words* are understood those *things*, which God promised to his people. And in the New Testament [*Mat.* 24.35.] *heaven and earth shal pass away, but my Words shal not pass*

The Word of God meta-phorically used, first, for the Decrees and Power of God

Secondly, for the effect of his Word

away; that is, there is nothing that I have promised or foretold, that shall not come to passe. And in this sense it is, that St. John the Evangelist,[46] and, I think, St. John onely calleth our Saviour himself as in the flesh *the Word of God* [as *Joh.* 1.14.] *the Word was made Flesh*; that is to say, the Word, or Promise that Christ should come into the world; *who in the beginning was with God*; that is to say, it was in the purpose of [224] God the Father, to send God the Son into the world, to enlighten men in the way of Eternall life; but it was not till then put in execution, and actually incarnate; So that our Saviour is there called *the Word*, not because he was the promise, but the thing promised. They that taking occasion from this place, doe commonly call him the Verbe of God, do but render the text more obscure. They might as well term him the Nown of God: for as by *Nown*, so also by *Verbe*, men understand nothing but a part of speech, a voice, a sound, that neither affirms, nor denies, nor commands, nor promiseth, nor is any substance corporeall, or spirituall; and therefore it cannot be said to bee either God, or Man; whereas our Saviour is both. And this *Word* which St. *John* in his Gospel saith was with God, is [in his 1 Epistle, verse 1.] called the *Word of life*; and [verse 2.] *the Eternall life, which was with the Father*: so that he can be in no other sense called the *Word*, then in that, wherein he is called Eternall life; that is, *he that hath procured us Eternall life*, by his comming in the flesh. So also [*Apocalypse* 19.13.] the Apostle speaking of Christ, clothed in a garment dipt in bloud, saith; his name is *the Word of God*; which is to be understood, as if he had said his name had been, *He that was come according to the purpose of God from the beginning, and according to his Word and promises delivered by the Prophets*. So that there is nothing here of the Incarnation of a Word, but of the Incarnation of God the Son, therefore called the *Word*, because his Incarnation was the Performance of the Promise; In like manner as the *Acts* 1. 4 Holy Ghost is called *the Promise*.   *Luke* 24. 49

Thirdly, for
the words of
reason and
equity

There are also places of the Scripture, where, by the *Word of God*, is signified such Words as are consonant to reason, and equity, though spoken sometimes neither by Prophet, nor by a holy man. For Pharaoh Necho was an Idolater; yet his Words to the good King Josiah, in which he advised him by Messengers, not to oppose him in his march against *Carchemish*, are said to have proceeded from the mouth of God; and that Josiah not hearkning to them, was slain in the battle; as is to be read 2 *Chron.* 35. vers. 21, 22, 23. It is true, that as the same History is related in the first Book of Esdras, not Pharaoh, but Jeremiah spake these words to Josiah, from the mouth of the Lord.[47] But wee are to give credit to the Canonicall Scripture, whatsoever be written in the Apocrypha.

The *Word of God*, is then also to be taken for the Dictates of reason, and equity, when the same is said in the Scriptures to bee written in mans heart; as *Psalm* 36.31. *Jerem.* 31.33. *Deut.* 30.11, 14. and many other like places.

Divers
acceptions
of the word
Prophet

The name of PROPHET, signifieth in Scripture sometimes *Prolocutor*; that is, he that speaketh from God to Man, or from man to God: And sometimes *Prædictor*, or a foreteller of things to come: And sometimes one that speaketh incoherently, as men that are distracted. It is most frequently used in the sense of speaking from God to the People. So *Moses, Samuel, Elijah, Isaiah, Jeremiah*, and others were *Prophets*. And in this sense the High Priest was a *Prophet*, for he only went into the *Sanctum Sanctorum*, to enquire of God; and was to de[225]clare his answer to the people. And therefore when Caiphas said, it was expedient that one man should die for the people,[48] St. John saith [chap. 11.51.] that *He spake not this of himselfe, but being High Priest that year, he prophesied that one man should dye for the nation.* Also they that in Christian Congregations taught the people [1 *Cor.* 14.3.] are said to Prophecy. In the like sense it is, that God saith to *Moses* [*Exod.*

4.16.] concerning *Aaron, He shall be thy Spokes-man to the People; and he shall be to thee a mouth, and thou shalt be to him in stead of God*: that which here is *Spokes-man*, is [chap. 7.1.] interpreted Prophet; *See* (saith God) *I have made thee a God to Pharaoh, and Aaron thy Brother shall be thy Prophet.* In the sense of speaking from man to God, Abraham is called a Prophet [*Genes*. 20.7.] where God in a Dream speaketh to Abimelech in this manner,[49] *Now therefore restore the man his wife, for he is a Prophet, and shall pray for thee*; whereby may be also gathered, that the name of Prophet may be given, not unproperly to them that in Christian Churches, have a Calling to say publique prayers for the Congregation. In the same sense, the Prophets that came down from the High place (or Hill of God) with a Psaltery, and a Tabret, and a Pipe, and a Harp [1 *Sam*. 10.5, 6.] and [vers. 10.] Saul amongst them, are said to Prophecy, in that they praised God, in that manner publiquely. In the like sense, is Miriam [*Exod*. 15.20.] called a Prophetesse.[50] So is it also to be taken [1 *Cor*. 11.4, 5.] where St. Paul saith, *Every man that prayeth or prophecyeth with his head covered, &c. and every woman that prayeth or prophecyeth with her head uncovered*: For Prophecy in that place, signifieth no more, but praising God in Psalmes, and Holy Songs; which women might doe in the Church, though it were not lawfull for them to speak to the Congregation. And in this signification it is, that the Poets of the Heathen, that composed Hymnes and other sorts of Poems in the honor of their Gods, were called *Vates* (Prophets) as is well enough known by all that are versed in the Books of the Gentiles, and as is evident [*Tit*. 1. 12.] where St. Paul saith of the Cretians, that a Prophet of their owne said, they were Liars; not that St. Paul held their Poets for Prophets, but acknowledgeth that the word Prophet was commonly used to signifie them that celebrated the honour of God in Verse.

When by Prophecy is meant Prædiction, or foretelling of future Contingents; not only they were Prophets,

Prædiction of future contingents, not alwaies Prophecy

who were Gods Spokesmen, and foretold those things to others, which God had foretold to them; but also all those Impostors, that pretend by the helpe of familiar spirits, or by superstitious divination of events past, from false causes, to foretell the like events in time to come: of which (as I have declared already in the 12. chapter of this Discourse) there be many kinds, who gain in the opinion of the common sort of men, a greater reputation of Prophecy, by one casuall event that may bee but wrested to their purpose, than can be lost again by never so many failings. Prophecy is not an Art, nor (when it is taken for Prædiction) a constant Vocation; but an extraordinary, and temporary Employment from God, most often of Good men, but sometimes also [226] of the Wicked. The woman of Endor,[51] who is said to have had a familiar spirit, and thereby to have raised a Phantasme of Samuel, and foretold Saul his death, was not therefore a Prophetesse; for neither had she any science, whereby she could raise such a Phantasme; nor does it appear that God commanded the raising of it; but onely guided that Imposture to be a means of Sauls terror and discouragement; and by consequent, of the discomfiture, by which he fell. And for Incoherent Speech, it was amongst the Gentiles taken for one sort of Prophecy, because the Prophets of their Oracles, intoxicated with a spirit, or vapour from the cave of the Pythian Oracle at Delphi,[52] were for the time really mad, and spake like mad-men; of whose loose words a sense might be made to fit any event, in such sort, as all bodies are said to be made of *Materia prima*.[53] In the Scripture I find it also so taken [1 *Sam.* 18. 10.] in these words, *And the Evill spirit came upon Saul, and he Prophecyed in the midst of the house.*

The manner how God hath spoken to the Prophets   And although there be so many significations in Scripture of the word *Prophet*; yet is that the most frequent, in which it is taken for him, to whom God speaketh immediately, that which the Prophet is to say from him, to some other man, or to the people. And hereupon a

question may be asked, in what manner God speaketh
to such a Prophet. Can it (may some say) be properly
said, that God hath voice and language, when it cannot be properly said, he hath a tongue, or other organs,
as a man? The Prophet David argueth thus,[54] *Shall he
that made the eye, not see? or he that made the ear, not
hear?* But this may be spoken, not (as usually) to signifie Gods nature, but to signifie our intention to honor
him. For to *see*, and *hear*, are Honorable Attributes,
and may be given to God, to declare (as far as our capacity can conceive) his Almighty power. But if it were
to be taken in the strict, and proper sense, one might
argue from his making of all other parts of mans body,
that he had also the same use of them which we have;
which would be many of them so uncomely, as it would
be the greatest contumely in the world to ascribe them
to him. Therefore we are to interpret Gods speaking to
men immediately, for that way (whatsoever it be), by
which God makes them understand his will: And the
wayes whereby he doth this, are many; and to be sought
onely in the Holy Scripture: where though many times
it be said, that God spake to this, and that person, without declaring in what manner; yet there be again many
places, that deliver also the signes by which they were
to acknowledge his presence, and commandement; and
by these may be understood, how he spake to many of
the rest.

In what manner God spake to *Adam*, and *Eve*, and *To the*
Cain, and *Noah*, is not expressed;[55] nor how he spake to *Extraordinary*
Abraham, till such time as he came out of his own coun- *Prophets*
trey to *Sichem* in the land of *Canaan*; and then [*Gen.* *of the Old*
12. 7.] God is said to have *appeared* to him. So there is *Testament*
one way, whereby God made his presence manifest; that *he spake by*
is, by an *Apparition*, or *Vision*. And again, [*Gen.* 15. 1.] *Dreams, or*
The Word of the Lord came to Abraham in a Vision; *Visions*
that is to say, somewhat, as a sign of Gods presence,
appeared as Gods Messenger, to speak to him. [227]
Again, the Lord appeared to Abraham [*Gen.* 18. 1.] by

an apparition of three Angels; and to Abimelech [*Gen.* 20. 3.] in a dream: To Lot [*Gen.* 19. 1.] by an apparition of two Angels: And to Hagar [*Gen.* 21. 17.] by the apparition of one Angel: And to Abraham again [*Gen.* 22. 11.] by the apparition of a voice from heaven: And [*Gen.* 26. 24.] to Isaac in the night; (that is, in his sleep, or by dream): And to Jacob [*Gen.* 18. 12.][56] in a dream; that is to say (as are the words of the text) *Jacob dreamed that he saw a ladder, &c.* And [*Gen.* 32. 1.] in a Vision of Angels: And to Moses [*Exod.* 3. 2.] in the apparition of a flame of fire out of the midst of a bush: And after the time of Moses, (where the manner how God spake immediately to man in the Old Testament, is expressed) hee spake alwaies by a Vision, or by a Dream; as to *Gideon, Samuel, Eliah, Elisha,*[57] *Isaiah, Ezekiel,* and the rest of the Prophets; and often in the New Testament, as to *Joseph,*[58] to St. *Peter,* to St. *Paul,* and to St. *John* the Evangelist in the Apocalypse.

Onely to Moses hee spake in a more extraordinary manner in Mount *Sinai,* and in the *Tabernacle*; and to the High Priest in the *Tabernacle,* and in the *Sanctum Sanctorum* of the Temple. But Moses, and after him the High Priests were Prophets of a more eminent place, and degree in Gods favour; And God himself in express words declareth, that to other Prophets hee spake in Dreams and Visions, but to his servant Moses, in such manner as a man speaketh to his friend. The words are these [*Numb.* 12. 6, 7, 8.] *If there be a Prophet among you, I the Lord will make my self known to him in a Vision, and will speak unto him in a Dream. My servant Moses is not so, who is faithfull in all my house; with him I will speak mouth to mouth, even apparently, not in dark speeches; and the similitude of the Lord shall he behold.* And [*Exod.* 33. 11.] *The Lord spake to Moses face to face, as a man speaketh to his friend.* And yet this speaking of God to Moses, was by mediation of an Angel, or Angels, as appears expressely, *Acts* 7. ver. 35. and 53. and *Gal.* 3. 19. and was

therefore a Vision, though a more cleer Vision than was
given to other Prophets. And conformable hereunto,
where God saith (*Deut.* 13. 1.) *If there arise amongst
you a Prophet, or Dreamer of Dreams*, the later word
is but the interpretation of the former. And [*Joel* 2. 28.]
*Your sons and your daughters shall Prophecy; your old
men shall dream Dreams, and your young men shall see
Visions*: where again, the word *Prophecy* is expounded
by *Dream*, and *Vision*. And in the same manner it was,
that God spake to Soloman, promising him Wisdome,
Riches, and Honor; for the text saith, [1 *Kings* 3. 15.]
And Solomon awoak, and behold it was a Dream: So
that generally the Prophets extraordinary in the Old
Testament took notice of the Word of God no otherwise,
than from their Dreams, or Visions; that is to say, from
the imaginations which they had in their sleep, or in an
Extasie: which imaginations in every true Prophet were
supernaturall; but in false Prophets were either naturall,
or feigned.

The same Prophets were neverthelesse said to speak
by the Spirit; [228] as [*Zach.* 7. 12.] where the Prophet
speaking of the Jewes, saith, *They made their hearts
hard as Adamant, lest they should hear the law, and the
words which the Lord of Hosts hath sent in his Spirit by
the former Prophets.* By which it is manifest, that speaking by the *Spirit*, or *Inspiration*, was not a particular
manner of Gods speaking, different from Vision, when *To Prophets*
they that were said to speak by the Spirit, were extraor- *of perpetuall*
dinary Prophets, such as for every new message, were *Calling, and*
to have a particular Commission, or (which is all one) a *Supreme, God*
new Dream, or Vision. *spake in the*

Of Prophets, that were so by a perpetuall Calling *Old Testa-*
in the Old Testament, some were *supreme*, and some *ment from*
subordinate: Supreme were first Moses; and after him *the Mercy*
the High Priest, every one for his time, as long as the *Seat, in a*
Priesthood was Royall; and after the people of the Jews, *manner not*
had rejected God, that he should no more reign over *expressed in*
them, those Kings which submitted themselves to Gods *the Scripture*

government, were also his chief Prophets; and the High
Priests office became Ministeriall. And when God was
to be consulted, they put on the holy vestments, and
enquired of the Lord, as the King commanded them,
and were deprived of their office, when the King thought
fit. For King Saul [1 *Sam.* 13. 9.] commanded the burnt
offering to be brought, and [1 *Sam.* 14. 18.] he commands the Priest to bring the Ark neer him; and [ver.
19.] again to let it alone, because he saw an advantage
upon his enemies. And in the same chapter Saul asketh
counsell of God. In like manner King David, after his
being anointed, though before he had possession of the
Kingdome, is said to *enquire of the Lord* [1 *Sam.* 23. 2.]
whether he should fight against the Philistines at *Keilah*;
and [verse 10.] David commandeth the Priest to bring
him the Ephod, to enquire whether he should stay in
Keilah, or not. And King Solomon [1 *Kings* 2. 27.] took
the Priesthood from *Abiathar*, and gave it [verse 35.] to
Zadoc.[59] Therefore Moses, and the High Priests, and the
pious Kings, who enquired of God on all extraordinary
occasions, how they were to carry themselves, or what
event they were to have, were all Soveraign Prophets.
But in what manner God spake unto them, is not manifest. To say that when Moses went up to God in Mount
Sinai, it was a Dream, or Vision, such as other Prophets had, is contrary to that distinction which God made
between Moses, and other Prophets, *Numb.* 12. 6, 7, 8.
To say God spake or appeared as he is in his own nature,
is to deny his Infinitenesse, Invisibility, Incomprehensibility. To say he spake by Inspiration, or Infusion of
the Holy Spirit, as the Holy Spirit signifieth the Deity,
is to make Moses equall with Christ, in whom onely
the Godhead [as St. Paul speaketh *Col.* 2. 9.] dwelleth
bodily. And lastly, to say he spake by the Holy Spirit,
as it signifieth the graces, or gifts of the Holy Spirit, is
to attribute nothing to him supernaturall. For God disposeth men to Piety, Justice, Mercy, Truth, Faith, and
all manner of Vertue, both Morall, and Intellectuall, by

doctrine, example, and by severall occasions, naturall, and ordinary.

And as these ways cannot be applyed to God, in his speaking to Moses, at Mount *Sinai*; so also, they cannot be applyed to him, in his [229] speaking to the High Priests, from the Mercy-Seat. Therefore in what manner God spake to those Soveraign Prophets of the Old Testament, whose office it was to enquire of him, is not intelligible. In the time of the New Testament, there was no Soveraign Prophet, but our Saviour; who was both God that spake, and the Prophet to whom he spake.

To subordinate Prophets of perpetuall Calling, I find not any place that proveth God spake to them supernaturally; but onely in such manner, as naturally he inclineth men to Piety, to Beleef, to Righteousnesse, and to other vertues all other Christian men. Which way, though it consist in Constitution, Instruction, Education, and the occasions and invitements men have to Christian vertues; yet it is truly attributed to the operation of the Spirit of God, or Holy Spirit, (which we in our language call the Holy Ghost): For there is no good inclination, that is not of the operation of God. But these operations are not alwaies supernaturall. When therefore a Prophet is said to speak in the Spirit, or by the Spirit of God, we are to understand no more, but that he speaks according to Gods will, declared by the supreme Prophet. For the most common acceptation of the word Spirit, is in the signification of a mans intention, mind, or disposition.

To Prophets of perpetuall Calling, but subordinate, God spake by the Spirit.

In the time of Moses, there were seventy men besides himself, that *Prophecyed* in the Campe of the Israelites. In what manner God spake to them, is declared in the 11 of *Numbers*, verse 25. *The Lord came down in a cloud, and spake unto Moses, and took of the Spirit that was upon him, and gave it to the seventy Elders. And it came to passe, when the Spirit rested upon them, they Prophecyed, and did not cease.* By which it is manifest, first, that their Prophecying to the people, was subservient, and subordinate to the Prophecying of Moses; for that God took of the Spirit of Moses, to put upon them; so that they Prophecyed as Moses would have them: otherwise they had not been suffered to Prophecy at all. For there was [verse 27.] a complaint made against them to Moses; and Joshua would have Moses to have forbidden them; which he did not, but said to Joshua, Bee not jealous in my behalf. Secondly, that the Spirit of God in that place, signifieth nothing but the Mind and Disposition to obey, and assist Moses in the administration of the Government. For if it were meant they had the substantial Spirit of God; that is, the Divine nature, inspired into them, then they had it in no lesse manner then Christ himself, in whom onely the Spirit of God dwelt bodily. It is meant therefore of the Gift and Grace of God, that guided them to co-operate with Moses; from whom their Spirit was derived. And it appeareth [verse 16.] that, they were such as Moses himself should appoint for Elders and Officers of the People: For the words are, *Gather unto me seventy men, whom thou knowest to be Elders and Officers of the people*: where, *thou knowest*, is the same with *thou appointest*, or *hast appointed to be such*. For we are told before [*Exod.* 18.] that Moses following the counsell of Jethro his Father-in-law, did appoint Judges, and Officers over the people, such as feared God; and of these, [230] were those Seventy, whom God by putting upon them Moses spirit, inclined to aid Moses in the Administration of the Kingdome: and in this sense the Spirit of God is said [1 *Sam.* 16. 13, 14.] presently upon the anointing of David, to have come upon David, and left Saul; God giving his graces to him he chose to govern his people, and taking them away from him, he rejected. So that by the Spirit is meant Inclination to Gods service; and not any supernaturall Revelation.

God sometimes also spake by Lots God spake also many times by the event of Lots; which were ordered by such as he had put in Authority over his people. So wee read that God manifested by the Lots which Saul caused to be drawn [1 *Sam.* 14. 43.] the fault that Jonathan had committed, in eating a honey-comb,[60] contrary to the oath taken by the people. And [*Josh.* 18. 10.] God divided the land of Canaan amongst the Israelite, by the *lots that Joshua did cast before the Lord in Shiloh*. In the same manner it seemeth to be, that God discovered [*Joshua* 7. 16, *&c.*] the crime of Achan. And these are the wayes whereby God declared his Will in the Old Testament.

All which ways he used also in the New Testament. To the *Virgin Mary*, by a Vision of an Angel:[61] To *Joseph* in a Dream:[62] again to *Paul* in the way to Damascus in a Vision of our Saviour:[63] and to *Peter* in the Vision of a sheet let down from heaven, with divers sorts of flesh, of clean, and unclean, beasts;[64] and in prison, by Vision of an Angel:[65] And to all the Apostles, and Writers of the New Testament, by the graces of his Spirit; and to the Apostles again (at the choosing of Matthias in the place of Judas Iscariot) by lot.[66]

Seeing then all Prophecy supposeth Vision, or Dream, (which two, when they be naturall, are the same,) or some especiall gift of God, so rarely observed in mankind, as to be admired where observed; And seeing as well such gifts, as the most extraordinary Dreams, and Visions, may proceed from God, not onely by his supernaturall, and immediate, but also by his naturall operation, and by mediation of second causes; there is need of Reason and Judgment to discern between naturall, and supernaturall Gifts, and between naturall, and supernaturall Visions, or Dreams. And consequently men had need to be very circumspect, and wary, in obeying the voice of man, that pretending himself to be a Prophet, requires us to obey God in that way, which he in Gods name telleth us to be the way to happinesse. For he that pretends to teach men the way of so great felicity, pretends to govern them; that is to say, to rule, and reign over them; which is a thing, that all men naturally desire, and is therefore worthy to be suspected of Ambition and Imposture; and consequently, ought to

Every man ought to examine the probability of a pretended Prophets Calling

be examined, and tryed by every man, before hee yeeld them obedience; unlesse he have yeelded it them already, in the institution of a Common-wealth; as when the Prophet is the Civill Soveraign, or by the Civil Soveraign Authorized. And if this examination of Prophets, and Spirits, were not allowed to every one of the people, it had been to no purpose, to set out the marks, by which every man might be able, to distinguish between those, whom they ought, and those whom they [231] ought not to follow. Seeing therefore such marks are set out [*Deut.* 13. 1, &c.] to know a Prophet by; and [1 *John* 4. 1. &c.] to know a Spirit by: and seeing there is so much Prophecying in the Old Testament; and so much Preaching in the New Testament against Prophets; and so much greater a number ordinarily of false Prophets, then of true; every one is to beware of obeying their directions, at their own perill. And first, that there were many more false then true Prophets, appears by this, that when Ahab[67] [1 *Kings* 12.] consulted four hundred Prophets, they were all false Impostors, but onely one Michaiah. And a little before the time of the Captivity, the Prophets were generally lyars. *The Prophets* (saith the Lord by *Jeremy*, cha. 14. verse 14.) *prophecy Lies in my name. I sent them not, neither have I commanded them, nor spake unto them, they prophecy to you a false Vision, a thing of naught; and the deceit of their heart.* In so much as God commanded the People by the mouth of the Prophet *Jeremiah* [chap. 23. 16.] not to obey them. *Thus saith the Lord of Hosts, hearken not unto the words of the Prophets, that prophecy to you. They make you vain, they speak a Vision of their own heart, and not out of the mouth of the Lord.*

All prophecy but of the Soveraign Prophet is to be examined by every Subject   Seeing then there was in the time of the Old Testament, such quarrells amongst the Visionary Prophets, one contesting with another, and asking, When departed the Spirit from me, to go to thee? as between Michaiah, and the rest of the four hundred; and such giving of the Lye to one another, [as in *Jerem.* 14. 14.] and such controversies in the New Testament at this day, amongst the Spirituall Prophets: Every man then was, and now is bound to make use of his Naturall Reason, to apply to all Prophecy those Rules which God hath given us, to discern the true from the false. Of which Rules, in the Old Testament, one was, conformable doctrine to that which Moses the Soveraign Prophet had taught them; and the other the miraculous power of foretelling what God would bring to passe, as I have already shewn out of *Deut.* 13. 1. &c. And in the New Testament there was but one onely mark; and that was the preaching of this Doctrine, *That Jesus is the Christ*, that is, the King of the Jews, promised in the Old Testament. Whosoever denyed that Article, he was a false Prophet, whatsoever miracles he might seem to work; and he that taught it was a true Prophet. For St. *John* [1 Epist. 4. 2, &c.] speaking expressely of the means to examine Spirits, whether they be of God, or not; after he had told them that there would arise false Prophets, saith thus, *Hereby know ye the Spirit of God. Every Spirit that confesseth that Jesus Christ is come in the flesh, is of God*; that is, is approved and allowed as a Prophet of God: not that he is a godly man, or one of the Elect, for this, that he confesseth, professeth, or preacheth Jesus to be the Christ; but for that he is a Prophet avowed. For God sometimes speaketh by Prophets, whose persons he hath not accepted; as he did by Baalam;[68] and as he foretold Saul of his death, by the Witch of Endor. Again in the next verse, *Every Spirit that confesseth not that Jesus Christ is come in the flesh, is not of Christ. And this is the Spirit of Antichrist.* So that the Rule is perfect on both [232] sides; that he is a true Prophet, which preacheth the Messiah already come, in the person of Jesus; and he a false one that denyeth him come, and looketh for him in some future Impostor, that shall take upon him that honour falsely, whom the Apostle there properly calleth Antichrist. Every man therefore ought to consider who is the Soveraign Prophet; that is to say,

who it is, that is Gods Vicegerent on Earth; and hath
next under God, the Authority of Governing Christian
men; and to observe for a Rule, that Doctrine, which in
the name of God, hee hath commanded to bee taught;
and thereby to examine and try out the truth of those
Doctrines, which pretended Prophets with miracle, or
without, shall at any time advance: and if they find it
contrary to that Rule, to doe as they did, that came
to Moses, and complained that there were some that
Prophecyed in the Campe,[69] whose Authority so to doe
they doubted of; and leave to the Soveraign, as they did
to Moses to uphold, or to forbid them, as hee should see
cause; and if hee disavow them, then no more to obey
their voice; or if he approve them, then to obey them,
as men to whom God hath given a part of the Spirit of
their Soveraigne. For when Christian men, take not their
Christian Soveraign, for Gods Prophet; they must either
take their owne Dreams, for the Prophecy they mean
to bee governed by, and the tumour of their own hearts
for the Spirit of God; or they must suffer themselves to
bee lead by some strange Prince; or by some of their
fellow subjects, that can bewitch them, by slander of
the government, into rebellion, without other miracle to
confirm their calling, then sometimes an extraordinary
successe, and Impunity; and by this means destroying all
laws, both divine, and humane, reduce all Order, Government, and Society, to the first Chaos of Violence, and
Civill warre. [233]

CHAP. XXXVII

Of MIRACLES, and their Use

*A Miracle
is a work
that causeth
Admiration*
By *Miracles* are signified the Admirable works of God:
& therefore they are also called *Wonders*. And because
they are for the most part, done, for a signification of

his commandement, in such occasions, as without them, men are apt to doubt, (following their private naturall reasoning,) what he hath commanded, and what not, they are commonly in Holy Scripture, called *Signes*, in the same sense, as they are called by the Latines, *Ostenta*, and *Portenta*, from shewing, and fore-signifying that, which the Almighty is about to bring to passe.

To understand therefore what is a Miracle, we must first understand what works they are, which men wonder at, and call Admirable. And there be but two things which make men wonder at any event: The one is, if it be strange, that is to say, such, as the like of it hath never, or very rarely been produced: The other is, if when it is produced, we cannot imagine it to have been done by naturall means, but onely by the immediate hand of God. But when wee see some possible, naturall cause of it, how rarely soever the like has been done; or if the like have been often done, how impossible soever it be to imagine a naturall means thereof, we no more wonder, nor esteem it for a Miracle. *And must therefore be rare, and whereof there is no naturall cause known*

Therefore, if a Horse, or Cow should speak, it were a Miracle; because both the thing is strange, & the naturall cause difficult to imagin: So also were it, to see a strange deviation of nature, in the production of some new shape of a living creature. But when a man, or other Animal, engenders his like, though we know no more how this is done, than the other; yet because 'tis usuall, it is no Miracle. In like manner, if a man be metamorphosed into a stone, or into a pillar, it is a Miracle; because strange: but if a peece of wood be so changed; because we see it often, it is no Miracle: and yet we know no more, by what operation of God, the one is brought to passe, than the other.

The first Rainbow that was seen in the world,[70] was a Miracle, because the first; and consequently strange; and served for a sign from God, placed in heaven, to assure his people, there should be no more an universall destruction of the world by Water. But at this day, because they are frequent, they are not Miracles, neither to them that know their naturall causes, nor to them who know them not. Again, there be many rare works produced by the Art of man: yet when we know they are done; because thereby wee know also the means how they are done, we count them not for Miracles, because not [234] wrought by the immediate hand of God, but by mediation of humane Industry.

That which seemeth a Miracle to one man, may seem otherwise to another Furthermore, seeing Admiration and Wonder, is consequent to the knowledge and experience, wherewith men are endued, some more, some lesse; it followeth, that the same thing, may be a Miracle to one, and not to another. And thence it is, that ignorant, and superstitious men make great Wonders of those works, which other men, knowing to proceed from Nature, (which is not the immediate, but the ordinary work of God,) admire not at all: As when Ecclipses of the Sun and Moon have been taken for supernaturall works, by the common people; when neverthelesse, there were others, could from their naturall causes, have foretold the very hour they should arrive: Or, as when a man, by confederacy, and secret intelligence, getting knowledge of the private actions of an ignorant, unwary man, thereby tells him, what he has done in former time; it seems to him a Miraculous thing; but amongst wise, and cautelous men, such Miracles as those, cannot easily be done.

The End of Miracles Again, it belongeth to the nature of a Miracle, that it be wrought for the procuring of credit to Gods Messengers, Ministers, and Prophets, that thereby men may know, they are called, sent, and employed by God, and thereby be the better inclined to obey them. And therefore, though the creation of the world, and after that the destruction of all living creatures in the universall deluge, were admirable works; yet because they were not done to procure credit to any Prophet, or other Minister of God, they use not to be called Miracles. For how admirable soever any work be, the Admiration consisteth not in that it could be done, because men naturally beleeve

the Almighty can doe all things, but because he does it
at the Prayer, or Word of a man. But the works of God
in Egypt, by the hand of Moses, were properly Miracles; because they were done with intention to make
the people of Israel beleeve, that Moses came unto them,
not out of any design of his owne interest, but as sent
from God. Therefore after God had commanded him to
deliver the Israelites from the Egyptian bondage, when
he said *They will not beleeve me, but will say, the Lord*
hath not appeared unto me, God gave him power, to
turn the Rod he had in his hand into a Serpent, and
again to return it into a Rod; and by putting his hand
into his bosome, to make it leprous; and again by pull-
ing it out to make it whole, to make the Children of
Israel beleeve (as it is verse 5.) that the God of their
Fathers had appeared unto him: And if that were not
enough, he gave him power to turn their waters into
bloud. And when hee had done these Miracles before
the people, it is said (verse 41.)[71] that *they beleeved him.* Exo. 4. 1, &c
Neverthelesse, for fear of Pharaoh, they durst not yet
obey him. Therefore the other works which were done
to plague Pharaoh, and the Egyptians, tended all to
make the Israelites beleeve in Moses, and were properly
Miracles. In like manner if we consider all the Miracles done by the hand of Moses, and all the rest of the
Prophets, till the Captivity; and those of our Saviour,
and his Apostles afterward; we shall find, their end
was alwaies to beget, or con[235]firm beleefe, that they
came not of their own motion, but were sent by God.
Wee may further observe in Scripture, that the end of
Miracles, was to beget beleef, not universally in all men,
elect, and reprobate; but in the elect only; that is to
say, in such as God had determined should become his
Subjects. For those miraculous plagues of Egypt, had not
for end, the conversation of Pharaoh; For God had told
Moses before, that he would harden the heart of Pharaoh, that he should not let the people goe: And when he
let them goe at last, not the Miracles perswaded him,

but the plagues forced him to it. So also of our Saviour, it is written, (*Mat.* 13.58.) that he wrought not many Miracles in his own countrey, because of their unbeleef; and (in *Marke* 6.5.) in stead of, *he wrought not many*, it is, *he could work none*. It was not because he wanted power; which to say, were blasphemy against God; nor that the end of Miracles was not to convert incredulous men to Christ; for the end of all the Miracles of Moses, of Prophets, of our Saviour, and of his Apostles was to adde men to the Church; but it was, because the end of their Miracles, was to adde to the Church (not all men, but) such as should be saved; that is to say, such as God had elected. Seeing therefore our Saviour was sent from his Father, hee could not use his power in the conversion of those, whom his Father had rejected. They that expounding this place of St. *Marke*,[72] say, that this word, *Hee could not*, is put for, *He would not*, do it without example in the Greek tongue, (where *Would not*, is put sometimes for *Could not*, in things inanimate, that have no will; but *Could not*, for *Would not*, never,) and thereby lay a stumbling block before weak Christians; as if Christ could doe no Miracles, but amongst the credulous.

The definition of a Miracle   From that which I have here set down, of the nature, and use of a Miracle, we may define it thus, *A* MIR-ACLE, *is a work of God, (besides his operation by the way of Nature, ordained in the Creation,) done for the making manifest to his elect, the mission of an extraordinary Minister for their salvation.*

And from this definition, we may inferre; First, that in all Miracles, the work done, is not the effect of any vertue in the Prophet; because it is the effect of the immediate hand of God; that is to say, God hath done it, without using the Prophet therein, as a subordinate cause.

Secondly, that no Devil, Angel, or other created Spirit, can do a Miracle. For it must either be by vertue of some naturall science, or by Incantation, that is, vertue of words. For if the Inchanters do it by their own power independent, there is some power that proceedeth not from God;

which all men deny: and if they doe it by power given them, then is the work not from the immediate hand of God, but naturall, and consequently no Miracle.

There be some texts of Scripture, that seem to attribute the power of working wonders (equall to some of those immediate Miracles, wrought by God himself,) to certain Arts of Magick, and Incantation. As for example, when we read that after the Rod of Moses be[236]ing cast on the ground became a Serpent, *the Magicians of* *Exod. 7. 11* *Egypt did the like by their Enchantments*; and that after Moses had turned the waters of the Egyptian Streams, Rivers, Ponds, and Pooles of water into blood, *the* *Magicians of Egypt did so likewise, with their Enchant-* *Exod. 7. 22* *ments*; and that after Moses had by the power of God brought frogs upon the land, *the Magicians also did so* *Exod. 8. 7* *with their Enchantments, and brought up frogs upon* *the land of Egypt*; will not a man be apt to attribute Miracles to Enchantments; that is to say, to the efficacy of the sound of Words; and think the same very well proved out of this, and other such places? and yet there is no place of Scripture, that telleth us what an Enchantment is. If therefore Enchantment be not, as many think it, a working of strange effects by spells, and words; but Imposture, and delusion, wrought by ordinary means; and so far from supernaturall, as the Impostors need not the study so much as of naturall causes, but the ordinary ignorance, stupidity, and superstition of mankind, to doe them; those texts that seem to countenance the power of Magick, Witchcraft, and Enchantment, must needs have another sense, than at first sight they seem to bear.

For it is evident enough, that Words have no effect, *That men* but on those that understand them; and then they have *are apt to be* no other, but to signifie the intentions, or passions of *deceived by* them that speak; and thereby produce, hope, fear, or *false Miracles* other passions, or conceptions in the hearer. Therefore when a Rod seemeth a Serpent, or the Waters Bloud, or any other Miracle seemeth done by Enchantment; if it be not to the edification of Gods people, not the Rod, nor the Water, nor any other thing is enchanted; that is to say, wrought upon by the Words, but the Spectator. So that all the Miracle consisteth in this, that the Enchanter has deceived a man; which is no Miracle, but a very easie matter to doe.

For such is the ignorance, and aptitude to error generally of all men, but especially of them that have not much knowledge of naturall causes, and of the nature, and interests of men; as by innumerable and easie tricks to be abused. What opinion of miraculous power, before it was known there was a Science of the course of the Stars, might a man have gained, that should have told the people, This hour, or day the Sun should be darkned? A Juggler by the handling of his goblets, and other trinkets, if it were not now ordinarily practised, would be thought to do his wonders by the power at least of the Devil. A man that hath practised to speak by drawing in of his breath, (which kind of men in antient time were called *Ventriloqui,*) and so make the weaknesse of his voice seem to proceed, not from the weak impulsion of the organs of Speech, but from distance of place, is able to make very many men beleeve it is a voice from Heaven, whatsoever he please to tell them. And for a crafty man, that hath enquired into the secrets, and familiar confessions that one man ordinarily maketh to another of his actions and adventures past, to tell them him again is no hard matter; and yet there be many, that by such means as that, obtain the reputation of being Conjurers. But it is too [237] long a businesse, to reckon up the severall sorts of those men, which the Greeks called *Thaumaturgi,* that is to say, workers of things wonderfull; and yet these do all they do, by their own single dexterity. But if we looke upon the Impostures wrought by Confederacy, there is nothing how impossible soever to be done, that is impossible to bee beleeved. For two men conspiring, one to seem lame, the other to cure him with a charme, will deceive many: but many conspiring, one to seem lame, another so to cure him, and all the rest to bear witnesse; will deceive many more.

In this aptitude of mankind, to give too hasty beleefe to pretended Miracles, there can be no better, nor I think any other caution, then that which God hath prescribed, first by Moses, (as I have said before in the precedent chapter,) in the beginning of the 13. and end of the 18. of *Deuteronomy*; That wee take not any for Prophets, that teach any other Religion, then that which Gods Lieutenant, (which at that time was Moses,) hath established; nor any, (though he teach the same Religion,) whose Prædiction we doe not see come to passe. Moses therefore in his time, and Aaron, and his successors in their times, and the Soveraign Governour of Gods people, next under God himself, that is to say, the Head of the Church in all times, are to be consulted, what doctrine he hath established, before wee give credit to a pretended Miracle, or Prophet. And when that is done, the thing they pretend to be a Miracle, we must both see it done, and use all means possible to consider, whether it be really done; and not onely so, but whether it be such, as no man can do the like by his naturall power, but that it requires the immediate hand of God. And in this also we must have recourse to Gods Lieutenant; to whom in all doubtfull cases, wee have submitted our private judgments. For example; if a man pretend, that after certain words spoken over a peece of bread, that presently God hath made it not bread, but a God, or a man, or both, and neverthelesse it looketh still as like bread as ever it did; there is no reason for any man to think it really done; nor consequently to fear him, till he enquire of God, by his Vicar, or Lieutenant, whether it be done, or not. If he say not, then followeth that which Moses saith, (*Deut.* 18.22.) *he hath spoken it presumptuously, thou shalt not fear him.* If he say 'tis done, then he is not to contradict it. So also if wee see not, but onely hear tell of a Miracle, we are to consult the Lawful Church; that is to say, the lawful Head thereof, how far we are to give

Cautions against the Imposture of Miracles

credit to the relators of it. And this is chiefly the case of men, that in these days live under Christian Soveraigns. For in these times, I do not know one man, that ever saw any such wondrous work, done by the charm, or at the word, or prayer of a man, that a man endued but with a mediocrity of reason, would think supernaturall: and the question is no more, whether what wee see done, be a Miracle; whether the Miracle we hear, or read of, were a reall work, and not the Act of a tongue, or pen; but in plain terms, whether the report be true, or a lye. In which question we are not every one, to make our own private Reason, or Conscience, but the Publique Reason, that is, the reason of Gods Supreme Lieutenant, Judge; and indeed we have made him Judge already, if wee have [238] given him a Soveraign power, to doe all that is necessary for our peace and defence. A private man has alwaies the liberty, (because thought is free,) to beleeve, or not beleeve in his heart, those acts that have been given out for Miracles, according as he shall see, what benefit can accrew by mens belief, to those that pretend, or countenance them, and thereby conjecture, whether they be Miracles, or Lies. But when it comes to confession of that faith, the Private Reason must submit to the Publique; that is to say, to Gods Lieutenant. But who is this Lieutenant of God, and Head of the Church, shall be considered in its proper place hereafter.

CHAP. XXXVIII

Of the Signification in Scripture of ETERNALL LIFE, HELL, SALVATION, THE WORLD TO COME, and REDEMPTION

The maintenance of Civill Society, depending on Justice; and Justice on the power of Life and Death, and other lesse Rewards and Punishments, residing in them

that have the Soveraignty of the Common-wealth; It
is impossible a Common-wealth should stand, where
any other than the Soveraign, hath a power of giving greater rewards than Life; and of inflicting greater
punishments, than Death. Now seeing *Eternall life* is a
greater reward, than the *life present*; and *Eternall torment* a greater punishment than the *death of Nature*; It
is a thing worthy to be well considered, of all men that
desire (by obeying Authority) to avoid the calamities of
Confusion, and Civill war, what is meant in holy Scripture, by *Life Eternall*, and *Torment Eternall*; and for
what offences, and against whom committed, men are
to be *Eternally tormented*; and for what actions, they
are to obtain *Eternall life*.

And first we find, that Adam was created in such a   *The place of*
condition of life, as had he not broken the commande-   *Adams*
ment of God, he had enjoyed it in the Paradise of Eden   *Eternity if*
Everlastingly. For there was the *Tree of life*; whereof he   *he had not*
was so long allowed to eat, as he should forbear to eat   *sinned, had*
of the tree of Knowledge of Good and Evill; which was   *been the*
not allowed him. And therefore as soon as he had eaten   *terrestriall*
of it, God thrust him out of Paradise, *lest he should*   *Paradise*
put forth his hand, and take also of the tree of life, and
live for ever. By which it seemeth to me, (with submis-   *Gen.* 3. 22
sion neverthelesse both in this, and in all questions,
whereof the determination dependeth on the Scriptures,
to the interpretation of the Bible authorized by the
Common-wealth, whose Subject I am,) that Adam if he
had not sinned, had had an Eternall Life on Earth: and
that Mortality entred upon himself, and his posterity,
by his first Sin. Not that actuall Death then entred; for
Adam then could never have had children; whereas he
lived long after, and saw a numerous posterity ere he
dyed. But where it is said, *In the day that thou eatest*
thereof, thou shalt surely die, it must needs bee meant of
his Mortality, and certitude of death. Seeing then Eternall life was lost by Adams forfeiture, in committing
sin, he that should cancell that forfeiture was to recover

thereby, that Life again. Now [239] Jesus Christ hath
satisfied for the sins of all that beleeve in him; and therefore recovered to all beleevers, that ETERNALL LIFE,
which was lost by the sin of Adam. And in this sense it
is, that the comparison of St. Paul holdeth (*Rom.* 5.18,
19.) *As by the offence of one, Judgment came upon all
men to condemnation, even so by the righteousnesse of
one, the free gift came upon all men to Justification of
Life.* Which is again (1 *Cor.* 15.21, 22.) more perspicuously delivered in these words, *For since by man came
death, by man came also the resurrection of the dead.
For as in Adam all die, even so in Christ shall all be
made alive.*

Texts   Concerning the place wherein men shall enjoy that
concerning Eternall Life, which Christ hath obtained for them, the
the place of texts next before alledged seem to make it on Earth. For
Life Eternall, if as in Adam, all die, that is, have forfeited Paradise,
for Beleevers and Eternall Life on Earth, even so in Christ all shall
bee made alive; then all men shall be made to live on
Earth; for else the comparison were not proper. Hereunto seemeth to agree that of the Psalmist, (*Psal.* 133.3.)[73]
*Upon Zion God commanded the blessing, even Life for
evermore*: for Zion, is in Jerusalem, upon Earth: as also
that of S. Joh. (*Rev.* 2.7.) *To him that overcommeth I
will give to eat of the tree of life, which is in the midst of
the Paradise of God.* This was the tree of Adams Eternall life; but his life was to have been on Earth. The same
seemeth to be confirmed again by St. Joh. (*Rev.* 21.2.)
where he saith, *I John saw the Holy City, New Jerusalem, coming down from God out of heaven, prepared
as a Bride adorned for her husband*: and again v. 10.
to the same effect: As if he should say, the new Jerusalem, the Paradise of God, at the coming again of Christ,
should come down to Gods people from Heaven, and
not they goe up to it from Earth. And this differs nothing from that, which the two men in white clothing (that
is, the two Angels) said to the Apostles, that were looking upon Christ ascending (*Acts* 1.11.) *This same Jesus,*

who is taken up from you into Heaven, shall so come,
as you have seen him go up into Heaven. Which sound-
eth as if they had said, he should come down to govern
them under his Father, Eternally here; and not take them
up to govern them in Heaven; and is conformable to
the Restauration of the Kingdom of God, instituted
under Moses; which was a Political government of the
Jews on Earth. Again, that saying of our Saviour (*Mat.*
22.30.) *that in the Resurrection they neither marry, nor*
are given in marriage, but are as the Angels of God in
heaven, is a description of an Eternall Life, resembling
that which we lost in Adam in the point of Marriage.
For seeing Adam, and Eve, if they had not sinned, had
lived on Earth Eternally, in their individuall persons; it
is manifest, they should not continually have procreated
their kind. For if Immortals should have generated, as
Mankind doth now; the Earth in a small time, would
not have been able to afford them place to stand on. The
Jews that asked our Saviour the question,[74] whose wife
the woman that had married many brothers, should be, in
the resurrection, knew not what were the consequences
of Life Eternall: and therefore our Saviour puts them
in mind of this consequence of Immortality; that there
shal be no Generation, and consequently no marriage,
no more than there is Marriage, or generation among
the Angels. The comparison between that Eternall life
which Adam lost, and our Saviour by his Victory over
death hath recovered; [240] holdeth also in this, that as
Adam lost Eternall Life by his sin, and yet lived after
it for a time; so the faithful Christian hath recovered
Eternal Life by Christs passion, though he die a natural death, and remaine dead for a time; namely, till the
Resurrection. For as Death is reckoned from the Condemnation of Adam, not from the Execution; so Life is
reckoned from the Absolution, not from the Resurrection of them that are elected in Christ.

That the place wherein men are to live Eternally, after *Ascension*
the Resurrection, is the Heavens, meaning by Heaven, *into heaven*

those parts of the world, which are the most remote
from Earth, as where the stars are, or above the stars,
in another Higher Heaven, called *Cœlum Empyreum*,[75]
(whereof there is no mention in Scripture, nor ground
in Reason) is not easily to be drawn from any text that
I can find. By the Kingdome of Heaven, is meant the
Kingdom of the King that dwelleth in Heaven; and his
Kingdome was the people of Israel, whom he ruled by
the Prophets his Lieutenants, first Moses, and after him
Eleazar, and the Soveraign Priests, till in the days of
Samuel they rebelled, and would have a mortall man
for their King, after the manner of other Nations. And
when our Saviour Christ, by the preaching of his Ministers, shall have perswaded the Jews to return, and called
the Gentiles to his obedience, then shall there be a new
Kingdome of Heaven; because our King shall then be
God, whose *throne* is Heaven; without any necessity
evident in the Scripture, that man shall ascend to his
happinesse any higher than Gods *footstool* the Earth.
On the contrary, we find written (*Joh.* 3.13.) that *no
man hath ascended into Heaven, but he that came down
from Heaven, even the Son of man, that is in Heaven.*
Where I observe by the way, that these words are not,
as those which go immediately before, the words of our
Saviour, but of St. John himself; for Christ was then not
in Heaven, but upon the Earth. The like is said of David
(*Acts* 2.34.) where St. Peter, to prove the Ascension of
Christ, using the words of the Psalmist, (*Psal.* 16.10.)
*Thou wilt not leave my soule in Hell, nor suffer thine
Holy one to see corruption*, saith, they were spoken (not
of David, but) of Christ; and to prove it, addeth this
Reason, *For David is not ascended into Heaven.* But to
this a man may easily answer, and say, that though their
bodies were not to ascend till the generall day of Judgment, yet their souls were in Heaven as soon as they
were departed from their bodies; which also seemeth to
be confirmed by the words of our Saviour (*Luke* 20.37,
38.) who proving the Resurrection out of the words of

Moses, saith thus, *That the dead are raised, even Moses shewed, at the bush, when he calleth the Lord, the God of Abraham, and the God of Isaac, and the God of Jacob. For he is not a God of the Dead, but of the Living; for they all live to him.* But if these words be to be understood only of the Immortality of the Soul, they prove not at all that which our Saviour intended to prove, which was the Resurrection of the Body, that is to say, the Immortality of the Man. Therefore our Saviour meaneth, that those Patriarchs were Immortall; not by a property consequent to the essence, and nature of mankind; but by the will of God, that was pleased of his mere grace, to bestow *Eternall life* upon the faithfull. [241] And though at that time the Patriarchs and many other faithfull men were *dead*, yet as it is in the text, they *lived to God*; that is, they were written in the Book of Life with them that were absolved of their sinnes, and ordained to Life eternall at the Resurrection. That the Soul of man is in its own nature Eternall, and a living Creature independent on the body; or that any meer man is Immortall, otherwise than by the Resurrection in the last day, (except *Enos* and *Elias*,)[76] is a doctrine not apparent in Scripture. The whole 14. Chapter of *Job*, which is the speech not of his friends, but of himselfe, is a complaint of this Mortality of Nature; and yet no contradiction of the Immortality at the Resurrection. *There is hope of a tree* (saith hee verse 7.) *if it be cast down, Though the root thereof wax old, and the stock thereof die in the ground, yet when it senteth the water it will bud, and bring forth boughes like a Plant. But man dyeth, and wasteth away, yea, man giveth up the Ghost, and where is he?* and (verse 12.) *man lyeth down, and riseth not, till the heavens be no more.* But when is it, that the heavens shall be no more? St. Peter tells us, that it is at the generall Resurrection. For in his 2. Epistle, 3. Chapter, and 7 verse, he saith, that *the Heavens and the Earth that are now, are reserved unto fire against the day of Judgment, and perdition of ungodly men*, and (verse 12.) *looking for, and hasting to the comming of God, wherein the Heavens shall be on fire, and shall be dissolved, and the Elements shall melt with fervent heat. Neverthelesse, we according to the promise look for new Heavens, and a new Earth, wherein dwelleth righteousnesse.* Therefore where Job saith, man riseth not till the Heavens be no more; it is all one,[77] as if he had said, the Immortall Life (and Soule and Life in the Scripture, do usually signifie the same thing) beginneth not in man, till the Resurrection, and day of Judgement; and hath for cause, not his specificall nature, and generation; but the Promise. For St. Peter saies not, *Wee look for new heavens, and a new earth, (from Nature,)* but *from Promise.*

Lastly, seeing it hath been already proved out of divers evident places of Scripture, in the 35. chapter of this book, that the Kingdom of God is a Civil Common-wealth, where God himself is Soveraign, by vertue first of the *Old*, and since of the *New* Covenant, wherein he reigneth by his Vicar, or Lieutenant; the same places do therefore also prove, that after the comming again of our Saviour in his Majesty, and glory, to reign actually, and Eternally; the Kingdom of God is to be on Earth. But because this doctrine (though proved out of places of Scripture not few, nor obscure) will appear to most men a novelty; I doe but propound it; maintaining nothing in this, or any other paradox of Religion; but attending the end of that dispute of the sword, concerning the Authority, (not yet amongst my Countrey-men decided,) by which all sorts of doctrine are to bee approved, or rejected; and whose commands, both in speech, and writing, (whatsoever be the opinions of private men) must by all men, that mean to be protected by their Laws, be obeyed. For the points of doctrine concerning the Kingdome [of] God, have so great influence [242] on the Kingdome of Man, as not to be determined, but by them, that under God have the Soveraign Power.

As the Kingdome of God, and Eternall Life, so also *The place* Gods Enemies, and their Torments after Judgment, *after Judg-* appear by the Scripture, to have their place on Earth. *ment, of* The name of the place, where all men remain till the *those who* Resurrection, that were either buryed, or swallowed up *were never in* of the Earth, is usually called in Scripture, by words that *the King-* signifie *under ground*; which the Latines read generally *dome of God,* *Infernus*, and *Inferi*, and the Greeks ᾅδης; that is to say, *or having* a place where men cannot see; and containeth as well *been in, are* the Grave, as any other deeper place. But for the place of *cast out* the damned after the Resurrection, it is not determined, neither in the Old, nor New Testament, by any note of situation; but onely by the company: as that it shall bee, where such wicked men were, as God in former times in extraordinary, and miraculous manner, had destroyed from off the face of the Earth: As for example, that they are *in Inferno*, in *Tartarus*, or in the bottomelesse pit; *Tartarus* because *Corah*, *Dathan*, and *Abirom*, were swallowed up alive into the earth.[78] Not that the Writers of the Scripture would have us beleeve, there could be in the globe of the Earth, which is not only finite, but also (compared to the height of the Stars) of no considerable magnitude, a pit without a bottome; that is, a hole of infinite depth, such as the Greeks in their *Dæmonologie* (that is to say, in their doctrine concerning *Dæmons*,) and after them the Romans called *Tartarus*; of which Virgill sayes,

> Bis patet in præceps, tantum tendítque sub umbras,
> Quantus ad æthereum cœli suspectus Olympum:[79]

for that is a thing the proportion of Earth to Heaven cannot bear: but that wee should beleeve them there, indefinitely, where those men are, on whom God inflicted that Exemplary punnishment.

Again, because those mighty men of the Earth, that *The* lived in the time of Noah, before the floud, (which the *congregation* Greeks called *Heroes*, and the Scripture *Giants*, and *of Giants* both say, were begotten, by copulation of the children of God, with the children of men,) were for their wicked life destroyed by the generall deluge; the place of the Damned, is therefore also sometimes marked out, by the company of those deceased Giants; as *Proverbs* 21.16. *The man that wandreth out of the way of understanding, shall remain in the congregation of the Giants,* and Job 26.5. *Behold the Giants groan under water, and they that dwell with them.* Here the place of the Damned, is under the water. And *Isaiah* 14.9. *Hell is troubled how to meet thee,* (that is, the King of Babylon) *and will displace the Giants for thee*: and here again the place of the Damned, (if the sense be literall,) is to be under water.

Lake of Fire   Thirdly, because the Cities of Sodom, and Gomorrah,[80] by the extraordinary wrath of God, were consumed for their wickednesse with Fire and Brimstone, and together with them the countrey about made a stinking bituminous Lake: the place of the Damned is sometimes expressed by Fire, and a Fiery Lake: as in the *Apocalypse* ch. 21. 8. *But the timorous, incredulous, and abominable, and Murderers, and* [243] *Whoremongers, and Sorcerers, and Idolaters, and all Lyars, shall have their part in the Lake that burneth with Fire, and Brimstone; which is the second Death.* So that it is manifest, that Hell Fire, which is here expressed by Metaphor, from the reall Fire of Sodome, signifieth not any certain kind, or place of Torment; but is to be taken indefinitely, for Destruction, as it is in the 20. Chapter, at the 14. verse; where it is said, that *Death and Hell were cast into the Lake of Fire*; that is to say, were abolished, and destroyed; as if after the day of Judgment, there shall be no more Dying, nor no more going into Hell; that is, no more going to *Hades* (from which word perhaps our word Hell is derived,) which is the same with no more Dying.

Utter   Fourthly, from the Plague of Darknesse inflicted on
Darknesse the Egyptians, of which it is written (*Exod.* 10.23.) *They saw not one another, neither rose any man from his place for three days; but all the Children of Israel had light in*

their dwellings; the place of the wicked after Judgment, is called *Utter Darknesse*, or (as it is in the originall) *Darknesse without*. And so it is expressed (*Mat.* 22.13.) where the King commandeth his Servants, *to bind hand and foot the man that had not on his Wedding garment, and to cast him out*, εἰς τὸ σκότος τὸ ἐξώτερον, *Externall darknesse*, or *Darknesse without*: which though translated *Utter darknesse*, does not signifie *how great*, but *where* that darknesse is to be; namely, *without the habitation* of Gods Elect.

Lastly, whereas there was a place neer Jerusalem, called the *Valley of the Children of Hinnon*; in a part whereof, called *Tophet*, the Jews had committed most grievous Idolatry, sacrificing their children to the Idol Moloch;[81] and wherein also God had afflicted his enemies with most grievous punishments; and wherein Josias had burnt the Priests of Moloch upon their own Altars, as appeareth at large in the 2 of *Kings* chap. 23. the place served afterwards, to receive the filth, and garbage which was carried thither, out of the City; and there used to be fires made, from time to time, to purifie the aire, and take away the stench of Carrion. From this abominable place, the Jews used ever after to call the place of the Damned, by the name of *Gehenna*, or *Valley of Hinnon*. And this *Gehenna*, is that word, which is usually now translated HELL; and from the fires from time to time there burning, we have the notion of *Everlasting*, and *Unquenchable Fire*. *Gehenna, and Tophet*

Seeing now there is none, that so interprets the Scripture, as that after the day of Judgment, the wicked are all Eternally to be punished in the Valley of Hinnon; or that they shall so rise again, as to be ever after under ground, or under water; or that after the Resurrection, they shall no more see one another; nor stir from one place to another; it followeth, me thinks, very necessarily, that that which is thus said concerning Hell Fire, is spoken metaphorically; and that therefore there is a proper sense to bee enquired *Of the literall sense of the Scripture concerning Hell*

after, (for of all Metaphors there is some reall ground,
that may be expressed in proper words) both of the
Place of *Hell*, and the nature of *Hellish Torments*, and
Tormenters.

Satan, Devill,   [244] And first for the Tormenters, wee have their
not Proper nature, and properties, exactly and properly delivered
names, but by the names of, *The Enemy*, or *Satan*; *The Accuser*,
Appellatives or *Diabolus*; *The Destroyer*, or *Abaddon*.[82] Which significant names, *Satan, Devill, Abaddon*, set not forth to
us any Individuall person, as proper names use to doe;
but onely an office, or quality; and are therefore Appellatives; which ought not to have been left untranslated,
as they are, in the Latine, and Modern Bibles; because
thereby they seem to be the proper names of *Dæmons*;
and men are the more easily seduced to beleeve the doctrine of Devills; which at that time was the Religion
of the Gentiles, and contrary to that of Moses, and of
Christ.

And because by the *Enemy*, the *Accuser*, and *Destroyer*, is meant, the Enemy of them that shall be in the
Kingdome of God; therefore if the Kingdome of God
after the Resurrection, bee upon the Earth, (as in the
former Chapter I have shewn by Scripture it seems to
be,) The Enemy, and his Kingdome must be on Earth
also. For so also was it, in the time before the Jews had
deposed God. For Gods Kingdome was in Palestine; and
the Nations round about, were the Kingdomes of the
Enemy; and consequently by *Satan*, is meant any Earthly
Enemy of the Church.

Torments of   The Torments of Hell, are expressed sometimes, by
Hell *weeping, and gnashing of teeth*, as *Mat.* 8.12. Sometimes, by *the worm of Conscience*; as *Isa.* 66.24. and
Mark 9.44, 46, 48: sometimes, by *Fire*, as in the place
now quoted, *where the worm dyeth not, and the fire is
not quenched*, and many places beside: sometimes by
shame, and contempt, as *Dan.* 12.2. *And many of them
that sleep in the dust of the Earth, shall awake; some
to Everlasting life; and some to shame, and everlasting*

contempt. All which places design metaphorically a grief, and discontent of mind, from the sight of that Eternall felicity in others, which they themselves through their own incredulity, and disobedience have lost. And because such felicity in others, is not sensible but by comparison with their own actuall miseries; it followeth that they are to suffer such bodily paines, and calamities, as are incident to those, who not onely live under evill and cruell Governours, but have also for Enemy, the Eternall King of the Saints, God Almighty. And amongst these bodily paines, is to be reckoned also to every one of the wicked a second Death. For though the Scripture bee clear for an universall Resurrection; yet wee do not read, that to any of the Reprobate is promised an Eternall life. For whereas St. *Paul* (1 *Cor.* 15.42, 43.) to the question concerning what bodies men shall rise with again, saith, that *the body is sown in corruption, and is raised in incorruption; It is sown in dishonour, it is raised in glory; it is sown in weaknesse, it is raised in power*; Glory and Power cannot be applyed to the bodies of the wicked: Nor can the name of *Second Death*, bee applyed to those that can never die but once: And although in Metaphoricall speech, a Calamitous life Everlasting, may bee called an Everlasting Death yet it cannot well be understood of a *Second Death*. [245] The fire prepared for the wicked, is an Everlasting Fire: that is to say, the estate wherein no man can be without torture, both of body and mind, after the Resurrection, shall endure for ever; and in that sense the Fire shall be unquenchable, and the torments Everlasting: but it cannot thence be inferred, that hee who shall be cast into that fire, or be tormented with those torments, shall endure, and resist them so, as to be eternally burnt, and tortured, and yet never be destroyed, nor die. And though there be many places that affirm Everlasting Fire, and Torments (into which men may be cast successively one after another for ever;) yet I find none that affirm there shall bee an Eternall Life therein of any individuall person; but to the contrary, an Everlasting Death, which *Apoc.* 20. 13, is the Second Death: *For after Death, and the Grave* 14 *shall have delivered up the dead which were in them, and every man be judged according to his works; Death and the Grave shall also be cast into the Lake of Fire. This is the Second Death.* Whereby it is evident, that there is to bee a Second Death of every one that shall bee condemned at the day of Judgement, after which hee shall die no more.

The Joyes of   The joyes of Life Eternall, are in Scripture compre-
Life Eternall, hended all under the name of SALVATION, or *being*
and Salvation *saved.* To be saved, is to be secured, either respectively,
the same thing against speciall Evills, or absolutely, against all Evill,
comprehending Want, Sicknesse, and Death it self. And
Salvation because man was created in a condition Immortall, not
from Sin, and subject to corruption, and consequently to nothing that
from Misery, tendeth to the dissolution of his nature; and fell from
all one that happinesse by the sin of Adam; it followeth, that
to be *saved* from Sin, is to be saved from all the Evill,
and Calamities that Sinne hath brought upon us. And
therefore in the Holy Scripture, Remission of Sinne, and
Salvation from Death and Misery, is the same thing, as it
appears by the words of our Saviour, who having cured
a man sick of the Palsey, by saying, (*Mat.* 9.2.) *Son be
of good cheer, thy Sins be forgiven thee*; and knowing
that the Scribes took for blasphemy, that a man should
pretend to forgive Sins, asked them (v. 5.) *whether it
were easier to say, Thy Sinnes be forgiven thee, or, Arise
and walk*; signifying thereby, that it was all one, as to
the saving of the sick, to say, *Thy Sins are forgiven*, and
Arise and walk; and that he used that form of speech,
onely to shew he had power to forgive Sins. And it is
besides evident in reason, that since Death and Misery,
were the punishments of Sin, the discharge of Sinne,
must also be a discharge of Death and Misery; that is to
say, Salvation absolute, such as the faithfull are to enjoy
after the day of Judgment, by the power, and favour of
Jesus Christ, who for that cause is called our SAVIOUR.

Concerning Particular Salvations, such as are understood, 1 *Sam.* 14.39. *as the Lord liveth that saveth Israel,*
that is, from their temporary enemies, and 2 *Sam.* 22.4.
Thou art my Saviour, thou savest me from violence; and
2 *Kings* 13.5. *God gave the Israelites a Saviour, and so
they were delivered from the hand of the Assyrians,* and
the [246] like, I need say nothing; there being neither
difficulty, nor interest, to corrupt the interpretation of
texts of that kind.

But concerning the Generall Salvation, because it *The Place*
must be in the Kingdome of Heaven, there is great dif- *of Eternall*
ficulty concerning the Place. On one side, by *Kingdome* *Salvation*
(which is an estate ordained by men for their perpetuall
security against enemies, and want) it seemeth that this
Salvation should be on Earth. For by Salvation is set
forth unto us, a glorious Reign of our King, by Conquest; not a safety by Escape: and therefore there where
we look for Salvation, we must look also for Triumph;
and before Triumph, for Victory; and before Victory,
for Battell; which cannot well be supposed, shall be in
Heaven. But how good soever this reason may be, I will
not trust to it, without very evident places of Scripture.
The state of Salvation is described at large, *Isaiah* 33.
ver. 20, 21, 22, 23, 24.

*Look upon Zion, the City of our solemnities; thine
eyes shall see Jerusalem a quiet habitation, a tabernacle
that shall not be taken down; not one of the stakes
thereof shall ever be removed, neither shall any of the
cords thereof be broken.*

*But there the glorious Lord will be unto us a place of
broad rivers, and streams; wherein shall goe no Gally
with oares; neither shall gallant ship passe thereby.*

*For the Lord is our Judge, the Lord is our Lawgiver,
the Lord is our King, he will save us.*

*Thy tacklings are loosed; they could not well
strengthen their mast; they could not spread the sail:
then is the prey of a great spoil divided; the lame take
the prey.*

And the Inhabitant shall not say, I am sicke; the people
that shall dwell therein shall be forgiven their Iniquity.

In which words wee have the place from whence
Salvation is to proceed, *Jerusalem, a quiet habitation*;
the Eternity of it, *a tabernacle that shall not be taken
down, &c.* The Saviour of it, *the Lord, their Judge,
their Lawgiver, their King, he will save us*; the Salvation, *the Lord shall be to them as a broad mote of swift
waters, &c.* the condition of their Enemies, *their tacklings are loose, their masts weak, the lame shal take the
spoil of them.* The condition of the Saved, *The Inhabitant shal not say, I am sick*: And lastly, all this is
comprehended in Forgivenesse of sin, *The people that
dwell therein shall be forgiven their iniquity.* By which it
is evident, that Salvation shall be on Earth, then, when
God shall reign, (at the coming again of Christ) in Jerusalem; and from Jerusalem shall proceed the Salvation
of the Gentiles that shall be received into Gods Kingdome: as is also more expressely declared by the same
Prophet, Chap. 65.20, 21. *And they* (that is, the Gentiles
who had any Jew in bondage) *shall bring all your brethren, for an offering to the Lord, out of all nations, upon
horses, and in charets, and in litters, and upon mules,
and upon swift beasts, to my holy mountain, Jerusalem,
saith the Lord, as the Children of Israel bring an offering in a clean vessell into the House of the Lord. And I
will also take of them for Priests and for Levites, saith
the Lord*: Whereby it is manifest, that the chief seat of
Gods Kingdome (which is the Place, [247] from whence
the Salvation of us that were Gentiles, shall proceed)
shall be Jerusalem: And the same is also confirmed by
our Saviour, in his discourse with the woman of Samaria, concerning the place of Gods worship; to whom he
saith, *John* 4.22. that the Samaritans worshipped they
knew not what, but the Jews worship what they knew,
For Salvation is of the Jews (*ex Iudæis*, that is, begins
at the Jews): as if he should say, you worship God, but
know not by whom he wil save you, as we doe, that

know it shall be by one of the tribe of Judah, a Jew, not a Samaritan. And therefore also the woman not impertinently answered him again, *We know the Messias shall come.* So that which our Saviour saith, *Salvation is from the Jews*, is the same that Paul sayes (*Rom.* 1.16, 17.) *The Gospel is the power of God to Salvation to every one that beleeveth: To the Jew first, and also to the Greek. For therein is the righteousnesse of God revealed from faith to faith*; from the faith of the Jew, to the faith of the Gentile. In the like sense the Prophet *Joel* describing the day of Judgment, (chap. 2.30, 31.) that God would *shew wonders in heaven, and in earth, bloud, and fire, and pillars of smoak. The Sun should be turned to darknesse, and the Moon into bloud, before the great and terrible day of the Lord come*, he addeth verse 32. *and it shall come to passe, that whosoever shall call upon the name of the Lord, shall be saved. For in Mount Zion, and in Jerusalem shall be Salvation.* And *Obadiah* verse 17. saith the same, *Upon Mount Zion shall be Deliverance; and there shall be holinesse, and the house of Jacob shall possesse their possessions*, that is, the possessions of the *Heathen*, which *possessions* he expresseth more particularly in the following verses, by the *mount of Esau*, the *Land of the Philistines*, the *fields of Ephraim*, of *Samaria*, *Gilead*, and the *Cities of the South*, and concludes with these words, *the Kingdom shall be the Lords.* All these places are for Salvation, and the Kingdome of God (after the day of Judgement) upon Earth. On the other side, I have not found any text that can probably be drawn, to prove any Ascension of the Saints into Heaven; that is to say, into any *Cœlum Empyreum*, or other ætheriall Region; saving that it is called the Kingdome of Heaven: which name it may have, because God, that was King of the Jews, governed them by his commands, sent to Moses by Angels from Heaven; and after their revolt, sent his Son from Heaven, to reduce them to their obedience; and shall send him thence again, to rule both them, and all other faithfull men, from the day of Judgment, Everlastingly: or from that, that the Throne of this our Great King is in Heaven; whereas the Earth is but his Footstoole. But that the Subjects of God should have any place as high as his Throne, or higher than his Footstoole, it seemeth not sutable to the dignity of a King, nor can I find any evident text for it in holy Scripture.

From this that hath been said of the Kingdom of God, and of Salvation, it is not hard to interpret what is meant by the WORLD TO COME. There are three worlds mentioned in Scripture, the *Old World*, the *Present World*, and the *World to come*. Of the first, St. Peter speaks, *2 Pet. 2. 5 If God spared not the Old World, but saved Noah the eighth person, a Preacher of righteousness, bringing the flood upon the world of* [248] *the ungodly, &c.* So the *first World*, was from Adam to the generall Flood. Of the present World, our Saviour speaks (*John* 18.36.) *My Kingdome is not of this World*. For he came onely to teach men the way of Salvation, and to renew the Kingdome of his Father, by his doctrine. Of the World *2 Pet. 3. 13* to come, St. Peter speaks, *Neverthelesse we according to his promise look for new Heavens, and a new Earth*. This is that WORLD, wherein Christ coming down from Heaven, in the clouds, with great power, and glory, shall send his Angels, and shall gather together his elect, from the four winds, and from the uttermost parts of the Earth, and thence forth reign over them, (under his Father) Everlastingly.

Redemption   *Salvation* of a sinner, supposeth a precedent REDEMPTION; for he that is once guilty of Sin, is obnoxious[83] to the Penalty of the same; and must pay (or some other for him) such Ransome, as he that is offended, and has him in his power, shall require. And seeing the person offended, is Almighty God, in whose power are all things; such Ransome is to be paid before Salvation can be acquired, as God hath been pleased to require. By this Ransome, is not intended a satisfaction for Sin, equivalent to the Offence; which no sinner for himselfe, nor righteous man can ever be able to make for another: The dammage a man does to another, he may make amends for by restitution, or recompence, but sin cannot be taken away by recompence; for that were to make the liberty to sin, a thing vendible. But sins may bee pardoned to the repentant, either *gratis*, or upon such penalty, as God is pleased to accept. That which God usually accepted in the Old Testament, was some Sacrifice, or Oblation. To forgive sin is not an act of Injustice, though the punishment have been threatned. Even amongst men, though the promise of Good, bind the promiser; yet threats, that is to say, promises of Evill, bind them not; much lesse shall they bind God, who is infinitely more mercifull then men. Our Saviour Christ therefore to *Redeem* us, did not in that sense satisfie for the Sins of men, as that his Death, of its own vertue, could make it unjust in God to punish sinners with Eternall death; but did make that Sacrifice, and Oblation of himself, at his first coming, which God was pleased to require, for the Salvation at his second coming, of such as in the mean time should repent, and beleeve in him. And though this act of our *Redemption*, be not alwaies in Scripture called a *Sacrifice*, and *Oblation*, but sometimes a *Price*; yet by *Price* we are not to understand any thing, by the value whereof, he could claim right to a pardon for us, from his offended Father; but that Price which God the Father was pleased in mercy to demand. [247]

CHAP. XXXIX

Of the signification in Scripture of the word CHURCH

The word *Church*, (*Ecclesia*) signifieth in the Books of Holy Scripture divers things. Sometimes (though not often) it is taken for *Gods House*, that is to say, for a

Church the Lords house

Temple, wherein Christians assemble to perform holy duties publiquely; as, 1 *Cor.* 14. ver. 34. *Let your women keep silence in the Churches*: but this is Metaphorically put, for the Congregation there assembled; and hath been since used for the Edifice it self, to distinguish between the Temples of Christians, and Idolaters. The Temple of Jerusalem was *Gods house*, and the House of Prayer; and so is any Edifice dedicated by Christians to the worship of Christ, *Christs house*: and therefore the Greek Fathers call it Κυριακὴ, *The Lords house*; and thence, in our language it came to be called *Kyrke*, and *Church*.

Ecclesia   Church (when not taken for a House) signifieth the
properly same that *Ecclesia* signified in the Grecian Common-
what wealths; that is to say, a Congregation, or an Assembly of Citizens, called forth, to hear the Magistrate speak unto them; and which in the Common-wealth of Rome was called *Concio*, as he that spake was called *Ecclesias-*
Acts 19. 39 *tes*, and *Concionator*. And when they were called forth by lawfull Authority, it was *Ecclesia legitima*, a *Lawfull Church*, ἔννομος ἐκκλησία. But when they were excited by tumultuous, and seditious clamor, then it was a confused Church, ἐκκλησία συγκεχυμένη.

It is taken also sometimes for the men that have right to be of the Congregation, though not actually assembled; that is to say, for the whole multitude of Christian men, how far soever they be dispersed: as (*Act.* 8.3.) where it is said, that *Saul made havock of the Church*: And in this sense is *Christ* said to be Head of the Church. And sometimes for a certain part of Christians, as (*Col.* 4.15.) *Salute the Church that is in his house.* Sometimes also for the Elect onely; as (*Ephes.* 5.27.) *A Glorious Church, without spot, or wrinkle, holy, and without blemish*; which is meant of the *Church triumphant*, or, *Church to come*. Sometimes, for a Congregation assembled, of professors of Christianity, whether their profession be true, or counterfeit, as it is understood, *Mat.* 18.17. where it is said, *Tell it to the Church, and*

if hee neglect to hear the Church, let him be to thee as a
Gentile, or Publican.

And in this last sense only it is that the *Church* can *In what sense*
be taken for one Person; that is to say, that it can be *the Church is*
said to have power to will, to pronounce, to command, *one Person*
to be obeyed, to make laws, or to doe any other action
whatsoever; For without authority from a lawfull Congregation, whatsoever act be done in a concourse of
people, it is the [248] particular act of every one of those
that were present, and gave their aid to the performance
of it; and not the act of them all in grosse, as of one
body; much lesse the act of them that were absent, or
that being present, were not willing it should be done.
According to this sense, I define a CHURCH to be, *A com-* *Church*
pany of men professing Christian Religion, united in the *defined*
person of one Soveraign; at whose command they ought
to assemble, and without whose authority they ought
not to assemble. And because in all Common-wealths,
that Assembly, which is without warrant from the
Civil Soveraign, is unlawful; that Church also, which is
assembled in any Common-wealth, that hath forbidden
them to assemble, is an unlawfull Assembly.

It followeth also, that there is on Earth, no such uni- *A Christian*
versall Church, as all Christians are bound to obey; *Common-*
because there is no power on Earth, to which all other *wealth, and*
Common-wealths are subject: There are Christians, in *a Church all*
the Dominions of severall Princes and States; but every *one*
one of them is subject to that Common-wealth, whereof
he is himself a member; and consequently, cannot be
subject to the commands of any other Person. And
therefore a Church, such a one as is capable to Command, to Judge, Absolve, Condemn, or do any other
act, is the same thing with a Civil Common-wealth,
consisting of Christian men; and is called a *Civill State*,
for that the subjects of it are *Men*; and a *Church*, for
that the subjects thereof are *Christians*. *Temporall* and
Spirituall Government, are but two words brought into
the world, to make men see double, and mistake their

Lawfull Soveraign. It is true, that the bodies of the faith-full, after the Resurrection, shall be not onely Spirituall, but Eternall: but in this life they are grosse, and cor-ruptible. There is therefore no other Government in this life, neither of State, nor Religion, but Temporall; nor teaching of any doctrine, lawfull to any Subject, which the Governour both of the State, and of the Religion, forbiddeth to be taught: And that Governor must be one; or else there must needs follow Faction, and Civil war in the Common-wealth, between the *Church* and *State*; between *Spiritualists*, and *Temporalists*; between the *Sword of Justice*, and the *Shield of Faith*; and (which is more) in every Christian mans own brest, between the *Christian*, and the *Man*. The Doctors of the Church, are called Pastors; so also are Civill Soveraignes: But if Pastors be not subordinate one to another, so as that there may bee one chief Pastor, men will be taught con-trary Doctrines, whereof both may be, and one must be false. Who that one chief Pastor is, according to the law of Nature, hath been already shewn; namely, that it is the Civill Soveraign: And to whom the Scripture hath assigned that Office, we shall see in the Chapters fol-lowing. [249]

CHAP. XL

Of the RIGHTS of the Kingdome of God, in Abraham, Moses, the High Priests, and the Kings of Judah

The Soveraign Rights of Abraham The Father of the Faithfull, and first in the Kingdome of God by Covenant, was *Abraham*. For with him was the Covenant first made; wherein he obliged himself, and his seed after him, to acknowledge and obey the com-mands of God; not onely such, as he could take notice of, (as Morall Laws,) by the light of Nature; but also

such, as God should in speciall manner deliver to him by
Dreams, and Visions. For as to the Morall law, they were
already obliged, and needed not have been contracted
withall, by promise of the Land of Canaan.[84] Nor was
there any Contract, that could adde to, or strengthen
the Obligation, by which both they, and all men else
were bound naturally to obey God Almighty: And therefore the Covenant which Abraham made with God, was
to take for the Commandement of God, that which in
the name of God was commanded him, in a Dream, or
Vision; and to deliver it to his family, and cause them to
observe the same.

In this Contract of God with Abraham, wee may
observe three points of important consequence in the
government of Gods people. First, that at the making
of this Covenant, God spake onely to Abraham; and
therefore contracted not with any of his family, or seed,
otherwise then as their wills (which make the essence
of all Covenants) were before the Contract involved in
the will of Abraham; who was therefore supposed to
have had a lawfull power, to make them perform all that
he covenanted for them. According whereunto (*Gen.*
18.18, 19.) God saith, *All the Nations of the Earth shall
be blessed in him, For I know him that he will command
his children and his houshold after him, and they shall
keep the way of the Lord.* From whence may be concluded this first point, that they to whom God hath not
spoken immediately, are to receive the positive commandements of God, from their Soveraign; as the family
and seed of Abraham did from Abraham their Father, and
Lord, and Civill Soveraign. And consequently in every
Common-wealth, they who have no supernaturall Revelation to the contrary, ought to obey the laws of their
own Soveraign, in the externall acts and profession of
Religion. As for the inward *thought*, and *beleef* of men,
which humane Governours can take no notice of, (for
God onely knoweth the heart) they are not voluntary,
nor the effect of the laws, but of the [250] unrevealed

*Abraham
had the sole
power of
ordering
the Religion
of his own
people*

will, and of the power of God; and consequently fall not under obligation.

No pretence of Private Spirit against the Religion of Abraham

From whence proceedeth another point, that it was not unlawfull for Abraham, when any of his Subjects should pretend Private Vision, or Spirit, or other Revelation from God, for the countenancing of any doctrine which Abraham should forbid, or when they followed, or adhered to any such pretender, to punish them; and consequently that it is lawfull now for the Soveraign to punish any man that shall oppose his Private Spirit against the Laws: For hee hath the same place in the Common-wealth, that Abraham had in his own Family.

Abraham sole Judge, and Interpreter of what God spake

There ariseth also from the same, a third point; that as none but Abraham in his family, so none but the Soveraign in a Christian Common-wealth, can take notice what is, or what is not the Word of God. For God spake onely to Abraham; and it was he onely, that was able to know what God said, and to interpret the same to his family: And therefore also, they that have the place of Abraham in a Common-wealth, are the onely Interpreters of what God hath spoken.

The authority of Moses whereon grounded

The same Covenant was renewed with Isaac; and afterwards with Jacob; but afterwards no more, till the Israelites were freed from the Egyptians, and arrived at the Foot of Mount Sinai: and then it was renewed by Moses (as I have said before, chap. 35.) in such manner, as they became from that time forward the Peculiar Kingdome of God; whose Lieutenant was Moses, for his owne time: and the succession to that office was setled upon Aaron, and his heirs after him, to bee to God a Sacerdotall Kingdome for ever.

By this constitution, a Kingdome is acquired to God. But seeing Moses had no authority to govern the Israelites, as a successor to the right of Abraham, because he could not claim it by inheritance; it appeareth not as yet, that the people were obliged to take him for Gods Lieutenant, longer than they beleeved that God spake unto him. And therefore his authority (notwithstanding

the Covenant they made with God) depended yet merely
upon the opinion they had of his Sanctity, and of the
reality of his Conferences with God, and the verity of his
Miracles; which opinion coming to change, they were
no more obliged to take any thing for the law of God,
which he propounded to them in Gods name. We are
therefore to consider, what other ground there was, of
their obligation to obey him. For it could not be the
commandement of God that could oblige them; because
God spake not to them immediately, but by the medi-
ation of Moses himself: And our Saviour saith of himself, *John 5. 31*
If I bear witnesse of my self, my witnesse is not true;
much lesse if Moses bear witnesse of himselfe, (especially
in a claim of Kingly power over Gods people) ought his
testimony to be received. His authority therefore, as the
authority of all other Princes, must be grounded on the
Consent of the People, and their Promise to obey him.
And so it was: For *the people (Exod. 20.18.) when they
saw the Thunderings, [251] and the Lightnings, and
the noyse of the Trumpet, and the mountaine smoak-
ing, removed, and stood a far off. And they said unto
Moses, speak thou with us, and we will hear, but let not
God speak with us lest we die.* Here was their promise
of obedience; and by this it was they obliged themselves
to obey whatsoever he should deliver unto them for the
Commandement of God.

And notwithstanding the Covenant constituteth *Moses was*
a Sacerdotall Kingdome, that is to say, a Kingdome *(under God)*
hereditary to Aaron; yet that is to be understood of the *Soveraign*
succession, after Moses should bee dead. For whosoever *of the Jews,*
ordereth, and establisheth the Policy, as first founder *all his own*
of a Common-wealth (be it Monarchy, Aristocracy, or *time, though*
Democracy) must needs have Soveraign Power over the *Aaron had*
people all the while he is doing of it. And that Moses *the Priest-*
had that power all his own time, is evidently affirmed *hood*
in the Scripture. First, in the text last before cited,
because the people promised obedience, not to Aaron
but to him. Secondly, (*Exod. 24.1, 2.*) *And God said*

*unto Moses, Come up unto the Lord, thou, and Aaron,
Nadab and Abihu, and seventy of the Elders of Israel.
And Moses alone shall come neer the Lord, but they
shall not come nigh, neither shall the people goe up with
him.* By which it is plain, that Moses who was alone
called up to God, (and not Aaron, nor the other Priests,
nor the Seventy Elders, nor the People who were forbidden to come up) was alone he, that represented to the
Israelites the Person of God; that is to say, was their sole
Soveraign under God. And though afterwards it be said
(verse 9.) *Then went up Moses, and Aaron, Nadab, and
Abihu, and seventy of the Elders of Israel, and they saw
the God of Israel, and there was under his feet, as it
were a paved work of a saphire stone, &c.* yet this was
not till after Moses had been with God before, and had
brought to the people the words which God had said to
him. He onely went for the businesse of the people; the
others, as the Nobles of his retinue, were admitted for
honour to that speciall grace, which was not allowed to
the people; which was, (as in the verse after appeareth)
to see God and live. *God laid not his hand upon them,
they saw God, and did eat and drink* (that is, did live),
but did not carry any commandement from him to the
people. Again, it is every where said, *The Lord spake
unto Moses*, as in all other occasions of Government;
so also in the ordering of the Ceremonies of Religion,
contained in the 25, 26, 27, 28, 29, 30, and 31 Chapters of *Exodus*, and throughout *Leviticus*: to Aaron
seldome. The Calfe that Aaron made, Moses threw into
the fire.[85] Lastly, the question of the Authority of Aaron,
by occasion of his and Miriams mutiny against Moses,
was (*Numbers* 12.) judged by God himself for Moses.
So also in the question between Moses, and the People,
who had the Right of Governing the People, when
Corah, Dathan, and Abiram, and two hundred and fifty
Princes of the Assembly *gathered themselves together*
(Numb. 16.3.) *against Moses, and against Aaron, and
said unto them, Ye take too much upon you, seeing all*

*the congregation are Holy, every one of them, and the
Lord is amongst them, why lift you up your selves above
the congregation of the Lord?* God caused the Earth to
swallow Corah, Dathan, and Abiram with [252] their
wives and children alive, and consumed those two hundred and fifty Princes with fire. Therefore neither Aaron,
nor the People, nor any Aristocracy of the chief Princes
of the People, but Moses alone had next under God the
Soveraignty over the Israelites: And that not onely in
causes of Civill Policy, but also of Religion: For Moses
onely spake with God, and therefore onely could tell the
People, what it was that God required at their hands.
No man upon pain of death might be so presumptuous
as to approach the Mountain where God talked with
Moses. *Thou shalt set bounds* (saith the Lord, *Exod.*
19.12.) *to the people round about, and say, Take heed to
your selves that you goe not up into the Mount, or touch
the border of it; whosoever toucheth the Mount shall
surely be put to death.* And again (verse 21.) *Goe down,
charge the people, lest they break through unto the Lord
to gaze.* Out of which we may conclude, that whosoever in a Christian Common-wealth holdeth the place of
Moses, is the sole Messenger of God, and Interpreter of
his Commandements. And according hereunto, no man
ought in the interpretation of the Scripture to proceed
further then the bounds which are set by their severall
Soveraigns. For the Scriptures since God now speaketh
in them, are the Mount Sinai; the bounds whereof are
the Laws of them that represent Gods Person on Earth.
To look upon them, and therein to behold the wondrous
works of God, and learn to fear him is allowed; but
to interpret them; that is, to pry into what God saith
to him whom he appointeth to govern under him, and
make themselves Judges whether he govern as God com-   *All spirits*
mandeth him, or not, is to transgresse the bounds God   *were sub-*
hath set us, and to gaze upon God irreverently.   *ordinate to*

    There was no Prophet in the time of Moses, nor pre-   *the spirit of*
tender to the Spirit of God, but such as Moses had   *Moses*

approved, and Authorized. For there were in his time but Seventy men, that are said to Prophecy by the Spirit of God, and these were of all Moses his election; concerning whom God saith to Moses (*Numb.* 11.16.) *Gather to mee Seventy of the Elders of Israel, whom thou knowest to be the Elders of the People.* To these God imparted his Spirit; but it was not a different Spirit from that of Moses; for it is said (verse 25.) *God came down in a cloud, and took of the Spirit that was upon Moses, and gave it to the Seventy Elders.* But as I have shewn before (chap. 36.) by *Spirit*, is understood the *Mind*; so that the sense of the place is no other than this, that God endued them with a mind conformable, and subordinate to that of Moses, that they might Prophecy, that is to say, speak to the people in Gods name, in such manner, as to set forward (as Ministers of Moses, and by his authority) such doctrine as was agreeable to Moses his doctrine. For they were but Ministers; and when two of them Prophecyed in the Camp, it was thought a new and unlawfull thing; and as it is in the 27. and 28. verses of the same Chapter, they were accused of it, and Joshua advised Moses to forbid them, as not knowing that it was by Moses his Spirit that they Prophecyed. By which it is manifest, that no Subject ought to pretend to Prophecy, or to the Spirit, in opposition to the doctrine [253] established by him, whom God hath set in the place of Moses.

After Moses the Sovereignty was in the High Priest   Aaron being dead, and after him also Moses, the Kingdome, as being a Sacerdotall Kingdome, descended by vertue of the Covenant, to Aarons Son, Eleazar the High Priest: And God declared him (next under himself) for Soveraign, at the same time that he appointed Joshua for the Generall of their Army. For thus God saith expressely (*Numb.* 27.21.) concerning Joshua; *He shall stand before Eleazar the Priest, who shall ask counsell for him, before the Lord, at his word shall they goe out, and at his word they shall come in, both he, and all the Children of Israel with him*: Therefore the Supreme

Power of making War and Peace, was in the Priest. The
Supreme Power of Judicature belonged also to the High
Priest: For the Book of the Law was in their keeping;
and the Priests and Levites onely, were the subordinate Judges in causes Civill, as appears in *Deut.* 17.8,
9, 10. And for the manner of Gods worship, there was
never doubt made, but that the High Priest till the time
of Saul, had the Supreme Authority. Therefore the Civill
and Ecclesiasticall Power were both joined together in
one and the same person, the High Priest; and ought to
bee so, in whosoever governeth by Divine Right; that is,
by Authority immediate from God.

After the death of Joshua, till the time of Saul, the *Of the*
time between is noted frequently in the Book of Judges, *Soveraign*
that there was in those dayes no King in Israel; and *power*
sometimes with this addition, that *every man did that* *between*
which was right in his own eyes.[86] By which is to bee *the time of*
understood, that where it is said, *there was no King,* *Joshua and*
is meant, *there was no Soveraign Power* in Israel. And *of Saul*
so it was, if we consider the Act, and Exercise of such
power. For after the death of Joshua, & Eleazar, *there
arose another generation* (Judges 2.10.) *that knew
not the Lord, nor the works which he had done for
Israel, but did evill in the sight of the Lord, and served
Baalim.*[87] And the Jews had that quality which St. Paul
noteth, *to look for a sign*, not onely before they would
submit themselves to the government of Moses, but also
after they had obliged themselves by their submission.
Whereas Signs, and Miracles had for End to procure
Faith, not to keep men from violating it, when they have
once given it; for to that men are obliged by the law
of Nature. But if we consider not the Exercise, but the
Right of Governing, the Soveraign power was still in
the High Priest. Therefore whatsoever obedience was
yeelded to any of the Judges (who were men chosen by
God extraordinarily, to save his rebellious subjects out
of the hands of the enemy,) it cannot bee drawn into
argument against the Right the High Priest had to the

Soveraign Power, in all matters, both of Policy and Religion. And neither the Judges, nor Samuel himselfe had an ordinary, but extraordinary calling to the Government; and were obeyed by the Israelites, not out of duty, but out of reverence to their favour with God, appearing in their wisdome, courage, or felicity. Hitherto therefore the Right of Regulating both the Policy, and the Religion, were inseparable.

Of the Rights   [254] To the Judges, succeeded Kings: And whereas
of the Kings before, all authority, both in Religion, and Policy, was
of Israel in the High Priest; so now it was all in the King. For the Soveraignty over the people, which was before, not onely by vertue of the Divine Power, but also by a particular pact of the Israelites in God, and next under him, in the High Priest, as his Vicegerent on earth, was cast off by the People, with the consent of God himselfe. For when they said to Samuel (1 *Sam.* 8.5.) *make us a King to judge us, like all the Nations*, they signified that they would no more bee governed by the commands that should bee laid upon them by the Priest, in the name of God; but by one that should command them in the same manner that all other nations were commanded; and consequently in deposing the High Priest of Royall authority, they deposed that peculiar Government of God. And yet God consented to it, saying to Samuel (verse 7.) *Hearken unto the voice of the People, in all that they shall say unto thee; for they have not rejected thee, but they have rejected mee, that I should not reign over them.* Having therefore rejected God, in whose Right the Priests governed, there was no authority left to the Priests, but such as the King was pleased to allow them; which was more, or lesse, according as the Kings were good, or evill. And for the Government of Civill affaires, it is manifest, it was all in the hands of the King. For in the same Chapter, verse 20. They say they will be like all the Nations; that their King shall be their Judge, and goe before them, and fight their battells; that is, he shall have the whole authority, both in Peace and War.

In which is contained also the ordering of Religion: for there was no other Word of God in that time, by which to regulate Religion, but the Law of Moses, which was their Civill Law. Besides, we read (1 *Kings* 2.27.) that Solomon *thrust out Abiathar from being Priest before the Lord*: He had therefore authority over the High Priest, as over any other Subject; which is a great mark of Supremacy in Religion. And we read also (1 *Kings* 8.) that hee dedicated the Temple; that he blessed the People; and that he himselfe in person made that excellent prayer, used in the Consecrations of all Churches, and houses of Prayer; which is another great mark of Supremacy in Religion. Again, we read (2 *Kings* 22.) that when there was question concerning the Book of the Law found in the Temple, the same was not decided by the High Priest, but Josiah sent both him, and others to enquire concerning it, of Hulda, the Prophetesse;[88] which is another mark of the Supremacy in Religion. Lastly, wee read (1 *Chron.* 26.30.) that David made Hashabiah and his brethren,[89] Hebronites, Officers of Israel among them Westward, *in all businesse of the Lord, and in the service of the King.* Likewise (verse 32.) that hee made other Hebronites, *rulers over the Reubenites, the Gadites, and the halfe tribe of Manasseh* (these were the rest of Israel that dwelt beyond Jordan)[90] *for every matter pertaining to God, and affairs of the King.* Is not this full Power, both *temporall* and *spirituall*, as they call it, that would divide it? To conclude; from the first institution of Gods [255] Kingdome, to the Captivity, the Supremacy of Religion, was in the same hand with that of the Civill Soveraignty; and the Priests office after the election of Saul, was not Magisteriall, but Ministeriall.

Notwithstanding the government both in Policy and Religion, were joined, first in the High Priests, and afterwards in the Kings, so far forth as concerned the Right; yet it appeareth by the same Holy History, that the people understood it not; but there being amongst them a great part, and probably the greatest part, that

The practice of Supremacy in Religion, was not in the time of the Kings, according to the Right thereof

no longer than they saw great miracles, or (which is equivalent to a miracle) great abilities, or great felicity in the enterprises of their Governours, gave sufficient credit, either to the fame of Moses, or to the Colloquies between God and the Priests; they took occasion as oft as their Governours displeased them, by blaming sometimes the Policy, sometimes the Religion, to change the Government, or revolt from their Obedience at their pleasure: And from thence proceeded from time to time the civill troubles, divisions, and calamities of the Nation. As for example, after the death of Eleazar and Joshua, the next generation which had not seen the wonders of God, but were left to their own weak reason, not knowing themselves obliged by the Covenant of a Sacerdotall Kingdome, regarded no more the Commandement of the Priest, nor any law of Moses, but did every man that which was right in his own eyes;[91] and obeyed in Civill affairs, such men, as from time to time they thought able to deliver them from the neighbour Nations that oppressed them; and consulted not with God (as they ought to doe,) but with such men, or women, as they guessed to bee Prophets by their Prædictions of things to come; and though they had an Idol in their Chappel, yet if they had a Levite for their Chaplain, they made account they worshipped the God of Israel.

And afterwards when they demanded a King, after the manner of the nations; yet it was not with a design to depart from the worship of God their King; but despairing of the justice of the sons of Samuel, they would have a King to judg them in Civill actions; but not that they would allow their King to change the Religion which they thought was recommended to them by Moses. So that they alwaies kept in store a pretext, either of Justice, or Religion, to discharge them selves of their obedience, whensoever they had hope to prevaile. Samuel was displeased with the people, for that they desired a King, (for God was their King already, and Samuel had but an authority under him); yet did Samuel, when Saul observed not his counsell, in destroying Agag as God had commanded, anoint another King, namely, David, to take the succession from his heirs.[92] Rehoboam[93] was no Idolater; but when the people thought him an Oppressor; that Civil pretence carried from him ten Tribes to Jeroboam an Idolater. And generally through the whole History of the Kings, as well of Judah, as of Israel, there were Prophets that alwaies controlled the Kings, for transgressing the Religion; and sometimes also for Errours of State; as Jehosaphat was reproved by the Prophet Jehu, for aiding [256] the King of Israel against the Syrians;[94] and Hezekiah, by Isaiah, for shewing his treasures to the Ambassadors of Babylon.[95] By all which it appeareth, that though the power both of State and Religion were in the Kings; yet none of them were uncontrolled in the use of it, but such as were gracious for their own naturall abilities, or felicities. So that from the practise of those times, there can no argument be drawn, that the Right of Supremacy in Religion was not in the Kings, unlesse we place it in the Prophets; and conclude, that because Hezekiah praying to the Lord before the Cherubins, was not answered from thence, nor then, but afterwards by the Prophet Isaiah, therefore Isaiah was supreme Head of the Church; or because Josiah consulted Hulda the Prophetesse, concerning the Book of the Law, that therefore neither he, nor the High Priest, but Hulda the Prophetesse had the Supreme authority in matter of Religion; which I thinke is not the opinion of any Doctor.

2 Chro. 19. 2

During the Captivity, the Jews had no Common-wealth at all: And after their return, though they renewed their Covenant with God, yet there was no promise made of obedience, neither to Esdras, nor to any other: And presently after they became subjects to the Greeks (from whose Customes, and Dæmonology, and from the doctrine of the Cabalists,[96] their Religion became much corrupted): In such sort as nothing can be gathered from

After the Captivity the Jews had no setled Common-wealth

their confusion, both in State and Religion, concerning the Supremacy in either. And therefore so far forth as concerneth the Old Testament, we may conclude, that whosoever had the Soveraignty of the Common-wealth amongst the Jews, the same had also the Supreme Authority in matter of Gods externall worship; and represented Gods Person; that is the person of God the Father; though he were not called by the name of Father, till such time as he sent into the world his Son Jesus Christ, to redeem mankind from their sins, and bring them into his Everlasting Kingdome, to be saved for evermore. Of which we are to speak in the Chapter following. [261]

CHAP. XLI

Of the OFFICE of our BLESSED SAVIOUR

Three parts of the Office of Christ We find in Holy Scripture three parts of the *Office* of the *Messiah*: The first of a *Redeemer*, or *Saviour*: The second of a *Pastor, Counsellor,* or *Teacher,* that is, of a *Prophet* sent from God, to convert such as God hath elected to Salvation: The third of a *King,* an *eternall King,* but under his Father, as Moses and the High Priests were in their severall times. And to these three parts are correspondent three times. For our Redemption he wrought at his first coming, by the Sacrifice, wherein he offered up himself for our sinnes upon the Crosse: our Conversion he wrought partly then in his own Person; and partly worketh now by his Ministers; and will continue to work till his coming again. And after his coming again, shall begin that his glorious Reign over his elect, which is to last eternally.

His Office as a Redeemer To the *Office* of a *Redeemer,* that is, of one that payeth the Ransome of Sin, (which Ransome is Death,) it appertaineth, that he was Sacrificed, and thereby bare

upon his own head, and carryed away from us our iniquities, in such sort as God had required. Not that the
death of one man, though without sinne, can satisfie for
the offences of all men, in the rigour of Justice, but in
the Mercy of God, that ordained such Sacrifices for sin,
as he was pleased in his mercy to accept. In the Old Law
(as we may read, *Leviticus* the 16.) the Lord required,
that there should every year once, bee made an Atone-
ment for the Sins of all Israel, both Priests, and others;
for the doing whereof, Aaron alone was to sacrifice for
himself and the Priests a young Bullock; and for the rest
of the people, he was to receive from them two young
Goates, of which he was to *sacrifice* one; but as for
the other, which was the *Scape Goat*, he was to lay his
hands on the head thereof, and by a confession of the
iniquities of the people, to lay them all on that head,
and then by some opportune man, to cause the Goat
to be led into the wildernesse, and there to *escape*, and
carry away with him the iniquities of the people. As the
Sacrifice of the one Goat was a sufficient (because an
acceptable) price for the Ransome of all Israel; so the
death of the Messiah, is a sufficient price, for the Sins
of all mankind, because there was no more required.
Our Saviour Christs sufferings seem to be here figured,
as cleerly, as in the oblation of Isaac, or in any other
type of him in the Old Testament: He was both the sacrificed Goat, and the Scape Goat; *Hee was oppressed,
and he was afflicted* (Esay 53.7.); *he opened not his
mouth; he is brought as a lamb to the slaughter, and as
a sheep is dumbe* [262] *before the shearer, so opened he
not his mouth*: Here he is the *sacrificed Goat. He hath
born our Griefs,* (ver. 4.) *and carried our sorrows*: And
again, (ver. 6.) *the Lord hath laid upon him the iniquities of us all*: And so he is the *Scape Goat. He was cut
off from the land of the living* (ver. 8.) *for the transgression of my People*: There again he is the *sacrificed
Goat.* And again, (ver. 11.) *he shall bear their sins*: Hee
is the *Scape Goat.* Thus is the Lamb of God equivalent

to both those Goates; sacrificed, in that he dyed; and
escaping, in his Resurrection; being raised opportunely
by his Father, and removed from the habitation of men
in his Ascension.

Christs   For as much therefore, as he that *redeemeth*, hath no
Kingdome title to the *thing redeemed*, before *the Redemption*, and
not of this Ransome paid; and this Ransome was the Death of the
world Redeemer; it is manifest, that our Saviour (as man) was
not King of those that he Redeemed, before hee suffered
death; that is, during that time hee conversed bodily on
the Earth. I say, he was not then King in present, by
vertue of the Pact, which the faithfull make with him
in Baptisme: Neverthelesse, by the renewing of their
Pact with God in Baptisme, they were obliged to obey
him for King, (under his Father) whensoever he should
be pleased to take the Kingdome upon him. According
whereunto, our Saviour himself expressely saith, (*John*
18.36.) *My Kingdome is not of this world.* Now seeing
the Scripture maketh mention but of two worlds; this
that is now, and shall remain to the day of Judgment,
(which is therefore also called, *the last day*;) and that
which shall bee after the day of Judgement, when there
shall bee a new Heaven, and a new Earth; the Kingdome
of Christ is not to begin till the generall Resurrection.
And that is it which our Saviour saith, (*Mat.* 16.27.)
*The Son of man shall come in the glory of his Father,
with his Angels; and then he shall reward every man
according to his works.* To reward every man according to his works, is to execute the Office of a King; and
this is not to be till he come in the glory of his Father,
with his Angells. When our Saviour saith, (*Mat.* 23.2.)
*The Scribes and Pharisees sit in Moses seat; All therefore
whatsoever they bid you doe, that observe and doe*; hee
declareth plainly, that hee ascribeth Kingly Power, for
that time, not to himselfe, but to them. And so hee doth
also, where he saith, (*Luke* 12.14.) *Who made mee a
Judge, or Divider over you?* And (*John* 12.47.) *I came
not to judge the world, but to save the world.* And yet

our Saviour came into this world that hee might bee a King, and a Judge in the world to come: For hee was the Messiah, that is, the Christ, that is, the Anointed Priest, and the Soveraign Prophet of God; that is to say, he was to have all the power that was in Moses the Prophet, in the High Priests that succeeded Moses, and in the Kings that succeeded the Priests. And St. *John* saies expressely (chap. 5. ver. 22.) *The Father judgeth no man, but hath committed all judgment to the Son.* And this is not repugnant to that other place, *I came not to judge the world*: for [263] this is spoken of the world present, the other of the world to come; as also where it is said, that at the second coming of Christ, (*Mat.* 19.28.) *Yee that have followed me in the Regeneration, when the Son of man shall sit in the throne of his Glory, yee shall also sit on twelve thrones, judging the twelve tribes of Israel.*

If then Christ whilest hee was on Earth, had no Kingdome in this world, to what end was his first coming? It was to restore unto God, by a new Covenant, the Kingdom, which being his by the Old Covenant, had been cut off by the rebellion of the Israelites in the election of Saul. Which to doe, he was to preach unto them, that he was the *Messiah*, that is, the King promised to them by the Prophets; and to offer himselfe in sacrifice for the sinnes of them that should by faith submit themselves thereto; and in case the nation generally should refuse him, to call to his obedience such as should beleeve in him amongst the Gentiles. So that there are two parts of our Saviours Office during his aboad upon the Earth: One to Proclaim himself the Christ; and another by Teaching, and by working of Miracles, to perswade, and prepare men to live so, as to be worthy of the Immortality Beleevers were to enjoy, at such time as he should come in majesty, to take possession of his Fathers Kingdome. And therefore it is, that the time of his preaching, is often by himself called the *Regeneration*; which is not properly a Kingdome, and thereby a warrant to deny obedience to the Magistrates that then were, (for

The End of Christs comming was to renew the Covenant of the Kingdome of God, and to perswade the Elect to imbrace it, which was the second part of his Office

hee commanded to obey those that sate then in Moses chaire, and to pay tribute to Cæsar;)[97] but onely an earnest of the Kingdome of God that was to come, to those to whom God had given the grace to be his disciples, and to beleeve in him; For which cause the Godly are said to bee already in the *Kingdome of Grace*, as naturalized in that heavenly Kingdome.

The preaching of Christ not contrary to the then law of the Jews, nor of Cæsar Hitherto therefore there is nothing done, or taught by Christ, that tendeth to the diminution of the Civill Right of the Jewes, or of Cæsar. For as touching the Common-wealth which then was amongst the Jews, both they that bare rule amongst them, and they that were governed, did all expect the Messiah, and Kingdome of God; which they could not have done if their Laws had forbidden him (when he came) to manifest, and declare himself. Seeing therefore he did nothing, but by Preaching, and Miracles go about to prove himselfe to be that Messiah, hee did therein nothing against their laws. The Kingdome hee claimed was to bee in another world: He taught all men to obey in the mean time them that sate in Moses seat: He allowed them to give Cæsar his tribute, and refused to take upon himselfe to be a Judg. How then could his words, or actions bee seditious, or tend to the overthrow of their then Civill Government? But God having determined his sacrifice, for the reduction of his elect to their former covenanted obedience, for the means, whereby he would bring the same to effect, made use of their malice, and ingratitude. Nor [264] was it contrary to the laws of Cæsar. For though Pilate himself (to gratifie the Jews) delivered him to be crucified; yet before he did so, he pronounced openly, that he found no fault in him: And put for title of his condemnation, not as the Jews required, *that he pretended to bee King*; but simply, *That hee was King of the Jews*; and notwithstanding their clamour, refused to alter it; saying, *What I have written, I have written.*[98]

The third part of his Office was to be King (under his Father) of the Elect As for the third part of his Office, which was to be *King*, I have already shewn that his Kingdome was not to begin till the Resurrection. But then he shall be King, not onely as God, in which sense he is King already, and ever shall be, of all the Earth, in vertue of his omnipotence; but also peculiarly of his own Elect, by vertue of the pact they make with him in their Baptisme. And therefore it is, that our Saviour saith (*Mat.* 19.28.) that his Apostles should sit upon twelve thrones, judging the twelve tribes of Israel, *When the Son of man shall sit in the throne of his glory*: whereby he signified that he should reign then in his humane nature; and (*Mat.* 16.27.) *The Son of man shall come in the glory of his Father, with his Angels, and then he shall reward every man according to his works*. The same we may read, *Marke* 13.26. and 14.26. and more expressely for the time, *Luke* 22.29, 30. *I appoint unto you a Kingdome, as my Father hath appointed to mee, that you may eat and drink at my table in my Kingdome, and sit on thrones judging the twelve tribes of Israel*. By which it is manifest, that the Kingdome of Christ appointed to him by his Father, is not to be before the Son of Man shall come in Glory, and make his Apostles Judges of the twelve tribes of Israel. But a man may here ask, seeing there is no marriage in the Kingdome of Heaven, whether men shall then eat, and drink; what eating therefore is meant in this place? This is expounded by our Saviour (*John* 6.27.) where he saith, *Labour not for the meat which perisheth, but for that meat which endureth unto everlasting life, which the Son of man shall give you*. So that by eating at Christs table, is meant the eating of the Tree of Life; that is to say, the enjoying of Immortality, in the Kingdome of the Son of Man. By which places, and many more, it is evident, that our Saviours Kingdome is to bee exercised by him in his humane nature. *Christs authority in*

Again, he is to be King then, no otherwise than as subordinate, or Vicegerent of God the Father, as Moses was in the wildernesse; and as the High Priests were before the reign of Saul: and as the Kings were after it. For it is one of the Prophecies concerning Christ, that he *the Kingdome of God subordinate to that of his Father* should be like (in Office) to Moses: *I will raise them up a Prophet* (saith the Lord, *Deut.* 18.18.) *from amongst their Brethren like unto thee, and will put my words into his mouth*, and this similitude with Moses, is also apparent in the actions of our Saviour himself, whilest he was conversant on Earth. For as Moses chose twelve Princes of the tribes, to govern under him;[99] so did our Saviour choose twelve Apostles, who shall sit on twelve [265] thrones, and judge the twelve tribes of Israel:[100] And as Moses authorized Seventy Elders,[101] to receive the Spirit of God, and to Prophecy to the people, that is, (as I have said before,) to speak unto them in the name of God; so our Saviour also ordained seventy Disciples, to preach his Kingdome, and Salvation to all Nations.[102] And as when a complaint was made to Moses, against those of the Seventy that prophecyed in the camp of Israel, he justified them in it, as being subservient therein to his government;[103] so also our Saviour, when St. John complained to him of a certain man that cast out Devills in his name, justified him therein, saying, (*Luke* 9.50.) *Forbid him not, for hee that is not against us, is on our part.*

Again, our Saviour resembled Moses in the institution of *Sacraments*, both of *Admission* into the Kingdome of God, and of *Commemoration* of his deliverance of his Elect from their miserable condition. As the Children of Israel had for Sacrament of their Reception into the Kingdome of God, before the time of Moses, the rite of *Circumcision*, which rite having been omitted in the Wildernesse, was again restored as soon as they came into the land of Promise;[104] so also the Jews, before the coming of our Saviour, had a rite of *Baptizing*, that is, of washing with water all those that being Gentiles, embraced the God of Israel. This rite St. John the Baptist used in the reception of all them that gave their names to the Christ, whom hee preached to bee already come into the world;[105] and our Saviour instituted the same for a Sacrament to be taken by all that beleeved in him. From what cause the rite of Baptisme first proceeded, is not expressed formally in the Scripture; but it may be probably thought to be an imitation of the law of Moses, concerning Leprousie; wherein the Leprous man was commanded to be kept out of the campe of Israel for a certain time; after which time being judged by the Priest to be clean, hee was admitted into the campe after a solemne Washing.[106] And this may therefore bee a type of the Washing in Baptisme; wherein such men as are cleansed of the Leprousie of Sin by Faith, are received into the Church with the solemnity of Baptisme. There is another conjecture drawn from the Ceremonies of the Gentiles, in a certain case that rarely happens; and that is, when a man that was thought dead, chanced to recover, other men made scruple to converse with him, as they would doe to converse with a Ghost, unlesse hee were received again into the number of men, by Washing, as Children new born were washed from the uncleannesse of their nativity, which was a kind of new birth. This ceremony of the Greeks, in the time that Judæa was under the Dominion of Alexander, and the Greeks his successors, may probably enough have crept into the Religion of the Jews. But seeing it is not likely our Saviour would countenance a Heathen rite, it is most likely it proceeded from the Legall Ceremony of Washing after Leprosie. And for the other Sacrament, [266] of eating the *Paschall Lambe*, it is manifestly imitated in the Sacrament of the *Lords Supper*; in which the Breaking of the Bread, and the pouring out of the Wine, do keep in memory our deliverance from the Misery of Sin, by Christs Passion, as the eating of the Paschall Lambe, kept in memory the deliverance of the Jewes out of the Bondage of Egypt. Seeing therefore the authority of Moses was but subordinate, and hee but a Lieutenant to God; it followeth, that Christ, whose authority, as man, was to bee like that of Moses, was no more but subordinate to the authority of his Father. The same is more expressely signified, by that that hee teacheth us to pray, *Our Father, Let thy Kingdome come*; and, *For*

thine is the Kingdome, the Power, and the Glory; and
by that it is said, that *Hee shall come in the Glory of his
Father*; and by that which St. Paul saith, (1 *Cor.* 15.24.)
*then commeth the end, when hee shall have delivered
up the Kingdome to God, even the Father*; and by many
other most expresse places.

One and the   Our Saviour therefore, both in Teaching, and Reign-
same God is ing, representeth (as Moses did) the Person of God; which
the Person God from that time forward, but not before, is called
represented the Father; and being still one and the same substance, is
by Moses, one Person as represented by Moses, and another Person
and by Christ as represented by his Sonne the Christ. For *Person* being
a relative to a *Representer*, it is consequent to plurality
of Representers, that there bee a plurality of Persons,
though of one and the same Substance. [267]

CHAP. XLII

Of POWER ECCLESIASTICALL

For the understanding of POWER ECCLESIASTICALL,
what, and in whom it is, we are to distinguish the time
from the Ascension of our Saviour, into two parts; one
before the Conversion of Kings, and men endued with
Soveraign Civill Power; the other after their Conversion.[107]
For it was long after the Ascension, before any King, or
Civill Soveraign embraced, and publiquely allowed the
teaching of Christian Religion.

Of the Holy   And for the time between, it is manifest, that the
Spirit that *Power Ecclesiasticall*, was in the Apostles; and after
fel on the them in such as were by them ordained to Preach the
Apostles Gospell, and to convert men to Christianity, and to
direct them that were converted in the way of Salvation; and after these the Power was delivered again to
others by these ordained, and this was done by Imposition of hands upon such as were ordained; by which

was signified the giving of the Holy Spirit, or Spirit of God, to those whom they ordained Ministers of God, to advance his Kingdome. So that Imposition of hands, was nothing else but the Seal of their Commission to Preach Christ, and teach his Doctrine; and the giving of the Holy Ghost by that ceremony of Imposition of hands, was an imitation of that which Moses did. For Moses used the same ceremony to his Minister Joshua, as wee read *Deuteronomy* 34. ver. 9. *And Joshua the Son of Nun was full of the Spirit of Wisdome; for Moses had laid his hands upon him.* Our Saviour therefore between his Resurrection, and Ascension, gave his Spirit to the Apostles; first, by *Breathing on them, and saying,* (*John* 20.22.) *Receive yee the Holy Spirit*; and after his Ascension (*Acts* 2.2, 3.) by sending down upon them, a *mighty wind, and Cloven tongues of fire*; and not by Imposition of hands; as neither did God lay his hands on Moses: and his Apostles afterward, transmitted the same Spirit by Imposition of hands, as Moses did to Joshua. So that it is manifest hereby, in whom the Power Ecclesiasticall continually remained, in those first times, where there was not any Christian Common-wealth; namely, in them that received the same from the Apostles, by successive laying on of hands.

Here wee have the Person of God born now the third time. For as Moses, and the High Priests, were Gods Representative in the Old Testament; and our Saviour himselfe as Man, during his abode on earth: So the Holy Ghost, that is to say, the Apostles, and their successors, in the Office of Preaching, and Teach[268]ing, that had received the Holy Spirit, have Represented him ever since. But a Person, (as I have shewn before, chapt. [16].) is he that is Represented, as often as hee is Represented; and therefore God, who has been Represented (that is, Personated) thrice, may properly enough be said to be three Persons; though neither the word *Person*, nor *Trinity* be ascribed to him in the Bible. St. *John* indeed (1 Epist. 5.7.) saith, *There be three that bear witnesse* *Of the Trinity*

*in heaven, the Father, the Word, and the Holy Spirit;
and these Three are One*: But this disagreeth not, but
accordeth fitly with three Persons in the proper significa-
cation of Persons; which is, that which is Represented
by another. For so God the Father, as Represented by
Moses, is one Person; and as Represented by his Sonne,
another Person; and as Represented by the Apostles,
and by the Doctors that taught by authority from them
derived, is a third Person; and yet every Person here, is
the Person of one and the same God. But a man may
here ask, what it was whereof these three bare witnesse.
St. *John* therefore tells us (verse 11.) that they bear witnesse, that *God hath given us eternall life in his Son.*
Again, if it should bee asked, wherein that testimony
appeareth, the Answer is easie; for he hath testified the
same by the miracles he wrought, first by Moses; secondly, by his Son himself; and lastly by his Apostles,
that had received the Holy Spirit; all which in their times
Represented the Person of God; and either prophecyed,
or preached Jesus Christ. And as for the Apostles, it
was the character of the Apostleship, in the twelve first
and great Apostles, to bear Witnesse of his Resurrection; as appeareth expressely (*Acts* 1. ver. 21, 22.) where
St. Peter, when a new Apostle was to be chosen in the
place of Judas Iscariot, useth these words, *Of these men
which have companied with us all the time that the Lord
Jesus went in and out amongst us, beginning at the Baptisme of John, unto that same day that hee was taken up
from us, must one bee ordained to be a Witnesse with us
of his Resurrection*: which words interpret the *bearing
of Witnesse*, mentioned by St. John. There is in the same
place mentioned another Trinity of Witnesses in Earth.
For (ver. 8.) he saith, *there are three that bear Witnesse
in Earth, the Spirit, and the Water, and the Bloud; and
these three agree in one*: that is to say, the graces of Gods
Spirit, and the two Sacraments, Baptisme, and the Lords
Supper, which all agree in one Testimony, to assure
the consciences of beleevers, of eternall life; of which

Testimony he saith (verse 10.) *He that beleeveth on the Son of man hath the Witnesse in himself.* In this Trinity on Earth, the Unity is not of the thing; for the Spirit, the Water, and the Bloud, are not the same substance, though they give the same testimony: But in the Trinity of Heaven, the Persons are the persons of one and the same God, though Represented in three different times and occasions. To conclude, the doctrine of the Trinity, as far as can be gathered directly from the Scripture, is in substance this; that God who is alwaies One and the same, was the Person Represented [269] by Moses; the Person Represented by his Son Incarnate; and the Person Represented by the Apostles. As Represented by the Apostles, the Holy Spirit by which they spake, is God; As Represented by his Son (that was God and Man), the Son is that God; As represented by Moses, and the High Priests, the Father, that is to say, the Father of our Lord Jesus Christ, is that God: From whence we may gather the reason why those names *Father*, *Son*, and *Holy Spirit* in the signification of the Godhead, are never used in the Old Testament: For they are Persons, that is, they have their names from Representing; which could not be, till divers men had Represented Gods Person in ruling, or in directing under him.

Thus wee see how the Power Ecclesiasticall was left by our Saviour to the Apostles; and how they were (to the end they might the better exercise that Power,) endued with the Holy Spirit, which is therefore called sometime in the New Testament *Paracletus* which signifieth an *Assister*,[108] or one called to for helpe, though it bee commonly translated a *Comforter.* Let us now consider the Power it selfe, what it was, and over whom.

Cardinall Bellarmine in his third generall Controversie, hath handled a great many questions concerning the Ecclesiasticall Power of the Pope of Rome;[109] and begins with this, Whether it ought to be Monarchicall, Aristocraticall, or Democraticall. All which sorts of Power, are Soveraign, and Coercive. If now it should appear, that

The Power Ecclesiasticall is but the power to teach

there is no Coercive Power left them by our Saviour; but onely a Power to proclaim the Kingdom of Christ, and to perswade men to submit themselves thereunto; and by precepts and good counsell, to teach them that have submitted, what they are to do, that they may be received into the Kingdom of God when it comes; and that the Apostles, and other Ministers of the Gospel, are our Schoolemasters, and not our Commanders, and their Precepts not Laws, but wholesome Counsells; then were all that dispute in vain.

An argument
thereof,
the Power
of Christ
himself:

I have shewn already (in the last Chapter,) that the Kingdome of Christ is not of this world: therefore neither can his Ministers (unlesse they be Kings,) require obedience in his name. For if the Supreme King, have not his Regall Power in this world; by what authority can obedience be required to his Officers? As my Father sent me, (so saith our Saviour) I send you.[110] But our Saviour was sent to perswade the Jews to return to, and to invite the Gentiles, to receive the Kingdome of his Father, and not to reign in Majesty, no not, as his Fathers Lieutenant, till the day of Judgment.

From the
name of
Regeneration:

The time between the Ascension, and the generall Resurrection, is called, not a Reigning, but a Regeneration; that is, a Preparation of men for the second and glorious coming of Christ, at the day of Judgment; as appeareth by the words of our Saviour, *Mat.* 19.28. *You that have followed me in the Regeneration, when the* [270] *Son of man shall sit in the throne of his glory, you shall also sit upon twelve Thrones*; And of St. Paul (*Ephes.* 6.15.) *Having your feet shod with the Preparation of the Gospell of Peace.*

From the
comparison
of it, with
Fishing,
Leaven, Seed

And is compared by our Saviour, to Fishing; that is, to winning men to obedience, not by Coercion, and Punishing; but by Perswasion: and therefore he said not to his Apostles, hee would make them so many Nimrods,[111] *Hunters of men; but Fishers of men.*[112] It is compared also to Leaven; to Sowing of Seed, and to the Multiplication of a grain of Mustard-seed; by all which Compulsion is excluded; and consequently there can in that time be no actual Reigning. The work of Christs Ministers, is Evangelization; that is, a Proclamation of Christ, and a preparation for his second comming; as the Evangelization of John Baptist, was a preparation to his first coming.

Again, the Office of Christs Ministers in this world, is to make men Beleeve, and have Faith in Christ: But Faith hath no relation to, nor dependence at all upon Compulsion, or Commandement; but onely upon certainty, or probability of Arguments drawn from Reason, or from something men beleeve already. Therefore the Ministers of Christ in this world, have no Power by that title, to Punish any man for not Beleeving, or for Contradicting what they say; they have I say no Power by that title of Christs Ministers, to Punish such: but if they have Soveraign Civill Power, by politick institution, then they may indeed lawfully Punish any Contradiction to their laws whatsoever: And St. Paul, of himselfe and other the then Preachers of the Gospell, saith in expresse words, *Wee have no Dominion over your Faith, but are Helpers of your Joy.* *From the nature of Faith:* *2 Cor. 1. 24*

Another Argument, that the Ministers of Christ in this present world have no right of Commanding, may be drawn from the lawfull Authority which Christ hath left to all Princes, as well Christians, as Infidels. St. Paul saith (*Col.* 3.20.) *Children obey your Parents in all things; for this is well pleasing to the Lord.* And ver. 22. *Servants obey in all things your Masters according to the flesh, not with eye-service, as men-pleasers, but in singlenesse of heart, as fearing the Lord*: This is spoken to them whose Masters were Infidells; and yet they are bidden to obey them *in all things.* And again, concerning obedience to Princes, (*Rom.* 13. the first 6. verses) exhorting *to be subject to the Higher Powers,* he saith, *that all Power is ordained of God*; and *that we ought to be subject to them, not onely for* fear *of incurring their wrath, but also for conscience sake.* And St. *Peter,* *From the Authority Christ hath left to Civill Princes*

(1 Epist. chap. 2. ver. 13, 14, 15.) *Submit your selves to*
every Ordinance of Man, for the Lords sake, whether
it bee to the King, as Supreme, or unto Governours, as
to them that be sent by him for the punishment of evill
doers, and for the praise of them that doe well; for so is
the will of God. And again St. Paul (*Tit.* 3.1.) *Put men in*
mind to be subject to Principalities, and Powers, and to
obey Magistrates. These Princes, and Powers, whereof
St. Peter, and St. Paul here speak, were all Infidels: much
[271] more therefore we are to obey those Christians,
whom God hath ordained to have Soveraign Power over
us. How then can wee be obliged to obey any Minister
of Christ, if he should command us to doe any thing
contrary to the Command of the King, or other Soveraign Representant of the Common-wealth, whereof we
are members, and by whom we look to be protected?
It is therefore manifest, that Christ hath not left to his
Ministers in this world, unlesse they be also endued with
Civill Authority, any authority to Command other men.

What But what (may some object) if a King, or a Senate, or
Christians other Soveraign Person forbid us to beleeve in Christ?
may do To this I answer, that such forbidding is of no effect;
to avoid because Beleef, and Unbeleef never follow mens Com-
persecution mands. Faith is a gift of God, which Man can neither
give, nor take away by promise of rewards, or men-
aces of torture. And if it be further asked, What if wee
bee commanded by our lawfull Prince, to say with our
tongue, wee beleeve not; must we obey such command?
Profession with the tongue is but an externall thing,
and no more then any other gesture whereby we signifie our obedience; and wherein a Christian, holding
firmely in his heart the Faith of Christ, hath the same
liberty which the Prophet Elisha allowed to Naaman
the Syrian.[113] Naaman was converted in his heart to the
God of Israel; For hee saith (2 *Kings* 5.17.) *Thy servant*
will henceforth offer neither burnt offering, nor sacrifice
unto other Gods but unto the Lord. In this thing the
Lord pardon thy servant, that when my Master goeth

into the house of Rimmon to worship there, and he leaneth on my hand; and I bow my selfe in the house of Rimmon; when I bow my selfe in the house of Rimmon, the Lord pardon thy servant in this thing. This the Prophet approved, and bid him *Goe in peace.* Here Naaman beleeved in his heart; but by bowing before the Idol Rimmon, he denyed the true God in effect, as much as if he had done it with his lips. But then what shall we answer to our Saviours saying, *Whosoever denyeth me before men, I will deny him before my Father which is in Heaven?*[114] This we may say, that whatsoever a Subject, as Naaman was, is compelled to in obedience to his Soveraign, and doth it not in order to his own mind, but in order to the laws of his country, that action is not his, but his Soveraigns; nor is it he that in this case denyeth Christ before men, but his Governour, and the law of his countrey. If any man shall accuse this doctrine, as repugnant to true, and unfeigned Christianity; I ask him, in case there should be a subject in any Christian Common-wealth, that should be inwardly in his heart of the Mahometan Religion, whether if his Soveraign command him to bee present at the divine service of the Christian Church, and that on pain of death, he think that Mahometan obliged in conscience to suffer death for that cause, rather than to obey that command of his lawful Prince. If he say, he ought rather to suffer death, then he authorizeth all private men, to disobey their Princes, in maintenance of their Religion, true, or false: if he say, he ought to bee [272] obedient, then he alloweth to himself, that which hee denyeth to another, contrary to the words of our Saviour, *Whatsoever you would that men should doe unto you, that doe yee unto them;*[115] and contrary to the Law of Nature, (which is the indubitable everlasting Law of God) *Do not to another, that which thou wouldest not he should doe unto thee.*

But what then shall we say of all those Martyrs we read of in the History of the Church, that they have needlessely cast away their lives? For answer hereunto, *Of Martyrs* we are to distinguish the persons that have been for that cause put to death; whereof some have received a Calling to preach, and professe the Kingdome of Christ openly; others have had no such Calling, nor more has been required of them than their owne faith. The former sort, if they have been put to death, for bearing witnesse to this point, that Jesus Christ is risen from the dead, were true Martyrs; For a *Martyr* is, (to give the true definition of the word) a Witnesse of the Resurrection of Jesus the Messiah; which none can be but those that conversed with him on earth, and saw him after he was risen: For a Witnesse must have seen what he testifieth, or else his testimony is not good. And that none but such, can properly be called Martyrs of Christ, is manifest out of the words of St. Peter, *Act.* 1.21, 22. *Wherefore of these men which have companyed with us all the time that the Lord Jesus went in and out amongst us, beginning from the Baptisme of John unto that same day hee was taken up from us, must one be ordained to be a Martyr* (that is a Witnesse) *with us of his Resurrection:* Where we may observe, that he which is to bee a Witnesse of the truth of the Resurrection of Christ, that is to say, of the truth of this fundamentall article of Christian Religion, that Jesus was the Christ, must be some Disciple that conversed with him, and saw him before, and after his Resurrection; and consequently must be one of his originall Disciples: whereas they which were not so, can Witnesse no more, but that their antecessors said it, and are therefore but Witnesses of other mens testimony; and are but second Martyrs, or Martyrs of Christs Witnesses.

He, that to maintain every doctrine which he himself draweth out of the History of our Saviours life, and of the Acts, or Epistles of the Apostles; or which he beleeveth upon the authority of a private man, wil oppose the Laws and Authority of the Civill State, is very far from being a Martyr of Christ, or a Martyr of his Martyrs. 'Tis one Article onely, which to die for, meriteth so honorable a name; and that Article is this, that *Jesus is the Christ*; that is to say, He that hath redeemed us, and shall come again to give us salvation, and eternall life in his glorious Kingdome. To die for every tenet that serveth the ambition, or profit of the Clergy, is not required; nor is it the Death of the Witnesse, but the Testimony it self that makes the Martyr: for the word signifieth nothing else, but the man that beareth Witnesse, whether he be put to death for his testimony, or not.

Also he that is not sent to preach this fundamentall article, but [273] taketh it upon him of his private authority, though he be a Witnesse, and consequently a Martyr, either primary of Christ, or secundary of his Apostles, Disciples, or their Successors; yet is he not obliged to suffer death for that cause; because being not called thereto, tis not required at his hands; nor ought hee to complain, if he loseth the reward he expecteth from those that never set him on work. None therefore can be a Martyr, neither of the first, nor second degree, that have not a warrant to preach Christ come in the flesh; that is to say, none, but such as are sent to the conversion of Infidels. For no man is a Witnesse to him that already beleeveth, and therefore needs no Witnesse; but to them that deny, or doubt, or have not heard it. Christ sent his Apostles, and his Seventy Disciples, with authority to preach; he sent not all that beleeved: And he sent them to unbeleevers; *I send you* (saith he) *as sheep amongst wolves*;[116] not as sheep to other sheep.

Lastly, the points of their Commission, as they are expressely set down in the Gospel, contain none of them any authority over the Congregation.   *Argument from the points of their Commission*

We have first (*Mat.* 10.) that the twelve Apostles were sent *to the lost sheep of the house of Israel*, and commanded to Preach, *that the Kingdome of God was at hand*. Now Preaching in the originall, is that act, which a Crier, Herald, or other Officer useth to doe publiquely in Proclaiming of a King. But a Crier hath not right to Command any man. And (*Luke* 10.2.) the seventy   *To Preach*

Disciples are sent out, as *Labourers, not as Lords of the Harvest*; and are bidden (verse 9.) to say, *The Kingdome of God is come nigh unto you*; and by Kingdom here is meant, not the Kingdome of Grace, but the Kingdome of Glory; for they are bidden to denounce it (ver. 11.) to those Cities which shall not receive them, as a threatning, that it shall be more tolerable in that day for *Sodome*, than for such a City. And (*Mat.* 20.28.) our Saviour telleth his Disciples, that sought Priority of place, their Office was to minister, even as the Son of man came, not to be ministred unto, but to minister. Preachers therefore have not Magisteriall, but Ministeriall power: *Bee not called Masters,* (saith our Saviour, *Mat.* 23.10.) *for one is your Master, even Christ.*

And Teach   Another point of their Commission, is, to *Teach all nations*; as it is in *Mat.* 28.19. or as in St. *Mark* 16.15. *Goe into all the world, and Preach the Gospel to every creature.* Teaching therefore, and Preaching is the same thing. For they that Proclaim the comming of a King, must withall make known by what right he commeth, if they mean men shall submit themselves unto him: As St. Paul did to the Jews of Thessalonica, when *three Sabbath days he reasoned with them out of the Scriptures, opening, and alledging that Christ must needs have suffered, and risen again from the dead, and that this Jesus is Christ.*[117] But to teach out of the Old Testament that Jesus was Christ, (that is to say, King,) and risen from the dead, is not to say, that men are bound after they beleeve it, to obey those that tell them so, against the laws, and commands of their Soveraigns; but that they shall doe [274] wisely, to expect the coming of Christ hereafter, in Patience, and Faith, with Obedience to their present Magistrates.

To Baptize;   Another point of their Commission, is to *Baptize, in the name of the Father, and of the Son, and of the Holy Ghost.* What is Baptisme? Dipping into water. But what is it to Dip a man into the water in the name of any thing? The meaning of these words of Baptisme is this.

He that is Baptized, is Dipped or Washed, as a sign of becomming a new man, and a loyall subject to that God, whose Person was represented in old time by Moses, and the High Priests, when he reigned over the Jews; and to Jesus Christ, his Sonne, God, and Man, that hath redeemed us, and shall in his humane nature Represent his Fathers Person in his eternall Kingdome after the Resurrection; and to acknowledge the Doctrine of the Apostles, who assisted by the Spirit of the Father, and of the Son, were left for guides to bring us into that Kingdome, to be the onely, and assured way thereunto. This, being our promise in Baptisme; and the Authority of Earthly Soveraigns being not to be put down till the day of Judgment; (for that is expressely affirmed by S. Paul 1 *Cor.* 15.22, 23, 24, where he saith, *As in Adam all die, so in Christ all shall be made alive. But every man in his owne order, Christ the first fruits, afterward they that are Christs, at his comming; Then commeth the end, when he shall have delivered up the Kingdom to God, even the Father, when he shall have put down all Rule, and all Authority and Power*) it is manifest, that we do not in Baptisme constitute over us another authority, by which our externall actions are to be governed in this life; but promise to take the doctrine of the Apostles for our direction in the way to life eternall.

The Power of *Remission, and Retention of Sinnes,* called also the Power of *Loosing,* and *Binding,* and sometimes the *Keyes of the Kingdome of Heaven,* is a consequence of the Authority to Baptize, or refuse to Baptize. For Baptisme is the Sacrament of Allegeance, of them that are to be received into the Kingdome of God; that is to say, into Eternall life; that is to say, to Remission of Sin: For as Eternall life was lost by the Committing, so it is recovered by the Remitting of mens Sins. The end of Baptisme is Remission of Sins: and therefore St. Peter, when they that were converted by his Sermon on the day of Pentecost, asked what they were to doe, advised them to *repent, and be Baptized* *And to Forgive, and Retain Sinnes*

in the name of Jesus, for the Remission of Sins.[118] And
therefore seeing to Baptize is to declare the Reception
of men into Gods Kingdome; and to refuse to Baptize
is to declare their Exclusion; it followeth, that the Power
to declare them Cast out, or Retained in it, was given
to the same Apostles, and their Substitutes, and Successors. And therefore after our Saviour had breathed upon
them, saying, (*John* 20.22.) *Receive the Holy Ghost,* hee
addeth in the next verse, *Whose soever Sins ye Remit,
they are Remitted unto them; and whose soever Sins
ye Retain, they are Retained.* By which words, is not
granted an Authority to Forgive, or Retain Sins, simply and absolutely, as God Forgiveth or Retaineth them,
who knoweth the [275] Heart of man, and truth of his
Penitence and Conversion; but conditionally, to the
Penitent: And this Forgivenesse, or Absolution, in case
the absolved have but a feigned Repentance, is thereby
without other act, or sentence of the Absolvent, made
void, and hath no effect at all to Salvation, but on the
contrary, to the Aggravation of his Sin. Therefore the
Apostles, and their Successors, are to follow but the outward marks of Repentance; which appearing, they have
no Authority to deny Absolution; and if they appeare
not, they have no authority to Absolve. The same also
is to be observed in Baptisme: for to a converted Jew, or
Gentile, the Apostles had not the Power to deny Baptisme; nor to grant it to the Un-penitent. But seeing no
man is able to discern the truth of another mans Repentance, further than by externall marks, taken from his
words, and actions, which are subject to hypocrisie;
another question will arise, Who it is that is constituted
Judge of those marks. And this question is decided by
our Saviour himself; *If thy Brother* (saith he) *shall tres-
passe against thee, go and tell him his fault between
thee, and him alone; if he shall hear thee, thou hast
gained thy Brother. But if he will not hear thee, then
take with thee one, or two more. And if he shall neglect
to hear them, tell it unto the Church; but if he neglect*

Mat. 18. 15,
16, 17

to hear the Church, let him be unto thee as an Heathen man, and a Publican. By which it is manifest, that the Judgment concerning the truth of Repentance, belonged not to any one Man, but to the Church, that is, to the Assembly of the Faithfull, or to them that have authority to bee their Representant. But besides the Judgment, there is necessary also the pronouncing of Sentence: And this belonged alwaies to the Apostle, or some Pastor of the Church, as Prolocutor; and of this our Saviour speaketh in the 18 verse, *Whatsoever ye shall bind on earth, shall be bound in heaven; and whatsoever ye shall loose on earth, shall be loosed in heaven.* And conformable hereunto was the practise of St. Paul (1 *Cor.* 5.3, 4, & 5.) where he saith, *For I verily, as absent in body, but present in spirit, have determined already, as though I were present, concerning him that hath so done this deed; In the name of our Lord Jesus Christ when ye are gathered together, and my spirit, with the power of our Lord Jesus Christ, To deliver such a one to Satan*; that is to say, to cast him out of the Church, as a man whose Sins are not Forgiven. Paul here pronounceth the Sentence; but the Assembly was first to hear the Cause, (for St. Paul was absent;) and by consequence to condemn him. But in the same chapter (ver. 11, 12.) the Judgment in such a case is more expressly attributed to the Assembly: *But now I have written unto you, not to keep company, if any man that is called a Brother be a Fornicator, &c. with such a one no not to eat. For what have I to do to judg them that are without? Do not ye judg them that are within?* The Sentence therefore by which a man was put out of the Church, was pronounced by the Apostle, or Pastor; but the Judgment concerning the merit of the cause, was in the Church; that is to say, (as the times were before the conversion of Kings, and men that had Soveraign Authority in the Common-wealth,) the Assembly of the Christians dwelling in the same City; [276] as in Corinth, in the Assembly of the Christians of Corinth.

Of Excom-
munication

This part of the Power of the Keyes, by which men were thrust out from the Kingdom of God, is that which is called *Excommunication*; and to *excommunicate*, is in the Originall, ἀποσυνάγωγον ποιεῖν, *to cast out of the Synagogue*; that is, out of the place of Divine service; a word drawn from the custome of the Jews, to cast out of their Synagogues, such as they thought in manners, or doctrine, contagious, as Lepers were by the Law of Moses separated from the congregation of Israel,[119] till such time as they should be by the Priest pronounced clean.

The use
of Excom-
munication
without Civill
Power,

The Use and Effect of Excommunication, whilest it was not yet strengthened with the Civill Power, was no more, than that they, who were not Excommunicate, were to avoid the company of them that were. It was not enough to repute them as Heathen, that never had been Christians; for with such they might eate, and drink; which with Excommunicate persons they might not do; as appeareth by the words of St. Paul, (1 *Cor.* 5. ver. 9, 10, *&c.*) where he telleth them, he had formerly forbidden them to *company with Fornicators*; but (because that could not bee without going out of the world,) he restraineth it to such Fornicators, and otherwise vicious persons, as were of the brethren; *with such a one* (he saith) they ought not to keep company, *no not to eat.* And this is no more than our Saviour saith (*Mat.* 18.17.) *Let him be to thee as a Heathen, and as a Publican.* For Publicans (which signifieth Farmers, and Receivers of the revenue of the Common-wealth) were so hated, and detested by the Jews that were to pay it, as that *Publican* and *Sinner* were taken amongst them for the same thing: Insomuch, as when our Saviour accepted the invitation of *Zacchæus* a Publican; though it were to Convert him, yet it was objected to him as a Crime.[120] And therefore, when our Saviour, to *Heathen*, added *Publican*, he did forbid them to eat with a man Excommunicate.

As for keeping them out of their Synagogues, or places of Assembly, they had no Power to do it, but that of the owner of the place, whether he were Christian, or Heathen. And because all places are by right, in the Dominion of the Common-wealth; as well hee that was Excommunicated, as hee that never was Baptized, might enter into them by Commission from the Civill Magistrate; as Paul before his conversion entred into their Synagogues at Damascus, to apprehend Christians, men and women, and to carry them bound to Jerusalem, by Commission from the High Priest. *Acts 9. 2*

By which it appears, that upon a Christian, that should become an Apostate, in a place where the Civill Power did persecute, or not assist the Church, the effect of Excommunication had nothing in it, neither of dammage in this world, nor of terrour: Not of terrour, because of their unbeleef; nor of dammage, because they returned thereby into the favour of the world; and in the world to come, were to be in no worse estate, then they which never had beleeved. The dammage redounded rather to the Church, by provocation [277] of them they cast out, to a freer execution of their malice. *Of no effect upon an Apostate*

Excommunication therefore had its effect onely upon those, that beleeved that Jesus Christ was to come again in Glory, to reign over, and to judge both the quick, and the dead, and should therefore refuse entrance into his Kingdom, to those whose Sins were Retained; that is, to those that were Excommunicated by the Church. And thence it is that St. Paul calleth Excommunication, a delivery of the Excommunicate person to Satan.[121] For without the Kingdom of Christ, all other Kingdomes after Judgment, are comprehended in the Kingdome of Satan. This is it that the faithfull stood in fear of, as long as they stood Excommunicate, that is to say, in an estate wherein their sins were not Forgiven. Whereby wee may understand, that Excommunication in the time that Christian Religion was not authorized by the Civill Power, was used onely for a correction of manners, not of errours in opinion: for it is a punishment, whereof none could be sensible but such as beleeved, *But upon the faithfull only* and expected the coming again of our Saviour to judge the world; and they who so beleeved, needed no other opinion, but onely uprightnesse of life, to be saved.

For what fault lyeth Excommunication There lyeth Excommunication for Injustice; as (*Mat.* 18.) If thy Brother offend thee, tell it him privately; then with Witnesses; lastly, tell the Church; and then if he obey not, *Let him be to thee as an Heathen man, and a Publican.* And there lieth Excommunication for a Scandalous Life, as (1 *Cor.* 5.11.) *If any man that is called a Brother, be a Fornicator, or Covetous, or an Idolater, or a Drunkard, or an Extortioner, with such a one yee are not to eat.* But to Excommunicate a man that held this foundation, that *Jesus was the Christ,* for difference of opinion in other points, by which that Foundation was not destroyed, there appeareth no authority in the Scripture, nor example in the Apostles. There is indeed in St. Paul (*Titus* 3.10.) a text that seemeth to be to the contrary. *A man that is an Hæretique, after the first and second admonition, reject.* For an Hæretique, is he, that being a member of the Church, teacheth neverthelesse some private opinion, which the Church has forbidden: and such a one, S. Paul adviseth *Titus,* after the first, and second admonition, to *Reject.* But to *Reject* (in this place) is not to *Excommunicate* the Man; But to *give over admonishing him, to let him alone, to set by disputing with him,* as one that is to be convinced onely by himselfe. The same Apostle saith (2 *Tim.* 2.23.) *Foolish and unlearned questions avoid*: The word *Avoid* in this place, and *Reject* in the former, is the same in the Originall, παραιτοῦ: but Foolish questions may bee set by without Excommunication. And again, (*Tit.* 3.9.) *Avoid Foolish questions,* where the Originall περιΐστασο, (*set them by*) is equivalent to the former word *Reject.* There is no other place that can so much as colourably be drawn, to countenance the Casting out of the Church faithfull men, such as beleeved the foundation, onely for a singular superstructure of their own, proceeding perhaps from a good & pious conscience. But on the contrary, all such places as command avoiding [278] such disputes, are written for a Lesson to Pastors, (such as Timothy and Titus were) not to make new Articles of Faith, by determining every small controversie, which oblige men to a needlesse burthen of Conscience, or provoke them to break the union of the Church. Which Lesson the Apostles themselves observed well. S. Peter, and S. Paul, though their controversie were great, (as we may read in *Gal.* 2.11.) yet they did not cast one another out of the Church. Neverthelesse, during the Apostles times, there were other Pastors that observed it not; As Diotrephes (3 *John* 9. *&c.*) who cast out of the Church, such as S. John himself thought fit to be received into it, out of a pride he took in Præeminence; so early it was, that Vainglory, and Ambition had found entrance into the Church of Christ.

That a man be liable to Excommunication, there be many conditions requisite; as First, that he be a member of some Commonalty, that is to say, of some lawfull Assembly, that is to say, of some Christian Church, that hath power to judge of the cause for which hee is to bee Excommunicated. For where there is no Community, there can bee no Excommunication; nor where there is no power to Judge, can there bee any power to give Sentence. *Of persons liable to Excommuni-cation*

From hence it followeth, that one Church cannot be Excommunicated by another: For either they have equall power to Excommunicate each other, in which case Excommunication is not Discipline, nor an act of Authority, but Schisme, and Dissolution of charity; or one is so subordinate to the other, as that they both have but one voice, and then they be but one Church; and the part Excommunicated, is no more a Church, but a dissolute number of individuall persons.

And because the sentence of Excommunication, importeth an advice, not to keep company, nor so much as to eat with him that is Excommunicate, if a Soveraign Prince, or Assembly bee Excommunicate, the sentence is of no effect. For all Subjects are bound to be in the company and presence of their own Soveraign (when he requireth it) by the law of Nature; nor can they lawfully either expell him from any place of his own Dominion, whether profane or holy; nor go out of his Dominion, without his leave; much lesse (if he call them to that honour,) refuse to eat with him. And as to other Princes and States, because they are not parts of one and the same congregation, they need not any other sentence to keep them from keeping company with the State Excommunicate: for the very Institution, as it uniteth many men into one Community; so it dissociateth one Community from another: so that Excommunication is not needfull for keeping Kings and States asunder; nor has any further effect then is in the nature of Policy it selfe; unlesse it be to instigate Princes to warre upon one another.

Nor is the Excommunication of a Christian Subject, that obeyeth the laws of his own Soveraign, whether Christian, or Heathen, of any effect. For if he beleeve that *Jesus is the Christ, he hath the* [279] *Spirit of God,* (1 Joh. 4.1.) *and God dwelleth in him, and he in God,* (1 Joh. 4.15.) But hee that hath the Spirit of God; hee that dwelleth in God; hee in whom God dwelleth, can receive no harm by the Excommunication of men. Therefore, he that beleeveth Jesus to be the Christ, is free from all the dangers threatned to persons Excommunicate. He that beleeveth it not, is no Christian. Therefore a true and unfeigned Christian is not liable to Excommunication: Nor he also that is a professed Christian, till his Hypocrisy appear in his Manners, that is, till his behaviour bee contrary to the law of his Soveraign, which is the rule of Manners, and which Christ and his Apostles have commanded us to be subject to. For the Church cannot judge of Manners but by externall Actions, which Actions can never bee unlawful, but when they are against the Law of the Common-wealth.

If a mans Father, or Mother, or Master bee Excommunicate, yet are not the Children forbidden to keep

them Company, nor to Eat with them; for that were (for
the most part) to oblige them not to eat at all, for want
of means to get food; and to authorise them to disobey
their Parents, and Masters, contrary to the Precept of
the Apostles.

In summe, the Power of Excommunication cannot be
extended further than to the end for which the Apostles and Pastors of the Church have their Commission
from our Saviour; which is not to rule by Command and
Coaction, but by Teaching and Direction of men in the
way of Salvation in the world to come. And as a Master
in any Science, may abandon his Scholar, when hee obstinately neglecteth the practise of his rules; but not accuse
him of Injustice, because he was never bound to obey
him: so a Teacher of Christian doctrine may abandon
his Disciples that obstinately continue in an unchristian
life; but he cannot say, they doe him wrong, because
they are not obliged to obey him: For to a Teacher that
shall so complain, may be applyed the Answer of God to
Samuel in the like place, *They have not rejected thee, but*   1 *Sam.* 8
mee. Excommunication therefore when it wanteth the
assistance of the Civill Power, as it doth, when a Christian
State, or Prince is Excommunicate by a forain Authority,
is without effect; and consequently ought to be without
terrour. The name of *Fulmen Excommunicationis* (that is,
the Thunderbolt of Excommunication) proceeded from
an imagination of the Bishop of Rome, which first used
it, that he was King of Kings, as the Heathen made Jupiter King of the Gods; and assigned him in their Poems,
and Pictures, a Thunderbolt, wherewith to subdue, and
punish the Giants, that should dare to deny his power:
Which imagination was grounded on two errours; one,
that the Kingdome of Christ is of this world, contrary to
our Saviours owne words, *My Kingdome is not of this
world*;[122] the other, that hee is Christs Vicar, not onely
over his owne Subjects, but over all the Christians of the
World; whereof there is no ground in Scrip[280]ture, and
the contrary shall bee proved in its due place.

Of the
Interpreter of
the Scriptures
before Civil
Soveraigns
became
Christians   *St. Paul* coming to *Thessalonica*, where was a Synagogue of the Jews, (*Acts* 17.2, 3.) *As his manner was,*
went in unto them, and three Sabbath dayes reasoned
with them out of the Scriptures, Opening and alledg-
ing, that Christ must needs have suffered and risen again
from the dead; and that this Jesus whom he preached
was the Christ. The Scriptures here mentioned were
the Scriptures of the Jews, that is, the Old Testament.
The men, to whom he was to prove that Jesus was the
Christ, and risen again from the dead, were also Jews,
and did beleeve already, that they were the Word of
God. Hereupon (as it is verse 4.) some of them beleeved,
and (as it is in the 5. ver.) some beleeved not. What was
the reason, when they all beleeved the Scripture, that
they did not all beleeve alike; but that some approved,
others disapproved the Interpretation of St. Paul that
cited them; and every one Interpreted them to himself?
It was this; S. Paul came to them without any Legall
Commission, and in the manner of one that would not
Command, but Perswade; which he must needs do,
either by Miracles, as Moses did to the Israelites in
Egypt, that they might see his Authority in Gods works;
or by Reasoning from the already received Scripture,
that they might see the truth of his doctrine in Gods
Word. But whosoever perswadeth by reasoning from
principles written, maketh him to whom hee speaketh
Judge, both of the meaning of those principles, and also
of the force of his inferences upon them. If these Jews
of Thessalonica were not, who else was the Judge of
what S. Paul alledged out of Scripture? If S. Paul, what
needed he to quote any places to prove his doctrine? It
had been enough to have said, I find it so in Scripture,
that is to say, in your Laws, of which I am Interpreter, as
sent by Christ. The Interpreter therefore of the Scripture,
to whose Interpretation the Jews of Thessalonica were
bound to stand, could be none: every one might beleeve,
or not beleeve, according as the Allegations seemed to
himselfe to be agreeable, or not agreeable to the meaning

of the places alledged. And generally in all cases of the world, hee that pretendeth any proofe, maketh Judge of his proofe him to whom he addresseth his speech. And as to the case of the Jews in particular, they were bound by expresse words (*Deut.* 17.) to receive the determination of all hard questions, from the Priests and Judges of Israel for the time being. But this is to bee understood of the Jews that were yet unconverted.

For the conversion of the Gentiles, there was no use of alledging the Scriptures, which they beleeved not. The Apostles therefore laboured by Reason to confute their Idolatry; and that done, to perswade them to the faith of Christ, by their testimony of his Life, and Resurrection. So that there could not yet bee any controversie concerning the authority to Interpret Scripture; seeing no man was obliged during his infidelity, to follow any mans Interpretation of any Scripture, except his Soveraigns Interpretation of the Laws of his countrey.

[281] Let us now consider the Conversion it self, and see what there was therein, that could be cause of such an obligation. Men were converted to no other thing then to the Beleef of that which the Apostles preached: And the Apostles preached nothing, but that Jesus was the Christ, that is to say, the King that was to save them, and reign over them eternally in the world to come; and consequently that hee was not dead, but risen again from the dead, and gone up into Heaven, and should come again one day to judg the world, (which also should rise again to be judged,) and reward every man according to his works. None of them preached that himselfe, or any other Apostle was such an Interpreter of the Scripture, as all that became Christians, ought to take their Interpretation for Law. For to Interpret the Laws, is part of the Administration of a present Kingdome; which the Apostles had not. They prayed then, and all other Pastors ever since, *Let thy Kingdome come*; and exhorted their Converts to obey their then Ethnique Princes. The New Testament was not yet published in

one Body. Every of the Evangelists was Interpreter of his own Gospel; and every Apostle of his own Epistle; And of the Old Testament, our Saviour himselfe saith to the Jews (*John* 5.39.) *Search the Scriptures; for in them yee thinke to have eternall life, and they are they that testifie of me.* If hee had not meant they should Interpret them, hee would not have bidden them take thence the proof of his being the Christ: he would either have Interpreted them himselfe, or referred them to the Interpretation of the Priests.

When a difficulty arose, the Apostles and Elders of the Church assembled themselves together, and determined what should bee preached, and taught, and how they should Interpret the Scriptures to the People; but took not from the People the liberty to read, and Interpret them to themselves. The Apostles sent divers Letters to the Churches, and other Writings for their instruction; which had been in vain, if they had not allowed them to Interpret, that is, to consider the meaning of them. And as it was in the Apostles time, it must be till such time as there should be Pastors, that could authorise an Interpreter, whose Interpretation should generally be stood to: But that could not be till Kings were Pastors, or Pastors Kings.

Of the Power to make Scripture Law There be two senses, wherein a Writing may be said to be *Canonicall*; for *Canon*, signifieth a *Rule*; and a Rule is a Precept, by which a man is guided, and directed in any action whatsoever. Such Precepts, though given by a Teacher to his Disciple, or a Counsellor to his friend, without power to Compell him to observe them, are neverthelesse Canons; because they are Rules: But when they are given by one, whom he that receiveth them is bound to obey, then are those Canons, not onely Rules, but Laws: The question therefore here, is of the Power to make the Scriptures (which are the Rules of Christian Faith) Laws.

Of the Ten Commandements That part of the Scripture, which was first Law, was the Ten Commandements, written in two Tables of

Stone,[123] and delivered by God [282] himselfe to Moses; and by Moses made known to the people. Before that time there was no written Law of God, who as yet having not chosen any people to bee his peculiar Kingdome, had given no Law to men, but the Law of Nature, that is to say, the Precepts of Naturall Reason, written in every mans own heart. Of these two Tables, the first containeth the law of Soveraignty; 1. That they should not obey, nor honour the Gods of other Nations, in these words, *Non habebis Deos alienos coram me*, that is, *Thou shalt not have for Gods, the Gods that other Nations worship; but onely me*: whereby they were forbidden to obey, or honor, as their King and Governour, any other God, than him that spake unto them then by Moses, and afterwards by the High Priest. 2. That they *should not make any Image to represent him*; that is to say, they were not to choose to themselves, neither in heaven, nor in earth, any Representative of their own fancying, but obey Moses and Aaron, whom he had appointed to that office. 3. That *they should not take the Name of God in vain*; that is, they should not speak rashly of their King, nor dispute his Right, nor the commissions of Moses and Aaron, his Lieutenants. 4. That *they should every Seventh day abstain from their ordinary labour*, and employ that time in doing him Publique Honor. The second Table containeth the Duty of one man towards another, as *To honor Parents; Not to kill; Not to Commit Adultery; Not to steale; Not to corrupt Judgment by false witnesse*; and finally, *Not so much as to designe in their heart the doing of any injury one to another*. The question now is, Who it was that gave to these written Tables the obligatory force of Lawes. There is no doubt but they were made Laws by God himselfe: But because a Law obliges not, nor is Law to any, but to them that acknowledge it to be the act of the Soveraign; how could the people of Israel that were forbidden to approach the Mountain to hear what God said to Moses, be obliged to obedience to all those laws which Moses propounded to them? Some of them were indeed the Laws of Nature, as all the Second Table; and therefore to be acknowledged for Gods Laws; not to the Israelites alone, but to all people: But of those that were peculiar to the Israelites, as those of the first Table, the question remains; saving that they had obliged themselves, presently after the propounding of them, to obey Moses, in these words (*Exod.* 20.19.) *Speak thou to us, and we will hear thee; but let not God speak to us, lest we dye.* It was therefore onely Moses then, and after him the High Priest, whom (by Moses) God declared should administer this his peculiar Kingdome, that had on Earth, the power to make this short Scripture of the Decalogue to bee Law in the Common-wealth of Israel. But Moses, and Aaron, and the succeeding High Priests were the Civill Soveraigns. Therefore hitherto, the Canonizing, or making of the Scripture Law, belonged to the Civill Soveraigne.

Of the Judiciall, and Leviticall Law The Judiciall Law, that is to say, the Laws that God prescribed to the Magistrates of Israel, for the rule of their administration of [283] Justice, and of the Sentences, or Judgments they should pronounce, in Pleas between man and man; and the Leviticall Law, that is to say, the rule that God prescribed touching the Rites and Ceremonies of the Priests and Levites, were all delivered to them by Moses onely; and therefore also became Lawes, by vertue of the same promise of obedience to Moses. Whether these laws were then written, or not written, but dictated to the People by Moses (after his forty dayes being with God in the Mount) by word of mouth, is not expressed in the Text; but they were all positive Laws, and equivalent to holy Scripture, and made Canonicall by Moses the Civill Soveraign.

The Second Law After the Israelites were come into the Plains of Moab over against Jericho, and ready to enter into the land of Promise, Moses to the former Laws added divers others; which therefore are called *Deuteronomy*; that is, *Second Laws*. And are (as it is written, *Deut.* 29.1.) *The words of a Covenant which the Lord commanded Moses to make with the Children of Israel, besides the Covenant which he made with them in Horeb.* For having explained those former Laws, in the beginning of the Book of *Deuteronomy*, he addeth others, that begin at the 12. Cha. and continue to the end of the 26. of the same Book. This Law (*Deut.* 27.1.) they were commanded to write upon great stones playstered over, at their passing over Jordan: This Law also was written by Moses himself in a Book; and delivered into the hands of the *Priests, and to the Elders of Israel*, (*Deut.* 31.9.) and commanded (ve. 26.) *to be put in the side of the Arke*; for in the Ark it selfe was nothing but the *Ten Commandements*. This was the Law, which Moses (*Deuteronomy* 17.18.) commanded the Kings of Israel should keep a copie of: And this is the Law, which having been long time lost, was found again in the Temple in the time of Josiah, and by his authority received for the Law of God. But both Moses at the writing, and Josiah at the recovery thereof, had both of them the Civill Soveraignty. Hitherto therefore the Power of making Scripture Canonicall, was in the Civill Soveraign.

Besides this Book of the Law, there was no other Book, from the time of Moses, till after the Captivity, received amongst the Jews for the Law of God. For the Prophets (except a few) lived in the time of the Captivity it selfe; and the rest lived but a little before it; and were so far from having their Prophecies generally received for Laws, as that their persons were persecuted, partly by false Prophets, and partly by the Kings which were seduced by them. And this Book it self, which was confirmed by Josiah for the Law of God, and with it all the History of the Works of God, was lost in the Captivity, and sack of the City of Jerusalem, as appears by that of 2 *Esdras* 14.21. *Thy Law is burnt; therefore no man knoweth the things that are done of thee, or the works that shall begin.* And before the Captivity, between the time when the Law was lost, (which is not mentioned

*1 Kings
14:26

in the Scripture, but may probably be thought to be the time of Rehoboam, when *Shishak King of Egypt[124] took the spoile of the Temple,) and the time of Josiah, when it was found againe, [284] they had no written Word of God, but ruled according to their own discretion, or by the direction of such, as each of them esteemed Prophets.

*The Old
Testament
when made
Canonicall*

From hence we may inferre, that the Scriptures of the Old Testament, which we have at this day, were not Canonicall, nor a Law unto the Jews, till the renovation of their Covenant with God at their return from the Captivity, and restauration of their Common-wealth under *Esdras*. But from that time forward they were accounted the Law of the Jews, and for such translated into Greek by Seventy Elders of Judæa, and put into the Library of Ptolemy at Alexandria, and approved for the Word of God.[125] Now seeing Esdras was the High Priest, and the High Priest was their Civill Soveraigne, it is manifest, that the Scriptures were never made Laws, but by the Soveraign Civill Power.

*The New
Testament
began to be
Canonicall
under
Christian
Soveraigns*

By the Writings of the Fathers that lived in the time before that Christian Religion was received, and authorised by Constantine the Emperour, we may find, that the Books wee now have of the New Testament, were held by the Christians of that time (except a few, in respect of whose paucity the rest were called the Catholique Church, and others Hæretiques) for the dictates of the Holy Ghost; and consequently for the Canon, or Rule of Faith: such was the reverence and opinion they had of their Teachers; as generally the reverence that the Disciples bear to their first Masters, in all manner of doctrine they receive from them, is not small. Therefore there is no doubt, but when S. Paul wrote to the Churches he had converted; or any other Apostle, or Disciple of Christ, to those which had then embraced Christ, they received those their Writings for the true Christian Doctrine. But in that time, when not the Power and Authority of the Teacher, but the Faith of the Hearer caused them to receive it, it was not the Apostles that made their own

Writings Canonicall, but every Convert made them so to himself.

But the question here, is not what any Christian made a Law, or Canon to himself, (which he might again reject, by the same right he received it;) but what was so made a Canon to them, as without injustice they could not doe any thing contrary thereunto. That the New Testament should in this sense be Canonicall, that is to say, a Law in any place where the Law of the Common-wealth had not made it so, is contrary to the nature of a Law. For a Law, (as hath been already shewn) is the Commandement of that Man, or Assembly, to whom we have given Soveraign Authority, to make such Rules for the direction of our actions, as hee shall think fit; and to punish us, when we doe any thing contrary to the same. When therefore any other man shall offer unto us any other Rules, which the Soveraign Ruler hath not prescribed, they are but Counsell, and Advice; which, whether good, or bad, hee that is counselled, may without injustice refuse to observe; and when cont[285]rary to the Laws already established, without injustice cannot observe, how good soever he conceiveth it to be. I say, he cannot in this case observe the same in his actions, nor in his discourse with other men; though he may without blame beleeve his private Teachers, and wish he had the liberty to practise their advice; and that it were publiquely received for Law. For internall Faith is in its own nature invisible, and consequently exempted from all humane jurisdiction; whereas the words, and actions that proceed from it, as breaches of our Civill obedience, are injustice both before God and Man. Seeing then our Saviour hath denyed his Kingdome to be in this world, seeing he hath said, he came not to judge, but to save the world, he hath not subjected us to other Laws than those of the Common-wealth; that is, the Jews to the Law of Moses, (which he saith (*Mat.* 5.) he came not to destroy, but to fulfill,) and other Nations to the Laws of their severall Soveraigns, and all men to the Laws of

Nature; the observing whereof, both he himselfe, and his Apostles have in their teaching recommended to us, as a necessary condition of being admitted by him in the last day into his eternall Kingdome, wherein shall be Protection, and Life everlasting. Seeing then our Saviour, and his Apostles, left not new Laws to oblige us in this world, but new Doctrine to prepare us for the next; the Books of the New Testament, which containe that Doctrine, untill obedience to them was commanded, by them that God had given power to on earth to be Legislators, were not obligatory Canons, that is, Laws, but onely good, and safe advice, for the direction of sinners in the way to salvation, which every man might take, and refuse at his owne perill, without injustice.

Again, our Saviour Christs Commission to his Apostles, and Disciples, was to Proclaim his Kingdome (not present, but) to come; and to Teach all Nations; and to Baptize them that should beleeve; and to enter into the houses of them that should receive them; and where they were not received, to shake off the dust of their feet against them;[126] but not to call for fire from heaven to destroy them,[127] nor to compell them to obedience by the Sword. In all which there is nothing of Power, but of Perswasion. He sent them out as Sheep unto Wolves, not as Kings to their Subjects. They had not in Commission to make Laws; but to obey, and teach obedience to Laws made; and consequently they could not make their Writings obligatory Canons, without the help of the Soveraign Civill Power. And therefore the Scripture of the New Testament is there only Law, where the lawfull Civill Power hath made it so. And there also the King, or Soveraign, maketh it a Law to himself; by which he subjecteth himselfe, not to the Doctor, or Apostle, that converted him, but to God himself, and his Son Jesus Christ, as immediately as did the Apostles themselves.

Of the Power of Councells to make the Scriptures Law That which may seem to give the New Testament, in respect of those that have embraced Christian Doctrine, the force of Laws, in the times, and places of persecution, is

the decrees they made amongst themselves in their
Synods. For we read (*Acts* 15.28.) the stile of the Councell
of the Apostles, the Elders, and the whole [286] Church,
in this manner, *It seemed good to the Holy Ghost, and to
us, to lay upon you no greater burthen than these necessary things, &c.* which is a stile that signifieth a Power to
lay a burthen on them that had received their Doctrine.
Now *to lay a burden on another*, seemeth the same that
to oblige; and therefore the Acts of that Councell were
Laws to the then Christians. Neverthelesse, they were
no more Laws than are these other Precepts, *Repent*; *Be
Baptized*; *Keep the Commandements*; *Beleeve the Gospel*; *Come unto me*; *Sell all that thou hast*; *Give it to the
poor*; and, *Follow me*; which are not Commands, but
Invitations, and Callings of men to Christianity, like that
of *Esay* 55.1.[128] Ho, *every man that thirsteth, come yee
to the waters, come, and buy wine and milke without
money.* For first, the Apostles power was no other than
that of our Saviour, to invite men to embrace the Kingdome of God; which they themselves acknowledged for
a Kingdome (not present, but) to come; and they that
have no Kingdome, can make no Laws. And secondly, if
their Acts of Councell, were Laws, they could not without sin be disobeyed. But we read not any where, that
they who received not the Doctrine of Christ, did therein
sin; but that they died in their sins; that is, that their sins
against the Laws to which they owed obedience, were
not pardoned. And those Laws were the Laws of Nature,
and the Civill Laws of the State, whereto every Christian
man had by pact submitted himself. And therefore by
the Burthen, which the Apostles might lay on such as
they had converted, are not to be understood Laws, but
Conditions, proposed to those that sought Salvation;
which they might accept, or refuse at their own perill,
without a new sin, though not without the hazard of
being condemned, and excluded out of the Kingdome of
God for their sins past. And therefore of Infidels, S. John
saith not, the wrath of God shall *come* upon them, but

John 3.36   *the wrath of God remaineth upon them*; and not that
John 3.18   they shall be condemned; but that *they are condemned already*. Nor can it be conceived, that the benefit of Faith, *is Remission of sins*, unlesse we conceive withall, that the dammage of Infidelity, is *the Retention of the same sins*.

But to what end is it (may some man aske), that the Apostles, and other Pastors of the Church, after their time, should meet together, to agree upon what Doctrine should be taught, both for Faith and Manners, if no man were obliged to observe their Decrees? To this may be answered, that the Apostles, and Elders of that Councell, were obliged even by their entrance into it, to teach the Doctrine therein concluded, and decreed to be taught, so far forth, as no precedent Law, to which they were obliged to yeeld obedience, was to the contrary; but not that all other Christians should be obliged to observe, what they taught. For though they might deliberate what each of them should teach; yet they could not deliberate what others should do, unless their Assembly had had a Legislative Power; which none could have but Civil Soveraigns. For though God be the Soveraign of all the world, we are not bound to take for his Law, whatsoever is propounded by every man in his name; nor any thing [287] contrary to the Civill Law, which God hath expressely commanded us to obey.

Seeing then the Acts of Councell of the Apostles, were then no Laws, but Counsells; much lesse are Laws the Acts of any other Doctors, or Councells since, if assembled without the Authority of the Civill Soveraign. And consequently, the Books of the New Testament, though most perfect Rules of Christian Doctrine, could not be made Laws by any other authority then that of Kings, or Soveraign Assemblies.

The first Councell, that made the Scriptures we now have, Canon, is not extant: For that Collection of the Canons of the Apostles, attributed to *Clemens*, the first Bishop of Rome after S. Peter, is subject to question: For though the Canonicall books bee there reckoned up; yet these words, *Sint vobis omnibus Clericis & Laicis Libri venerandi,*[129] *&c.* containe a distinction of Clergy, and Laity, that was not in use so neer St. Peters time. The first Councell for setling the Canonicall Scripture, that is extant, is that of Laodicea, *Can. 59.* which forbids the reading of other Books then those in the Churches; which is a Mandate that is not addressed to every Christian, but to those onely that had authority to read any thing publiquely in the Church; that is, to Ecclesiastiques onely.

Of Ecclesiasticall Officers in the time of the Apostles, some were Magisteriall, some Ministeriall. Magisteriall were the Offices of preaching of the Gospel of the Kingdom of God to Infidels; of administring the Sacraments, and Divine Service; and of teaching the Rules of Faith and Manners to those that were converted. Ministeriall was the Office of Deacons, that is, of them that were appointed to the administration of the secular necessities of the Church, at such time as they lived upon a common stock of mony, raised out of the voluntary contributions of the faithfull. *Of the Right of constituting Ecclesiasticall Officers in the time of the Apostles*

Amongst the Officers Magisteriall, the first, and principall were the Apostles; whereof there were at first but twelve; and these were chosen and constituted by our Saviour himselfe; and their Office was not onely to Preach, Teach, and Baptize, but also to be Martyrs, (Witnesses of our Saviours Resurrection.) This Testimony, was the specificall, and essentiall mark; whereby the Apostleship was distinguished from other Magistracy Ecclesiasticall; as being necessary for an Apostle, either to have seen our Saviour after his Resurrection, or to have conversed with him before, and seen his works, and other arguments of his Divinity, whereby they might be taken for sufficient Witnesses. And therefore at the election of a new Apostle in the place of Judas Iscariot, S. Peter saith (*Acts 1.21, 22.*) *Of these men that have companyed with us, all the time that the Lord Jesus went in and out among us, beginning from the Baptisme of John unto that same day that he was taken up from us,* must *one be ordained to be a* Witnesse *with us of his Resurrection*: where, by this word *must,* is implyed a necessary pro[288]perty of an Apostle, to have companyed with the first and prime Apostles in the time that our Saviour manifested himself in the flesh.

Matthias made Apostle by the Congregation The first Apostle, of those which were not constituted by Christ in the time he was upon the Earth, was *Matthias,* chosen in this manner: There were assembled together in Jerusalem about 120 Christians (*Acts* 1.15.) These appointed two, *Joseph* the *Just,* and *Matthias* (ver. 23.) and caused lots to be drawn; *and* (ver. 26.) *the Lot fell on Matthias, and he was numbred with the Apostles.* So that here we see the ordination of this Apostle, was the act of the Congregation, and not of St. Peter, nor of the eleven, otherwise then as Members of the Assembly.

Paul and Barnabas made Apostles by the Church of Antioch After him there was never any other Apostle ordained, but Paul and Barnabas; which was done (as we read (*Acts* 13.1, 2, 3.)) in this manner. *There were in the Church that was at Antioch, certaine Prophets, and Teachers; as Barnabas, and Simeon that was called Niger, and Lucius of Cyrene, and Manaen; which had been brought up with Herod the Tetrarch,*[130] *and Saul. As they ministred unto the Lord, and fasted, the Holy Ghost said, Separate mee Barnabas, and Saul for the worke whereunto I have called them. And when they had fasted, and prayed, and laid their hands on them, they sent them away.*

By which it is manifest, that though they were called by the Holy Ghost, their Calling was declared unto them, and their Mission authorized by the particular Church of Antioch. And that this their calling was to the Apostleship, is apparent by that, that they are both called (*Acts* 14.14.) Apostles: And that it was by vertue of this act of the Church of Antioch, that they were Apostles, S. Paul declareth plainly (*Rom.* 1.1.) in that hee useth the word, which the Holy Ghost used at his calling: For hee stileth himself, *An Apostle separated unto the Gospel of God*; alluding to the words of the Holy Ghost, *Separate me Barnabas and Saul, &c.* But seeing the work of an Apostle, was to be a Witnesse of the Resurrection of Christ, a man may here aske, how S. Paul, that conversed not with our Saviour before his passion, could know he was risen. To which is easily answered, that our Saviour himself appeared to him in the way to Damascus, from Heaven, after his Ascension; *and chose him for a vessell to bear his name before the Gentiles, and Kings, and Children of Israel*;[131] and consequently (having seen the Lord after his passion) was a competent Witnesse of his Resurrection: And as for Barnabas, he was a Disciple before the Passion. It is therefore evident that Paul, and Barnabas were Apostles; and yet chosen, and authorized (not by the first Apostles alone, but) by the Church of Antioch; as Matthias was chosen, and authorized by the Church of Jerusalem.

Bishop, a word formed in our language, out of the Greek *Episcopus*, signifieth an overseer, or Superintendent of any businesse, and particularly a Pastor, or Shepherd; and thence by metaphor was taken, not only amongst the Jews that were originally Shepherds, [289] but also amongst the Heathen, to signifie the Office of a King, or any other Ruler, or Guide of People, whether he ruled by Laws, or Doctrine. And so the Apostles were the first Christian Bishops, instituted by Christ himselfe: in which sense the Apostleship of Judas is called (*Acts* 1. 20.) *his Bishoprick*. And afterwards, when there were constituted Elders in the Christian Churches, with charge to guide Christs flock by their doctrine, and advice; these Elders were also called Bishops. Timothy was an Elder (which word *Elder*, in the New Testament is a name of Office, as well as of Age;) yet he was also a Bishop. And Bishops were then content with the Title of Elders. Nay S. John himselfe, the Apostle beloved of our Lord, beginneth his Second Epistle with these words, *The Elder to the Elect Lady.* By which it

What Offices in the Church are Magisteriall

is evident, that *Bishop*, *Pastor*, *Elder*, *Doctor*, that is to say, *Teacher*, were but so many divers names of the same Office in the time of the Apostles. For there was then no government by Coercion, but only by Doctrine, and Perswading. The Kingdome of God was yet to come, in a new world; so that there could be no authority to compell in any Church, till the Common-wealth had embraced the Christian Faith; and consequently no diversity of Authority, though there were diversity of Employments.

Besides these Magisteriall employments in the Church; namely, Apostles, Bishops, Elders, Pastors, and Doctors, whose calling was to proclaim Christ to the Jews, and Infidels, and to direct, and teach those that beleeved we read in the New Testament of no other. For by the names of *Evangelists* and *Prophets*, is not signified any Office, but severall Gifts, by which severall men were profitable to the Church: as Evangelists, by writing the life and acts of our Saviour; such as were S. *Matthew* and S. *John* Apostles, and S. *Marke* and S. *Luke* Disciples, and whosoever else wrote of that subject, (as S. *Thomas*, and S. *Barnabas* are said to have done,[132] though the Church have not received the Books that have gone under their names:) and as Prophets, by the gift of interpreting the Old Testament; and sometimes by declaring their speciall Revelations to the Church. For neither these gifts, nor the gifts of Languages, nor the gift of Casting out Devils, or of Curing other diseases, nor any thing else did make an Officer in the Church, save onely the due calling and election to the charge of Teaching.

Ordination of Teachers As the Apostles, Matthias, Paul, and Barnabas, were not made by our Saviour himself, but were elected by the Church, that is, by the Assembly of Christians; namely, Matthias by the Church of Jerusalem, and Paul, and Barnabas by the Church of Antioch; so were also the *Presbyters*, and *Pastors* in other Cities, elected by the Churches of those Cities. For proof whereof, let us consider, first, how S. Paul proceeded in the Ordination

of Presbyters, in the Cities where he had converted men
to the Christian Faith, immediately after he and Barnabas had received their Apostleship. We read (*Acts* 14.
23.) that *they ordained Elders in every Church*; which
at [290] first sight may be taken for an Argument, that
they themselves chose, and gave them their authority:
But if we consider the Originall text, it will be manifest, that they were authorized, and chosen by the
Assembly of the Christians of each City. For the words
there are, χειροτονήσαντες αὐτοῖς πρεσβυτέρους κατ'
ἐκκλησίαν, that is, *When they had Ordained them Elders
by the Holding up of Hands in every Congregation.*
Now it is well enough known, that in all those Cities,
the manner of choosing Magistrates, and Officers, was
by plurality of suffrages; and (because the ordinary way
of distinguishing the Affirmative Votes from the Negatives, was by Holding up of Hands) to ordain an Officer
in any of the Cities, was no more but to bring the people
together, to elect them by plurality of Votes, whether it
were by plurality of elevated hands, or by plurality of
voices, or plurality of balls, or beans, or small stones, of
which every man cast in one, into a vessell marked for
the Affirmative, or Negative; for divers Cities had divers
customes in that point. It was therefore the Assembly
that elected their own Elders: the Apostles were onely
Presidents of the Assembly to call them together for such
Election, and to pronounce them Elected, and to give
them the benediction, which now is called Consecration. And for this cause they that were Presidents of the
Assemblies, as (in the absence of the Apostles) the Elders
were, were called προεστῶτες, and in Latin *Antistities*;
which words signifie the Principall Person of the Assembly, whose office was to number the Votes, and to declare
thereby who was chosen; and where the Votes were
equall, to decide the matter in question, by adding his
own; which is the Office of a President in Councell. And
(because all the Churches had their Presbyters ordained
in the same manner,) where the word is *Constitute*, (as

Titus 1. 5.) ἵνα καταστήσης κατὰ πόλιν πρεσβυτέρους,
*For this cause left I thee in Crete, that thou shouldest
constitute Elders in every City*, we are to understand
the same thing; namely, that hee should call the faithfull
together, and ordain them Presbyters by plurality of suffrages. It had been a strange thing, if in a Town, where
men perhaps had never seen any Magistrate otherwise
chosen then by an Assembly, those of the Town becomming Christians, should so much as have thought on any
other way of Election of their Teachers, and Guides, that
is to say, of their Presbyters, (otherwise called Bishops,)
then this of plurality of suffrages, intimated by S. Paul
(*Acts* 14. 23.) in the word χειροτονήσαντες: Nor was
there ever any choosing of Bishops, (before the Emperors found it necessary to regulate them in order to the
keeping of the peace amongst them,) but by the Assemblies of the Christians in every severall Town.

The same is also confirmed by the continuall practise
even to this day, in the Election of the Bishops of Rome.
For if the Bishop of any place, had the right of choosing
another, to the succession of the Pastorall Office, in any
City, at such time as he went from thence, to plant the
same in another place; much more had he had the Right,
to appoint his successour in that place, in which he last
resided and [291] dyed: And we find not, that ever any
Bishop of Rome appointed his successor. For they were
a long time chosen by the People, as we may see by the
sedition raised about the Election, between *Damasus*,
and *Ursicinus*; which Ammianus Marcellinus saith was
so great, that *Juventius* the Præfect, unable to keep the
peace between them, was forced to goe out of the City;
and that there were above an hundred men found dead
upon that occasion in the Church it self.[133] And though
they afterwards were chosen, first, by the whole Clergy
of Rome, and afterwards by the Cardinalls; yet never
any was appointed to the succession by his predecessor. If therefore they pretended no right to appoint their
own successors, I think I may reasonably conclude, they

had no right to appoint the successors of other Bishops, without receiving some new power; which none could take from the Church to bestow on them, but such as had a lawfull authority, not onely to Teach, but to Command the Church; which none could doe, but the Civill Soveraign.

The word *Minister* in the Originall Διάκονος, signifieth one that voluntarily doth the businesse of another man; and differeth from a Servant onely in this, that Servants are obliged by their condition, to what is commanded them; whereas Ministers are obliged onely by their undertaking, and bound therefore to no more than that they have undertaken: So that both they that teach the Word of God, and they that administer the secular affairs of the Church, are both Ministers, but they are Ministers of different Persons. For the Pastors of the Church, called (*Acts 6. 4.*) *The Ministers of the Word*, are Ministers of Christ, whose Word it is: But the Ministery of a *Deacon*, which is called (verse 2. of the same Chapter) *Serving of Tables*, is a service done to the Church, or Congregation: So that neither any one man, nor the whole Church, could ever of their Pastor say, he was their Minister; but of a Deacon, whether the charge he undertook were to serve tables, or distribute maintenance to the Christians, when they lived in each City on a common stock, or upon collections, as in the first times, or to take a care of the House of Prayer, or of the Revenue, or other worldly businesse of the Church, the whole Congregation might properly call him their Minister.

Ministers of the Church what:

For their employment, as Deacons, was to serve the Congregation; though upon occasion they omitted not to preach the Gospel, and maintain the Doctrine of Christ, every one according to his gifts, as S. Steven did; and both to Preach, and Baptize, as Philip did:[134] For that Philip, which (*Act. 8. 5.*) Preached the Gospell at Samaria, and (verse 38.) Baptized the Eunuch, was Philip the Deacon, not Philip the Apostle. For it is manifest (verse 1.)

that when Philip preached in Samaria, the Apostles were at Jerusalem, and (verse 14.) *when they heard that Samaria had received the Word of God, sent Peter and John to them*; by imposition of whose hands, they that were Baptized, (verse 15.) received (which before by the Baptisme of Philip they had not received) the Holy Ghost. For it [292] was necessary for the conferring of the Holy Ghost, that their Baptisme should be administred, or confirmed by a Minister of the Word, not by a Minister of the Church. And therefore to confirm the Baptisme of those that Philip the Deacon had Baptized, the Apostles sent out of their own number from Jerusalem to Samaria, Peter, and John; who conferred on them that before were but Baptized, those graces that were signs of the Holy Spirit, which at that time did accompany all true Beleevers; which what they were may be understood by that which S. *Marke* saith (chap. 16. 17.) *These signes follow them that beleeve in my Name; they shall cast out Devills; they shall speak with new tongues; They shall take up Serpents, and if they drink any deadly thing, it shall not hurt them; They shall lay hands on the sick, and they shall recover.* This to doe, was it that Philip could not give; but the Apostles could, and (as appears by this place) effectually did to every man that truly beleeved, and was by a Minister of Christ himself Baptized: which power either Christs Ministers in this age cannot conferre, or else there are very few true Beleevers, or Christ hath very few Ministers.

And how chosen what: That the first Deacons were chosen, not by the Apostles, but by a Congregation of the Disciples; that is, of Christian men of all sorts, is manifest out of *Acts* 6. where we read that the *Twelve*, after the number of Disciples was multiplyed, called them together, and having told them, that it was not fit that the Apostles should leave the Word of God, and serve tables, said unto them (verse 3.) *Brethren looke you out among you seven men of honest report, full of the Holy Ghost, and of Wisdome, whom we may appoint over this businesse.*

Here it is manifest, that though the Apostles declared them elected; yet the Congregation chose them; which also, (verse the fift) is more expressely said, where it is written, that *the saying pleased the multitude, and they chose seven, &c.*

Under the Old Testament, the Tribe of Levi were onely capable of the Priesthood, and other inferiour Offices of the Church. The land was divided amongst the other Tribes (Levi excepted,) which by the subdivision of the Tribe of Joseph, into Ephraim and Manasses, were still twelve.[135] To the Tribe of Levi were assigned certain Cities for their habitation, with the suburbs for their cattell: but for their portion, they were to have the tenth of the fruits of the land of their Brethren. Again, the Priests for their maintenance had the tenth of that tenth, together with part of the oblations, and sacrifices. For God had said to Aaron (*Numb.* 18. 20.) *Thou shalt have no inheritance in their land, neither shalt thou have any part amongst them, I am thy part, and thine inheritance amongst the Children of Israel.* For God being then King, and having constituted the Tribe of Levi to be his Publique Ministers, he allowed them for their maintenance, the Publique revenue, that is to say, the part that God had reserved to himself; which were Tythes, and Offerings: and that is it which is meant, where God saith, I am thine inheritance. And therefore to the Levites might not unfitly be attributed [293] the name of *Clergy* from Κλῆρος, which signifieth Lot, or Inheritance; not that they were heirs of the Kingdome of God, more than other; but that Gods inheritance, was their maintenance. Now seeing in this time God himself was their King, and Moses, Aaron, and the succeeding High Priests were his Lieutenants; it is manifest, that the Right of Tythes, and Offerings was constituted by the Civill Power.

After their rejection of God in the demanding of a King, they enjoyed still the same revenue; but the Right thereof was derived from that, that the Kings did never take it from them: for the Publique Revenue was at the

disposing of him that was the Publique Person; and
that (till the Captivity) was the King. And again, after
the return from the Captivity, they paid their Tythes as
before to the Priest. Hitherto therefore Church Livings
were determined by the Civill Soveraign.

In our   Of the maintenance of our Saviour, and his Apostles,
Saviours time, we read onely they had a Purse, (which was carried by
and after Judas Iscariot;)[136] and, that of the Apostles, such as were
Fisher-men, did sometimes use their trade; and that
when our Saviour sent the Twelve Apostles to Preach,
Mat. 10. 9, he forbad them *to carry Gold, and Silver, and Brasse in*
10 *their purses, for that the workman is worthy of his hire*:
By which it is probable, their ordinary maintenance was
not unsuitable to their employment; for their employment was (ver. 8.) *freely to give, because they had freely
received*; and their maintenance was the *free gift* of
those that beleeved the good tyding they carryed about
of the coming of the Messiah their Saviour. To which we
may adde, that which was contributed out of gratitude;
by such as our Saviour had healed of diseases; of which
are mentioned *Certain women* (Luke 8. 2, 3.) *which had
been healed of evill spirits and infirmities; Mary Magdalen, out of whom went seven Devills; and Joanna the
wife of Chuza, Herods Steward; and Susanna, and many
others,*[137] *which ministred unto him of their substance.*

After our Saviours Ascension, the Christians of every
Acts 4. 34 City lived in Common, upon the mony which was
made of the sale of their lands and possessions, and
laid down at the feet of the Apostles, of good will, not
of duty; for *whilest the Land remained* (saith S. Peter
to Ananias[138] (*Acts* 5. 4.)) *was it not thine? and after
it was sold, was it not in thy power?* which sheweth
he needed not have saved his land, nor his money by
lying, as not being bound to contribute any thing at
all, unlesse he had pleased. And as in the time of the
Apostles, so also all the time downward, till after Constantine the Great, we shall find, that the maintenance
of the Bishops, and Pastors of the Christian Church, was

nothing but the voluntary contribution of them that had embraced their Doctrine. There was yet no mention of Tythes: but such was in the time of Constantine, and his Sons, the affection of Christians to their Pastors, as Ammianus Marcellinus saith (describing the sedition of *Damasus* and *Ursicinus* about the Bishopricke,) that it was worth their contention, in that the Bishops of those times by the liberality of their flock, and [294] especially of Matrons, lived splendidly, were carryed in Coaches, and were sumptuous in their fare and apparell.

But here may some ask, whether the Pastor were then bound to live upon voluntary contribution, as upon almes, *For who* (saith S. Paul 1 *Cor.* 9. 7.) *goeth to war at his own charges? or who feedeth a flock, and eateth not of the milke of the flock?* And again, *Doe ye not know that they which minister about holy things, live of the things of the Temple; and they which wait at the Altar, partake with the Altar*; that is to say, have part of that which is offered at the Altar for their mainten-ance? And then he concludeth, *Even so hath the Lord appointed, that they which preach the Gospel should live of the Gospel.* From which place may be inferred indeed, that the Pastors of the Church ought to be main-tained by their flocks; but not that the Pastors were to determine, either the quantity, or the kind of their own allowance, and be (as it were) their own Carvers. Their allowance must needs therefore be determined, either by the gratitude, and liberality of every particular man of their flock, or by the whole Congregation. By the whole Congregation it could not be, because their Acts were then no Laws: Therefore the maintenance of Pas-tors, before Emperours and Civill Soveraigns had made Laws to settle it, was nothing but Benevolence. They that served at the Altar lived on what was offered. So may the Pastors also take what is offered them by their flock; but not exact what is not offered. In what Court should they sue for it, who had no Tribunalls? Or if they had Arbitrators amongst themselves, who should

The Ministers of the Gospel lived on the Benevolence of their flocks
1 Cor. 9. 13

execute their Judgments, when they had no power to arme their Officers? It remaineth therefore, that there could be no certaine maintenance assigned to any Pastors of the Church, but by the whole Congregation; and then onely, when their Decrees should have the force (not onely of *Canons*, but also) of *Laws*; which Laws could not be made, but by Emperours, Kings, or other Civill Soveraignes. The Right of Tythes in Moses Law, could not be applyed to the then Ministers of the Gospell; because Moses and the High Priests were the Civill Soveraigns of the people under God, whose Kingdom amongst the Jews was present; whereas the Kingdome of God by Christ is yet to come.

Hitherto hath been shewn what the Pastors of the Church are; what are the points of their Commission (as that they were to Preach, to Teach, to Baptize, to be Presidents in their severall Congregations;) what is Ecclesiasticall Censure, *viz.* Excommunication, that is to say, in those places where Christianity was forbidden by the Civill Laws, a putting of themselves out of the company of the Excommunicate, and where Christianity was by the Civill Law commanded, a putting the Excommunicate out of the Congregations of Christians; who elected the Pastors and Ministers of the Church, (that it was the Congregation); who consecrated and blessed them, (that it was the Pastor); what was their due revenue, (that it was none but their own possessions, and their own labour, and the voluntary contributions of devout and gratefull Christians). We are [295] to consider now, what Office in the Church those persons have, who being Civill Soveraignes, have embraced also the Christian Faith.

That the Civill   And first, we are to remember, that the Right of Judg-
Soveraign   ing what Doctrines are fit for Peace, and to be taught the
being a   Subjects, is in all Common-wealths inseparably annexed
Christian hath   (as hath been already proved cha. 18.) to the Soveraign
the Right of   Power Civill, whether it be in one Man, or in one Assem-
appointing   bly of men. For it is evident to the meanest capacity,
Pastors

that mens actions are derived from the opinions they have of the Good, or Evill, which from those actions redound unto themselves; and consequently, men that are once possessed of an opinion, that their obedience to the Soveraign Power, will bee more hurtfull to them, than their disobedience, will disobey the Laws, and thereby overthrow the Common-wealth, and introduce confusion, and Civil war; for the avoiding whereof, all Civill Government was ordained. And therefore in all Common-wealths of the Heathen, the Soveraigns have had the name of Pastors of the People, because there was no Subject that could lawfully Teach the people, but by their permission and authority.

This Right of the Heathen Kings, cannot bee thought taken from them by their conversion to the Faith of Christ; who never ordained, that Kings for beleeving in him, should be deposed, that is, subjected to any but himself, or (which is all one) be deprived of the power necessary for the conservation of Peace amongst their Subjects, and for their defence against foraign Enemies. And therefore Christian Kings are still the Supreme Pastors of their people, and have power to ordain what Pastors they please, to teach the Church, that is, to teach the People committed to their charge.

Again, let the right of choosing them be (as before the conversion of Kings) in the Church, for so it was in the time of the Apostles themselves (as hath been shewn already in this chapter); even so also the Right will be in the Civill Soveraign, Christian. For in that he is a Christian, he allowes the Teaching; and in that he is the Soveraign (which is as much as to say, the Church by Representation,) the Teachers hee elects, are elected by the Church. And when an Assembly of Christians choose their Pastor in a Christian Common-wealth, it is the Soveraign that electeth him, because tis done by his Authority; In the same manner, as when a Town choose their Maior, it is the act of him that hath the Soveraign Power: For every act done, is the act of him, without

whose consent it is invalid. And therefore whatsoever
examples may be drawn out of History, concerning the
Election of Pastors, by the People, or by the Clergy,
they are no arguments against the Right of any Civill
Soveraign, because they that elected them did it by his
Authority.

Seeing then in every Christian Common-wealth, the
Civill Soveraign is the Supreme Pastor, to whose charge
the whole flock of [296] his Subjects is committed, and
consequently that it is by his authority, that all other
Pastors are made, and have power to teach, and performe all other Pastorall offices; it followeth also, that it
is from the Civill Soveraign, that all other Pastors derive
their right of Teaching, Preaching, and other functions
pertaining to that Office; and that they are but his Ministers; in the same manner as the Magistrates of Towns,
Judges in Courts of Justice, and Commanders of Armies,
are all but Ministers of him that is the Magistrate of
the whole Common-wealth, Judge of all Causes, and
Commander of the whole Militia, which is alwaies the
Civill Soveraign. And the reason hereof, is not because
they that Teach, but because they that are to Learn, are
his Subjects. For let it be supposed, that a Christian
King commit the Authority of Ordaining Pastors in his
Dominions to another King, (as divers Christian Kings
allow that power to the Pope;) he doth not thereby constitute a Pastor over himself, nor a Soveraign Pastor
over his People; for that were to deprive himself of the
Civill Power; which depending on the opinion men have
of their Duty to him, and the fear they have of Punishment in another world, would depend also on the skill,
and loyalty of Doctors, who are no lesse subject, not
only to Ambition, but also to Ignorance, than any other
sort of men. So that where a stranger hath authority
to appoint Teachers, it is given him by the Soveraign
in whose Dominions he teacheth. Christian Doctors are
our Schoolmasters to Christianity; But Kings are Fathers
of Families, and may receive Schoolmasters for their

Subjects from the recommendation of a stranger, but
not from the command; especially when the ill teaching
them shall redound to the great and manifest profit of
him that recommends them: nor can they be obliged to
retain them, longer than it is for the Publique good; the
care of which they stand so long charged withall, as they
retain any other essentiall Right of the Soveraignty.

If a man therefore should ask a Pastor, in the execution of his Office, as the chief Priests and Elders of
the people (*Mat.* 21.23.) asked our Saviour, *By what
authority dost thou these things, and who gave thee
this authority*: he can make no other just Answer, but
that he doth it by the Authority of the Common-wealth,
given him by the King, or Assembly that representeth it.
All Pastors, except the Supreme, execute their charges
in the Right, that is by the Authority of the Civill Soveraign, that is, *Jure Civili*. But the King, and every other
Soveraign, executeth his Office of Supreme Pastor, by
immediate Authority from God, that is to say, *in Gods
Right*, or *Jure Divino*. And therefore none but Kings
can put into their Titles (a mark of their submission to
God onely) *Dei gratiâ Rex, &c.* Bishops ought to say in
the beginning of their Mandates, *By the favour of the
Kings Majesty, Bishop of such a Diocesse*; or as Civill
Ministers, *In his Majesties Name*. For in saying, *Divinâ
providentiâ*, which is the same with *Dei gratiâ*, though
disguised, they deny to have received their authority
from the Civill State; and sliely [297] slip off the Col-
lar of their Civill Subjection, contrary to the unity and
defence of the Common-wealth.

But if every Christian Soveraign be the Supreme Pastor of his own Subjects, it seemeth that he hath also
the Authority, not only to Preach (which perhaps no
man will deny;) but also to Baptize, and to Administer
the Sacrament of the Lords Supper; and to Consecrate
both Temples, and Pastors to Gods service; which
most men deny; partly because they use not to do it;
and partly because the Administration of Sacraments,

*The Pastorall
Authority of
Soveraigns
only is de
Jure Divino,
that of other
Pastors is
Jure Civili*

*Christian
Kings have
Power to
execute all
manner of
Pastoral
function*

and Consecration of Persons, and Places to holy uses, requireth the Imposition of such mens hands, as by the like Imposition successively from the time of the Apostles have been ordained to the like Ministery. For proof therefore that Christian Kings have power to Baptize, and to Consecrate, I am to render a reason, both why they use not to doe it, and how, without the ordinary ceremony of Imposition of hands, they are made capable of doing it, when they will.

There is no doubt but any King, in case he were skilfull in the Sciences, might by the same Right of his Office, read Lectures of them himself, by which he authorizeth others to read them in the Universities. Neverthelesse, because the care of the summe of the businesse of the Common-wealth taketh up his whole time, it were not convenient for him to apply himself in Person to that particular. A King may also if he please, sit in Judgment, to hear and determine all manner of Causes, as well as give others authority to doe it in his name; but that the charge that lyeth upon him of Command and Government, constrain him to bee continually at the Helm, and to commit the Ministeriall Offices to others under him. In the like manner our Saviour (who surely had *John 4. 2 power to Baptize) Baptized none* himselfe, but sent his Apostles and Disciples to Baptize. So also S. Paul, by the necessity of Preaching in divers and far distant places, *1 Cor. 1. 14, Baptized few: Amongst all the Corinthians he Baptized 16 only* Crispus, Cajus, and Stephanus; and the reason *1 Cor. 1. 17 was, because his principall* Charge was to Preach. Whereby it is manifest, that the greater Charge, (such as is the Government of the Church,) is a dispensation for the lesse. The reason therefore why Christian Kings use not to Baptize, is evident, and the same, for which at this day there are few Baptized by Bishops, and by the Pope fewer.

And as concerning Imposition of Hands, whether it be needfull, for the authorizing of a King to Baptize, and Consecrate, we may consider thus.

Imposition of Hands, was a most ancient publique ceremony amongst the Jews, by which was designed, and made certain, the person, or other thing intended in a mans prayer, blessing, sacrifice, consecration, condemnation, or other speech. So Jacob in blessing the children of Joseph (*Gen.* 48.14.) *Laid his right Hand on Ephraim the younger, and his left Hand on Manasseh the first born*; and [298] this he did *wittingly* (though they were so presented to him by Joseph, as he was forced in doing it to stretch out his arms acrosse) to design to whom he intended the greater blessing. So also in the sacrificing of the Burnt offering, Aaron is commanded [*Exod.* 29.10.] *to Lay his Hands on the head of the bullock*; and [ver. 15.] *to Lay his Hand on the head of the ramme.* The same is also said again, *Levit.* 1.4. & 8.14. Likewise Moses when he ordained Joshua to be Captain of the Israelites, that is, consecrated him to Gods service, [*Numb.* 27.23.] *Laid his Hands upon him, and gave him his Charge*, designing, and rendring certain, who it was they were to obey in war. And in the consecration of the Levites [*Numb.* 8.10.] God commanded that *the Children of Israel should Put their Hands upon the Levites.* And in the condemnation of him that had blasphemed the Lord [*Levit.* 24.14.] God commanded that *all that heard him should Lay their Hands on his head, and that all the Congregation should stone him.* And why should they only that heard him, Lay their Hands upon him, and not rather a Priest, Levite, or other Minister of Justice, but that none else were able to design, and demonstrate to the eyes of the Congregation, who it was that had blasphemed, and ought to die? And to design a man, or any other thing, by the Hand to the Eye, is lesse subject to mistake, than when it is done to the Eare by a Name.

And so much was this ceremony observed, that in blessing the whole Congregation at once, which cannot be done by Laying on of Hands, yet *Aaron* [*Levit.* 9.22.] *did lift up his Hand towards the people when he blessed them.* And we read also of the like ceremony of Consecration of Temples amongst the Heathen, as that the Priest laid his Hands on some post of the Temple, all the while he was uttering the words of Consecration. So naturall it is to design any individuall thing, rather by the Hand, to assure the Eyes, than by Words to inform the Eare in matters of Gods Publique service.

This ceremony was not therefore new in our Saviours time. For Jairus [*Mark* 5.23.] whose daughter was sick, besought our Saviour (not to heal her, but) *to Lay his Hands upon her, that shee might bee healed.* And [*Matth.* 19.13.] *they brought unto him little children, that hee should Put his Hands on them, and Pray.*

According to this ancient Rite, the Apostles, and Presbyters, and the Presbytery it self, Laid Hands on them whom they ordained Pastors, and withall prayed for them that they might receive the Holy Ghost; and that not only once, but sometimes oftner, when a new occasion was presented: but the end was still the same, namely a punctuall, and religious designation of the person, ordained either to the Pastorall Charge in general, or to a particular Mission: so [*Act.* 6.6.] *The Apostles Prayed, and Laid their Hands* on the seven Deacons; which was done, not to give them the Holy Ghost, (for they were full of the Holy Ghost before they were chosen, as appeareth im[299]mediately before, verse 3.) but to design them to that Office. And after Philip the Deacon had converted certain persons in Samaria, Peter and John went down [*Act* 8.17.] *and Laid their Hands on them, and they received the Holy Ghost.* And not only an Apostle, but a Presbyter had this power: For S. Paul adviseth Timothy [1 *Tim.* 5.22.] *Lay Hands suddenly on no man*; that is, designe no man rashly to the Office of a Pastor. The whole Presbytery Laid their Hands on Timothy, as we read 1 *Tim.* 4.14. but this is to be understood, as that some did it by the appointment of the Presbytery, and most likely their προεστώς, or Prolocutor, which it may be was St. Paul himself. For in his

2 Epist. to *Tim.* ver. 6.[139] he saith to him, *Stirre up the gift of God which is in thee, by the Laying on of my Hands*: where note by the way, that by the Holy Ghost, is not meant the third Person in the Trinity, but the Gifts necessary to the Pastorall Office. We read also, that St. Paul had Imposition of Hands twice; once from Ananias at Damascus [*Acts* 9.17, 18.] at the time of his Baptisme; and again [*Acts* 13.3.] at Antioch, when he was first sent out to Preach. The use then of this ceremony considered in the Ordination of Pastors, was to design the Person to whom they gave such Power. But if there had been then any Christian, that had had the Power of Teaching before; the Baptizing of him, that is, the making him a Christian, had given him no new Power, but had onely caused him to preach true Doctrine, that is, to use his Power aright; and therefore the Imposition of Hands had been unnecessary; Baptisme it selfe had been sufficient. But every Soveraign, before Christianity, had the power of Teaching, and Ordaining Teachers; and therefore Christianity gave them no new Right, but only directed them in the way of teaching Truth; and consequently they needed no Imposition of Hands (besides that which is done in Baptisme) to authorize them to exercise any part of the Pastorall Function, as namely, to Baptize, and Consecrate. And in the Old Testament, though the Priest only had right to Consecrate, during the time that the Soveraignty was in the High Priest; yet it was not so when the Soveraignty was in the King: For we read [1 *Kings* 8.] That Solomon Blessed the People, Consecrated the Temple, and pronounced that Publique Prayer, which is the pattern now for Consecration of all Christian Churches, and Chappels: whereby it appears, he had not only the right of Ecclesiasticall Government; but also of exercising Ecclesiasticall Functions.

From this consolidation of the Right Politique, and Ecclesiastique in Christian Soveraigns, it is evident, they have all manner of Power over their Subjects, that can be given to man, for the government of mens externall

The Civill Soveraigne if a Christian, is head of the Church in his own Dominions

actions, both in Policy, and Religion; and may make such Laws, as themselves shall judge fittest, for the government of their own Subjects, both as they are the Common-wealth, and as they are the Church: for both State, and Church are the same men.

[300] If they please therefore, they may (as many Christian Kings now doe) commit the government of their Subjects in matters of Religion to the Pope; but then the Pope is in that point Subordinate to them, and exerciseth that Charge in anothers Dominion *Jure Civili*, in the Right of the Civill Soveraign; not *Jure Divino*, in Gods Right; and may therefore be discharged of that Office, when the Soveraign for the good of his Subjects shall think it necessary. They may also if they please, commit the care of Religion to one Supreme Pastor, or to an Assembly of Pastors; and give them what power over the Church, or one over another, they think most convenient; and what titles of honor, as of Bishops, Archbishops, Priests, or Presbyters, they will; and make such Laws for their maintenance, either by Tithes, or otherwise, as they please, so they doe it out of a sincere conscience, of which God onely is the Judge. It is the Civill Soveraign, that is to appoint Judges, and Interpreters of the Canonicall Scriptures; for it is he that maketh them Laws. It is he also that giveth strength to Excommunications; which but for such Laws and Punishments, as may humble obstinate Libertines, and reduce them to union with the rest of the Church, would bee contemned. In summe, he hath the Supreme Power in all causes, as well Ecclesiasticall, as Civill, as far as concerneth actions, and words, for those onely are known, and may be accused; and of that which cannot be accused, there is no Judg at all, but God, that knoweth the heart. And these Rights are incident to all Soveraigns, whether Monarchs, or Assemblies: for they that are the Representants of a Christian People, are Representants of the Church: for a Church, and a Commonwealth of Christian People, are the same thing.

Though this that I have here said, and in other places *Cardinal* of this Book, seem cleer enough for the asserting of the *Bellarmines* Supreme Ecclesiasticall Power to Christian Soveraigns; *Books* De yet because the Pope of Romes challenge to that Power *Summo* universally, hath been maintained chiefly, and I think *Pontifice* as strongly as is possible, by Cardinall Bellarmine, in *considered* his Controversie *De Summo Pontifice*; I have thought it necessary, as briefly as I can, to examine the grounds, and strength of his Discourse.

Of five Books he hath written of this subject, the first *The first* containeth three Questions: One, Which is simply the *book* best government, *Monarchy*, *Aristocracy*, or *Democracy*; and concludeth for neither, but for a government mixt of all three: Another, which of these is the best Government of the Church; and concludeth for the mixt, but which should most participate of Monarchy: The third, whether in this mixt Monarchy, St. Peter had the place of Monarch. Concerning his first Conclusion, I have already sufficiently proved (chapt. 18.) that all Governments, which men are bound to obey, are Simple, and Absolute. In Monarchy there is but One Man Supreme; and all other men that have any kind of Power in the State, have it by his Commission, during his pleasure; and execute it in his name: And in Aristocracy, and Democracy, but One Supreme Assembly, [301] with the same Power that in Monarchy belongeth to the Monarch, which is not a Mixt, but an Absolute Soveraignty. And of the three sorts, which is the best, is not to be disputed, where any one of them is already established; but the present ought alwaies to be preferred, maintained, and accounted best; because it is against both the Law of Nature, and the Divine positive Law, to doe any thing tending to the subversion thereof. Besides, it maketh nothing to the Power of any Pastor, (unlesse he have the Civill Soveraignty,) what kind of Government is the best; because their Calling is not to govern men by Commandement, but to teach them, and perswade them by Arguments, and leave it to them to consider, whether they shall embrace, or reject the Doctrine taught. For Monarchy, Aristocracy, and Democracy, do mark out unto us three sorts of Soveraigns, not of Pastors; or, as we may say, three sorts of Masters of Families, not three sorts of Schoolmasters for their children.

And therefore the second Conclusion, concerning the best form of Government of the Church, is nothing to the question of the Popes Power without his own Dominions: For in all other Common-wealths his Power (if hee have any at all) is that of the Schoolmaster onely, and not of the Master of the Family.

For the third Conclusion, which is, that St. Peter was Monarch of the Church, he bringeth for his chiefe argument the place of S. *Matth.* (chap. 16. 18, 19.) *Thou art Peter, And upon this rock I will build my Church, &c. And I will give thee the keyes of Heaven; whatsoever thou shalt bind on Earth, shall be bound in Heaven, and whatsoever thou shalt loose on Earth, shall be loosed in Heaven.* Which place well considered, proveth no more, but that the Church of Christ hath for foundation one onely Article; namely, that which Peter in the name of all the Apostles professing, gave occasion to our Saviour to speak the words here cited; which that wee may cleerly understand, we are to consider, that our Saviour preached by himself, by John Baptist, and by his Apostles, nothing but this Article of Faith, *that he was the Christ*; all other Articles requiring faith no otherwise, than as founded on that. John began first, (*Mat.* 3.2.) preaching only this, *The Kingdome of God is at hand.* Then our Saviour himself (*Mat.* 4.17.) preached the same: And to his Twelve Apostles, when he gave them their Commission (*Mat.* 10.7.) there is no mention of preaching any other Article but that. This was the fundamentall Article, that is the Foundation of the Churches Faith. Afterwards the Apostles being returned to him, he asketh them all, (*Mat.* 16.13.) not Peter onely, *Who men said he was*; and they answered, that *some said he was John the Baptist, some Elias, and*

others Jeremias, or one of the Prophets: Then (ver. 15.)
he asked them all again, (not Peter onely) *Whom say
yee that I am?* Therefore S. Peter answered (for them
all) *Thou art Christ, the Son of the Living God*; which I
said is the Foundation of the Faith of the whole Church;
from which our Saviour takes the oc[302]casion of
saying, *Upon this stone I will build my Church*: By
which it is manifest, that by the Foundation-Stone of
the Church, was meant the Fundamentall Article of the
Churches Faith. But why then (will some object) doth
our Saviour interpose these words, *Thou art Peter?* If
the originall of this text had been rigidly translated, the
reason would easily have appeared: We are therefore to
consider, that the Apostle Simon, was surnamed *Stone*,
(which is the signification of the Syriacke word *Cephas*,
and of the Greek word *Petrus*). Our Saviour therefore
after the confession of that Fundamentall Article, alluding
to his name, said (as if it were in English) thus, Thou art
Stone, and upon this Stone I will build my Church: which
is as much as to say, this Article, that *I am the Christ*, is
the Foundation of all the Faith I require in those that are
to bee members of my Church: Neither is this allusion to
a name, an unusuall thing in common speech: But it had
been a strange, and obscure speech, if our Saviour intending to build his Church on the Person of S. Peter, had
said, *thou art a Stone, and upon this Stone I will build
my Church*, when it was so obvious without ambiguity to
have said, *I will build my Church on thee*; and yet there
had been still the same allusion to his name.

And for the following words, *I will give thee the Keyes
of Heaven, &c.* it is no more than what our Saviour
gave also to all the rest of his Disciples [*Matth.* 18.18.]
*Whatsoever yee shall bind on Earth, shall be bound in
Heaven. And whatsoever ye shall loose on Earth, shall
be loosed in Heaven.* But howsoever this be interpreted,
there is no doubt but the Power here granted belongs
to all Supreme Pastors; such as are all Christian Civill Soveraignes in their own Dominions. In so much, as

if St. Peter, or our Saviour himself had converted any of them to beleeve him, and to acknowledge his Kingdome; yet because his Kingdome is not of this world, he had left the supreme care of converting his subjects to none but him; or else hee must have deprived him of the Soveraignty, to which the Right of Teaching is inseparably annexed. And thus much in refutation of his first Book, wherein hee would prove St. Peter to have been the Monarch Universall of the Church, that is to say, of all the Christians in the world.

The second **The second Book hath two Conclusions: One, that**
Book S. Peter was Bishop of Rome, and there dyed: The other, that the Popes of Rome are his Successors. Both which have been disputed by others. But supposing them true; yet if by Bishop of Rome, bee understood either the Monarch of the Church, or the Supreme Pastor of it; not Silvester, but Constantine[140] (who was the first Christian Emperour) was that Bishop; and as Constantine, so all other Christian Emperors were of Right supreme Bishops of the Roman Empire; I say of the Roman Empire, not of all Christendome: For other Christian Soveraigns had the same Right in their severall Territories, as to an Office essentially adhærent to their Soveraignty. Which shall serve for answer to his second Book.

The third [303] In the third Book, he handleth the question
Book whether the Pope be Antichrist. For my part, I see no argument that proves he is so, in that sense the Scripture useth the name: nor will I take any argument from the quality of Antichrist, to contradict the Authority he exerciseth, or hath heretofore exercised in the Dominions of any other Prince, or State.

It is evident that the Prophets of the Old Testament foretold, and the Jews expected a Messiah, that is, a Christ, that should re-establish amongst them the kingdom of God, which had been rejected by them in the time of Samuel, when they required a King after the manner of other Nations. This expectation of theirs, made them obnoxious to the Imposture of all such, as had both the ambition to attempt the attaining of the Kingdome, and the art to deceive the People by counterfeit miracles, by hypocriticall life, or by orations and doctrine plausible. Our Saviour therefore, and his Apostles forewarned men of False Prophets, and of False Christs. False Christs, are such as pretend to be the *Christ*, but are not, and are called properly *Antichrists*, in such sense, as when there happeneth a Schisme in the Church by the election of two Popes, the one calleth the other *Antipapa*, or the false Pope. And therefore Antichrist in the proper signification hath two essentiall marks; One, that he denyeth Jesus to be Christ; and another that he professeth himselfe to bee Christ. The first Mark is set down by S. *John* in his 1 Epist. 4. ch. 3. ver. *Every Spirit that confesseth not that Jesus Christ is come in the flesh, is not of God; And this is the Spirit of Antichrist.* The other Mark is expressed in the words of our Saviour, (*Mat.* 24.5.) *Many shall come in my name, saying, I am Christ*; and again, *If any man shall say unto you, Loe, here is Christ, there is Christ, beleeve it not.* And therefore Antichrist must be a False Christ, that is, some one of them that shall pretend themselves to be Christ. And out of these two Marks, *to deny Jesus to be the Christ*, and to *affirm himselfe to be the Christ*, it followeth, that he must also be an *Adversary of Jesus the true Christ*, which is another usuall signification of the word Antichrist. But of these many Antichrists, there is one speciall one, ὁ Ἀντίχριστος, *The Antichrist*, or *Antichrist* definitely, as one certaine person; not indefinitely *an Antichrist.* Now seeing the Pope of Rome, neither pretendeth himself, nor denyeth Jesus to bee the Christ, I perceive not how he can be called Antichrist; by which word is not meant, one that falsely pretendeth to be *His* Lieutenant, or Vicar generall, but to be *Hee.* There is also some Mark of the time of this speciall Antichrist, as (*Mat.* 24.15.) when that abominable Destroyer, spoken of by Daniel,* shall stand in the Holy place, and such tribulation as was not since the beginning of the world, *Dan. 9. 27

nor ever shall be again, insomuch as if it were to last long, (ver. 22.) *no flesh could be saved; but for the elects sake those days shall be shortened* (made fewer). But that tribulation is not yet come; for it is to be followed immediately (ver. 29.) by a darkening of the Sun and Moon, a falling of the Stars, a concussion of the Heavens, and the glorious coming again of our Saviour in the cloudes. And [304] therefore *The Antichrist* is not yet come; whereas, many Popes are both come and gone. It is true, the Pope in taking upon him to give Laws to all Christian Kings, and Nations, usurpeth a Kingdome in this world, which Christ took not on him: but he doth it not *as Christ*, but as *for Christ*, wherein there is nothing of *The Antichrist*.

The fourth Book   In the fourth Book, to prove the Pope to be the supreme Judg in all questions of Faith and Manners, (*which is as much as to be the absolute Monarch of all Christians in the world,*) he bringeth three Propositions: The first, that his Judgments are Infallible: The second, that he can make very Laws, and punish those that observe them not: The third, that our Saviour conferred all Jurisdiction Ecclesiasticall on the Pope of Rome.

Texts for the Infallibility of the Popes Judgement in points of Faith   For the Infallibility of his Judgments, he alledgeth the Scriptures: and first, that of *Luke* 22.31. *Simon, Simon, Satan hath desired you that hee may sift you as wheat; but I have prayed for thee, that thy faith faile not; and when thou art converted, strengthen thy Brethren*. This, according to Bellarmines exposition, is, that Christ gave here to Simon Peter two priviledges: one, that neither his Faith should fail, nor the Faith of any of his successors: the other, that neither he, nor any of his successors should ever define any point concerning Faith, or Manners erroneously, or contrary to the definition of a former Pope: Which is a strange, and very much strained interpretation. But he that with attention readeth that chapter, shall find there is no place in the whole Scripture, that maketh more against the Popes Authority, than this very place. The Priests and Scribes seeking to kill our Saviour

at the Passeover, and Judas possessed with a resolution
to betray him, and the day of killing the Passeover being
come, our Saviour celebrated the same with his Apostles, which he said, till the Kingdome of God was come
hee would doe no more; and withall told them, that one
of them was to betray him: Hereupon they questioned,
which of them it should be; and withall (seeing the next
Passeover their Master would celebrate should be when
he was King) entred into a contention, who should then
be the greatest man. Our Saviour therefore told them,
that the Kings of the Nations had Dominion over their
Subjects, and are called by a name (in Hebrew) that signifies Bountifull; but I cannot be so to you, you must
endeavour to serve one another; I ordain you a Kingdome, but it is such as my Father hath ordained mee; a
Kingdome that I am now to purchase with my blood,
and not to possesse till my second coming; then yee shall
eat and drink at my Table, and sit on Thrones, judging
the twelve Tribes of Israel: And then addressing himself
to St. Peter, he saith, *Simon, Simon*, Satan seeks by sug-
gesting a present domination, to weaken your faith of
the future; but I have prayed for thee, that thy faith shall
not fail; Thou therefore (Note this,) being converted,
and understanding my Kingdome as of another world,
confirm the same faith in thy Brethren: To which S. Peter
answered (as one that no more expected any authority
in this world) *Lord I am ready to goe with thee, not
onely* [305] *to Prison, but to Death.* Whereby it is manifest, S. Peter had not onely no jurisdiction given him in
this world, but a charge to teach all the other Apostles,
that they also should have none. And for the Infallibility
of St. Peters sentence definitive in matter of Faith, there
is no more to be attributed to it out of this Text, than
that Peter should continue in the beleef of this point,
namely, that Christ should come again, and possesse the
Kingdome at the day of Judgement; which was not given
by this Text to all his Successors; for wee see they claime
it in the World that now is.

The second place is that of *Matth.* 16. *Thou art Peter, and upon this rocke I will build my Church, and the gates of Hell shall not prevail against it.* By which (as I have already shewn in this chapter) is proved no more, than that the gates of Hell shall not prevail against the confession of Peter, which gave occasion to that speech; namely this, that *Jesus is Christ the Sonne of God.*

The third Text is *John* 21. ver. 16, 17. *Feed my sheep*; which contains no more but a Commission of Teaching: And if we grant the rest of the Apostles to be contained in that name of *Sheep*; then it is the supreme Power of Teaching: but it was onely for the time that there were no Christian Soveraigns already possessed of that Supremacy. But I have already proved, that Christian Soveraignes are in their owne Dominions the supreme Pastors, and instituted thereto, by vertue of their being Baptized, though without other Imposition of Hands. For such Imposition being a Ceremony of designing the person, is needlesse, when hee is already designed to the Power of Teaching what Doctrine he will, by his institution to an Absolute Power over his Subjects. For as I have proved before, Soveraigns are supreme Teachers (in generall) by their Office; and therefore oblige themselves (by their Baptisme) to teach the Doctrine of Christ: And when they suffer others to teach their people, they doe it at the perill of their own souls; for it is at the hands of the Heads of Families that God will require the account of the instruction of his Children and Servants. It is of Abraham himself, not of a hireling, that God saith (*Gen.* 18.19.) *I know him that he will command his Children, and his houshold after him, that they keep the way of the Lord, and do justice and judgement.*

The fourth place is that of *Exod.* 28.30. *Thou shalt put in the Breastplate of Judgment, the Urim and the Thummin*: which hee saith is interpreted by the Septuagint δήλωσιν καὶ ἀλήθειαν, that is, *Evidence* and *Truth*: And thence concludeth, God had given Evidence, and Truth, (which is almost Infallibility,) to the High

Priest. But be it Evidence and Truth it selfe that was given; or be it but Admonition to the Priest to endeavour to inform himself cleerly, and give judgment uprightly; yet in that it was given to the High Priest, it was given to the Civill Soveraign: For such next under God was the High Priest in the Common-wealth of Israel; and is an argument [306] for Evidence and Truth, that is, for the Ecclesiasticall Supremacy of Civill Soveraigns over their own Subjects, against the pretended Power of the Pope. These are all the Texts hee bringeth for the Infallibility of the Judgement of the Pope, in point of Faith.

For the Infallibility of his Judgment concerning Manners, hee bringeth one Text, which is that of *John* 16.13. *When the Spirit of truth is come, hee will lead you into all truth*: where (saith he) by *all truth*, is meant, at least, *all truth necessary to salvation*. But with this mitigation, he attributeth no more Infallibility to the Pope, than to any man that professeth Christianity, and is not to be damned: For if any man erre in any point, wherein not to erre is necessary to Salvation, it is impossible he should be saved; for that onely is necessary to Salvation, without which to be saved is impossible. What points these are, I shall declare out of the Scripture in the Chapter following. In this place I say no more, but that though it were granted, the Pope could not possibly teach any error at all, yet doth not this entitle him to any Jurisdiction in the Dominions of another Prince, unlesse we shall also say, a man is obliged in conscience to set on work upon all occasions the best workman, even then also when he hath formerly promised his work to another.

Besides the Text, he argueth from Reason, thus. If the Pope could erre in necessaries, then Christ hath not sufficiently provided for the Churches Salvation; because he hath commanded her to follow the Popes directions. But this Reason is invalid, unlesse he shew when, and where Christ commanded that, or took at all any notice of a Pope: Nay granting whatsoever was given

Texts for the same in point of Manners

to S. Peter, was given to the Pope; yet seeing there is in the Scripture no command to any man to obey St. Peter, no man can bee just, that obeyeth him, when his commands are contrary to those of his lawfull Soveraign.

Lastly, it hath not been declared by the Church, nor by the Pope himselfe, that he is the Civill Soveraign of all the Christians in the world; and therefore all Christians are not bound to acknowledge his Jurisdiction in point of Manners. For the Civill Soveraignty, and supreme Judicature in controversies of Manners, are the same thing: And the Makers of Civill Laws, are not onely Declarers, but also Makers of the justice, and injustice of actions; there being nothing in mens Manners that makes them righteous, or unrighteous, but their conformity with the Law of the Soveraign. And therefore when the Pope challengeth Supremacy in controversies of Manners, hee teacheth men to disobey the Civill Soveraign; which is an erroneous Doctrine, contrary to the many precepts of our Saviour and his Apostles, delivered to us in the Scripture.

To prove the Pope has Power to make Laws, he alledgeth many places; as first, *Deut.* 17.12. *The man that will doe presumptuously, and will not hearken unto the Priest, (that standeth to Minister there before the Lord thy God, or unto the Judge,) even that man* [307] *shall die, and thou shalt put away the evill from Israel.* For answer whereunto, we are to remember that the High Priest (next and immediately under God) was the Civill Soveraign; and all Judges were to be constituted by him. The words alledged sound therefore thus. *The man that will presume to disobey the Civill Soveraign for the time being, or any of his Officers in the execution of their places, that man shall die, &c.* which is cleerly for the Civill Soveraignty, against the Universall power of the Pope.

Secondly, he alledgeth that of *Matth.* 16. *Whatsoever yee shall bind, &c.* and interpreteth it for such *binding* as is attributed (*Matth.* 23.4.) to the Scribes and Pharisees,

They bind heavy burthens, and grievous to be born, and lay them on mens shoulders; by which is meant (he sayes) Making of Laws; and concludes thence, that the Pope can make Laws. But this also maketh onely for the Legislative power of Civill Soveraigns: For the Scribes, and Pharisees sat in Moses Chaire, but Moses next under God was Soveraign of the People of Israel: and therefore our Saviour commanded them to doe all that they should say, but not all that they should do. That is, to obey their Laws, but not follow their Example.

The third place, is *John* 21.16. *Feed my sheep*; which is not a Power to make Laws, but a command to Teach. Making Laws belongs to the Lord of the Family; who by his owne discretion chooseth his Chaplain, as also a Schoolmaster to Teach his children.

The fourth place *John* 20.21. is against him. The words are, *As my Father sent me, so send I you.* But our Saviour was sent to Redeem (by his Death) such as should Beleeve; and by his own, and his Apostles preaching to prepare them for their entrance into his Kingdome; which he himself saith, is not of this world, and hath taught us to pray for the coming of it here-after, though hee refused (*Acts* 1.6, 7.) to tell his Apostles when it should come; and in which, when it comes, the twelve Apostles shall sit on twelve Thrones (every one perhaps as high as that of St. Peter) to judge the twelve tribes of Israel.[141] Seeing then God the Father sent not our Saviour to make Laws in this present world, wee may conclude from the Text, that neither did our Saviour send S. Peter to make Laws here, but to perswade men to expect his second comming with a stedfast faith; and in the mean time, if Subjects, to obey their Princes; and if Princes, both to beleeve it themselves, and to do their best to make their Subjects doe the same; which is the Office of a Bishop. Therefore this place maketh most strongly for the joining of the Ecclesiasticall Supremacy to the Civill Soveraignty, contrary to that which Cardinall Bellarmine alledgeth it for.

The fift place is *Acts* 15.28. *It hath seemed good to the Holy Spirit, and to us, to lay upon you no greater burden, than these necessary things, that yee abstaine from meats offered to Idols, and from bloud, and from things strangled, and from fornication.* Here hee notes the word *Laying of burdens* for the Legislative [308] Power. But who is there, that reading this Text, can say, this stile of the Apostles may not as properly be used in giving Counsell, as in making Laws? The stile of a Law is, *We command*: But, *We think good*, is the ordinary stile of them, that but give Advice; and they lay a Burthen that give Advice, though it bee conditionall, that is, if they to whom they give it, will attain their ends: And such is the Burthen, of abstaining from things strangled, and from bloud; not absolute, but in case they will not erre. I have shewn before (chap. 25.) that Law, is distinguished from Counsell, in this, that the reason of a Law, is taken from the designe, and benefit of him that prescribeth it; but the reason of a Counsell, from the designe, and benefit of him, to whom the Counsell is given. But here, the Apostles aime onely at the benefit of the converted Gentiles, namely their Salvation; not at their own benefit; for having done their endeavour, they shall have their reward, whether they be obeyed, or not. And therefore the Acts of this Councell, were not Laws, but Counsells.

The sixt place is that of *Rom.* 13. *Let every Soul be subject to the Higher Powers, for there is no Power but of God*; which is meant, he saith not onely of Secular, but also of Ecclesiasticall Princes. To which I answer, first, that there are no Ecclesiasticall Princes but those that are also Civill Soveraignes; and their Principalities exceed not the compasse of their Civill Soveraignty; without those bounds though they may be received for Doctors, they cannot be acknowledged for Princes. For if the Apostle had meant, we should be subject both to our own Princes, and also to the Pope, he had taught us a doctrine, which Christ himself hath told us is impossible, namely, *to serve two Masters.*[142] And though the Apostle say in another place,[143] *I write these things being absent, lest being present I should use sharpnesse, according to the Power which the Lord hath given me*; it is not, that he challenged a Power either to put to death, imprison, banish, whip, or fine any of them, which are Punishments; but onely to Excommunicate, which (without the Civill Power) is no more but a leaving of their company, and having no more to doe with them, than with a Heathen man, or a Publican; which in many occasions might be a greater pain to the Excommunicant, than to the Excommunicate.

The seventh place is 1 *Cor.* 4.21. *Shall I come unto you with a Rod, or in love, and the spirit of lenity?* But here again, it is not the Power of a Magistrate to punish offenders, that is meant by a Rod; but onely the Power of Excommunication, which is not in its owne nature a Punishment, but onely a Denouncing of punishment, that Christ shall inflict, when he shall be in possession of his Kingdome, at the day of Judgment. Nor then also shall it bee properly a Punishment, as upon a Subject that hath broken the Law; but a Revenge, as upon an Enemy, or Revolter, that denyeth the Right of our Saviour to the Kingdome: And therefore this proveth not the Legislative Power of any Bishop, that has not also the Civill Power.

[309] The eighth place is, *Timothy* 3.2.[144] *A Bishop must be the husband but of one wife, vigilant, sober, &c.* which he saith was a Law. I thought that none could make a Law in the Church, but the Monarch of the Church, St. Peter. But suppose this Precept made by the authority of St. Peter; yet I see no reason why to call it a Law, rather than an Advice, seeing Timothy was not a Subject, but a Disciple of S. Paul; nor the flock under the charge of Timothy, his Subjects in the Kingdome, but his Scholars in the Schoole of Christ: If all the Precepts he giveth Timothy, be Laws, why is not this also a Law, *Drink no longer water, but use a little wine for*

thy healths sake?[145] And why are not also the Precepts of good Physitians, so many Laws? but that it is not the Imperative manner of speaking, but an absolute Subjection to a Person, that maketh his Precepts Laws.

In like manner, the ninth place, 1 *Tim.* 5.19. *Against an Elder receive not an accusation, but before two or three Witnesses*, is a wise Precept, but not a Law.

The tenth place is, *Luke* 10.16. *He that heareth you, heareth mee; and he that despiseth you, despiseth me.* And there is no doubt, but he that despiseth the Counsell of those that are sent by Christ, despiseth the Counsell of Christ himself. But who are those now that are sent by Christ, but such as are ordained Pastors by lawfull Authority? and who are lawfully ordained, that are not ordained by the Soveraign Pastor? and who is ordained by the Soveraign Pastor in a Christian Common-wealth, that is not ordained by the authority of the Soveraign thereof? Out of this place therefore it followeth, that he which heareth his Soveraign being a Christian, heareth Christ; and hee that despiseth the Doctrine which his King being a Christian, authorizeth, despiseth the Doctrine of Christ (which is not that which Bellarmine intendeth here to prove, but the contrary). But all this is nothing to a Law. Nay more, a Christian King, as a Pastor, and Teacher of his Subjects, makes not thereby his Doctrines Laws. He cannot oblige men to beleeve; though as a Civill Soveraign he may make Laws suitable to his Doctrine, which may oblige men to certain actions, and sometimes to such as they would not otherwise do, and which he ought not to command; and yet when they are commanded, they are Laws; and the externall actions done in obedience to them, without the inward approbation, are the actions of the Soveraign, and not of the Subject, which is in that case but as an instrument, without any motion of his owne at all; because God hath commanded to obey them.

The eleventh, is every place, where the Apostle for Counsell, putteth some word, by which men use to

signifie Command; or calleth the following of his Counsell, by the name of Obedience. And therefore they are
alledged out of 1 *Cor.* 11.2. *I commend you for keeping
my Precepts as I delivered them to you.* The Greek is,
*I commend you for keeping those things I delivered to
you, as I delivered them.* Which is far from signifying
that they were Laws, or any [310] thing else, but good
Counsell. And that of 1 *Thess.* 4.2. *You know what
commandements we gave you*: where the Greek word
is παραγγελίας ἐδώκαμεν, equivalent to παρεδώκαμεν,
what wee delivered to you, as in the place next before
alledged, which does not prove the Traditions of the
Apostles, to be any more than Counsells; though as is
said in the 8 verse, *he that despiseth them, despiseth
not man, but God*: For our Saviour himself came not to
Judge, that is, to be King in this world; but to Sacrifice
himself for Sinners, and leave Doctors in his Church, to
lead, not to drive men to Christ, who never accepteth
forced actions, (which is all the Law produceth,) but the
inward conversion of the heart; which is not the work of
Laws, but of Counsell, and Doctrine.

And that of 2 *Thess.* 3.14. *If any man Obey not our
word by this Epistle, note that man, and have no company with him, that he may bee ashamed*: where from
the word *Obey,* he would inferre, that this Epistle was a
Law to the Thessalonians. The Epistles of the Emperours
were indeed Laws. If therefore the Epistle of S. Paul were
also a Law, they were to obey two Masters. But the word
Obey, as it is in the Greek ὑπακούει, signifieth *heark-
ening to,* or *putting in practice,* not onely that which is
Commanded by him that has right to punish, but also
that which is delivered in a way of Counsell for our good;
and therefore St. Paul does not bid kill him that disobeys,
nor beat, nor imprison, nor amerce him, which Legislators may all do; but avoid his company, that he may bee
ashamed: whereby it is evident, it was not the Empire
of an Apostle, but his Reputation amongst the Faithfull,
which the Christians stood in awe of.

The last place is that of *Heb.* 13.17. *Obey your Leaders, and submit your selves to them, for they watch for your souls, as they that must give account*: And here also is intended by Obedience, a following of their Counsell: For the reason of our Obedience, is not drawn from the will and command of our Pastors, but from our own benefit, as being the Salvation of our Souls they watch for, and not for the Exaltation of their own Power, and Authority. If it were meant here, that all they teach were Laws, then not onely the Pope, but every Pastor in his Parish should have Legislative Power. Again, they that are bound to obey their Pastors, have no power to examine their commands. What then shall wee say to St. *John* who bids us (1 Epist. chap. 4. ver. 1.) *Not to beleeve every Spirit, but to try the Spirits whether they are of God, because many false Prophets are gone out into the world*? It is therefore manifest, that wee may dispute the Doctrine of our Pastors; but no man can dispute a Law. The Commands of Civill Soveraigns are on all sides granted to be Laws: if any else can make a Law besides himselfe, all Common-wealth, and consequently all Peace, and Justice must cease; which is contrary to all Laws, both Divine and Humane. Nothing therefore can be drawn from these, or any other places of Scripture, to prove the Decrees of the Pope, where he has not also the Civill Soveraignty, to be Laws.

The question of Superiority between the Pope and other Bishops [311] The last point hee would prove, is this, *That our Saviour Christ has committed Ecclesiasticall Jurisdiction immediately to none but the Pope.* Wherein he handleth not the Question of Supremacy between the Pope and Christian Kings, but between the Pope and other Bishops. And first, he sayes it is agreed, that the Jurisdiction of Bishops, is at least in the generall *de Jure Divino*, that is, in the Right of God; for which he alledges S. Paul, *Ephes.* 4.11. where hee sayes, that Christ after his Ascension into heaven, *gave gifts to men, some Apostles, some Prophets, and some Evangelists, and some Pastors, and some Teachers*: And thence inferres, they have indeed their Jurisdiction in Gods Right; but will not grant they have it immediately from God, but derived through the Pope. But if a man may be said to have his Jurisdiction *de Jure Divino*, and yet not immediately; what lawfull Jurisdiction, though but Civ-ill, is there in a Christian Common-wealth, that is not also *de Jure Divino*? For Christian Kings have their Civ-ill Power from God immediately; and the Magistrates under him exercise their severall charges in vertue of his Commission; wherein that which they doe, is no lesse *de Jure Divino mediato*, than that which the Bishops doe, in vertue of the Popes Ordination. All lawfull Power is of God, immediately in the Supreme Governour, and medi-ately in those that have Authority under him: So that either hee must grant every Constable in the State, to hold his Office in the Right of God; or he must not hold that any Bishop holds his so, besides the Pope himselfe.

But this whole Dispute, whether Christ left the Juris-diction to the Pope onely, or to other Bishops also, if considered out of those places where the Pope has the Civill Soveraignty, is a contention *de lana Caprina*:[146] For none of them (where they are not Soveraigns) has any Jurisdiction at all. For Jurisdiction is the Power of hearing and determining Causes between man and man; and can belong to none, but him that hath the Power to prescribe the Rules of Right and Wrong; that is, to make Laws; and with the Sword of Justice to compell men to obey his Decisions, pronounced either by himself, or by the Judges he ordaineth thereunto; which none can law-fully do, but the Civill Soveraign.

Therefore when he alledgeth out of the 6 of *Luke*, that our Saviour called his Disciples together, and chose twelve of them which he named Apostles, he proveth that he Elected them (all, except Matthias, Paul and Barnabas,) and gave them Power and Command to Preach, but not to Judge of Causes between man and man: for that is a Power which he refused to take upon himselfe, saying, *Who made me a Judge, or a Divider,*[147] *amongst you?* and in another place, *My Kingdome is not of this world.* But hee that hath not the Power to hear, and determine Causes between man and man, cannot be said to have any Jurisdiction at all. And yet this hinders not, but that our Saviour gave them Power to Preach and Baptize in all parts of the world, supposing they were not by their own lawfull Soveraign forbidden: For to our own Soveraigns Christ himself, and his Apo[312]stles have in sundry places expressely commanded us in all things to be obedient.

The arguments by which he would prove, that Bishops receive their Jurisdiction from the Pope (seeing the Pope in the Dominions of other Princes hath no Jurisdiction himself,) are all in vain. Yet because they prove, on the contrary, that all Bishops receive Jurisdiction when they have it from their Civill Soveraigns, I will not omit the recitall of them.

The first, is from *Numbers* 11. where Moses not being able alone to undergoe the whole burthen of administring the affairs of the People of Israel, God commanded him to choose Seventy Elders, and took part of the spirit of Moses, to put it upon those Seventy Elders: by which is understood, not that God weakned the spirit of Moses, for that had not eased him at all; but that they had all of them their authority from him; wherein he doth truly, and ingenuously interpret that place. But seeing Moses had the entire Soveraignty in the Common-wealth of the Jews, it is manifest, that it is thereby signified, that they had their Authority from the Civill Soveraign: and therefore that place proveth, that Bishops in every Christian Common-wealth have their Authority from the Civill Soveraign; and from the Pope in his own Territories only, and not in the Territories of any other State.

The second argument, is from the nature of Monarchy; wherein all Authority is in one Man, and in others by derivation from him: But the Government of the Church, he says, is Monarchicall. This also makes for Christian Monarchs. For they are really Monarchs of their own people; that is, of their own Church (for the Church is the same thing with a Christian people;) whereas the Power of the Pope, though hee were S. Peter, is neither Monarchy, nor hath any thing of *Archicall*, nor *Craticall*, but onely of *Didacticall*;[148] For God accepteth not a forced, but a willing obedience.

The third, is, from that the *Sea* of S. Peter is called by S. Cyprian,[149] the *Head*, the *Source*, the *Roote*, the *Sun*, from whence the Authority of Bishops is derived. But by the Law of Nature (which is a better Principle of Right and Wrong, than the word of any Doctor that is but a man) the Civill Soveraign in every Common-wealth, is the *Head*, the *Source*, the *Root*, and the *Sun*, from which all Jurisdiction is derived. And therefore the Jurisdiction of Bishops, is derived from the Civill Soveraign.

The fourth, is taken from the Inequality of their Jurisdictions: For if God (saith he) had given it them immediately, he had given aswell Equality of Jurisdiction, as of Order: But wee see, some are Bishops but of one Town, some of a hundred Towns, and some of many whole Provinces; which differences were not determined by the command of God; their Jurisdiction therefore is not of God, but of Man; and one has a greater, another a lesse, as it pleaseth the Prince of the Church. Which argument, if he had proved before, that the Pope had had an Universall Jurisdiction over all Christians, had [313] been for his purpose. But seeing that hath not been proved, and that it is notoriously known, the large Jurisdiction of the Pope was given him by those that had it, that is, by the Emperours of Rome, (for the Patriarch of Constantinople, upon the same title, namely, of being Bishop of the Capitall City of the Empire, and Seat of the Emperour, claimed to be equall to him,) it followeth, that all other Bishops have their Jurisdiction from the Soveraigns of the place wherein they exercise the same: And as for that cause they have not their Authority *de Jure Divino*; so neither hath the Pope his *de Jure Divino*, except onely where hee is also the Civill Soveraign.

His fift argument is this, *If Bishops have their Jurisdiction immediately from God, the Pope could not take it from them, for he can doe nothing contrary to Gods ordination*; And this consequence is good, and well proved. *But* (saith he) *the Pope can do this, and has done it*. This also is granted, so he doe it in his own Dominions, or in the Dominions of any other Prince that hath given him that Power; but not universally, in Right of the Popedome: For that power belongeth to every Christian Soveraign, within the bounds of his owne Empire, and is inseparable from the Soveraignty. Before the People of Israel had (by the commandment of God to Samuel) set over themselves a King, after the manner of other Nations, the High Priest had the Civill Government; and none but he could make, nor depose an inferiour Priest: But that Power was afterwards in the King, as may be proved by this same argument of Bellarmine; For if the Priest (be he the High Priest or any other) had his Jursidiction immediately from God, then the King could not take it from him; *for he could doe nothing contrary to Gods ordinance*: But it is certain, that King Solomon (1 *Kings* 2.26.) deprived Abiathar the High Priest of his Office, and placed Zadok (verse 35.) in his room. Kings therefore may in the like manner Ordaine, and Deprive Bishops, as they shall thinke fit, for the well governing of their Subjects.

His sixth argument is this, If Bishops have their Jurisdiction *de Jure Divino* (that is, *immediately from God,*) they that maintain it, should bring some Word of God to prove it: But they can bring none. The argument is good; I have therefore nothing to say against it. But it is an argument no lesse good, to prove the Pope himself to have no Jurisdiction in the Dominion of any other Prince.

Lastly, hee bringeth for argument, the testimony of two Popes, *Innocent*, and *Leo*;[150] and I doubt not but hee might have alledged, with as good reason, the testimonies of all the Popes almost since S. Peter: For considering the love of Power naturally implanted in mankind, whosoever were made Pope, he would be tempted to uphold the same opinion. Neverthelesse, they should therein but doe, as *Innocent*, and *Leo* did, bear witnesse of themselves, and therefore their witnesse should not be good.

[314] In the fift Book he hath four Conclusions. The first is, *That the Pope is not Lord of all the world*: The second, *That the Pope is not Lord of all the Christian world*: The third, *That the Pope* (without his owne Territory) *has not any Temporall Jurisdiction DIRECTLY*: These three Conclusions are easily granted. The fourth is, *That the Pope has* (in the Dominions of other Princes) the Supreme *Temporall Power INDIRECTLY*: which is denyed; unlesse hee mean by *Indirectly*, that he has gotten it by Indirect means; then is that also granted. But I understand, that when he saith he hath it *Indirectly*, he means, that such Temporall Jurisdiction belongeth to him of Right, but that this Right is but a Consequence of his Pastorall Authority, the which he could not exercise, unlesse he have the other with it: And therefore to the Pastorall Power (which he calls Spirituall) the Supreme Power Civill is necessarily annexed; and that thereby hee hath a Right to change Kingdomes, giving them to one, and taking them from another, when he shall think it conduces to the Salvation of Souls.

Of the Popes Temporall Power

Before I come to consider the Arguments by which hee would prove this Doctrine, it will not bee amisse to lay open the Consequences of it; that Princes, and States, that have the Civill Soveraignty in their severall Common-wealths, may bethink themselves, whether it bee convenient for them, and conducing to the good of their Subjects, of whom they are to give an account at the day of Judgment, to admit the same.

When it is said, the Pope hath not (in the Territories of other States) the Supreme Civill Power *Directly*; we are to understand, he doth not challenge it, as other Civill Soveraigns doe, from the originall submission thereto of those that are to be governed. For it is evident, and has already been sufficiently in this Treatise demonstrated, that the Right of all Soveraigns, is derived originally from the consent of every one of those that are to bee governed; whether they that choose him, doe it for their common defence against an Enemy, as when they agree amongst themselves to appoint a Man, or an Assembly of men to protect them; or whether they doe it, to save their lives, by submission to a conquering Enemy. The Pope therefore, when he disclaimeth the Supreme Civill Power over other States *Directly*, denyeth no more, but that his Right cometh to him by that way; He ceaseth not for all that, to claime it another way; and that is, (without the consent of them that are to be governed) by a Right given him by God, (which hee calleth *Indirectly*,) in his Assumption to the Papacy. But by what way soever he pretend, the Power is the same; and he may (if it bee granted to be his Right) depose Princes and States, as often as it is for the Salvation of Soules, that is, as often as he will; for he claimeth also the Sole Power to Judge, whether it be to the Salvation of mens Souls, or not. And this is the Doctrine, not onely that Bellarmine here, and many other Doctors teach in their Sermons and Books, but also that some Councells have decreed, and [315] the Popes have accordingly, when the occasion hath served them, put in practise. For the fourth Councell of Lateran held under Pope *Innocent* the third,[151] (in the third Chap. *De Hæreticis*,) hath this Canon. *If a King at the Popes admonition, doe not purge his Kingdome of Hæretiques, and being Excommunicate for the same, make not satisfaction within a year, his subjects are absolved of their Obedience.* And the practise hereof hath been seen on divers occasions; as in the Deposing of *Chilperique*, King of France; in the Translation of the Roman Empire to *Charlemaine*;[152] in the Oppression of *John* King of England;[153] in Transferring the Kingdome of *Navarre*;[154] and of late years, in the League against *Henry* the third of France,[155] and in many more occurrences. I think there be few Princes that consider not this as Injust, and Inconvenient; but I wish they would all resolve to be Kings, or Subjects. Men cannot serve two Masters: They ought therefore to ease them, either by holding the Reins of Government wholly in their own hands; or by wholly delivering them into the hands of the Pope; that such men as are willing to be obedient, may be protected in their obedience. For this distinction of Temporall, and Spirituall Power is but words. Power is as really divided, and as dangerously to all purposes, by sharing with another *Indirect* Power, as with a *Direct* one. But to come now to his Arguments.

The first is this, *The Civill Power is subject to the Spirituall: Therefore he that hath the Supreme Power Spirituall, hath right to command Temporall Princes, and dispose of their Temporalls in order to the Spirituall.* As for the distinction of Temporall, and Spirituall, let us consider in what sense it may be said intelligibly, that the Temporall, or Civill Power is subject to the Spirituall. There be but two ways that those words can be made sense. For when wee say, one Power is subject to another Power, the meaning either is, that he which hath the one, is subject to him that hath the other; or that the one Power is to the other, as the means to the end. For wee cannot understand, that one Power hath Power over another Power; or that one Power can have Right or Command over another: For Subjection, Command, Right, and Power are accidents, not of Powers, but of Persons: One Power may be subordinate to another, as the art of a Sadler, to the art of a Rider. If then it bee granted, that the Civill Government be ordained as a means to bring us to a Spirituall felicity; yet it does not follow, that if a King have the Civill Power, and the Pope the Spirituall, that therefore the King is bound to obey the Pope, more then every Sadler is bound to obey every Rider. Therefore as from Subordination of an Art, cannot be inferred the Subjection of the Professor; so from the Subordination of a Government, cannot be inferred the Subjection of the Governor. When therefore he saith, the Civill Power is Subject to the Spirituall, his meaning is, that the Civill Soveraign, is Subject to the Spirituall Soveraign. And the Argument stands thus, *The Civil Soveraign, is subject to the Spirituall; Therefore the Spirituall Prince may command Temporall Princes.* Where the Conclusion is the same, [316] with the Antecedent he should have proved. But to prove it, he alledgeth first, this reason, *Kings and Popes, Clergy and Laity make but one Common-wealth; that is to say, but one Church: And in all Bodies the Members depend one upon another: But things Spirituall depend not of things Temporall: Therefore Temporall depend on Spirituall. And therefore are Subject to them.* In which Argumentation there be two grosse errours: one is, that all Christian Kings, Popes, Clergy, and all other Christian men, make but one Common-wealth: For it is evident that France is one Common-wealth, Spain another, and Venice a third, &c. And these consist of Christians; and therefore also are severall Bodies of Christians; that is to say, severall Churches: And their severall Soveraigns Represent them, whereby they are capable of commanding and obeying, of doing and suffering, as a naturall man; which no Generall or Universall Church is, till it have a Representant; which it hath not on Earth: for if it had, there is no doubt but that all Christendome were one Common-wealth, whose Soveraign were that Representant, both in things Spirituall and Temporall: And the Pope, to make himself this Representant, wanteth three things that our Saviour hath not given him, to *Command*, and to *Judge*, and to *Punish*, otherwise than (by Excommunication) to run from those that will not Learn of him: For though the Pope were Christs onely Vicar, yet he cannot exercise his government, till our Saviours second coming: And then also it is not the

Pope, but St. Peter himselfe, with the other Apostles, that are to be Judges of the world.

The other errour in this his first Argument is, that he sayes, the Members of every Common-wealth, as of a naturall Body, depend one of another: It is true, they cohære together; but they depend onely on the Soveraign, which is the Soul of the Common-wealth; which failing, the Common-wealth is dissolved into a Civill war, no one man so much as cohæring to another, for want of a common Dependance on a known Soveraign; Just as the Members of the naturall Body dissolve into Earth, for want of a Soul to hold them together. Therefore there is nothing in this similitude, from whence to inferre a dependance of the Laity on the Clergy, or of the Temporall Officers on the Spirituall; but of both on the Civill Soveraign; which ought indeed to direct his Civill commands to the Salvation of Souls; but is not therefore subject to any but God himselfe. And thus you see the laboured fallacy of the first Argument, to deceive such men as distinguish not between the Subordination of Actions in the way to the End; and the Subjection of Persons one to another in the administration of the Means. For to every End, the Means are determined by Nature, or by God himselfe supernaturally: but the Power to make men use the Means, is in every nation resigned (by the Law of Nature, which forbiddeth men to violate their Faith given) to the Civill Soveraign.

[317] His second Argument is this, *Every Common-wealth, (because it is supposed to be perfect and sufficient in it self,) may command any other Common-wealth, not subject to it, and force it to change the administration of the Government; nay depose the Prince, and set another in his room, if it cannot otherwise defend it selfe against the injuries he goes about to doe them: much more may a Spirituall Common-wealth command a Temporall one to change the administration of their Government, and may depose Princes, and institute others, when they cannot otherwise defend the Spirituall Good.*

That a Common-wealth, to defend it selfe against injuries, may lawfully doe all that he hath here said, is very true; and hath already in that which hath gone before been sufficiently demonstrated. And if it were also true, that there is now in this world a Spirituall Common-wealth, distinct from a Civill Common-wealth, then might the Prince thereof, upon injury done him, or upon want of caution that injury be not done him in time to come, repaire, and secure himself by Warre; which is in summe, deposing, killing, or subduing, or doing any act of Hostility. But by the same reason, it would be no lesse lawfull for a Civill Soveraign, upon the like injuries done, or feared, to make warre upon the Spirituall Soveraign; which I beleeve is more than Cardinall Bellarmine would have inferred from his own proposition.

But Spirituall Common-wealth there is none in this world: for it is the same thing with the Kingdome of Christ; which he himselfe saith, is not of this world; but shall be in the next world, at the Resurrection, when they that have lived justly, and beleeved that he was the Christ, shall (though they died *Naturall* bodies) rise *Spirituall* bodies; and then it is, that our Saviour shall judge the world, and conquer his Adversaries, and make a Spirituall Common-wealth. In the mean time, seeing there are no men on earth, whose bodies are Spirituall; there can be no Spirituall Common-wealth amongst men that are yet in the flesh; unlesse wee call Preachers, that have Commission to Teach, and prepare men for their reception into the Kingdome of Christ at the Resurrection, a Common-wealth; which I have proved to bee none.

The third Argument is this; *It is not lawfull for Christians to tolerate an Infidel, or Hæreticall King, in case he endeavour to draw them to his Hæresie, or Infidelity. But to judge whether a King draw his subjects to Hæresie, or not, belongeth to the Pope. Therefore hath the Pope Right, to determine whether the Prince be to be deposed, or not deposed.*

To this I answer, that both these assertions are false. For Christians, (or men of what Religion soever,) if they tolerate not their King, whatsoever law hee maketh, though it bee concerning Religion, doe violate their faith, contrary to the Divine Law, both *Naturall* and *Positive*: Nor is there any Judge of Hæresie amongst Subjects, but their owne Civill Soveraign: For *Hæresie is nothing else, but a private opinion, obstinately maintained, contrary* [318] *to the opinion which the Publique Person* (that is to say, the Representant of the Common-wealth) *hath commanded to bee taught*. By which it is manifest, that an opinion publiquely appointed to bee taught, cannot be Hæresie; nor the Soveraign Princes that authorize them, Hæretiques. For Hæretiques are none but private men, that stubbornly defend some Doctrine, prohibited by their lawfull Soveraigns.

But to prove that Christians are not to tolerate Infidell, or Hæreticall Kings, he alledgeth a place in *Deut.* 17. where God forbiddeth the Jews, when they shall set a King over themselves, to choose a stranger: And from thence inferreth, that it is unlawfull for a Christian, to choose a King, that is not a Christian. And 'tis true, that he that is a Christian, that is, hee that hath already obliged himself to receive our Saviour when he shall come, for his King, shal tempt God too much in choosing for King in this world, one that hee knoweth will endeavour, both by terrour, and perswasion to make him violate his faith. But, it is (saith hee) the same danger, to choose one that is not a Christian, for King, and not to depose him, when hee is chosen. To this I say, the question is not of the danger of not deposing; but of the Justice of deposing him. To choose him, may in some cases bee unjust; but to depose him, when he is chosen, is in no case Just. For it is alwaies violation of faith, and consequently against the Law of Nature, which is the eternall Law of God. Nor doe wee read, that any such Doctrine was accounted Christian in the time of the Apostles; nor in the time of the Romane Emperours, till the Popes had the Civill Soveraignty of

Rome. But to this he hath replyed, that the Christians of old, deposed not *Nero*, nor *Dioclesian*, nor *Julian*, nor *Valens* an Arrian,[156] for this cause onely, that they wanted Temporall forces. Perhaps so. But did our Saviour, who for calling for, might have had twelve Legions of immortall, invulnerable Angels to assist him,[157] want forces to depose *Cæsar*, or at least *Pilate*, that unjustly, without finding fault in him, delivered him to the Jews to bee crucified? Or if the Apostles wanted Temporall forces to depose *Nero*, was it therefore necessary for them in their Epistles to the new made Christians, to teach them (as they did) to obey the Powers constituted over them, (whereof *Nero* in that time was one,) and that they ought to obey them, not for fear of their wrath, but for conscience sake?[158] Shall we say they did not onely obey, but also teach what they meant not, for want of strength? It is not therefore for want of strength, but for conscience sake, that Christians are to tolerate their Heathen Princes, or Princes (for I cannot call any one whose Doctrine is the Publique Doctrine, an Hæretique) that authorize the teaching of an Errour. And whereas for the Temporall Power of the Pope, he alledgeth further, that St. Paul (1 *Cor.* 6.) appointed Judges under the Heathen Princes of those times, such as were not ordained by those Princes; it is not true. For St. Paul does but advise them, to take some of their Brethren to compound their differences, as Arbitrators, [319] rather than to goe to law one with another before the Heathen Judges; which is a wholsome Precept, and full of Charity, fit to bee practised also in the best Christian Common-wealths. And for the danger that may arise to Religion, by the Subjects tolerating of an Heathen, or an Erring Prince, it is a point, of which a Subject is no competent Judge; or if hee bee, the Popes Temporall Subjects may judge also of the Popes Doctrine. For every Christian Prince, as I have formerly proved, is no lesse Supreme Pastor of his own Subjects, than the Pope of his.

The fourth Argument, is taken from the Baptisme

of Kings; wherein, that they may be made Christians they submit their Scepters to Christ; and promise to keep, and defend the Christian Faith. This is true; for Christian Kings are no more but Christs Subjects: but they may, for all that, bee the Popes Fellowes; for they are Supreme Pastors of their own Subjects; and the Pope is no more but King, and Pastor, even in Rome it selfe.

The fifth Argument, is drawn from the words spoken by our Saviour, *Feed my sheep*; by which was given all Power necessary for a Pastor; as the Power to chase away Wolves, such as are Hæretiques; the Power to shut up Rammes, if they be mad, or push at the other Sheep with their Hornes, such as are Evill (though Christian) Kings; and Power to give the Flock convenient food: From whence hee inferreth, that St. Peter had these three Powers given him by Christ. To which I answer, that the last of these Powers, is no more than the Power, or rather Command to Teach. For the first, which is to chase away Wolves, that is, Hæretiques, the place hee quoteth is (*Matth.* 7.15.) *Beware of false Prophets which come to you in Sheeps clothing, but inwardly are ravening Wolves.* But neither are Hæretiques false Prophets, or at all Prophets: nor (admitting Hæretiques for the Wolves there meant,) were the Apostles commanded to kill them, or if they were Kings, to depose them; but to beware of, fly, and avoid them: nor was it to St. Peter, nor to any of the Apostles, but to the multitude of the Jews that followed him into the mountain, men for the most part not yet converted, that hee gave this Counsell, to Beware of false Prophets: which therefore if it conferre a Power of chasing away Kings, was given, not onely to private men; but to men that were not at all Christians. And as to the Power of Separating, and Shutting up of furious Rammes, (by which hee meaneth Christian Kings that refuse to submit themselves to the Roman Pastor,) our Saviour refused to take upon him that Power in this world himself, but advised to let the Corn and Tares grow up together[159] till the day of Judgment: much lesse did hee give it to St. Peter, or can S. Peter give it to the Popes. St. Peter, and all other Pastors, are bidden to esteem those Christians that disobey the Church, that is, (that disobey the Christian Soveraigne) as [320] Heathen men, and as Publicans. Seeing then men challenge to the Pope no authority over Heathen Princes, they ought to challenge none over those that are to bee esteemed as Heathen.

But from the Power to Teach onely, hee inferreth also a Coercive Power in the Pope, over Kings. The Pastor (saith he) must give his flock convenient food: Therefore the Pope may, and ought to compell Kings to doe their duty. Out of which it followeth, that the Pope, as Pastor of Christian men, is King of Kings: which all Christian Kings ought indeed either to Confesse, or else they ought to take upon themselves the Supreme Pastorall Charge, every one in his own Dominion.

His sixth, and last Argument, is from Examples. To which I answer, first, that Examples prove nothing: Secondly, that the Examples he alledgeth make not so much as a probability of Right. The fact of Jehoi-ada, in Killing Athaliah (2 *Kings* 11.) was either by the Authority of King Joash, or it was a horrible Crime in the High Priest, which (ever after the election of King Saul) was a mere Subject.[160] The fact of St. Ambrose, in Excommunicating Theodosius the Emperour, (if it were true hee did so,) was a Capitall Crime.[161] And for the Popes, Gregory 1. Greg. 2. Zachary, and Leo 3. their Judgments are void, as given in their own Cause;[162] and the Acts done by them conformably to this Doctrine, are the greatest Crimes (especially that of Zachary) that are incident to Humane Nature. And thus much of *Power Ecclesiasticall*; wherein I had been more briefe, forbear-ing to examine these Arguments of Bellarmine, if they had been his, as a Private man, and not as the Champion of the Papacy, against all other Christian Princes, and States. [321]

Of what is NECESSARY for a Mans
Reception into the Kingdome of Heaven

The most frequent prætext of Sedition, and Civill Warre, *The difficulty* in Christian Common-wealths hath a long time pro- *of obeying* ceeded from a difficulty, not yet sufficiently resolved, of *God and* obeying at once, both God, and Man, then when their *Man both at* Commandements are one contrary to the other. It is *once,* manifest enough, that when a man receiveth two con- trary Commands, and knows that one of them is Gods, he ought to obey that, and not the other, though it be the command even of his lawfull Soveraign (whether a Monarch, or a soveraign Assembly,) or the command of his Father. The difficulty therefore consisteth in this, that men when they are commanded in the name of God, know not in divers Cases, whether the com- mand be from God, or whether he that commandeth, doe but abuse Gods name for some private ends of his own. For as there were in the Church of the Jews, many false Prophets, that sought reputation with the people, by feigned Dreams, and Visions; so there have been in all times in the Church of Christ, false Teachers, that seek reputation with the people, by phantasticall and false Doctrines; and by such reputation (as is the nature of Ambition,) to govern them for their private benefit.

But this difficulty of obeying both God, and the Civ- *Is none to* ill Soveraign on earth, to those that can distinguish *them that* between what is *Necessary*, and what is not *Necessary* *distinguish* for their *Reception* into the *Kingdome of God*, is of no *between* moment. For if the command of the Civill Soveraign bee *what is, and* such, as that it may be obeyed, without the forfeiture *what is not* of life Eternall; not to obey it is unjust; and the precept *Necessary to* of the Apostle takes place; *Servants obey your Masters* *Salvation* *in all things*; and, *Children obey your Parents in all* *things*; and the precept of our Saviour, *The Scribes and*

Pharisees sit in Moses Chaire,[163] *All therefore they shall say, that observe, and doe.* But if the command be such, as cannot be obeyed, without being damned to Eternall Death, then it were madnesse to obey it, and the Counsell of our Saviour takes place, (*Mat.* 10. 28.) *Fear not those that kill the body, but cannot kill the soule.* All men therefore that would avoid, both the punishments that are to be in this world inflicted, for disobedience to their earthly Soveraign, and those that shall be inflicted in the world to come for disobedience to God, have need be taught to distinguish well between what is, and what is not Necessary to Eternall Salvation.

[322] All that is NECESSARY *to Salvation*, is contained in two Vertues, *Faith in Christ*, and *Obedience to Laws*. The latter of these, if it were perfect, were enough to us. But because wee are all guilty of disobedience to Gods Law, not onely originally in Adam, but also actually by our own transgressions, there is required at our hands now, not onely *Obedience* for the rest of our time, but also a *Remission* of sins for the time past; which Remission is the reward of our Faith in Christ. That nothing else is Necessarily required to Salvation, is manifest from this, that the Kingdome of Heaven is shut to none but to Sinners; that is to say, to the disobedient, or transgressors of the Law; nor to them, in case they Repent, and Beleeve all the Articles of Christian Faith, Necessary to Salvation.

The Obedience required at our hands by God, that accepteth in all our actions the Will for the Deed, is a serious Endeavour to Obey him; and is called also by all such names as signifie that Endeavour. And therefore Obedience, is sometimes called by the names of *Charity*, and *Love*, because they imply a Will to Obey; and our Saviour himself maketh our Love to God, and to one another, a Fulfilling of the whole Law: and sometimes by the name of *Righteousnesse*; for Righteousnesse is but the will to give to every one his owne, that is to say, the will to obey the Laws: and sometimes by the name of *Repentance*; because to Repent, implyeth a turning away from sinne, which is the same, with the return of the will to Obedience. Whosoever therefore unfeignedly desireth to fulfill the Commandements of God, or repenteth him truely of his transgressions, or that loveth God with all his heart, and his neighbor as himself, hath all the Obedience Necessary to his Reception into the Kingdom of God: For if God should require perfect Innocence, there could no flesh be saved.

But what Commandements are those that God hath *And to what* given us? Are all those Laws which were given to the *Laws* Jews by the hand of Moses, the Commandements of God? If they bee, why are not Christians taught to Obey them? If they be not, what others are so, besides the Law of Nature? For our Saviour Christ hath not given us new Laws, but Counsell to observe those wee are subject to; that is to say, the Laws of Nature, and the Laws of our severall Soveraigns: Nor did he make any new Law to the Jews in his Sermon on the Mount, but onely expounded the Laws of Moses, to which they were subject before. The Laws of God therefore are none but the Laws of Nature, whereof the principall is, that we should not violate our Faith, that is, a commandement to obey our Civill Soveraigns, which wee constituted over us, by mutuall pact one with another. And this Law of God, that commandeth Obedience to the Law Civill, commandeth by consequence Obedience to all the Precepts of the Bible; which (as I have proved in the precedent Chapter) is there onely Law, where the Civill Soveraign hath made it so; and in other places but Counsell; which a man at his own perill, may without injustice refuse to obey.

[323] Knowing now what is the Obedience Necessary *In the Faith* to Salvation, and to whom it is due; we are to consider *of a Christian,* next concerning Faith, whom, and why we beleeve; *who is the* and what are the Articles, or Points necessarily to be *Person* beleeved by them that shall be saved. And first, for the *beleeved* Person whom we beleeve, because it is impossible to

beleeve any Person, before we know what he saith, it is
necessary he be one that wee have heard speak. The Person therefore, whom Abraham, Isaac, Jacob, Moses and
the Prophets beleeved, was God himself, that spake unto
them supernaturally: And the Person, whom the Apostles and Disciples that conversed with Christ beleeved,
was our Saviour himself. But of them, to whom neither
God the Father, nor our Saviour ever spake, it cannot
be said, that the Person whom they beleeved, was God.
They beleeved the Apostles, and after them the Pastors
and Doctors of the Church, that recommended to their
faith the History of the Old and New Testament: so that
the Faith of Christians ever since our Saviours time, hath
had for foundation, first, the reputation of their Pastors,
and afterward, the authority of those that made the
Old and New Testament to be received for the Rule of
Faith; which none could do but Christian Soveraignes;
who are therefore the Supreme Pastors, and the onely
Persons, whom Christians now hear speak from God;
except such as God speaketh to, in these days supernaturally. But because there be many false Prophets *gone
out into the world*, other men are to examine such Spirits (as St. *John* adviseth us, 1 Epistle, Chap. 4. ver. 1.)
whether they be of God, or not. And therefore, seeing
the Examination of Doctrines belongeth to the Supreme
Pastor, the Person which all they that have no speciall
revelation are to beleeve, is (in every Common-wealth)
the Supreme Pastor, that is to say, the Civill Soveraigne.

The causes   The causes why men beleeve any Christian Doctrine,
of Christian are various: For Faith is the gift of God; and he worketh
Faith it in each severall man, by such wayes, as it seemeth
good unto himself. The most ordinary immediate cause
of our beleef, concerning any point of Christian Faith,
is, that wee beleeve the Bible to be the Word of God.
But why wee beleeve the Bible to be the Word of God,
is much disputed, as all questions must needs bee, that
are not well stated. For they make not the question to
be, *Why we Beleeve it*, but, *How wee Know it*; as if

Beleeving and *Knowing* were all one. And thence while one side ground their Knowledge upon the Infallibility of the Church, and the other side, on the Testimony of the Private Spirit, neither side concludeth what it pretends. For how shall a man know the Infallibility of the Church, but by knowing first the Infallibility of the Scripture? Or how shall a man know his own Private spirit to be other than a beleef, grounded upon the Authority, and Arguments of his Teachers; or upon a Presumption of his own Gifts? Besides, there is nothing in the Scripture, from which can be inferred the Infallibility of the Church; much lesse, of any particular Church; and least of all, the Infallibility of any particular man.

[324] It is manifest therefore, that Christian men *Faith comes* doe not know, but onely beleeve the Scripture to be *by Hearing* the Word of God; and that the means of making them beleeve which God is pleased to afford men ordinarily, is according to the way of Nature, that is to say, from their Teachers. It is the Doctrine of St. Paul concerning Christian Faith in generall, (*Rom.* 10. 17.) *Faith cometh by Hearing*, that is, by Hearing our lawfull Pastors. He saith also (ver. 14, 15. of the same Chapter) *How shall they beleeve in him of whom they have not heard? and how shall they hear without a Preacher? and how shall they Preach, except they be sent?* Whereby it is evident, that the ordinary cause of beleeving that the Scriptures are the Word of God, is the same with the cause of the beleeving of all other Articles of our Faith, namely, the Hearing of those that are by the Law allowed and appointed to Teach us, as our Parents in their Houses, and our Pastors in the Churches: Which also is made more manifest by experience. For what other cause can there bee assigned, why in Christian Common-wealths all men either beleeve, or at least professe the Scripture to bee the Word of God, and in other Common-wealths scarce any; but that in Christian Common-wealths they are taught it from their infancy; and in other places they are taught otherwise?

But if Teaching be the cause of Faith, why doe not all beleeve? It is certain therefore that Faith is the gift of God, and hee giveth it to whom he will. Neverthelesse, because to them to whom he giveth it, he giveth it by the means of Teachers, the immediate cause of Faith is Hearing. In a School, where many are taught, and some profit, others profit not, the cause of learning in them that profit, is the Master; yet it cannot be thence inferred, that learning is not the gift of God. All good things proceed from God; yet cannot all that have them, say they are Inspired; for that implies a gift supernaturall, and the immediate hand of God; which he that pretends to, pretends to be a Prophet, and is subject to the examination of the Church.

But whether men *Know*, or *Beleeve*, or *Grant* the Scriptures to be the Word of God; if out of such places of them, as are without obscurity, I shall shew what Articles of Faith are necessary, and onely necessary for Salvation, those men must needs *Know*, *Beleeve*, or *Grant* the same.

The onely Necessary Article of Christian Faith; The (*Unum Necessarium*) Onely Article of Faith, which the Scripture maketh simply Necessary to Salvation, is this, that JESUS IS THE CHRIST. By the name of *Christ*, is understood the King, which God had before promised by the Prophets of the Old Testament, to send into the world, to reign (over the Jews, and over such of other nations as should beleeve in him) under himself eternally; and to give them that eternall life, which was lost by the sin of Adam. Which when I have proved out of Scripture, I will further shew when, and in what sense some other Articles may bee also called *Necessary*.

Proved from the Scope of the Evangelists: [325] For Proof that the Beleef of this Article, *Jesus is the Christ*, is all the Faith required to Salvation, my first Argument shall bee from the Scope of the Evangelists; which was by the description of the life of our Saviour, to establish that one Article, *Jesus is the Christ*. The summe of St. Matthews Gospell is this, That Jesus was of the stock of David; Born of a Virgin; which are the

Marks of the true Christ: That the *Magi* came to worship him as King of the Jews: That Herod for the same
cause sought to kill him:[164] That John Baptist proclaimed
him: That he preached by himselfe, and his Apostles
that he was that King: That he taught the Law, not as
a Scribe, but as a man of Authority: That he cured diseases by his Word onely, and did many other Miracles,
which were foretold the Christ should doe: That he was
saluted King when hee entered into Jerusalem: That he
fore-warned them to beware of all others that should
pretend to be Christ: That he was taken, accused, and
put to death, for saying, hee was King: That the cause
of his condemnation written on the Crosse, was JESUS
OF NAZARETH, THE KING OF THE JEWES. All which
tend to no other end than this, that men should beleeve,
that *Jesus is the Christ*. Such therefore was the Scope
of St. Matthews Gospel. But the Scope of all the Evangelists (as may appear by reading them) was the same.
Therefore the Scope of the whole Gospell, was the
establishing of that onely Article. And St. John expressely makes it his conclusion, *John* 20. 31. *These things
are written, that you may know that Jesus is the Christ,
the Son of the living God.*

My second Argument is taken from the Subject of the *From the*
Sermons of the Apostles, both whilest our Saviour lived *Sermons of*
on earth, and after his Ascension. The Apostles in our *the Apostles:*
Saviours time were sent, *Luke* 9. 2. to Preach the Kingdome of God: For neither there, nor *Mat.* 10. 7. giveth
he any Commission to them, other than this, *As ye go,
Preach, saying, the Kingdome of Heaven is at hand*; that
is, that *Jesus* is the *Messiah*, the *Christ*, the *King* which
was to come. That their Preaching also after his ascension was the same, is manifest out of *Acts* 17. 6. *They
drew* (saith St. Luke) *Jason and certain Brethren unto
the Rulers of the City, crying, These that have turned
the world upside down are come hither also, whom
Jason hath received. And these all do contrary to the
Decrees of Cæsar, saying, that there is another King, one*

Jesus: And out of the 2. & 3. verses of the same Chapter, where it is said, that St. *Paul as his manner was, went in unto them; and three Sabbath dayes reasoned with them out of the Scriptures; opening and alledging, that Christ must needs have suffered, and risen againe from the dead, and that this Jesus (whom hee preached) is Christ.*

From the Easinesse of the Doctrine: The third Argument is, from those places of Scripture, by which all the Faith required to Salvation is declared to be Easie. For if an inward assent of the mind to all the Doctrines concerning Christian Faith now taught, (whereof the greatest part are disputed,) were necessary to Salvation, there would be nothing in the world so hard, as to be a Christian. The Thief upon the Crosse though repenting, [326] could not have been saved for saying, *Lord remember me when thou commest into thy Kingdome;*[165] by which he testified no beleefe of any other Article, but this, That *Jesus was the King.* Nor could it bee said (as it is *Mat.* 11. 30.) that *Christs yoke is Easy, and his burthen Light*: Nor that *Little Children beleeve in him,* as it is *Matth.* 18. 6. Nor could St. Paul have said (1 *Cor.* 1. 21.) *It pleased God by the Foolishnesse of preaching, to save them that beleeve*: Nor could St. Paul himself have been saved, much lesse have been so great a Doctor of the Church so suddenly, that never perhaps thought of Transubstantiation, nor Purgatory, nor many other Articles now obtruded.

From formall and cleer texts The fourth Argument is taken from places expresse, and such as receive no controversie of Interpretation; as first, *John* 5. 39. *Search the Scriptures, for in them yee thinke yee have eternall life; and they are they that testifie of mee.* Our Saviour here speaketh of the Scriptures onely of the Old Testament; for the Jews at that time could not search the Scriptures of the New Testament, which were not written. But the Old Testament hath nothing of Christ, but the Markes by which men might know him when hee came; as that he should descend from David; be born at Bethlem, and of a Virgin; doe great Miracles, and the like. Therefore to beleeve that this Jesus was He, was sufficient to eternall life: but more than sufficient is not Necessary; and consequently no other Article is required. Again, (*John* 11. 26.) *Whosoever liveth and beleeveth in mee, shall not die eternally*, Therefore to beleeve in Christ, is faith sufficient to eternall life; and consequently no more faith than that is Necessary, But to beleeve in Jesus, and to beleeve that Jesus is the Christ, is all one, as appeareth in the verses immediately following. For when our Saviour (verse 26.) had said to Martha,[166] *Beelevest thou this?* she answereth (verse 27.) *Yea Lord, I beleeve that thou art the Christ, the Son of God, which should come into the world*: Therefore this Article alone is faith sufficient to life eternall; and more than sufficient is not Necessary. Thirdly, *John* 20. 31. *These things are written that yee might beleeve, that Jesus is the Christ, the Son of God, and that beleeving yee might have life through his name.* There, to beleeve that *Jesus is the Christ*, is faith sufficient to the obtaining of life; and therefore no other Article is Necessary. Fourthly, 1 *John* 4. 2. *Every spirit that confesseth that Jesus Christ is come in the flesh, is of God.* And 1 *Joh.* 5. 1. *Whosoever beleeveth that Jesus is the Christ, is born of God.* And verse 5. *Who is hee that overcommeth the world, but he that beleeveth that Jesus is the Son of God?* Fiftly, *Act.* 8. ver. 36, 37. See (saith the Eunuch) *here is water, what doth hinder me to be baptized? And Philip said, If thou beleevest with all thy heart thou mayst. And hee answered and said, I beleeve that Jesus Christ is the Son of God.* Therefore this Article beleeved, *Jesus is the Christ*, is sufficient to Baptisme, that is to say, to our Reception into the Kingdome of God, and by consequence, onely Necessary. And generally in all places where our Saviour saith to any man, *Thy* [327] *faith hath saved thee*, the cause he saith it, is some Confession, which directly, or by consequence, implyeth a beleef, that *Jesus is the Christ*.

The last Argument is from the places, where this Article is made the Foundation of Faith: For he that

From that it is the Foundation of all other Articles

holdeth the Foundation shall bee saved. Which places
are first, *Mat.* 24.23. *If any man shall say unto you,
Loe, here is Christ, or there, beleeve it not, for there
shall arise false Christs, and false Prophets, and shall
shew great signes and wonders, &c.* Here wee see, this
Article *Jesus is the Christ,* must bee held, though hee
that shall teach the contrary should doe great miracles.
The second place is, *Gal.* 1.8. *Though we, or an Angell
from Heaven preach any other Gospell unto you, than
that wee have preached unto you, let him bee accursed.*
But the Gospell which Paul, and the other Apostles,
preached, was onely this Article, that *Jesus is the Christ*:
Therefore for the Beleef of this Article, we are to reject
the Authority of an Angell from heaven; much more of
any mortall man, if he teach the contrary. This is therefore the Fundamentall Article of Christian Faith. A third
place is, 1 *Joh.* 4.1. *Beloved, beleeve not every spirit.
Hereby yee shall know the Spirit of God; every spirit
that confesseth that Jesus Christ is come in the flesh, is
of God.* By which it is evident, that this Article, is the
measure, and rule, by which to estimate, and examine
all other Articles; and is therefore onely Fundamentall.
A fourth is, *Matt.* 16.18. where after St. Peter had professed this Article, saying to our Saviour, *Thou art Christ
the Son of the living God,* Our Saviour answered, *Thou
art Peter, and upon this Rock I will build my Church*:
from whence I inferre, that this Article is that, on which
all other Doctrines of the Church are built, as on their
Foundation. A fift is (1 *Cor.* 3. ver. 11, 12, &c.) *Other
Foundation can no man lay, than that which is laid, Jesus
is the Christ. Now if any man build upon this Foundation, Gold, Silver, pretious Stones, Wood, Hay, Stubble;
Every mans work shall be made manifest; For the Day
shall declare it, because it shall be revealed by fire, and
the fire shall try every mans work, of what sort it is. If
any mans work abide, which he hath built thereupon, he
shall receive a reward: If any mans work shall bee burnt,
he shall suffer losse; but he himself shall be saved, yet so*

as by fire. Which words, being partly plain and easie to understand, and partly allegoricall and difficult; out of that which is plain, may be inferred, that Pastors that teach this Foundation, that *Jesus is the Christ*, though they draw from it false consequences, (which all men are sometimes subject to,) they may neverthelesse bee saved; much more that they may bee saved, who being no Pastors, but Hearers, beleeve that which is by their lawfull Pastors taught them. Therefore the beleef of this Article is sufficient; and by consequence, there is no other Article of Faith Necessarily required to Salvation.

[328] Now for the part which is Allegoricall, as *That the fire shall try every mans work*, and that *They shall be saved, but so as by fire*, or *through fire*, (for the originall is διὰ πυρός,) it maketh nothing against this conclusion which I have drawn from the other words, that are plain. Neverthelesse, because upon this place there hath been an argument taken, to prove the fire of Purgatory, I will also here offer you my conjecture concerning the meaning of this triall of Doctrines, and saving of men as by Fire. The Apostle here seemeth to allude to the words of the Prophet Zachary,[167] Ch. 13.8, 9. who speaking of the Restauration of the Kingdome of God, saith thus, *Two parts therein shall be cut off, and die, but the third shall be left therein; And I will bring the third part through the Fire, and will refine them as Silver is refined, and will try them as Gold is tryed; they shall call on the name of the Lord, and I will hear them.* The day of Judgment, is the day of the Restauration of the Kingdome of God; and at that day it is, that St. Peter tells us * shall be the Conflagration of the world, wherein the wicked shall perish; but the remnant which God will save, shall passe through that Fire, unhurt, and be therein (as Silver and Gold are refined by the fire from their drosse) tryed, and refined from their Idolatry, and be made to call upon the name of the true God. Alluding whereto St. Paul here saith, That *the Day* (that is, the Day of Judgment, the Great Day of our

*2 Pet. 3. v. 7, 10, 12

Saviours comming to restore the Kingdome of God in
Israel) shall try every mans doctrine, by Judging, which
are Gold, Silver, Pretious Stones, Wood, Hay, Stubble;
And then they that have built false Consequences on the
true Foundation, shall see their Doctrines condemned;
neverthelesse they themselves shall be saved, and passe
unhurt through this universall Fire, and live eternally, to
call upon the name of the true and onely God. In which
sense there is nothing that accordeth not with the rest of
Holy Scripture, or any glimpse of the fire of Purgatory.

In what sense   But a man may here aske, whether it bee not as neces-
other Articles sary to Salvation, to beleeve, that God is Omnipotent;
may be called Creator of the world; that Jesus Christ is risen; and that
Necessary   all men else shall rise again from the dead at the last day;
as to beleeve, that *Jesus is the Christ*. To which I answer,
they are; and so are many more Articles: but they are
such, as are contained in this one, and may be deduced
from it, with more, or lesse difficulty. For who is there
that does not see, that they who beleeve Jesus to be the
Son of the God of Israel, and that the Israelites had for
God the Omnipotent Creator of all things, doe therein
also beleeve, that God is the Omnipotent Creator of all
things? Or how can a man beleeve, that Jesus is the King
that shall reign eternally, unlesse hee beleeve him also
risen again from the dead? For a dead man cannot exercise the Office of a King. In summe, he that holdeth this
Foundation, *Jesus is the Christ*, holdeth Expressely all
that hee seeth rightly deduced from it, and Implicitely all
that is consequent thereunto, though he have not skill
enough to discern the consequence. And [329] therefore
it holdeth still good, that the beleef of this one Article
is sufficient faith to obtain remission of sinnes to the
That Faith,   *Penitent*, and consequently to bring them into the King-
and Obedi- dome of Heaven.
ence are   Now that I have shewn, that all the Obedience required
both of them to Salvation, consisteth in the will to obey the Law of
Necessary to God, that is to say, in Repentance; and all the Faith
Salvation   required to the same, is comprehended in the beleef

of this Article *Jesus is the Christ*; I will further alledge those places of the Gospell, that prove, that all that is Necessary to Salvation is contained in both these joined together. The men to whom St. Peter preached on the day of Pentecost, next after the Ascension of our Saviour, asked him, and the rest of the Apostles, saying, (*Act.* 2.37.) *Men and Brethren what shall we doe?* To whom St. Peter answered (in the next verse) *Repent, and be Baptized every one of you, for the remission of sins, and ye shall receive the gift of the Holy Ghost.* Therefore Repentance, and Baptisme, that is, beleeving that *Jesus is the Christ*, is all that is Necessary to Salvation. Again, our Saviour being asked by a certain Ruler, (*Luke* 18.18.) *What shall I doe to inherite eternall life?* Answered (verse 20.) *Thou knowest the Commandements, Doe not commit Adultery, Doe not Kill, Doe not Steal, Doe not bear false witnesse, Honor thy Father, and thy Mother*: which when he said he had observed, our Saviour added, *Sell all thou hast, give it to the Poor, and come and follow me*: which was as much as to say, Relye on me that am the King: Therefore to fulfill the Law, and to beleeve that Jesus is the King, is all that is required to bring a man to eternall life. Thirdly, St. Paul saith (*Rom.* 1.17.) *The Just shall live by Faith*; not every one, but the *Just*; therefore *Faith* and *Justice* (that is, the *will to be Just*, or *Repentance*) are all that is Necessary to life eternall. And (*Mark* 1.15.) our Saviour preached, saying, *The time is fulfilled, and the Kingdom of God is at hand, Repent and Beleeve the Evangile*, that is, the Good news that the Christ was come. Therefore to Repent, and to Beleeve that Jesus is the Christ, is all that is required to Salvation.

Seeing then it is Necessary that Faith, and Obedience (implyed in the word Repentance) do both concurre to our Salvation; the question by which of the two we are Justified, is impertinently disputed. Neverthelesse, it will not be impertinent, to make manifest in what manner each of them contributes thereunto; and in what sense

What each of them contributes thereunto

it is said, that we are to be Justified by the one, and
by the other. And first, if by Righteousnesse be understood the Justice of the Works themselves, there is no
man that can be saved; for there is none that hath not
transgressed the Law of God. And therefore when wee
are said to be Justified by Works, it is to be understood
of the Will, which God doth alwaies accept for the Work
it selfe, as well in good, as in evill men. And in this sense
onely it is, that a man is called *Just*, or *Unjust*; and that
his Justice Justifies him, that is, gives him the title, in
Gods acceptation, of *Just*; and renders him capable of
living by his Faith, which before he was not. So that
Justice Justi[330]fies in that sense, in which to *Justifie*, is
the same that to *Denominate a man Just*; and not in the
signification of discharging the Law; whereby the punishment of his sins should be unjust.

But a man is then also said to be Justified, when his
Plea, though in it selfe unsufficient, is accepted; as when
we Plead our Will, our Endeavour to fulfill the Law, and
Repent us of our failings, and God accepteth it for the
Performance it selfe: And because God accepteth not the
Will for the Deed, but onely in the Faithfull; it is therefore Faith that makes good our Plea; and in this sense
it is, that Faith onely Justifies: So that *Faith* and *Obedience* are both Necessary to Salvation; yet in severall
senses each of them is said to Justifie.

Obedience   Having thus shewn what is Necessary to Salvation;
to God and it is not hard to reconcile our Obedience to God, with
to the Civill our Obedience to the Civill Soveraign; who is either
Soveraign   Christian, or Infidel. If he bee a Christian, he alloweth
not inconsis- the beleefe of this Article, that *Jesus is the Christ*; and
tent, whether of all the Articles that are contained in, or are by evi-
Christian,   dent consequence deduced from it: which is all the Faith
Necessary to Salvation. And because he is a Soveraign,
he requireth Obedience to all his owne, that is, to all the
Civill Laws; in which also are contained all the Laws of
Nature, that is, all the Laws of God: for besides the Laws
of Nature, and the Laws of the Church, which are part

of the Civill Law, (for the Church that can make Laws is the Common-wealth,) there bee no other Laws Divine. Whosoever therefore obeyeth his Christian Soveraign, is not thereby hindred, neither from beleeving, nor from obeying God. But suppose that a Christian King should from this Foundation *Jesus is the Christ*, draw some false consequences, that is to say, make some superstructions of Hay, or Stubble, and command the teaching of the same; yet seeing St. Paul says, he shal be saved;[168] much more shall he be saved, that teacheth them by his command; and much more yet, he that teaches not, but onely beleeves his lawfull Teacher. And in case a Subject be forbidden by the Civill Soveraign to professe some of those his opinions, upon what just ground can he disobey? Christian Kings may erre in deducing a Consequence, but who shall Judge? Shall a private man Judge, when the question is of his own obedience? or shall any man Judg but he that is appointed thereto by the Church, that is, by the Civill Soveraign that representeth it? or if the Pope, or an Apostle Judge, may he not erre in deducing of a consequence? did not one of the two, St. Peter, or St. Paul erre in a superstructure, when St. Paul withstood St. Peter to his face?[169] There can therefore be no contradiction between the Laws of God, and the Laws of a Christian Common-wealth.

And when the Civill Soveraign is an Infidel, every one *Or Infidel* of his own Subjects that resisteth him, sinneth against the Laws of God (for such as are the Laws of Nature,) and rejecteth the counsell of the Apostles, that admonisheth all Christians to obey their Princes, and all Children and Servants to obey their Parents, and Masters, in all [331] things. And for their *Faith*, it is internall, and invisible; They have the licence that Naaman had,[170] and need not put themselves into danger for it. But if they do, they ought to expect their reward in Heaven, and not complain of their Lawfull Soveraign; much lesse make warre upon him. For he that is not glad of any just occasion of Martyrdome, has not the faith he professeth, but pretends it onely, to set some colour upon his own contumacy. But what Infidel King is so unreasonable, as knowing he has a Subject, that waiteth for the second comming of Christ, after the present world shall bee burnt, and intendeth then to obey him (which is the intent of beleeving that Jesus is the Christ,) and in the mean time thinketh himself bound to obey the Laws of that Infidel King, (which all Christians are obliged in conscience to doe,) to put to death, or to persecute such a Subject?

And thus much shall suffice, concerning the Kingdome of God, and Policy Ecclesiasticall. Wherein I pretend not to advance any Position of my own, but onely to shew what are the Consequences that seem to me deducible from the Principles of Christian Politiques, (which are the holy Scriptures,) in confirmation of the Power of Civill Soverains, and the Duty of their Subjects. And in the allegation of Scripture, I have endeavoured to avoid such texts as are of obscure, or controverted Interpretation; and to alledge none, but in such sense as is most plain, and agreeable to the harmony and scope of the whole Bible; which was written for the re-establishment of the Kingdome of God in Christ. For it is not the bare Words, but the Scope of the writer that giveth the true light, by which any writing is to bee interpreted; and they that insist upon single Texts, without considering the main Designe, can derive no thing from them cleerly; but rather by casting atomes of Scripture, as dust before mens eyes, make every thing more obscure than it is; an ordinary artifice of those that seek not the truth, but their own advantage. [333]

PART FOUR

OF THE KINGDOME
OF DARKNESSE

CHAP. XLIV

Of Spirituall Darknesse from
MISINTERPRETATION of Scripture

Besides these Soveraign Powers, *Divine*, and *Humane*,
of which I have hitherto discoursed, there is mention in
Scripture of another Power, namely, * that of *the Rulers
of the Darknesse of this world,* * *the Kingdome of Satan,*
and * *the Principality of Beelzebub over Dæmons,* that
is to say, over Phantasmes that appear in the Air: For
which cause Satan is also called * *the Prince of the
Power of the Air*; and (because he ruleth in the darknesse of this world) * *The Prince of this world*: And in
consequence hereunto, they who are under his Dominion, in opposition to the faithfull (who are the *Children
of the Light*) are called the *Children of Darknesse.* For
seeing Beelzebub is Prince of Phantasmes, Inhabitants
of his Dominion of Air and Darknesse, the Children of
Darknesse, and these Dæmons, Phantasmes, or Spirits
of Illusion, signifie allegorically the same thing. This
considered, the Kingdome of Darknesse, as it is set forth
in these, and other places of the Scripture, is nothing
else but a *Confederacy of Deceivers, that to obtain
dominion over men in this present world, endeavour by
dark, and erroneous Doctrines, to extinguish in them
the Light, both of Nature, and of the Gospell; and so
to dis-prepare them for the Kingdome of God to come.*

*The Kingdom
of Darkness
what*

*Eph. 6. 12

*Mat. 12. 26

*Mat. 9. 34

*Eph. 2. 2

*Joh. 16. 11

The Church [334] As men that are utterly deprived from their
not yet fully Nativity, of the light of the bodily Eye, have no Idea
freed of at all, of any such light; and no man conceives in his
Darknesse imagination any greater light, than he hath at some
time, or other, perceived by his outward Senses: so also
is it of the light of the Gospel, and of the light of the
Understanding, that no man can conceive there is any
greater degree of it, than that which he hath already
attained unto. And from hence it comes to passe, that
men have no other means to acknowledge their owne
Darknesse, but onely by reasoning from the un-foreseen
mischances, that befall them in their ways; The Darkest
part of the Kingdom of Satan, is that which is without
the Church of God; that is to say, amongst them that
beleeve not in Jesus Christ. But we cannot say, that
therefore the Church enjoyeth (as the land of Goshen)[1]
all the light, which to the performance of the work
enjoined us by God, is necessary. Whence comes it, that
in Christendome there has been, almost from the time
of the Apostles, such justling of one another out of their
places, both by forraign, and Civill war? such stumbling
at every little asperity of their own fortune, and every
little eminence of that of other men? and such diversity
of ways in running to the same mark, *Felicity*, if it be not
Night amongst us, or at least a Mist? wee are therefore
yet in the Dark.

Four Causes The Enemy has been here in the Night of our naturall
of Spiritual Ignorance, and sown the tares of Spirituall Errors; and
Darknesse that, First, by abusing, and putting out the light of the
Scriptures: For we erre, not knowing the Scriptures. Secondly, by introducing the Dæmonology of the Heathen
Poets, that is to say, their fabulous Doctrine concerning Dæmons, which are but Idols, or Phantasms of the
braine, without any reall nature of their own, distinct
from humane fancy; such as are dead mens Ghosts, and
Fairies, and other matter of old Wives tales. Thirdly, by
mixing with the Scripture divers reliques of the Religion, and much of the vain and erroneous Philosophy

of the Greeks, especially of Aristotle. Fourthly, by min-
gling with both these, false, or uncertain Traditions, and
fained, or uncertain History. And so we come to erre, by
giving heed to seducing Spirits, and the Dæmonology of
such *as speak lies in Hypocrisie*, (or as it is in the Originall, 1 *Tim.* 4.1, 2. *of those that play the part of lyars*)
with a seared conscience, that is, contrary to their own
knowledge. Concerning the first of these, which is the
Seducing of men by abuse of Scripture, I intend to speak
briefly in this Chapter.

The greatest, and main abuse of Scripture, and to
which almost all the rest are either consequent, or subservient, is the wresting of it, to prove that the Kingdome
of God, mentioned so often in the Scripture, is the present Church, or multitude of Christian men now living, or
that being dead, are to rise again at the last day: whereas
the Kingdome of God was first instituted by the Ministery of Moses, over the Jews onely; who were therefore
called his Peculiar People; and ceased afterward, in the
election of Saul, when they refused to be governed by
God any more, and demanded a King after the [335]
manner of the nations; which God himself consented
unto, as I have more at large proved before, in the 35.
Chapter. After that time, there was no other Kingdome
of God in the world, by any Pact, or otherwise, than
he ever was, is, and shall be King, of all men, and of
all creatures, as governing according to his Will, by his
infinite Power. Neverthelesse, he promised by his Prophets to restore this his Government to them again, when
the time he hath in his secret counsell appointed for it
shall bee fully come, and when they shall turn unto him
by repentance, and amendment of life: and not onely so,
but he invited also the Gentiles to come in, and enjoy
the happinesse of his Reign, on the same conditions of
conversion and repentance; and hee promised also to
send his Son into the world, to expiate the sins of them
all by his death, and to prepare them by his Doctrine, to
receive him at his second coming: Which second coming

Errors from
misinter-
preting the
Scriptures,
concerning
the Kingdome
of God

not yet being, the Kingdome of God is not yet come, and wee are not now under any other Kings by Pact, but our Civill Soveraigns; saving onely, that Christian men are already in the Kingdome of Grace, in as much as they have already the Promise of being received at his comming againe.

As that the Kingdome of God is the present Church: Consequent to this Errour, that the present Church is Christs Kingdome, there ought to be some one Man, or Assembly, by whose mouth our Saviour (now in heaven) speaketh, giveth law, and which representeth his Person to all Christians, or divers Men, or divers Assemblies that doe the same to divers parts of Christendome. This power Regal under Christ, being challenged, universally by the Pope, and in particular Common-wealths by Assemblies of the Pastors of the place, (when the Scripture gives it to none but to Civill Soveraigns,) comes to be so passionately disputed, that it putteth out the Light of Nature, and causeth so great a Darknesse in mens understanding, that they see not who it is to whom they have engaged their obedience.

And that the Pope is his Vicar generall: Consequent to this claim of the Pope to Vicar Generall of Christ in the present Church, (supposed to be that Kingdom of his, to which we are addressed in the Gospel,) is the Doctrine, that it is necessary for a Christian King, to receive his Crown by a Bishop; as if it were from that Ceremony, that he derives the clause of *Dei gratiâ* in his title; and that then onely he is made King by the favour of God, when he is crowned by the authority of Gods universall Vicegerent on earth; and that every Bishop whosoever be his Soveraign, taketh at his Consecration an oath of absolute Obedience to the Pope. Consequent to the same, is the Doctrine of the fourth Councell of Lateran, held under Pope *Innocent* the third, (Chap. 3. de Hæreticis.) *That if a King at the Popes admonition, doe not purge his Kingdome of Hæresies, and being excommunicate for the same, doe not give satisfaction within a year, his Subjects are absolved of the bond of their obedience.* Where, by Hæresies are understood all opinions which the Church of Rome hath forbidden to be maintained. And by this means, as often as [336] there is any repugnancy between the Politicall designes of the Pope, and other Christian Princes, as there is very often, there ariseth such a Mist amongst their Subjects, that they know not a stranger that thrusteth himself into the throne of their lawfull Prince, from him whom they had themselves placed there; and in this Darknesse of mind, are made to fight one against another, without discerning their enemies from their friends, under the conduct of another mans ambition.

From the same opinion, that the present Church is the Kingdome of God, it proceeds that Pastours, Deacons, and all other Ministers of the Church, take the name to themselves of the *Clergy*; giving to other Christians the name of *Laity*, that is, simply *People*. For Clergy signifies those, whose maintenance is that Revenue, which God having reserved to himselfe during his Reigne over the Israelites, assigned to the tribe of Levi (who were to be his publique Ministers, and had no portion of land set them out to live on, as their brethren) to be their inheritance.[2] The Pope therefore, (pretending the present Church to be, as the Realme of Israel, the Kingdome of God) challenging to himselfe and his subordinate Ministers, the like revenue, as the Inheritance of God, the name of Clergy was sutable to that claime. And thence it is, that Tithes, and other tributes paid to the Levites, as Gods Right, amongst the Israelites, have a long time been demanded, and taken of Christians, by Ecclesiastiques, *Jure divino*, that is, in Gods Right. By which meanes, the people every where were obliged to a double tribute; one to the State, another to the Clergy; whereof, that to the Clergy, being the tenth of their revenue, is double to that which a King of Athens (and esteemed a Tyrant) exacted of his subjects for the defraying of all publique charges: For he demanded no more but the twentieth part; and yet abundantly maintained therewith the Commonwealth. And in the Kingdome of the

And that the Pastors are the Clergy

Jewes, during the Sacerdotall Reigne of God, the Tithes and Offerings were the whole Publique Revenue.

From the same mistaking of the present Church for the Kingdom of God, came in the distinction betweene the *Civill* and the *Canon* Laws: The Civil Law being the Acts of *Soveraigns* in their own Dominions, and the Canon Law being the Acts of the *Pope* in the same Dominions. Which Canons, though they were but Canons, that is, *Rules Propounded*, and but voluntarily received by Christian Princes, till the translation of the Empire to *Charlemain*; yet afterwards, as the power of the Pope encreased, became *Rules Commanded*, and the Emperours themselves (to avoyd greater mischiefes, which the people blinded might be led into) were forced to let them passe for Laws.

From hence it is, that in all Dominions, where the Popes Ecclesiasticall power is entirely received, Jewes, Turkes, and Gentiles, are in the Roman Church tolerated in their Religion, as farre forth, as in the exercise and profession thereof they offend not against the civill power: whereas in a Christian, though a stranger, not to be of the Roman Religion, is Capitall; because the Pope pretendeth that all [337] Christians are his Subjects. For otherwise it were as much against the law of Nations, to persecute a Christian stranger, for professing the Religion of his owne country, as an Infidell; or rather more, in as much as they that are not against Christ, are with him.

From the same it is, that in every Christian State there are certaine men, that are exempt, by Ecclesiasticall liberty, from the tributes, and from the tribunals of the Civil State; for so are the secular Clergy, besides Monks and Friars, which in many places, bear so great a proportion to the common people, as if need were, there might be raised out of them alone, an Army, sufficient for any warre the Church militant should imploy them in, against their owne, or other Princes.

A second generall abuse of Scripture, is the turning

of Consecration into Conjuration, or Enchantment. To *Error from* Consecrate, is in Scripture, to Offer, Give, or Dedicate, *mistaking* in pious and decent language and gesture, a man, or any *Consecration* other thing to God, by separating of it from common *for* use; that is to say, to Sanctifie, or make it Gods, and to *Conjuration* be used only by those, whom God hath appointed to be his Publike Ministers, (as I have already proved at large in the 35. Chapter;) and thereby to change, not the thing Consecrated, but onely the use of it, from being Profane and common, to be Holy, and peculiar to Gods service. But when by such words, the nature or qualitie of the thing it selfe, is pretended to be changed, it is not Consecration, but either an extraordinary worke of God, or a vaine and impious Conjuration. But seeing (for the frequency of pretending the change of Nature in their Consecrations,) it cannot be esteemed a work extraordinary, it is no other than a *Conjuration* or *Incantation*, whereby they would have men to beleeve an alteration of Nature that is not, contrary to the testimony of mans Sight, and of all the rest of his Senses. As for example, when the Priest, in stead of Consecrating Bread and Wine to Gods peculiar service in the Sacrament of the Lords Supper, (which is but a separation of it from the common use, to signifie, that is, to put men in mind of their Redemption, by the Passion of Christ, whose body was broken, and blood shed upon the Crosse for our transgressions,) pretends, that by saying of the words of our Saviour, *This is my Body*, and *This is my Blood*, the nature of Bread is no more there, but his very Body; notwithstanding there appeared not to the Sight, or other Sense of the Receiver, any thing that appeareth not before the Consecration. The Egyptian Conjurers, that are said to have turned their Rods to Serpents, and the Water into Bloud,[3] are thought but to have deluded the senses of the Spectators by a false shew of things, yet are esteemed Enchanters: But what should wee have thought of them, if there had appeared in their Rods nothing like a Serpent, and in the Water enchanted, nothing like Bloud, nor like any thing else but Water, but that they had faced down the King, that they were Serpents that looked like Rods, and that it was Bloud that seemed Water? That had been both Enchantment, and Lying. And yet in this daily act of the Priest, they doe the very same, by [338] turning the holy words into the manner of a Charme, which produceth nothing new to the Sense; but they face us down, that it hath turned the Bread into a Man; nay more, into a God; and require men to worship it, as if it were our Saviour himself present God and Man, and thereby to commit most grosse Idolatry. For if it bee enough to excuse it of Idolatry, to say it is no more Bread, but God; why should not the same excuse serve the Egyptians, in case they had the faces to say, the Leeks, and Onyons they worshipped, were not very Leeks, and Onyons, but a Divinity under their *species*, or likenesse. The words, *This is my Body*, are æquivalent to these, *This signifies, or represents my Body*; and it is an ordinary figure of Speech: but to take it literally, is an abuse; nor though so taken, can it extend any further, than to the Bread which Christ himself with his own hands Consecrated. For hee never said, that of what Bread soever, any Priest whatsoever, should say, *This is my Body*, or, *This is Christs Body*, the same should presently be transubstantiated. Nor did the Church of Rome ever establish this Transubstantiation, till the time of *Innocent* the third; which was not above 500. years agoe, when the Power of Popes was at the Highest, and the Darknesse of the time grown so great, as men discerned not the Bread that was given them to eat, especially when it was stamped with the figure of Christ upon the Crosse, as if they would have men beleeve it were Transubstantiated, not onely into the Body of Christ, but also into the Wood of his Crosse, and that they did eat both together in the Sacrament.

Incantation in the Ceremonies of Baptisme   The like Incantation, in stead of Consecration, is used also in the Sacrament of Baptisme: Where the abuse of Gods name in each severall Person, and in the whole

Trinity, with the sign of the Crosse at each name, maketh up the Charm: As first, when they make the Holy water, the Priest saith, *I Conjure thee, thou Creature of Water, in the name of God the Father Almighty, and in the name of Jesus Christ his onely Son our Lord, and in vertue of the Holy Ghost, that thou become Conjured water, to drive away all the Powers of the Enemy, and to eradicate, and supplant the Enemy, &c.* And the same in the Benediction of the Salt to be mingled with it; *That thou become Conjured Salt, that all Phantasmes, and Knavery of the Devills fraud may fly and depart from the place wherein thou art sprinkled; and every unclean Spirit bee Conjured by Him that shall come to judge the quicke and the dead.* The same in the Benediction of the Oyle, *That all the Power of the Enemy, all the Host of the Devill, all Assaults and Phantasmes of Satan, may be driven away by this Creature of Oyle.* And for the Infant that is to be Baptized, he is subject to many Charms: First, at the Church dore the Priest blows thrice in the Childs face, and sayes, *Goe out of him unclean Spirit, and give place to the Holy Ghost the Comforter.* As if all Children, till blown on by the Priest were Dæmoniaques: Again, before his entrance into the Church, he saith as before, *I Conjure thee, &c. to goe out, and depart from this Servant of* [339] *God*: And again the same Exorcisme is repeated once more before he be Baptized. These, and some other Incantations, are those that are used in stead of Benedictions, and Consecrations, in administration of the Sacraments of Baptisme, and the Lords Supper; wherein every thing that serveth to those holy uses (except the unhallowed Spittle of the Priest) hath some set form of Exorcisme.

Nor are the other rites, as of Marriage, of Extreme Unction, of Visitation of the Sick, of Consecrating Churches, and Church-yards, and the like, exempt from Charms; in as much as there is in them the use of Enchanted Oyle, and Water, with the abuse of the Crosse, and of the holy word of David, *Asperges me*

And in Marriage, in Visitation of the Sick, and in Consecration of Places

Domine Hyssopo,[4] as things of efficacy to drive away Phantasmes, and Imaginery Spirits.

Another generall Error, is from the Misinterpretation of the words *Eternall Life, Everlasting Death*, and the *Second Death*. For though we read plainly in holy Scripture, that God created Adam in an estate of Living for Ever, which was conditionall, that is to say, if he disobeyed not his Commandement;[5] which was not essentiall to Humane Nature, but consequent to the vertue of the Tree of Life; whereof hee had liberty to eat, as long as hee had not sinned; and that hee was thrust out of Paradise after he had sinned, lest hee should eate thereof, and live for ever; and that Christs Passion is a Discharge of sin to all that beleeve on him; and by consequence, a restitution of Eternall Life, to all the Faithfull, and to them onely: yet the Doctrine is now, and hath been a long time far otherwise; namely, that every man hath Eternity of Life by Nature, in as much as his Soul is Immortall: So that the flaming Sword at the entrance of Paradise,[6] though it hinder a man from coming to the Tree of Life, hinders him not from the Immortality which God took from him for his Sin; nor makes him to need the sacrificing of Christ, for the recovering of the same; and consequently, not onely the faithfull and righteous, but also the wicked, and the Heathen, shall enjoy Eternall Life, without any Death at all; much lesse a Second, and Everlasting Death. To salve this, it is said, that by *Second*, and *Everlasting Death*, is meant a Second, and Everlasting Life, but in Torments; a Figure never used, but in this very Case.

All which Doctrine is founded onely on some of the obscurer places of the New Testament; which neverthelesse, the whole scope of the Scripture considered, are cleer enough in a different sense, and unnecessary to the Christian Faith. For supposing that when a man dies, there remaineth nothing of him but his carkasse; cannot God that raised inanimated dust and clay into a living creature by his Word, as easily raise a dead carkasse to life again, and continue him alive for Ever, or make him die again, by another Word? The *Soule* in Scripture, signifieth alwaies, either the Life, or the Living Creature; and the Body and Soule jointly, the *Body* [340] *alive.* In the fift day of the Creation, God said, Let the waters produce *Reptile animæ viventis,* the creeping thing that hath in it a Living Soule; the English translate it, *that hath Life:* And again, God created Whales, *&* *omnem animam viventem*; which in the English is, *every Living Creature:* And likewise of Man, God made him of the dust of the earth, and breathed in his face the breath of Life, *& factus est Homo in animam viventem,* that is, *and Man was made a Living Creature:*[7] And after *Noah* came out of the Arke, God saith, hee will no more smite *omnem animam viventem,* that is, *every Living Creature:*[8] And Deut. 12.23. *Eate not the Bloud, for the Bloud is the Soule*; that is, *the Life.* From which places, if by *Soule* were meant a *Substance Incorporeall,* with an existence separated from the Body, it might as well be inferred of any other living Creature, as of Man. But that the Souls of the Faithfull, are not of their own Nature, but by Gods speciall Grace, to remaine in their Bodies, from the Resurrection to all Eternity, I have already I think sufficiently proved out of the Scriptures, in the 38. Chapter. And for the places of the New Testament, where it is said that any man shall be cast Body and Soul into Hell fire, it is no more than Body and Life; that is to say, they shall be cast alive into the perpetuall fire of Gehenna.[9]

This window it is, that gives entrance to the Dark Doctrine, first, of Eternall Torments; and afterwards of Purgatory, and consequently of the walking abroad, especially in places Consecrated, Solitary, or Dark, of the Ghosts of men deceased; and thereby to the pretences of Exorcisme and Conjuration of Phantasmes; as also of Invocation of men dead; and to the Doctrine of Indulgences; that is to say, of exemption for a time, or for ever, from the fire of Purgatory, wherein these

As the Doctrine of Purgatory, and Exorcismes, and Invocation of Saints

Incorporeall Substances are pretended by burning to
be cleansed, and made fit for Heaven. For men being
generally possessed before the time of our Saviour, by
contagion of the Dæmonology of the Greeks, of an
opinion, that the Souls of men were substances distinct
from their Bodies, and therefore that when the Body was
dead, the Soule of every man, whether godly, or wicked,
must subsist somewhere by vertue of its own nature,
without acknowledging therein any supernaturall gift of
Gods; the Doctors of the Church doubted a long time,
what was the place, which they were to abide in, till they
should be re-united to their Bodies in the Resurrection;
supposing for a while, they lay under the Altars: but
afterward the Church of Rome found it more profitable,
to build for them this place of Purgatory; which by some
other Churches in this later age, has been demolished.

The Texts   Let us now consider, what texts of Scripture seem
alledged for   most to confirm these three generall Errors, I have here
the Doctrines touched. As for those which Cardinall Bellarmine hath
aforemen-   alledged, for the present Kingdome of God administred
tioned   by the Pope, (than which there are none that make a
have been   better shew of proof,) I have already answered [341]
answered   them; and made it evident, that the Kingdome of God,
before   instituted by Moses, ended in the election of Saul: After
which time the Priest of his own authority never deposed
any King. That which the High Priest did to Athaliah,
was not done in his owne right, but in the right of the
young King Joash her Son: But Solomon in his own right
deposed the High Priest Abiathar, and set up another in
his place.[10] The most difficult place to answer, of all those
that can be brought, to prove the Kingdome of God
by Christ is already in this world, is alledged, not by
Bellarmine, nor any other of the Church of Rome; but
by Beza;[11] that will have it to begin from the Resurrection of Christ. But whether hee intend thereby, to entitle
the Presbytery to the Supreme Power Ecclesiasticall in
the Common-wealth of Geneva, (and consequently to
every Presbytery in every other Common-wealth,) or

to Princes, and other Civill Soveraigns, I doe not know. For the Presbytery hath challenged the power to Excommunicate their owne Kings, and to bee the Supreme Moderators in Religion, in the places where they have that form of Church government, no lesse then the Pope challengeth it universally.

The words are (Marke 9.1.) *Verily I say unto you, that there be some of them that stand here, which shall not tast of death, till they have seene the Kingdome of God come with power.* Which words, if taken grammatically, make it certaine, that either some of those men that stood by Christ at that time, are yet alive; or else, that the Kingdome of God must be now in this present world. And then there is another place more difficult: For when the Apostles after our Saviours Resurrection, and immediately before his Ascension, asked our Saviour, saying, (Acts 1.6.) *Wilt thou at this time restore again the Kingdome to Israel,* he answered them, *It is not for you to know the times and the seasons, which the Father hath put in his own power; But ye shall receive power by the comming of the Holy Ghost upon you, and yee shall be my (Martyrs) witnesses both in Jerusalem, & in all Judæa, and in Samaria, and unto the uttermost part of the Earth*: Which is as much as to say, My Kingdome is not yet come, nor shall you foreknow when it shall come; for it shall come as a theefe in the night;[12] But I will send you the Holy Ghost, and by him you shall have power to beare witnesse to all the world (by your preaching) of my Resurrection, and the workes I have done, and the doctrine I have taught, that they may beleeve in me, and expect eternall life, at my comming againe: How does this agree with the comming of Christs Kingdome at the Resurrection? And that which St. *Paul* saies (1 *Thessal.* 1.9, 10.) *That they turned from Idols, to serve the living and true God, and to waite for his Sonne from Heaven*; Where to waite for his Sonne from Heaven, is to wait for his comming to be King in power; which were not necessary, if this

Answer to the text on which Beza infereth that the Kingdome of Christ began at the Resurrection

Kingdome had beene then present. Againe, if the Kingdome of God began (as *Beza* on that place (*Mark* 9.1.)
would have it) at the Resurrection; what reason is there
for Christians ever since the Resurrection to say in their
prayers, *Let thy Kingdome Come?* It is therefore manifest, that the words of St. *Mark* are not so [342] to be
interpreted. There be some of them that stand here (saith
our Saviour) that shall not tast of death till they have
seen the Kingdome of God come in power. If then this
Kingdome were to come at the Resurrection of Christ,
why is it said, *some of them*, rather than *all*? For they all
lived till after Christ was risen.

Explication   But they that require an exact interpretation of this
of the Place text, let them interpret first the like words of our Saviour
in Mark 9. 1 to St. *Peter* concerning St. John, (chap. 21.22.) *If I will
that he tarry till I come, what is that to thee?* upon
which was grounded a report that hee should not dye:
Neverthelesse the truth of that report was neither confirmed, as well grounded; nor refuted, as ill grounded
on those words; but left as a saying not understood. The
same difficulty is also in the place of St. Marke. And if it
be lawfull to conjecture at their meaning, by that which
immediately followes, both here, and in St. Luke, where
the same is againe repeated,[13] it is not unprobable, to
say they have relation to the Transfiguration, which is
described in the verses immediately following; where it
is said, that *After six dayes Jesus taketh with him Peter,
and James, and John* (not all, but some of his Disciples)[14]
*and leadeth them up into an high mountaine apart by
themselves, and was transfigured before them. And his
rayment became shining, exceeding white as snow; so as
no Fuller on earth can white them. And there appeared
unto them Elias with Moses, and they were talking with
Jesus, &c.* So that they saw Christ in Glory and Majes-
tie, as he is to come; insomuch as *They were sore afraid.*
And thus the promise of our Saviour was accomplished
by way of *Vision*: For it was a Vision, as may probably
bee inferred out of St. Luke, that reciteth the same story

(ch. 9. ve. 28.) and saith, that Peter and they that were with him, were heavy with sleep: But most certainly out of Matth. 17.9. (where the same is again related;) for our Saviour charged them, saying, *Tell no man the Vision untill the Son of man be Risen from the dead.* Howsoever it be, yet there can from thence be taken no argument, to prove that the Kingdome of God taketh beginning till the day of Judgement.

As for some other texts, to prove the Popes Power over civill Soveraignes (besides those of *Bellarmine*;) as that the two Swords that Christ and his Apostles had amongst them, were the Spirituall and the Temporall Sword, which they say St. Peter had given him by Christ: And, that of the two Luminaries, the greater signifies the Pope, and the lesser the King; One might as well inferre out of the first verse of the Bible, that by Heaven is meant the Pope, and by Earth the King: Which is not arguing from Scripture, but a wanton insulting over Princes, that came in fashion after the time the Popes were growne so secure of their greatnesse, as to contemne all Christian Kings; and Treading on the necks of Emperours, to mocke both them, and the Scripture, in the words of the 91. Psalm, *Thou shalt Tread upon the Lion and the Adder, the young Lion and the Dragon thou shalt Trample under thy feet.* *Abuse of some other texts in defence of the Power of the Pope*

As for the rites of Consecration, though they depend for the most part upon the discretion and judgement of the governors of the Church, and not upon the Scriptures; yet those governors are obli[343]ged to such direction, as the nature of the action it selfe requireth; as that the ceremonies, words, and gestures, be both decent, and significant, or at least conformable to the action. When Moses consecrated the Tabernacle, the Altar, and the Vessels belonging to them, (*Exod.* 40.) he anointed them with the Oyle which God had commanded to bee made for that purpose; and they were holy: There was nothing Exorcized, to drive away Phantasmes. The same Moses (the civill Soveraigne of Israel) when he consecrated *The manner of Consecrations in the Scripture, was without Exorcisms*

Aaron (the High Priest,) and his Sons, did wash them with Water, (not Exorcized water,) put their Garments upon them, and anointed them with Oyle; and they were sanctified, to minister unto the Lord in the Priests office; which was a simple and decent cleansing, and adorning them, before hee presented them to God, to be his servants. When King *Solomon*, (the civill Soveraigne of Israel) consecrated the Temple hee had built, (2 *Kings* 8.)[15] he stood before all the Congregation of Israel; and having blessed them, he gave thankes to God, for putting into the heart of his father, to build it; and for giving to himselfe the grace to accomplish the same; and then prayed unto him, first, to accept that House, though it were not sutable to his infinite Greatnesse; and to hear the prayers of his Servants that should pray therein, or (if they were absent,) towards it; and lastly, he offered a sacrifice of Peace-offering, and the House was dedicated. Here was no Procession; the King stood still in his first place; no Exorcised Water; no *Asperges me*, nor other impertinent application of words spoken upon another occasion; but a decent, and rationall speech, and such as in making to God a present of his new built House, was most conformable to the occasion.

We read not that St. John did Exorcize the Water of Jordan; nor Philip the Water of the river wherein he baptized the Eunuch;[16] nor that any Pastor in the time of the Apostles, did take his spittle, and put it to the nose of the person to be Baptized, and say, *In odorem suavitatis*, that is, *for a sweet savour unto the Lord*; wherein neither the Ceremony of Spittle, for the uncleannesse; nor the application of that Scripture for the levity, can by any authority of man be justified.

The immor-tality of mans Soule, not proved by Scripture to be of Nature, but of Grace

To prove that the Soule separated from the Body, liveth eternally, not onely the Soules of the Elect, by especiall grace, and restauration of the Eternall Life which Adam lost by Sinne, and our Saviour restored by the Sacrifice of himself, to the Faithfull; but also the Soules of Reprobates, as a property naturally consequent to the essence of mankind, without other grace of God, but that which is universally given to all mankind; there are divers places, which at the first sight seem sufficiently to serve the turn: but such, as when I compare them with that which I have before (Chapter 38.) alledged out of the 14 of *Job*, seem to mee much more subject to a divers interpretation, than the words of *Job*.

And first there are the words of Solomon (*Ecclesiastes* 12.7.) *Then shall the Dust return to Dust, as it was, and the Spirit shall* [344] *return to God that gave it.* Which may bear well enough (if there be no other text directly against it) this interpretation, that God onely knows, (but Man not,) what becomes of a mans spirit, when he expireth; and the same Solomon, in the same Book, (Chap. 3. ver. 20, 21.) delivereth the same sentence in the sense I have given it: His words are, *All goe* (man and beast) *to the same place; all are of the dust, and all turn to dust again; who knoweth that the spirit of Man goeth upward, and that the spirit of the Beast goeth downward to the earth?* That is, none knows but God; Nor is it an unusuall phrase to say of things we understand not, *God Knows what*, and *God Knows where*. That of *Gen.* 5.24. *Enoch walked with God, and he was not; for God took him*; which is expounded Heb. 13.5. *He was translated, that he should not die; and was not found, because God had translated him.* For before his *Translation, he had this testimony, that he pleased God,* making as much for the Immortality of the Body, as of the Soule, proveth, that this his translation was peculiar to them that please God; not common to them with the wicked; and depending on Grace, not on Nature. But on the contrary, what interpretation shall we give, besides the literall sense of the words of Solomon (*Eccles.* 3.19.) *That which befalleth the Sons of Men, befalleth Beasts, even one thing befalleth them; as the one dyeth, so doth the other; yea, they have all one breath* (one spirit;) *so that a Man hath no præeminence above a Beast, for all is vanity.* By the literall sense, here is no Naturall

Immortality of the Soule; nor yet any repugnancy with the Life Eternall, which the Elect shall enjoy by Grace. And (chap. 4. ver. 3.) *Better is he that hath not yet been, than both they*; that is, than they that live, or have lived; which, if the Soule of all them that have lived, were Immortall, were a hard saying; for then to have an Immortall Soule, were worse than to have no Soule at all. And againe, (Chapt. 9.5.) *The living know they shall die, but the dead know not any thing*; that is, Naturally, and before the resurrection of the body.

Another place which seems to make for a Naturall Immortality of the Soule, is that, where our Saviour saith, that Abraham, Isaac, and Jacob are living:[17] but this is spoken of the promise of God, and of their certitude to rise again, not of a Life then actuall; and in the same sense that God said to Adam, that on the day hee should eate of the forbidden fruit, he should certainly die;[18] from that time forward he was a dead man by sentence; but not by execution, till almost a thousand years after. So Abraham, Isaac, and Jacob were alive by promise, then, when Christ spake; but are not actually till the Resurrection. And the History of Dives and Lazarus, make nothing against this, if wee take it (as it is) for a Parable.[19]

But there be other places of the New Testament, where an Immortality seemeth to be directly attributed to the wicked. For it is evident, that they shall all rise to Judgement. And it is said besides in many places, that they shall goe into *Everlasting fire, Everlasting* [345] *torments, Everlasting punishments; and that the worm of conscience never dyeth*;[20] and all this is comprehended in the word *Everlasting Death*, which is ordinarily interpreted *Everlasting Life in torments*: And yet I can find no where that any man shall live in torments Everlastingly. Also, it seemeth hard, to say, that God who is the Father of Mercies, that doth in Heaven and Earth all that hee will; that hath the hearts of all men in his disposing; that worketh in men both to doe, and to will; and without whose free gift a man hath neither inclination to good, nor repentance of evill, should punish mens transgressions without any end of time, and with all the extremity of torture, that men can imagine, and more. We are therefore to consider, what the meaning is, of *Everlasting Fire*, and other the like phrases of Scripture.

I have shewed already, that the Kingdome of God by Christ beginneth at the day of Judgment: That in that day, the Faithfull shall rise again, with glorious, and spirituall Bodies, and bee his Subjects in that his Kingdome, which shall be Eternall: That they shall neither marry, nor be given in marriage, nor eate and drink, as they did in their naturall bodies; but live for ever in their individuall persons, without the specificall eternity of generation: And that the Reprobates also shall rise again, to receive punishments for their sins: As also, that those of the Elect, which shall be alive in their earthly bodies at that day, shall have their bodies suddenly changed, and made spirituall, and Immortall. But that the bodies of the Reprobate, who make the Kingdome of Satan, shall also be glorious, or spirituall bodies, or that they shall bee as the Angels of God, neither eating, nor drinking, nor engendring; or that their life shall be Eternall in their individuall persons, as the life of every faithfull man is, or as the life of Adam had been if hee had not sinned, there is no place of Scripture to prove it; save onely these places concerning Eternall Torments; which may otherwise be interpreted.

From whence may be inferred, that as the Elect after the Resurrection shall be restored to the estate, wherein Adam was before he had sinned; so the Reprobate shall be in the estate, that Adam, and his posterity were in after the sin committed; saving that God promised a Redeemer to Adam, and such of his seed as should trust in him, and repent; but not to them that should die in their sins, as do the Reprobate.

These things considered, the texts that mention *Eter-* *Eternall* *nall Fire, Eternall Torments, or the Worm that never* *Torments* *dieth*, contradict not the Doctrine of a Second, and *what*

Everlasting Death, in the proper and naturall sense of the word *Death*. The Fire, or Torments prepared for the wicked in *Gehenna, Tophet*, or in what place soever, may continue for ever; and there may never want wicked men to be tormented in them; though not every, nor any one Eternally. For the wicked being left in the estate they were in after Adams sin, may at the Resurrection live as they did, marry, and give in marriage, and have grosse and corruptible bodies, as all mankind now [346] have; and consequently may engender perpetually, after the Resurrection, as they did before: For there is no place of Scripture to the contrary. For St. Paul, speaking of the Resurrection (*1 Cor.* 15.) understandeth it onely of the Resurrection to Life Eternall; and not the Resurrection to Punishment. And of the first, he saith that the Body is *Sown in Corruption, raised in Incorruption; sown in Dishonour, raised in Honour; sown in Weaknesse, raised in Power; sown a Naturall body, raised a Spirituall body*: There is no such thing can be said of the bodies of them that rise to Punishment. So also our Saviour, when hee speaketh of the Nature of Man after the Resurrection, meaneth, the Resurrection to Life Eternall, not to Punishment. The text is *Luke* 20. verses 34. 35, 36. a fertile text. *The Children of this world marry, and are given in marriage; but they that shall be counted worthy to obtaine that world, and the Resurrection from the dead, neither marry, nor are given in marriage: Neither can they die any more; for they are equall to the Angells, and are the Children of God, being the Children of the Resurrection*: The Children of this world, that are in the estate which Adam left them in, shall marry, and be given in marriage; that is, corrupt, and generate successively; which is an Immortality of the Kind, but not of the Persons of men: They are not worthy to be counted amongst them that shall obtain the next world, and an absolute Resurrection from the dead; but onely a short time, as inmates of that world; and to the end onely to receive condign punishment for their contumacy. The

Elect are the onely children of the Resurrection; that is to say, the sole heirs of Eternall Life: they only can die no more: it is they that are equall to the Angels, and that are the children of God; and not the Reprobate. To the Reprobate there remaineth after the Resurrection, a *Second*, and *Eternall* Death: between which Resurrection, and their Second, and Eternall death, is but a time of Punishment and Torment; and to last by succession of sinners thereunto, as long as the kind of Man by propagation shall endure; which is Eternally.

Upon this Doctrine of the Naturall Eternity of separated Soules, is founded (as I said) the Doctrine of Purgatory. For supposing Eternall Life by Grace onely, there is no Life, but the Life of the Body; and no Immortality till the Resurrection. The texts for Purgatory alledged by Bellarmine out of the Canonicall Scripture of the old Testament, are first, the Fasting of *David* for *Saul* and *Jonathan*, mentioned (2 *Kings*, 1. 12.);[21] and againe, (2 *Sam.* 3. 35.) for the death of *Abner*.[22] This Fasting of *David*, he saith, was for the obtaining of something for them at Gods hands, after their death; because after he had Fasted to procure the recovery of his owne child, assoone as he knew it was dead, he called for meate. Seeing then the Soule hath an existence separate from the Body, and nothing can be obtained by mens Fasting for the Soules that are already either in Heaven, or Hell, it followeth that there be some Soules of dead men, that are neither in Heaven, nor in Hell; and therefore they must bee in some third place, which must be Purgatory. And thus with hard straining, hee has wre[347]sted those places to the proofe of a Purgatory: whereas it is manifest, that the ceremonies of Mourning, and Fasting, when they are used for the death of men, whose life was not profitable to the Mourners, they are used for honours sake to their persons; and when tis done for the death of them by whose life the Mourners had benefit, it proceeds from their particular dammage: And so *David* honoured *Saul*, and *Abner*, with his Fasting; and

Answer of the Texts alledged for Purgatory

in the death of his owne child, recomforted himselfe, by receiving his ordinary food.

In the other places, which he alledgeth out of the old Testament, there is not so much as any shew, or colour of proofe. He brings in every text wherein there is the word *Anger*, or *Fire*, or *Burning*, or *Purging*, or *Clensing*, in case any of the Fathers have but in a Sermon rhetorically applied it to the Doctrine of Purgatory, already beleeved. The first verse of *Psalme*, 37.[23] *O Lord rebuke me not in thy wrath, nor chasten me in thy hot displeasure*: What were this to Purgatory, if Augustine had not applied the *Wrath* to the fire of Hell, and the *Displeasure* to that of Purgatory?[24] And what is it to Purgatory, that of *Psalme*, 66. 12. *Wee went through fire and water, and thou broughtest us to a moist place*; and other the like texts, (with which the Doctors of those times entended to adorne, or extend their Sermons, or Commentaries) haled to their purposes by force of wit?

Places of the New Testament for Purgatory answered   But he alledgeth other places of the New Testament, that are not so easie to be answered: And first that of *Matth.* 12. 32. *Whosoever speaketh a word against the Sonne of man, it shall be forgiven him; but whosoever speaketh against the Holy Ghost, it shall not bee forgiven him neither in this world, nor in the world to come*: Where he will have Purgatory to be the World to come, wherein some sinnes may be forgiven, which in this World were not forgiven: notwithstanding that it is manifest, there are but three Worlds; one from the Creation to the Flood, which was destroyed by Water, and is called in Scripture *the Old World*; another from the Flood, to the day of Judgement, which is *the Present World*, and shall bee destroyed by Fire; and the third, which shall bee from the day of Judgement forward, everlasting, which is called *the World to come*; and in which it is agreed by all, there shall be no Purgatory: And therefore the World to come, and Purgatory, are inconsistent. But what then can bee the meaning of those our Saviours words? I confesse they are very hardly to bee reconciled with all the Doctrines now unanimously received: Nor is it any shame, to confesse the profoundnesse of the Scripture, to bee too great to be sounded by the shortnesse of humane understanding. Neverthelesse, I may propound such things to the consideration of more learned Divines, as the text it selfe suggesteth. And first, seeing to speake against the Holy Ghost, as being the third Person of the Trinity, is to speake against the Church, in which the Holy Ghost resideth; it seemeth the comparison is made, betweene the Easinesse of our Saviour, in bearing with offences done to him while hee himselfe taught the world, that is, when he was on earth, and the Severity of the Pastors after him, against those which should deny their authority, which was from the Holy Ghost: As if he should say, You that deny [348] my Power; nay you that shall crucifie me, shall be pardoned by mee, as often as you turne unto mee by Repentance: But if you deny the Power of them that teach you hereafter, by vertue of the Holy Ghost, they shall be inexorable, and shall not forgive you, but persecute you in this World, and leave you without absolution, (though you turn to me, unlesse you turn also to them,) to the punishments (as much as lies in them) of the World to come: And so the words may be taken as a Prophecy, or Prædiction concerning the times, as they have along been in the Christian Church: Or if this be not the meaning, (for I am not peremptory in such difficult places,) perhaps there may be place left after the Resurrection for the Repentance of some sinners: And there is also another place, that seemeth to agree therewith. For considering the words of St. Paul (1 *Cor.* 15. 29.) *What shall they doe which are Baptized for the dead, if the dead rise not at all? why also are they Baptized for the dead?* a man may probably inferre, as some have done, that in St. Pauls time, there was a custome by receiving Baptisme for the dead, (as men that now beleeve, are Sureties and Undertakers for the Faith of Infants, that are not capable of beleeving,) to undertake for the persons of their deceased friends, that they should be ready to obey, and receive our Saviour for their King, at his coming again; and then the forgivenesse of sins in the world to come, has no need of a Purgatory. But in both these interpretations, there is so much of paradox, that I trust not to them; but propound them to those that are throughly versed in the Scripture, to inquire if there be no clearer place that contradicts them. Onely of thus much, I see evident Scripture, to perswade me, that there is neither the word, nor the thing of Purgatory, neither in this, nor any other text; nor any thing that can prove a necessity of a place for the Soule without the Body; neither for the Soule of Lazarus during the four days he was dead;[25] nor for the Soules of them which the Romane Church pretend to be tormented now in Purgatory. For God, that could give a life to a peece of clay, hath the same power to give life again to a dead man, and renew his inanimate, and rotten Carkasse, into a glorious, spirituall, and immortall Body.

Another place is that of 1 *Cor.* 3. where it is said, that they which built Stubble, Hay, &c. on the true Foundation, their work shall perish; but *they themselves shall be saved; but as through Fire*: This Fire, he will have to be the Fire of Purgatory. The words, as I have said before, are an allusion to those of *Zach.* 13. 9. where he saith, *I will bring the third part through the Fire, and refine them as Silver is refined, and will try them as Gold is tryed*: Which is spoken of the comming of the Messiah in Power and Glory; that is, at the day of Judgment, and Conflagration of the present world; wherein the Elect shall not be consumed, but be refined; that is, depose their erroneous Doctrines, and Traditions, and have them as it were sindged off; and shall afterwards call upon the name of the true God. In like manner, the Apostle saith of them, that holding this Foundation *Jesus is the Christ*, shall build thereon some other [349] Doctrines that be erroneous, that they shall not be consumed in that fire which reneweth the world, but shall passe through it to Salvation; but so, as to see, and relinquish their former Errours. The Builders, are the *Pastors*; the Foundation, that *Jesus is the Christ*; the Stubble and Hay, *False Consequences drawn from it through Ignorance, or Frailty*; the Gold, Silver, and pretious Stones, are their *True Doctrines*; and their Refining or Purging, the *Relinquishing of their Errors*. In all which there is no colour at all for the burning of Incorporeall, that is to say, Impatible Souls.

A third place is that of 1 *Cor.* 15. before mentioned, concerning Baptisme for the Dead: out of which he concludeth, first, that Prayers for the Dead are not unprofitable; and out of that, that there is a Fire of Purgatory: But neither of them rightly. For of many interpretations of the word Baptisme, he approveth this in the first place, that by Baptisme is meant (metaphorically) a Baptisme of Penance; and that men are in this sense Baptized, when they Fast, and Pray, and give Almes: And so Baptisme for the Dead, and Prayer for the Dead, is the same thing. But this is a Metaphor, of which there is no example, neither in the Scripture, nor in any other use of language; and which is also discordant to the harmony, and scope of the Scripture. The word Baptisme is used (*Mar.* 10. 38. & *Luk.* 12. 50.) for being Dipped in ones own bloud, as Christ was upon the Cross, and as most of the Apostles were, for giving testimony of him. But it is hard to say, that Prayer, Fasting, and Almes, have any similitude with Dipping. The same is used also *Mat.* 3. 11. (which seemeth to make somewhat for Purgatory) for a Purging with Fire. But it is evident the Fire and Purging here mentioned, is the same whereof the Prophet *Zachary* speaketh (chap. 13. v. 9.) *I will bring the third part through the Fire, and will Refine them, &c.* And St. Peter after him (1 Epist. 1. 7.) *That the triall of your Faith, which is much more precious than of Gold that perisheth, though it be tryed with Fire, might be found unto praise, and honour, and glory at the Appearing of Jesus Christ*; And St. Paul

Baptisme for the Dead, how understood

(1 *Cor.* 3. 13.) *The Fire shall trie every mans work of what sort it is.* But St. Peter, and St. Paul speak of the Fire that shall be at the Second Appearing of Christ; and the Prophet Zachary of the Day of Judgment: And therefore this place of S. Mat. may be interpreted of the same; and then there will be no necessity of the Fire of Purgatory.

Another interpretation of Baptisme for the Dead, is that which I have before mentioned, which he preferreth to the second place of probability: And thence also he inferreth the utility of Prayer for the Dead. For if after the Resurrection, such as have not heard of Christ, or not beleeved in him, may be received into Christs Kingdome; it is not in vain, after their death, that their friends should pray for them, till they should be risen. But granting that God, at the prayers of the faithfull, may convert unto him some of those that have not heard Christ preached, and consequently cannot have rejected Christ, and that the charity of men in that point, cannot be blamed; yet this concludeth nothing for Purgatory, be[350]cause to rise from Death to Life, is one thing; to rise from Purgatory to Life is another; as being a rising from Life to Life, from a Life in torments to a Life in joy.

A fourth place is that of *Mat.* 5. 25. *Agree with thine Adversary quickly, whilest thou art in the way with him, lest at any time the Adversary deliver thee to the Judge, and the Judge deliver thee to the Officer, and thou be cast into prison. Verily I say unto thee, thou shalt by no means come out thence, till thou hast paid the uttermost farthing.* In which Allegory, the Offender is the *Sinner*; both the Adversary and the Judge is *God*; the Way is this *Life*; the Prison is the *Grave*; the Officer, *Death*; from which, the sinner shall not rise again to life eternall, but to a second Death, till he have paid the utmost farthing, or Christ pay it for him by his Passion, which is a full Ransome for all manner of sin, as well lesser sins, as greater crimes; both being made by the passion of Christ equally veniall.

The fift place, is that of *Matth.* 5. 22. *Whosoever is angry with his Brother without a cause, shall be guilty in Judgment. And whosoever shall say to his Brother, RACHA, shall be guilty in the Councel. But whosoever shall say, Thou Foole, shall be guilty to hell fire.* From which words he inferreth three sorts of Sins, and three sorts of Punishments; and that none of those sins, but the last, shall be punished with hell fire; and consequently, that after this life, there is punishment of lesser sins in Purgatory. Of which inference, there is no colour in any interpretation that hath yet been given of them: Shall there be a distinction after this life of Courts of Justice, as there was amongst the Jews in our Saviours time, to hear, and determine divers sorts of Crimes; as the Judges, and the Councell? Shall not all Judicature appertain to Christ, and his Apostles? To understand therefore this text, we are not to consider it solitarily, but jointly with the words precedent, and subsequent. Our Saviour in this Chapter interpreteth the Law of Moses; which the Jews thought was then fulfilled, when they had not transgressed the Grammaticall sense thereof, howsoever they had transgressed against the sentence, or meaning of the Legislator. Therefore whereas they thought the Sixth Commandement was not broken, but by Killing a man; nor the Seventh, but when a man lay with a woman, not his wife; our Saviour tells them, the inward Anger of a man against his brother, if it be without just cause, is Homicide: You have heard (saith hee) the Law of Moses, *Thou shalt not Kill,* and the *Whosoever shall Kill, shall bee condemned before the Judges,* or before the Session of the Seventy: But I say unto you, to be Angry with ones Brother without cause; or to say unto him *Racha,* or *Foole,* is Homicide, and shall be punished at the day of Judgment, and Session of Christ, and his Apostles, with Hell fire: so that those words were not used to distinguish between divers Crimes, and divers Courts of Justice, and divers Punishments; but to taxe the distinction between sin, and sin, which the Jews drew not from the difference of the Will in Obeying God, but from the [351] difference of their Temporall Courts of Justice; and to shew them that he that had the Will to hurt his Brother, though the effect appear but in Reviling, or not at all, shall be cast into hell fire, by the Judges, and by the Session, which shall be the same, not different Courts at the day of Judgment. This considered, what can be drawn from this text, to maintain Purgatory, I cannot imagine.

The sixth place is *Luke* 16. 9. *Make yee friends of the unrighteous Mammon, that when yee faile, they may receive you into Everlasting Tabernacles.* This he alledges to prove Invocation of Saints departed. But the sense is plain, That we should make friends with our Riches, of the Poore; and thereby obtain their Prayers whilest they live. *He that giveth to the Poore, lendeth to the Lord.*[26]

The seventh is *Luke* 23. 42. *Lord remember me when thou commest into thy Kingdome*: Therefore, saith hee, there is Remission of sins after this life. But the consequence is not good. Our Saviour then forgave him; and at his comming againe in Glory, will remember to raise him againe to Life Eternall.

The Eight is *Acts* 2. 24. where St. Peter saith of Christ, *that God had raised him up, and loosed the Paines of Death, because it was not possible he should be holden of it*: Which hee interprets to bee a descent of Christ into Purgatory, to loose some Soules there from their torments: whereas it is manifest, that it was Christ that was loosed; it was hee that could not bee holden of Death, or the Grave; and not the Souls in Purgatory. But if that which Beza sayes in his notes on this place be well observed, there is none that will not see, that in stead of *Paynes*, it should be *Bands*; and then there is no further cause to seek for Purgatory in this Text. [352]

Of Dæmonology, *and other Reliques of the Religion of the Gentiles*

The impression made on the organs of Sight, by lucide Bodies, either in one direct line, or in many lines, reflected from Opaque, or refracted in the passage through Diaphanous Bodies, produceth in living Creatures, in whom God hath placed such Organs, an Imagination of the Object, from whence the Impression proceedeth; which Imagination is called *Sight*; and seemeth not to bee a meer Imagination, but the Body it selfe without us; in the same manner, as when a man violently presseth his eye, there appears to him a light without, and before him, which no man perceiveth but himselfe; because there is indeed no such thing without him, but onely a motion in the interiour organs, pressing by resistance outward, that makes him think so. And the motion made by this pressure, continuing after the object which caused it is removed, is that we call *Imagination*, and *Memory*, and (in sleep, and sometimes in great distemper of the organs by Sicknesse, or Violence) a *Dream*: of which things I have already spoken briefly, in the second and third Chapters.

The Originall of Dæmonology

This nature of Sight having never been discovered by the ancient pretenders to Naturall Knowledge; much lesse by those that consider not things so remote (as that Knowledge is) from their present use; it was hard for men to conceive of those Images in the Fancy, and in the Sense, otherwise, than of things really without us: Which some (because they vanish away, they know not whither, nor how,) will have to be absolutely Incorporeall, that is to say Immateriall, or Formes without Matter; Colour and Figure, without any coloured or figured Body; and that they can put on Aiery bodies (as a garment) to make them Visible when they will to our bodily Eyes;

and others say, are Bodies, and living Creatures, but
made of Air, or other more subtile and æthereall Matter,
which is, then, when they will be seen, condensed. But
Both of them agree on one generall appellation of them,
DÆMONS. As if the Dead of whom they Dreamed, were
not Inhabitants of their own Brain, but of the Air, or of
Heaven, or Hell; not Phantasmes, but Ghosts; with just
as much reason, as if one should say, he saw his own
Ghost in a Looking-Glasse, or the Ghosts of the Stars
in a River; or call the ordinary apparition of the Sun, of
the quantity of about a foot, the *Dæmon*, or Ghost of
that great Sun that enlighteneth the whole visible world:
And by that means have feared them, as things of an
unknown, that is, of an unlimited power to doe them
good, or [353] harme; and consequently, given occasion
to the Governours of the Heathen Common-wealths to
regulate this their fear, by establishing that DÆMON-
OLOGY (in which the Poets, as Principall Priests of the
Heathen Religion, were specially employed, or reverenced) to the Publique Peace, and to the Obedience of
Subjects necessary thereunto; and to make some of them
Good *Dæmons*, and others Evill; the one as a Spurre to
the Observance, the other, as Reines to withhold them
from Violation of the Laws.

What were   What kind of things they were, to whom they attrib-
the Dæmons uted the name of *Dæmons*, appeareth partly in the
of the Genealogie of their Gods, written by *Hesiod*,[27] one of
Ancients the most ancient Poets of the Græcians; and partly in
other Histories; of which I have observed some few
before, in the 12. Chapter of this discourse.

How that   The Græcians, by their Colonies and Conquests,
Doctrine was communicated their Language and Writings into Asia,
spread Egypt, and Italy; and therein, by necessary consequence
their *Dæmonology*, or (as St. *Paul* calles it) *their Doctrines of Devils*:[28] And by that meanes, the contagion
was derived also to the Jewes, both of *Judæa*, and *Alexandria*, and other parts, whereinto they were dispersed.
But the name of *Dæmon* they did not (as the Græcians)

attribute to Spirits both Good, and Evill; but to the Evill How far
onely: And to the Good *Dæmons* they gave the name of received by
the Spirit of God; and esteemed those into whose bodies the Jews
they entred to be Prophets. In summe, all singularity if
Good, they attributed to the Spirit of God; and if Evill,
to some *Dæmon*, but a κακοδάιμων, an Evill *Dæmon*,
that is, a *Devill*. And therefore, they called *Dæmoniaques*, that is, *possessed by the Devill*, such as we call
madmen or Lunatiques; or such as had the Falling Sicknesse;[29] or that spoke any thing, which they for want of
understanding, thought absurd: As also of an Unclean
person in a notorious degree, they used to say he had an
Unclean Spirit; of a Dumbe man, that he had a Dumbe
Devill; and of *John Baptist* (*Math.* 11. 18.) for the singularity of his fasting, that he had a Devill; and of our
Saviour, because he said, hee that keepeth his sayings
should not see Death *in æternum, Now we know thou* John 8. 52
hast a Devill; Abraham is dead, and the Prophets are
dead: And again, because he said (*John* 7. 20.) *They*
went about to kill him, the people answered, *Thou hast*
a Devill, who goeth about to kill thee? Whereby it is
manifest, that the Jewes had the same opinions concerning Phantasmes, namely, that they were not Phantasmes
that is, Idols of the braine, but things reall, and independent on the Fancy.

Which doctrine if it be not true, why (may some say) Why our
did not our Saviour contradict it, and teach the contrary? Saviour
nay why does he use on diverse occasions, such forms of controlled
speech as seem to confirm it? To this I answer, that first, it not
where Christ saith, *A spirit hath not flesh and bone,*[30]
though hee shew that there be Spirits, yet hee denies not
that they are Bodies: And where St. *Paul* sais, *We shall*
rise spirituall Bodies,[31] he acknowledgeth the nature of
Spirits, but that they are Bodily Spirits; which is not difficult to understand. For Air and many other things are
Bodies, though not Flesh and Bone, or any other grosse
body, to bee [354] discerned by the eye. But when our
Saviour speaketh to the Devill, and commandeth him

to go out of a man, if by the Devill, be meant a Disease, as Phrenesy, or Lunacy, or a corporeal Spirit, is
not the speech improper? can Diseases heare? or can
there be a corporeall Spirit in a Body of Flesh and Bone,
full already of vitall and animall Spirits? Are there not
therefore Spirits, that neither have Bodies, nor are meer
Imaginations? To the first I answer, that the addressing
of our Saviours command to the Madnesse, or Lunacy
he cureth, is no more improper, then was his rebuking of
the Fever, or of the Wind, and Sea; for neither do these
hear: Or than was the command of God, to the Light, to
the Firmament, to the Sunne, and Starres, when he commanded them to bee: for they could not heare before
they had a beeing. But those speeches are not improper,
because they signifie the power of Gods Word: no more
therefore is it improper, to command Madnesse, or
Lunacy (under the appellation of Devils, by which they
were then commonly understood,) to depart out of a
mans body. To the second, concerning their being Incorporeall, I have not yet observed any place of Scripture,
from whence it can be gathered, that any man was ever
possessed with any other Corporeall Spirit, but that of
his owne, by which his body is naturally moved.

The Scrip-   Our Saviour, immediately after the Holy Ghost
tures doe not descended upon him in the form of a Dove, is said by
teach that   St. *Matthew* (Chapt. 4. 1.) to have been *led up by the*
Spirits are   *Spirit into the Wildernesse*; and the same is recited (*Luke*
Incorporeall   4. 1.) in these words, *Jesus being full of the Holy Ghost,*
was led in the Spirit into the Wildernesse: Whereby
it is evident, that by *Spirit* there, is meant the Holy
Ghost. This cannot be interpreted for a Possession: For
Christ, and the Holy Ghost, are but one and the same
substance; which is no possession of one substance, or
body, by another. And whereas in the verses following,
he is said *to have been taken up by the Devill into the*
Holy City, and set upon a pinnacle of the Temple, shall
we conclude thence that hee was possessed of the Devill, or carried thither by violence? And again, *carryed*

thence by the Devill into an exceeding high mountain, who shewed him them thence all the Kingdomes of the world: Wherein, wee are not to beleeve he was either possessed, or forced by the Devill; nor that any Mountaine is high enough, (according to the literall sense,) to shew him one whole Hemisphere. What then can be the meaning of this place, other than that he went of himself into the Wildernesse; and that this carrying of him up and down, from the Wildernesse to the City, and from thence into a Mountaine, was a Vision? Conformable whereunto, is also the phrase of St. Luke, that hee was led into the Wildernesse, not *by*, but *in* the Spirit: whereas concerning His being Taken up into the Mountaine, and unto the Pinnacle of the Temple, hee speaketh as St. Matthew doth. Which suiteth with the nature of a Vision.

Again, where St. Luke sayes of Judas Iscariot, that *Satan entred into him, and thereupon that he went and communed with the Chief Priests, and Captaines, how he might betray Christ unto them*:[32] it [355] may be answered, that by the Entring of *Satan* (that is the *Enemy*) into him, is meant, the hostile and traiterous intention of selling his Lord and Master. For as by the Holy Ghost, is frequently in Scripture understood, the Graces and good Inclinations given by the Holy Ghost; so by the Entring of Satan, may bee understood the wicked Cogitations, and Designes of the Adversaries of Christ, and his Disciples. For as it is hard to say, that the Devill was entred into Judas, before he had any such hostile designe; so it is impertinent to say, he was first Christs Enemy in his heart, and that the Devill entred into him afterwards. Therefore the Entring of Satan, and his Wicked Purpose, was one and the same thing.

But if there be no Immateriall Spirit, nor any Possession of mens bodies by any Spirit Corporeall, it may again be asked, why our Saviour and his Apostles did not teach the People so; and in such cleer words, as they might no more doubt thereof. But such questions as these, are more curious, than necessary for a Christian mans Salvation. Men may as well aske, why Christ that could have given to all men Faith, Piety, and all manner of morall Vertues, gave it to some onely, and not to all: and why he left the search of naturall Causes, and Sciences, to the naturall Reason and Industry of men, and did not reveal it to all, or any man supernaturally; and many other such questions: Of which neverthelesse there may be alledged probable and pious reasons. For as God, when he brought the Israelites into the Land of Promise, did not secure them therein, by subduing all the Nations round about them; but left many of them, as thornes in their sides, to awaken from time to time their Piety and Industry: so our Saviour, in conducting us toward his heavenly Kingdome, did not destroy all the difficulties of Naturall Questions; but left them to exercise our Industry, and Reason; the Scope of his preaching, being onely to shew us this plain and direct way to Salvation, namely, the beleef of this Article, *that he was the Christ, the Son of the living God, sent into the world to sacrifice himselfe for our Sins, and at his comming again, gloriously to reign over his Elect, and to save them from their Enemies eternally*: To which, the opinion of Possession by Spirits, or Phantasmes, are no impediment in the way; though it be to some an occasion of going out of the way, and to follow their own Inventions. If wee require of the Scripture an account of all questions, which may be raised to trouble us in the performance of Gods commands; we may as well complaine of Moses for not having set downe the time of the creation of such Spirits, as well as of the Creation of the Earth, and Sea, and of Men, and Beasts. To conclude, I find in Scripture that there be Angels, and Spirits, good and evill; but not that they are Incorporeall, as are the Apparitions men see in the Dark, or in a Dream, or Vision; which the Latines call *Spectra*, and took for *Dæmons*. And I find that there are Spirits Corporeall, (though subtile and Invisible;) but not that any mans body was possessed, or inhabited by them; And that the Bodies of [356] the Saints shall be such, namely, Spirituall Bodies, as St. Paul calls them.

Neverthelesse, the contrary Doctrine, namely, that there be Incorporeall Spirits, hath hitherto so prevailed in the Church, that the use of Exorcisme, (that is to say, of ejection of Devills by Conjuration) is thereupon built; and (though rarely and faintly practised) is not yet totally given over. That there were many Dæmoniaques in the Primitive Church, and few Mad-men, and other such singular diseases; whereas in these times we hear of, and see many Mad-men, and few Dæmoniaques, proceeds not from the change of Nature; but of Names. But how it comes to passe, that whereas heretofore the Apostles, and after them for a time, the Pastors of the Church, did cure those singular Diseases, which now they are not seen to doe; as likewise, why it is not in the power of every true Beleever now, to doe all that the Faithfull did then, that is to say, as we read (*Mark* 16. 17.) *In Christs name to cast out Devills, to speak with new Tongues, to take up Serpents, to drink deadly Poison without harm taking, and to cure the Sick by the laying on of their hands*, and all this without other words, but *in the Name of Jesus*, is another question. And it is probable, that those extraordinary gifts were given to the Church, for no longer a time, than men trusted wholly to Christ, and looked for their felicity onely in his Kingdome to come; and consequently, that when they sought Authority, and Riches, and trusted to their own Subtilty for a Kingdome of this world, these supernaturall gifts of God were again taken from them.

The Power of Casting out Devills, not the same it was in the Primitive Church

Another relique of Gentilisme, is the *Worship of Images*, neither instituted by Moses in the Old, nor by Christ in the New Testament; nor yet brought in from the Gentiles; but left amongst them, after they had given their names to Christ. Before our Saviour preached, it was the generall Religion of the Gentiles, to worship for Gods, those Apparences that remain in the Brain from

Another relique of Gentilisme, Worshipping of Images, left in the Church, not brought into it

the impression of externall Bodies upon the organs of their Senses, which are commonly called *Ideas*, *Idols*, *Phantasmes*, *Conceits*, as being Representations of those externall Bodies, which cause them, and have nothing in them of reality, no more than there is in the things that seem to stand before us in a Dream: And this is the reason why St. Paul says, *Wee know that an Idol is Nothing*:[33] Not that he thought that an Image of Metall, Stone, or Wood, was nothing; but that the thing which they honored, or feared in the Image, and held for a God, was a meer Figment, without place, habitation, motion, or existence, but in the motions of the Brain. And the worship of these with Divine Honour, is that which is in the Scripture called Idolatry, and Rebellion against God. For God being King of the Jews, and his Lieutenant being first Moses, and afterward the High Priest; if the people had been permitted to worship, and pray to Images, (which are Representations of their own Fancies,) they had had no farther dependence on the true God, of whom there can be no similitude; nor on his [357] prime Ministers, Moses, and the High Priests; but every man had governed himself according to his own appetite, to the utter eversion of the Common-wealth, and their own destruction for want of Union. And therefore the first Law of God was, *They should not take for Gods*, ALIENOS DEOS, that is, *the Gods of other nations, but that onely true God, who vouchsafed to commune with Moses, and by him to give them laws and directions, for their peace, and for their salvation from their enemies*. And the second was, that *they should not make to themselves any Image to Worship, of their own Invention*. For it is the same deposing of a King, to submit to another King, whether he be set up by a neighbour nation, or by our selves.

Answer to certain seeming texts for Images   The places of Scripture pretended to countenance the setting up of Images, to worship them; or to set them up at all in the places where God is worshipped, are First, two Examples; one of the Cherubins over the Ark of

God; the other of the Brazen Serpent:[34] Secondly, some
texts whereby we are commanded to worship certain
Creatures for their relation to God; as to worship his
Footstool:[35] And lastly, some other texts, by which is
authorized, a religious honoring of Holy things. But
before I examine the force of those places, to prove that
which is pretended, I must first explain what is to be
understood by *Worshipping*, and what by *Images*, and
Idols.

I have already shewn in the 20 Chapter of this Dis- *What is*
course, that to Honor, is to value highly the Power of *Worship*
any person: and that such value is measured, by our
comparing him with others. But because there is nothing
to be compared with God in Power; we Honor him not
but Dishonour him by any Value lesse than Infinite. And
thus Honor is properly of its own nature, secret, and
internall in the heart. But the inward thoughts of men,
which appeare outwardly in their words and actions,
are the signes of our Honoring, and these goe by the
name of WORSHIP, in Latine CULTUS. Therefore, to
Pray to, to Swear by, to Obey, to bee Diligent, and Offi-
cious in Serving: in summe, all words and actions that
betoken Fear to Offend, or Desire to Please, is *Worship*,
whether those words and actions be sincere, or feigned:
and because they appear as signes of Honoring, are
ordinarily also called *Honor*.

The Worship we exhibit to those we esteem to be *Distinction*
but men, as to Kings, and men in Authority, is *Civill* *between*
Worship: But the worship we exhibit to that which we *Divine and*
think to bee God, whatsoever the words, ceremonies, *Civill Worship*
gestures, or other actions be, is *Divine Worship*. To fall
prostrate before a King, in him that thinks him but a
Man, is but Civill Worship: And he that but putteth off
his hat in the Church, for this cause, that he thinketh
it the House of God, worshippeth with Divine Worship. They that seek the distinction of Divine and Civill
Worship, not in the intention of the Worshipper, but in
the Words δουλεία, and λατρεία, deceive themselves.

For whereas there be two sorts of Servants; that sort, which is of those that [358] are absolutely in the power of their Masters, as Slaves taken in war, and their Issue, whose bodies are not in their own power, (their lives depending on the Will of their Masters, in such manner as to forfeit them upon the least disobedience,) and that are bought and sold as Beasts, were called Δοῦλοι, that is properly, Slaves, and their Service Δουλεία: The other, which is of those that serve (for hire, or in hope of benefit from their Masters) voluntarily; are called Θῆτες; that is, Domestique Servants; to whose service the Masters have no further right, than is contained in the Covenants made betwixt them. These two kinds of Servants have thus much common to them both, that their labour is appointed them by another: And the word Λάτεις, is the generall name of both, signifying him that worketh for another, whether, as a Slave, or a voluntary Servant: So that Λατρεία signifieth generally all Service; but Δουλεία the service of Bondmen onely, and the condition of Slavery: And both are used in Scripture (to signifie our Service of God) promiscuously. Δουλεία, because we are Gods Slaves; Λατρεία, because wee Serve him: and in all kinds of Service is contained, not onely Obedience, but also Worship, that is, such actions, gestures, and words, as signifie Honor.

An Image what. An IMAGE (in the most strict signification of the word) is the Resemblance of some thing visible: In which sense *Phantasmes* the Phantasticall Formes, Apparitions, or Seemings of visible Bodies to the Sight, are onely *Images*; such as are the Shew of a man, or other thing in the Water, by Reflexion, or Refraction; or of the Sun, or Stars by Direct Vision in the Air; which are nothing reall in the things seen, nor in the place where they seem to bee; nor are their magnitudes and figures the same with that of the object; but changeable, by the variation of the organs of Sight, or by glasses; and are present often-times in our Imagination, and in our Dreams, when the object is absent; or changed into other colours, and shapes, as things that depend onely upon the Fancy. And these are the Images which are originally and most properly called *Ideas*, and IDOLS, and derived from the language of the Græcians, with whom the word Εἴδω signifieth to *See*. They are also called PHANTASMES, which is in the same language, *Apparitions*. And from these Images it is that one of the faculties of mans Nature, is called the *Imagination*. And from hence it is manifest, that there neither is, nor can bee any Image made of a thing Invisible.

It is also evident, that there can be no Image of a thing Infinite: for all the Images, and Phantasmes that are made by the Impression of things visible, are figured: but Figure is a quantity every way determined: And therefore there can bee no Image of God; nor of the Soule of Man; nor of Spirits; but onely of Bodies Visible, that is, Bodies that have light in themselves, or are by such enlightened.

And whereas a man can fancy Shapes he never saw; *Fictions* making up a Figure out of the parts of divers creatures; as the Poets make their [359] Centaures, Chimæras,[36] and other Monsters never seen: So can he also give Matter to those Shapes, and make them in Wood, Clay or *Materiall* Metall. And these are also called Images, not for the *Images* resemblance of any corporeall thing, but for the resemblance of some Phantasticall Inhabitants of the Brain of the Maker. But in these Idols, as they are originally in the Brain, and as they are painted, carved, moulded, or moulten in matter, there is a similitude of the one to the other, for which the Materiall Body made by Art, may be said to be the Image of the Phantasticall Idoll made by Nature.

But in a larger use of the word Image, is contained also, any Representation of one thing by another. So an earthly Soveraign may be called the Image of God: And an inferiour Magistrate the Image of an earthly Soveraign. And many times in the Idolatry of the Gentiles there was little regard to the similitude of their Materiall Idol to the Idol in their fancy, and yet it was called the

Image of it. For a Stone unhewn has been set up for Neptune,[37] and divers other shapes far different from the shapes they conceived of their Gods. And at this day we see many Images of the Virgin Mary, and other Saints, unlike one another, and without correspondence to any one mans Fancy; and yet serve well enough for the purpose they were erected for; which was no more but by the Names onely, to represent the Persons mentioned in the History; to which every man applyeth a Mentall Image of his owne making, or none at all. And thus an Image in the largest sense, is either the Resemblance, or the Representation of some thing Visible; or both together, as it happeneth for the most part.

But the name of Idoll is extended yet further in Scripture, to signifie also the Sunne, or a Starre, or any other Creature, visible or invisible, when they are worshipped for Gods.

Idolatry what   Having shewn what is *Worship*, and what an *Image*; I will now put them together, and examine what that IDOLATRY is, which is forbidden in the Second Commandement, and other places of the Scripture.

To worship an Image, is voluntarily to doe those externall acts, which are signes of honoring either the matter of the Image, which is Wood, Stone, Metall, or some other visible creature; or the Phantasme of the brain, for the resemblance, or representation whereof, the matter was formed and figured; or both together, as one animate Body, composed of the Matter and the Phantasme, as of a Body and Soule.

To be uncovered, before a man of Power and Authority, or before the Throne of a Prince, or in such other places as hee ordaineth to that purpose in his absence, is to Worship that man, or Prince with Civill Worship; as being a signe, not of honoring the stoole, or place, but the Person; and is not Idolatry. But if hee that doth it, should suppose the Soule of the Prince to be in the Stool, or should present a Petition to the Stool, it were Divine Worship, and Idolatry.

OF THE KINGDOME OF DARKNESSE

[360] To pray to a King for such things, as hee is able to doe for us, though we prostrate our selves before him, is but Civill Worship; because we acknowledge no other power in him, but humane: But voluntarily to pray unto him for fair weather, or for any thing which God onely can doe for us, is Divine Worship, and Idolatry. On the other side, if a King compell a man to it by the terrour of Death, or other great corporall punishment, it is not Idolatry: For the Worship which the Soveraign commandeth to bee done unto himself by the terrour of his Laws, is not a sign that he that obeyeth him, does inwardly honour him as a God, but that he is desirous to save himselfe from death, or from a miserable life; and that which is not a sign of internall honor, is no Worship; and therefore no Idolatry. Neither can it bee said, that hee that does it, scandalizeth, or layeth any stumbling block before his Brother; because how wise, or learned soever he be that worshippeth in that manner, another man cannot from thence argue, that he approveth it; but that he doth it for fear; and that it is not his act, but the act of his Soveraign.

To worship God, in some peculiar Place, or turning a mans face towards an Image, or determinate Place, is not to worship, or honor the Place, or Image; but to acknowledge it Holy, that is to say, to acknowledge the Image, or the Place to be set apart from common use: for that is the meaning of the word *Holy*; which implies no new quality in the Place, or Image; but onely a new Relation by Appropriation to God; and therefore is not Idolatry; no more than it was Idolatry to worship God before the Brazen Serpent; or for the Jews when they were out of their owne countrey, to turn their faces (when they prayed) toward the Temple of Jerusalem; or for Moses to put off his Shoes when he was before the Flaming Bush, the ground appertaining to Mount Sinai;[38] which place God had chosen to appear in, and to give his Laws to the People of Israel, and was therefore Holy ground, not by inhærent sanctity, but by separation to

Gods use; or for Christians to worship in the Churches, which are once solemnly dedicated to God for that purpose, by the Authority of the King, or other true Representant of the Church. But to worship God, as inanimating, or inhabiting, such Image, or place; that is to say, an infinite substance in a finite place, is Idolatry: for such finite Gods, are but Idols of the brain, nothing reall; and are commonly called in the Scripture by the names of *Vanity*, and *Lyes*, and *Nothing*. Also to worship God, not as inanimating, or present in the place, or Image; but to the end to be put in mind of him, or of some works of his, in case the Place, or Image be dedicated, or set up by private authority, and not by the authority of them that are our Soveraign Pastors, is Idolatry. For the Commandement is, *Thou shalt not make to thy selfe any graven Image*. God commanded Moses to set up the Brazen Serpent; hee did not make it to himselfe; it was not therefore against the Commandement. But the making of the Golden Calfe by Aaron, and the People, as being done without [361] authority from God, was Idolatry;[39] not onely because they held it for God, but also because they made it for a Religious use, without warrant either from God their Soveraign, or from Moses, that was his Lieutenant.

The Gentiles worshipped for Gods, Jupiter, and others; that living, were men perhaps that had done great and glorious Acts; and for the Children of God, divers men and women, supposing them gotten between an Immortall Deity, and a mortall man. This was Idolatry, because they made them so to themselves, having no authority from God, neither in his eternall Law of Reason, nor in his positive and revealed Will. But though our Saviour was a man, whom wee also beleeve to bee God Immortall, and the Son of God; yet this is no Idolatry; because wee build not that beleef upon our own fancy, or judgment, but upon the Word of God revealed in the Scriptures. And for the adoration of the Eucharist, if the words of Christ, *This is my Body*, signifie, *that he himselfe, and the seeming bread in his hand; and not onely so, but that all the seeming morsells of bread that have ever since been, and any time hereafter shall bee consecrated by Priests, bee so many Christs bodies, and yet all of them but one body,* then is that no Idolatry, because it is authorized by our Saviour: but if that text doe not signifie that, (for there is no other that can be alledged for it,) then, because it is a worship of humane institution, it is Idolatry. For it is not enough to say, God can transubstantiate the Bread into Christs Body: For the Gentiles also held God to be Omnipotent; and might upon that ground no lesse excuse their Idolatry, by pretending, as well as others, a transubstantiation of their Wood, and Stone into God Almighty.

Whereas there be, that pretend Divine Inspiration, to be a supernaturall entring of the Holy Ghost into a man, and not an acquisition of Gods graces, by doctrine, and study; I think they are in a very dangerous Dilemma. For if they worship not the men whom they beleeve to be so inspired, they fall into Impiety; as not adoring Gods supernaturall Presence. And again, if they worship them, they commit Idolatry; for the Apostles would never permit themselves to be so worshipped. Therefore the safest way is to beleeve, that by the Descending of the Dove upon the Apostles; and by Christs Breathing on them, when hee gave them the Holy Ghost; and by the giving of it by Imposition of Hands, are understood the signes which God hath been pleased to use, or ordain to bee used, of his promise to assist those persons in their study to Preach his Kingdome, and in their Conversation, that it might not be Scandalous, but Edifying to others.

Besides the Idolatrous Worship of Images, there is also a Scandalous Worship of them; which is also a sin; but not Idolatry. For *Idolatry* is to worship by signes of an internall, and reall honour: but *Scandalous Worship*, is but Seeming Worship; and may sometimes bee joined with an inward, and hearty detestation, both of the [362] Image, and of the Phantasticall *Dæmon*, or

Scandalous worship of Images

Idol, to which it is dedicated; and proceed onely from the fear of death, or other grievous punishment; and is neverthelesse a sin in them that so worship, in case they be men whose actions are looked at by others, as lights to guide them by; because following their ways, they cannot but stumble, and fall in the way of Religion: Whereas the example of those we regard not, works not on us at all, but leaves us to our own diligence and caution; and consequently are no causes of our falling.

If therefore a Pastor lawfully called to teach and direct others, or any other, of whose knowledge there is a great opinion, doe externall honor to an Idol for fear; unlesse he make his feare, and unwillingnesse to it, as evident as the worship; he Scandalizeth his Brother, by seeming to approve Idolatry. For his Brother arguing from the action of his teacher, or of him whose knowledge he esteemeth great, concludes it to bee lawfull in it selfe. And this Scandall, is Sin, and a *Scandall given*. But if one being no Pastor, nor of eminent reputation for knowledge in Christian Doctrine, doe the same, and another follow him; this is no Scandall given; for he had no cause to follow such example: but is a pretence of Scandall which hee taketh of himselfe for an excuse before men: For an unlearned man, that is in the power of an Idolatrous King, or State, if commanded on pain of death to worship before an Idoll, hee detesteth the Idoll in his heart, hee doth well; though if he had the fortitude to suffer death, rather than worship it, he should doe better. But if a Pastor, who as Christs Messenger, has undertaken to teach Christs Doctrine to all nations, should doe the same, it were not onely a sinfull Scandall, in respect of other Christian mens consiences, but a perfidious forsaking of his charge.

The summe of that which I have said hitherto, concerning the Worship of Images, is this, that he that worshippeth in an Image, or any Creature, either the Matter thereof, or any Fancy of his own, which he thinketh to dwell in it; or both together; or beleeveth that such things hear his Prayers, or see his Devotions, without Ears, or Eyes, committeth Idolatry: and he that counterfeiteth such Worship for fear of punishment, if he bee a man whose example hath power amongst his Brethren, committeth a sin: But he that worshippeth the Creator of the world before such an Image, or in such a place as he hath not made, or chosen of himselfe, but taken from the commandement of Gods Word, as the Jewes did in worshipping God before the Cherubins, and before the Brazen Serpent for a time, and in, or towards the Temple of Jerusalem, which was also but for a time, committeth not Idolatry.

Now for the Worship of Saints, and Images, and Reliques, and other things at this day practised in the Church of Rome, I say they are not allowed by the Word of God, not brought into the Church of Rome, from the Doctrine there taught; but partly left [363] in it at the first conversion of the Gentiles; and afterwards countenanced, and confirmed, and augmented by the Bishops of Rome.

As for the proofs alledged out of Scripture, namely, those examples of Images appointed by God to bee set up; They were not set up for the people, or any man to worship; but that they should worship God himselfe before them; as before the Cherubins over the Ark, and the Brazen Serpent. For we read not, that the Priest, or any other did worship the Cherubins; but contrarily wee read (2 *Kings* 18.4.) that Hezekiah brake in pieces the Brazen Serpent which Moses had set up, because the People burnt incense to it. Besides, those examples are not put for our Imitation, that we also should set up Images, under pretence of worshipping God before them; because the words of the second Commandement, *Thou shalt not make to thy selfe any graven Image, &c.* distinguish between the Images that God commanded to be set up, and those which wee set up to our selves. And therefore from the Cherubins, or Brazen Serpent, to the Images of mans devising; and from the Worship

Answer to the Argument from the Cherubins, and Brazen Serpent

commanded by God, to the Will-Worship of men, the argument is not good. This also is to bee considered, that as Hezekiah brake in pieces the Brazen Serpent, because the Jews did worship it, to the end they should doe so no more; so also Christian Soveraigns ought to break down the Images which their Subjects have been accustomed to worship; that there be no more occasion of such Idolatry. For at this day, the ignorant People, where Images are worshipped, doe really beleeve there is a Divine Power in the Images; and are told by their Pastors, that some of them have spoken; and have bled; and that miracles have been done by them; which they apprehend as done by the Saint, which they think either is the Image it self, or in it. The Israelites, when they worshipped the Calfe, did think they worshipped the God that brought them out of Egypt; and yet it was Idolatry, because they thought the Calfe either was that God, or had him in his belly. And though some man may think it impossible for people to be so stupid, as to think the Image to be God, or a Saint; or to worship it in that notion; yet it is manifest in Scripture to the contrary; where when the Golden Calfe was made, *Exod. 32. 2 the people said, *These are thy Gods O Israel; and *Gen. 31. 30 where the Images of Laban* are called his Gods.[40] And wee see daily by experience in all sorts of People, that such men as study nothing but their food and ease, are content to beleeve any absurdity, rather than to trouble themselves to examine it; holding their faith as it were by entaile unalienable, except by an expresse and new Law.

Painting of Fancies no Idolatry: but abusing them to Religious Worship is But they inferre from some other places, that it is lawfull to paint Angels, and also God himself: as from Gods walking in the Garden; from Jacobs seeing God at the top of the ladder; and from other Visions, and Dreams. But Visions, and Dreams, whether naturall, or supernaturall, are but Phantasmes: and he that painteth an [364] Image of any of them, maketh not an Image of God, but of his own Phantasm, which is, making of an Idol. I say not, that to draw a Picture after a fancy, is a

Sin; but when it is drawn, to hold it for a Representation of God, is against the second Commandement; and can be of no use, but to worship. And the same may be said of the Images of Angels, and of men dead; unlesse as Monuments of friends, or of men worthy of remembrance: For such use of an Image, is not Worship of the Image; but a civill honoring of the Person, not that is, but that was: But when it is done to the Image which we make of a Saint, for no other reason, but that we think he heareth our prayers, and is pleased with the honour wee doe him, when dead, and without sense, wee attribute to him more than humane power; and therefore it is Idolatry.

Seeing therefore there is no authority, neither in the Law of Moses, nor in the Gospel, for the religious Worship of Images, or other Representations of God, which men set up to themselves; or for the Worship of the Image of any Creature in Heaven, or Earth, or under the Earth: And whereas Christian Kings, who are living Representants of God, are not to be worshipped by their Subjects, by any act, that signifieth a greater esteem of his power, than the nature of mortall man is capable of; It cannot be imagined, that the Religious Worship now in use, was brought into the Church, by misunderstanding of the Scripture. It resteth therefore, that it was left in it, by not destroying the Images themselves, in the conversion of the Gentiles that worshipped them.

The cause whereof, was the immoderate esteem, and prices set upon the workmanship of them, which made the owners (though converted, from worshipping them as they had done Religiously for Dæmons) to retain them still in their houses, upon pretence of doing it in the honor of *Christ*, of the *Virgin Mary*, and of the *Apostles*, and other the Pastors of the Primitive Church; as being easie, by giving them new names, to make that an Image of the *Virgin Mary*, and of her *Sonne* our Saviour, which before perhaps was called the Image of *Venus*, and *Cupid*; and so of a *Jupiter* to make a *Barnabas*, and

How Idolatry was left in the Church

of *Mercury* a *Paul*, and the like. And as worldly ambition creeping by degrees into the Pastors, drew them to an endeavour of pleasing the new made Christians; and also to a liking of this kind of honour, which they also might hope for after their decease, as well as those that had already gained it: so the worshipping of the Images of Christ and his Apostles, grew more and more Idolatrous; save that somewhat after the time of Constantine, divers Emperors, and Bishops, and generall Councells observed, and opposed the unlawfulnesse thereof; but too late, or too weakly.

Canonizing   The *Canonizing of Saints*, is another Relique of Gen-
of Saints   tilisme: It is neither a misunderstanding of Scripture, nor a new invention of the Roman Church, but a custome as ancient as the Common-wealth of *Rome* it self. The first that ever was canonized at Rome, was *Romulus*, and that upon the narration of *Julius Proculus*, that swore before the Senate, he spake with him after his death, and was assured by him, he [365] dwelt in Heaven, and was there called *Quirinus*, and would be propitious to the State of their new City:[41] And thereupon the Senate gave *publique testimony* of his Sanctity. *Julius Cæsar*, and other Emperors after him, had the like *testimony*; that is, were Canonized for Saints; for by such testimony is CANONIZATION, now defined; and is the same with the Ἀποθέωσις of the Heathen.

The name of   It is also from the Roman Heathen, that the Popes
Pontifex   have received the name, and power of PONTIFEX MAXIMUS. This was the name of him that in the ancient Common-wealth of Rome, had the Supreme Authority under the Senate and People, of regulating all Ceremonies, and Doctrines concerning their Religion: And when *Augustus Cæsar* changed the State into a Monarchy, he took to himself no more but this office, and that of Tribune of the People, (that is to say, the Supreme Power both in State, and Religion;) and the succeeding Emperors enjoyed the same. But when the Emperour Constantine lived, who was the first that professed and

authorized Christian Religion, it was consonant to his
profession, to cause Religion to be regulated (under
his authority) by the Bishop of Rome: Though it doe
not appear they had so soon the name of *Pontifex*; but
rather, that the succeeding Bishops took it of themselves, to countenance the power they exercised over the
Bishops of the Roman Provinces. For it is not any Priviledge of St. Peter, but the Priviledge of the City of Rome,
which the Emperors were alwaies willing to uphold, that
gave them such authority over other Bishops; as may be
evidently seen by that, that the Bishop of Constantinople, when the Emperour made that City the Seat of the
Empire, pretended to bee equall to the Bishop of Rome;
though at last, not without contention, the Pope carryed it, and became the *Pontifex Maximus*; but in right
onely of the Emperour; and not without the bounds of
the Empire; nor any where, after the Emperour had lost
his power in Rome; though it were the Pope himself that
took his power from him. From whence wee may by the
way observe, that there is no place for the superiority
of the Pope over other Bishops, except in the territories
whereof he is himself the Civill Soveraign; and where the
Emperour having Soveraign Power Civill, hath expressely chosen the Pope for the chief Pastor under himselfe,
of his Christian Subjects.

The carrying about of Images in *Procession*, is *Procession of*
another Relique of the Religion of the Greeks, and *Images*
Romans: For they also carried their Idols from place to
place, in a kind of Chariot, which was peculiarly dedicated to that use, which the Latines called *Thensa*, and
Vehiculum Deorum;[42] and the Image was placed in a
frame, or Shrine, which they called *Ferculum*: And that
which they called *Pompa*, is the same that now is named
Procession: According whereunto, amongst the Divine
Honors which were given to *Julius Cæsar* by the Senate,
this was one, that in the Pompe (or Procession) at the
Circæan games, he should have *Thensam & Ferculum*, a
sacred Chariot, and a Shrine; which was as much, as to

be carried up and down as a God: Just as at this day the Popes are carried by Switzers under a Canopie.[43]

Wax Candles, and Torches lighted   [366] To these Processions also belonged the bearing of burning Torches, and Candles, before the Images of the Gods, both amongst the Greeks, and Romans. For afterwards the Emperors of Rome received the same honor; as we read of *Caligula*, that at his reception to the Empire, he was carried from *Misenum* to *Rome*, in the midst of a throng of People, the wayes beset with Altars, and Beasts for Sacrifice, and burning *Torches*:[44] And of *Caracalla* that was received into *Alexandria* with Incense, and with casting of Flowers,[45] and δαδουχίαις, that is, with Torches; for Δαδοῦχοι were they that amongst the Greeks carried Torches lighted in the Processions of their Gods: And in processe of time, the devout, but ignorant People, did many times honor their Bishops with the like pompe of Wax Candles, and the Images of our Saviour, and the Saints, constantly, in the Church it self. And thus came in the use of Wax Candles; and was also established by some of the ancient Councells.

The Heathens had also their *Aqua Lustralis*, that is to say, *Holy Water*. The Church of Rome imitates them also in their *Holy Dayes*. They had their *Bacchanalia*; and we have our *Wakes*, answering to them: They their *Saturnalia*, and we our *Carnevalls*, and Shrove-tuesdays liberty of Servants: They their Procession of *Priapus*; wee our fetching in, erection, and dancing about *May-poles*; and Dancing is one kind of Worship: They had their Procession called *Ambarvalia*; and we our Procession about the fields in the *Rogation week*. Nor do I think that these are all the Ceremonies that have been left in the Church, from the first conversion of the Gentiles: but they are all that I can for the present call to mind; and if a man would wel observe that which is delivered in the Histories, concerning the Religious Rites of the Greeks and Romanes, I doubt not but he might find many more of these old empty Bottles of

Gentilisme, which the Doctors of the Romane Church, either by Negligence, or Ambition, have filled up again with the new Wine of Christianity, that will not faile in time to break them. [367]

CHAP. XLVI

Of DARKNESSE *from* VAIN PHILOSOPHY, *and* FABULOUS TRADITIONS

By PHILOSOPHY, is understood *the Knowledge acquired* *by Reasoning, from the Manner of the Generation of* *any thing, to the Properties; or from the Properties, to* *some possible Way of Generation of the same; to the* *end to bee able to produce, as far as matter, and humane* *force permit, such Effects, as humane life requireth.* So the Geometrician, from the Construction of Figures, findeth out many Properties thereof; and from the Properties, new Ways of their Construction, by Reasoning; to the end to be able to measure Land, and Water; and for infinite other uses. So the Astronomer, from the Rising, Setting, and Moving of the Sun, and Starres, in divers parts of the Heavens, findeth out the Causes of Day, and Night, and of the different Seasons of the Year; whereby he keepeth an account of Time: And the like of other Sciences. *What Philosophy is*

By which Definition it is evident, that we are not to account as any part thereof, that originall knowledge called Experience, in which consisteth Prudence: Because it is not attained by Reasoning, but found as well in Brute Beasts, as in Man; and is but a Memory of successions of events in times past, wherein the omission of every little circumstance altering the effect, frustrateth the expectation of the most Prudent: whereas nothing is produced by Reasoning aright, but generall, eternall, and immutable Truth. *Prudence no part of Philosophy*

No false
Doctrine is
part of
Philosophy:

Nor are we therefore to give that name to any false Conclusions: For he that Reasoneth aright in words he understandeth, can never conclude an Error:

Nor to that which any man knows by supernaturall Revelation; because it is not acquired by Reasoning:

No more is
Revelation
supernaturall:

Nor that which is gotten by Reasoning from the Authority of Books; because it is not by Reasoning from the Cause to the Effect, nor from the Effect to the Cause; and is not Knowledge, but Faith.

Nor learning
taken upon
credit of
Authors

The faculty of Reasoning being consequent to the use of Speech, it was not possible, but that there should have been some generall Truthes found out by Reasoning, as ancient almost as Language it selfe. The Savages of America, are not without some good Morall Sentences; also they have a little Arithmetick, to adde, and divide in Numbers not too great: but they are not therefore Philosophers. For as there were Plants of Corn and Wine in small quantity disper[368]sed in the Fields and Woods, before men knew their vertue, or made use of them for their nourishment, or planted them apart in Fields, and Vineyards; in which time they fed on Akorns, and drank Water: so also there have been divers true, generall, and profitable Speculations from the beginning; as being the naturall plants of humane Reason: But they were at first but few in number; men lived upon grosse Experience; there was no Method; that is to say, no Sowing, nor Planting of Knowledge by it self, apart from the Weeds, and common Plants of Errour and Conjecture: And the cause of it being the want of leasure from procuring the necessities of life, and defending themselves against their neighbors, it was impossible, till the erecting of great Common-wealths, it should be otherwise. *Leasure* is the mother of *Philosophy*; and *Common-wealth*, the mother of *Peace*, and *Leasure*: Where first were great and flourishing *Cities*, there was first the study of *Philosophy*. The *Gymnosophists* of *India*,[46] the *Magi* of *Persia*, and the *Priests* of *Chaldæa* and *Egypt*, are counted the most ancient Philosophers; and those Countreys were

Of the
Beginnings
and Progresse
of Philosophy

the most ancient of Kingdomes. *Philosophy* was not
risen to the *Græcians*, and other people of the West,
whose *Common-wealths* (no greater perhaps then
Lucca, or *Geneva*) had never *Peace*, but when their fears
of one another were equall; nor the *Leasure* to observe
any thing but one another. At length, when Warre had
united many of these *Græcian* lesser Cities, into fewer,
and greater; then began *Seven men*, of severall parts of
Greece, to get the reputation of being *Wise*;[47] some of
them for *Morall* and *Politique* sentences; and others for
the learning of the *Chaldæans* and *Egyptians*, which
was *Astronomy*, and *Geometry*. But we hear not yet of
any *Schools* of *Philosophy*.

After the *Athenians* by the overthrow of the *Per-* *Of the*
sian Armies, had gotten the Dominion of the Sea; and *Schools of*
thereby, of all the Islands, and Maritime Cities of the *Philosophy*
Archipelago, as well of *Asia* as *Europe*; and were grown *amongst the*
wealthy; they that had no employment, neither at home, *Athenians*
nor abroad, had little else to employ themselves in, but
either (as St. *Luke* says, *Acts* 17.21.) *in telling and hear-*
ing news, or in discoursing of *Philosophy* publiquely to
the youth of the City. Every Master took some place
for that purpose. *Plato* in certain publique Walks called
Academia, from one *Academus*: *Aristotle* in the Walk of
the Temple of *Pan*, called *Lycæum*: others in the *Stoa*,
or covered Walk, wherein the Merchants Goods were
brought to land: others in other places; where they spent
the time of their Leasure, in teaching or in disputing of
their Opinions: and some in any place, where they could
get the youth of the City together to hear them talk. And
this was it which *Carneades* also did at *Rome*, when
he was Ambassadour: which caused *Cato* to advise the
Senate to dispatch him quickly, for feare of corrupting
the manners of the young men that delighted to hear
him speak (as they thought) fine things.[48]

From this it was, that the place where any of them
taught, and disputed, was called *Schola*, which in
their Tongue signifieth *Leasure*; and their Disputations,

Diatribæ, that is to say, *Passing of the* [369] *time*. Also
the Philosophers themselves had the name of their Sects,
some of them from these their Schools: For they that followed *Plato*'s Doctrine, were called *Academiques*; The
followers of *Aristotle*, *Peripatetiques*, from the Walk
hee taught in; and those that *Zeno* taught,[49] *Stoiques*,
from the *Stoa*: as if we should denominate men from
More-fields, from *Pauls-Church*, and from the *Exchange*,
because they meet there often, to prate and loyter.

Neverthelesse, men were so much taken with this
custome, that in time it spread it selfe over all Europe,
and the best part of Afrique; so as there were Schools
publiquely erected, and maintained for Lectures, and
Disputations, almost in every Common-wealth.

Of the   There were also Schools, anciently, both before, and
Schools of after the time of our Saviour, amongst the *Jews*: but they
the Jews were Schools of their Law. For though they were called
Synagogues, that is to say, Congregations of the People;
yet in as much as the Law was every Sabbath day read,
expounded, and disputed in them, they differed not in
nature, but in name onely from Publique Schools; and
were not onely in Jerusalem, but in every City of the
Gentiles, where the Jews inhabited. There was such a
Schoole at *Damascus*, whereinto *Paul* entred, to persecute. There were others at *Antioch*, *Iconium* and
Thessalonica, whereinto he entred, to dispute: And such
was the Synagogue of the *Libertines*, *Cyrenians*, *Alex-
andrians*, *Cilicians*, and those of *Asia*; that is to say, the
Schoole of *Libertines*, and of *Jewes*, that were strangers
in *Jerusalem*: And of this Schoole they were that disputed (*Act.* 6.9.) with *Saint Steven*.

The Schoole   But what has been the Utility of those Schools? what
of the Science is there at this day acquired by their Readings
Græcians and Disputings? That wee have of Geometry, which is
unprofitable the Mother of all Naturall Science, wee are not indebted
for it to the Schools. *Plato* that was the best Philosopher
of the Greeks, forbad entrance into his Schoole, to all
that were not already in some measure Geometricians.

There were many that studied that Science to the great advantage of mankind: but there is no mention of their Schools; nor was there any Sect of Geometricians; nor did they then passe under the name of Philosophers. The naturall Philosophy of those Schools, was rather a Dream than Science, and set forth in senselesse and insignificant Language; which cannot be avoided by those that will teach Philosophy, without having first attained great knowledge in Geometry: For Nature worketh by Motion; the Wayes, and Degrees whereof cannot be known, without the knowledge of the Proportions and Properties of Lines, and Figures. Their Morall Philosophy is but a description of their own Passions. For the rule of Manners, without Civill Government, is the Law of Nature; and in it, the Law Civill; that determineth what is *Honest*, and *Dishonest*; what is *Just*, and *Unjust*; and generally what is *Good*, and *Evill*: whereas they make the Rules of *Good*, and *Bad*, by their own *Liking*, and *Disliking*: By which means, in so great di[370]versity of taste, there is nothing generally agreed on; but every one doth (as far as he dares) whatsoever seemeth good in his owne eyes, to the subversion of Common-wealth. Their *Logique* which should bee the Method of Reasoning, is nothing else but Captions of Words, and Inventions how to puzzle such as should goe about to pose them. To conclude, there is nothing so absurd, that the old Philosophers (as *Cicero* saith, who was one of them) have not some of them maintained. And I beleeve that scarce any thing can be more absurdly said in naturall Philosophy, than that which now is called *Aristotles Metaphysiques*; nor more repugnant to Government, than much of that hee hath said in his *Politiques*; nor more ignorantly, than a great part of his *Ethiques*.

The Schoole of the Jews, was originally a Schoole of the Law of *Moses*; who commanded (*Deut.* 31.10.) that at the end of every seventh year, at the Feast of the Tabernacles, it should be read to all the people, that they might hear, and learn it: Therefore the reading of the Law

The Schools of the Jews unprofitable

(which was in use after the Captivity) every Sabbath day, ought to have had no other end, but the acquainting of the people with the Commandements which they were to obey, and to expound unto them the writings of the Prophets. But it is manifest, by the many reprehensions of them by our Saviour, that they corrupted the Text of the Law with their false Commentaries, and vain Traditions; and so little understood the Prophets, that they did neither acknowledge Christ, nor the works he did; of which the Prophets prophecyed. So that by their Lectures and Disputations in their Synagogues, they turned the Doctrine of their Law into a Phantasticall kind of Philosophy, concerning the incomprehensible nature of God, and of Spirits; which they compounded of the Vain Philosophy and Theology of the Græcians, mingled with their own fancies, drawn from the obscurer places of the Scripture, and which might most easily bee wrested to their purpose; and from the Fabulous Traditions of their Ancestors.

University what it is   That which is now called an *University*, is a Joyning together, and an Incorporation under one Government of many Publique Schools, in one and the same Town or City. In which, the principall Schools were ordained for the three Professions, that is to say, of the Romane Religion, of the Romane Law, and of the Art of Medicine. And for the study of Philosophy it hath no otherwise place, then as a handmaid to the Romane Religion: And since the Authority of Aristotle is onely current there, that study is not properly Philosophy, (the nature whereof dependeth not on Authors,) but Aristotelity. And for Geometry, till of very late times it had no place at all; as being subservient to nothing but rigide Truth. And if any man by the ingenuity of his owne nature, *Errors brought into Religion from Aristotles Metaphysiques* had attained to any degree of perfection therein, hee was commonly thought a Magician, and his Art Diabolicall.

[371] Now to descend to the particular Tenets of Vain Philosophy, derived to the Universities, and thence into the Church, partly from Aristotle, partly from Blindnesse

of understanding; I shall first consider their Principles. There is a certain *Philosophia prima*, on which all other Philosophy ought to depend; and consisteth principally, in right limiting of the significations of such Appellations, or Names, as are of all others the most Universall: Which Limitations serve to avoid ambiguity, and æquivocation in Reasoning; and are commonly called Definitions; such as are the Definitions of Body, Time, Place, Matter, Forme, Essence, Subject, Substance, Accident, Power, Act, Finite, Infinite, Quantity, Quality, Motion, Action, Passion, and divers others, necessary to the explaining of a mans Conceptions concerning the Nature and Generation of Bodies. The Explication (that is, the setling of the meaning) of which, and the like Terms, is commonly in the Schools called *Metaphysiques*; as being a part of the Philosophy of Aristotle, which hath that for title: but it is in another sense; for there it signifieth as much, as *Books written, or placed after his naturall Philosophy*: But the Schools take them for *Books of supernaturall Philosophy*: for the word *Metaphysiques* will bear both these senses. And indeed that which is there written, is for the most part so far from the possibility of being understood, and so repugnant to naturall Reason, that whosoever thinketh there is any thing to bee understood by it, must needs think it supernaturall.

From these Metaphysiques, which are mingled with the Scripture to make Schoole Divinity, wee are told, there be in the world certaine Essences separated from Bodies, which they call *Abstract Essences, and Substantiall Formes*: For the Interpreting of which *Jargon*, there is need of somewhat more than ordinary attention in this place. Also I ask pardon of those that are not used to this kind of Discourse, for applying my selfe to those that are. The World, (I mean not the Earth onely, that denominates the Lovers of it *Worldly men*, but the *Universe*, that is, the whole masse of all things that are) is Corporeall, that is to say, Body; and hath the dimensions of Magnitude, namely, Length, Bredth, and

Errors concerning Abstract Essences

Depth: also every part of Body, is likewise Body, and hath the like dimensions; and consequently every part of the Universe, is Body, and that which is not Body, is no part of the Universe: And because the Universe is All, that which is no part of it, is *Nothing*; and consequently *no where*. Nor does it follow from hence, that Spirits are *nothing*: for they have dimensions, and are therefore really *Bodies*; though that name in common Speech be given to such Bodies onely, as are visible, or palpable; that is, that have some degree of Opacity: But for Spirits, they call them Incorporeall; which is a name of more honour, and may therefore with more piety bee attributed to God himselfe; in whom wee consider not what Attribute expresseth best his Nature, which is Incomprehensible; but what best expresseth our desire to honour Him.

[372] To know now upon what grounds they say there be *Essences Abstract*, or *Substantiall Formes*, wee are to consider what those words do properly signifie. The use of Words, is to register to our selves, and make manifest to others the Thoughts and Conceptions of our Minds. Of which Words, some are the names of the Things conceived; as the names of all sorts of Bodies, that work upon the Senses, and leave an Impression in the Imagination: Others are the names of the Imaginations themselves; that is to say, of those Ideas, or mentall Images we have of all things wee see, or remember: And others againe are names of Names; or of different sorts of Speech: As *Universall*, *Plurall*, *Singular*, are the names of Names; and *Definition*, *Affirmation*, *Negation*, *True*, *False*, *Syllogisme*, *Interrogation*, *Promise*, *Covenant*, are the names of certain Forms of Speech. Others serve to shew the Consequence, or Repugnance of one name to another; as when one saith, *A Man is a Body*, hee intendeth that the name of *Body* is necessarily consequent to the name of *Man*; as being but severall names of the same thing, *Man*; which Consequence is signified by coupling them together with the word *Is*. And as wee use the Verbe *Is*; so the Latines use their Verbe *Est*,

and the Greeks their Ἔστι through all its Declinations.
Whether all other Nations of the world have in their
severall languages a word that answereth to it, or not, I
cannot tell; but I am sure they have not need of it: For
the placing of two names in order may serve to signifie
their Consequence, if it were the custome, (for Custome
is it, that give words their force,) as well as the words *Is*,
or *Bee*, or *Are*, and the like.

And if it were so, that there were a Language without any verb answerable to *Est*, or *Is*, or *Bee*; yet the
men that used it would bee not a jot the lesse capable
of Inferring, Concluding, and of all kind of Reasoning, than were the Greeks, and Latines. But what then
would become of these Terms, of *Entity*, *Essence*, *Essentiall*, *Essentiality*, that are derived from it, and of many
more that depend on these, applyed as most commonly
they are? They are therefore no Names of Things; but
Signes, by which wee make known, that wee conceive
the Consequence of one name or Attribute to another:
as when we say, *a Man, is, a living Body*, wee mean not
that the *Man* is one thing, the *Living Body* another, and
the *Is*, or *Beeing* a third: but that the *Man*, and the *Living Body*, is the same thing; because the Consequence,
If hee bee a Man, hee is a living Body, is a true Consequence, signified by that word *Is*. Therefore, *to bee a
Body, to Walke, to bee Speaking, to Live, to See*, and
the like Infinitives; also *Corporeity, Walking, Speaking,
Life, Sight*, and the like, that signifie just the same, are
the names of *Nothing*; as I have elsewhere more amply
expressed.

But to what purpose (may some man say) is such subtilty in a work of this nature, where I pretend to nothing
but what is necessary to the doctrine of Government and
Obedience? It is to this purpose, that men may no longer
suffer themselves to be abused, [373] by them, that by
this doctrine of *Separated Essences*, built on the Vain
Philosophy of Aristotle, would fright them from Obeying the Laws of their Countrey, with empty names; as

men fright Birds from the Corn with an empty doublet, a hat, and a crooked stick. For it is upon this ground, that when a Man is dead and buried, they say his Soule (that is his Life) can walk separated from his Body, and is seen by night amongst the graves. Upon the same ground they say, that the Figure, and Colour, and Tast of a peece of Bread, has a being, there, where they say there is no Bread: And upon the same ground they say, that Faith, and Wisdome, and other Vertues are sometimes *powred* into a man, sometimes *blown* into him from Heaven; as if the Vertuous, and their Vertues could be asunder; and a great many other things that serve to lessen the dependance of Subjects on the Soveraign Power of their Countrey. For who will endeavour to obey the Laws, if he expect Obedience to be Powred or Blown into him? Or who will not obey a Priest, that can make God, rather than his Soveraign; nay than God himselfe? Or who, that is in fear of Ghosts, will not bear great respect to those that can make the Holy Water, that drives them from him? And this shall suffice for an example of the Errors, which are brought into the Church, from the *Entities*, and *Essences* of Aristotle: which it may be he knew to be false Philosophy; but writ it as a thing consonant to, and corroborative of their Religion; and fearing the fate of Socrates.[50]

Being once fallen into this Error of *Separated Essences*, they are thereby necessarily involved in many other absurdities that follow it. For seeing they will have these Forms to be reall, they are obliged to assign them *some place*. But because they hold them Incorporeall, without all dimension of Quantity, and all men know that Place is Dimension, and not to be filled, but by that which is Corporeall; they are driven to uphold their credit with a distinction, that they are not indeed any where *Circumscriptivè*, but *Definitivè*: Which Terms being meer Words, and in this occasion insignificant, passe onely in Latine, that the vanity of them may bee concealed. For the Circumscription of a thing, is nothing else but the Determination, or Defining of its Place; and so both the Terms of the Distinction are the same. And in particular, of the Essence of a Man, which (they say) is his Soule, they affirm it, to be All of it in his little Finger, and All of it in every other Part (how small soever) of his Body; and yet no more Soule in the Whole Body, than in any one of those Parts. Can any man think that God is served with such absurdities? And yet all this is necessary to beleeve, to those that will beleeve the Existence of an Incorporeall Soule, Separated from the Body.

And when they come to give account, how an Incorporeall Substance can be capable of Pain, and be tormented in the fire of Hell, or Purgatory, they have nothing at all to answer, but that it cannot be known how fire can burn Soules.

[374] Again, whereas Motion is change of Place, and Incorporeall Substances are not capable of Place, they are troubled to make it seem possible, how a Soule can goe hence, without the Body to Heaven, Hell, or Purgatory; and how the Ghosts of men (and I may adde of their clothes which they appear in) can walk by night in Churches, Church-yards, and other places of Sepulture. To which I know not what they can answer, unlesse they will say, they walke *definitivè*, not *circumscriptivè*, or *spiritually*, not *temporally*: for such egregious distinctions are equally applicable to any difficulty whatsoever.

For the meaning of *Eternity*, they will not have it to be an Endlesse Succession of Time; for then they should not be able to render a reason how Gods Will, and Præordaining of things to come, should not be before his Præscience of the same, as the Efficient Cause before the Effect, or Agent before the Action; nor of many other their bold opinions concerning the Incomprehensible Nature of God. But they will teach us, that Eternity is the Standing still of the Present Time, a *Nunc-stans* (as the Schools call it;) which neither they, nor any else understand, no more than they would a *Hic-stans* for an Infinite greatnesse of Place. *Nunc-stans*

One Body in   And whereas men divide a Body in their thought,
many places, by numbring parts of it, and in numbring those parts,
and many   number also the parts of the Place it filled; it cannot
Bodies in one be, but in making many parts, wee make also many places
place at once of those parts; whereby there cannot bee conceived in
the mind of any man, more, or fewer parts, than there
are places for: yet they will have us beleeve, that by the
Almighty power of God, one body may be at one and
the same time in many places; and many bodies at one
and the same time in one place; as if it were an acknowledgment of the Divine Power, to say, that which is, is
not; or that which has been, has not been. And these are
but a small part of the Incongruities they are forced to,
from their disputing Philosophically, in stead of admir-
ing, and adoring of the Divine and Incomprehensible
Nature; whose Attributes cannot signifie what he is, but
ought to signifie our desire to honour him, with the best
Appellations we can think on. But they that venture to
reason of his Nature, from these Attributes of Honour,
losing their understanding in the very first attempt, fall
from one Inconvenience into another, without end, and
without number; in the same manner, as when a man
ignorant of the Ceremonies of Court, comming into the
presence of a greater Person than he is used to speak
to, and stumbling at his entrance, to save himselfe from
falling, lets slip his Cloake; to recover his Cloake, lets
fall his Hat; and with one disorder after another, discov-
ers his astonishment and rusticity.

Absurdities   Then for *Physiques*, that is, the knowledge of the
in naturall   subordinate, and secundary causes of naturall events;
Philosophy,   they render none at all, but empty words. If you desire
as Gravity   to know why some kind of bodies sink naturally down-
the Cause of wards toward the Earth, and others goe naturally from it;
Heavinesse   The Schools will tell you out of Aristotle, that the bodies
[375] that sink downwards, are *Heavy*; and that this
Heavinesse is it that causes them to descend: But if you
ask what they mean by *Heavinesse*, they will define it to
bee an endeavour to goe to the center of the Earth: so that

the cause why things sink downward, is an Endeavour to be below: which is as much as to say, that bodies descend, or ascend, because they doe. Or they will tell you the center of the Earth is the place of Rest, and Conservation for Heavy things; and therefore they endeavour to be there: As if Stones, and Metalls had a desire, or could discern the place they would bee at, as Man does; or loved Rest, as Man does not; or that a peece of Glasse were lesse safe in the Window, than falling into the Street.

If we would know why the same Body seems greater (without adding to it) one time, than another; they say, when it seems lesse, it is *Condensed*; when greater, *Rarefied*. What is that *Condensed*, and *Rarefied*? Condensed, is when there is in the very same Matter, lesse Quantity than before; and Rarefied, when more. As if there could be Matter, that had not some determined Quantity; when Quantity is nothing else but the Determination of Matter; that is to say of Body, by which we say one Body is greater, or lesser than another, by thus, or thus much. Or as if a Body were made without any Quantity at all, and that afterwards more, or lesse were put into it, according as it is intended the Body should be more, or lesse Dense. *Quantity put into Body already made*

For the cause of the Soule of Man, they say, *Creatur Infundendo*, and *Creando Infunditur*: that is, *It is Created by Powring it in*, and *Powred in by Creation*. *Powring in of Soules*

For the Cause of Sense, an ubiquity of *Species*; that is, of the *Shews* or *Apparitions* of objects; which when they be Apparitions to the Eye, is *Sight*; when to the Eare, *Hearing*; to the Palate, *Tast*; to the Nostrill, *Smelling*; and to the rest of the Body, *Feeling*. *Ubiquity of Apparition.*

For cause of the Will, to doe any particular action, which is called *Volitio*, they assign the Faculty, that is to say, the Capacity in generall, that men have, to will sometimes one thing, sometimes another, which is called *Voluntas*; making the *Power* the cause of the *Act*: As if one should assign for cause of the good or evill Acts of men, their Ability to doe them. *Will, the Cause of Willing*

Ignorance an occult Cause   And in many occasions they put for cause of Naturall events, their own Ignorance, but disguised in other words: As when they say, Fortune is the cause of things contingent; that is, of things whereof they know no cause: And as when they attribute many Effects to *occult qualities*; that is, qualities not known to them; and therefore also (as they thinke) to no Man else. And to *Sympathy, Antipathy, Antiperistasis,*[51] *Specificall Qualities*, and other like Termes, which signifie neither the Agent that produceth them, nor the Operation by which they are produced.

[376] If such *Metaphysiques*, and *Physiques* as this, be not *Vain Philosophy*, there was never any; nor needed St. Paul to give us warning to avoid it.

One makes the things incongruent, another the Incongruity   And for their Morall, and Civill Philosophy, it hath the same, or greater absurdities. If a man doe an action of Injustice, that is to say, an action contrary to the Law, God they say is the prime cause of the Law, and also the prime cause of that, and all other Actions; but no cause at all of the Injustice; which is the Inconformity of the Action to the Law. This is Vain Philosophy. A man might as well say, that one man maketh both a streight line, and a crooked, and another maketh their Incongruity. And such is the Philosophy of all men that resolve of their Conclusions, before they know their Premises; pretending to comprehend, that which is Incomprehensible; and of Attributes of Honour to make Attributes of Nature; as this distinction was made to maintain the Doctrine of Free-Will, that is, of a Will of man, not subject to the Will of God.

Private Appetite the rule of Publique good: Aristotle, and other Heathen Philosophers define Good, and Evill, by the Appetite of men; and well enough, as long as we consider them governed every one by his own Law: For in the condition of men that have no other Law but their own Appetites, there can be no generall Rule of Good, and Evil Actions. But in a Common-wealth this measure is false: Not the Appetite of Private men, but the Law, which is the Will and

Appetite of the State is the measure. And yet is this Doctrine still practised; and men judge the Goodnesse, or Wickednesse of their own, and of other mens actions, and of the actions of the Common-wealth it selfe, by their own Passions; and no man calleth Good or Evill, but that which is so in his own eyes, without any regard at all to the Publique Laws; except onely Monks, and Friers, that are bound by Vow to that simple obedience to their Superiour, to which every Subject ought to think himself bound by the Law of Nature to the Civill Soveraign. And this private measure of Good, is a Doctrine, not onely Vain, but also Pernicious to the Publique State.

It is also Vain and false Philosophy, to say the work of Marriage is repugnant to Chastity, or Continence, and by consequence to make them Morall Vices; as they doe, that pretend Chastity, and Continence, for the ground of denying Marriage to the Clergy. For they confesse it is no more, but a Constitution of the Church, that requireth in those holy Orders that continually attend the Altar, and administration of the Eucharist, a continuall Abstinence from women, under the name of continuall Chastity, Continence, and Purity. Therefore they call the lawfull use of Wives, want of Chastity, and Continence; and so make Marriage a Sin, or at least a thing so impure, and unclean, as to render a man unfit for the Altar. If the Law were made because the use of Wives is Incontinence, and contrary to Chastity, then all Marriage is vice: If because it is a thing too impure, and unclean for a man consecrated to God; much more should other naturall, necessary, and daily works which all men doe, [377] render men unworthy to bee Priests, because they are more unclean.

And that lawfull Marriage is Unchastity:

But the secret foundation of this prohibition of Marriage of Priests, is not likely to have been laid so slightly, as upon such errours in Morall Philosophy; nor yet upon the preference of single life, to the estate of Matrimony; which proceeded from the wisdome of St. Paul, who perceived how inconvenient a thing it was, for those that in those times of persecution were Preachers of the Gospel, and forced to fly from one countrey to another, to be clogged with the care of wife and children; but upon the designe of the Popes, and Priests of after times, to make themselves the Clergy, that is to say, sole Heirs of the Kingdome of God in this world; to which it was necessary to take from them the use of Marriage, because our Saviour saith, that at the coming of his Kingdome the Children of God *shall neither Marry, nor bee given in Marriage, but shall bee as the Angels in heaven;*[52] that is to say, Spirituall. Seeing then they had taken on them the name of Spirituall, to have allowed themselves (when there was no need) the propriety of Wives, had been an Incongruity.

And that all Government but Popular, is Tyranny: From Aristotles Civill Philosophy, they have learned, to call all manner of Common-wealths but the Popular, (such as was at that time the state of Athens,) *Tyranny.* All Kings they called Tyrants; and the Aristocracy of the thirty Governours set up there by the Lacedemonians that subdued them, the thirty Tyrants:[53] As also to call the condition of the people under the Democracy, *Liberty.* A *Tyrant* originally signified no more simply, but a *Monarch*: But when afterwards in most parts of Greece that kind of government was abolished, the name began to signifie, not onely the thing it did before, but with it, the hatred which the Popular States bare towards it: As also the name of King became odious after the deposing of the Kings in Rome, as being a thing naturall to all men, to conceive some great Fault to be signified in any Attribute, that is given in despight, and to a great Enemy. And when the same men shall be displeased with those that have the administration of the Democracy, or Aristocracy, they are not to seek for disgracefull names to expresse their anger in; but call readily the one *Anarchy*, and the other, *Oligarchy*, or the *Tyranny of a Few.* And that which offendeth the People, is no other thing, but that they are governed, not as every one of them would himselfe, but as the Publique Representant, be it one Man, or an Assembly of men thinks fit; that is, by an Arbitrary government: for which they give evill names to their Superiors; never knowing (till perhaps a little after a Civill warre) that without such Arbitrary government, such Warre must be perpetuall; and that it is Men, and Arms, not Words, and Promises, that make the Force and Power of the Laws.

And therefore this is another Errour of Aristotles Poli- *That not Men,* tiques, that in a wel ordered Common-wealth, not Men *but Law* should govern, but the Laws.[54] What man, that has *governs* his naturall Senses, though he can nei[378]-ther write nor read, does not find himself governed by them he fears, and beleeves can kill or hurt him when he obeyeth not? or that beleeves the Law can hurt him; that is, Words, and Paper, without the Hands, and Swords of men? And this is of the number of pernicious Errors: for they induce men, as oft as they like not their Gover- nours, to adhære to those that call them Tyrants, and to think it lawfull to raise warre against them: And yet they are many times cherished from the Pulpit, by the Clergy.

There is another Errour in their Civill Philosophy *Laws* (which they never learned of Aristotle, nor Cicero, nor *over the* any other of the Heathen,) to extend the power of the *Conscience* Law, which is the Rule of Actions onely, to the very Thoughts, and Consciences of men, by Examination, and *Inquisition* of what they Hold, notwithstanding the Conformity of their Speech and Actions: By which, men are either punished for answering the truth of their thoughts, or constrained to answer an untruth for fear of punishment. It is true, that the Civill Magistrate, intend- ing to employ a Minister in the charge of Teaching, may enquire of him, if hee bee content to Preach such, and such Doctrines; and in case of refusall, may deny him the employment: But to force him to accuse himselfe of Opinions, when his Actions are not by Law forbidden, is against the Law of Nature; and especially in them, who teach, that a man shall bee damned to Eternall and extream torments, if he die in a false opinion concerning an Article of the Christian Faith. For who is there, that knowing there is so great danger in an error, whom the naturall care of himself, compelleth not to hazard his Soule upon his own judgement, rather than that of any other man that is unconcerned in his damnation?

*Private Inter-
pretation of
Law* For a Private man, without the Authority of the Common-wealth, that is to say, without permission from the Representant thereof, to Interpret the Law by his own Spirit, is another Error in the Politiques; but not drawn from Aristotle, nor from any other of the Heathen Philosophers. For none of them deny, but that in the Power of making Laws, is comprehended also the Power of Explaining them when there is need. And are not the Scriptures, in all places where they are Law, made Law by the Authority of the Common-wealth, and consequently, a part of the Civill Law?

Of the same kind it is also, when any but the Soveraign restraineth in any man that power which the Common-wealth hath not restrained; as they do, that impropriate the Preaching of the Gospell to one certain Order of men, where the Laws have left it free. If the State give me leave to preach, or teach; that is, if it forbid me not, no man can forbid me. If I find my selfe amongst the Idolaters of America, shall I that am a Christian, though not in Orders, think it a sin to preach Jesus Christ, till I have received Orders from Rome? or when I have preached, shall not I answer their doubts, and expound the Scriptures to them; that is, shall I not Teach? But for this may some say, as also for administring to them [379] the Sacraments, the necessity shall be esteemed for a sufficient Mission; which is true: But this is true also, that for whatsoever, a dispensation is due for the necessity, for the same there needs no dispensation, when there is no Law that forbids it. Therefore to deny these Functions to those, to whom the Civill Soveraigne hath not denyed them, is a taking away of a lawfull Liberty, which is contrary to the Doctrine of Civill Government.

More examples of Vain Philosophy, brought into Religion by the Doctors of Schoole-Divinity, might be produced; but other men may if they please observe them of themselves. I shall onely adde this, that the Writings of *Language of* Schoole-Divines, are nothing else for the most part, but *Schoole-* insignificant Traines of strange and barbarous words, or *Divines* words otherwise used, then in the common use of the Latine tongue; such as would pose Cicero, and Varro, and all the Grammarians of ancient Rome.[55] Which if any man would see proved, let him (as I have said once before) see whether he can translate any Schoole-Divine into any of the Modern tongues, as French, English, or any other copious language: for that which cannot in most of these be made Intelligible, is not Intelligible in the Latine. Which Insignificancy of language, though I cannot note it for false Philosophy; yet it hath a quality, not onely to hide the Truth, but also to make men think they have it, and desist from further search.

Lastly, for the Errors brought in from false, or *Errors from* uncertain History, what is all the Legend of fictitious *Tradition* Miracles, in the lives of the Saints; and all the Histories of Apparitions, and Ghosts, alledged by the Doctors of the Romane Church, to make good their Doctrines of Hell, and Purgatory, the power of Exorcisme, and other Doctrines which have no warrant, neither in Reason, nor Scripture; as also all those Traditions which they call the unwritten Word of God; but old Wives Fables? Whereof, though they find dispersed somewhat in the Writings of the ancient Fathers; yet those Fathers were men, that might too easily beleeve false reports; and the producing of their opinions for testimony of the truth of what they beleeved, hath no other force with them that (according to the Counsell of St. *John* 1 Epist. chap. 4. verse 1.) examine Spirits, than in all things that concern the power of the Romane Church, (the abuse whereof either they suspected not, or had benefit by it,) to discredit their testimony, in respect of too rash beleef of reports; which the most sincere men, without great knowledge of naturall causes, (such as the Fathers were) are commonly the most subject to: For naturally, the best men are the least suspicious of fraudulent purposes. Gregory the Pope, and S. Bernard have somewhat of Apparitions of Ghosts, that said they were in Purgatory; and so has our Beda:[56] but no where, I beleeve, but by report from others. But if they, or any other, relate any such stories of their own knowledge, they shall not thereby confirm the more such vain reports; but discover their own Infirmity, or Fraud.

Suppression [380] With the Introduction of False, we may joyn *of Reason* also the suppression of True Philosophy, by such men, as neither by lawfull authority, nor sufficient study, are competent Judges of the truth. Our own Navigations make manifest, and all men learned in humane Sciences, now acknowledge there are Antipodes: And every day it appeareth more and more, that Years, and Dayes are determined by Motions of the Earth. Neverthelesse, men that have in their Writings but supposed such Doctrine, as an occasion to lay open the reasons for, and against it, have been punished for it by Authority Ecclesiasticall. But what reason is there for it? Is it because such opinions are contrary to true Religion? that cannot be, if they be true. Let therefore the truth be first examined by competent Judges, or confuted by them that pretend to know the contrary. Is it because they be contrary to the Religion established? Let them be silenced by the Laws of those, to whom the Teachers of them are subject; that is, by the Laws Civill: For disobedience may lawfully be punished in them, that against the Laws teach even true Philosophy. Is it because they tend to disorder in Government, as countenancing Rebellion, or Sedition? then let them be silenced, and the Teachers punished by vertue of his Power to whom the care of the Publique quiet is committed; which is the Authority Civill. For whatsoever Power Ecclesiastiques take upon themselves (in any place where they are subject to the State) in their own Right, though they call it Gods Right, is but Usurpation. [381]

Of the BENEFIT that proceedeth from such Darknesse, and to whom it accreweth

Cicero maketh honorable mention of one of the *Cassii*, a severe Judge amongst the Romans, for a custome he had, in Criminall causes, (when the testimony of the witnesses was not sufficient,) to ask the Accusers, *Cui bono*;[57] that is to say, what Profit, Honor, or other Contentment, the accused obtained, or expected by the Fact. For amongst Præsumptions, there is none that so evidently declareth the Author, as doth the BENEFIT of the Action. By the same rule I intend in this place to examine, who they may be, that have possessed the People so long in this part of Christendome, with these Doctrines, contrary to the Peaceable Societies of Mankind.

He that receiveth Benefit by a Fact, is presumed to be the Author

And first, to this Error, *that the present Church now Militant on Earth, is the Kingdome of God,* (that is, the Kingdome of Glory, or the Land of Promise; not the Kingdome of Grace, which is but a Promise of the Land,) are annexed these worldly Benefits; First, that the Pastors, and Teachers of the Church, are entitled thereby, as Gods Publique Ministers, to a Right of Governing the Church; and consequently (because the Church, and Common-wealth are the same Persons) to be Rectors, and Governours of the Common-wealth. By this title it is, that the Pope prevailed with the subjects of all Christian Princes, to beleeve, that to disobey him, was to disobey Christ himselfe; and in all differences between him and other Princes, (charmed with the word *Power Spirituall*,) to abandon their lawfull Soveraigns; which is in effect an universall Monarchy over all Christendome. For though they were first invested in the right of being Supreme Teachers of Christian Doctrine, by, and under Christian Emperors, within the limits of the Romane Empire (as is acknowledged by themselves) by the title

That the Church Militant is the Kingdome of God, was first taught by the Church of Rome

of *Pontifex Maximus*, who was an Officer subject to the Civill State; yet after the Empire was divided, and dissolved, it was not hard to obtrude upon the people already subject to them, another Title, namely, the Right of St. Peter; not onely to save entire their pretended Power; but also to extend the same over the same Christian Provinces, though no more united in the Empire of Rome. This Benefit of an Universall Monarchy, (considering the desire of men to bear Rule) is a sufficient Presumption, that the Popes that pretended to it, and for a long time enjoyed it, were the Authors of the Doctrine, by which it was obtained; namely, that the Church now on Earth, is the Kingdome of Christ. For that granted, it must be understood, that Christ hath some Lieutenant amongst us, by whom we are to be told what are his Commandements.

[382] After that certain Churches had renounced this universall Power of the Pope, one would expect in reason, that the Civill Soveraigns in all those Churches, should have recovered so much of it, as (before they had unadvisedly let it goe) was their own Right, and in their own hands. And in England it was so in effect; saving that they, by whom the Kings administred the Government of Religion, by maintaining their imployment to be in Gods Right, seemed to usurp, if not a Supremacy, yet an Independency on the Civill Power; and they but seemed to usurpe it, in as much as they acknowledged a Right in the King, to deprive them of the Exercise of their Functions at his pleasure.

And maintained also by the Presbytery   But in those places where the Presbytery took that Office, though many other Doctrines of the Church of Rome were forbidden to be taught; yet this Doctrine, that the Kingdome of Christ is already come, and that it began at the Resurrection of our Saviour, was still retained. But *cui bono?* What Profit did they expect from it? The same which the Popes expected: to have a Soveraign Power over the People. For what is it for men to excommunicate their lawful King, but to

keep him from all places of Gods publique Service in
his own Kingdom? and with force to resist him, when
he with force endeavoureth to correct them? Or what
is it, without Authority from the Civill Soveraign, to
excommunicate any person, but to take from him his
Lawfull Liberty, that is, to usurpe an unlawfull Power
over their Brethren? The Authors therefore of this Darknesse in Religion, are the Romane, and the Presbyterian
Clergy.

To this head, I referre also all those Doctrines, that *Infallibility*
serve them to keep the possession of this spirituall Soveraignty after it is gotten. As first, that the *Pope in his
publique capacity cannot erre.* For who is there, that
beleeving this to be true, will not readily obey him in
whatsoever he commands?

Secondly, that all other Bishops, in what Common- *Subjection of*
wealth soever, have not their Right, neither immediately *Bishops*
from God, nor mediately from their Civill Soveraigns,
but from the Pope, is a Doctrine, by which there comes
to be in every Christian Common-wealth many potent
men, (for so are Bishops,) that have their dependance
on the Pope, and owe obedience to him, though he be a
forraign Prince; by which means he is able, (as he hath
done many times) to raise a Civill War against the State
that submits not it self to be governed according to his
pleasure and Interest.

Thirdly, the exemption of these, and of all other *Exemptions*
Priests, and of all Monkes, and Fryers, from the Power *of the Clergy*
of the Civill Laws. For by this means, there is a great
part of every Common-wealth, that enjoy the benefit of
the Laws, and are protected by the Power of the Civill
State, which neverthelesse pay no part of the Publique
expence; nor are lyable to the penalties, as other Subjects, due to their crimes; and consequently, stand not in
fear of any man, but the Pope; and adhere to him onely,
to uphold his universall Monarchy.

Fourthly, the giving to their Priests (which is no more *The names of*
in the New Testament but Presbyters, that is, Elders) the *Sacerdotes,*
and Sacrifices

name of *Sacerdotes*, [383] that is, Sacrificers, which was the title of the Civill Soveraign, and his publique Ministers, amongst the Jews, whilest God was their King. Also, the making the Lords Supper a Sacrifice, serveth to make the People beleeve the Pope hath the same power over all Christians, that Moses and Aaron had over the Jews; that is to say, all Power, both Civill and Ecclesiasticall, as the High Priest then had.

The Sacramentation of Marriage Fiftly, the teaching that Matrimony is a Sacrament, giveth to the Clergy the Judging of the lawfulnesse of Marriages; and thereby, of what Children are Legitimate; and consequently, of the Right of Succession to hæreditary Kingdomes.

The single life of Priests Sixtly, the Deniall of Marriage to Priests, serveth to assure this Power of the Pope over Kings. For if a King be a Priest, he cannot Marry, and transmit his Kingdome to his Posterity; If he be not a Priest then the Pope pretendeth this Authority Ecclesiasticall over him, and over his people.

Auricular Confession Seventhly, from Auricular Confession, they obtain, for the assurance of their Power, better intelligence of the designs of Princes, and great persons in the Civill State, than these can have of the designs of the State Ecclesiasticall.

Canonization of Saints, and declaring of Martyrs Eighthly, by the Canonization of Saints, and declaring who are Martyrs, they assure their Power, in that they induce simple men into an obstinacy against the Laws and Commands of their Civill Soveraigns even to death, if by the Popes excommunication, they be declared Heretiques or Enemies to the Church; that is, (as they interpret it,) to the Pope.

Transubstantiation, Pennance, Absolution Ninthly, they assure the same, by the Power they ascribe to every Priest, of making Christ; and by the Power of ordaining Pennance; and of Remitting, and Retaining of sins.

Purgatory, Indulgences, Externall works Tenthly, by the Doctrine of Purgatory, of Justification by externall works, and of Indulgences, the Clergy is enriched.

Eleventhly, by their Dæmonology, and the use of Exorcisme, and other things appertaining thereto, they keep (or thinke they keep) the People more in awe of their Power. *Dæmonology and Exorcism*

Lastly, the Metaphysiques, Ethiques, and Politiques of Aristotle, the frivolous Distinctions, barbarous Terms, and obscure Language of the Schoolmen, taught in the Universities, (which have been all erected and regulated by the Popes Authority,) serve them to keep these Errors from being detected, and to make men mistake the *Ignis fatuus* of Vain Philosophy, for the Light of the Gospell. *School-Divinity*

To these, if they sufficed not, might be added other of their dark Doctrines, the profit whereof redoundeth manifestly, to the setting up of an unlawfull Power over the lawfull Soveraigns of Christian People; or for the sustaining of the same, when it is set up; or to the worldly Riches, Honour, and Authority of those that sustain it. And therefore by the aforesaid rule, of *Cui bono*, we may justly pronounce for the Authors of all this Spirituall Darknesse, the Pope, and Roman Clergy, and all those besides that endeavour to settle in the mindes of men this erroneous Doctrine, that the Church now on Earth, is that Kingdome of God mentioned in the Old and New Testament. *The Authors of spirituall Darknesse, who they be*

[384] But the Emperours, and other Christian Soveraigns, under whose Government these Errours, and the like encroachments of Ecclesiastiques upon their Office, at first crept in, to the disturbance of their possessions, and of the tranquillity of their Subjects, though they suffered the same for want of foresight of the Sequel, and of insight into the designs of their Teachers, may neverthelesse bee esteemed accessaries to their own, and the Publique dammage: For without their Authority there could at first no seditious Doctrine have been publiquely preached. I say they might have hindred the same in the beginning: But when the people were once possessed by those spirituall men, there was no humane remedy to be applyed, that any man could invent: And

for the remedies that God should provide, who never faileth in his good time to destroy all the Machinations of men against the Truth, wee are to attend his good pleasure, that suffereth many times the prosperity of his enemies, together with their ambition, to grow to such a height, as the violence thereof openeth the eyes, which the warinesse of their predecessours had before sealed up, and makes men by too much grasping let goe all, as Peters net was broken, by the struggling of too great a multitude of Fishes;[58] whereas the Impatience of those, that strive to resist such encroachment, before their Subjects eyes were opened, did but encrease the power they resisted. I doe not therefore blame the Emperour Frederick for holding the stirrop to our countryman Pope Adrian;[59] for such was the disposition of his subjects then, as if hee had not done it, hee was not likely to have succeeded in the Empire: But I blame those, that in the beginning, when their power was entire, by suffering such Doctrines to be forged in the Universities of their own Dominions, have holden the Stirrop to all the succeeding Popes, whilest they mounted into the Thrones of all Christian Soveraigns, to ride, and tire, both them, and their people, at their pleasure.

But as the Inventions of men are woven, so also are they ravelled out; the way is the same, but the order is inverted: The web begins at the first Elements of Power, which are Wisdom, Humility, Sincerity, and other vertues of the Apostles, whom the people converted, obeyed, out of Reverence, not by Obligation: Their Consciences were free, and their Words and Actions subject to none but the Civill Power. Afterwards the Presbyters (as the Flocks of Christ encreased) assembling to consider what they should teach, and thereby obliging themselves to teach nothing against the Decrees of their Assemblies, made it to be thought the people were thereby obliged to follow their Doctrine, and when they refused, refused to keep them company, (that was then called Excommunication,) not as being Infidels, but as being disobedient:

And this was the first knot upon their Liberty. And the number of Presbyters encreasing, the Presbyters of the chief City or Province, got themselves an authority over the Parochiall Presbyters, and appropriated to themselves the names of Bishops: And this was a second knot on Christian Liberty. Last[385]ly, the Bishop of Rome, in regard of the Imperiall City, took upon him an Authority (partly by the wills of the Emperours themselves, and by the title of *Pontifex Maximus*, and at last when the Emperours were grown weak, by the priviledges of St. Peter) over all other Bishops of the Empire: Which was the third and last knot, and the whole *Synthesis* and *Construction* of the Pontificall Power.

And therefore the *Analysis*, or *Resolution* is by the same way; but beginneth with the knot that was last tyed; as wee may see in the dissolution of the præterpoliticall[60] Church Government in England. First, the Power of the Popes was dissolved totally by Queen Elizabeth;[61] and the Bishops, who before exercised their Functions in Right of the Pope, did afterwards exercise the same in Right of the Queen and her Successours; though by retaining the phrase of *Jure Divino*, they were thought to demand it by immediate Right from God: And so was untyed the first knot. After this, the Presbyterians lately in England obtained the putting down of Episcopacy:[62] And so was the second knot dissolved: And almost at the same time, the Power was taken also from the Presbyterians:[63] And so we are reduced to the Independency of the Primitive Christians to follow Paul, or Cephas, or Apollos, every man as he liketh best:[64] Which, if it be without contention, and without measuring the Doctrine of Christ, by our affection to the Person of his Minister, (the fault which the Apostle reprehended in the Corinthians,) is perhaps the best: First, because there ought to be no Power over the Consciences of men, but of the Word it selfe, working Faith in every one, not alwayes according to the purpose of them that Plant and Water, but of God himself, that giveth the Increase: and secondly, because it is unreasonable in them, who teach there is such danger in every little Errour, to require of a man endued with Reason of his own, to follow the Reason of any other man, or of the most voices of many other men; Which is little better, then to venture his Salvation at crosse and pile. Nor ought those Teachers to be displeased with this losse of their antient Authority: For there is none should know better then they, that power is preserved by the same Vertues by which it is acquired; that is to say, by Wisdome, Humility, Clearnesse of Doctrine, and sincerity of Conversation; and not by suppression of the Naturall Sciences, and of the Morality of Naturall Reason; nor by obscure Language; nor by Arrogating to themselves more Knowledge than they make appear; nor by Pious Frauds; nor by such other faults, as in the Pastors of Gods Church are not only Faults, but also scandalls, apt to make men stumble one time or other upon the suppression of their Authority.

Comparison of the Papacy with the Kingdome of Fayries But after this Doctrine, *that the Church now Militant, is the Kingdome of God spoken of in the Old and New Testament,* was received in the World; the ambition, and canvasing for the Offices that belong thereunto, and especially for that great Office of being [386] Christs Lieutenant, and the Pompe of them that obtained therein the principall Publique Charges, became by degrees so evident, that they lost the inward Reverence due to the Pastorall Function: in so much as the Wisest men, of them that had any power in the Civill State, needed nothing but the authority of their Princes, to deny them any further Obedience. For, from the time that the Bishop of Rome had gotten to be acknowledged for Bishop Universall, by pretence of Succession to St. Peter, their whole Hierarchy, or Kingdome of Darknesse, may be compared not unfitly to the *Kingdome of Fairies*; that is, to the old wives *Fables* in England, concerning *Ghosts* and *Spirits,* and the feats they play in the night. And if a man consider the originall of this great Ecclesiasticall Dominion, he will easily perceive, that the *Papacy,* is no other, than the *Ghost* of the deceased *Romane Empire*, sitting crowned upon the grave thereof: For so did the Papacy start up on a Sudden out of the Ruines of that Heathen Power.

The *Language* also, which they use, both in the Churches, and in their Publique Acts, being *Latine*, which is not commonly used by any Nation now in the world, what is it but the *Ghost* of the Old *Romane Language*?

The *Fairies* in what Nation soever they converse, have but one Universall King, which some Poets of ours call King *Oberon*; but the Scripture calls *Beelzebub*, Prince of *Dæmons*. The *Ecclesiastiques* likewise, in whose Dominions soever they be found, acknowledge but one Universall King, the *Pope*.

The *Ecclesiastiques* are *Spirituall* men, and *Ghostly* Fathers. The Fairies are *Spirits*, and *Ghosts*. *Fairies* and *Ghosts* inhabite Darknesse, Solitudes, and Graves. The *Ecclesiastiques* walke in Obscurity of Doctrine, in Monasteries, Churches, and Church-yards.

The *Ecclesiastiques* have their Cathedrall Churches; which, in what Towne soever they be erected, by vertue of Holy Water, and certain Charmes called Exorcismes, have the power to make those Townes, Cities, that is to say, Seats of Empire. The *Fairies* also have their enchanted Castles, and certain Gigantique Ghosts, that domineer over the Regions round about them.

The *Fairies* are not to be seized on; and brought to answer for the hurt they do. So also the *Ecclesiastiques* vanish away from the Tribunals of Civill Justice.

The *Ecclesiastiques* take from young men, the use of Reason, by certain Charms compounded of Metaphysiques, and Miracles, and Traditions, and Abused Scripture, whereby they are good for nothing else, but to execute what they command them. The *Fairies* likewise are said to take young Children out of their Cradles, and to change them into Naturall Fools, which Common people do therefore call *Elves*, and are apt to mischief.

In what Shop, or Operatory the Fairies make their Enchantment, the old Wives have not determined. But the Operatories of the *Clergy*, are well enough known to be the Universities, that received their Discipline from Authority Pontificiall.

[387] When the *Fairies* are displeased with any body, they are said to send their Elves, to pinch them. The *Ecclesiastiques*, when they are displeased with any Civill State, make also their Elves, that is, Superstitious, Enchanted Subjects, to pinch their Princes, by preaching Sedition; or one Prince enchanted with promises, to pinch another.

The *Fairies* marry not; but there be amongst them *Incubi*, that have copulation with flesh and bloud. The *Priests* also marry not.

The *Ecclesiastiques* take the Cream of the Land, by Donations of ignorant men, that stand in aw of them, and by Tythes: So also it is in the Fable of *Fairies*, that they enter into the Dairies, and Feast upon the Cream, which they skim from the Milk.

What kind of Money is currant in the Kingdome of *Fairies*, is not recorded in the Story. But the *Ecclesiastiques* in their Receipts accept of the same Money that we doe; though when they are to make any Payment, it is in Canonizations, Indulgences, and Masses.

To this, and such like resemblances between the *Papacy*, and the Kingdome of *Fairies*, may be added this, that as the *Fairies* have no existence, but in the Fancies of ignorant people, rising from the Traditions of old Wives, or old Poets: so the Spirituall Power of the *Pope* (without the bounds of his own Civill Dominion) consisteth onely in the Fear that Seduced people stand in, of their Excommunications; upon hearing of false Miracles, false Traditions, and false Interpretations of the Scripture.

It was not therefore a very difficult matter, for Henry 8. by his Exorcisme; nor for Qu. Elizabeth by hers, to cast them out. But who knows that this Spirit of Rome, now gone out, and walking by Missions through the dry places of China, Japan, and the Indies, that yeeld him little fruit, may not return, or rather an Assembly of Spirits worse than he, enter, and inhabite this clean swept house, and make the End thereof worse than the Beginning? For it is not the Romane Clergy onely, that pretends the Kingdome of God to be of this World, and thereby to have a Power therein, distinct from that of the Civill State. And this is all I had a designe to say, concerning the Doctrine of the POLITIQUES. Which when I have reviewed, I shall willingly expose it to the censure of my Countrey. [389]

A REVIEW, and
CONCLUSION

From the contrariety of some of the Naturall Faculties
of the Mind, one to another, as also of one Passion to
another, and from their reference to Conversation, there
has been an argument taken, to inferre an impossibility
that any one man should be sufficiently disposed to all
sorts of Civill duty. The Severity of Judgment, they say,
makes men Censorious, and unapt to pardon the Errours and Infirmities of other men: and on the other side,
Celerity of Fancy, makes the thoughts lesse steddy than is
necessary, to discern exactly between Right and Wrong.
Again, in all Deliberations, and in all Pleadings, the faculty of solid Reasoning, is necessary: for without it, the
Resolutions of men are rash, and their Sentences unjust:
and yet if there be not powerfull Eloquence, which
procureth attention and Consent, the effect of Reason
will be little. But these are contrary Faculties; the former being grounded upon principles of Truth; the other
upon Opinions already received, true, or false; and upon
the Passions and Interests of men, which are different,
and mutable.

And amongst the Passions, *Courage*, (by which I
mean the Contempt of Wounds, and violent Death)
enclineth men to private Revenges, and sometimes to
endeavour the unsetling of the Publique Peace: And
Timorousnesse, many times disposeth to the desertion
of the Publique Defence. Both these they say cannot
stand together in the same person.

And to consider the contrariety of mens Opinions,

and Manners in generall, It is they say, impossible to entertain a constant Civill Amity with all those, with whom the Businesse of the world constrains us to converse: Which Businesse, consisteth almost in nothing else but a perpetuall contention for Honor, Riches, and Authority.

To which I answer, that these are indeed great difficulties, but not Impossibilities: For by Education, and Discipline, they may bee, and are sometimes reconciled. Judgment, and Fancy may have place in the same man; but by turnes; as the end which he aimeth at requireth. As the Israelites in Egypt, were sometimes fastened to their labour of making Bricks, and other times were ranging abroad to gather Straw:[1] So also may the Judgement sometimes be fixed upon one certain Consideration, and the Fancy at another time wandring about the world. So also Reason, and Eloquence, (though not perhaps in the Naturall Sciences, yet in the Morall) may stand very well together. For wheresoever [390] there is place for adorning and preferring of Errour, there is much more place for adorning and preferring of Truth, if they have it to adorn. Nor is there any repugnancy between fearing the Laws, and not fearing a publique Enemy; nor between abstaining from Injury, and pardoning it in others. There is therefore no such Inconsistence of Humane Nature, with Civill Duties, as some think. I have known cleernesse of Judgment, and largenesse of Fancy; strength of Reason, and gracefull Elocution; a Courage for the Warre, and a Fear for the Laws, and all eminently in one man; and that was my most noble and honored friend Mr. *Sidney Godolphin*; who hating no man, nor hated of any, was unfortunately slain in the beginning of the late Civill warre, in the Publique quarrell, by an undiscerned, and an undiscerning hand.

To the Laws of Nature, declared in the 15. Chapter, I would have this added, *That every man is bound by Nature, as much as in him lieth, to protect in Warre, the Authority, by which he is himself protected in time of*

Peace. For he that pretendeth a Right of Nature to preserve his owne body, cannot pretend a Right of Nature
to destroy him, by whose strength he is preserved: It is
a manifest contradiction of himselfe. And though this
Law may bee drawn by consequence, from some of
those that are there already mentioned; yet the Times
require to have it inculcated, and remembred.

And because I find by divers English Books lately
printed,[2] that the Civill warres have not yet sufficiently
taught men, in what point of time it is, that a Subject
becomes obliged to the Conquerour; nor what is Conquest; nor how it comes about, that it obliges men to
obey his Laws: Therefore for farther satisfaction of
men therein, I say, the point of time, wherein a man
becomes subject to a Conquerour, is that point, wherein
having liberty to submit to him, he consenteth, either
by expresse words, or by other sufficient sign, to be
his Subject. When it is that a man hath the liberty to
submit, I have shewed before in the end of the 21. Chapter; namely, that for him that hath no obligation to his
former Soveraign but that of an ordinary Subject, it is
then, when the means of his life is within the Guards
and Garrisons of the Enemy; for it is then, that he hath
no longer Protection from him, but is protected by the
adverse party for his Contribution. Seeing therefore such
contribution is every where, as a thing inevitable, (notwithstanding it be an assistance to the Enemy,) esteemed
lawfull; a totall Submission, which is but an assistance
to the Enemy, cannot be esteemed unlawful. Besides, if
a man consider that they who submit, assist the Enemy
but with part of their estates, whereas they that refuse,
assist him with the whole, there is no reason to call their
Submission, or Composition an Assistance; but rather a
Detriment to the Enemy. But if a man, besides the obligation of a Subject, hath taken upon him a new obligation
of a Souldier, then he hath not the liberty to submit to
a new Power, as long as the old one keeps the field, and
giveth him means of subsistence, either in his Armies, or

Garrisons: for in this case, he cannot complain of want of Protection, and means to [391] live as a Souldier: But when that also failes, a Souldier also may seek his Protection wheresoever he has most hope to have it; and may lawfully submit himself to his new Master. And so much for the Time when he may do it lawfully, if hee will. If therefore he doe it, he is undoubtedly bound to be a true Subject: For a Contract lawfully made, cannot lawfully be broken.

By this also a man may understand, when it is, that men may be said to be Conquered; and in what the nature of Conquest, and the Right of a Conquerour consisteth: For this Submission is it implyeth them all. Conquest, is not the Victory it self; but the Acquisition by Victory, of a Right, over the persons of men. He therefore that is slain, is Overcome, but not Conquered: He that is taken, and put into prison, or chaines, is not Conquered, though Overcome; for he is still an Enemy, and may save himself if hee can: But he that upon promise of Obedience, hath his Life and Liberty allowed him, is then Conquered, and a Subject; and not before. The Romanes used to say, that their Generall had *Pacified* such a *Province*, that is to say, in English, *Conquered* it; and that the Countrey was *Pacified* by Victory, when the people of it had promised *Imperata facere*, that is, *To doe what the Romane People commanded them*: this was to be Conquered. But this promise may be either expresse, or tacite: Expresse, by Promise: Tacite, by other signes. As for example, a man that hath not been called to make such an expresse Promise, (because he is one whose power perhaps is not considerable;) yet if he live under their Protection openly, hee is understood to submit himselfe to the Government: But if he live there secretly, he is lyable to any thing that may bee done to a Spie, and Enemy of the State. I say not, hee does any Injustice, (for acts of open Hostility bear not that name); but that he may be justly put to death. Likewise, if a man, when his Country is conquered, be out of it, he is not Conquered, nor Subject: but if at his return, he submit to the Government, he is bound to obey it. So that *Conquest* (to define it) is the Acquiring of the Right of Soveraignty by Victory. Which Right, is acquired, in the peoples Submission, by which they contract with the Victor, promising Obedience, for Life and Liberty.

In the 29. Chapter I have set down for one of the causes of the Dissolutions of Common-wealths, their Imperfect Generation, consisting in the want of an Absolute and Arbitrary Legislative Power; for want whereof, the Civill Soveraign is fain to handle the Sword of Justice unconstantly, and as if it were too hot for him to hold: One reason whereof (which I have not there mentioned) is this, That they will all of them justifie the War, by which their Power was at first gotten, and whereon (as they think) their Right dependeth, and not on the Possession. As if, for example, the Right of the Kings of England did depend on the goodnesse of the cause of *William* the Conquerour, and upon their lineall, and directest Descent from him; by which means, there would perhaps be no tie of the Subjects obedience to their Soveraign at this day in all the world: wherein [392] whilest they needlessely think to justifie themselves, they justifie all the successefull Rebellions that Ambition shall at any time raise against them, and their Successors. Therefore I put down for one of the most effectuall seeds of the Death of any State, that the Conquerors require not onely a Submission of mens actions to them for the future, but also an Approbation of all their actions past; when there is scarce a Common-wealth in the world, whose beginnings can in conscience be justified.

And because the name of Tyranny, signifieth nothing more, nor lesse, than the name of Soveraignty, be it in one, or many men, saving that they that use the former word, are understood to bee angry with them they call Tyrants; I think the toleration of a professed hatred of Tyranny, is a Toleration of hatred to Common-wealth in general, and another evill seed, not differing much from the former. For to the Justification of the Cause of a Conqueror, the Reproach of the Cause of the Conquered, is for the most part necessary: but neither of them necessary for the Obligation of the Conquered. And thus much I have thought fit to say upon the Review of the first and second part of this Discourse.

In the 35. Chapter, I have sufficiently declared out of the Scripture, that in the Common-wealth of the Jewes, God himselfe was made the Soveraign, by Pact with the People; who were therefore called his *Peculiar People*, to distinguish them from the rest of the world, over whom God reigned not by their Consent, but by his own Power: And that in this Kingdome Moses was Gods Lieutenant on Earth; and that it was he that told them what Laws God appointed them to be ruled by. But I have omitted to set down who were the Officers appointed to doe Execution; especially in Capitall Punishments; not then thinking it a matter of so necessary consideration, as I find it since. Wee know that generally in all Common-wealths, the Execution of Corporeall Punishments, was either put upon the Guards, or other Souldiers of the Soveraign Power; or given to those, in whom want of means, contempt of honour, and hardnesse of heart, concurred, to make them sue for such an Office. But amongst the Israelites it was a Positive Law of God their Soveraign, that he that was convicted of a capitall Crime, should be stoned to death by the People; and that the Witnesses should cast the first Stone, and after the Witnesses, then the rest of the People. This was a Law that designed who were to be the Executioners; but not that any one should throw a Stone at him before Conviction and Sentence, where the Congregation was Judge. The Witnesses were neverthelesse to be heard before they proceeded to Execution, unlesse the Fact were committed in the presence of the Congregation it self, or in sight of the lawfull Judges; for then there needed no other Witnesses but the Judges themselves. Nevertheless, this manner of proceeding being not throughly understood, hath given occasion to a dangerous opinion, that any man may kill another, in some cases, by a Right of Zeal; as if the Executions done upon Offenders in the Kingdome of God in old time, proceeded not from [393] the Soveraign Command, but from the Authority of Private Zeal: which, if we consider the texts that seem to favour it, is quite contrary.

First, where the Levites fell upon the People, that had made and worshipped the Golden Calfe, and slew three thousand of them; it was by the Commandement of Moses, from the mouth of God; as is manifest, *Exod.* 32.27. And when the Son of a woman of Israel had blasphemed God, they that heard it, did not kill him, but brought him before Moses, who put him under custody, till God should give Sentence against him; as appears, *Levit.* 25.11, 12. Again, (*Numbers* 25.6, 7.) when Phinehas killed Zimri and Cosbi, it was not by right of Private Zeale: Their Crime was committed in the sight of the Assembly; there needed no Witnesse; the Law was known, and he the heir apparent to the Soveraignty; and which is the principall point, the Lawfulnesse of his Act depended wholly upon a subsequent Ratification by Moses, whereof he had no cause to doubt. And this Presumption of a future Ratification, is sometimes necessary to the safety [of] a Common-wealth; as in a sudden Rebellion, any man that can suppresse it by his own Power in the Countrey where it begins, without expresse Law or Commission, may lawfully doe it, and provide to have it Ratified, or Pardoned, whilest it is in doing, or after it is done. Also *Numb.* 35.30. it is expressely said, *Whosoever shall kill the Murtherer, shall kill him upon the word of Witnesses*: but Witnesses suppose a formall Judicature, and consequently condemn that pretence of *Jus Zelotarum*. The Law of Moses concerning him that enticeth to Idolatry, (that is to say, in the Kingdome of God to a renouncing of his Allegiance (*Deut.* 13. 8.)) forbids to conceal him, and commands the Accuser to cause him to be put to death, and to cast the first stone at him; but not to kill him before he be Condemned. And (*Deut.* 17. ver. 4, 5, 6.) the Processe against Idolatry is exactly set down: For God there speaketh to the People, as Judge, and commandeth them, when a man is Accused of Idolatry, to Enquire diligently of the Fact, and finding it true, then to Stone him; but still the hand of the Witnesse throweth the first stone. This is not Private Zeale, but Publique Condemnation. In like manner when a Father hath a rebellious Son, the Law is (*Deut.* 21.18.) that he shall bring him before the Judges of the Town, and all the people of the Town shall Stone him. Lastly, by pretence of these Laws it was, that St. Steven was Stoned, and not by pretence of Private Zeal: for before hee was carried away to Execution, he had Pleaded his Cause before the High Priest.[3] There is nothing in all this, nor in any other part of the Bible, to countenance Executions by Private Zeal; which being oftentimes but a conjunction of Ignorance and Passion, is against both the Justice and Peace of a Common-wealth.

In the 36. Chapter I have said, that it is not declared in what manner God spake supernaturally to Moses: Not that he spake not to him sometimes by Dreams and Visions, and by a supernaturall Voice, as to other Prophets: For the manner how he spake unto him from the Mercy-Seat, is expressely set down *Numbers* 7.89. in [394] these words, *From that time forward, when Moses entred into the Tabernacle of the Congregation to speak with God, he heard a Voice which spake unto him from over the Mercy-Seate, which is over the Arke of the Testimony, from between the Cherubins he spake unto him.* But it is not declared in what consisted the præeminence of the manner of Gods speaking to Moses, above that of his speaking to other Prophets, as to Samuel, and to Abraham, to whom he also spake by a Voice, (that is, by Vision) Unlesse the difference consist in the cleernesse of the Vision. For *Face to Face*, and *Mouth to Mouth*, cannot be literally understood of the Infinitenesse, and Incomprehensibility of the Divine Nature.

And as to the whole Doctrine, I see not yet, but the Principles of it are true and proper; and the Ratiocination solid. For I ground the Civill Right of Soveraigns, and both the Duty and Liberty of Subjects, upon the known naturall Inclinations of Mankind, and upon the Articles of the Law of Nature; of which no man, that pretends but reason enough to govern his private family, ought to be ignorant. And for the Power Ecclesiasticall of the same Soveraigns, I ground it on such Texts, as are both evident in themselves, and consonant to the Scope of the whole Scripture. And therefore am perswaded, that he that shall read it with a purpose onely to be informed, shall be informed by it. But for those that by Writing, or Publique Discourse, or by their eminent actions, have already engaged themselves to the maintaining of contrary opinions, they will not bee so easily satisfied. For in such cases, it is naturall for men, at one and the same time, both to proceed in reading, and to lose their attention, in the search of objections to that they had read before: Of which, in a time wherein the interests of men are changed (seeing much of that Doctrine, which serveth to the establishing of a new Government, must needs be contrary to that which conduced to the dissolution of the old,) there cannot choose but be very many.

In that part which treateth of a Christian Commonwealth, there are some new Doctrines, which, it may be, in a State where the contrary were already fully determined, were a fault for a Subject without leave to divulge, as being an usurpation of the place of a Teacher. But in this time, that men call not onely for Peace, but also for Truth, to offer such Doctrines as I think True, and that manifestly tend to Peace and Loyalty, to the consideration of those that are yet in deliberation, is no more, but to offer New Wine, to bee put into New Cask, that both may be preserved together. And I suppose, that then, when Novelty can breed no trouble, nor disorder in a State, men are not generally so much inclined to the reverence of Antiquity, as to preferre Ancient Errors, before New and well proved Truth.

There is nothing I distrust more than my Elocution; which nevertheless I am confident (excepting the Mischances of the Presse) is not obscure. That I have neglected the Ornament of quoting ancient Poets, Orators, and Philosophers, contrary to the custome of late time, (whether I have done well or ill in it,) proceedeth from my [395] judgment, grounded on many reasons. For first, all Truth of Doctrine dependeth either upon *Reason*, or upon *Scripture*; both which give credit to many, but never receive it from any Writer. Secondly, the matters in question are not of *Fact*, but of *Right*, wherein there is no place for *Witnesses*. There is scarce any of those old Writers, that contradicteth not sometimes both himself, and others; which makes their Testimonies insufficient. Fourthly, such Opinions as are taken onely upon Credit of Antiquity, are not intrinsecally the Judgment of those that cite them, but Words that passe (like gaping) from mouth to mouth. Fiftly, it is many times with a fraudulent Designe that men stick their corrupt Doctrine with the Cloves of other mens Wit. Sixtly, I find not that the Ancients they cite, took it for an Ornament, to doe the like with those that wrote before them. Seventhly, it is an argument of Indigestion, when Greek and Latine Sentences unchewed come up again, as they use to doe, unchanged. Lastly, though I reverence those men of Ancient time, that either have written Truth perspicuously, or set us in a better way to find it out our selves; yet to the Antiquity it self I think nothing due: For if we will reverence the Age, the Present is the Oldest. If the Antiquity of the Writer, I am not sure, that generally they to whom such honor is given, were more Ancient when they wrote, than I am that am Writing: But if it bee well considered, the praise of Ancient Authors, proceeds not from the reverence of the Dead, but from the competition, and mutuall envy of the Living.

To conclude, there is nothing in this whole Discourse, nor in that I writ before of the same Subject in Latine,[4] as far as I can perceive, contrary either to the Word of God, or to good Manners; or to the disturbance of the Publique Tranquillity. Therefore I think it may be profitably printed, and more profitably taught in the Universities, in case they also think so, to whom the judgment of the same belongeth. For seeing the Universities are the Fountains of Civill, and Morall Doctrine, from whence the Preachers, and the Gentry, drawing such water as they find, use to sprinkle the same (both from the Pulpit, and in their Conversation) upon the People, there ought certainly to be great care taken, to have it pure, both from the Venime of Heathen Politicians, and from the Incantation of Deceiving Spirits. And by that means the most men, knowing their Duties, will be the less subject to serve the Ambition of a few discontented persons, in their purposes against the State; and be the lesse grieved with the Contributions necessary for their Peace, and Defence; and the Governours themselves have the lesse cause, to maintain at the Common charge any greater Army, than is necessary to make good the Publique Liberty, against the Invasions and Encroachments of forraign Enemies.

And thus I have brought to an end my Discourse of Civill and Ecclesiasticall Government, occasioned by the disorders of the present time, without partiality, without application, and without other designe, than to set before mens eyes the mutuall Relation be[396]-tween Protection and Obedience; of which the condition of Humane Nature, and the Laws Divine, (both Naturall and Positive) require an inviolable observation. And though in the revolution of States, there can be no very good Constellation for Truths of this nature to be born under, (as having an angry aspect from the dissolvers of an old Government, and seeing but the backs of them that erect a new;) yet I cannot think it will be condemned at this time, either by the Publique Judge of

Doctrine, or by any that desires the continuance of Publique Peace. And in this hope I return to my interrupted
Speculation of Bodies Naturall; wherein, (if God give
me health to finish it,) I hope the Novelty will as much
please, as in the Doctrine of this Artificiall Body it useth
to offend. For such Truth, as opposeth no mans profit,
nor pleasure, is to all men welcome.

FINIS

Notes

Epistle Dedicatory

1. *FRANCIS GODOLPHIN . . . Sidney Godolphin*:
   Francis and Sidney Godolphin were both elected to the
   House of Commons in 1640 to represent Helston in
   Cornwall. Sidney was a minor court poet, who fought
   for the King in the Civil War and was killed in an ambush
   in Devon in February 1643. In his will, he left £200 to
   'my worthie friend' Hobbes, and his older brother Francis (1605–67) – who as his executor could have exploited
   the political situation to pocket much of the money himself – made sure that Hobbes received it.

2. *Civill Society*: In the seventeenth century, 'civil society'
   referred to political society (to be juxtaposed with the
   'natural society' of the family or the state of nature – on
   which see ch. 13) rather than to what we tend to think
   about when we use the term today (where the implicit
   juxtaposition, often enough, is with the state itself).

3. *like to those simple and unpartiall creatures in the Roman
   Capitol*: In 390 BCE, the city of Rome was supposed
   to have been saved by the goddess Juno's sacred geese,
   whose honks alerted the Romans to the invading Gauls,
   clambering up the side of the Capitoline Hill while the
   dogs slept. Thereafter, the Romans held an annual fes-
   tival to mark the occasion at which geese were paraded
   on cushions and dogs were crucified. The story is told by
   Livy, *Ab urbe condita* 5.47 and Plutarch, *Of the Fortune
   of the Romans* 12.

4. *with due submission*: With these words Hobbes indicates
   that he does not think anything in *Leviathan* contradicts
   the established doctrine of the Church of England.

The Introduction

1. Nosce teipsum, Read thy self: *Nosce teipsum* is the Latin for the Greek γνῶθι σεαυτόν, 'Know yourself', which was inscribed in the forecourt of the temple of Apollo at Delphi. See Pausanias, *Description of Greece* 10.24.

Part I: Of Man

1. *and I have else-where written of the same at large*: This is probably a reference to *The Elements of Law* ch. 2.
2. *But the Philosophy-schooles . . . teach another doctrine*: Aristotle (384–322 BCE) was a philosopher from Stagira in northern Greece who came to Athens to study under Plato and subsequently set up his own school, the Lyceum. Many of his works survive, and came to exercise a huge influence on intellectual life in Western Europe after being translated into Latin in the twelfth and thirteenth centuries.
3. *For men measure . . . by themselves*: Hobbes here refers to a maxim associated with the Greek philosopher Protagoras in the fifth century BCE that 'man is the measure of all things'. See, e.g., Plato, *Theaetetus* 160d.
4. *a Centaure*: Centaurs were creatures from Greek mythology, half human (head, arms and torso) and half horse (body, legs and tail).
5. *a Hercules, or an Alexander*: Hercules is the Roman name for the Greek mythological hero Herakles, best known for his prodigious strength. Alexander (356–323 BCE), known as 'the Great', was king of Macedonia and a pupil of Aristotle. He led an army into Asia and conquered the Persian Empire.
6. *In the same manner*: What follows is Hobbes's explanation of sex dreams.
7. *We read of Marcus Brutus . . . but a short dream*: Marcus Junius Brutus (*c*. 85–42 BCE) was one of the assassins of the Roman dictator Julius Caesar (100–44 BCE). In the civil war that followed Caesar's murder, Brutus committed suicide after his forces were defeated at Philippi in northern Greece by those of Caesar's great-nephew and adopted son Octavian (63 BCE–14 CE). After triumphing

over his former ally Mark Antony in 31 BCE, Octavian became master of the Roman world – he is regarded as the first of the Roman Emperors – and took on the name Augustus in 27 BCE. See Plutarch, *Life of Brutus* 36 and 48, and *Life of Caesar* 69. The apparition is dramatized by William Shakespeare in *Julius Caesar*, Act 4, Scene 3.

8.   *Ghostly men*: Priests.

9.   *For in a Discourse of our present civill warre . . . Thought is quick*: King Charles became a prisoner of the Scottish Presbyterian army in May 1646, and was held at Newcastle upon Tyne before being sold to the Parliamentarians in January 1647. The '30 pence' refers to the thirty pieces of silver for which Judas Iscariot betrayed Jesus of Nazareth (Matthew 26:15).

10.   Respice finem: 'Consider the end'. Solon of Athens (*c.* 630–*c.* 560 BCE), one of the 'seven sages' of ancient Greece, is supposed to have refrained from judging that Croesus, king of Lydia, was happy, on the grounds that one cannot make that kind of judgement until you know how someone met their end. See Herodotus, *Histories* 1.32–3, 86–7; Plutarch, *Life of Solon* 28. The Latin formulation comes from a mediaeval compilation, the *Gesta Romanorum* ch. 103.

11.   *He that first brought them into* Greece: For the introduction of the alphabet to Greece, see Herodotus, *Histories* 5.58.

12.   *The first author of Speech . . . presented to his sight*: Genesis 2:19–20. Adam was the first human to be created by God.

13.   *the Tower of Babel*: Genesis 11:1–9.

14.   *as a bird in lime-twiggs*: A method of trapping birds: the 'lime', a sticky substance, is pasted on twigs, on which a bird might be induced to perch, whereupon the bird's instinct on making contact with the lime is to dig in with its claws, thus becoming more stuck.

15.   *a* Cicero, *or a* Thomas: Marcus Tullius Cicero (106–43 BCE) was a leading politician in the final decades of the Roman Republic, whose contributions to Latin literature include speeches and letters, as well as a body of philosophical writing which is significant both in its own right and for Cicero's translation of Greek philosophical vocabulary into Latin. Thomas Aquinas (1225–74) was a

Dominican friar who taught at the University of Paris and elsewhere, and whose philosophical writings – both his commentaries on Aristotle and the *Summa Theologiae* – are among the masterpieces of mediaeval philosophy.

16. *pusled*: An archaic spelling of 'puzzled'.

17. *as it is in play . . . most in their hand*: This card-playing simile illustrates what is perhaps the central idea of *Leviathan*, that if there is an established procedure for resolving disagreements, it cannot be overridden just because someone is convinced, for whatever reason, that their own opinion is superior.

18. *or accidents of Bread in Cheese . . . A free-Will*: 'Accidents of Bread in Cheese' mocks the way scholastic philosophers write about transubstantiation, the Roman Catholic doctrine according to which bread and wine are transformed through the sacrament of the Eucharist into the body and the blood of Christ. 'Immateriall Substances' mocks the view of Hobbes's contemporary René Descartes (1596–1650) that there is, in addition to material substance, such a thing as the immaterial substance of the mind. (Descartes' *Meditations on First Philosophy* were first published in 1641 in a volume containing a set of objections by Hobbes, alongside those of other critics, together with Descartes' replies.) For Hobbes's further thoughts on freedom, see ch. 21.

19. *For it is most true that* Cicero *. . . the books of Philosophers*: Cicero, *De divinatione* 2.119.

20. *As they do, that say,* Faith is infused, *or* inspired: Aquinas considers 'whether faith is infused into man by God' in his *Summa Theologiae* IIa-IIae, Q. 6, Art. 1.

21. *The seventh . . . Schoolemen*: 'Hypostatical', 'transubstantiate' and 'consubstantiate' are technical terms relating to claims about the nature of Christ and to the question of what happens to the bread and wine during the Eucharist. For the 'eternal-Now', see Aquinas, *Summa Theologiae* I, Q. 10, Art. 2.

22. *ignes fatui*: Will-o'-the-wisps.

23. *But they that trusting onely to the authority of books . . . the master of Fence*: Hobbes himself had written a short essay in the mid-1640s on 'The mathematical demonstration of the sword' (British Library, Harleian MS 5219).

24. *Concoction*: Digestion.

25. *exoneration*: Emptying of the bowels.

26. *Onerations*: Filling of the stomach.

27. *Constant* Despayre, DIFFIDENCE *of our selves*: This is the first appearance of 'diffidence', meaning mistrustfulness, in *Leviathan*; it becomes a keyword in ch. 13.

28. Pan: The goat-like Greek god of flocks, shepherds and the wildness of nature. For 'panic', see Pausanias, *Description of Greece* 10.23.7.

29. *The Definition of the* Will . . . *is not good*: See, e.g., Aquinas, *Summa Theologiae* Ia–IIae, Q. 8, Art. 1.

30. *For there is no such thing . . . while we live here*: Hobbes here rejects a great deal of ancient Greek philosophy – including that of the Epicureans, Sceptics and Stoics – that held one could aspire to a state of ἀταραξία, or of having a tranquil soul.

31. *And that whereby they signifie the opinion . . . no name in our tongue*: μακαρισμός is sometimes translated as a state of blessedness. For biblical uses, see Romans 4:6, 9 and Galatians 4:15.

32. *If* Livy *say . . . wee distrust not God therein, but* Livy: Livy (59 BCE–17 CE) wrote a history of Rome, *Ab urbe condita* ('from the founding of the city'), significant chunks of which have survived. Talking cows make brief appearances at 3.10 and 41.13.

33. *Gingling*: The *Oxford English Dictionary* offers, 'to play with words for the sake of sound'.

34. *If some man in Bedlam*: The psychiatric hospital of St Mary of Bethlehem at Bishopsgate in London was colloquially known as Bedlam.

35. *There was once . . . the Tragedy of* Andromeda: *Andromeda* was a play by the Athenian tragedian Euripides, only fragments of which survive, in which the mythological hero Perseus defeats a sea monster, thereby preventing it from eating Andromeda, who had been chained to a rock on the order of her father, the king of Ethiopia. The story Hobbes reports here comes from the second-century satirist Lucian, *How History Ought to be Written* 1.

36. *Likewise there raigned a fit of madnesse . . . hang themselves*: See Plutarch, *Moralia*, 'Virtues of Women' 11, and Aulus Gellius, *Attic Nights* 15.10.

37. *But on the other side . . . and other Gods*: The ancient Greek Furies – goddesses of vengeance – were alternatively

known as the 'Eumenides', or 'kindly ones'. Ceres was the Roman goddess of corn. Phoebus is another name for Apollo, the Greek god of music, poetry and healing.

38. *For neither* Moses, *nor* Abraham: Moses led the Jews out of bondage in Egypt and received the Ten Commandments from God on Mount Sinai. Abraham was the first of the Jewish Patriarchs, who migrated from Ur to Canaan, and made a covenant with God.

39. *Aaron*: Moses' older brother.

40. *Burthen of the Lord*: See Jeremiah 23:33.

41. *So in the old Testament he that came to anoynt* Jehu: There are two Jehus in *Leviathan*. This one was the tenth king of Israel, whose reign is described at 2 Kings 9–10.

42. *except by the Sadduces*: Acts 23:8. The Sadducees were a Jewish sect that was active at the time of the ministry of Jesus of Nazareth.

43. *They are the Translation of the Title . . .* Of the Concourse, Motion, and Help of God: Francisco Suárez (1548–1617) was a Jesuit philosopher and theologian, and one of the most important early modern Aristotelians.

44. *THE TABLE OF THE SCIENCES*: '*Sciography*': The art of using a sundial.

45. *The King of* Persia, *Honoured* Mordecay: Esther 6:1–11. Mordecai was a Jewish exile at the Persian court, where he had thwarted a plot to assassinate the king.

46. *And yet another King of* Persia . . . *and then it was Dishonour*: Plutarch, *Life of Artaxerxes* 5.2.

47. *Scutchions*: I.e., 'escutcheons', a shield on which is painted a heraldic coat of arms.

48. *In so much as nothing is so much celebrated in* Jupiter . . . *from his Herdsmen*: Jupiter was the sky god and king of the gods in the Roman pantheon. Mercury was the messenger god, and the god of commerce, known to the Greeks as Hermes. Hobbes refers here to the fourth *Homeric Hymn*, 'To Hermes' 17–19. (These are not thought to be by Homer, the poet of the *Iliad* and the *Odyssey*.)

49. *in Dutch*: 'Dutch' here means 'German'.

50. *about the time of* Constantine *the Great*: Constantine I (272/3–337) became Emperor of Rome in 306, and founded Constantinople in 324. He was the first Christian Emperor, supposedly converted following a vision

before the Battle of the Milvian Bridge in 312, and being baptized shortly before his death.

51. *in Mr.* Seldens *most excellent Treatise*: John Selden (1584–1654) was an English scholar and politician. The treatise mentioned here is his *Titles of Honor* (1614).

52. *For there is no such* Finis ultimus . . . *in the Books of the old Morall Philosophers*: Ancient ethical theories – such as are discussed in Cicero's *De finibus* – were often organized around the pursuit of a *summum bonum* (highest good), such as virtue for the Stoics or pleasure for the Epicureans. Hobbes here denies that such a thing exists.

53. *as for example . . . in killing Catiline*: Lucius Sergius Catilina (108–62 BCE), known in English as Catiline, was the central figure in a conspiracy against the Roman Republic, opposed by Cicero, in 63 BCE. The Roman Senate passed a number of resolutions against the conspirators, including '*Senatus consultum ultimum*' (the 'final decree of the Senate', authorizing extraordinary powers to the consuls in defence of the state), a declaration that Catiline was an enemy of the republic and an order for the execution without trial of a number of his associates. See Sallust, *The Conspiracy of Catiline* 29, 36, 50–3.

54. Prometheus: In Greek mythology Prometheus was a Titan who stole fire from Olympus in a hollow fennel stalk and passed it on to humans for their use, and was punished by Zeus as Hobbes describes. The story is told by Hesiod, *Theogony* 507–69.

55. *In which sense . . . is very true*: E.g., Statius, *Thebaid* 3.661.

56. *As the Athenians . . . another* Scipio: Phormio was an Athenian general during the Peloponnesian War, who defeated the Spartans at Naupactus, later known as Lepanto, in 429 BCE. A subsequent naval expedition to the same place was commanded by his son Asopius. See Thucydides, *History of the Peloponnesian War* 2.83–4, 3.7. Publius Cornelius Scipio Africanus (236–183 BCE) was the Roman general who defeated the Carthaginian general Hannibal at the Battle of Zama in 202 BCE; Scipio Aemilianus (185/4–129 BCE) presided over the destruction of Carthage in 146 BCE. Gnaeus Pompeius

Magnus (106–48 BCE) was a Roman general, who fought a civil war against Julius Caesar from 49 BCE. After being defeated at Pharsalus in 48 BCE Pompey was murdered in Egypt, but his supporters continued to fight, with Metellus Scipio commanding the Pompeian armies in Africa during the civil war in 47–46 BCE. He committed suicide after being defeated by Julius Caesar's forces at Thapsus, in modern Tunisia. See Plutarch, *Life of Cato the Younger* 57.3.

57. *Men, Women . . . a Leeke, Deified*: Juvenal, *Satire* 15.1–9.

58. *as* Charon, Cerberus: In Greek mythology, Charon ferried the souls of the recently dead across the river Acheron into the underworld, where Cerberus was the multi-headed dog who guarded its gates.

59. *They invoked also their own Wit . . . and* Succubæ: In Greek and Roman mythology, the nine Muses were the goddesses of various arts, such as Clio for history or Terpsichore for dance; Cupid (in Greek: Eros) was the god of love, armed with his trademark bow and arrow; and Priapus was a fertility god, whose very large penis was in a state of permanent erection. Incubi and succubae are demons, male and female respectively, who have sex with people while they sleep.

60. *ascribing the cause of Fœcundity . . . to* Æolus: Venus was the Roman goddess of love; Aeolus the ruler of the winds in Greek mythology.

61. Bacchus: The Roman god of wine.

62. *in the ambiguous or senslesse answers . . . and other famous Oracles*: Delphi, on the Greek mainland, and Delos, an island in the Aegean, were both locations of oracles of Apollo. The Siwa oasis in the Libyan desert was home to the oracle of the Egyptian god Amun, whom the Greeks identified with their Zeus.

63. *Sometimes in the leaves of the Sibills . . .* Nostradamus: The Sibyls were female oracles. Michel de Nostredame (1503–66), known as Nostradamus, was a French astrologer whose 1555 volume of enigmatic prophecies in verse, *Les Propheties*, remains popular down to the present time.

64. *Crosse and Pile*: Heads or tails – with reference to the images that used to appear on French coins.

65. Virgil: Publius Vergilius Maro (70–19 BCE), known as Virgil, was a Roman poet, the author of the *Eclogues*, the *Georgics* and the *Aeneid*.

66. *So Numa Pompilius . . . with the Holy Ghost, in forme of a Dove*: Numa Pompilius was the second king of Rome, after Romulus, who is supposed to have reigned 715–673 BCE, and who established the Roman religion. The story of Numa and Egeria is told by Livy, *Ab urbe condita* 1.19. Manco Cápac was the founder of the Inca kingdom; he and his wife Mama Uqllu were held to be the children of the sun god Inti and the moon goddess Mama Killa. 'Mahomet' is a variant spelling of Muhammad, the Islamic prophet (570–632). The involvement of a dove in Muhammad's prophecies was a commonplace in European literature, e.g. Shakespeare, *Henry VI, Part I*, Act 1, Scene 2.

67. *nor do we read . . . subjection to any mortall King or State whatsoever*: Cf. Suetonius, *Life of Tiberius* 36.

68. Joshua: Israelite military commander who led the invasion of Canaan after the death of Moses.

69. Baal: A Levantine god.

70. *the sons of* Samuel: Samuel was a judge and a prophet in ancient Israel, who presided over the transition to monarchy after the Jews rejected the rule of his wicked sons, Joel and Abijah.

71. *That a King . . . one of his Subjects?*: Childeric III was king of Francia from 743 until 751, when he was ousted by Pepin the Short (Charlemagne's father), with the support of Zachary (679–752), who was Pope from 741.

72. *dommage*: I.e., damage.

73. *nasty, brutish, and short*: This is the most famous phrase Hobbes ever wrote, but it is striking that he did not straightforwardly translate it into Latin. The Latin *Leviathan* has 'bruta & brevis'.

74. *This is that Law of the Gospell . . . alteri ne feceris*: Matthew 7:12; Luke 6:31. Lampridius, *Life of Severus Alexander* 51.

75. *And this I think . . . Meritum condigni*: See Aquinas, *Summa Theologiae* Ia-IIae, Q. 114, Arts. 3, 6.

76. *the Herbage*: The right to pasture cattle on a piece of land.

77. *Such was the Heathen Forme . . . as I kill this Beast*: Livy, *Ab urbe condita* 1.24.

78. *For they say . . . every man his own*: Justinian, *Institutes* 1.1.

79. *The Foole hath sayd in his heart . . . no such thing as Justice*: cf. Psalm 14:1.

80. *And the Heathen that believed . . . the avenger of Injustice*: For the story of the god Kronos (= Saturn) and his son Zeus (= Jupiter), see Hesiod, *Theogony* 453-506.

81. *Somewhat like to a piece of Law . . . the Atteynder be voyd*: Sir Edward Coke (1552-1634) was a leading jurist and author of *The Institutes of the Lawes of England*, whose first part (published in 1628) was *A Commentarie upon Littleton*, i.e., on the *Treatise on Tenures* by Sir Thomas Littleton (d. 1481). Hobbes here refers to a passage towards the end of 1.1.8 of that first part. '*Eo instante*' means 'at that instant'.

82. *Justice of Actions . . . And Distributive*: See, e.g., Aquinas, *Summa Theologiae* IIa-IIae, Q. 61, Art. 1, which refers back to Aristotle, *Nicomachean Ethics* 1130b-1131a.

83. *I know that* Aristotle *. . . of his doctrine*: Aristotle, *Politics* 1253b-1255b.

84. *The Greeks call the violation of this law . . . more than their share*: See Aristotle, *Nicomachean Ethics* 1130a.

85. Προσωποληψία: See Romans 2:11.

86. in foro interno . . . in foro externo: 'In the internal court', i.e. in conscience; 'in the external court', i.e. with respect to action.

87. *in which sence . . . and the Judges*: Cicero, *De oratore* 2.102.

88. *not in his own name . . . with* Hoc dicit Dominus: I.e., 'Thus says Moses', 'Thus says the Lord'. Hobbes seems to refer to Exodus 32:27 here; he returns to this verse explicitly in the 'Review, and Conclusion' (p. 593).

Part II: Of Common-wealth

1. *It is true . . . Politicall creatures*: Cranes, ants and bees are all discussed in Aristotle, *History of Animals* 1.1. For bees, see also *Politics* 1253a.

2. *(or Meum and Tuum)*: Mine and thine.

3. *And this division is it, whereof it is said,* a Kingdome divided in it selfe cannot stand: Mark 3:24.

4. *multiplying glasses . . . prospective glasses*: Magnifying glasses; and telescopes or binoculars.

5. *There be other names of Government . . . Formes misliked*: See Aristotle, *Politics* 1279ab; also Polybius, *Histories* 6.3–9.

6. *but the Soveraignty was in the* Ephori: The ephors were five magistrates, elected each year by the popular assembly, who supervised the conduct of the kings.

7. *And this was it our most wise King . . . of* England *and* Scotland: James (1566–1625) succeeded to the Scottish throne as an infant in 1567 on the abdication of his mother Mary, Queen of Scots, and to the English throne in 1603 following the death of his cousin Elizabeth. The early years of his reign in England saw an attempt to unify the two kingdoms, which was effectively blocked by the House of Commons in 1607.

8. *We find in History . . . the dominion of the Females was in the Mother*: Strabo, *Geography* 11.5.1.

9. Salomon: Solomon was the third king of ancient Israel, after Saul and David, who oversaw the construction of the Temple of Jerusalem.

10. Saul *sought the life of* David: Saul was the first king of ancient Israel, and David the second.

11. *St.* Paul: Paul – originally Saul of Tarsus – underwent a conversion experience on the road to Damascus to become one of the most important of the early Christian apostles and the author of a number of the letters that are included in the New Testament. He was executed in Rome under Nero.

12. Give to Cæsar that which is Cæsars: Matthew 22:21.

13. *As when* Jeptha *caused his daughter to be sacrificed*: Jephtha was one of the judges of ancient Israel. See Judges 11:29–40.

14. *(as was the killing of* Uriah, *by* David*)*: 2 Samuel 11.

15. To thee only have I sinned: Psalm 51:4.

16. *sometimes banished an* Aristides *. . . to make a Jest of it*: For Aristides and Hyperbolus, both Athenian politicians of the fifth century BCE, see Plutarch, *Life of Aristides* 7.

17. *As for Example . . . in Parliament*: The legislation to which Hobbes refers, such as the Forcible Entry Act of 1381, was repealed by section 13 of the Criminal Law Act 1977.

18. Virginia, *and* Sommer-Ilands: The Sommer-Ilands are better known as Bermuda. Hobbes was personally involved with both the Virginia Company of London and the Somers Islands Company.

19. *not by obligation*: This 'not' does not appear in some versions of the text of *Leviathan*.

20. Demetrius: A silversmith at Ephesus. Acts 19:24.

21. Dei gratiâ & Regis; *or* Dei providentiâ & voluntate Regis: 'By the grace of God and the king', 'by the providence of God and the will of the king'.

22. Let the Civill Law . . . what another mans: Cicero, *Pro Caecina* 74, 70.

23. *but by the discretion of* Eleazar *the Priest*: Eleazar was the son of Aaron, his successor as high priest, and, according to Hobbes (p. 394), sovereign over the Israelites.

24. *the Tribe of* Joseph . . . *the Tribe of* Levi: Joseph and Levi were two of the twelve sons of Jacob, after whom the tribes of Israel were named. For the division of the land amongst the tribes, see Joshua 13:1–14:5, also 18:7, and Numbers 18:21.

25. *And though a People comming into possession of a Land by warre . . . their Estates*: See Joshua 8:18–11:23.

26. William *the* Conquerour: William, duke of Normandy (1027/8–1087) conquered England in 1066 and became king.

27. *expresse them in Holy Scripture*: Exodus 20:1–17.

28. *But these words*: Matthew 19:21.

29. *These words*: Matthew 21:2.

30. *but these words*: Acts 2:38.

31. *yet in a Wheele-barrough*: One of Hobbes's French correspondents, François du Verdus, wrote in 1656 to ask whether tennis was played in wheel-barrows in England, as he had himself not seen anyone playing that way. *The Correspondence of Thomas Hobbes*, Noel Malcolm, ed. (Oxford: Clarendon Press, 1994), letter #100, vol. 1, p. 350.

32. Plato: Plato (*c.* 429–347 BCE) was a pupil of Socrates and the teacher of Aristotle, the founder of the Academy

in Athens, and the author of a number of philosophical dialogues, including *Republic*, which have survived.

33. *(as* Alexander *did with his sword in the Gordian knot)*: Whoever untied the Gordian knot was supposed to become ruler of the world. See, e.g., Plutarch, *Life of Alexander* 18.

34. *nay, Heaven and Earth shall passe . . . the Eternall Law of God*: cf. Matthew 5:18.

35. *Yet this is set down by a great Lawyer for the common Law* of England: Coke, *The First Part of the Institutes of the Lawes of England* 3.13.709.

36. *In the Institutions of* Justinian, *we find seven sorts of Civill Lawes*: Justinian (*c.* 482–565) was Emperor of Byzantium, 527–65. Under his reign, much of the Western Empire was reconquered and various codifications of law issued, including the *Institutes* in 533. The reference here is to *Institutes* 1.2.3–9.

37. *Againe, where God saith to* Abraham: Genesis 18:18–19.

38. *At Mount* Sinai Moses *only went up to God*: Exodus 19:16–21, 20:19.

39. *Thou shalt not covet*: Exodus 20:17.

40. *so that what* Marius *makes a Crime,* Sylla *shall make meritorious*: Gaius Marius (157–86 BCE) and Lucius Cornelius Sulla (138–78 BCE) were Roman politicians and military commanders who fought a civil war in 88–87 BCE, with Marius declaring Sulla's reforms invalid during his own seventh consulate.

41. *From these different sources of Crimes . . . the same allay*: The Stoics held that all sins were equal; this is the third of the six 'paradoxes of the Stoics' discussed by Cicero, *Paradoxa Stoicorum* 20–26.

42. *he is totally Excused*: For the right of necessity and right of self-defence, see, e.g., Aquinas, *Summa Theologiae* IIa-IIae, Q. 66, Art. 7 and Q. 64, Art. 7 respectively.

43. *which Crimes . . . a Fundamentall Law*: See, e.g., Justinian, *Digest* 48.4.

44. *And* Cicero *sayes . . . a refuge of men in danger*: Cicero, *Pro Caecina* 100.

45. *the last two verses of the one and fortieth of* Job: Job 41:33–4.

46. *So was* Thomas Becket *. . . by the Pope*: Thomas Becket (1120?–70) was Archbishop of Canterbury from 1162

until he was murdered by four knights in Canterbury Cathedral. Henry II (1133–89) succeeded to the English throne in 1154, and was widely blamed for Becket's murder, for which he subsequently did penance. The Pope mentioned here is Alexander III.

47. *And so were the* Barons . . . *the Succession from his Elder brother, to himselfe*: William Rufus (*c.* 1060–1100) was William the Conqueror's third son, who succeeded his father to the English throne in 1087, reigning as William II, while his older brother Robert (*c.* 1050–1134) became Duke of Normandy.

48. *maintained in their Rebellion against King* John, *by the French*: John (1167–1216) was king of England 1199–1216. Hobbes refers here to the First Barons' War, 1215–17, in which the rebellious barons were supported by a French army under Prince Louis (later Louis VIII of France).

49. *the seditions, of* Tiberius Gracchus, Caius Gracchus, Lucius Saturninus: The Gracchi were Roman politicians in the second century BCE. Tiberius Sempronius Gracchus (*c.* 163–133 BCE) championed land reform and was murdered along with many of his supporters by a crowd of Roman senators. Gaius Sempronius Gracchus (*c.* 154–121 BCE) continued with his brother's programme, but committed suicide to avoid death at the hands of a mob. Lucius Saturninus (d. 100 BCE) was an ally of Marius and was killed in mob violence.

50. *The people of* Athens *bound themselves but from one onely Action*: Plutarch, *Life of Solon* 8.1–2.

51. *So the people of the Jewes were stirred up to reject God . . . the Nations*: 1 Samuel 8:4–7.

52. *Lacedæmonians*: Spartans.

53. *From the reading, I say, of such books, men have undertaken to kill their Kings*: E.g., Cicero, *De officiis* 3.32.

54. *which is a Kingdome divided in it selfe, and cannot stand*: Mark 3:24, again.

55. *And this is a Disease which not unfitly may be compared to the Epilepsie*: See, e.g., Luke 9:38–42.

56. *like the foolish daughters of* Peleus . . . *cut him in pieces*: In Greek mythology, Medea was the daughter of the king of Colchis on the Black Sea, who eloped with Jason and

later (according to Euripides) killed their children. Pelias was king of Iolcos in Thessaly. Ovid, *Metamorphoses* 7:297–349.

57. *For there God sayes . . . Though shalt not have the Gods of other Nations*: Exodus 20:3.

58. *but openly . . . the ten Commandements*: Exodus 20:4. *'In facie Ecclesiae'* = 'in the presence of the church'.

59. *Which doctrine the third Commandement by resemblance pointeth to*: Exodus 20:7.

60. *To this end had the* Jewes *every seventh day, a* Sabbath *. . . by lawfull recreation*: Exodus 20:8–11.

61. *it is necessary that they should be obedient to them*: Exodus 20:12.

62. *all of which things are intimated in the sixth, seventh, eighth, and ninth Commandements*: Exodus 20:13–16.

63. *And this is the intention of the tenth Commandement*: Exodus 20:17.

64. Thou shalt love thy neighbour as thy selfe: Matthew 19:19.

65. Henry the eighth: Henry VIII (1491–1547) was King of England from 1509. He broke with the Roman Church over the question of his marriage to Catherine of Aragon (1485–1536), whom he divorced in 1533, and became head of the Church of England. Five other wives followed, two of whom were executed.

66. *They must either do as the Jewes did . . . hold the Sword in the other*: Nehemiah 4:17.

67. *as in the case of* Tarquin *. . . the Monarchy it selfe dissolved*: Tarquinius Superbus was the seventh and last of the legendary kings of Rome. In 510 BCE his son Sextus Tarquinius is supposed to have raped Lucretia, and the monarchy was overthrown in the upheaval that followed. Livy, *Ab urbe condita* 1.57–60.

68. *It is a contention with Ambition . . . there grew up three*: Servius, *Commentary on the Aeneid* 6.287.

69. Psal. 96.1: Hobbes here uses a different numbering system to that most commonly used today. See Psalms 97.1.

70. Psal. 98.1: Psalms 99.1.

71. Psal. 72. ver. *1, 2, 3*: Psalms 73:1–3.

72. *in these words*: John 9:3.

73. *And though it be said*: Romans 5:12.

74. It is better to obey God than men: Acts 5:29.
75. *For he also is of opinion that it is impossible for the disorders of State . . . till Soveraigns be Philosophers*: Plato, *Republic* 473c–e.
76. *(as by* Plato *they are)*: Plato, *Republic* 525b.

Part III: Of a Christian Common-wealth

1. *the warre he made against* Ramoth Gilead, *only* Micaiah *was a true one*: Micaiah is a prophet in the Hebrew Bible.
2. Jeroboam: Jeroboam was the first king of Israel after the partition of the kingdom *c.* 930 BCE into Israel (in the north) and Judah (in the south).
3. *For the works of the* Egyptian *Sorcerers . . . great miracles*: Exodus 7:11–12.
4. *and they are the same that are acknowledged by St.* Jerome: Jerome (*c.* 347–420) produced the Latin translation of the Bible known as the Vulgate.
5. *Of the Canonicall . . . the* Hebrew *Alphabet*: Flavius Josephus (*c.* 37–*c.* 101) took part in the Jewish Revolt, later settling in Rome. He wrote extensively on Jewish history and religion. Titus Flavius Domitian (51–96) was Emperor of Rome from 81.
6. *sent for by* Ptolemy *King of* Egypt: Ptolemy II Philadelphus (308–246 BCE), king of Ptolemaic Egypt from 282 BCE.
7. *The* History of Livy *. . . denominated from the subject*: Livy's history of Rome is referred to in these notes as *Ab urbe condita*. Gjergj Kastrioti (1405–68), known as Skanderbeg, was an Albanian military leader in the fifteenth century, celebrated for his resistance against the Ottoman Turks.
8. *was long time after found again by* Hilkiah, *and sent to King* Josias: Josiah (*c.* 649–609 BCE) was king of Judah, succeeding to the throne aged eight after the murder of his father Amon. Hilkiah was the high priest during Josiah's reign.
9. *from the trouble that* Achan *raised in the Camp*: Achan was stoned to death for stealing from Jericho, in contravention of a divine command.

10. *where it is said, that Jonathan:* Jonathan was one of Moses' grandsons.

11. *called the place* Perez-Uzzah: 1 Chronicles 13:11.

12. *of the Prophet* Nathan . . . *and of the Prophet* Addo: Nathan was a prophet from the time of David who features in Samuel, Kings and Chronicles. For the others, see 2 Chronicles 9:29, 12:15, 13:22. 'Serveiah' seems to be a garbled rendering of 'Shemaiah'.

13. *partly of* Agur *the son of* Jakeh; *and partly of the Mother of King* Lemuel: Proverbs 30:1, 31:1-4.

14. *Of the Prophets . . . Kings of* Judah: 'Sophoniah' is better known as Zephaniah, 'Jonas' as Jonah, who was swallowed by a large fish, and 'Ozias' / 'Azariah' as Uzziah, who was king of Judah in the eighth century BCE, as was Amaziah, who was his father. Isaiah and Michaiah are the only prophets in this list who appear in other passages of *Leviathan*. Isaiah's prophecies are recorded in the book of Isaiah. For the story of Michaiah, see 1 Kings 22:1-40.

15. *Fourty dayes and* Ninivy *shall be destroyed:* Jonah 3:4.

16. Jeremiah, Abdias: Jeremiah was active in the late seventh and early sixth centuries BCE, a period which included the destruction of the Temple of Solomon *c.* 586 BCE. 'Abdias' is better known as Obadiah.

17. Ezekiel, Daniel, Aggeus, *and* Zacharias, *in the Captivity*: 'Aggeus' is better known as Haggai, 'Zacharias' as Zechariah. Daniel and Ezekiel appear elsewhere in *Leviathan*, both were prophets who lived in Babylon during the Jewish Capitivity there in the sixth century BCE.

18. *When* Joel *and* Malachi *prophecyed:* The dating of the book of Joel is, as Hobbes remarks, uncertain. The book of Malachi is usually thought to have been written in the fifth century BCE.

19. Esdras: Esdras, also known as Ezra, was a Jewish priest who played a key role in the reorganization of Jewish religion in Jerusalem following the Babylonian Captivity. Hobbes was one of those who argued that the Pentateuch – the first five books of the Hebrew Bible – were written not by Moses, as tradition held, but by Ezra.

20. *except St.* Paul *and St.* Luke: Luke (d. *c.* 84) was a disciple of Paul, and the author of one of the Gospels and of the Acts of the Apostles.

21. *supposed to be collected by* Clement *the first (after St. Peter) Bishop of* Rome: Peter (d. *c.* 64) was one of the disciples of Jesus, and the first bishop of Rome. Clement (d. 99) was one of his earliest successors as bishop of Rome (though not the first, as Hobbes remarks). The Canons of the Apostles Hobbes mentions are widely thought to be a much later collection. Hobbes discusses the attribution problem on p. 438.

22. Philo: Philo of Alexandria (d. 50) was a Jewish scholar of the first century, who attempted a synthesis of Greek philosophy and Jewish religion.

23. *(as the Apostle saith generally of all Idols)*: 1 Corinthians 8:4.

24. *as when it excited Othoniel . . .* Judg. *3.10. 6.34. 11.29. 13.25. 14.6, 19*: Othniel was the first of the judges of ancient Israel. Gideon was a judge, who defeated the Midianites. Samson was a judge of prodigious strength, as long as he did not cut his hair, who was betrayed by Delilah to the Philistines, and who died when he tore down the pillars of the temple of Dagon.

25. *The false Prophet* Zedekiah: Zedekiah, son of Chenaanah, was a false prophet at the court of King Ahab.

26. *(Ezek. 2.30.)*: This is an error, for Ezekiel 2:2.

27. *such as was the Spirit of Python*: Acts 16:16–18. Python was the mythological serpent, slain by Apollo, who was associated with the oracle at Delphi. See, e.g., *Homeric Hymn* 3:300–74.

28. *in the tenth verse, saith to Agar*: Hagar was the Egyptian servant of Sarah, Abraham's wife.

29. *Why therefore may not the Angels that appeared to Lot, and are called* Gen. *19.13.* Men: Lot was Abraham's nephew, who escaped the destruction of Sodom (after which his wife was turned into a pillar of salt), and subsequently impregnated both of his daughters.

30. *When the Angel called to Abraham . . . from slaying Isaac*: Isaac was one of the Jewish Patriarchs. He was the son of Abraham, who attempted to sacrifice him when he was young, and the father of Jacob and Esau.

31. *The Angels which Jacob saw on the Ladder of Heaven*: Jacob was one of the Jewish Patriarchs, later given the name Israel by God. He was the son of Isaac, and the brother of Esau, and the father of twelve sons, from

whom the various tribes of Israel are held to have descended.

32. *Also (Exod. 14.9) the Angel that went before the Army of Israel . . . and* Angel *promised to Moses (Exod. 14. 9) for the Armies guide*: Hobbes's biblical references here are imprecise, but most of what he presents here is found in Exodus 14, especially verses 19 and 24.

33. *for Messenger; as John Baptist is called an Angel*: John the Baptist appears as the forerunner of Jesus Christ in the Gospels, whom he baptized in the river Jordan. He was later beheaded on the order of Herod Antipas.

34. *Though we find in Daniel two names of Angels,* Gabriel, *and Michael*: E.g., Daniel 8:16 (Gabriel) and 12:1 (Michael).

35. *impatible*: The *Oxford English Dictionary* offers, 'Incapable of suffering, or of sustaining injury'.

36. *and gave him commandement to abstaine from the tree of cognizance of Good and Evill*: Genesis 2:16–17.

37. *And afterwards God punished his posterity, for their vices, all but eight persons, with an universall deluge*: Genesis 6:18.

38. *(as in the Lords Prayer)*: Matthew 6:11.

39. *by which no man might enter into the* Sanctum Sanctorum: The holiest part of the Temple, where the Ark of the Covenant stood. 1 Kings 6:16–19.

40. *the title of his crosse . . . with a crown of Thornes*: John 19:19, 2.

41. *when we say,* For thine is the Kingdome, the Power, and Glory: Matthew 6:13.

42. *should deliver to them from before the* Cherubins *in the* Sanctum Sanctorum: Exodus 25:18–20.

43. *In which sense, when we say, the Gospel of St. Matthew . . . and sometimes of the Subject*: Matthew was a tax-collector who became one of Jesus's disciples and is reputed as the author of one of the Gospels.

44. *For example, though these words,* I am the Lord thy God, &c. . . . *the holy History*: Exodus 20:1–2.

45. *So also . . . Elijah saith to God*: Elijah was a prophet in the ninth century BCE, who ascended to heaven in a fiery chariot.

46. *that St. John the Evangelist, and, I think, St. John onely calleth*: John was the author of one of the Gospels,

traditionally identified with the John who was one of
Jesus' twelve disciples.

47. *It is true, that as the same History is related in the first
     Book of Esdras . . . from the mouth of the Lord*: 1 Esdras
     25–8.

48. *And therefore when Caiphas said, it was expedient that
     one man should die for the people*: Caiaphas was the
     high priest when Jesus was arrested and put on trial.

49. *In the sense of speaking from man to God . . . in this
     manner*: Abimelech was king of Gerar.

50. *In the like sense, is Miriam [Exod. 15.20.] called a
     Prophetesse*: Miriam was the sister of Moses and Aaron.

51. *The woman of Endor*: 1 Samuel 28:7–25.

52. *vapor from the cave of the Pythian Oracle at Delphi*:
     The Pythian Oracle was the priestess of Apollo at
     Delphi.

53. Materia prima: Primal, formless matter.

54. *The Prophet David argueth thus*: Psalm 94:9.

55. *In what manner God spake to Adam, and Eve, and Cain,
     and Noah, is not expressed*: Eve was the first woman cre-
     ated by God, and the wife of Adam. Cain, who killed his
     brother Abel, was their son. Noah built an ark.

56. *[Gen. 18.12]*: This is an incorrect reference, which should
     be 28:12.

57. Elisha: Elisha was a prophet in the ninth century BCE.

58. Joseph: Joseph was the husband of Mary.

59. *took the Priesthood from Abiathar, and gave it [verse
     35.] to Zadoc*: Abiathar was the high priest during the
     reign of David. Zadok was the first high priest of the
     Temple of Solomon.

60. *the fault that Jonathan had committed, in eating a
     honey-comb*: Jonathan was the son of Saul and a friend
     of David.

61. *To the Virgin Mary, by a Vision of an Angel*: Luke 1:26–
     38. Mary was the mother of Jesus.

62. *To Joseph in a Dream*: Matthew 1:20–21.

63. *again to Paul in the way to Damascus in a Vision of our
     Saviour*: Acts 9:3–9.

64. *and to Peter in the Vision of a sheet let down from
     heaven, with divers sorts of flesh, of clean, and unclean,
     beasts*: Acts 10:9–16.

65. *and in prison, by Vision of an Angel*: Acts 12:5–9.

66.   *and to the Apostles again . . . (at the choosing of Mat-
      thias in the place of Judas Iscariot) by lot*: Acts 1: 21–6.
      Judas Iscariot was one of Jesus's disciples, who betrayed
      him, and was replaced as an apostle by Matthias, about
      whom next to nothing else is known.

67.   *Ahab*: Ahab was king of Israel in the ninth century BCE.
      He was married to Jezebel. The reference Hobbes provides
      is incorrect; it should be to 1 Kings 22, around verse 6.

68.   *as he did by Baalam*: Balaam was a prophet during the
      final phase of the Israelites' wandering in the wilderness.
      See Numbers 23:5, 23:16, 24:2–9.

69.   *and complained that there were some that Prophecyed in
      the Campe*: Numbers 11:27–8.

70.   *The first Rainbow that was seen in the world*: Genesis
      9:12–16.

71.   *(verse 41.)*: This verse does not exist. Exodus 4:31 is
      better.

72.   *St. Marke*: Mark (d. 68) was one of the early followers
      of Jesus. He was the author of one of the Gospels, and is
      held to have founded the church in Alexandria, where he
      was martyred.

73.   *(Psal. 133.3)*: Psalms 134:3.

74.   *The Jews that asked our Saviour the question*: Luke
      20:27–38.

75.   *Cœlum Empyreum*: The fiery heaven.

76.   *otherwise than by the Resurrection in the last day, (except
      Enos and Elias)*: Enoch, the father of Methuselah, was
      'taken' one day by God (Genesis 5:24). For Elijah's
      ascent into heaven, 2 Kings 2:11.

77.   *Therefore where Job saith, man riseth not till the Heav-
      ens be no more; it is all one*: Job 14:12.

78.   *because Corah, Dathan, and Abirom, were swallowed
      up alive into the earth*: Korah, Dathan and Abiram rose
      up against Moses and Aaron and were swallowed up by
      the earth. Numbers 16:1–35.

79.   Bis patet in præceps, tantum tendítque sub umbras /
      Quantus ad æthereum cœli suspectus Olympum: Virgil,
      Aeneid 6.578–9. Then Tartarus itself 'opens precipi-
      tously, and extends down into the shadows, twice as far
      as the view of the sky does towards heavenly Olympus'.

80.   *Thirdly, because the Cities of Sodom, and Gomorrah*:
      Genesis 19:24–5.

81. *Lastly, whereas there was a place neer Jerusalem . . . sacrificing their children to the Idol Moloch*: Jeremiah 7:31–2. In the seventeenth century, 'Moloch' was believed to be the name of a Levantine god. Nowadays the word is thought to refer instead to a kind of sacrifice.

82. Abaddon: Revelation 9:11.

83. *Obnoxious*: 'Obnoxious' here means 'liable'.

84. *by promise of the Land of Canaan*: Genesis 17:8.

85. *The Calfe that Aaron made, Moses threw into the fire*: Exodus 32:20.

86. *After the death of Joshua . . . that every man did that which was right in his own eyes*: Judges 17:6, 18:1, 19:1, 21:25.

87. *but did evil in the sight of the Lord, and served Baalim*: 'Baalim' is the plural of 'Baal'.

88. *Hulda, the Prophetesse*: Huldah was a prophet. This is the only biblical story in which she features. (It is repeated at 2 Chronicles 34.)

89. *Lastly, wee read . . . that David made Hashabiah and his brethren*: Hashabiah, son of Kemuel, was a Levite.

90. *Likewise (verse 32.) . . . and the halfe tribe of Manasseh (these were the rest of Israel that dwelt beyond Jordan)*: Manasseh was, along with Ephraim, one of the sons of Joseph, and gave his name to one of the tribes of Israel (as did Joseph's brothers, Reuben and Gad).

91. *As for example, after the death of Eleazar and Joshua . . . but did every man that which was right in his own eyes*: Judges, 2:8–10.

92. *yet did Samuel . . . anoint another King, namely David, to take the succession from his heirs*: Agag was the king of Amalek, 1 Samuel, 15:8–33. The anointing of David, 1 Samuel 16:13.

93. *Rehoboam*: Rehoboam was the son of Solomon and king of Judah in the tenth century BCE. 1 Kings 12:3–20.

94. *as Jehosaphat was reproved by the Prophet Jehu, for aiding the King of Israel against the Syrians*: Jehoshaphat was king of Judah in the ninth century BCE. This Jehu is not the same as the one mentioned earlier. 2 Chronicles 19:2.

95. *and Hezekiah, by Isaiah, for shewing his treasures to the Ambassadors of Babylon*: Hezekiah was king of Judah in the late eighth and early seventh centuries BCE. Isaiah 39.

96. *the Cabalists*: Practitioners of the Kabbalah, an esoteric Jewish tradition.

97. *(for hee commanded to obey those that sate then in Moses chaire, and to pay tribute to Cæsar;)*: Moses' chair: Matthew 23:1–3; paying tribute to Caesar, Matthew 22:21.

98. *For though Pilate himself . . . What I have written, I have written*: Pontius Pilate was prefect of Judaea at the time of the trial and execution of Jesus. John 19:6, 19–22.

99. *For as Moses chose twelve Princes of the tribes, to govern under him*: This may be a reference to Deuteronomy 1:13, or a slightly garbled reference to 1:23.

100. *so did our Saviour choose twelve Apostles, who shall sit on twelve thrones, and judge the twelve tribes of Israel*: Luke 6:13, 22:30.

101. *And as Moses authorized Seventy Elders*: Numbers 11:24.

102. *so our Saviour also ordained seventy Disciples, to preach his Kingdome, and Salvation to all Nations*: Luke 10:1.

103. *And as when a complaint was made to Moses . . . he justified them in it, as being subservient therein to his government*: Numbers 11:26–9.

104. *As the Children of Israel . . . they came into the land of Promise*: Joshua 5:1–8.

105. *This rite St. John the Baptist . . . whom hee preached to bee already come into the world*: Luke 3:1–18.

106. *after a solemne Washing*: Leviticus 14:1–9.

107. *the other after their Conversion*: The conversion of Constantine is usually held to have been in 312, on the occasion of his vision before the Battle of the Milvian Bridge.

108. *which is therefore called sometime in the New Testament* Paracletus *which signifieth an* Assister: e.g., John 14:26.

109. *Cardinall Bellarmine . . . the Ecclesiasticall Power of the Pope of Rome*: Roberto Bellarmino (1542–1621) was a Jesuit theologian, who became rector of the Collegio Romano in 1592 and cardinal and an inquisitor in 1599, playing an important role in the cases of both Giordano Bruno (1548–1600) and Galileo Galilei (1564–1642). His *Disputationes de Controversiis Christianae Fidei Adversus Huius Temporis Haereticos* (1581–92) defended the Catholic Church against the Protestants.

110. *As my Father sent me, (so saith our Saviour) I send you*: John 20:21.

111. *hee would make them so many Nimrods*: Nimrod was a mighty hunter. Genesis 10:8–9.

112. Fishers of men: Matthew 4:19.

113. *which the Prophet Elisha allowed to Naaman the Syrian*: Naaman was an army commander and leper.

114. *to our Saviours saying . . . my Father which is in Heaven?*: Matthew 10:33.

115. *to the words of our Saviour,* Whatsoever you would that men should doe unto you, that doe yee unto them: Luke 6:31.

116. I send you *(saith he) . . . as sheep amongst wolves*: Matthew 10:16.

117. *As St. Paul did to the Jews of Thessalonica . . .* and that this Jesus is Christ: Acts 17:2–3.

118. repent, and be Baptized in the name of Jesus, for the Remission of Sins: Acts 2:38.

119. *as Lepers were by the Law of Moses separated from the congregation of Israel*: Leviticus 14.

120. *Insomuch, as when our Saviour accepted the invitation of Zacchæus . . . as a Crime*: Zacchaeus was a tax-collector in Jericho. Luke 19:1–10.

121. *And thence it is that St. Paul calleth Excommunication, a delivery of the Excommunicate person to Satan*: 1 Corinthians 5:1–8.

122. My Kingdome is not of this world: John 18:36.

123. *written in two Tables of Stone*: Exodus 34:28.

124. *Shishak King of Egypt*: Shishak was an Egyptian pharaoh who made war against Judah in the tenth century BCE.

125. *and put into the Library of Ptolemy at Alexandria, and approved for the Word of God*: Ptolemy I Soter (*c.* 367–282 BCE) was one of Alexander's generals, who established the Hellenistic kingdom of Egypt.

126. *and where they were not received, to shake off the dust of their feet against them*: Mark 6:11.

127. *but not to call for fire from heaven to destroy them*: Luke 9:54.

128. *like that of Esay 55.1*: 'Esay' is Isaiah.

129. Sint vobis omnibus Clericis & Laicis Libri venerandi: 'May the books be venerated by all of you, priests and laity.' Apostolic canons 85.

130. Herod the Tetrarch: Herod Antipas was the ruler, or 'tetrarch', of Galilee and Perea at the time of Jesus's ministry and execution.

131. and chose him for a vessell to bear his name before the Gentiles, and Kings, and Children of Israel: Acts 9:15.

132. (as S. Thomas, and S. Barnabas are said to have done: Thomas was one of Jesus's disciples, best known for his disinclination to believe in the resurrected Christ until he had personally examined his wounds. Barnabas was an apostle who travelled with St Paul and is celebrated by the Cypriot Orthodox Church.

133. as we may see by the sedition raised about the Election ... there were above an hundred men found dead upon that occasion in the Church it self: Ammianus Marcellinus was a fourth-century historian who wrote a history of the Roman empire covering the period 353–78. The story described here involving Damasus (who was Pope, 366–84), Ursinus (the defeated candidate in the papal election) and Viventius (not 'Juventius') is at Res Gestae 27.3.12–13.

134. every one according to his gifts, as S. Steven did; and both to Preach, and Baptize, as Philip did: Stephen, along with the Philip mentioned in this passage, was one of seven deacons appointed by Jesus's disciples after his death to assist with charitable work (Acts 6:1–5). He was charged with blasphemy and stoned to death, and is regarded as the first Christian martyr. The other Philip was one of Jesus's, twelve disciples, from Bethsaida.

135. which by the subdivision of the Tribe of Joseph, into Ephraim and Manasses, were still twelve: Ephraim was, along with Manasseh, one of the sons of Joseph, and gave his name to one of the tribes of Israel.

136. (which was carried by Judas Iscariot;): John 12:6, 13:29.

137. Mary Magdalen ... and many others: Mary Magdalen was witness to Christ's crucifixion, burial and resurrection. Chuza was the steward of Herod Antipas.

138. Ananias: Ananias (not to be confused with Ananias of Damascus) was an early Christian who was struck dead for telling a lie in front of Peter, as was his wife Sapphira.

139. 2 Epist. to Tim. ver. 6: 2 Timothy 1:6.

140. not Silvester, but Constantine: Sylvester I was Pope 314–35, during much of Constantine's reign.

141. *the twelve Apostles shall sit on twelve Thrones . . . to judge the twelve tribes of Israel*: Luke 22:30.

142. *to serve two Masters*: Matthew 6:24.

143. *And though the Apostle say in another place*: 2 Corinthians 13:10.

144. *The eighth place is,* Timothy 3:2: 1 Timothy 3:2.

145. *Drink no longer water, but use a little wine for thy healths sake*: 1 Timothy 5:23.

146. *de lana Caprina*: 'about a goat's wool', here meaning irrelevant or beside the point.

147. *Who made me a Judge, or a Divider*: Luke 12:14.

148. *nor hath any thing of* Archicall, *nor* Craticall, *but onely of* Didacticall: 'Archicall' and 'Craticall' are words made up by Hobbes, on the model of words like 'monarchical' or 'aristocratical': the authority of the Popes is to teach, not to govern.

149. *S. Cyprian*: Cyprian (*c.* 200–258) was bishop of Carthage and a martyr.

150. *two Popes, Innocent, and* Leo: Innocent I was Pope 401–17, at the time of Alaric the Visigoth's sack of Rome. Leo I, known as Leo the Great, was Pope 440–61, at the time of Attila the Hun's invasion of Italy.

151. *For the fourth Councell of Lateran held under Pope Innocent the third*: Innocent III (1160/1–1216) was elected Pope in 1198. He excommunicated King John of England, and convoked the Fourth Lateran Council, which met in 1215.

152. *in the Translation of the Roman Empire to* Charlemaine: Charlemagne (740s–814) became king of the Franks in 768, and was crowned Emperor of the Romans by Pope Leo III on Christmas Day 800.

153. *in the Oppression of* John *King of England*: Pope Innocent III placed England under interdict in 1208, suspending the administration of most sacraments, in a dispute over the appointment of the Archbishop of Canterbury. The Pope then proceeded to excommunicate John in 1209. The excommunication was lifted in 1213, and the interdict in 1214.

154. *in Transferring the Kingdome of* Navarre: Pope Julius II in 1512–13 collaborated with Ferdinand II of Aragon's ambitions for territorial expansion with rulings against Catherine and John III of Navarre.

155. *and of late years, in the League against* Henry *the third of France*: Henry III (1551–89) was King of Poland from 1573 and of France from 1574. He was opposed by the Duke of Guise's Catholic League, which had the support of Pope Sixtus V, and was assassinated in 1589.

156. *But to this he hath replyed, that the Christians of old, deposed not* Nero, *nor* Dioclesian, *nor* Julian, *nor* Valens *an Arrian*: A list of rulers who were believed to have persecuted Christians. Nero (37–68) was Emperor from 54, in succession to Claudius, and is supposed to have blamed the Christians for the Great Fire of Rome in 64. Diocletian (*c.* 244–*c.* 312) was Emperor from 284 until 305, famous for his reorganization of the Roman Empire. Julian (*c.* 331–63) known as 'the Apostate', was Emperor from 361 and the last non-Christian ruler of the empire. Valens was Emperor 364–78, killed fighting the Goths at Adrianople. He was an Arian, i.e. one who did not consider Christ sufficiently divine, by the standards of official Catholic doctrine.

157. *who for calling for, might have had twelve Legions of immortall, invulnerable Angels to assist him*: Matthew 26:53.

158. *to obey the Powers constituted over them . . . and that they ought to obey them, not for fear of their wrath, but for conscience sake?*: Romans 13:1–5.

159. *let the Corn and Tares grow up together*: Matthew 13:24–30.

160. *The fact of Jehoiada . . . was a mere Subject*: In the ninth century BCE, Jehoiada was the high priest. When Athaliah, the queen mother, sought to wipe out the rest of the royal family in order to hold on to power, Jehoiada rescued her infant grandson Joash and, six years later, had her killed.

161. *The fact of St. Ambrose . . . was a Capitall Crime*: Ambrose (*c.* 340–97) was bishop of Milan, where he baptized Augustine of Hippo in 387. Theodosius I (*c.* 346–95) became Emperor in 379. After a massacre in Thessalonica, Ambrose is supposed to have barred him from entering the church until he had done penance. The scene was painted by both Peter Paul Rubens and Anthony van Dyck. See Theodoret, *Ecclesiastical History* 5.17.

162. *And for the Popes, Gregory 1. Greg. 2. Zachary, and Leo 3. their Judgments are void, as given in their own Cause*: Gregory I, known as 'the Great' (*c.* 540–604), was elected Pope in 590. A vigorous administrator, he expanded the authority of the Papacy, and launched the mission for the conversion of England. Gregory II (669–731) became Pope in 715 and contributed to the development of the Papacy as a temporal power. Leo III (750–816) was elected Pope in 795, and crowned Charlemagne as Emperor in 800.

163. Servants obey your Masters in all things . . . The Scribes and Pharisees sit in Moses Chaire: Colossians 3:22. Colossians 3:20. Matthew 23:2–3.

164. *That Herod for the same cause sought to kill him*: Herod I, known as 'the Great' (*c.* 73–4 BCE, not to be confused with Herod Antipas), was the Roman client king of Judaea at the time of the birth of Jesus.

165. Lord remember me when thou commest into thy Kingdome: Luke 23:42.

166. *For when our Saviour . . . had said to Martha*: Martha was the sister of Lazarus (whom Jesus raised from the dead) and Mary (whom some traditions identify with Mary Magdalen).

167. *Zachary*: Zechariah.

168. *yet seeing St. Paul says, he shal be saved*: 1 Corinthians 3:12–15.

169. *when St. Paul withstood St. Peter to his face*: Galatians 2:11.

170. *the licence that Naaman had*: See 2 Kings 5.

Part IV: Of the Kingdome of Darknesse

1. *(as the land of Goshen)*: Exodus 10:21–3.

2. *which God having reserved to himselfe during his Reigne over the Israelites, assigned to the tribe of Levi . . . to be their inheritance*: Numbers 18:20–24.

3. *The Egyptian Conjurers . . . the Water into Bloud*: Rods becoming serpents, Exodus 7:11–12. Water becoming blood, Exodus 7:22.

4. Asperges me Domine Hyssopo: 'Sprinkle me with hyssop, Lord', from Psalm 51:7.

5. *that is to say, if he disobeyed not his Commandement*: Genesis 2:16–17.

6. *So that the flaming Sword at the entrance of Paradise*: Genesis 3:24.

7. *In the fift day of the Creation . . .* made a Living Creature: Genesis 1:20–7, with Hobbes quoting (and translating) phrases from the Latin Vulgate.

8. *And after* Noah *came out of the Arke, God saith . . .* every Living Creature: Genesis 8:21.

9. *that is to say, they shall be cast alive into the perpetuall fire of Gehenna*: E.g. Matthew 10:28.

10. *That which the High Priest did to Athaliah . . . and set up another in his place*: For Athaliah, 2 Kings 11: 13–16. For Abiathar, 1 Kings 2:26–7. Joash was Athaliah's grandson, not her son.

11. *Beza*: Theodore Beza (1519–1605) was professor of theology at Geneva, at the heart of the Calvinist Reformation.

12. *for it shall come as a theefe in the night*: 2 Peter 3:10.

13. *and in St. Luke, where the same is againe repeated*: Luke 9:27.

14. After six dayes Jesus taketh with him Peter, and James, and John *(not all, but some of his Disciples)*: James (d. 44), son of Zebedee, was one of Jesus's disciples. The passage is Mark 9:2–4.

15. *(2 Kings 8)*: This should be 1 Kings 8.

16. *nor Philip the Water of the river wherein he baptized the Eunuch*: Acts 8:38.

17. *that Abraham, Isaac, and Jacob are living*: Matthew 22:32.

18. *and in the same sense that God said to Adam, that on the day hee should eate of the forbidden fruit, he should certainly die*: Genesis 2:17.

19. *And the History of Dives and Lazarus, make nothing against this, if wee take it (as it is) for a Parable*: Luke 16:19–31.

20. *And it is said besides in many places . . . and that the worm of conscience never dyeth*: Everlasting fire, e.g. Matthew 18:8. Everlasting torments, e.g. Revelation 14:11. Everlasting punishments, e.g. Matthew 25:46. Worm that does not die, Mark 9:44, 46.

21. *(2 Kings 1. 12)*: This should be 2 Samuel 1:12.

22. Abner: Abner was a cousin of Saul, and a captain in his army.

23. *The first verse of* Psalme, *37*: Psalm 38:1.

24. *What were this to Purgatory, if Augustine had not applied the* Wrath *to the fire of Hell, and the* Displeasure, *to that of Purgatory?*: Augustine (354–430) was bishop of Hippo and author of many books, including his *Confessions* and *The City of God against the Pagans*.

25. *for the Soule of Lazarus during the four days he was dead*: John 11:39.

26. He that giveth to the Poore, lendeth to the Lord: Proverbs 19:17.

27. *written by* Hesiod: There have been references to Hesiod before in these notes; this is the first time he is mentioned in the text of *Leviathan*. An archaic Greek poet, around 700 BCE, he was the author of the *Theogony*, to which Hobbes here refers, as well as the *Works and Days*.

28. *and therein, by necessary consequence their* Dæmonology, *or (as St.* Paul *calles it)* their Doctrines of Devils: 1 Timothy 4:1.

29. *Falling Sicknesse*: Epilepsy.

30. A spirit hath not flesh and bone: Luke 24:39.

31. We shall rise spirituall Bodies: 1 Corinthians 15:44 (approx.).

32. *Again, where St. Luke sayes of Judas Iscariot . . .* how he might betray Christ unto them: Luke 22:3–4.

33. Wee know that an Idol is Nothing: 1 Corinthians 8:4.

34. *are First, two Examples; one of the Cherubins over the Ark of God; the other of the Brazen Serpent*: Cherubim: Exodus 37:7–9. Brazen serpent: Numbers 21:9.

35. *as to worship his Footstool*: E.g. Psalm 99:5.

36. *Chimæras*: For a description of this monster, see Hesiod, *Theogony* 319–24.

37. *Neptune*: Neptune was the Roman god of the sea.

38. *or for Moses to put off his Shoes when he was before the Flaming Bush, the ground appertaining to Mount Sinai*: Exodus 3:5.

39. *But the making of the Golden Calfe by Aaron . . . was Idolatry*: Exodus 32:1–4.

40. *and where the Images of Laban are called his Gods*: Laban was the uncle of Jacob and Esau.

41. *The first that ever was canonized at Rome, was* Romulus . . . *to the State of their new City*: Romulus was the legendary founder of Rome. He was raised by a she-wolf along with his brother Remus, whom he later killed. His ghost subsequently appeared to Julius Proculus, a Roman senator. Livy, *Ab urbe condita* 1.16.5–8.

42. Vehiculum Deorum: 'Vehicle of the gods'.

43. *Just as at this day the Popes are carried by Switzers under a Canopie*: The Swiss Guard continue to serve the Pope down to the present day.

44. *as we read of* Caligula . . . *and burning* Torches: Caligula (12–41; the name means 'little boots') was Roman Emperor 37–41, in a reign marked by violence and excess. He was murdered by the Praetorian Guard. Suetonius, *Life of Caligula* 13.

45. *And of* Caracalla *that was received into* Alexandria *with Incense, and with casting of Flowers*: Caracalla (188–217) was Roman Emperor from 198, who extended citizenship to almost all free men throughout the empire and had the Baths of Caracalla built in Rome. He was murdered by a soldier.

46. *The* Gymnosophists *of* India: Plutarch, *Life of Alexander* 64.

47. *At length, when* Warre *had united many of these* Græcian *lesser Cities . . . to get the reputation of being* Wise: Diogenes Laertius, *Lives and Opinions of Eminent Philosophers* 1.40–1.

48. *And this was it which* Carneades *also did at* Rome . . . *that delighted to hear him speak (as they thought) fine things*: Carneades (214–*c.* 129 BCE) was a Greek Sceptic who came to Rome in 155 BCE as an ambassador from Athens. On that occasion, he spoke on successive days both for and against justice, provoking Cato to have him expelled from the city. Marcus Porcius Cato 'the Elder' (234–149 BCE) was a Roman senator, celebrated for his stern moralism, defence of traditional Roman values and opposition to Carthage. Plutarch, *Life of Cato the Elder* 22.

49. *and those that* Zeno *taught*: Zeno of Citium (334–262 BCE) was the founder of Stoicism, one of the major post-Aristotelian traditions in Greek philosophy.

50. *and fearing the fate of Socrates*: Socrates (*c.* 470–399 BCE) was Plato's teacher, and the central character in many of Plato's dialogues. He was found guilty of impiety and corrupting the young and was condemned to death by drinking hemlock.

51. Antiperistasis: Antiperistasis is an Aristotelian term describing the tendency for opposing qualities (e.g. heat and cold) to intensify one another.

52. shall neither Marry, nor bee given in Marriage, but shall bee as the Angels in heaven: Matthew 22:30.

53. *and the Aristocracy of the thirty Governours set up there by the Lacedemonians that subdued them, the thirty Tyrants*: The 'thirty tyrants' were installed in Athens by the Spartans after their victory in the Peloponnesian War in 404 BCE.

54. *And therefore this is another Errour of Aristotles Politiques . . . but the Laws*: Aristotle, *Politics* 1282b.

55. *such as would pose Cicero, and Varro, and all the Grammarians of ancient Rome*: Marcus Terentius Varro (116–27 BCE) was a prolific Roman scholar, the great bulk of whose works are now lost, though we still possess a complete work on agriculture, and a sizeable portion of his treatise on Latin.

56. *S. Bernard . . . and so has our Beda*: Bernard of Clairvaux (1090–1153) was a monk and, later, abbot, who reformed the Cistercian order. Bede (*c.* 673–735), known as 'the Venerable Bede', was a monk whose major work was *The Ecclesiastical History of the English People*.

57. *Cicero maketh honorable mention of one of the* Cassii *. . . Cui bono*: Cicero, *Pro S. Roscio Amerino* 84.

58. *as Peters net was broken, by the struggling of too great a multitude of Fishes*: Luke 5:6.

59. *I doe not therefore blame the Emperour Frederick for holding the stirrop to our countryman Pope Adrian*: Frederick 'Barbarossa' (1122–90) was elected Holy Roman Emperor in 1155. He died en route to Palestine on the Third Crusade. Adrian IV (*c.* 1100–59) was Pope from 1154. Born Nicholas Breakspear, he remains the only Englishman to have held that office. In 1155, when the two met at Sutri, north of Rome, the Emperor-elect declined to hold the Pope's stirrup as he dismounted, lest

anyone think he was his vassal, though after negotiations he agreed to do so, and a second meeting was arranged.

60. *Præterpoliticall*: The *Oxford English Dictonary* offers 'outside the sphere of politics'.

61. *First, the Power of the Popes was dissolved totally by Queen Elizabeth*: Elizabeth (1533–1603) became Queen of England in 1558 and was the last of the Tudor monarchs. Hobbes here refers to the Act of Supremacy 1558, which re-established the Church of England as independent of Rome, reversing her sister Mary's religious policy.

62. *After this, the Presbyterians lately in England obtained the putting down of Episcopacy*: Episcopacy was abolished by an ordinance of Parliament in October 1646.

63. *And almost at the same time, the Power was taken also from the Presbyterians*: This may be a reference to the repeal of the Act of Uniformity in September 1650, which removed the penalties for non-attendance at church.

64. *And so we are reduced to the Independency of the Primitive Christians . . . every man as he liketh best*: The 'primitive' Christians are the early Christians, before the establishment of ecclesiastical hierarchies. For Paul, Cephas and Apollos, see 1 Corinthians 1:12.

A Review, and Conclusion

1. *As the Israelites in Egypt . . . and other times were ranging abroad to gather Straw*: Exodus 5:7.

2. *And because I find by divers English Books lately printed*: Hobbes seems to have in mind in particular Anthony Ascham's *Of the Confusions and Revolutions of Governments* (1649) and Marchamont Nedham, *The Case of the Common-wealth of England, Stated* (1650). See Kinch Hoekstra, 'The de facto turn in Hobbes's political philosophy', in Tom Sorell and Luc Foisneau, eds., *Leviathan After 350 Years* (Oxford: Clarendon Press, 2004).

3. *Lastly, by pretence of these Laws it was . . . he had Pleaded his Cause before the High Priest*: Acts 6:8–15, 7:1–60.

4. *nor in that I writ before of the same Subject in Latine*: Hobbes here refers to his earlier treatment of political philosophy, *De Cive* (1642).

PARADISE LOST

John Milton

'Better to reign in Hell, than serve in Heav'n'

In *Paradise Lost* John Milton produced a poem of epic scale, conjuring up a vast, awe-inspiring cosmos and ranging across huge tracts of space and time. And yet, in putting a charismatic Satan and naked Adam and Eve at the centre of this story, he also created an intensely human tragedy on the Fall of Man. Written when Milton was in his fifties – blind; bitterly disappointed by the Restoration and briefly in danger of execution – *Paradise Lost's* apparent ambivalence towards authority has led to immense debate about whether it manages to 'justify the ways of God to men' or exposes the cruelty of Christianity.

Edited with Notes and an Introduction by John Leonard

ISBN: 978 0 14 042 439 3

AN ESSAY CONCERNING HUMAN UNDERSTANDING

John Locke

'It matters not what men's fancies are, 'tis the knowledge of
things that is only to be prized'

In *An Essay Concerning Human Understanding*, first published
in 1690, John Locke (1632–1704) provides a complete account
of how we acquire mathematical, natural, scientific, religious and
ethical knowledge. Rejecting the theory that some knowledge is
innate, Locke argues that it derives from sense perceptions and
experience, as analysed and developed by reason. While defending
these central claims with vigorous common sense, Locke offers
many incidental – and highly influential – reflections on space and
time, meaning, free will and personal identity. The result is a
powerful, pioneering work, which, together with Descartes's works,
largely set the agenda for modern philosophy.

Edited with an introduction and notes by Roger Woolhouse

ISBN: 978 0 14 143 482 8

OROONOKO

Aphra Behn

'We are bought and sold like apes or monkeys, to be the sport of women, fools, and cowards, and the support of rogues'

When Prince Oroonoko's passion for the virtuous Imoinda arouses the jealousy of his grandfather, the lovers are cast into slavery and transported from Africa to the colony of Surinam. Oroonoko's noble bearing soon wins the respect of his English captors, but his struggle for freedom brings about his destruction. Inspired by Aphra Behn's visit to Surinam, *Oroonoko* reflects the author's romantic view of native peoples as in 'the first state of innocence, before man knew how to sin.' The novel also reveals Behn's ambiguous attitude to African slavery – while she favoured it as a means to strengthen England's rule, her powerful and moving work conveys its injustice and brutality.

Edited with an Introduction and Notes by Janet Todd

ISBN: 978 0 14 043 988 5

A TREATISE OF HUMAN NATURE

David Hume

'Human Nature is the only science of man, and yet has hitherto
been the most neglected'

One of the most significant works of Western philosophy, Hume's
Treatise was published in 1739–40, before he was thirty years
old. A pinnacle of English empiricism, it is a comprehensive attempt
to apply scientific methods of observation to a study of human
nature, and a vigorous attack upon the principles of traditional
metaphysical thought. With masterly eloquence, Hume denies the
immortality of the soul and the reality of space; considers the
manner in which we form concepts of identity and cause and
effect; and speculates upon the nature of freedom, virtue and
emotion. Opposed both to metaphysics and to rationalism, Hume's
philosophy of informed scepticism sees man not as a religious
creation, nor as a machine, but as a creature dominated by senti-
ment, passion and appetite.

Edited with an introduction by Ernest C. Mossner

ISBN: 978 0 14 043 244 2

CRITIQUE OF PURE REASON

Immanuel Kant

'The purpose of this critique of pure speculative reason consists
in the attempt to change the old procedure of metaphysics and to
bring about a complete revolution'

Kant's *Critique of Pure Reason* (1781) is the central text of modern
philosophy. It presents a profound and challenging investigation
into the nature of human reason, its knowledge and its illusions.
Reason, Kant argues, is the seat of certain concepts that precede
experience and make it possible, but we are not therefore entitled
to draw conclusions about the natural world from these concepts.
The *Critique* brings together two opposing schools of philosophy:
rationalism, which grounds all our knowledge in reason, and
empiricism, which traces all our knowledge to experience. Kant's
transcendental idealism indicates a third way that goes beyond
these alternatives.

Translated, edited and with an introduction by Marcus Weigelt
Based on the translation by Max Müller

ISBN: 978 0 14 044 747 7

DEMOCRACY IN AMERICA

Alexis de Tocqueville

'A new political science is needed for a totally new world'

In 1831 Alexis de Tocqueville, a young French aristocrat and civil servant, made a nine-month journey through eastern America. The result was *Democracy in America*, a monumental study of the strengths and weaknesses of the nation's evolving politics. Tocqueville looked to the flourishing democratic system in America as a possible model for post-revolutionary France, believing its egalitarian ideals reflected the spirit of the age – even that they were the will of God. His insightful work has become one of the most influential political texts ever written on America and an indispensable authority for anyone interested in the future of democracy. This volume includes the rarely translated 'Two Weeks in the Wilderness', an evocative account of Tocqueville's travels among the Iroquois and Chippeway and 'Exclusion to Lake Oneida'.

Translated by Gerald Bevan
with an Introduction and Notes by Isaac Kram

ISBN: 978 0 14 044 760 6

FEAR AND TREMBLING

Søren Kierkegaard

'He who loved himself became great in himself, and he who loved
others became great through his devotion, but he who loved God
became greater than all'

In *Fear and Trembling* Kierkegaard, writing under the pseudonym
Johannes de silentio, expounds his personal view of religion
through a discussion of the scene in Genesis in which Abraham
prepares to sacrifice his son at God's command. Believing Abraham's unreserved obedience to be the essential leap of faith needed
to make a full commitment to his religion. Kierkegaard himself
made great sacrifices in order to dedicate his life entirely to his
philosophy and to God. The conviction shown in this religious
polemic – that a man can have an exceptional mission in his life
– informed all Kierkegaard's later writings, and was also hugely
influential for both Protestant theology and the existentialist
movement.

Translated with an Introduction by Alastair Hannay

ISBN: 978 0 14 044 449 0

THUS SPOKE ZARATHUSTRA

Friedrich Nietzsche

'Yes! I am Zarathustra the Godless'

Nietzsche was one of the most revolutionary and subversive thinkers in Western philosophy, and *Thus Spoke Zarathustra* remains his most famous and influential work. It describes how the ancient Persian prophet Zarathustra descends from his solitude in the mountains to tell the world that God is dead and that the Superman, the human embodiment of divinity, is his successor. With blazing intensity and poetic brilliance, Nietzsche argues that the meaning of existence is not to be found in religious pieties or meek submission, but in all-powerful life force: passionate, chaotic and free.

Translated and edited with an Introduction by R. J. Hollingdale

ISBN: 978 0 14 044 118 5

THE STATE AND REVOLUTION

Vladimir Lenin

'The replacement of the bourgeois state by the proletarian state is impossible without a violent revolution'

In July 1917, when the Provisional Government issued a warrant for his arrest, Lenin fled from Petrograd; later than year, the October Revolution swept him to supreme power. In the short intervening period he spent in Finland, he wrote his impassioned, never-completed masterwork *The State and Revolution*. This powerfully argued book offers both the rationale for the new regime and a wealth of insights into Leninist politics. It was here that Lenin justified his personal interpretation of Marxism, savaged his opponents and set out his trenchant views on class conflict, the lessons of earlier revolutions, the dismantling of the bourgeois state and the replacement of capitalism by the dictatorship of the proletariat. As both historical document and political statement, its importance can hardly be exaggerated.

Translated and edited with an Introduction by Robert Service

ISBN: 978 0 14 018 435 8

A ROOM OF ONE'S OWN

Virginia Woolf

'But, you may say, we asked you to speak about women and fiction – what has that got to do with a room of one's own?'

A Room of One's Own grew out of a lecture that Virginia Woolf had been invited to give at Girton College, Cambridge in 1928 and became a landmark work of feminist thought. Covering everything from why a woman must have money and a room of her own if she is to write, to authors such as Jane Austen, Aphra Behn and the Brontë sisters, and the tragic story of Shakespeare's fictional sister Judith, it remains a passionate assertion for female creativity and independence in a world dominated by men.

ISBN: 978 0 24 138 752 8